Joseph P. Kennedy Presents

# Joseph P. Kennedy Presents

## HIS HOLLYWOOD YEARS

## Cari Beauchamp

Alfred A. Knopf · NEW YORK · 2009

THIS IS A BORZOI BOOK
PUBLISHED BY ALFRED A. KNOPF

*Copyright © 2009 by Cari Beauchamp*

*All rights reserved. Published in the United States by Alfred A. Knopf, a division of Random House, Inc., New York, and in Canada by Random House of Canada Limited, Toronto.*
*www.aaknopf.com*

*Knopf, Borzoi Books, and the colophon are registered trademarks of Random House, Inc.*

*Library of Congress Cataloging-in-Publication Data*
*Beauchamp, Cari.*
*Joseph P. Kennedy presents : his Hollywood years / by Cari Beauchamp. — 1st ed.*
*p. cm.*
*ISBN 978-1-4000-4000-1*
*Includes bibliographical references and index.*
*1. Kennedy, Joseph P. (Joseph Patrick), 1888–1969 — Career in the motion picture industry.*
*2. Irish Americans — California — Los Angeles — Biography.   3. Capitalists and financiers —*
*California — Los Angeles — Biography.   4. Businessmen — California — Los Angeles — Biography.*
*5. Hollywood (Los Angeles, Calif.) — Biography.   6. Los Angeles (Calif.) — Biography.*
*7. Kennedy family.   I. Title.*
*E748.K376B43 2009*
*973.9092 — dc22*
*{B}       2008032828*

*Manufactured in the United States of America*
*First Edition*

*This book is adapted and expanded from an article that originally appeared in* Vanity Fair.

*This book was supported by a grant from the Academy Film Scholars Program*
*of the Academy of Motion Picture Arts and Sciences.*

*For Tom Flynn*

All arrogance will reap a harvest rich in tears. God calls men to a heavy reckoning for overweening pride.

— HERODOTUS (underlined by Robert Kennedy
in his copy of Edith Hamilton's *The Greek Way*)

# CONTENTS

# ILLUSTRATIONS

# PREFACE

*M*ention the name Joseph P. Kennedy, the patriarch of America's royal family, and it evokes a mental picture: an older man smiling out from a photograph surrounded by numerous family members, or perhaps he is gaunt and wheelchair-bound, felled by a stroke. Erase those images.

Visualize, instead, a young man in his mid-thirties, a "wickedly handsome six footer, exuding vitality and roguish charm." He strides confidently into a room wearing "the most wonderful smile that seemed to light up his entire face," impressing everyone he met with "his warm handshake and his friendly volubility." His vibrant energy fuels a head-turning charisma that commands attention. "You felt not just that you were the only one in the room that mattered," recalls Joan Fontaine, "but the only one in the world." With bright blue eyes behind wire-rimmed glasses, a frequent laugh, and a tendency to slap his thigh when amused, he is strikingly different from the typical Wall Street banker or studio mogul.

This is the man who took Hollywood by storm, at one point running four companies simultaneously when no one before or since ran more than one. He was profiled in national magazines and newspapers as a brilliant financial wunderkind, "the most intriguing personality in the motion picture world" and "the person who now monopolizes conversation in the studios and on location." Kennedy was "the blonde Moses" leading film companies into profitable territory as they faced the pivotal years of converting from silent films to sound. In the process he was instrumental in killing vaudeville. The mystique around him grew so thick that *Fortune* magazine warned "the legends are so luxuriant that when you see Joe Kennedy you are likely to be startled to find him as plain and matter of fact as he is—a healthy hardy good natured sandy haired Irish family man—athletic, unperplexed, easily pleased, hot tempered, independent and restless as they come."

Louella Parsons hailed Joe Kennedy as "the coming Napoleon" of the movies, the white knight with the wherewithal to save film studios by bringing bankers and corporate representatives onto their boards of directors. He was the architect of the mergers that laid the groundwork for today's Hollywood. While even he might be surprised to find that United Artists, Metro-Goldwyn-Mayer, and Columbia are now all partially owned by the same multinational conglomerate, he was the one who designed that very blueprint.

Kennedy was the first financier to simply buy a studio. *Fortune* used the metaphor of a chess game to describe his Hollywood climb: taking "small pawns" such as Robertson-Cole and FBO and methodically knocking down the knights and bishops of Pathé and Keith-Albee-Orpheum to create "the queen of R-K-O" in less than four years. They concluded that "Kennedy moved so fast that opinions still differ as to whether he left a string of reorganized companies or a heap of wreckage behind him."

Over one hundred films were released under the banner of "Joseph P. Kennedy Presents" during which time he influenced the careers and personal lives of Gloria Swanson, Marlene Dietrich, and the cowboy stars Fred Thomson and Tom Mix, as well as dozens of other investors, executives, and underlings. Kennedy was a multifaceted, magnetic charmer, a devious visionary with exquisite timing and more than a flash of genius. And nothing, including the destruction of other people's careers, deterred his consuming passion to increase his personal bank accounts.

"Not a half dozen men have been able to keep the whole equation of pictures in their heads," F. Scott Fitzgerald noted in his final novel, *The Last Tycoon*. Joe Kennedy was not one of those men, for he had no appreciation of the nuances of storytelling or an ability to spark true creative collaboration. However, to paraphrase Fitzgerald, Kennedy may have been the only one to have the whole economic equation in his head and that is a key to understanding him. He saw everything and everyone, from Gloria Swanson to Adolf Hitler, through a lens of dollars and cents.

When he first arrived in Hollywood in 1926, no one knew Joe Kennedy as the man he would become; he wasn't that man yet. He was already more than well off, always meticulously dressed and chauffeured in his Rolls-Royce, but he had yet to accumulate his fortune. His wealth was estimated at a little over a million dollars and he would increase that tenfold over the five years he was immersed in the film industry. When Kennedy left Hollywood, "he already had so much money that making the rest of it, which must have been many many millions, was almost a routine affair."

He caught the wave at exactly the right moment, and, perhaps more important, the timing of his departure was perfect. By 1932, he was "the richest Irish American in the world," and while he would continue to build capital through other ventures, it was Hollywood that provided the foundation of his wealth. It was also Hollywood where he learned how to perform as a public personality and where he came to believe that how you were perceived was more important than who you were. The skills and knowledge he gained would affect everything he did and influenced from then on, from how he presented his family to the world to his son's election to the presidency.

This is the story of those Hollywood years.

Joseph P. Kennedy Presents

# CHAPTER I

# "America's Youngest Bank President"
## (1888–1919)

*T*he family that Joseph Patrick Kennedy was born into on September 6, 1888, was more comfortable than that of most Boston Irish Catholics. His father, Patrick Joseph (known to everyone as P.J.), was a thirty-year-old member of the Massachusetts House of Representatives and his mother, Mary Augusta Hickey Kennedy, was the daughter of a relatively well-to-do family. Although Boston in 1888 was heavily populated by Irish Catholics, it was dominated by the Protestants who had founded it two hundred and fifty years before. John Winthrop and John Cotton, along with the Quincys and the Saltonstalls, had arrived with the strict and codified purpose of establishing their "City upon a Hill." The churches and schools they had built and their streets and the common ground remained the city's defining touchstones, and their descendants still ruled Boston society. The Irish population had skyrocketed with the potato famines of the late 1840s, and one of their own was elected mayor in 1885, yet when openings for work were advertised, "Protestant only" or "Irish need not apply" were all too familiar provisos.

P. J. Kennedy's father, Patrick, had immigrated to Boston from Ireland after the second potato famine in 1848. Unlike those fleeing poverty and starvation in "coffin ships," Patrick was a younger son of a landed family, and he arrived as a passenger on a scheduled liner. Half of the Boston Irish were tagged as "laborers," but Patrick was a skilled artisan, much in demand as a cooper, making the kegs and barrels used for storing and shipping everything from china to produce. He married fellow émigrée Bridget Murphy, and they were already the parents of three daughters when P.J. was born on January 15, 1858. A few months later, Patrick died at the age of thirty-five, a victim of cholera or consumption, without leaving a will. Bridget put up the $600 bond the court required for her to be named executor of Patrick's estate and was left with a home large enough to take in a boarder. Though the story is often told of her working at a notions shop on the docks, she may actually have owned the store. The family was far from wealthy, but P.J.'s older sisters all "married well." By the time he had finished his schooling in his late teens, P.J. was working on the docks as a stevedore. He soon saved enough to buy his own "lager bar" on Elbow Street in East Boston, and two years later, P.J. joined with a partner to open Kennedy & Quigley's Saloon on Border Street. Then, combining his knowledge of the docks and saloons, he formed his own liquor import company.

P.J. was firmly established and in his second year in the Massachusetts House of Representatives when he married Mary Hickey in 1887. The following year brought the birth of their first child, and instead of giving him the potential burden of being a "Junior," Mary reversed her husband's given names and christened the boy Joseph Patrick. "Pat" was a typical Irish name; "Joseph" transcended ethnicity. A daughter, Margaret, was born the next year and then came another son they named Francis. Loretta was born in 1892, completing the family, but Frank died before reaching his third birthday. Just as P.J. had been the revered only boy in an Irish Catholic family of girls, Joe held the same familial rank, made all the more precious by the loss of Frank. And this time it was in a household with an assured income and a very successful, very present father.

When Joe was four, P.J. became a founding partner in Columbia Trust, an East Boston bank created to serve the growing ethnically mixed neighborhood. That same year, he was elected to the Massachusetts Senate, but in turn-of-the-century Boston, power was exercised more overtly in the precincts than in the statehouse. Being a ward boss in East Boston meant "running a pocket sized welfare state," and P.J., most comfortable behind the bar, was in a unique position to know the personal concerns and professional troubles of his constituents. He was smart and calculating, but he was also patient and sympathetic to the problems of others.

Boston was the home of both the American League Red Sox and the National League Braves and father and son went to games together and then played ball in the yard at home. Joe occasionally accompanied P.J. to his parades and precinct meetings, or to his liquor dealership on High Street. Time and attention were lavished on Joe and neither parent was a harsh disciplinarian. He described his father as "the sweetest, gentlest man I've ever known; he never raised his voice and was never other than kind." Respect was assumed, and Joe said that all it took was a cer-

Joe with his sisters, Loretta and Margaret, 1895

tain look from his mother, given at a telling moment, to get the message across. Joe also saw that look when supplicants came to their door and P.J. willingly left the dining-room table to hear their pleas. Mary thought such discussions should take place elsewhere and for Joe, who "worshipped" his mother, those scenes deepened his belief that his father was being taken advantage of.

Whereas P.J. found great personal satisfaction in aiding those who genuinely needed his help, his son looked at the same people and "all I could see was their predatory stare." P.J. accrued business and political success as well as legions of friends, yet his eldest child saw him as suffering financially and emotionally by giving too much to his acquaintances and his community. Joe watched his father ride the wins and losses of elected officialdom, and it was as a young witness to those realities that he developed his own personality. "Joe decided early on," says Doris Kearns Goodwin, author of *The Fitzgeralds and the Kennedys,* "that he would build his life on his own foundation without depending on the loyalty of any place or institution."

Unlike his father, who had worked as a young man because he needed to, Joe worked because of his own ambition and his parents' belief that it encouraged discipline. While his mother, in particular, set high expectations, no one pushed Joe harder than he pushed himself. He later told tales of hawking newspapers, clerking in a candy store, selling peanuts to tourists at the wharf, and making department store deliveries.

P.J. occasionally eased the way for Joe's entry into various economic ventures, but it was his mother who provided the steady hand that ensured the damask cloths on the table, the lace curtains, and the "Irish hospitality" that made the children feel comfortable bringing their friends home. Mary was also an active supporter of "social welfare," church charities, and suffrage for women. Her brother was a doctor who had graduated from Harvard Medical School, and her daughters went to college, but she wanted more for her only son.

It was Mary who determined that Joe would attend Boston Latin, established by the colony's founders in 1635, with alumni such as Samuel Adams and John Hancock. Each morning Joe put a penny down to cross the harbor on the ferry. He played forward in basketball and first base on the school's baseball team, batting over .500 his senior year. Though it took him five years instead of the usual four to graduate, Joe was elected president of his senior class and chaired the debating society. Prophetically, his classmates predicted that Joe Kennedy "will make [his] mark on the world," but "will earn his living in a very round about way."

Confident and almost cocky, Joe was accepted at Harvard University, ready to prove himself capable of cracking through the economic, religious, and social segregation that had for so long held Bostonians in its

Up front and in the middle, president of his graduating class of Boston Latin, 1908

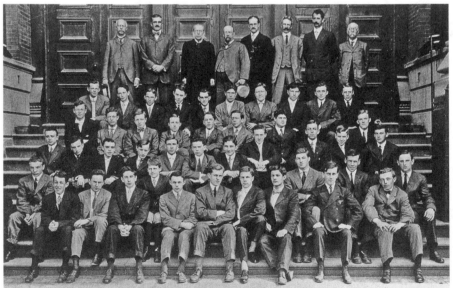

grip. He received a regular and "adequate allowance," but he developed an eye for shortcuts and making money off the needs and wants of others. He enjoyed the scouting and the planning as much as the financial results, and partnered with his college friend Joe Donovan to purchase a sightseeing bus to ferry summer tourists around the monuments of Boston. The city controlled the routes, and the story goes that Joe went straight to the mayor to request they be allowed to take on passengers at the premium spot, the railroad station. The mayor assumed he was getting both Joe and his father in his debt by granting the request, but there is no record showing that P.J. knew anything about it, and Joe did not see it as a debt at all. From the start, he was not a politician looking for favors, he was an entrepreneur looking for profit. With Donovan behind the wheel and Kennedy polishing his verbal skills by recounting historical anecdotes, Joe boasted that in less than three years, he netted $5,000 on his $300 investment.

A witness to his early achievements was fellow Harvard student Hugh Nawn, two years Joe's senior and the son of a successful contractor. He remembered Joe's "wanted to be on his own" and was struck that "here was this sophomore in college already planning his life's work; always a long range thinker. Early in life, he had charted his course."

Academic success did not come easily, but Joe wasn't about to let schoolwork deter him from an active social life. His classmates included the future humorist Robert Benchley and Joe joined several associations, including Hasty Pudding. Harvard wasn't just overwhelmingly Protestant; one friend recalled that "Democrats were as scarce as orange trees in Labrador." And Joe learned the hard way that even if a few Catholics and Jews were allowed to attend, they were barred from the most exclusive "final" clubs on campus. This highest echelon of social life was the equivalent of private gentlemen's clubs, where undergraduates gathered for meals, reading, and playing pool. Fewer than one tenth of the students were chosen. Most wouldn't even apply, but Joe did, and when he was rejected, the seeds of resentment were deeply planted. When he learned that the men he thought were his friends were to enter those hallowed halls and he was not, "he looked at himself in a different way." Joe later told his wife "that he would perpetually be an outsider."

"A Harvard man knows who he is," said Edmund Quincy, a descendant of one of the founding families of Boston. "If he isn't a Harvard man, who is he?" The Quincys personified the Protestant elite that Kennedy saw as scorning him but when, in 2002, John Quincy, Jr., current scion and eleventh generation of the family, was asked about Joe

Kennedy, he heaved a sigh of noblesse oblige and said, "We tire of the Kennedys." It was that impenetrable indifference that most infuriated Joe: he didn't matter. The outside world could see him as "a Harvard man," yet while he had one foot in that domain, he knew he would never fully be accepted by those within; "these were not his people."

"Joe Kennedy saw early what made the power and gentility he wanted," his friend Tom Corcoran explained. "Power came from money. Joe had a keen mind; it was honed against the great cynicism underlying rank and station in Brahmin Boston." Joe himself put it more bluntly: "You can go to Harvard and it doesn't mean a damn thing. The only thing these people understand is money."

Another incident at Harvard bears recounting. When several of his classmates were interviewed in the late 1950s, they volunteered the tale of Joe's making the varsity baseball team in his junior year but not play- ing until the final game against Yale. It was the biggest game of the sea- son and if he saw action, he would win a coveted letter "H" for all the world to see. It wasn't until the final inning, with Harvard in the lead 4 to 1 and Yale down to one more out, that the team captain and pitcher, Charles McLaughlin, put Joe and two other players in to assure them their letter. The Yale batter hit a grounder that was fielded to Joe at first for the final out of the game. While his teammates surrounded the victo- rious pitcher, Kennedy put the game ball in his pocket and walked off the field. Confronted by McLaughlin with a request for the ball, Joe refused and kept walking. He could talk about being excluded, but the story was told as an example of how he brought exclusion on himself. As one of his former classmates summarized, "If he wanted something bad enough, [he] would get it and he didn't much care how he got it. He'd run right over anybody."

Joe saw it differently. He had tried to play by Brahmin rules and still it was not enough. He wasn't making that mistake again. And succeed- ing was no longer enough; he set out to best them.

Outwardly, Kennedy was his "very outgoing, gregarious, vibrant" self and continued his studies and his moneymaking activities. He lived on campus to be a part of it all, returning home to visit his parents on week- ends, occasionally bringing friends with him for Sunday dinner. The family had moved to a larger house with a wraparound veranda in Winthrop, the more prosperous neighborhood. The home was complete with luxuries such as a Steinway baby grand and P.J.'s sixty-foot pleasure boat. Joe went to church fairly regularly, didn't smoke or drink liquor or coffee, but he made time for a vigorous and bifurcated love life: pursuing chorus girls on one side and courting Rose Fitzgerald on the other.

Rose (third from left) and Joe (second from right) among family
and friends at the beach, Maine, 1907

In retrospect, Rose Elizabeth Fitzgerald and Joseph Patrick Kennedy appear destined for each other. As children of political, popular, and well-known fathers, Rose and the Kennedy boy first met at Old Orchard Beach in Maine, where the "sociable Irish" summered, and the families of Boston powers like P. J. Kennedy and John "Honey Fitz" Fitzgerald played together on the beach.

Their fathers had risen to the top tier of influence in Irish Catholic Boston. Fitzgerald is often painted as a boisterous, backslapping buffoon, but that was only one side of his personality. A graduate of Boston Latin, Fitzgerald left Harvard Medical School after his parents' deaths to care for his six younger siblings. He was taken under the wing of the North End boss Matthew Keany, and within a few years Fitzgerald won a seat in the State Senate. At thirty-one, he was elected to Congress, but it was when he was inaugurated as mayor of Boston in January 1906 that Honey Fitz came into his own, with all the vices and virtues of a turn-of-the-century big-city politician.

The Fitzgerald and Kennedy patriarchs had their disagreements and rapprochements, but they could not have been more different in style. Honey Fitz was effusive, short, and roundish, busy telling people what they wanted to hear. P.J., on the other hand, was much more reticent, tall with glasses and a distinguished handlebar mustache; "intelligent, shrewd and impeccably fair and honest." Both were active in politics for decades, but while P.J. "kept himself free of taint," the same cannot be said of Fitzgerald.

Late in life, Rose said her father's determination to keep her apart from Joe Kennedy shaped her teenage years. Much has been written about Honey Fitz's disapproval of Joe as a suitor, yet many of those stories were promoted by Joe and Rose themselves, fueling Joe's tales of being a poor Irish kid who had pulled himself up by his bootstraps and providing her with a solace that they had made it in spite of the world being against them.

Two years younger than Joe, Rose was being publicly linked with him by the time he graduated from Boston Latin. After finishing at Dorchester High School at the age of sixteen, Rose wanted to go to Wellesley, but her father insisted she attend Sacred Heart Convent College in Boston. Her consolation was that she was often at her father's side as he attended an average of "two dinners and three dances a night." Her shy mother had turned reclusive, staying at home and growing bitter over her husband's long absences, so it was Rose, as the eldest of the six children, who took her mother's place, enjoying the public life that being the mayor's daughter opened for her.

Any remaining hope of going to Wellesley was crushed when her father announced that Rose and her sister Agnes would spend a year at the Convent of the Sacred Heart in Blumenthal in (then) Prussia. At the stark religious school, the girls wore long dark dresses with high white collars and were taught primarily by French nuns. Rose spoke French and German and had the opportunity to interact with other girls from all over Europe, but there is no record of her maintaining any friendships from that year. While she found a new satisfaction in the daily structure of prayer, meditation, and confession, her emotional life remained in Boston. She told a close friend that among the few possessions she brought with her was a picture of Joe Kennedy, and she continued writing him throughout the months she was abroad.

Rose was nineteen when she returned home; her father was reelected mayor and her interest in Joe, now a junior at Harvard, was stronger than ever. Along with the governor and four hundred other guests, Joe attended her elaborate debut, but when he asked Rose to his junior prom, her father informed her she was accompanying him to Palm Beach instead. Her education continued the next fall at yet another convent school, Sacred Heart in Manhattanville, New York. She saw Joe whenever possible, often on the sly. Rose was frequently on the road with her father, accompanying him to Chicago, to the White House to meet President William Howard Taft, and to the Democratic National Convention. They took another grand tour of Europe together, when Mayor Fitzgerald headed a Chamber of Commerce delegation. Father and daughter returned home to pack again, this time for Panama. Rose thrived on these public outings and extensive travels, but the more challenging it was for her to see Joe, the more intriguing the relationship became.

In the spring of 1912, as Joe was preparing to graduate from Harvard, President Taft and former president Theodore Roosevelt were battling over the White House, giving scant attention to the Democratic candidate, the former president of Princeton, Woodrow Wilson. Only twenty-five miles north of Boston, thousands of women were demonstrating in the streets of Lawrence, Massachusetts, demanding "bread and roses" in a strike that was shaking the textile industry. Yet Joe Kennedy's eyes were focused close to home and on his own immediate future. Sixty percent of America's personal wealth was in the hands of 2 percent of its population and he knew which side he wanted to be on. Since concluding "the only thing these people understand is money," it was natural that Joe methodically decided to enter banking. "Sooner or later, [it is] the source of all business," he told a reporter several years later. "I was careful to choose a ladder with more than one rung because I knew banking could lead a man anywhere." Or as he more brusquely put it to a friend, "If you want to make money, go where the money is."

Banking, like just about everything else in Boston, was the jurisdiction of the Brahmins, but among the hundreds of financial institutions operating in the state were small single-branch banks such as Columbia Trust, serving local residents and small businesses. With only $100,000 plus in capital, its primary attraction for Joe was that P. J. Kennedy was a member of the board of directors and was currently serving as vice president.

Joe began at the family bank as a clerk under the guidance of Columbia Trust's veteran treasurer, Alfred Wellington. Joe immediately set his sights on becoming a bank examiner and when he passed his civil service exam, he didn't leave anything to chance. Once again he went to see the mayor, this time armed with statistics showing that Massachusetts had never had an Irish Catholic bank examiner. Fitzgerald may have looked askance at Kennedy as a suitor for his beloved Rose, but he shared his resentment at being treated as less than a first-class citizen. With the influence of Fitzgerald and Wellington behind him, Kennedy was appointed a state bank examiner in September after working at Columbia Trust for only three months.

There were over five hundred banks in Massachusetts and Joe crisscrossed the state, analyzing thousands of records. It was the equivalent of a crash course in financial structure, operations, and loan criteria, and it would serve him well the rest of his life. He disciplined himself to be impressed with nothing except the bottom line and claimed the most important lesson he learned was "we make a mistake when we call money hard cash. It's lively and fluid—the blood of business."

After working for less than a year, Joe took his own trip to Europe during the summer of 1913 with several college friends. He was a curious traveler, eager to see how others lived and carefully noting what the wealthier passengers wore and how they conducted themselves. One of his companions recalled how Joe befriended the ship's purser and arranged to take over one of the premier suites for a reduced rate. From then on, "there was nothing to do but travel to Europe like Kings."

Even if his continental travels fell short of the ease that Rose Fitzgerald was used to, Joe returned with a deeper sense of self-assurance and a determination to marry her. They were both ambitious, confident, and "born to conquer," in some ways, Rose even more so than Joe. She was, however, content within her world as "the leader of the young Catholic set in Boston." If she wasn't welcome in the highest echelon of women's clubs, Rose simply started her own. Yet she also had a sense of entitlement, such as her assumption that as the mayor's daughter, she shouldn't have to pay the fare when taking the streetcar. Joe never thought he deserved something for nothing: little was off-limits, but nothing was assumed.

Rose saw in Joe someone very much like her father, a man who was the star of every room he walked into and, just as important, one who was proud to have her on his arm. Both men made a habit of being immaculately dressed; "dapper, debonair and bubbling with good cheer."

Honey Fitz must have seen himself in Joe too, but a different reflection than the one Rose perceived. He saw a man willing to pull strings and take shortcuts as well as a womanizer with a bifurcated life, one lived to the fullest in the outside world and one lived very separately, and only occasionally, at home. Joe may well have been dedicated in his courting of Rose, but he was also already known as a man about town and the mayor did not have to go far to find that out.

Up to that point, both men had kept their extracurricular love lives out of the public arena, but that was about to change for the mayor. In the midst of Fitzgerald's reelection campaign, his opponent, the man he had once mentored, James Michael Curley, had a letter sent to the mayor's wife, detailing her husband's affair with a beautiful young "cigarette girl," one Elizabeth "Toodles" Ryan. Curley threatened to go public with the information if Fitzgerald stayed in the race. To show he was serious about spreading the story, he announced a series of lectures including one entitled "Great Lovers of History: From Cleopatra to Toodles."

Even in her self-imposed isolation, Josie Fitzgerald must have heard stories about her husband and other women, but she had suffered in relative silence. This time, however, she confronted him over the potentially acute public embarrassment and the possible ruination of her daughters' futures. Whatever Josie said to Honey Fitz, it worked. Reporters who had been writing that Fitzgerald had the race won in a landslide were shocked when Edward Moore, the mayor's secretary, announced that exhaustion from overwork was forcing Fitzgerald to withdraw "under the advice of my physician."

Another immediate repercussion of the Toodles episode was that whatever moral authority Honey Fitz had held over Rose and Joe evaporated. Less than two weeks after the now lame-duck mayor's announcement, the *Boston Herald* reported that Rose was rumored to be engaged to a "well known businessman" and within several more weeks, Joe was given the opportunity of proving his worth.

IN LATE 1913, Columbia Trust found itself threatened with an attempted takeover by a larger East Boston bank. Columbia Trust's president, Frank Wood, was in favor of selling out, but P. J. Kennedy wanted to remain independent. Joe stepped in to lead the effort to gather enough stock to keep the bank and yet even with the help of several maternal uncles, a few other relatives, and a Harvard friend or two, he was $15,000 short. For that, he went to Eugene Thayer, president of Merchants National, one of Boston's largest banks. Kennedy's passion and obvious knowledge persuaded Thayer to come through with the loan and when the smoke cleared, Wood obviously needed to be replaced. After P.J. and Wellington withdrew their names from consideration, Joe was elected president of Columbia Trust. On January 21, 1914, the *Boston Herald* ran a picture of a smiling twenty-five-year-old Kennedy above the heading "Youngest President of Massachusetts Bank."

"Things don't happen, they are made to happen in the public relations field," Joe would later tell his sons "a thousand times," and he made things happen after he took over Columbia Trust. Newspapers throughout the country were soon reporting the rise of "America's youngest bank president" and then "The youngest bank president in the world." Columbia Trust might have been one of the smallest banks in the state,

America's youngest bank president, 1914

but turning an accident into destiny, assuming no one would look too deeply, was becoming another of Kennedy's areas of expertise. He also trusted his relatives to keep quiet when he failed to pay back their accounts that he had accessed to retain control of the bank.

The official announcement of Rose and Joe's engagement was made that June and finally, at the age of twenty-four, Rose could bask in the anticipation of her marriage. She had enjoyed being her father's "hostess, companion, helper" and looked forward to taking on a similar role with Joe, but this time at his side as an equal partner.

Fitzgerald's fall from grace was reflected in the size and scope of the wedding. In contrast to Rose's coming-out party, which had been hailed as "the most gala event of the season," her nuptials were attended by both sets of parents and a few siblings and friends. Rose's sister Agnes was maid of honor, and Joe's Harvard friend Joe Donovan was best man. While it was nine on a Wednesday morning when Cardinal O'Connell performed the private ceremony in the chapel in his home, Rose was beautifully dressed in full white satin bridal regalia. After a simple reception at the Fitzgerald home, Joe and Rose caught the one o'clock train to New York to begin their long-planned honeymoon.

The newlyweds checked into the Belmont Hotel and then went to see *He Comes Up Smiling* starring Douglas Fairbanks. After two nights in New York, they headed for Philadelphia, where their "Miracle Boston Braves" were taking on the heavily favored Athletics in the World Series. Rose, who had become a fan attending games with her father, now cheered with her husband as the Braves won both the

Rose in her wedding dress, 1914

Friday and Saturday games. Rose and Joe then took the night train to White Sulphur Springs, West Virginia, where they had reserved a suite at the luxurious Greenbrier Hotel. They rode horses in the morning and played tennis and golf together in the afternoon, enjoying each other and the couples they met at the exclusive resort. After eleven days and nights, Joe and Rose headed north to Atlantic City, where they saw Nazimova in a Broadway-bound play before returning to New York for more theater and dining and dancing at the Biltmore.

They moved into their new home at 83 Beals Street in "overwhelmingly Protestant" Brookline, twenty minutes west of downtown Boston. Joe had put $2,000 down on the $6,000 house several months before and while Rose described it as "common looking," it had three bedrooms in addition to two maids' rooms. From the beginning of their marriage, they had hired help, the first being "a gay neat Irish girl who cooked and served and made the beds at 7 [dollars] a week." Their first child, Joseph Patrick, Jr., was born nine months and eighteen days after their wedding.

A Brookline residence meant Joe was again taking the ferry each day, albeit in the opposite direction than when he was going to Boston Latin. As soon as he arrived at the bank each morning, everyone could feel the electricity, his longtime secretary, Ethel Turner, remembered. "His voice would boom out for whomever he needed at that moment." It would be fifteen years until Herbert Hoover became the first president to have a telephone on his desk, but Kennedy was already living by his phone. He took the then revolutionary step of installing a "silencer" on the mouthpiece so others could not overhear his conversations. From his perch as president of Columbia Trust, he invested in real estate as well as serving on several boards of directors, making friends, contacts, and money. Saturday nights were for the symphony and the Kennedys were among the youngest patrons of the Boston orchestra. On Sundays, Joe put his young son in their new Ford Sedan and drove out to visit his parents in Winthrop.

The American economy was booming, in part because of the war that had been raging in Europe since 1914. Citizens could tell themselves they had little at stake in what happened across the ocean and reelect President Wilson on his promise of keeping their boys out of harm's way, yet by April of 1917, U.S. banks had committed more than $2 billion in loans to the Allies. The financiers' growing belief that their prosperity was intrinsically tied to an Allied victory helped push Wilson to sign a declaration of war and, a month later, the Selective Service Act, requiring all men between eighteen and thirty to register for the draft. A vehement isolationist, Kennedy may well have genuinely agonized as he watched his friends and business colleagues enlist for a cause he believed America had no reason to join, but Doris Kearns Goodwin concluded "the truth is that his abstract feelings of patriotism and justice were simply not as strong as his fundamental principle of self interest."

Joe was determined to avoid serving and claimed exemption by virtue of "Dependency." He was now the father of two with the birth that very month of his second son, named John Fitzgerald after Rose's father, and immediately dubbed Jack. No matter how Joe justified his deferment request to himself and the Selective Service, his granddaughter Amanda Smith says that his failure to enlist "resulted in cooled relations between himself and a number of his friends and contemporaries."

Now twenty-eight years old and perfectly healthy, Joe was notified he was listed "Class 1"; being a father and presiding over a bank were insufficient reasons for a deferment. By the time he appealed, he was able to explain that he had resigned from the presidency of Columbia Trust in October of 1917 to take on the "public service" of being the assistant general manager of Bethlehem's Fore River Ship Building Corporation.

On the porch with Joe Junior, 1916

The man responsible for Joe's career change was Guy Currier, a wealthy Episcopalian who had graduated from the Massachusetts Institute of Technology in 1888, the same year Kennedy was born. Currier went to California after finishing college, but when his father was killed in an accident a few years later, Guy returned home to take over the family finances. He graduated from Boston University School of Law in 1895, was elected to a term in the Massachusetts House, and then moved to the Senate. Confident he had learned all he could after six years in the legislature, Currier returned to the business world, combining his experiences and contacts to become a powerful lawyer, lobbyist, and trustee for a variety of companies.

Currier was a Renaissance man who traveled extensively in Europe and amassed an impressive library of first editions. He was a progressive Democrat who was a confidant of Republicans such as President Taft and Massachusetts's Governor Calvin Coolidge. Currier shunned the limelight and methodically refrained from befriending the press. He took to studying the art of employment negotiations, wrote a book on the subject, and grew to be respected by both management and labor.

Kennedy's new mentor was a magnet for accomplished, smart individuals no matter what their backgrounds, and he firmly believed that prejudice only served to reduce the talent pool. Currier took the time and energy to foster potential whenever he found it and he liked what he saw in Joe Kennedy. Perhaps Joe was a little too anxious to please, but Cur-

Young Guy Currier

rier thought he had "an excellent brain" and took him on as a protégé. Twice before, Joe had tried and failed to become a member of the board of Massachusetts Electric, but when Guy Currier put the word out, Kennedy was elected. Just as he believed he should be, Joe was sitting at the same table with the great-grandson of John Quincy Adams, and other descendants of the state's founding fathers as well as the powerful Gordon Abbott, head of the Old Colony Trust Company, and the financier Galen Stone. And once again, Joe promoted himself in the press with the announcement he was now "one of the youngest trustees of a big corporation as well as the youngest bank president in the country."

One of the hats Currier wore in 1917 was counsel to Bethlehem Shipbuilding. When their vice president, Joseph Powell, was looking for a savvy administrator to be the number two man at Bethlehem's newly organized Fore River shipyards in Quincy, Currier set up a lunch for Powell to meet Kennedy.

America's entry into the war resulted in a quantum growth in the government's control of the economy and money flowed into shipbuilding. Joe's work in Quincy consumed him as the steep increase in shipbuilding eventually required 25,000 workers, who in turn needed to be transported, housed, fed, and pushed to produce. As the chief financial officer, he often put in sixty hours a week overseeing the extensive agreements necessary to run the plant and the company's wide-ranging insurance businesses. His salary and bonus would reap him $20,000 a year, but he also personally profited by contracting to run the Fore River cafeteria and restaurant. Still, he made time to help organize the company baseball team, which played in a league composed of other Bethlehem plants.

When the professional baseball season was cut short because all "able bodied men" were needed for war work, Kennedy and one of his accountants, Clinton "Pat" Scollard, who also served as the in-house team manager, came up with a plan to hire athletes "worried not about salary but about the draft." Dangling the possibility of an industrial deferment, Kennedy recruited Boston Red Sox pitcher Hub Leonard, but when he reported for his first day of work just in time to pitch that afternoon, complaints were heard from other plants. While Joseph Powell lamented that "this amateur stuff is no good in the Bethlehem league this year" and was tempted to allow the pros to immediately enter the fray, he ultimately ruled that men had to work for the company for a given amount of time before being put on the roster.

Even though shipbuilding was considered essential to the war effort, Joe's latest request for a draft deferment was denied. Almost frantic, he went directly to Powell for help. The Bethlehem vice president made two separate pleas to the draft board and then personally cabled friends in Washington with the claim that to put Kennedy "in Class 1 is inexcusable." Joe received his deferment in the late spring of 1918.

The war was over by mid-November, but Kennedy stayed on at Fore River and then took several months off to recuperate "from nervous and physical exhaustion." After putting in almost inhuman hours, he rested at company expense while giving a hard look at what to do next. His father had stepped in as president of Columbia Trust and while Joe kept abreast of the bank's activities, he didn't want to return in an official capacity. Instead, he decided the best roost was one where he could learn while having the flexibility to continue his own investments, so he officially resigned from Fore River in June of 1920 and accepted an offer from the banking and brokerage firm Hayden, Stone.

Kennedy knew Galen Stone, co-founder of the firm, as a fellow trustee of Massachusetts Electric, a friend of Guy Currier's, and a man who had been doing business with Mayor Fitzgerald for years. Twenty years Kennedy's senior, Stone not only hired Joe, but took the young man under his wing. Their offices were located in the heart of downtown Boston and occupied almost half of the seven-story New England Mutual Life Insurance Building. The lobby "resembled a gracious library in an exclusive men's club," complete with original paintings and oriental rugs and Kennedy liked the feeling of belonging in such surroundings. No more ferries for him.

Joe's base pay was $10,000 a year, well above the national average but hardly sufficient for a man dreaming of becoming a millionaire. Yet one of the attractions of Hayden, Stone was that the earning potential was unlimited because employees were free to invest in whatever caught their fancy along the way. Kennedy soon mastered the fine art of making quick profits through the then legal practice of stock pools. A group of brokers came together and appointed a manager to oversee the buying of a particular stock to push the price upward. When the ticker tapes in more than two dozen stock exchanges throughout the nation reflected the rise in activity, many smaller investors assumed that it was time to jump on the gravy train, pushing the price still higher. The press could help with the illusion, and Kennedy learned which reporters were the most malleable and cultivated them. At what was gauged to be a top price, the pool manager then sold the pool's shares en masse, taking a nice profit, usually sending the stock price downward and leaving the unattached investors with the losses.

Kennedy worked so intensely on establishing himself and expanding his holdings that "his sense of well being was profoundly associated with his ability to smell the market." Traveling often between New York and Boston, Joe was becoming known as a whip-smart loner who kept his business close to the vest.

# CHAPTER 2

# "This Is Another Telephone"

## (1919–1920)

*K*ennedy's banking experience heavily influenced his work at Hayden, Stone. His eyes never wavered from the bottom line of the investments he explored, but that obsession didn't stop him from combining profits with entertainment. His appreciation of chorus girls went along with his enjoyment of theater in general and the acrobatic comic Fred Stone was a particular favorite. Kennedy had first seen him in 1914 when Stone was partnering with Dave Montgomery, performing their songs and dances in blackface. After Montgomery's death in 1917, Stone developed a solo musical comedy act in which he walked a tightrope, danced in ice skates, and performed on horseback. He was headlining on the vaudeville circuit, but looking for a way to keep his name in lights during the off-season.

As Kennedy became friendly with Stone and his manager, Arthur Houghton, he asked if they had thought about making films. Joe had never made a movie, but he had seen people lined up outside theaters waiting to put their money down to get in. On the stage, profits were limited to the capacity of one theater, but put Fred Stone on the screen and he could be seen in hundreds of theaters throughout the country. Stone's name was already established and Joe was convinced his fame as a vaudevillian would translate into that of a movie personality. Films could be made in the summer when the stages were dark and, to put his money where his mouth was, or more accurately, his associate Daniel Gurnett's money, Kennedy would produce the films. By May of 1919, Joe had Stone's signature on a contract committing him to make films that were essentially recordings of his various vaudeville acts for the next five summers. Stone agreed to work for an advance of $1,000 a week while he was filming and that "salary" was to be paid back through his own percentage of the net profits.

"Joe Kennedy knew as much about movies as I know about flying a plane," Gloria Swanson later claimed, but he did know enough about accounting to ensure that every possible production and distribution cost was taken out of the gross before calculating the net profits. If, for some reason, there wasn't enough left after one film to repay the advance, the charges were to be rolled over and taken out of the next film. Kennedy didn't have to pay Stone his percentage until a year after the release date and Joe gave himself a salary of $100 a week as well as an expense account. His responsibility was to arrange with a company to make and distribute the films; to give himself an added safety net, Joe was not only the producer for Fred Stone Productions, he was also the treasurer.

Fred Stone was one of many irons Kennedy had in the fire. He leased a summer beach house for his family, but the schedule he kept usually allowed him to join them only on weekends, if that. Other priorities kept taking precedence, such as the weekend in the late summer of 1919 when he mixed business with pleasure on a 150-mile road trip to Maine with his friend Joe Conway. Their destination was William Gray's lakeside cabin to enjoy the outdoors and discuss Gray's expanding theater business.

Bill Gray was in his mid-thirties and had been through most states and tried many jobs by the time he landed in Lewiston, Maine, in 1914. Running a dance hall in Portsmouth, New Hampshire, he spotted the growing popularity of the one-reel movies shown between dances. Gray turned the hall into a full-time movie theater and proceeded to buy and refurbish sites in Portland, Lewiston, and other nearby towns. By the time Kennedy and Conway arrived at Gray's house, the Maine and New Hampshire Theatres Company boasted several dozen venues throughout New England.

Joe assumed that the company was in need of a loan or at least financial advice, yet as they sat out on Gray's front porch, nothing of the kind was mentioned. In fact, as Bill Gray talked about his business, it sounded too good to be true. "What's this fellow giving me?" Kennedy whispered to Conway, who assured him he "never knew him to exaggerate." Gray took his doubts as a friendly challenge and insisted they go to his office, where he kept the books. There was no arguing with him, so the three men headed for downtown Lewiston.

Kennedy took his time going over the ledgers. He was always willing to ask for information if he thought the man across the table knew more than he did, and Gray clearly knew about exhibition. Joe pummeled him with questions. The numbers told him that while the entire company was valued at a little over $300,000, it was grossing almost $200,000 a year. Kennedy didn't declare his conclusions until he was back in the car with Conway, but by then he couldn't restrain his enthusiasm. If the accounts were accurate, and he had no reason to doubt that they were, the profits were "astounding." He set a new course when he told Conway, "This is another telephone and we must get into this business."

With new determination, Kennedy began studying "the trades," the journals that had sprung up to cover the business side of film. *Variety* had originated to report on vaudeville but started writing about movies in 1907 because one-reelers were shown between stage acts. *Moving Picture World* began printing that same year, and by 1919, there were half a dozen chroniclers of the film business, including *Motion Picture News, Film Daily,* and the *Motion Picture Herald.* Not only were there huge profits at stake, but other bankers and investors didn't seem to realize it.

Kennedy liked what he saw and told a fellow broker, "Look at that bunch of pants pressers in Hollywood making themselves millionaires. I could take the whole business away from them."

"Pants pressers" was his euphemism for the almost exclusively Jewish immigrants who had begun as glove salesmen, furriers, or junk dealers and through hard work, foresight, luck, and timing had risen to run burgeoning studios. Moviemaking in 1919 was still coming into its own, built to that point primarily by immigrants, women, and those not welcome, let alone allowed, in "legitimate" professions. Films were a magnet for creative entrepreneurs and soon there were hundreds of small companies making movies, most of them financed by the profits of the last one.

Kennedy might have just discovered films, but the medium had been evolving for over twenty-five years. The Lumière brothers in France are credited with the first public screening of short films in late 1895, and the following spring, Thomas Edison, who had introduced the peepshow Kinetoscope, displayed a film in which waves pounded toward the audience from the screen, followed by a larger-than-life Annabelle Sun dancing seductively for a few minutes. Edison's primary focus was on the equipment, cameras, and projectors, but at Gaumont in Paris, Alice Guy was fashioning dramatic film stories each evening after she finished her secretarial duties. In 1903, Edwin Porter in New Jersey filmed and then edited over a dozen shots into a several-minute narrative he called *The Great Train Robbery.* Short films were soon being used as "chasers" to clear out vaudeville customers before the next live performance, yet their popularity pushed proprietors to build separate halls, dubbed nickelodeons because of the entrance fee. When audiences wanted to know the names of the actors they were beginning to recognize from one film to the next, fan magazines, starting with *Photoplay* in 1912, spawned an auxiliary industry.

Movies were a cheap form of entertainment aimed primarily at the lower classes until Adolph Zukor, a Hungarian immigrant furrier turned arcade owner, had the bright idea to import a French film, *Queen Elizabeth*, starring Sarah Bernhardt. By carefully presenting the almost hour-long film as a prestigious event and then selling the rights to distribute it state by state, Zukor quadrupled his investment. Then George Kleine screened the Italian eight-reeler *Quo Vadis?* at the Astor in New York, and it ran for several months at a dollar a ticket. It didn't take long before first-class theaters were built exclusively to show movies and the Strand in New York opened its doors in 1914 with the premiere of one of the first American-made feature length films, *The Spoilers.* The next year, there were lines around the block to see D. W. Griffith's *The Birth of a Nation,* which President Wilson heralded as "history written in lightning." While the earlier epics all attracted a growing, wide-ranging audience, it was the technically brilliant and shockingly racist *The Birth of a Nation* that brought audiences from all classes into movie theaters.

Films also played a pivotal role in turning an isolation-inclined nation into one that proactively supported America's entry into World War I. Blatantly promoting the Allied cause, *Johanna Enlists* encouraged soldiers not to stop "until we've taken the 'Germ' out of Germany." The enemy was demonized in the none-too-subtle *To Hell with the Kaiser* and *The Kaiser—The Beast of Berlin,* with audiences urged to "come and hiss." Newsreels informed the hinterlands of the war's progress and when Mary Pickford, Douglas Fairbanks, Marie Dressler, and Charlie Chaplin made public appearances, they caused near riots while selling millions of dollars in war bonds. With the Armistice in November 1918, there was no doubting either the power or the patriotism of the film industry. As historian Kevin Brownlow summarizes it, "The movies had clearly shown the effectiveness with which they could exploit a nation's latent hatred and the box office had shown its profitability."

World War I also had a cataclysmic effect on the business of films. Before the assassination in Sarajevo that sparked the war, the quality of French and Italian films far surpassed that of those made in America. As the war progressed, production facilities were shut down and theaters taken over by occupying armies. At the war's end, European filmmaking was crippled and American movies dominated the world market.

An armistice of a different sort had been declared by the courts, ending Edison's attempt to monopolize the rights to filmmaking equipment and thereby control who made and exhibited movies. Independent companies that had fled to Cuba, Mexico, and California were now free to grow and they were booming. While filmmakers were operating all over the country, there were more than one hundred movie companies in Los Angeles in 1919.

It was a cash-on-the-barrelhead business, precarious in the best of times. Theater owners routinely paid a quarter of their rental fees in advance and the remainder when the film was delivered so everyone was dealt a devastating blow by the flu epidemic of 1918. Two thirds of the country's theaters were closed for at least a week and, as a result, many small companies went out of business.

Even though over a million movie tickets were sold in 1919, traditional bankers willing to make conventional loans to filmmakers were scarce. One exception was A. H. Giannini, the brother of Bank of Italy founder A. P. Giannini, who had been extending credit to filmmakers for a decade.

Kennedy let it be known there was another investor open to discussing film financing. He approached William Gray about buying his Maine and New Hampshire Theatres Company outright, but Gray had no desire to sell. He did agree to put Joe on retainer as an advisor and to look for appropriate real estate to enlarge the circuit. Aside from the salary, the Maine and New Hampshire connection gave Kennedy continued access to the books and a title with a going concern that enhanced his entrée to other companies.

With Gray making such good money screening films, Kennedy looked for ways to grab a percentage of the production end. Confident in his belief that well-known personalities were brand names begging to be exploited on the screen, Joe sought out famous figures to sign. Sam Goldwyn had Will Rogers under contract and Jesse Lasky was producing films starring Harry Houdini, so Joe found Babe Ruth, the twenty-four-year-old left-hander who had led the Boston Red Sox to victory in three of the last four World Series. Joe was so sure he had a winner that he bought an option on Ruth for $100 to start making a movie within the next three weeks. The agreement guaranteed the ballplayer $10,000 for his appearance in the completed film, the same salary he had earned for the entire 1919 season. With the clock ticking, Joe set up appointments with various production companies, but after ten days of waiting, William Fox personally turned down the idea and no one else was biting.

Ruth was seen as a Boston phenomenon, but at the moment he was enjoying Los Angeles, playing golf and attending meetings about other possible deals. In late October, Ruth cabled Kennedy that if he didn't have full payment for a picture immediately, he was ending the option. If that wasn't disappointing enough, Joe, the baseball fan, must have been devastated when less than two months later Ruth's Red Sox contract was sold to the New York Yankees. Coincidentally, Red Sox owner Harry Frazee was also in the entertainment business and it was reported he needed the cash to finance a new Broadway play.

Kennedy was not about to be discouraged for long. If so much work went into individual productions that then had to be distributed, why not create an umbrella organization to distribute other people's films? He brought together half a dozen local investors, including the attorney Daniel Lyne, who had handled the Ruth contract for him, and created a Boston-based distributing company he called Columbia Films Incorporated. Joe held stock in the company, put himself on salary, and established the company's bank accounts at Columbia Trust. Columbia Films soon had commitments from production companies such as the newly formed Mayflower Photoplay Company and the American Feature Film Company.

The Columbia Films board of directors was a disparate mix of lawyers, diamond importers, and professional investors and they were often mired in a "tangle of tattling," calls for audits, and charges of underhanded payments made to theater owners. When Kennedy missed a meeting, Lyne kept him informed and occasionally joined him in his search for other ventures.

Joe spent months investigating film companies to invest in, but he found his prospective partners demanding "altogether too much for their end of the deal." Kennedy and Lyne then called on Carl Laemmle, head of Universal, a studio known for ten- to twenty-minute films, low budget westerns, serials, and comedies, and the occasional "special" such as Erich von Stroheim's *Blind Husbands.*

Laemmle found in Kennedy "a disposition to be perfectly fair" and told him there was "a keen desirability of getting men of your type" into films; "God knows it needs them." Laemmle, however, was referring to bankers and businessmen who would simply invest and Kennedy had no intention of being anyone's silent partner. He wanted his own slice of the pie so he began negotiating for Universal's New England franchise. A deal with Universal opened new possibilities and gave Joe access to hundreds of theaters for Fred Stone films as well as those distributed by

Columbia Films. Kennedy could not resist making comments about the quality of some of Universal's films, but he called on Guy Currier, who agreed to invest. Then, adding a few small loans to the package, Joe structured the deal to purchase the rights to distribute Universal films in New England for $135,000.

All the while, Kennedy not only kept up his work with Hayden, Stone, but continued to serve on the board of Columbia Trust where he reviewed weekly statements and gave advice on investments and loans. He remained on the lookout for new opportunities and methodically expanded his contacts through a flow of letters and telephone calls as well as frequent trips to New York.

Kennedy did not limit himself to cultivating those in power. Believing "it's the little people in key spots who determine whether you will be successful," he developed a lifelong habit of charming the women behind the men. He sent flowers to secretaries and invited them to dinner. He attached handwritten notes on top of his letters to their bosses, laced with endearing comments before asking them to be sure his requests were handled quickly. He treated them like attractive, entertaining women worthy of attention on their own, and the gossip, genuine information, and consideration he received in return was priceless.

When Kennedy went on the road, he rarely traveled alone. Sometimes he brought along business associates who were also friends such as Joe Conway or Daniel Lyne, but the man most often at Joe's side was Eddie Moore. They had first met when Moore was Mayor Fitzgerald's personal secretary and Kennedy was courting Rose. A native of Somerville, Massachusetts, Eddie served Fitzgerald for four full years and stayed on a few months after Mayor Curley took over, all the while sharpening his diplomatic skills and his dry sense of humor. Moore began investing in real estate with Kennedy as early as 1915, was appointed to the city's Election Department, and tried his hand at running his own poultry business, but he returned to his role as the mayor's secretary after Andrew Peters was elected in 1918. When Joe left Fore River, he arranged for Eddie to become the assistant to the general manager, a perfect position to keep his eyes on Kennedy's continuing interests in Quincy.

Whenever possible, Eddie made himself available to travel with Joe and, if there was extra time in the day, the men might get in a round of golf. Evenings in New York, Chicago, and even Boston were often for being entertained by friends such as the impresario Charles Dillingham and Arthur Houghton, who in turn introduced Kennedy to their friends such as the actor John Barrymore. It was heady stuff to say nothing of the

Joe and Eddie Moore at White Sulphur Springs, 1921

joys of the attendant chorus girls. As Joe wrote to Arthur in response to an invitation to a party, "count on me and let me know the details so we can work up an appetite." Eagerly awaiting another night on the town, Joe told him, "I hope you have all those good looking girls in your company looking forward, with anticipation, to meeting the high Irish of Boston, because I have a gang around me who must be fed on wild meat (lately, they are so bad). As for me, I have too many troubles around me to bother with such things at the present time. Everything may be better, however, when you arrive."

Joe may have feigned fatigue to his friends, but back home in Brookline, it was Rose Kennedy who was getting tired. It was shortly after Christmas of 1919 and Rose was seven months pregnant with her fourth child when she decided she just couldn't take it anymore. Only five years earlier, she and Joe had been planning their future together and she had envisioned a life as his active partner in a stimulating community. That, she was now realizing, had been a romantic fantasy. Before the Toodles revelation, it hadn't occurred to Rose that her mother's misery was the result of anything her beloved father had done. She had watched her mother become resentful, bitter, and isolated over Honey Fitz's absences and yet blamed her mother for choosing to respond the way she did. Now Rose had to wonder. She was in a fine home, but with few friends in the neighborhood. She had three young children, Joe Junior (four), Jack (two), and Rosemary (one), and another on the way. Her husband leased a beach house for the family for four months each summer, but Rose, never making herself fully aware of Joe's finances, considered that "a great extravagance." For Joe, it was tangible evidence he was providing the best for his family while he was off working or on his own. He was gone most of the time and when he was at home, he often didn't want to talk about his work. He played with the children, listened to music, or buried himself in Wall Street news or detective novels. And though Rose would never publicly acknowledge her awareness of her husband's infidelity, a relative told a family biographer, "Even in the early years of their marriage, Joe had a reputation for being a ladies' man and some of this gossip must have caught up with Rose."

A series of women was one thing; one in particular was something else again. Now the word was that there was one specific New York actress whom Joe was seeing on a regular basis. The beautiful blonde who was galvanizing his attention was the twenty-two-year-old star of *The Miracle Man,* Betty Compson. She found him romantic and generous as he lavished her with flowers, "diamonds and furs." Eventually, it was Compson who ended the relationship because she heard so many stories of Joe and chorus girls that his "promiscuity was too much for her."

Home alone with her children and the hired help, Rose was feeling so diminished that she "simply couldn't go on living with a man who treated her with such contempt," says Jack Kennedy biographer Nigel Hamilton. She packed

Betty Compson

her bags, left the staff in charge of the children, and moved back into her old room at her parents' house.

Doris Kearns Goodwin believes Rose suffered "a mini breakdown at that time. She couldn't cope with it any more. She had lost her roots, her place in the world and her only answer was to go home to her father and somehow hope to recapture who she was; Rosie Fitzgerald not just Mrs. Kennedy." Yet once Rose was in Dorchester, it was as if no one noticed. Joe didn't come to see her, but still she waited. Finally, after three long weeks, her father confronted her. "Go back where you belong," he told her. "The old days are gone. Your children need you and your husband needs you. You can make things work."

If Rose did suffer a breakdown, she certainly didn't receive the support she needed. Her mother was as remote as ever and the father who had opened the doors to the public life she craved was now telling her she had no alternative but to return to the permanently subservient role she found stifling, degrading, and unfulfilling.

Nationally, women were finally being "given" the vote with the ratification of the Nineteenth Amendment, and the Jazz Age was beginning. "We got the vote and the barbers got our hair," young women chanted as they cut off their long tresses and traded in their corsets for loose-fitting chemises. Though Rose was only in her late twenties, she identified with the previous Victorian generation.

Betrayed by the two most important men in her life, Rose reached back to the satisfaction she had found in meditation and prayer at her European convent. Searching to make the best of a difficult situation, she sought out an alternative reality at a local Catholic retreat. She emerged with a determination to take her father's command as a challenge and make his words work for her. "You have made your commitment and you must honor it." That she would do, not as her mother had done with resentment or martyrdom, but as a higher calling, as a manager of the family she now thought of as "my enterprise."

Joe was taken aback by the separation; he didn't understand it. "Rosie," he asked in all sincerity, "what's the matter with you? You are a mother." To his mind, that should have been more than enough to make her happy. He tried to be more present and attentive, but within weeks of her return they faced a crisis that shook him more deeply than his wife's absence.

As Rose was at home giving birth to their daughter Kathleen on February 20, 1920, two-year-old Jack was showing the early symptoms of scarlet fever. His condition worsened quickly, and with the help of Joe's father-in-law and Mayor Peters, Joe was successful in getting Jack admitted to Boston Hospital, which had only a fraction of the beds necessary for the number of stricken children. For the two months Jack was hospitalized, sometimes improving, often worse, Joe cut his work time in half, went to Mass every morning, and spent his afternoons at Jack's bedside. Almost willing Jack to recover, Joe went through his own familial conversion and made his own bargain with God, vowing to be more charitable and put a new emphasis on his family. Joe supported his wife in anything financial or material she needed and, for a while, he was even home more often. Rose must have been encouraged when Joe was appointed the manager of the Stock Exchange Department of the Hayden, Stone Boston office, assuming it would keep him in town. They went out together to the theater and dined with friends more frequently. Rose exacted the promise from Joe that he would try harder to be home for dinner, a time she sought to ritualize with the children. As Rose put it, Joe's acquiescence "made me feel I had a partner in my enterprise."

Joe arranged for Columbia Trust to buy him a larger and more imposing home, but instead of relocating closer to downtown or near Rose's parents and friends in Dorchester, they moved only a block from their other Brookline residence. Still, the two-and-a-half-story house on the corner of Naples and Abbotsford was imposing with its bay windows and wide wraparound porch. It featured three bathrooms and four fireplaces, an intercom system throughout, and, for Rose, a bedroom of her own. The size of their household staff increased as well. They now had a baby nurse, a governess, and a full-time housekeeper. And even though Eddie Moore was still officially working at Fore River in Quincy, he and his wife, Mary, moved into the Kennedys' old house on Beals Street, close at hand whenever they were needed.

Eddie was Rosemary's godfather and he checked regularly on Jack's progress when the boy was sent with his governess to Poland Spring in Maine for two months of continued recovery. It was also Eddie who took Rose to the theater or the movies in Joe's absence. And it was Eddie who coordinated the letters of support for Kennedy when he lobbied to become President Wilson's assistant secretary of the treasury in the spring of 1920.

While a national appointment would have been a feather in his cap and a ticket out of parochial Boston, it is difficult to imagine Joe being all that serious about public service in 1920, as so much of his attention was given to accumulating wealth. First and foremost, Joe saw his primary duty to his family as providing for them financially, not just sufficiently, but substantially. With the birth of each child, he opened a Columbia Trust bank account in their name and bought Rose an impressive piece of jewelry. At the age of thirty-two, Joe spoke of becoming a millionaire within the next few years and, increasingly, he saw movies as the way to do it.

# CHAPTER 3

# "I Have Just Reorganized the Company"

## (1920–1921)

There is no question Kennedy entered films because of his financial interest," says his granddaughter Amanda Smith, "but he immediately delved into every minute detail of production." By early 1920, Kennedy had his hand in Maine and New Hampshire Theaters, Columbia Films, Fred Stone Productions, and the New England Universal film franchise. He picked up commissions or stockholdings with each deal as well as cash flow from salaries, dividends, and expense accounts, but he was still looking for the big ticket. Joe put out the word that if any film-related proposals came in to Hayden, Stone, he wanted to handle them and he was soon inundated with requests for financing everything from individual theaters to distribution syndicates; he even fielded casting suggestions.

Hayden, Stone as a company appears to have been hesitant to invest in the film business, but Joe wasn't. He was careful to keep the records separate, but there were times when his interests and the company's threatened to conflict such as when Phil Boyer in the New York office suggested Joe call on Frank Hall, president of Hallmark Pictures Corporation. Only a few months before, Hall had merged his own interests with half a dozen smaller distribution and production companies to offer "better and more efficient service, better pictures and assistance from an exploitation office" on a national scale.

Kennedy met with Hall and was intrigued, but when he heard that Charles Hayden might be interested, Joe told him that he believed Hallmark wasn't a proposition "that would interest the firm at all." Hallmark was too small for Hayden, Stone to bother with and any investment would be "entirely speculative." Hallmark had already been through most of the $500,000 the company had raised and was using its stock to pay for services and salaries. At best, it was breaking even.

Yet within days of telling Hayden, Stone all the reasons to forget

Hallmark, Kennedy was doing business with Frank Hall. Hallmark appeared to have everything Joe wanted in his own film investments: production capabilities, a distribution network, and the marketing ability to sell the films. It was a national, "on going concern" offering expansion into production and distribution beyond his New England contacts. Hall's plan was to release a film a week, twelve of which would be "special features." He admitted that he still needed to get his hands on a few good films to pull it off, but he convinced Joe that Hallmark was in a unique position to distribute both the films it bought and films from its associated production companies.

Kennedy's apprehension over Hallmark's indebtedness was allayed by Hall's proposal to create a separate financing arm. It would raise money for "several high class productions" without carrying the debts of the original company and minimizing the participation of his now "dissatisfied" partners. And Hall put on the pressure, telling Joe he had to decide immediately, both to take advantage of the films that were available and because J. P. Morgan was "very much interested in the proposition."

Kennedy bit and between December of 1919 and June of 1920, he put over $80,000 into Hallmark. He had been assured that he was to receive the grosses from Hallmark's "Willard-Dempsey Bout Pictures," but by August, both Hallmark and its new financing arm were in receivership. A consolidation of failing companies had added up to a larger failing company and Kennedy's money had done little but buy time before the inevitable collapse.

Joe didn't give up without a fight. He spent time and money entangled in court, trying to collect on promissory notes. Yet the failure of Hallmark was a humbling experience. He had never lost that much of his own money in a single investment and he chastised himself for his "ignorance of the business."

There were dozens of companies like Hallmark, flailing in the wave of credit crunches and mergers. The business was a challenge even for those most familiar with the personalities and the economics, let alone someone such as Kennedy for whom film was just one of many interests. More movie theaters were being built and the demand for films was increasing, but audiences were becoming discerning and most movies were in and out of theaters within a week. For companies with outstanding high-interest loans or without a steady supply of salable films, it took only a bad month or two to spell bankruptcy.

While Joe knew he had much to learn, he believed that the heart of Hallmark's problem was that he had not been the one in charge. He certainly wasn't looking to repeat his role as a minority financier, so when Rufus Cole, whom he had met through Frank Hall, came calling, Kennedy was less than encouraging. Cole was a tall, good-looking Britisher who, along with his partner, Harry Robertson, had formed Robertson-Cole of America to export American cars to India and the United Kingdom. They were soon distributing movies as well and R-C grew into a national distribution network by buying independent films and absorbing vestiges of failing companies such as Hallmark. To expand into production, they were building their own seventeen-acre Hollywood studio. They were not yet ready to begin filming, but Cole went ahead and announced plans to distribute a feature film every week in hopes of attracting new, much needed investors.

"My experience in the picture business with my own money and in some instances with that of my friends has been disastrous," Kennedy told Cole, but he wasn't taking no for an answer. Cole was so desperate for even a small amount of hard cash, he tried to sell Kennedy one or two R-C films to distribute, but Joe wasn't interested in anything if he wasn't in control. Was Cole willing to sell off the New England portion of R-C's distribution network?

Since its inception, R-C had been a national network, but now Cole agreed to separate out New England to reinvigorate the rest of his company. Then the haggling began. Cole claimed they had over $130,000 in "unplayed business," films they had already bought or contracted to distribute in the region but had yet to book. Joe believed the value was half that and then reproached Cole for booking some films into Boston theaters for far less than the going rate. All the give-and-take was hardnosed, but quite civil, and by December it was agreed that Kennedy would form his own wholly owned company, Robertson-Cole Distributing Corporation of New England.

While the majority of Kennedy's surviving papers are now open, those that contain specific monetary amounts, mention stock held in his family's name, or refer to dealings perceived as tainted with illegality usually remain withheld. Because of that, and Joe's propensity to handle so much by telephone, the exact methods he used at key moments in deal making are often difficult to pinpoint. Therefore the following letter is worth reprinting in full for it reveals Kennedy's keen ability to juggle the breadth of his holdings, his access to his extended family members' bank accounts, and how very convenient it was to have a bank in the family to handle these complicated transactions. On December 23, 1920, he wrote his secretary at Columbia Trust the following instructions:

My dear Miss Turner:

I put through a deal yesterday, which I will outline to you so that your records may be clear.

I have formed a Massachusetts corporation called the Robertson-Cole Distributing Corporation of New England, with $100,000 preferred and $200,000 common stock. Yesterday I bought $60,000 worth of the preferred. The $40,000 in the preferred is still in the treasury and I have not decided how the common will be divided.

To get the $60,000 I made the following arrangements:

With the Brookline Trust Company: I withdrew from my loan there 100 Eastern Steamship Preferred, and substituted therefor, 2,100 shares of Columbia Trust and 10 shares United States Envelope Company. With the 200 Todd which you sent me, I took this 100 Eastern Steamship, Preferred, and placed it as part of the collateral in a loan that John F. [Fitzgerald, his father-in-law] has at the Shawmut Bank and received a check from his account with Hayden Stone & Co. with the understanding that when I either sold some of my Robertson-Cole Preferred, or got some additional cash, I should pay back the $20,000 to his account and take back my 200 Todd and 100 Eastern Steamship, Pfd.

In addition to that, I withdrew $5,000 from the account of Mary A. Kennedy [his mother] and placed it to her account in the Columbia Trust Company and then put through a charge ticket against it for $5,000.

I also put through a charge ticket against my own account in the Columbia Trust Company for $5,000.

I also arranged to borrow from the Columbia Trust company $20,000 with miscellaneous collateral furnished by Mr. Fitzgerald, not signed by J. J. Shinkwin.

After you understand this transaction thoroughly, and make out your records, kindly destroy this letter.

Sincerely yours,

Kennedy had assured himself control of Robertson-Cole of New England (RCNE) by owning over half of the preferred stock, yet he had put in only $5,000 of his own money to create a company with an on-paper value of $300,000. Over the next month, he would sell some of the remaining stock to his father-in-law and Joe Conway and then repay himself and some of the loans from his family members' accounts.

The deal's structure is a classic example of the template Kennedy would use throughout his life. Parting with even a small amount of his own money was anathema to him and he resisted it whenever possible. Instead, he made his own expertise and guidance his contribution, using other people's money to bring him profits.

Joe's investments outside of Hayden, Stone were now significant enough to justify opening a separate office at 39 Church Street. He hired Stephen Fitzgibbon, who had been one of his assistants at Fore River, to be the RCNE day-to-day man, supervising film rentals and keeping the accounts. Kennedy also moved his Maine and New Hampshire business to the new office and, at William Gray's request, added one of Gray's associates to his staff. Gray, in turn, agreed to bring on Johnnie Ford, an accountant Joe recommended from Fore River, as his executive assistant at Maine and New Hampshire. Kennedy was confident that everything was in order and took off with several men friends for his January Palm Beach vacation, but he was back in early February to personally supervise the Boston opening of *Kismet,* the first feature film completed at R-C's Hollywood studio.

Starring Otis Skinner, *Kismet* was an epic compared with R-C's usual fare and Joe pulled out all the stops. He arranged for the premiere to be held at the Majestic Theatre, which was usually reserved for live performances, and enlisted his father-in-law to use his "influence with the Boston newspapers" to publicize the event. He also asked Fitzgerald to "drop in on the Shuberts" to see if they would reduce the $3,500 a week rent on the theater.

Advertising began a month in advance and R-C's public relations staff sent over a dozen memos with promotion ideas: hire men "dressed as Arabs" to give away *Kismet* desk blotters, have "attractive girls" hand out flyers, and find music stores willing to put *Kismet* sheet music in their windows. They also proposed camels be paraded down the street in front of the theater, but while all these suggestions came under the guise of support, each had a price tag attached. For instance, one camel was available to be rented and transported to Boston for "only" $150.

Kennedy eventually agreed to buy several hundred blotters and twenty thousand gold and black printed programs to be given to the first run customers. He also rented eight oil paintings of different *Kismet* scenes to hang in the Majestic lobby in advance of the opening. He had been promised Otis Skinner for the premiere, but only days before he was informed "other business" prevented his appearance in Boston. Even Rufus Cole canceled at the last minute, saying his wife was ill and the cable he sent Joe was backhanded at best: "Every wish that the opening of Kismet tonight may have the same success that has been experienced in other large cities."

In the end, the two-week exclusive run was a smash and the people whose opinions Joe did value, such as William Gray, told him it was "a magnificent presentation" and he should be proud.

Kennedy noted each little slight, but continued to use Rufus Cole as best he could. R-C agreed to take over the foreign distribution of Fred Stone films and then the production costs as well, a weight off Joe's mind. And when improbable propositions came to him at Hayden, Stone, he sent them on to Cole in New York asking for his advice. If something came of it, he could share the wealth and if it didn't, he was not the one to say no. With each new contact, Joe expanded his network while offending no one in the process.

Within days of signing off on RCNE, Cole sought Kennedy's help to finance a new corporation to fund future productions. His idea to separate out the company's debt by creating another entity was similar to Hall's attempt to save Hallmark, and Kennedy still felt the tinge of that burn. But Cole had a twist. His new company would buy the old company's Hollywood studio for its cost of $600,000.

Cole bombarded Kennedy with numbers and information and, after a bit of hedging, Joe put the financing plan before Hayden, Stone and advertised it to attract other investors but refused to put in any of his own money. He focused his attention on RCNE and, in the process, found himself with growing doubts about Cole. Joe discovered the relationship between R-C and the local theaters was "not nearly as good" as he had been led to believe and the monies owed were half of what he had been told. He was confident enough in his own abilities (and his belief that the franchise had been mishandled) that he forged ahead, but Cole had gone down another few notches in his estimation. Kennedy concluded that he was a "very good salesman and a pretty good organizer," but he was in over his head.

Cole's biggest concern at the moment was the English bankers to whom he was still very much indebted. Two Anglo banking houses, Graham's and Co., and Cox and Co., had already invested over $5 million in R-C and the drain was continuing. The main offices of many Hollywood studios were in New York, but monitoring finances from London was close to impossible, so the English bankers sent Sir Erskine Crum to America to investigate. Crum arrived with little faith in Rufus Cole, but what he heard about Kennedy intrigued him. Crum asked Joe to come to New York, but then decided that since he didn't want "the present management" to know they were meeting, he would come to Boston for confidential discussions. Kennedy agreed and, in order to divert any suspicions Cole might have, sent Crum a cable he could show Cole stating he was unable to come to New York.

Before even meeting the man, Kennedy had proven his loyalty to Crum, and trading up paid off. Crum appointed Joe to serve on the R-C board of directors and gave him a $1,500 a month salary as an advisor in addition to his director's fees and expenses. As a member of the board, all the books were open to him, and to Kennedy's banker-trained eyes, Cole's balance sheets were a joke. Real value was impossible to grasp when items such as posters were counted as assets to be depreciated. With their numbers changing every week, how could the figures be trusted?

By mid-April of 1921, Crum was threatening to give Cole sixty days to settle his debts or have his company taken over by the bankers. Joe's allegiance had completely shifted to Crum, and in the process, the two men grew closer, trading tidbits about the different personalities they were dealing with and discussing everything from local distribution to potential script problems. Crum depended upon Kennedy for honest assessments and assistance in understanding company budgets, projections, and proposals. Joe spent his time appeasing and cajoling all the involved parties. While telling outsiders that the company was "in excellent financial condition and prospering very successfully," he assured Crum of his "desire to see you out of this situation."

Crum came to the conclusion there was no choice but to sell R-C. He named Kennedy the company's agent and promised him a $75,000 commision. However, Joe soon realized that Cole was also trying to market the company and as R-C's official representative, Joe judiciously complained to Crum. He sympathized, but was not particularly helpful, claiming he just wanted to find a buyer. And he had a complaint of his own. Why did Joe have to show the balance sheets to potential buyers? Then Crum further frustrated Kennedy by making himself unavailable to meet with possible investors.

Selling R-C was clearly going to be an uphill battle, yet Kennedy fought on, reaching out to old friends and making new ones such as the film pioneer William W. Hodkinson. Back in 1908, Hodkinson had noticed the strain on the backs and eyes of customers looking through the peep-show machines to watch one-reel movies, so he opened Chicago's first theater with a large screen and comfortable chairs. He formed Progressive Films, became a prime organizer of Paramount, and claimed that just before the company's first meeting, he sketched the mountain encircled by stars, the logo still used by Paramount today.

Hodkinson was a character with firm ideas who didn't hesitate to call himself a man of "foresight and genius." He was adamant that the business of making films and the business of distributing them were apples and oranges. Paramount initially had been created to distribute other companies' films, beginning with those produced by Bosworth, the Jesse Lasky Feature Play Company, and Adolph Zukor's Famous Players. Within two years, Lasky and Zukor joined forces to push Hodkinson out of Paramount. After a bit of kicking and screaming, he formed his own distribution firm, which went through several incarnations before being renamed the W. W. Hodkinson Corporation, his base when he met with Kennedy in the summer of 1921.

Kennedy was intrigued by Hodkinson and his theories, and he loved sitting across the table, as an equal, with someone who had seen it all. Hodkinson's pitch was that it was "practically impossible" to make enough successful films to justify the costs of carrying a distribution arm. If R-C worked with him, they would be free to concentrate on making good films. He would take care of the rest.

Yet Kennedy knew that Hodkinson's offering price was nowhere near enough to fund productions for the next year. It was true that distribution was a financial drain for R-C, but there were no guarantees that Hodkinson could get more for their films than R-C did now. With a new middleman, they might get even less. Most of all, Joe didn't want to enter into a situation that could threaten his own role at R-C or his New England franchise. Kennedy advised Crum and Cole that Hodkinson had "not much to offer" and warned them that if word got out R-C was dumping their distribution unit, "it would give rise to further suspicion on our ability" to survive as a company. Joe then implied to Hodkinson that it was others who declined his offer, keeping himself in the pioneer's good graces.

Kennedy and Hodkinson spent the next few months discussing taking over each other's distribution interests in New England. In the end, Joe decided that while Hodkinson was interesting to know, he "strikes me as a smart fellow but one with a personality that would be difficult to get along with," and no deal was made.

Joe continued to attend the R-C board meetings, where the company's steady losses dominated the discussions. Declaring bankruptcy was an option that came up often only to be dismissed, since little could be salvaged and it would put the parent company's automobile business at risk. That left two real choices: either severely reduce the asking price or resign themselves to investing even more money. Kennedy declared "we should either go all the way through and do it right or else not put any more money in than we have today," but the rest of the board continued to wallow in micromanagement that revealed how lost they really were. Hours were spent debating issues that staff should have been handling: whether to bring in a coproducer for individual films, if a director should have casting approval on a particular film, the length of actors' contracts, the plot lines of different scripts, and even the potential for success of various titles. They flailed in their attempts to increase income in small but creative ways such as selling scripts they had bought but couldn't afford to produce, reissuing old films, and offering bonuses to the region with the largest increase in sales.

New England was the only franchise in private hands, and the Board discussed selling off other regions. Joe looked at the possibility of expanding his RCNE into a national enterprise, but when he approached Guy Currier and Joe Conway about investing, they agreed that without an increase in the number and quality of R-C productions, whoever was distributing them was doomed to continued failure.

While being the one to sell the company would give Kennedy a nice commission, it would also leave him without a national toehold in the industry. Revisiting all his options, he came up with the idea of masterminding a merger. He was convinced "all these smaller companies are on their way to the poorhouse and nothing can stop them unless a consolidation goes through," and he saw himself as the man to accomplish it.

Claiming "I have just reorganized the company," Joe told the chairman of Goldwyn Pictures that he was meeting with the publisher William Randolph Hearst and then told Hearst he had talked with Goldwyn. His plan was to "get hold of an organization that would consist of Goldwyn, Metro, Robertson-Cole and [Lewis] Selznick."

Hearst, for one, was willing to listen but saw no reason to make a move. When asked why Hearst didn't bite, his biographer David Nasaw says, "He recognized Kennedy was a real businessman, in contrast to the rest of the movie people who he thought had just been lucky, but he also realized how competitive and complex the business was. And his priority was Marion Davies." Hearst's Cosmopolitan Pictures produced a wide variety of films, but his priority was indeed the love of his life, the chorus girl turned accomplished actress, Marion Davies. Hearst would later make a deal to distribute Marion's films through MGM, a studio formed in a merger several years later along the very lines Kennedy envisioned.

If Kennedy had been able to pull it off, he would have created the largest film company of the day. He was absolutely right, but R-C did not have enough real assets relative to debt to make it attractive at the bargaining table. And Joe wasn't a big enough player . . . yet.

# CHAPTER 4

# "Fight like Hell to Win"

## (1921–1923)

Sir Erskine Crum returned to England in the fall of 1921 without declaring a decisive course of action, and Kennedy's frustration was ready to boil over. While he was still receiving his advisor's fees, R-C was also costing him money because until the company turned around, his own RCNE continued to struggle. What he had envisioned as a $300,000 company now had a net worth of a little over $60,000. It had made a profit of only $5,000 over the past nine months and they had less than $100 in ready cash.

Then, to add to his annoyance, Joe heard that Crum was holding meetings in England to sell the company without consulting him. Joe lost his temper, protesting that he had been working "unceasingly" to make R-C a going concern, and the service he was providing "was worth lots more than the monthly salary." If he wasn't going to get his commission on the sale, then the least they could do was let him match any offer on the table. Crum returned to America in December and called Joe on his bluff, telling him that there was "nothing sufficiently definite" from any other buyer and he would be happy to listen to his proposal.

R-C's real assets were its New York office building and the Hollywood studio, but mortgage payments were due on both. With more money going out each month than was coming in, Joe knew the English bankers were desperate. He offered $100,000 in cash for 25 percent of the business with a guarantee that they would receive 75 percent of future income or the profits from a sale. Crum took the offer seriously enough to send it to London for consideration, but in the end it was determined that the amount was insufficient to make a dent in their losses. Once again, the board of directors decided not to decide, hoping that somehow, something would change.

Kennedy was too action-oriented to agree, but he had lost nothing from making his attempt to take over the company except that now he and Crum were a bit more wary of each other. Joe stayed on the board, learning from both the positives and negatives, and turned his time and energy to his other, more profitable, interests. He was working hours on end, busy on all fronts expanding and massaging his contacts and walking the tightrope of representing and investing for Hayden, Stone while serving on the boards of Robertson-Cole and Columbia Trust, being on retainer to Maine New Hampshire, as well as making and protecting his own, separate investments.

In spite of his promises to Rose, Joe was rarely home two nights in a row, but he was amassing the wealth that was so important to him. He bought his first Rolls-Royce and hired a chauffeur to go with it. He positioned himself as a presence in the Boston community where he was ecumenical if not overly generous in his charitable activities. He gave to the Catholic Church, local hospitals, and Harvard as well as the Irish Relief Fund, the Boston Police Fund, the Red Cross, Jewish War Relief, and the Boston American Christmas Basket Fund. He was also a joiner, becoming a member of the Harvard Club in New York, the Boston Athletic Club, the Woodland Golf Club, and the Exchange Club of Boston. Shortly after President Warren G. Harding's election in 1920 Kennedy had joined the Middlesex Club, "the oldest Republican club in New England and one of the three best known Republican clubs in the United States." Henry Cabot Lodge was one of the vice presidents and Joe socialized with members with last names of Bates and Proctor. He also used his membership to advocate that "Irish Catholics are not discriminated against just because they are Irish Catholics."

He was on the entertainment committee for his Harvard reunion and arranged to provide the liquor as well as a screening of the recent Jack Dempsey championship fight. Away from Harvard, Joe could claim he didn't care about his old college, but he thoroughly enjoyed the bonhomie of the all-male reunion and the awareness that anyone who cared to notice had to acknowledge he had done very well indeed over the last ten years.

In 1922, Kennedy attempted to elevate his social standing by moving the family's summer rental from the Catholic-dominated retreat of Nantasket where Rose's parents stayed to the WASP enclave of Cohasset. His name was submitted for membership in the local country club and he was given a list of the members and a five-day guest pass so he could golf and mingle to make his case in person. While some of the members liked "his cut and his attitude," enough others did not and his "application was not found acceptable."

Biographers have speculated that his rejection in Cohasset, following his failure to be accepted in a prestigious club at Harvard, explains his bitterness against Boston and her Brahmins. It certainly is true that it was a deeply held antipathy and one that he released in angry flashes of indignation throughout his life. Joe's tendency was to blame any such rebuffs on the fact he was Irish Catholic and never on the possibility that questions could be raised about his methods of doing business or his reputation as a ladies' man. Without debating the depths of hypocrisy, self-righteousness, and prejudice on both sides, one can easily envision a wealthy Episcopalian's knee-jerk disdain for the man J. P. Morgan, Jr., dismissed as "an Irish Papist and a Wall Street punter," or a society matron's sense of superiority to the daughter of a discredited mayor. Whatever the cause of his defeat or the extent of the wound, Kennedy knew that to dwell on it would accomplish nothing. As he later told his sons, "fight like hell to win, but if you don't, forget about it."

One of the advantages of being engaged in so many interests was that there was always something new around the next corner. The summer and fall of 1922 found Joe involved in two political campaigns, the first being his father-in-law's run for governor. After withdrawing from the mayor's race in 1914, Honey Fitz had tried and failed to be elected to Congress in 1916. He won the same race two years later, but when a congressional investigation revealed blatant and massive voter fraud, "the House voted overwhelmingly to unseat Fitzgerald and swear in his opponent on the spot." None of this discouraged him for long and, through it all, the correspondence with his son-in-law reveals a convivial relationship. Joe regularly asked Fitzgerald for small favors, often involving their mutual financial investments of which Joe was clearly in charge. Now that Fitzgerald was running again, Kennedy didn't record any objections and even used his show business contacts to have Honey Fitz's name woven into the scripts of vaudeville performances. Joe Junior and Jack Kennedy, eight and six, accompanied their grandfather to parades and rallies. He also made time to take them to Red Sox games, visibly reveling in his role as grandfather.

The other campaign that galvanized Joe's attention was the Massachusetts referendum against film censorship. Cries for censorship, at varying decibels, had been with the movies practically since their inception, but they were now at an all-time high, and several dozen laws were pending before voters and legislators throughout the country.

Since the end of the war, righteousness in many forms had been thriving. The Ohio legislature was considering a law to forbid women from wearing skirts a few inches above the ankle and a bill was pending in Virginia to prohibit a woman from showing "more than three inches of her throat." On a far more serious level, the anti-German campaign of the war years had fanned a hatred of foreigners and immigrants that culminated in the full-fledged Red Scare. Attorney General A. Mitchell Palmer led raids that blurred any distinction between lawful union organizers, anarchists, communists, and actual illegal activity; hundreds were deported and thousands jailed without formal charges being filed.

Prohibition was enacted in 1920 after being debated for over seventy-five years. With this victory, the most vociferous reformers were ripe for a new cause when the popular three-hundred-plus-pound comedian Roscoe "Fatty" Arbuckle was arrested for manslaughter in the death of Virginia Rappe following a Labor Day party in San Francisco in 1921. Anyone who had ever blamed Hollywood for postwar cultural changes, loosening morals, or sins of any kind had a new focal point.

Arbuckle was making a million dollars a year because his screen antics were adored by children as well as adults and so his arrest was tinged with a sense of betrayal that increased the outrage. The comedian's size aggravated his dilemma; as Earl Rogers, the prominent attorney and the father of writer Adela Rogers St. Johns, said when he was approached to defend Arbuckle, "The idea of a man of that enormous fatness being charged with the rape of a young girl will prejudice them . . . just the thought of it."

That visceral reaction shot terror through the hearts of the studio bosses. Between the jingoism that was bubbling throughout the country and this latest scandal, they feared a "deepening resentment toward the immigrant Jewish moguls who controlled the industry." Could it threaten all they had built? Paramount's Adolph Zukor, who released Arbuckle's films, and Joe Schenck, who produced them, joined together in the fall of 1921 with William Fox, Rufus Cole, and half a dozen others in deciding something drastic had to be done. The only equivalent infamy that had threatened an entire industry was the Black Sox baseball scandal of 1919. Seeking a neutral third party of unquestionable character to give the game a clean bill of health and nominally oversee the business of baseball, the team owners had turned to Kenesaw Mountain Landis, a judge known for cracking down on securities fraud, to be baseball's "czar." The studio heads needed a similar savior and they quickly agreed their man was Will Hays, President Hoover's postmaster general.

If they were searching for an astute accomplished politician, they could not have made a better choice than William Harrison Hays. He might have looked like a little mouse with oversized ears, but he was born and bred to become the canny lobbyist the film industry thought they needed. The son of an Indiana Republican, Hays was committed to the party at birth by being named for President William Henry Harrison. After graduating from college, Hays joined his father's law firm and quickly showed his skill at cultivating contacts through his involvement in the Presbyterian Church, the Shriners, the Elks, and just about every community organization in the state. By 1918, Hays was the chairman of the National Republican Party, masterminding its takeover of Congress, the same Congress that would refuse to ratify the Versailles Treaty and leave President Wilson's League of Nations dead on arrival. While Hays was mentioned as a presidential candidate himself, no one was more supportive of the party's eventual 1920 nominee, Ohio senator Warren G. Harding. Hays supervised the raising of over $8 million, four times the amount spent by their Democratic opponents, James Cox and Franklin Delano Roosevelt. Hays was one of the architects of the campaign that kept Harding out of the public eye and urged the country, weary of Wilson, to go "Back to Normalcy." When Harding and his running mate, Calvin Coolidge, won in a landslide, Hays was rewarded with a cabinet post.

Will Hays had been postmaster general for less than a year when the movie chieftains came calling with the $100,000-a-year job offer. Hays told them he had to think about it, but as much as he enjoyed being a Washington power, the opportunity was too alluring to resist. In January of 1922, he announced he was accepting the position as head of the new Motion Picture Producers and Distributors Association just weeks before Fatty Arbuckle's third and final trial came to an end.

After two hung juries, yet another dozen San Franciscans had spent a month listening to more than seventy witnesses. It took them only six minutes to declare Arbuckle innocent and issue an extraordinary pronouncement: "Acquittal is not enough for Roscoe Arbuckle. We feel that a great injustice has been done him. . . . Roscoe Arbuckle is entirely innocent and free from all blame." It was straightforward and heartfelt, but Will Hays knew what he had to do, regardless of the jurors' plea. A week after his acquittal, Fatty Arbuckle, whose salary had been cut off with his arrest on the grounds he had failed to show up to work, was permanently banned from the screen by the MPPDA.

"A Real Leader—He Knows and Loves America!" declared *Photoplay* in a flurry of accolades for the new "Movie Czar." When Hays made his first trip to Hollywood in July, he was greeted like a conquering hero

Irving Thalberg, Louis B. Mayer, and
Will Hays, 1925

with a parade down bunting-lined streets and a star-studded dinner of 1,500 at the Ambassador Hotel. Still, what Hays referred to as "the unsavory incidents" (the Arbuckle trial, the unsolved murder of director William Desmond Taylor in February, and the rumors of matinee idol Wallace Reid's drug addiction), were threatening to jeopardize the box office. The loose coalition of outraged reformers, women's organizations, and the Catholic Church that had come together after Arbuckle's arrest was now growing into a full-fledged censorship movement.

Hays had not realized how serious the threat was or how disastrous the economic ramifications could be until he was established in his new office. He sought to promote "self-regulation" of the industry and the studio bosses were ready to agree to almost anything, yet first they had to survive the upcoming elections. Reading through all of the pending legislation, Hays decided the most important one to win was in Massachusetts. The Committee of Massachusetts Citizens Against Censorship was already at work to put a referendum on the fall ballot. Hays strategically decided that it was crucial to turn censorship back before it was allowed to spread and put the full weight of the MPPDA behind the campaign.

Hays framed the question, If movies could be censored, were newspapers next? He put the case before the editors of Massachusetts's more than three hundred newspapers, whose publishers' pocketbooks were also threatened because a key element of the reformers' cause was the "salacious and sensational [film] advertising in the newspapers, especially on Sunday."

As he had done throughout his life as a political organizer, Hays worked community groups and sought out "prominent figures" such as Joe Kennedy. Knowing the state like the back of his hand from his bank examining days, being a film distributor, and serving on the Board of R-C, as well as being friendly with several of the key newspaper editors, put Kennedy in a position to be helpful. He made the most of his opportunity to work with Hays and when the votes were counted that November, Fitzgerald lost his governor's race, but censorship was rejected by a margin of three to one. The win was so decisive that Hays claimed "the people's victory in Massachusetts turned the national tide" against censorship and concluded "we never made a wiser decision nor won a more important test." For an organization that had been in place for less than a year, the victory was a crucial step in cementing the credibility of the MPPDA and Hays let Kennedy know his help was appreciated. Even though Hays was knee-deep in the Teapot Dome scandal, by the time the corruption of the Harding administration was becoming public knowledge, the irony that they had provided America with its king of film morality was mute. Hays's power was firmly entrenched and Kennedy's was on the rise.

AT THE END OF 1922, Galen Stone announced his retirement from Hayden, Stone and Kennedy decided it was the opportune time to officially go out on his own. Without Stone there for support, protection, and as a sounding board, staying with the company looked to be more of a hindrance than a help. Joe claimed he "never had any ambition to be a partner" in the company and he had learned his lessons well. While he still had his R-C office on Church Street, he needed more palatial surroundings for himself and he didn't have to go far to find them. He opened an office in the same building where Hayden, Stone was housed and put a sign on his door reading "J. P. Kennedy, Banker."

"Banker" was a very loose term in the early 1920s and Joe took on private "clients," individuals who gave him money to invest on their behalf. If a person entrusted Kennedy with $5,000 (and he requested cash) he committed to pay them $25 a month in interest, a guaranteed return of 6 percent, the going rate for loans and mortgages. Yet he never had to reveal what he did with the money and any return over the 6 percent went straight into his own pocket, unaccounted for. The one-page, single-spaced agreements were unlimited in duration, but Kennedy could resign and return the base amount at any time. It was a mutually advantageous arrangement, for the client couldn't lose and Joe was provided with a pot of funds to invest, once again creating profits without touching his own money.

Being on his own meant Kennedy needed a support staff beyond those already working out of his Church Street office and Columbia Trust. He turned to Eddie Moore, who readily agreed to leave Fore River and join him on a full-time basis. For the past several years, Joe had counted on Eddie for his discretion and follow-through, to make inquiries on his behalf and generally expand his reach. Now Eddie was there on a daily basis to handle the minutiae and be his "auxiliary memory." With his "infinite capacity to make friends," Moore buffered Joe's occasional hard edges. Kennedy summed up Moore's affability by pointing out that he had "served as secretary to three former mayors of Boston, no one of whom talks to the others, but each speaks affectionately to Eddie."

Moore was twelve years older than Kennedy, but the role Eddie was to play was most akin to that of a devoted younger brother. They knew every detail of each other's lives, yet there was never any doubt about who was in charge. Eddie had a sixth sense for knowing what buttons he could push and, with his dry sense of humor, got away with needling Joe in a way no one else dared, in part because of his total, unconditional acceptance of and support for everything Joe did.

Having Eddie on the job gave Joe new freedom. He was in and out of New York often with intermittent trips to Chicago where, in his constant search for contacts and talent, he met a young tenor who impressed him named Morton Downey. They would become lifelong friends, and Downey remembered being a bit awed by Kennedy, "the intangible something . . . radiating knowledge, success, perception and an excitement in living."

Through his R-C connections, Joe took advantage of the opportunity to meet Frances Marion, the highest-paid screenwriter in Hollywood, and her husband, Fred Thomson. Joe knew Frances had written the dozen films that had defined Mary Pickford's stardom, including *Poor Little Rich Girl, Pollyanna,* and *Rebecca of Sunnybrook Farm,* but he was also a passionate sports fan and remembered Fred as the college athlete who had set world records when he attended Occidental and Princeton. An ordained Presbyterian minister, Fred served as an Army chaplain overseas during the war and won medals in the Inter-Allied Games for the javelin throw, shot put, and, paradoxically for a man of the cloth, set an international record by hurling a hand grenade eighty-five yards. Yet he had refused a trip to the Olympics because it would interfere with his church work and mandate competition on the Sabbath.

As they walked through the door, Kennedy had to be a bit bemused by the impressive-looking couple. Frances and Fred were both in their mid-thirties; she was as beautiful as the stars she wrote for and, at six feet three with chiseled cheekbones and a strong chin, he radiated the good looks of a matinee idol. The Thomsons were also surprised. "Accustomed to the squinty eyed appraisal of those in power who sat behind big desks and merely grunted or nodded when you entered their offices, we were taken aback by Kennedy's sudden leap from behind his desk, his warm handshake and his friendly volubility." Here was a man their own age who lavished both of them with praise for their accomplishments and led them to three equally comfortable chairs saying, "Now sit down and tell me how I happen to be honored by this visit."

Fred began the conversation by talking about his plans to make "clean cut Westerns for young America." As a minister and former head of the Boy Scouts in Nevada, he had seen the way young boys worshipped their cowboy heroes, so he was looking for a backer for films that promoted clean living, kindness to animals, and the Golden Rule.

For more than a year, Fred had been training a dapple gray hunter he named Silver King to do an impressive array of tricks. Thomson became animated as he described the horse's ability to "kneel and bow his head in prayer; dance, swinging his big rump rhythmically; roll over and play dead; bare his teeth in a menacing threat or a self conscious grin." Taking his cue from his friend Doug Fairbanks, whose athletic hijinks had catapulted him to stardom, Fred planned to combine his own physical prowess and the singular abilities of his horse into a pulpit to teach young people compassion while entertaining them in the process. Fred closed his passionate appeal with, "Now you can understand why I think he's worthy of being starred, Mr. Kennedy."

Joe brushed aside Thomson's formality. "Joe, please. Joe, Frances, Fred. That could be a good, sound working trio one of these days." Yet Kennedy had to wonder why they were coming to him when Frances knew every important producer in the business. What became clear in the course of their conversation was that these two people from very different backgrounds valued their marriage above all else. If Frances were to be the one to overtly make the financing connection or use her own money, the imbalance in the relationship would be set. What she would say out loud was that they had seen too many friends, such as Clara Kimball Young and Charles Ray, back their own productions with disastrous results. While she was accompanying him on this visit, Fred insisted on making his own success on his own merits.

It was an admirable, if naive, position, but that was Fred. When they first met on the set of *Johanna Enlists* in 1917, Frances was a twice-divorced screenwriter making more than $50,000 a year and Fred was a

Frances Marion

widowed Army chaplain. He was forced to leave his ministry when he married a divorcée and appeared in his first film only because he was a handy replacement for an actor who failed to show up on the set of a film his wife was directing. Mary Pickford was sufficiently impressed with Fred as an actor that she tapped him to be her co-star in another film Frances Marion wrote and directed, *The Love Light.* If his wife had doubts about Fred's screen persona, they were assuaged when she saw the rushes. After all, the agnostic Frances concluded, what great preacher wasn't a good actor?

Only Fred was less than enthusiastic because he wanted his work to serve a larger purpose. Universal was now offering to star him in a serial highlighting his athleticism, but he believed he had found that higher calling in his Silver King westerns.

What was Kennedy to make of this man who looked like a matinee idol but was a Boy Scout underneath? Action-packed westerns starring a world-class athlete and a horse "with a personality" sounded like a sure-fire package. Yet Joe wasn't about to single-handedly underwrite films and R-C was hardly in a position to take on new projects, so he ingratiated himself without committing. While Frances remained skeptical, Fred broke into a broad smile, assuming that Joe's general encouragement meant a deal was near. Instead, Joe told Fred he should accept the offer on the table from Universal. From his experience distributing their product, he knew they were very successful with serials. Fred started to reiterate his reasons for not wanting to "just act," but Kennedy interrupted him. "This will give you experience in how to handle stunts, study camera angles, build sets without entailing too great a cost and in finding the best locations for Western backgrounds. After you finish that chore, you'll be ready to start your own productions." Universal would be footing the bill for all this education as well as the cost of promoting him as a star. Everyone now agreed the serial was a logical next step and while no promises were made, the Thomsons left assuming that Kennedy would be there to help when the time came.

Fred was walking on air, declaring Kennedy "a brilliant man." By far the more sophisticated of the two, Frances was less impressed and unable to shake her suspicion that he was "a rascal," but in the end she concluded, "I was so thunderstruck by the way he had swayed my handsome stubborn husband that I could only nod in agreement."

Kennedy had made two important friends without spending a cent or calling in a single chit.

# CHAPTER 5

# "We Have Valued Your Advice and Assistance"

## (1923–JULY 1925)

One of the keys to Kennedy's success in handling a multitude of activities was his remarkable ability to be absolutely present, to give his "whole souled concentration," to whatever task was at hand. And that was just as true when he was with his children as it was in his business dealings.

For the holidays, Christmas Day was spent at home and then the family packed up for Poland Spring, Maine. That is, Rose, their now five children (Eunice was born in July 1921), some hired help, and usually Mary Moore, all headed north. Joe and Eddie followed a few days later and once they arrived, the men simply took another room and bunked together, and joined in family activities full throttle. Time was also made to dine with William Gray and catch up on Maine New Hampshire business. Joe and Eddie went to Boston for the workweek and then reunited with the family for another weekend of play before leaving on what was becoming Joe's annual pilgrimage to Palm Beach. He went south with "the boys," a group that almost always included Eddie Moore, and occasionally his college friend Ted O'Leary, or men from the press such as William Spargo, publisher of the *Quincy Telegram*. No matter how many irons he had in the fire, Kennedy made time for periods of serious relaxation.

Joe depended upon his old Boston friend Chris Dunphy to make the arrangements. They had met when Dunphy was assistant manager of the Copley Hotel in Boston, and he was now managing the Mount Pleasant Hotel in Bretton Woods, New Hampshire, in the summer and the Royal Poinciana Hotel in Palm Beach during the winter season. Over the years, Kennedy helped Dunphy with his stock portfolio, even guaranteeing his account when necessary, and Dunphy, among other things, was on call to serve as an ad hoc travel agent, assuring Kennedy the finest suites and reserving private rail cars and other accoutrements of luxurious travel.

Dunphy was also the secretary of the Palm Beach Oasis Club where he arranged for Kennedy and his friends to stay.

The Oasis Club was a men-only private resort on par with the Everglades or the Breakers and the place to see and be seen by the likes of E. F. Hutton, the Biddles, and the du Ponts. The Oasis's claim to fame was that it attracted members who usually did not join clubs, particularly ironic in light of the fact that Kennedy would not be welcomed as a member in their clubs in Boston or New York. Wealth, more than class or religion, was the determining factor for a positive reception in Palm Beach and Joe was comfortable relaxing while cultivating the financial elite.

Rose stayed in New England, going back and forth between Maine and Boston, sometimes taking a child with her, sometimes leaving them all under the supervision of governesses and Mary Moore. Since 1920, when the Moores had moved into the Kennedys' old Beals Street home, the lives of the two families had grown entwined. Eddie had long been flanking Joe, but now Mary too joined in as an adjunct, sometimes with Eddie, often without.

The Moores had married in 1904 and Mary had to adjust to life with a man whose job it was to be at the beck and call of others, first with various mayors and now Joe. Eddie was dubbed "Doc" or "the Doctor" because of his reputation for fixing things, but Mary called her husband "The Hopper" since he was constantly on the go. Her attitude, however, was one of tolerance and acquiescence. Early in their marriage she realized it was hopeless to fight Eddie's propensity for telling her when he'd be home and then arriving much later, if at all. Mary discovered Eddie was never "at a loss for an excuse," but "I gave up trying to catch him for whenever I thought I had him cornered, he always had another good excuse for telling me the first one. So I said to myself, 'Why should I make him tell more lies?' " Mary chose to accept rather than resist, laugh instead of cry, and go along for the ride.

Rose, on the other hand, adapted to her familial situation by leaving it. She appeared to be understanding of Joe's absences, but took off on extended trips of her own. In the spring of 1923, Rose and her sister Agnes were gone for nearly two months, traveling west together to Chicago, the Grand Canyon, Yosemite, the missions of California, and a brief foray into Mexico. If most of the family chose to regard Rose's trips as routine, one child dared to verbally object. "You're a great mother to go away and leave your children all alone," six-year-old Jack is reported to have said to Rose's face as she was walking out the door. She gave him

Mary and P. J. Kennedy, flanked by their daughters, Margaret and Loretta

a frozen look in response and he learned the hard way that his tears only resulted in his mother withdrawing further from him. The other children had to see that as well; cheerful waving and acceptance of whatever their parents did was the way to keep peace.

One or the other parent being absent was the norm in the Kennedy household from early on, but the children were hardly left alone. Mary Moore stepped in to assist the plethora of hired help and Joe made a point of staying close to home when Rose was away. He visited the boys' school and met with their teachers, arranged the children's visits with their grandparents, and took them all out to dinner on the cook's night off.

Rose sent home picture postcards and Joe and the children sent her loving notes and cables at her various stops. This time Joe was staying in Boston not just to be close to the children, but because his mother had been in and out of the hospital for several months. After being operated on in the spring of 1923, Mary Kennedy died of uremia on May 20, the day after Rose's return from California. More than a thousand mourners packed St. John the Evangelist Church in Winthrop. Three priests officiated and over a dozen local reverends, pastors, and deacons were in attendance. The newspapers claimed "never before in the history of the town has there been such an outpouring of people." Fitzgerald was a pallbearer and Eddie Moore one of the ushers as Joe sat with his family, his father, and his sisters surrounded by current and former congressmen, mayors, and council members.

P. J. Kennedy had been financially successful, yet Joe had already accumulated more wealth than his father. It was he who paid his mother's remaining doctor and hospital bills, took over all the administrative duties on his mother's estate, and then made arrangements for his father to take a trip to Europe.

THAT SUMMER OF 1923 was one of decision for Joe Kennedy. It had been almost three years since Rufus Cole had first come to call and Joe had managed to rise to the board of directors as well as establish his own regional distribution network. Yet he had failed to sell R-C or package it to create a mega-company and now he found himself fighting just to be heard.

Sir Erskine Crum might not have been ready or able to stick to his decisions, but he was running out of patience with Rufus Cole. Cole had failed to bring in new money and was spreading irritation at both the California studio and the New York office by telling everyone else what to do. Finally, Crum confronted Cole and asked for his resignation by the next board meeting. Cole was shocked, believing he had bent over backward to bring in potential investors, and be the positive, public face of the company that bore his name but over which he had little control. As he began to realize his days were numbered, Cole asked if he could at least take over foreign distribution or be given a production deal to make it look like an "amicable settlement." Crum said no; a six-month salary with no stock was the best he was going to get.

Crum explained his decision to Kennedy, saying "I am very very sorry about it, but if ever a man has had a chance, he has had it and he has indeed made a mess of it." Joe agreed, but if the decision had already been made, there was no reason for him to make an enemy, even a discredited one. He stayed away from the board meeting where Cole was the lone negative voice at every turn. Cole was out of the company he had founded, but not before complaining loudly that "the treatment I have received has been unkind, unfair, unbusinesslike and absolutely repudiating every promise made to me."

While he was still trying to save himself, Cole had brought in Pat Powers as a potential savior, but Crum had latched on to him and personally taken over the discussions. Born in Ireland and raised in Buffalo, New York, Powers had already been in the picture business for several years when he joined forces with the tiny German immigrant Carl Laemmle to form Universal Pictures in 1912. As the two major stockholders, Powers and Laemmle bought up a half dozen smaller companies, fought Edison's trust, and opened the several-hundred-acre Universal City outside Los Angeles, but their nearly constant power struggle threatened to overwhelm the company's accomplishments. At least once, police were called in to break up a brawl between them. Laemmle eventually triumphed, buying out his partner for over $1 million, and now Powers was looking for a new roost.

Powers already had the reputation of being "one of the most aggressive, belligerently active men" in the business, but he had been producing and distributing films for over ten years. That experience, along with his cash, was enough to convince Crum that he was the man to take over R-C. For his several hundred thousand dollars, Powers was named administrative director of the company, given four thousand shares of stock, and control of the Los Angeles studio. He brought with him another investor and experienced movie man, Joseph Schnitzer, who was given an equal number of shares and made vice president of the company based in New York.

Powers was a physically huge man, six foot five with a voice to match, and he commanded attention by just walking into a room. Joe Schnitzer, if not quite Mutt to Powers's Jeff, was slight and bespectacled with a quiet demeanor. In his own way, he was just as knowledgeable, having worked for a variety of film companies since 1907. He had risen to general manager of Universal before joining forces with Powers.

Powers replaced Cole on the board of directors, but it was Schnitzer who turned to dealing with Kennedy. Schnitzer knew his way around film company budgets, and he wanted more money from Joe, both as an investor and as the man responsible for distribution in New England.

Joe Schnitzer

Instead, Kennedy complained that the quality of films he was given was so poor, theaters wouldn't pay good money for them. Schnitzer countered that the other regions were doubling their profits for the quarter while the Boston office had a 35 percent decrease over the same period. They quibbled back and forth, with Joe protesting that New York should pay for the promotion of his films and that they were holding income far too long before forwarding it. He alternated between sulking that he was imposed upon and reaching out with claims he wanted to be helpful. He made it obvious he didn't want to deal with anyone but the head man, and Schnitzer was clearly number two. It couldn't have been too pleasant for Schnitzer either, for the usually thorough Kennedy continued to misspell his name for months. Unfazed, Schnitzer kept asking for new investments in any form, down to advancing cash on individual films. "I am all through with putting money into the picture business," Kennedy told him with finality. Of course he wasn't, but he was getting fed up with R-C. With his own franchise not doing as well as he thought it should, Joe was all the more susceptible to irritation, and he didn't have to look far to find it.

As Crum was the first to admit, he had arrived in America "knowing no one in the film business" and had depended heavily upon Kennedy for advice and direction. However, from the moment the Powers deal had been accepted, he was running the show. Joe remained on the board, but Powers was the first among equals. He was not above standing next to Kennedy and staring down at him, imposing in both size and authority. Joe didn't even have Crum to turn to, as he had returned to London leaving Major Thomson as the English bank's representative. Both Thomson in New York and Crum, by long-distance mail, sympathized with Joe but said their "hands were tied." They claimed to "absolutely agree that it is exceedingly galling to have Powers's view considered at all times," particularly when the rest of the board opposed some of his actions, but it "is the only policy to follow at the present moment." Kennedy tolerated the new situation as long as he could, but after they cut his salary and director's fees, he settled his contract, sold his New England franchise back to R-C "at a substantial profit," and then, after several pique-filled missives, resigned from the board in July of 1923. Crum responded that while "we have valued your advice and assistance," his resignation was "regrettably accepted and understood."

Whether he wanted to be or not, Kennedy was now free of his R-C commitments and he went into high gear creating several corporations over which he did have control. He still had his interest in Columbia Films, and it was continuing to profit, but Joe was only one of six board members. He created his own Motion Picture Finance Corporation, a broad umbrella organization to funnel his buying, selling, and producing "without limit or restriction." The address of the corporation was his personal office and the two other board members, Eddie Moore and Ted O'Leary, had already proven their loyalty. Joe wasn't taking any chances.

Kennedy's growing sophistication and understanding of the business was showing in a multitude of ways. When he invested in or loaned money on individual films, he arranged for R-C to distribute them, keeping their books open to him. With each new contract, clauses were added and more bases were covered. For instance, he was now assured possession of the film's negatives if the companies went into receivership. And the attorney who was handling his film-related legal work was none other than Benjamin DeWitt, the court-appointed receiver Joe had wrangled with during the Hallmark bankruptcy but who had impressed him with his acumen.

Ever since placing Mayor Fitzgerald's name into vaudeville performances, Kennedy had been thinking of the money to be made in putting the company's names into stage shows. He was convinced the idea was so effective it was worth incorporating yet another entity, and so Columbia Advertising was born. Buying the rights to the curtains in both stage and movie theaters, the company turned around and sold space to hotels and restaurants to have their names painted on them.

Steve Fitzgibbon, who had been running the RCNE office, now became the day-to-day man for Columbia Advertising. They took a small office on Fifth Avenue in New York and hired several salesmen on a commission basis to promote "theatrical scenic advertising." Cafés, lumber companies, and cigar manufacturers were just some of the businesses willing to pay a weekly fee to have their names on curtains in theaters in Boston, New York, and New Jersey. Amanda Smith looks back on Columbia Advertising and says "Kennedy may have been one of the earliest practitioners of product placement."

Joe stayed on top of Columbia Advertising's accounts receivable, billing summaries, and the status of each theater's curtain. By cable, he encouraged the salesmen and reminded them to watch their travel expenses. Columbia Advertising was soon in Chicago, St. Louis, and Memphis, covering the eastern half of the United States with ad-laced theater curtains. With his expanding domain, Kennedy needed a full-time, top-rate accountant he could trust, so he brought in his old Fore River accountant and company baseball team manager, Pat Scollard, to monitor the financial end of the business. Scollard's large ears, small eyes, strong jaw, and long nose gave him a bit of a horse face, but his quiet, self-deprecating sense of humor endeared him to his co-workers and his talent for ferreting out the last penny endeared him to Kennedy. As was becoming his pattern, Joe limited the board of directors of Columbia Advertising to those in his employ, in this case, Steve Fitzgibbon, Pat Scollard, and the ever faithful Eddie Moore.

ON THE NATIONAL FRONT, President Harding died suddenly in August 1923. His vice president, Calvin Coolidge, had come to national fame when, as governor of Massachusetts, he refused to arbitrate a Boston police strike, claiming they had no right to strike in the first place. Labor issues were one of the questions that Coolidge discussed with his friend Guy Currier, and at the moment he was notified of Harding's death, Coolidge was leaving his father's home to visit Currier in New Hampshire. Instead, Coolidge was sworn in as president on the spot and headed straight to Washington.

The ubiquitous corruption of the Harding administration was slowly revealing itself, but the taciturn Coolidge wasn't held responsible. He was perceived as a man who led by not interfering and that was good news for business. It went beyond that; with Coolidge and a Republican-controlled House and Senate, *The Wall Street Journal* found that government was "completely fused with business." Kennedy backed Coolidge for election in his own right, believing he was the best man for Wall Street and, more to the point, to Joe's own continuing good fortune. With a Supreme Court that overturned child labor laws and a Congress that opposed regulations and cut the maximum surtax on the richest Americans to 20 percent, the stock market was running wild.

Banking and brokering were so intermingled and unrestricted that the historian William Leuchtenburg says "bankers provided their customers with everything but the roulette wheel." The phrase "insider information" had only positive connotations, and Joe worked hard to stay on top of trends, proving himself to be "by all accounts, a brilliant corporate predator and an expert manipulator of both Wall Street and his fellow investors."

In the spring of 1924, Walter Howey, the editor of the *Boston American,* turned to Joe for help. Two years before, when Fitzgerald was running for governor, Kennedy and Howey had come to a reported understanding: Howey's paper would support Fitzgerald, and Kennedy would supply useful information. The relationship had grown from there and now Howey found himself in the position of having sunk much of his own money into the Chicago-based Yellow Cab Company, which was being threatened by a hostile takeover. With encouragement and a borrowed $5 million from Yellow Cab's president, John Hertz, Kennedy, along with Eddie Moore, went into seclusion at the Waldorf. Installing ticker tape machines and several phone lines in the room, Kennedy began exercising the skills he had learned at Hayden, Stone in reverse;

instead of riding a pool's upward surge and cashing in, he confused and discouraged others from pooling Yellow Cab stock by methodically increasing and decreasing the stock's value in what appeared to be random actions. While Hertz later speculated that Kennedy had "carried out such a raid against the stock himself," after six solid weeks, Joe emerged from the Waldorf victorious. He was several pounds lighter and suffering from neuritis, but with the stock stabilized, Hertz and Howey in his debt, and another healthy commission to add to his bank account. He returned to Boston to meet his sixth child, Patricia, born while he was in New York.

The Yellow Cab story was one that Joe told, positioning himself as a skillful manipulator who used his talents as a friend and savior. One can also assume that his expertise was used dozens of times, if less dramatically, for no greater purpose than to increase his personal wealth. A decade later, a *Fortune* magazine reporter used the Yellow Cab story to illuminate the building blocks of the "pure personal politics" with which Joe created his web of influence: "Kennedy saves his father in law with Howey; Howey's deal is productive with Kennedy; Kennedy aids his friend Howey; Howey helps himself and his friend Hertz; Hertz has been saved by Kennedy. This is the house that Joe builds."

Yellow Cab was a micro-example of Kennedy's broadening interests. He was now serving as a trustee of several enterprises, including the New England Fuel and Transportation Company and the Fenway Building Trust. He continued to be active with Columbia Trust, soliciting institutional investors such as Boston College as well as reviewing the bank's mortgages and active loans. P. J. Kennedy remained the president and Alfred Wellington the treasurer, but Joe was the one who approved the new bylaws before they were disseminated. Ethel Turner sent him regular updates on the status of all their accounts and Joe didn't hesitate to encourage his father to seek additional collateral on loans he considered vulnerable. While he willingly cut through the red tape for friends such as Joe Conway, he required assurance that "the collateral is ample." The sole exception was Eugene Thayer, the banker who had come through with the last-minute loan in 1914 that allowed Kennedy to keep Columbia Trust in the family and thereby, Joe said, "make all the rest of the things possible." When he heard that Thayer, now in New York as head of Chase National Bank, was in personal financial trouble, he told him $75,000 was "yours for the asking on 72 hours notice."

With multiple sources of income, many of which required a minimum of personal attention, Kennedy was accumulating real wealth and was not averse to spending it in ways that enhanced his image. Joe dressed in the finest, often imported, clothes, and his chauffeur-driven Rolls-Royce announced his importance upon arrival. He was always looking for new opportunities. He seriously investigated buying into the Florida land boom, but after consulting the men who were becoming his mentors, Guy Currier and Matt Brush, Kennedy resisted the temptation to jump on a train that had already left the station, no matter how much steam it still appeared to have.

It has been reported that another source of income for Kennedy during these years was liquor. Joe Kennedy being a bootlegger is taken almost as common knowledge, as if that explains everything: his fortune, his presumed involvement with illegal activities, and his contacts with the underworld. Gus Russo, in his book on the Chicago mob, *The Outfit,* goes so far as to say, "It is all but universally accepted as historical fact that in the 1920s Joe Kennedy was up to his eyes in illegal alcohol." But was he?

The Eighteenth Amendment to the Constitution, making it illegal "to manufacture, sell or transport intoxicating liquor," was ratified in 1919 and went into effect early the next year. If pre-Prohibition Americans could take or leave their liquor, they were suddenly insatiable. The surge in the popularity of speakeasies was bolstered by the fact that while bars of the past had been primarily male bastions, the illicit variation welcomed both sexes. In the fine tradition of capitalism, this surging demand had to be supplied and Kennedy was in an enviable position to take advantage of it: a banker surrounded by friends and relatives in the liquor business. His father owned several saloons as well as the wholesale business that had been importing liquor for years. Rose's uncles, Edward and James Fitzgerald, had been in the brewing and saloon business all their professional lives, and now James turned to opening a soda fountain with a drugstore that serviced those with prescriptions for liquor and the back room became a speakeasy. Two of Joe's close friends in Boston were liquor wholesaler Ambrose Dowling and John Murray, the manager of a large brewing company.

The law clearly stated that liquor could be stored for "personal use," and it appears P. J. Kennedy increased his stock under the assumption it could be legally locked away. Then, only two days before the new law was to go into force, the courts ruled that any liquor outside private homes could be seized. Suddenly, there was a frantic rush by the Kennedys to move P.J.'s supply of hard liquor into his basement and the wines into Joe's cellar.

"Evasion of the law began immediately," Frederick Lewis Allen reports, and that evasion took on many forms. The relatively straitlaced governor of New York, Al Smith, discreetly "served liquor at public receptions," while New York's freewheeling Mayor Jimmy Walker flaunted his disregard for the law. In Hollywood, Mary Pickford's mother, Charlotte, just bought out a liquor store and had the contents moved to her basement. Sam Goldwyn's secretary saw it as a sign of her boss's growing trust when he gave her the responsibility of dealing with his bootlegger. Director George Hill's assistant, Joe Newman, counted among his duties his four o'clock run to the drugstore to pick up Hill's medically prescribed daily pint of liquor. Doctor's prescriptions were so prevalent that in Chicago alone, 300,000 prescriptions were written for "patients" who required liquor for "medicinal" purposes.

Prohibition was to last for thirteen years, but the first few were very different from the last few. An enormous, complex industry was created that required many levels of activity, not all of which was conducted by gun-toting men in loud ties. "New York's Italians were not as quick off the mark as the city's Jews and Irish and several years would pass before they felt emboldened to expand beyond their Italian colonies," notes Mafia historian Thomas Reppetto. By 1929, when the infamous St. Valentine's Day Massacre occurred, Al Capone and his minions had made bloodshed and Prohibition synonymous, but that combination evolved over time. It was when the law initially went into effect in January of 1920 that Joe was uniquely positioned to profit.

Kennedy would do business wherever and whenever there was a good chance for a safe profit and among the people he associated with over the years were members of the mob. Gore Vidal believes that the family connection goes back to 1914 when Mayor Fitzgerald had "his hand in the cookie jar" and Kennedy became president of Columbia Trust. "After all," asks Vidal, "what is a bank besides a great money laundromat?"

Members of the underworld who flourished during Prohibition, such as Meyer Lansky, Joe Bonanno, Lucky Luciano, and Frank Costello, told writers over the years that they had "bought booze that had been shipped into the country by Joseph Kennedy."

Precious little remains in Joe Kennedy's files that alludes directly to liquor. His father's papers do not survive and in Joe's own files, there is a record of a one-page "Accounts Receivable/Whiskey" in a closed Columbia Trust file for 1922–1925. There are letters to a number of people regarding the several hundred dollars they owed for their "orders," a reference to getting the figures "from my father's head man," and notes thanking Joe for providing the liquor for his college reunion in 1922. There are also half a dozen cables from the early and mid-1920s between Joe and his father and to Joe from Ted O'Leary concerning vague business in Buffalo, an important hub for transferring still legal Canadian liquor.

Picturing Joe Kennedy standing on the shores unloading crates from boats or hopping on the running board of a car speeding from a raid stretches the imagination beyond credulity. However, put him at a dining room table, cajoling and thoroughly enjoying himself with men of the underworld in an atmosphere of mutual respect, or on the phone, finding, allocating, and financing an activity offering real and immediate profits, and the image comes into clearer focus.

Seymour Hersh examined "hundreds of pages" of FBI files and found "no mention of any link between Joseph Kennedy, organized crime and the bootlegging industry." While acknowledging the circumstantial evidence, Doris Kearns Goodwin thinks that it is "possible" that Joe was involved in financing shipments, but says that "it is harder to imagine Kennedy still involved during the middle to late twenties, after the large criminal gangs had taken over and fundamentally changed the nature of the illicit trade." And John Kennedy biographer Nigel Hamilton, who spent years looking, concluded, "I've never seen any documentary evidence [that Joe Kennedy was a bootlegger] myself. And I rather doubt it. I mean there's no doubt that this man really is a swindler. There's no doubt that this man manipulates the stock market. There's no doubt that this man is a master of insider trading. There's no doubt this man is one of the great mavericks of the twentieth century. But I see him as a man who was far too smart actually to get deeply embroiled in something like bootlegging. He looked at a far bigger balance sheet."

And by mid-1925, as the illegal liquor trade shifted to deeper gangland control, Kennedy was turning his eyes to that "far bigger balance sheet" and that meant his own film company.

# CHAPTER 6

# "I'm Beginning to Think I'm a 'Picture' Man"

## (AUGUST 1925–MARCH 1926)

Robertson-Cole had been shopped around, off and on, for three years. Since Kennedy's departure from the board, the distribution arm had been renamed Film Booking Offices and, for a short while, the Hollywood studio had boasted a sign that read "Powers Studio." Pat Powers had lasted less than two years in active management and left to produce his own films, but Joe Schnitzer stayed on as vice president in charge of production. The company was now commonly referred to as R-C/FBO or just FBO. While the names had changed, the problems they faced were the same. One of their primary financiers, Cox and Co., had been absorbed by Lloyd's Bank, and in the summer of 1925, Lloyd's, along with Graham's and Co., let it be known they were ready to recoup some of their losses.

Kennedy knew it was time to make his move. He met with his mentor of almost ten years, Guy Currier, who agreed to be his silent partner in the enterprise if Joe could purchase the entire company for a bargain price. Though Kennedy was said to be worth over $1 million at this point, he wasn't about to volunteer any of his own money, even for a deal he had wanted for so long. Instead, Guy Currier brought in investors.

Currier's best friend was Frederick Prince, a Boston mayor's son who had dropped out of Harvard to earn a fortune in railroads and rise to chairman of the board of Union Stock Yards and Transit Company of Chicago. Prince, along with other Currier colleagues such as Gordon Abbott, chairman of Boston's Old Colony Trust, and Louis Kirstein, head of Boston's Filene's Department Store, were not men who normally would have considered investing in films, but on Currier's recommendation they each put in between $25,000 and $100,000, more than enough to secure the necessary initial financing. Kennedy and Currier created Reserved Assets Company, Limited, to hold the investors' commitments; to make the offer in person, Joe sailed for England on August 18, 1925.

The story was later repeated that the English bankers refused to see Kennedy because they didn't know who he was. To conquer that situation, the saga goes, he went to Paris where he bribed a waiter to seat him next to the Prince of Wales from whom he finagled a "letter of introduction" that so impressed the bankers, Joe was allowed entrée in their hallowed halls. That tale, however, has all the earmarks of "a Joe Kennedy special," the kind of story he told to show that no one, not British bankers or even a prince, was going to intimidate him.

Of course, the English bankers knew full well who Kennedy was. He had been taking a salary from them for years, all the while learning everything about their finances and their losses. They had been paying him to find a buyer, not to be one, so they must have been infuriated when he offered $1 million for the entire company, less than the value of the Hollywood studio alone.

Kennedy did go to Paris, but according to his own records, he spent most of his time shopping. He purchased underwear and pajamas from Dallère, silk socks, ties, and monogrammed handkerchiefs from A. Sulka, an umbrella with a mother-of-pearl handle from Delpeut, and cuff links from Maubussin. He had ordered hand-tailored suits in London so the bankers must have at least been impressed with his wardrobe when he eventually appeared before them. Joe met with Lord Inverforth of Lloyd's and enjoyed what he called "extensive palaver," but the bankers still had one more card to play. Their Hollywood studio was worth $1,250,000 and now they sent Joe Schnitzer to Los Angeles to try to sell or lease it.

First National was making their films at the United Studios, adjacent to FBO on Melrose, but Famous Players-Lasky/Paramount had expressed an interest in buying the United property. If that sale went through, First National would need a new operating base quickly and what could be easier than moving next door? Schnitzer was not enthusiastic at the prospect of selling the studio they needed to stay in production, but he spent the second week of December holed up in meetings with First National. The United Studio/Paramount sale went through, but First National still wasn't interested in moving to FBO. Schnitzer reported to London that if he was to ensure the minimum flow of films vital to maintaining the basic value of the company, he had to focus on their upcoming production schedule. To the best of his knowledge, there were no other buyers on the horizon.

No buyer, that is, except Joe Kennedy, who had returned home to Boston in time for the birth of his seventh child, Robert. Joe bided his time and stayed in touch with Major Thomson who was readying to go to London to meet with Lloyd's and Graham's about the future of the company.

The bankers were looking at accumulated losses of between $7 and $9 million. Without Powers or Kennedy or even Cole to spur them, the company had sunk to new depths. They let their membership in Hays's MPPDA lapse and even added a man to their board who gave them a discount on printing. It was time to get out and Kennedy's was the only offer on the table. Thomson and Lord Inverforth were dispatched to America in January to negotiate a deal.

The Englishmen stayed in New York and conferred on the phone with Kennedy, who remained in Boston. In between conversations with the bankers, Joe consulted with Guy Currier as well as William Gray and Will Hays. There was talk of "plenty of competition" arising at the last minute, but on Friday, February 5, 1926, agreement was formally reached for Kennedy to put down $200,000 on the $1.1 million purchase price, $400,000 less than they were asking five years before. He had worked and waited for almost seven years to make this day a reality, but his patience and persistence had finally been rewarded.

"BOSTON FINANCIER PURCHASES CONTROL OF FBO" headlined *Moving Picture World* that February of 1926 and similar banners were posted across the pages of *Variety, Exhibitors Herald,* and the other trades. *The New York Times* made note of the "Boston banker" taking over a film studio and other newspapers variously identified Kennedy as a financier, an associate of Hayden, Stone, a former executive at Bethlehem Shipbuilding, and the "youngest bank president in America."

Kennedy was the first outsider to simply purchase a studio outright, and much was later made of film pioneer Marcus Loew's comment upon hearing of the buyout: "A banker? I thought this was a business for furriers." While some Hollywood veterans may have looked askance, it didn't immediately affect them. FBO was known for the B pictures that showed for a week at a time in smaller theaters, not in the large "picture palaces" with full orchestras where MGM and Paramount showed their films. Yet Kennedy's acquisition made for good press in the larger world and with a photogenic wife and seven children, he presented the appearance of "home and family life and all those fireside virtues" that was manna to Will Hays, still combating the image of Hollywood as Sodom and Gomorrah. With most film companies being run by self-educated immigrant Jews, Hays greeted Kennedy with hosannas and hailed the Catholic Harvard graduate as "exceedingly American."

The trades encouraged the wide coverage of Kennedy's ascension to studio chief because it "proved that the picture business is an ideal business for bankers." His "lofty and conservative financial connections" were seen as evidence that the film business was finally "coming of age among the nation's industries."

There was also a large amount of misinformation in those initial announcements. Many newspapers simply reprinted the English bank's press release, quoting Major Thomson as saying they had sold because of their belief FBO needed to be "under resident control." No mention was made of their massive losses or of Kennedy's longtime association with the company.

Some reports assumed that the purchase was backed by Hayden, Stone because of Joe's past connection and while it was true that his father-in-law had a small amount invested in the deal, it hardly justified the dominating *Boston Post* front page headline: "Fitzgerald a Film Magnate." The former mayor had grabbed the local microphone to announce that he would be "actively interested in the 10 million motion picture venture" that would bring "a profit of a million dollars a year." Only in small print was it noted that it was Honey Fitz's son-in-law who was to actually head the company. If Joe was irked at his presumption, he had to love the lines that claimed that "since the day Joe Kennedy received his degree at Harvard, he has been the marvel of the Boston financial world" and now he was to "take his place alongside the great movie magnates of the world."

When Kennedy talked directly to the press, he was methodically self-deprecating and made the entire enterprise sound like a fluke instead of the culmination of seven difficult and challenging years. He told *Photoplay* he was leaving the Harvard Club in Manhattan and heading to the train station for a long-planned vacation in Palm Beach when he was suddenly called back to take a phone call. A few minutes later he returned to tell his waiting friends, "You'll have to go on without me. . . . I seem to have bought a motion picture company." Of course it hadn't happened that way at all.

Joe and Eddie Moore did board a train on Sunday, February 7, but it was from Boston to New York, where they checked in to the Harvard Club. Before he even went to his new office, Kennedy solidified his relationships with old friends. He wrote William Gray what he told others he thought might be useful: that he was counting on them for advice and "I hope I may call on you from time to time for further suggestions." There was nothing like being needed to make people feel appreciated.

E. B. Derr

Kennedy also paid a call on Will Hays, whom he had taken to addressing as "General." Joe assured him he was looking forward to being "a real honest to goodness member" of the MPPDA as soon as "our finances are properly adjusted." Just as Joe had ached to serve on the board of Massachusetts Electric to sit with the scions of society, he wanted to do the same with the heads of MGM, Paramount, and Universal. He told Hays how much he needed and valued his support and Hays, in turn, assured Joe he was "delighted" to have him as a studio owner. "Really," Hays said, "it is going to be a great satisfaction, comfort and pleasure to me." They were both natural-born politicians who could be of great benefit to each other.

Only weeks before Kennedy's takeover, FBO had moved their New York headquarters to the new, eleven-story Embassy Building at 1560 Broadway. The trades called their offices "one of the most efficient and attractive in the country" and it included their own projection room. Kennedy recognized many of the employees as he walked in and out of the various rooms with his trademark smile, shaking hands and telling everyone he was "much impressed with everything I have seen."

"The executives and operating personnel will remain unchanged" was an oft-repeated phrase in the coverage of the purchase, but it was a quote from the Lloyd's press release. While Joe had definite plans to the contrary, there was no reason to let anyone else know about them at the moment. His immediate task was to create his own team and he called in two of his former Fore River shipyard colleagues who had proved their loyalty under fire. Edward Derr, known as "E.B.," and Charlie Sullivan had also exhibited other crucial traits: brilliant minds for money, a willingness to work long and hard when the occasion called for it, and the ability to keep their mouths shut.

E. B. Derr was a Pennsylvania native a few years Kennedy's junior, a short, good-looking man with dark wavy hair and piercing eyes. He had a smile that revealed dimples and a walk that revealed the fact he was pigeon-toed. He was also an impressive, accomplished accountant who "could work out any mathematical problem in an instant and give the answer off the top of his head." By the time Kennedy left Fore River, Derr had risen to comptroller. For the past several years, he had been thriving in Boston as a consultant to several New England banks, specializing in large manufacturing loans, and Joe had called on him for advice when he was buying RCNE several years before. Derr was the only one of the group who had previous experience in the entertainment business. When he was in his early twenties, in Bethlehem, Pennsylvania, he put his savings into building and managing the Broad Theater. He learned the hard way when he paid too much for renting films, but it was a measles epidemic in 1917 that closed many theaters and forced him out of the business entirely. Setting his dreams aside, he joined Bethlehem Steel and when Kennedy called after buying FBO, Derr came running.

Charlie Sullivan was a very quiet man, at least with outsiders. With his brown hair parted down the middle and dark-frame glasses, he was quick to smile, but rarely spoke unless spoken to, and even then his shyness got the best of him. As one friend who saw him at work put it, Charlie "never seemed to be able to express himself until a pile of papers with digits on them were dropped in his lap. Then he became a wizard."

Pat Scollard, whom Kennedy had recruited several years before to join him at Columbia Advertising, was also a Fore River veteran and now he was reunited with Derr, Sullivan, and Eddie Moore. Together, they became the core group around Kennedy, forming a cordon of loyalty to protect him, to keep him informed, and to be in the places he couldn't be. Each man served different purposes at different times, but they were there to keep the information flowing, ensure that all transactions were as legal as possible, and know when they could handle things and when to bring in Kennedy. They double-checked each other's work and gave each other a bad time if they were a nickel off. But they also took care of each other and, most of all, they took care of Joe Kennedy. They were all married and Derr had a young daughter, but home was where the work took them.

At first glance, some assumed they were sycophants, yet while they were generally deferential, they were anything but yes-men. Joe counted on them to tell him the truth as they found it. One secretary expressed

Charlie Sullivan

concern when they walked in the room together because "they looked like gangsters," but what mattered most to Kennedy was their total loyalty. They were willing to, as Derr put it, "take the gloves off and get down in the gutter to fight. Collectively, we can lick anybody." They called each other "the gang" and they called Kennedy "Boss." It was a clear and simple world-view: if you weren't one of them, you were "an outsider." There was no middle ground.

The gang moved into the new FBO offices and Joe Schnitzer, still in California working on the upcoming production schedule, was left wondering where he fit in the new regime. Kennedy took over Schnitzer's office, used his secretary, and waited five full days to be in contact with him. If that made Schnitzer nervous, and it did, the reality was that he was no threat to Kennedy and it was a good idea to have someone on hand with institutional knowledge. Besides, Schnitzer had just signed a four-year contract and he still held some stock from when he and Pat Powers had run the company. He had shown himself willing and able to work with a variety of administrations as a nose-to-the-grindstone executive. While there had been little love lost between the two men in the over three years they had known each other, Kennedy wanted Schnitzer inside his tent and assured him he had "the greatest confidence in the world in your ability." For the time being, though, he needed Schnitzer to remain in California to keep his eye on production and stay away from the New York office while Joe was making changes.

Kennedy's pride in his new position was obvious as he told friends, "I'm beginning to think I'm a 'picture' man." As the news spread, he heard from a variety of well-wishers as well as from those who hoped to do business with him, including Rufus Cole, who was now with Hupp Motor Cars in Detroit. Joe politely brushed him off but kept the lines of communication open with the likes of Pat Powers, claiming he would "be glad of" any suggestions he might have.

In between his glad-handing and communicating with dozens of people in and out of the company, Kennedy set Derr, Scollard, and Sullivan to the task of assessing the company's books and hemorrhaging budgets. He knew that credit squeezes and high interest payments had plagued the company for years. Overhead was running at $100,000 a week and, over the past two years, incoming cash had fluctuated between $35,000 to $150,000 a week. All the accounting was done in the New York office and Hollywood sent their needs in on a monthly basis. Nothing was in the detailed format Kennedy expected.

First, Joe needed to secure ongoing funding. His answer was to internalize the financing and he did that by creating a new company, the Cinema Credits Corporation. Once again, he turned to Guy Currier and his friends who had already backed the purchase of FBO. Investors were promised a return of 7 percent annually and, in a $100 per share, cash-for-stock transaction, Frederick Prince put in $100,000, Joseph Powell $50,000, and Louis Kirstein $25,000. Four other friends of Currier's combined for an additional $200,000. Kennedy's father-in-law was good for $75,000, but Joe himself was once again putting his brains to work instead of his own money in exchange for his share of the business. Within weeks, $500,000 worth of CCC stock had been sold and Kennedy turned that into lines of credit of more than $1 million at four different banks.

Cinema Credits Corporation was a simple, but brilliant, creation. The ebb and flow of cash was no longer a concern. It was the equivalent of a private bank providing a revolving fund that kept financing in-house and it was the key to putting FBO on solid footing. CCC also gave Kennedy total control. There were no external financiers to placate or superiors to cajole. As Budd Schulberg, son of the Paramount production chief B. P. Schulberg, remembered, "All you had to say was 'New York'" to make other studio heads shudder. It meant they had to justify their spending. "It meant trouble. 'New York' was bad news." By creating Cinema Credits Corporation, Kennedy didn't have a "New York" to worry about. There was no one to check with or wait on, let alone to question him. He *was* "New York" and so he was free to concentrate on the task at hand: making and distributing movies at a profit.

Cinema Credits' only employee was the Harvard-educated Ted Streibert, who served as accountant as well as treasurer for $216 a month. He signed as the company's secretary on the formal Delaware incorporation forms and the only other officer listed was Kennedy's New York attorney, Benjamin DeWitt, as president.

Scollard, Sullivan, and Derr reported back with a new accounting system. No more money in advance because someone in Los Angeles thought they might need it. Now each film's supervisor had to provide a weekly accounting of every penny spent, listed under a dozen different categories. Funds were allocated only after expenses were approved and verified, again on a weekly basis. The gang could be counted on to check and double-check the money as it was transferred between accounts.

Kennedy's new procedures were just being put into place when the first board of directors meeting under his leadership was held in early March. The initial order of business was to elect Joe as chairman. Major Thomson, representing Graham's, and W. W. Lancaster of Lloyd's would remain on the board until over half the money for the purchase actually changed hands, but several others were out, including H. J. Yates, who owned the printing company that gave FBO discount rates. He was replaced by E. B. Derr, who was elected treasurer. Benjamin DeWitt also joined the board as general counsel. Pat Scollard was named assistant treasurer and overseer of the distribution offices. So much for the idea that the personnel would "remain unchanged."

Another major shift was occurring in the business at large: the slow but sure movement of film production from east to west. While the financial center remained New York, moviemaking was increasingly concentrated in California and business was booming. Over four hundred features would be made during the 1926–1927 season and 90 percent of them were made in the Los Angeles area. There was no doubt about it; it was time for Joe to head to Hollywood.

## CHAPTER 7

# "I Never Needed a Vacation Less"

### (APRIL–DECEMBER 1926)

*J*oe Kennedy, with Eddie Moore at his side, boarded the train to Chicago and, for the first time in his life, continued on to California. The snowcapped Rockies, the desert, and the Sierra Nevada were all glimpsed before the last leg into Los Angeles where ribbons of wildflowers, aided by years of porters and conductors tossing out seeds, paralleled the tracks. Then came the palm trees with fronds like feather dusters; they weren't in Boston anymore.

They checked in to the finest hotel in town, the Ambassador on Wilshire Boulevard. The six-story main building was surrounded by bungalows on more than twenty beautifully landscaped acres. With an Olympic-sized swimming pool, tennis courts, and its own golf course, the Ambassador rivaled the best hotels in the east. An ornate fountain graced the middle of the massive lobby and arched hallways led to the dining room, ballrooms, and the Cocoanut Grove nightclub. If for any reason every need was not met within the hotel walls, the Brown Derby, a restaurant designed in the shape of a giant bowler, was just going up across the street.

As Joe and Eddie acclimated themselves to the sunshine, two of Hollywood's most famous names were heading out of town. Buster Keaton was on his way to Oregon for location shots on *The General* and Rudolph Valentino was heading to Yuma, Arizona, which was to pass for Arabian sands in *The Son of the Sheik.* Yet many other celebrated citizens were right down the street, such as Charlie Chaplin, busy at his own studio on La Brea directing and starring in *The Circus,* and Aimee Semple McPherson, who in a matter of weeks would disappear from her Echo Park Church of the Foursquare Gospel and be the cause of a nationwide search, ending in a scandal when she was discovered hiding in Carmel with a married lover.

Mary Pickford and Douglas Fairbanks were the reigning monarchs of

Hollywood, but they had reduced their personal output to one film a year. The Big Three companies were MGM, First National, and Paramount. The next tier was known as the Little Five: Warner Brothers, Fox, Producers Distributing Corporation, Universal, and FBO. Perhaps "middle-sized" would have been a better tag, because there were over thirty-five studios in the greater Los Angeles area. Universal City was over the hill in Burbank and to the southwest, in remote Culver City, Cecil B. De Mille was putting the finishing touches on *The Volga Boatman.*

Down the street from De Mille's studio was the much larger Metro-Goldwyn-Mayer, created in 1924 in the first major merger of the budding industry. With Louis B. Mayer as studio boss and Irving Thalberg as head of production, they systematically put enough writers, directors, and actors under contract to allow up to twenty films at a time to be in their production assembly line. At the moment, William Randolph Hearst was preparing to oversee Marion Davies dressed as a Dutch girl in *The Red Mill* and her personal choice for director was Fatty Arbuckle, still banned from the screen but trying his hand behind the camera under the name of William Goodrich. MGM's resident class act, Lillian Gish, was filming *The Scarlet Letter* on the impressive back lot. And the very week of Kennedy's arrival, critics were praising "the find of the year," a young Swedish actress Mayer had signed two years earlier who was only now making her American film debut in *Torrent,* Greta Garbo.

Los Angeles was thriving because of the movies. In 1910, a little more than 300,000 people lived there, but by the time Joe arrived, a million called it home. Since 1920, filmmaking had been the area's largest employer and the ripple effect on hotels, restaurants, and tourism was incalculable. What had been disdained only a decade earlier was now appreciated for the business it was and the business it brought in.

It was all a new world to Joe Kennedy as he was driven to his new domain, seventeen acres on the corner of Gower and Melrose. Only a thin fence separated FBO from the much larger United Studios that was about to become Paramount, but Joe was the proverbial kid in the candy store as he walked through the gracious lobby and climbed the stairs of the arched two-story administration building that fronted on Gower. Today stuccoed walls block the studio from public view, but in 1926 a garden courtyard with landscaped lawns centered by a fountain welcomed guests to the FBO studio.

The main office building was bookended by two large rectangular structures housing the carpenter shop and storage for the sets, furniture, props, and wardrobes. There were a plaster and paint shop, a nine-car

FBO's main office and lot, with Paramount in the background

garage, and cutting rooms. Filming was done on stages of various levels of construction, many with movable glass roofs to take full advantage of the sun to light the actors. The back lot was laced with an assortment of constantly changing sets, except for the tall minaret that remained from *Kismet,* the first major film shot at the studio five years earlier.

Before spending serious time at his own new corner office, Kennedy went calling. Just as one of his first visits upon buying FBO was to Will Hays, Joe now went to see Hays's top man in Los Angeles, Fred Beetson, at his office on Hollywood Boulevard. Beetson's presence at almost every meeting where two or more studio heads were gathered testified to the power of the Motion Picture Producers and Distributors Association. He was referred to as "Fred Beetson of the Hays Office" as if it were his full name. A hail-fellow-well-met, Beetson was social to the point that Budd Schulberg called him the " 'drink and let drink custodian of motion picture morality.' He always seemed to have a Scotch highball somehow permanently attached to his right hand" yet managed to never appear "altogether drunk." The important thing to Kennedy was that a few positive remarks from Beetson could open many doors.

Joe impressed him to the point that Beetson reported back to Hays

Kennedy, center, at his first FBO sales convention dinner, 1926

"while you spoke beautifully of him in your letter to me, it wasn't half enough. I found him to be not only one of the most delightful men in the picture industry but one of the most delightful men I have ever met in my life." Beetson's conclusion that "FBO should go far under his guidance" helped spread the word that Kennedy was a man worthy of attention. Beetson's generous comments were soon followed by the announcement that FBO had joined the MPPDA and Joe had been elected to the board of directors, underscoring the message that he was here to stay.

Kennedy's trip coincided with the previously planned FBO annual sales convention so he played host to more than seventy-five executives and branch managers who poured in from all over the country. The convention opened at the Ambassador on Thursday, the 1st of April, and then Joe walked his men through the lots he himself had seen for the first time only a week before. Not that he pretended to know anything about making films; he went out of his way to let them know he didn't. He told the story on himself that when he watched the director Ralph Ince film a circus performer fall from a trapeze several times, his frustration led him to ask Ince why he didn't get an actor who could do the stunt correctly. "I can," Kennedy said Ince told him, "but you see it would spoil the story which calls for a flop."

For Kennedy, the three-day convention was an opportunity to size up the men working under him. He also used the time to bombard them

Fred Thomson and Silver King

(and the trades) with a guarantee of great films to come. Promoting them with a straight face was no small feat when their biggest films included the likes of *Kosher Kitty Kelly* with its "Irish-Jewish theme" and a promise of "a deluge of laughs in an ocean of sentiment." The convention concluded with a Saturday night dance on FBO's Stage 3 where the executives and sales force mingled with the movie stars.

For many, however, the highlight of the weekend was the welcoming reception hosted by the studio's top attraction, Fred Thomson. After their initial meeting, Fred had taken Joe's advice and starred in Universal's fifteen-part serial *The Eagle's Talons*. Billed as the "World's Champion Athlete," Fred co-starred with Ann Little and stuntman Al Wilson in the "super thrilling chapter play" used in theaters throughout the country to get patrons to return week after week. Just as Kennedy had predicted, Fred drew enough attention that he graced his own lobby posters and the trades soon proclaimed him "new but already popular." And as Joe had suggested, Fred used the opportunity to study every aspect of making outdoor action films. He continued Silver King's daily training and if anything, *The Eagle's Talons* increased his commitment to making westerns.

As the Universal serial was hitting the nation's screens, Fred and Silver King found their backers in producer Harry Joe Brown and his silent partner, the actor Lew Cody. In August of 1923, Thomson signed with them to make six westerns, with budgets of $10,000 each. He was to receive $300 a week and 5 percent of the profits, but after three films were in the can, there were neither profits nor money to continue filming. Monogram Pictures was trying to distribute the westerns on a state-by-state basis, but with only marginal success. With good words from Monogram head Andrew Callaghan and Joe Kennedy, FBO, with sales offices throughout the country and Canada, picked up the national distribution rights. The first Fred and Silver King western, *The Mask of Lopez,* was released in January of 1924 and one year and nine films later, Fred and Silver King had, in the words of *Moving Picture World,* "skyrocketed to fame."

Fred turned down approaches from bigger studios and, in the spring of 1925, renegotiated his FBO contract to include the creation of his own production unit and a salary of $6,000 a week. He was Hollywood's second highest paid western star after Tom Mix and Silver King, whose "box office value almost equals his famous master," now had several doubles and a $100,000 life insurance policy. The cost of making a Fred Thomson western had risen to close to $75,000 each, but by grossing an average of $250,000, they were by far the studio's "biggest money getter."

The other important numbers as far as Kennedy was concerned were the almost twenty thousand theaters throughout the country. Over half of them were in towns with populations under five thousand and that is where Thomson's films were becoming legend. In theaters with two to five hundred seats, children, often with their parents in tow, paid 10 to 50 cents apiece to pack the house on Saturdays to watch Fred and Silver King catch the bad guy and get the girl.

Praise for Thomson's films came in from grateful theater owners and columns such as "What this film did for me" reported tales of seats being filled week after week. The *Exhibitors Herald* ran an article headlined "Thomson Pictures Kept House Open" about the Bristol, Colorado, theater owner who had been ready to close his doors permanently before Fred and Silver King brought in enough profit to keep him in business. Thousands of fan letters arrived each week, some addressed simply: Silver King, Hollywood, USA.

There was no arguing with Thomson's popularity, and since he had first come to Joe's attention as a sports hero, the new studio head looked for another famous figure to put in front of the camera. He found him in Harold "Red" Grange, the impressive running back whom sportswriter Grantland Rice dubbed "the Galloping Ghost" because no tackler seemed to be able to touch him on the field. Grange had been playing in

Fred Thomson, seated, far left, was the only FBO star to have his own crew.

front of as many as 85,000 fans at the University of Illinois and within a week of his last college game in November of 1925, George Halas signed him for his Chicago Bears of the nascent National Football League. Until then, the largest crowd the league had attracted was six thousand. Grange increased that tenfold and was given a percentage of the gate. While contemporaries described him as "very modest" and "humble," Grange was a natural promoter who heard opportunity when it knocked. He had already made a small fortune endorsing products such as the milk he claimed helped him run fast, a clothing line, and even cigarettes that "he would smoke if he ever decided to take up smoking."

Grange was so well known that the actor John Gilbert, the director King Vidor, and a dozen other male guests at Marion Davies's lavish, spring costume ball had all reddened their hair and dressed up as the football star. As *Variety* put it, "three years of more publicity than any other football player has ever received has made Grange synonymous with the gridiron sport."

Proven fame and the drawing power that went with it impressed Kennedy and at five feet eleven and a powerfully built 170 pounds, the handsome twenty-three-year-old Grange looked like a natural for the screen. The two men met following the Bears game at the Los Angeles Coliseum and agreed Grange would make one film in which he played himself. As soon as Grange signed on the dotted line and promised to move to Los Angeles within the month, ads announced that Joseph P. Kennedy was presenting Red Grange in FBO's upcoming *The Halfback.*

Kennedy was pleased to be the one to nab Grange; once again Joe received a burst of press coverage and it certainly impressed his children, especially Joe and Jack, now in the fourth and third grades at the Dexter School in Boston. Having a bona fide sports hero working for your father was something to be proud of, as were the Fred Thomson chaps and spurs that he sent home to them.

Yet now Joe had two highly paid actors on the payroll and that ran counter to his plan to cut costs. Just weeks before his takeover, FBO had announced increased budgets for a series of "Super Specials" in which "star, cast and story value will be the most pretentious yet." As far as Kennedy was concerned, those were press releases for the likes of Paramount or MGM. FBO wouldn't and shouldn't compete on that level. His vision was to create basic entertainment for small-town America. "In other words," he proudly told the press, "we are trying to be the Woolworth and Ford of the motion picture industry rather than the Tiffany."

To follow his own mandate, Kennedy looked to clone a cheaper version of Fred Thomson and turned to a Detroit weightlifter who had hitchhiked his way to Hollywood and found a few bit parts under his birth name, Vincent Markowski. The twenty-two-year-old six-footer was renamed Tom Tyler, put on a horse for the first time in his life, and started churning out westerns that even copied Thomson's titles. Tyler's first FBO film was *Let's Go, Gallagher* after Thomson's earlier success, *Galloping Gallagher.* Best of all, from Kennedy's point of view, the Tyler films were produced for under $10,000 each and the star was happy with his $175-a-week salary. While Tyler's westerns would never begin to match Thomson's in popularity, such a small investment guaranteed a profit.

To make sure he touched every base of the sports craze, Kennedy signed the French tennis champion Suzanne Lenglen and the American tennis star Mary Browne for a series of low-cost "Racquet Girls" pictures. And almost every studio had a German shepherd dog on the payroll and FBO had Ranger and counted on him to bring his popular films in under budget.

With the production schedule set for the next six months, Kennedy decided to eliminate a policy that had kept the FBO lot busy, but did not maximize profits. A variety of independent producers were hanging their shingles at FBO and their films brought in a steady if relatively small cash flow. That might have impressed others, but Joe saw the arrangement as sharing income with unnecessary middlemen. Within weeks of his arrival in Hollywood, the independents were notified that when they finished their film currently in production, they could start packing.

Someone had to oversee the studio lot and Joe Schnitzer didn't intend to be the one to do it. He had been in Hollywood since November and wanted to go home to his family. He also knew that he needed to be in the East if he was to successfully integrate himself into Kennedy's operation. The two men made their peace and together chose Edwin King, the general manager of the Famous Players-Lasky studios in New York, to be the new FBO head of production. His charge was to produce forty-two feature films and a dozen specials and only Fred Thomson, who had his own production unit, was outside King's purview.

After all the years of red ink, FBO was now operating in the black. The new accounting system gave a "weekly picture and finance report" for every film in production. Columns listed the original budget for each item, what had been spent so far, the estimated cost needed for completion, and the amount of overhead applicable to that particular film. Anyone having anything to do with the production soon learned to keep the report in his desk drawer, available at a moment's notice. As E. B. Derr

Edwin King, Kennedy's first FBO production chief

put it in one of his pep talks, it "will show you where you're coming from and where you have been." The underlying message was clear: profits were the engine that was driving the company.

All the while, Eddie Moore was serving Joe's interests, sometimes at his side, but more often following up on loose ends and getting to know the personnel. His "grave, graying and urbane" manner was welcomed in the office suites and it was soon clear that he "can and does assume complete command whenever necessary." Few made "the mistake of thinking of Mr. Moore as supercargo."

After a full month in California, Kennedy returned to New York feeling good about the policy changes he had instituted. The trades praised him for his business acumen, but soon the ripple effects of eliminating the independent producers began to be felt. One of the first actors to raise questions was Maurice "Lefty" Flynn, who was known as an FBO star, but his films were actually produced under Harry Garson's purview and Garson's contract was cut in Kennedy's purge. Flynn entered negotiations to stay with FBO, and he did for a short time, but the top female star, Evelyn Brent, was not as easy to appease. Brent had been a steady moneymaker and Kennedy picked up her option for another year, but she was not pleased by the cost cutting that she saw affecting the quality of the scripts and her crew. She agreed to make *Flame of the Argentine,* but balked at *Princess Pro Tem* and *The Adorable Deceiver,* with their predictable storylines and minimal production values. When her objections were quickly followed by several directors announcing they would not accept what they considered inferior stories, Edwin King was told to lay down the law: Anyone could either film what they were given or leave. Brent asked for her release and after several days of meetings, her request was granted. Kennedy wasn't worried; he believed there was always someone else eager to work and for less money. Viola Dana, who had proven her appeal and cooperation in *Bigger than Barnum's,* was groomed to take Brent's place as FBO's leading female star. Dana signed a six-film deal and promotion on her about-to-be-released *Kosher Kitty Kelly* was increased to play up her name. It was cheaper to build a star than to pay an established one and Kennedy had faith in his ability to build.

From his New York office, Joe kept in daily touch with Hollywood and lit fires under any section of the company that he felt was lagging. He had been unimpressed by FBO's publicist, Edward McNamee, whose idea of clever promotion at a theater owners' convention was to park a dilapidated old Ford outside with a sign reading "I Didn't Buy FBO Pictures." Kennedy was looking for someone to publicize him in addition to his company and his inspired choice was Joe O'Neill. A former reporter for the *New York World,* O'Neill had also served as assistant to Will Hays and knew the reporters who covered the business. Soon "Joseph P. Kennedy Presents" was strung across the ads for FBO films and Joe's name began appearing more regularly in the columns.

Since the April convention, it had come to Kennedy's attention that FBO's salesmen, who were scattered throughout the country in more than thirty branch offices, did most of their selling by mail or telephone. Joe ordered the sales force to hit the road and get to know the theater owners, find out what they liked, and make them believe they had partners in their success. The results were close to immediate: orders for FBO films set new records that summer.

Another simple, but effective, way of boosting sales was snappier film titles. Red Grange's debut was changed from the stagnant *The Halfback* to the more rousing *One Minute to Play.* Even Ranger's dog films could be made more exciting and so *Always Faithful* became *Flashing Fangs.* The word went out to look for opportunities for tie-ins as a film was being conceived and soon it was announced that Fred Thomson's next was to be *A Regular Scout,* with the Boy Scouts of America signed on as a supporter of the movie and "real scouts" used as extras. With that imprimatur, a story version of *A Regular Scout* was then serialized in over two hundred newspapers throughout the country.

As hard as Kennedy worked, he had his share of fun as well. He told his eldest son to send him the names of his best friends to be included in Krazy Kat cartoons. Then, to herald his new status to his hometown, Kennedy chose to premiere *Bigger than Barnum's,* the first major film released under his aegis, in Boston. He hosted a lunch for the local press and reporters surrounded him later that night as he waved to the crowds outside the Olympia Theatre on Washington Street. "Joseph P. Kennedy Presents" was prominently printed on the film's posters and he took advantage of the attention to emphasize his commitment to making films "worthy of being witnessed by every member of an American family." In case anyone thought he had gone completely "Hollywood," he pointed out that filmmaking was now a "well balanced conservatively operated enterprise." The fact that Ringling Brothers was threatening legal action over the film's tag line, "The Greatest Show on Earth," and the use of "the Wrangling Brothers" in their plot line didn't seem to faze Joe in the slightest. He was too busy thoroughly enjoying his new role as the public face of moviemaking.

Kennedy hit pay dirt in the columns when he invited New York's

*A throbbing love story shot with the blazing lights of the* **Great City!**

**JOSEPH P. KENNEDY** *presents* **A Glamorous Melodrama of New York Life!**

**Rose of the Tenements**

*Distributed by* **GREATER FBO** FILM BOOKING OFFICES OF AMERICA, INC. **Starring SHIRLEY MASON** and **JOHNNY HARRON** *Directed by* **PHIL ROSEN**

In spite of his vow to produce only family fare, many titles, such as *Rose of the Tenements,* promised a sexy theme.

Mayor Jimmy Walker to be his guest at a private preview of *One Minute to Play.* The mayor's viewing of the Red Grange film was hailed as an "unusual tribute to a motion picture and its producers" and then Walker was quoted as proclaiming the film "thrilling entertainment" that was "bound to please everyone."

While Joe spent most weeks, and many weekends, in New York, the family summered at a rented home on Cape Cod. Both Rose's and Joe's fathers visited their grandchildren frequently and Joe and Rose set aside one weekend to visit Joe Junior at camp. They returned home to pack for their first long trip together since their honeymoon twelve years before, a much postponed voyage to Europe.

It had been exactly one year since Joe had gone to London to try to buy FBO and he had owned the studio for less than six months. Not that this trip was just for pleasure; Europe was a solid source of income, but Kennedy knew they could do better. Eighty-five percent of the world's films were being made in America and a large portion of their receipts came from abroad.

Colvin Brown, who had started in the business working for the producer-director Thomas Ince and was acting as FBO's general sales manager when Kennedy bought the company, had impressed Joe with his efforts to reenergize the sales force. Now Kennedy sent Brown to Europe ahead of him to visit their current distributors in Paris, London, and Berlin. If the contacts were not impressive, Kennedy wouldn't have to bother with a visit and if there were new deals to make, Brown was to initiate discussions and lay the groundwork. As Guy Currier put it in a letter of introduction he sent to a friend in Paris on Kennedy's behalf, "we do a substantial business in France, but not as much as we would like."

The Kennedys spent almost a month abroad; Joe was in and out of Paris, in meetings and buying clothes, while Rose saw the sights. They celebrated his thirty-eighth birthday at the luxurious Hôtel du Palais in Biarritz. Joe was so geared up to do business, he kept in daily touch with FBO and told Eddie Moore, "I never needed a vacation less." After five nights at Brown's Hotel in London, Rose and Joe departed for home on the 21st of September.

Many of the cables Joe received during his travels concerned the release of *One Minute to Play.* He heard good things about the Grange picture from Johnnie Ford at Maine New Hampshire and Martin Quigley, publisher of *Exhibitors Herald,* told him it was sure to be "a great money-maker." *Photoplay* proclaimed "You'll like Red and you'll like the picture," calling Grange "a real screen personality who wins you from the start." FBO was giving *One Minute to Play* the biggest promotional boost of any film yet with over-the-top ads comparing Grange to the gladiators of Rome.

The box office was going wild, but Grange's off-screen personality left much to be desired. Sitting around waiting for the cameras to roll was not his idea of a good time. He complained to the press that he was "fed up with the picture business" and Hollywood stars that "kissed like a bunch of amateurs, nothing like the coeds back in Illinois." Production chief Ed King should have been able to stifle such remarks, but increasingly Joe was receiving reports that King was too weak to deal effectively with grumbling actors and directors.

Of the men closest to Kennedy, E. B. Derr was emerging as the one to be groomed for active production duties. Derr joined Joe Schnitzer and Lee Marcus, the general sales manager, on a tour of FBO's distributing centers, holding meetings with salesmen in San Francisco and New Orleans and points in between. He was getting to know the players while learning how their product was selling and how they were selling it. Now Derr was sent to California to be the eyes and ears on the lot and he quickly concluded that King was in over his head. Still, they weren't ready to make a change so the gang would have to share the duty of being on the scene at all times. Kennedy would return in late October, but first he had a few things to take care of in New York.

The sports mania that was sweeping the country and filling the theaters to see Red Grange had spawned another passion: championship boxing. Jack Dempsey had held the heavyweight championship title for seven years and was the choice of most sportswriters to beat his latest challenger, Gene Tunney. Dempsey was a Hollywood favorite, in part because he was married to the popular actress Estelle Taylor, but one Hollywood star who was rooting for Tunney was his old friend Fred Thomson.

Thomson and Tunney had grown close during the war while training together for the Inter-Allied Games. When Tunney came to Los Angeles to star in a ten-part serial for Pathé, *The Fighting Marine,* he stayed with the Thomsons when he wasn't at the Hollywood Athletic Club. Both men actively disliked the accoutrements of stardom such as performing "asinine gestures for publicity." Fred had learned to live with such necessities by keeping them to a minimum, but his wife chided them that their idea of a great evening out was a horseback ride through the Beverly Hills followed by dinner at home with no other company. After several months, Gene had had enough of Hollywood and began training in earnest for his match against Dempsey.

Thomson, who lived almost exclusively for work, family, and church, wanted to go to Philadelphia to witness his friend's match, but was concerned about leaving Frances, who was seven months pregnant with their first child. She insisted he go and encouraged him to do some business while he was there. His FBO contract was ending in March and he needed to have a serious talk with Kennedy, who had been urging Fred to come to New York to promote his films.

Thomson took the train to Philadelphia where, as big a star as he was, he was almost lost in the crowd of over 120,000 people gathering at the open-air Sesquicentennial Stadium. Charlie Chaplin, Tom Mix, William Randolph Hearst, and Joe Schenck and his wife, Norma Talmadge, were just a few of the other famous faces; the excitement was electric. Despite the rain that began to fall halfway through the fight, almost everyone stayed for the full ten rounds to witness Gene Tunney become the new heavyweight champion.

Fred was exhilarated by Tunney's victory, but when he went on to New York and walked into the Astor Hotel, he found that what had been billed as a small lunch for theater owners had become several hundred exhibitors in a large ballroom. Kennedy jovially presided as host and on the dais next to Fred were two "surprise guests," Will Hays and Gene Tunney. Arthur James of *Motion Pictures Today* was the master of ceremonies. Clearly, the event wasn't just to prime exhibitors to buy Thomson's westerns, but to promote all FBO movies and Kennedy as well. When he rose to speak, Joe nodded in Fred's direction and then read his rather bulky prepared remarks, telling the crowd that "the pleasure of association with real men like this is one of the greatest regards to be obtained from the motion picture business." But if his praises of Fred sounded stilted, Joe became eloquent when he turned his attention to Will Hays. Speaking of his recent trip to Europe, Kennedy claimed it was Hays who had "placed us on a strong footing" throughout the world and instilled the confidence that made their prosperity possible.

Hays responded in kind by actually thanking Joe for buying FBO, saying, "You have honored the motion picture business by coming into it and it is better for your presence." The highest praise Hays could think of for Fred Thomson was that, to the best of his knowledge, "There has never been a single shot in a single picture you have turned out" that had to be censored. In the end, only Gene Tunney spoke at length about Fred, telling of training with his "modest and retiring" friend during the war. Finally, it was Fred's turn to talk and he kept it very short, saying nothing at all about his own films but thanking Gene for coming and for the satisfaction of watching him win the championship. Hays the booster was not about to let the afternoon end on that note so he returned to the microphone and announced, "I see three champions here—Champion Gene Tunney, Champion Fred Thomson and Champion Joe Kennedy—all champions in their lines." When the master of ceremonies quickly added, "And Champion Will Hays," the room went wild in a burst of self-approval.

It was the type of event Fred detested, but he still felt a strong loyalty to Kennedy and listened when he asked him to not sign with any other company until they had a chance to talk at length when he came to California in a few weeks. Fred agreed and returned home to Frances and to begin his next FBO film, *Don Mike.*

Kennedy knew full well that other companies had approached his star, but he was determined to continue profiting from him, one way or another. Fred was certainly a pleasure to deal with, compared to Red Grange's public grousing. Joe had announced the football player would be back for a second FBO film, but his off-screen antics made Kennedy all the more appreciative of what he had in Fred Thomson.

When Joe arrived in Hollywood that October, one of his first orders of business was to meet with Thomson. He proposed what he described as a mutually beneficial solution: if Fred signed a personal contract with him, Kennedy would represent the cowboy star in talks with various studios, and cut the best deal. Fred could keep his crew together, expand his budgets into "super westerns," and do nothing but concentrate on making the best films possible. Joe would take care of everything else. It sounded perfect to Fred, who had come to depend on Kennedy for his advice,

Fred Thomson

trusted him completely, and wanted to keep his friendship. After all, he was the man who had encouraged him long before he had "skyrocketed to fame."

Thomson had already talked seriously with Joe Schenck about signing with United Artists where he would work alongside Mary Pickford and Doug Fairbanks, friends since he and Frances had shared a double European honeymoon with them seven years before. Schenck was also a friend of long standing; Frances had been writing films for his wife, Norma, and his sister-in-law, Constance Talmadge, for years and Fred and Frances often went to his home for Saturday night barbecues. Yet at United Artists, Fred would have to be his own producer, responsible for his own financing. Paramount was also looking for a cowboy star to compete with Fox's Tom Mix, MGM's Tim McCoy, and First National's Ken Maynard and the studio had approached Fred with an offer of $15,000 a week, doubling his current salary. Now Kennedy could be the one to compare these deals and, if United Artists still looked the best, Joe would handle the financing. Thomson signed the personal contract in late October 1926 and, because Joe told him it was best "for tax purposes as well as having a convenient medium for handling the transaction," Fred signed a waiver approving the assignment of the contract to a newly formed Delaware corporation called Fred Thomson Productions. With that, Fred went back to finishing out his FBO contract, relieved and confident he was in the best of hands. And Joe was relieved as well, knowing he was now going to personally and directly profit off the success of Fred Thomson.

KENNEDY CONTINUED to cultivate the press, often putting on the self-deprecating front that was becoming familiar. He was getting used to seeing his name in the trades, but now he increased his visibility by giving a lengthy interview to the *Los Angeles Examiner.* He predicted that mergers were in the offing because a "period of consolidation" was the only economical way for the film industry to continue to grow. The trades reprinted the story, but several columnists asked if Kennedy's comments meant his own studio was for sale. While he consistently denied FBO was on the block, there was a flurry of rumors such as the report that FBO was going to acquire Universal and then Paramount would buy FBO. Kennedy was said to be turning the offer down even though it meant a $2 million profit. Yet it was Joe who was feeding the press many of these tales that were eventually followed by denials. If others were irked by having their studios being the subject of conjecture, Kennedy's name was being bandied about as a player and it marked the beginning of his image as a "mystery man."

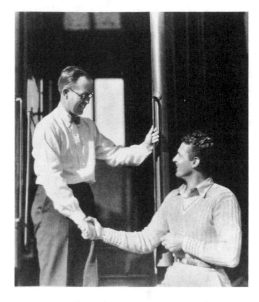
Kennedy and Thomson seal the deal.

The FBO lot was bustling with activity, and the films in production were the cheap and quick type he advocated. *Her Father Said No* and *California or Bust* were under way, as were the low-budget westerns *Lightning Lariats, Cactus Trails,* and Ranger's *For the Love of a Mutt.* This time, Joe left Eddie in Los Angeles to keep his eye on things and Mary Moore came out to be with her husband. Eddie had managed to quickly immerse himself in the business and the relationships that were key to being effective in Hollywood. Joe claimed there was no one like Eddie when it came to making a refusal a "pleasant" experience for the supplicant. He was "an artist in personal relations," leaving most everyone with a favorable and affectionate feeling.

The end of the year brought annual reviews that took the temperature of the business and rated the status of its leaders. *Variety* acknowledged that FBO was "making strides in production since taken over by Joseph P. Kennedy" and credited him with getting a few of their films into the bigger Broadway theaters for the first time, yet FBO remained a second-tier studio. And when *Film Daily* polled over thirty "leaders of the industry" on their predictions for the year ahead, Kennedy was not among them. In spite of the announcement that FBO would gross $9 million and increase their production to fifty-four feature films and forty-eight two-reelers, the studio did not warrant the attention lavished on the majors.

If there wasn't anything Kennedy could do about that at the moment, he was determined to find a way to have himself taken more seriously. And he would do it by offering the studio bosses, who almost to a man were without extended formal education, one of the ultimate imprimaturs of respectability: Harvard University.

# CHAPTER 8

# "The Inner Cabinet of the Film Industry"

## (EARLY 1927)

*I*n Boston for Christmas, Kennedy approached Wallace Donham, the dean of Harvard's Graduate School of Business Administration, with an idea for a series of lectures by "the inner cabinet of the film industry." Donham believed in courses that studied specific businesses, and he and Kennedy quickly roughed out a curriculum featuring nine speakers over a period of three weeks. It was hardly a major commitment of time, yet it would make Harvard the first Ivy League school to sanction and promote a course on the business of filmmaking.

Joe Kennedy was the man to deliver it. To ensure the acceptance of his plan by others at Harvard, he promised to donate $30,000 to the university. To ensure that all the seats were filled, the course was to be required for all second-year students. And to ensure the appearance of Hollywood's elite, Joe turned to Will Hays to issue the invitations.

When Kennedy first mentioned the idea, Hays embraced it as a wonderful way to elevate the industry, but he was surprised to receive a cable from Joe confirming he had "completed negotiations" and the lecture series was to begin in two months. Kennedy threw out names such as Zukor, Schenck, and Lloyd and told "the General" that Harvard wanted the speakers confirmed immediately so they could announce it in three days' time. Hays's innate caution didn't allow him to move that quickly, and besides, at the moment he was on the *Sunset Limited,* heading west to Hollywood.

Hays wired his response from a stop in Texas, and while he was effusive in his praise of the plan, he had some concerns. Invitations should be spread throughout the various studios so there weren't "too many from any one company." Speakers should represent "every important phase of the industry" and he cautioned it might not be easy to find men willing to travel as far as Boston. Harold Lloyd didn't give speeches, but Hays suggested Doug Fairbanks, Bill Hart, or Fred Thomson as the actor representative. Zukor would be great on "executive management" and De Mille was the "best selection for directing." Hays readily agreed to be a participant and added, "Obviously among the nine should be yourself and a good subject for you would be motion picture financing or any other subject you select."

Hays need not have worried; Kennedy was planning to speak. He deferred to Hays's suggestions and then quietly molded the course into what he envisioned. The two men conferred regularly by phone and Joe assigned Ted Streibert, still in Boston and on salary with Cinema Credits Corporation, to handle the details; Hays asked his New York assistant, Carl Milliken, to be his representative. Both Milliken and Streibert were Harvard men who easily interacted with the faculty and staff, but it was Joe who laid all the groundwork and made the assignments behind the scenes with Hays as the front man, sending the invitations over his signature on his office stationery.

Kennedy was determined to minimize the number of speakers with heavy accents and viewed an émigré such as Universal's chief Carl Laemmle as inappropriate for Harvard. Instead, Universal's vice president, Robert Cochrane, was invited. Kennedy and Hays settled on Milton Sills, a University of Chicago graduate, to speak on acting. A. H. Giannini, Sidney Kent of Paramount, and Samuel Katz, president of Publix Theaters, were also added to the roster. De Mille was the director both Kennedy and Hays wanted, but he protested that such a trip would interfere with his all-important filming.

Harvard was finally able to send out its press release, approved and punched up by the MPPA, at the end of January 1927. Everything was set to the point that Joe felt comfortable spending several weeks at the Oasis Club in Palm Beach. E. B. Derr was in Los Angeles overseeing FBO business and, as usual, Kennedy was in regular touch with both the studio and New York. He was able to sit back, relax, and quietly celebrate his one-year anniversary of being a Hollywood mogul.

By the time Joe returned from his vacation, the Harvard initiative was expanding beyond the Business School. Telling Hays they had the support of "Dr. Kennedy," James Seymour, head of publicity and alumni affairs at Harvard, wanted to create an ongoing link between the film industry and Harvard's Fine Arts Department, their Fogg Museum, and the university library. He suggested a jury of Harvard faculty choose a dozen films each year to be housed at the museum. Perhaps older films could be surveyed for their merit and then new ones added annually to preserve as "works of art."

*Photoplay* had been naming a best film of the year since the early 1920s, but the idea of awards had not been discussed at the "Plan and Scope Committee" meeting Will Hays attended during his recent trip to Hollywood. This new organization, initiated over dinner at Louis B. Mayer's house with the director Fred Niblo and the actor Conrad Nagel, was now investigating the possibility of bringing together the five "creative branches" of filmmaking "to organize for the common benefit." Hays expressed apprehension that their mission might duplicate work "well in hand" by the MPPA, but his Hollywood representative, Fred Beetson, was included in all the meetings and was acting as secretary. Besides, the Hays Office represented the companies to the outside world, whereas this new association sought to promote "harmony and solidarity" from within. Hays acknowledged such a group could "be most beneficial to the industry," for their unnamed catalyst, alluded to in the minutes only as "the menace," was the rising threat of unionization. That was the immediate concern of the group that would become the Academy of Motion Picture Arts and Sciences later that summer; the bestowing of awards was still several years in the future.

Kennedy could not have been more pleased with the way his Harvard plans were progressing and he promised to donate two projectors, one for the museum and one for a juror's home, so the committee could screen films in comfort. He also offered to arrange summer jobs at the studios for Harvard students. When Hays arrived in Cambridge in advance of his lecture, the agreements were finalized and announced as "Youngest of Arts Recognized by Oldest of American Universities." Here was the revered Harvard labeling movies as integral to "the cultural development of the country" and Hays was so enthusiastic that he sent copies of the release to his full mailing list.

The course opened on Tuesday, March 14, 1927, with Donham introducing Kennedy, who delivered the first lecture to the more than a hundred graduate students. After an effusively flattering sketch of each of the speakers to come, Joe gave an interesting and fairly thorough overview of the business. He surprised some by claiming he had no problem with million-dollar salaries so long as those stars brought in more than that in return. The next day, Will Hays spoke on what he called "supervision from within," painstakingly differentiating that from "censorship in any sense of the word." Each of the speeches was followed by question-and-answer sessions that were remarkably on point and elevated the program to more than a lecture series.

Kennedy had been successful beyond Hays's hopes in finding the highest caliber speakers willing to trek to Boston. Only Cecil B. De Mille had balked, but then Joe personally appealed, telling the director that he had "spent most of my first lecture at Harvard telling them about the marvelous work you have done," that his latest, *The King of Kings,* was "the greatest motion picture ever," and how anxious Harvard's president was to meet him. De Mille eventually agreed to come, but his late arrival resulted in the lecture series lasting until the end of April.

Joe introduced each of his guests to the class and was their host on campus. He squired them through the Common and into the Fogg Museum to show them where their films were to be archived. They were clearly being courted—for their films and quite possibly their contributions as well. The Harvard administrators had to see the initiative as a potential fund-raising boon. Joe had already committed $30,000 and the people he was bringing to campus were almost all millionaires several times over.

Hays, Sills, and Kennedy held college degrees, but Joe had opened the doors of Harvard to men who, in the main, had little schooling. Pioneers such as William Fox, Adolph Zukor, and Harry Warner personified the history of the business and their stories underscored the rapidity of change and growth. Marcus Loew, the venerable creator and head of the MGM Corporation, contradicted doctor's orders to travel from New York to Cambridge because, as he told the students, "I cannot begin to tell you how it impresses me, coming to a great college such as this to deliver a lecture when I have never even seen the inside of one before."

It was exactly the response Kennedy had hoped for. In one stroke he gained instant access to the established leaders of Hollywood while picking up chits at the same time. As Joe wrote in his letters thanking the participants, the Harvard series had given him "the opportunity to meet you more

With Adolph Zukor at Harvard, 1927

intimately than I might have done in many years in the business." If he was a bit obsequious in his introductions, his guests could hardly find fault in the flattery and the end result was that "in a matter of weeks," Jesse Lasky's daughter recalled, Joe's telephone started to ring with "invitations to play golf and dine with his important new friends."

The press coverage of the Harvard series was spectacular, both in the trades and in newspapers such as *The Washington Post*. Several articles referred to the momentous nature of the encounter, declaring that historians would proclaim it as "the date the motion picture was given official recognition as a business and as an art." Kennedy's name was prominently displayed; he was described as the facilitator and quoted extensively, predicting that this course was just the beginning of the permanent study of film at Harvard and other universities. The publicity was a result of having made himself available as the spokesperson, but also because Harvard's James Seymour had promoted him. Seymour's efforts and his effectiveness were soon rewarded: a month after the final lecture, he resigned his Harvard position for a berth in FBO's publicity department.

Joe offered his continued support to both Hays and Harvard, but removed himself from active participation in any follow-up. (In fact, the college would have to remind him often of his pledge of $30,000 and wait four more years to collect all of it.) He had accomplished his goal of joining that "inner cabinet of the film industry." Still, he wanted more.

To ensure that posterity appreciated his role and to provide a permanent and tangible tribute to the course and to himself, he decided to publish the lectures in book form under the all-inclusive title, *The Story of the Films*. He told the Harvard administrators that he hoped it "would be a comprehensive study of a major industry and a series of intimate personal histories with numerous prophetic passages. It would supplement a textbook of the movie industry (if there were one) or serve as the basis for one." Yet for Joe it was much more than that. It was his name being stamped, figuratively on the industry and literally on the cover of the book, as a member of the elite.

Kennedy had planned to be in California in early April, but with the Harvard series still going on and FBO's upcoming sales meetings scheduled to begin in a few weeks, he handled the company business from New York. Moore, Sullivan, Scollard, and Derr were fulfilling their roles, keeping their collective eye on the other personnel and knowing where every penny was going. None of them wanted to spend all his time in California, but they were willing to take turns doing whatever Joe

William LeBaron, Kennedy's proudest hire at FBO

needed. After Derr had stepped in to oversee the disappointing Ed King, Kennedy knew he needed to replace the production chief with an experienced film man and he found him in William LeBaron.

Bill LeBaron, a ten-year film veteran in his early forties, was Kennedy's first big hire outside his own sphere. Born and raised in Illinois, LeBaron graduated from New York University, where he teamed with Deems Taylor to write several musicals, including the Broadway hit *The Echo*. In 1918, LeBaron was the managing editor of *Collier's* magazine and, showing a flair for story selection and editing, he was hired away by William Randolph Hearst to produce for Cosmopolitan Pictures. He oversaw the *Photoplay* award-winning *Humoresque* and Marion Davies's big-budget films such as *When Knighthood Was in Flower* before Hearst moved his filmmaking to California in 1924. LeBaron wanted to stay in New York, so he moved to Paramount's Long Island studio, where he supervised films starring Gloria Swanson, Thomas Meighan, and Louise Brooks. When Paramount announced it too was closing its East Coast production facilities in favor of Hollywood, LeBaron became an executive at its home office. Yet after only a few months, he was missing hands-on production, and so he was intrigued when a call came from FBO.

LeBaron's story sense and his experience as both a writer and producer as well as a studio supervisor all impressed Kennedy. Everyone seemed to have good things to say about the man who was charming and authoritative both on a movie set or off the lot with a martini in his hand.

LeBaron was a few years older than Kennedy and an inch shorter but had the same bright blue eyes, and the two men hit it off. In their discussions, LeBaron told Joe he thought the look of the films coming out of Gower Street could be improved. With better people running the lab, he could get a higher quality of prints without spending more money and so Kennedy agreed to bring John Swain, who had run the Paramount lab, to FBO. When LeBaron was assured of a wide breadth in decision making and given some stock, he accepted the position of vice president of FBO in charge of production.

Along with Eddie Moore, E. B. Derr, and Charlie Sullivan, Kennedy went to Atlantic City for the eastern sales convention, the first of three across the country. The big news was Bill LeBaron's appointment, and photographs and articles about him were displayed throughout the hotel lobby. Here was a man who had been with the major studios putting his faith in FBO.

Plans for the new season included fifty feature films, and Joe and his team promised each one was "a wallop." *Kosher Kitty Kelly* had been a box office bonanza so now they were following it with *Clancy's Jewish Wedding*. There were plenty of other features to promote as well: *The Great Air Mail Robbery, The Devil's Trademark,* and Patsy Ruth Miller in *Shanghaied.*

Kennedy genuinely impressed his salespeople with his enthusiasm, his strong handshake, and his ability to remember their names after just one or two meetings. Throughout the convention, Kennedy was a natural at making the men feel valued and appreciated. After the closing night banquet, Joe and the gang were off to Chicago to repeat their presentations at their mid-country sales convention.

# CHAPTER 9

## "All Records Have Been Broken"

### (APRIL–OCTOBER 1927)

Joe Kennedy's life was in New York, Los Angeles, and on the road. For a man absent for weeks if not months at a time, he was a remarkably involved father. He was a constant writer of notes to his children throughout their lives; he prodded them, assured them, and challenged them. He was clearly on top of their schedules, their school reports, and their work habits. As Ted Kennedy put it later in life, "he kept the blow torch on us." They felt his passion for them and kept it in their hearts. That might be fine for the children, who knew nothing else, but by the spring of 1927, that was not enough for Rose.

Joe Junior, eleven, and Jack, nine, were both enrolled at the private Dexter School in Brookline. After attending kindergarten at Devotion Elementary, Rosemary had not been recommended for promotion to first grade. Was it the fact she had been born at the height of the flu epidemic or some other affliction that made her slower to develop than other children? Rose knew her eldest daughter had trouble completing simple tasks, but when the teachers suggested that the child be institutionalized, Rose rebelled. She sought out expert opinions, yet while everyone seemed to be able to point out what Rosemary could not do, no one could improve the situation. Convinced no institution would be more constructive than her own home, Rose hired private tutors to teach the now eight-year-old Rosemary academics as well as dancing and sports. And while Rose supervised the other children's activities and dutifully monitored their monthly weight gain, illnesses, and doctor's visits on note cards, she physically played with Rosemary.

As overwhelmed as Rose must have felt at times, she knew that Kathleen, just seven, Eunice, six, Patricia, almost three, and Robert, the baby born the previous November, were all still young enough to have developed few strong ties outside the home. She had resisted the idea of moving, but if her husband was to be a physical presence in their lives, it seemed to be the only viable solution. While they rarely traveled

together, Rose decided to meet Joe in California to evaluate the possibility of relocating. Even though it meant missing Joe Junior's confirmation by Cardinal O'Connell and Kathleen's instructions for First
Communion, Rose arrived at the Ambassador Hotel in Los Angeles in
time for Joe's West Coast FBO sales convention.

After their Atlantic City and Chicago appearances, Joe and the top
members of his team had honed their performances. Lee Marcus sang the
praises of the upcoming films, E. B. Derr sang the praises of their solid
finances, and Joe Kennedy sang the praises of the sales force and the
product they had to sell. A dinner dance at the Ambassador closed the
three days of backslapping, hard selling, and general reverie and for most
of the FBO employees, it was also the only time they would have the
opportunity to catch a glimpse of the boss's wife.

Rose had either been kept away or stayed away from nearly all Joe's
business activities, but this time she accompanied him to dinner at the
home of Fred Thomson and Frances Marion. Rose and Joe were driven up
through Beverly Hills where the road narrowed and turned as they
approached the very top of Angelo Drive, taking in the 360-degree view.
The car continued along a fruit-tree-lined driveway, past the tennis
court, the five-car garage, and the house for the ranch hands and on past
the swimming pool with its freestanding dressing rooms and aviary.
Finally, they entered its cobbled front courtyard with a spouting tiled
fountain in the center.

Aerial view of the Thomsons' Enchanted Hill

Visiting Fred Thomson and Frances Marion at their home
with an unidentified woman far right

Fred and Frances had entertained Joe at their home before and were used to his bringing other women with him. Being married to a "minister" had not changed Frances's attitudes. Before her marriage to Fred, she had had two husbands and a series of lovers and was never one to judge others. Hollywood had rubbed off on Fred to the extent that while he lived a straight-and-narrow life, he adopted a laissez-faire outlook when it came to how others chose to conduct themselves.

Now they were meeting Rose for the first time and couldn't have been more genial. Frances was still grateful to Kennedy for his early encouragement of Fred and was excited about the arrangements Joe had just made with Paramount, a four-picture deal that promised to "establish a new standard in the field of Westerns." Fred would keep his own company and crew together, be paid $100,000 for each film, and maintain his association with Kennedy. Joe had arranged Fred's release from his tentative agreement with United Artists and, after various discussions, decided that Paramount gave them the best "break in publicity, advertising and distribution." They already had their subject for the first grand-scale western: Jesse James.

Will Hays had been "a bit disturbed" that they might be "glorifying the bandit," but Joe had gone to bat for them. While Hays had refused others who wanted to put Jesse James on the screen, he trusted Fred and gave his approval. Frances was in the process of writing the script with the bandit as a victim of circumstances fighting the invading carpetbaggers.

Frances showed Rose and Joe into the atrium and then down a few steps to the oversized living room where arched windows revealed views of the city on one side and the ocean on the other. Before dinner, Fred walked the Kennedys down the path to the mahogany-floored stable that housed Silver King and the family's other horses and then Frances took Rose upstairs to meet Fred Junior, not yet six months old.

Joe was at ease in the home and was most enamored with the basement theater with its concrete-walled projection room and overstuffed chairs for comfortable viewing. Yet even with the public life and servants she had been accustomed to since childhood, Rose was taken aback by the vastness and opulence. Frances dismissed the surroundings (and, in the process, her own talent) by calling the estate "the house that bunk built," even though she was tremendously proud of what she and Fred had created. Rose told her she found the home "magnificent," but she "would never want to surround her children with such an over abundance of luxuries."

Rose returned to the Thomsons' a few days later when Frances hosted a lunch for the woman she still called "the boss's wife." Colleen Moore, who epitomized the screen flapper, the comedienne Polly Moran, and the actress Hedda Hopper (her powerful column still a decade away) were among the dozen guests. Rose held her own in such company and charmed the Hollywood women with her "poise, gracious manners and flashes of Irish wit," but when it was mentioned in passing that the young, bobbed Colleen Moore made $10,000 a week "with that lousy haircut," Rose was shocked. She was always a bit in the dark about her husband's money and such sums seemed astronomical.

If Rose felt isolated as an Irish Catholic in Brookline, she had to admit that, relatively speaking, Los Angeles was an open society. Almost everyone came from somewhere else and many had experienced some kind of prejudice. As the writer Anita Loos pointed out, it was a town where the wealthiest and most prestigious social leaders were the "peers [of their hired help] in everything but sex appeal." A class system like Boston's simply did not exist. Yet Los Angeles, with its near-constant sunny weather, its culture or lack of it, and its paucity of a traditional society was a place that Rose was happy to visit, but she wouldn't want to live there.

It is difficult to imagine Joe seriously thinking of moving his family to California. While Kennedy found himself needing to be in Hollywood more than he had initially thought, some of his business, and his father and sisters, were still in Boston. Joe also had to know that if they all moved to Los Angeles, Rose would become more dependent upon him and more demanding of his time. He wanted to keep her appeased, but maintain a separate life as well.

Rose knew some compromise had to be made, but for now it was back to Brookline and Jack's tenth birthday party, for which a projector and large movie screen were set up in the middle of the living room for a private viewing of Fred Thomson's yet-to-be-released *Silver Comes Through.* If that wasn't special enough, Joe had cowboy outfits delivered for all the children.

Kennedy spent much of that week in his FBO office in Hollywood, reviewing the studio's commitments and meeting with his top aides, including Bill LeBaron. One of the issues on the table was whether to make an offer to Charles Lindbergh, who had captured the world's imagination when he soloed across the Atlantic and landed in Paris on May 21. Studios were scrambling to lay a fortune at Lindbergh's feet for the rights to his story. Paramount offered him $300,000 to appear in a film, First National upped the ante to $500,000, and a variety of companies and theaters wanted him for personal appearances. After some debate, Kennedy determined that even if they could get the innately shy Lindbergh to agree to play himself in a film, by the time that was accomplished "I have grave doubts we could get the kind of picture we want or it would sell as well as we hoped." Kennedy knew profits required exclusive rights, and that was impossible with someone of Lindbergh's unprecedented fame. Joe was proven right when over five hundred news and motion picture photographers showed up to record the pilot's every move upon his return to America. The trades were riddled with ads claiming unique angles on Lindbergh, but there was just too much out there for anyone to corner the market. Still, the coverage underscored the growing impact and importance of newsreels. As *Film Daily* put it, "There is more of a genuine thrill in a hundred feet of Lindy on the screen than in one hundred pages of cold type."

With the completion of Red Grange's second and final film, *A Racing Romeo,* and Fred Thomson's salary taken care of through Paramount, FBO was free from the burden of high-priced talent. In spite of E. B. Derr wincing over what "a terrible actor" Tom Tyler was, he was boosted to the position of lead western star and Kennedy looked for another, even lower priced cowboy to put under long-term contract. He found him in Robert Bradbury, a teenager who had acted with his twin brother,

William, in a series of one-reelers directed by their father, Robert North Bradbury. When Bill decided to go to medical school, Kennedy renamed young Robert "Bob Steele" and put him on a horse.

Bob Steele was nineteen years old when he made his first FBO western, *The Mojave Kid,* yet the audiences who packed the small-town theaters on Saturday were mostly young boys, so Kennedy would give them one of their own as well. Thirteen-year-old Buzz Barton was spotted in a featured role in Tom Tyler's *Splitting the Breeze* and signed to his own seven-picture deal. Playing a character named Red, Barton joined Tyler and Steele as the FBO cowboys. Their plots blurred together as the good guys chased the bad, and the beautiful girl was rescued, all with guns blazing and hooves thundering. Their film titles verged on redundancy as well; Thomson had hit box office gold in *The Bandit's Baby,* so Tom Tyler headlined *The Masquerade Bandit* and Bob Steele's second FBO western was *The Bandit's Son.*

With the troika of Tyler, Steele, and Barton working alongside Ranger on the lot, a new action movie was due to be released almost every week for the rest of the year. Other FBO films in various stages of production included those with "pull 'em in" titles such as *Chicago After Midnight, Not for Publication,* and *In a Moment of Temptation.* If the names belied Kennedy's original claims of only making wholesome films for the entire family, they all shared the same mantra that was the key to profits: a minimum spent on production while maximizing sales.

FBO no longer had independent producers at the studio, but they did distribute films made elsewhere. Kennedy personally picked up the American and Canadian rights to the German film *Moon of Israel,* directed by the then unknown Hungarian Michael Curtiz. It had been made several years earlier in a Zeppelin hangar where the space allowed for mob scenes and even the parting of the sea on a scale that rivaled De Mille's epic *The Ten Commandments.* With the insertion of English title cards, *Moon of Israel* was the surprise hit of the summer.

With the experienced LeBaron overseeing production, E. B. Derr spending months at a time at the studio, and the recalcitrant Ed King shunted to the side, Kennedy left for the East feeling firmly in control of the company. To add a flurry to his departure, he announced that "all records have been broken" for FBO sales and he took care of a housekeeping issue as well: Film Booking Offices, long referred to as FBO, would now officially take that name, without periods between the letters, for both the studio and distribution arm.

Kennedy returned to Boston after an absence of almost two months, yet summer meant the family was in their rented house on Cape Cod while Joe spent most of his days in New York. E. B. Derr was back home after three long months in Hollywood and Bill LeBaron came east for several weeks of meetings in July. Joe took a suite at the Waldorf, his hotel of choice, and when Rose came into the city, she began a lifelong habit of staying at the Plaza.

While they were still discussing whether to move or stay in Boston, Joe made the decision to purchase their Hyannisport summer home for $25,000. It had been built at the turn of the century and Kennedy brought back the original architect to increase the size to fourteen rooms and nine bathrooms. To complete his needs, Kennedy had a private stock ticker machine installed, small enough to be brought out onto the sun porch for easy tracking. If that seems extraordinary, another change in the structure would make a bigger impression on visitors for years to come. He had the cellar converted into a movie theater similar to the one he had admired at the Thomsons'. While still a rarity in Hollywood, private screening rooms were unheard of on the Cape. The finest commercial projectors were installed behind a steel door for fire protection and there was plenty of room for the audience to view the films in comfort.

Joe knew that he and his family would never be fully accepted in Boston and even if he could learn to live with it, he couldn't abide his children being raised in an atmosphere of discrimination. He had the house on the Cape and Massachusetts would always be "home," but he and Rose made the decision to move to New York. Eddie Moore was assigned to the task and he found an estate to lease overlooking the Hudson in Riverdale, north of Manhattan and overlooking the Hudson. There was no way Joe was going to let his "grandly defiant" departure from Boston go unnoticed; he made arrangements worthy of press coverage by leasing private railroad cars to transport his family to their new home.

# CHAPTER 10

# "The Reigning Queen of the Movies"

By the fall of 1927, the family was ensconced in Riverdale, adjusting happily to Joe's more regular presence, at least on the weekends. He spent just as many hours as ever at his desk in New York and it was there one morning in early November he received a request from Robert Kane, a major independent producer. They had known each other since 1919 when Kane was seeking film financing, but he was also a founder of United Studios, the former manager of the Famous Players-Lasky studio, and had produced dozens of films on both coasts. He was an experienced player and Kennedy would have paid attention to any appeal from him, but this time the business was also a distinct pleasure.

Kane had a friend he thought Joe might enjoy meeting, "the reigning queen of the movies," Gloria Swanson. Kane explained that she had just finished filming *Sadie Thompson* and was planning a trip to New York. She was, he said, in rather dire financial straits and in need of advice. Kane suggested they might help her out together; he could produce her films and Kennedy could finance them. Joe had plenty on his plate at the moment, but he cleared it to set a lunch date with the woman *Photoplay* called "the most interesting feminine personality of the present generation."

At twenty-eight years old, Gloria Swanson had been making films for almost half her life. Barely five feet tall, with a large head, diminutive feet, huge sapphire blue eyes, and "dazzling white teeth," she was every inch a star. "She was tiny, almost bird boned," observed the screenwriter Lenore Coffee, who appreciated Gloria's refusal to be typecast. Swanson had proven herself capable of playing the comedienne, the ingenue, and the drama queen, everything from sophisticated matrons to shopgirls, waifs to royalty. Her friend Frances Marion compared her to Greta Garbo, with their "Nordic faces, the passionate gravity of their expression, deep throated laughter and luminous eyes that reflected every emotion."

The only child of Joseph Swanson, an Army officer, and his wife, Addie, the Chicago-born Gloria May Josephine Swanson had moved with her parents to Florida and then to Puerto Rico. She was a young teenager on a summer visit to Chicago when her aunt took her to Essanay Studios, the largest film company in the city. Dressed to the nines in the clothes handmade by her talented mother, Gloria was immediately recruited as an extra and was soon playing larger roles. When it evolved into a steady position at $13.50 a week, fifteen-year-old Gloria willingly left school to act full time. Playing opposite much older men such as Edmund Lowe, Wallace Beery, Frances X. Bushman, and Charlie Chaplin, she taught herself to cry on cue and became friendly with one of the staff writers, Louella Parsons. As much as Gloria enjoyed the work, her independence, and the studio's communal atmosphere, she wasn't all that disappointed when her mother informed her they were leaving Chicago to join her father, who had been stationed in Manila for over a year. On the train west, Addie changed her mind and confided to her daughter that she wasn't really all that sure she wanted to stay married. Perhaps they should stop in Los Angeles so she could think things over.

There was hardly time for quiet reflection, however, for Wallace Beery was there to meet their train. The thirty-year-old bachelor had been moved to Essanay's Northern California studio following complaints of inappropriate behavior with underage females, but either Addie didn't know or didn't care, for Wally was soon helping them find an apartment, driving down to visit almost every weekend, and encouraging Gloria to go out to Glendale where Mack Sennett was making his comedies. At Sennett's Keystone studios, she was paired with the actor Bobby Vernon in a series of romantic comedies where she finally was playing a girl her own age on the screen. Off-camera, she was a sixteen-year-old making $100 a week and just learning to drive when she married Wallace Beery in Pasadena, with her mother as their witness.

Gloria later reported that Wally literally raped her on their wedding night, then fell soundly to sleep as she writhed in pain and blood. The newlyweds moved in with his parents and Wally joined her at Keystone where he began picking up her paycheck along with his own and spending the money on other women. When Gloria told her husband she was pregnant, he gave her "medicine" that induced an abortion. That was more than enough for Gloria. She left both Wally and Keystone and went to live with her mother and to work at Triangle Studios in Culver City.

Swanson had been making films for over three years, but at Triangle she read her first script and was introduced to the technical aspects of filmmaking by her directors Jack Conway and Frank Borzage. Shifting from light comedies to sophisticated romances, she was noticed by the "Director General" of Famous Players-Lasky, Cecil B. De Mille, who had been in the lead of California filmmaking since arriving to make the acclaimed *Squaw Man* in 1913. Five years later, De Mille was nearing a creative power on par with Griffith and Chaplin. The World War was over, the Jazz Age was about to begin, and together Swanson and De Mille (assisted by his screenwriter Jeanie Macpherson) caught the wave of changing mores. In films that De Mille's brother William dubbed "sex a la mode" such as *Don't Change Your Husband, For Better, for Worse,* and *The Affairs of Anatol,* Swanson portrayed a flirt, a restless wife, a seductive innocent. With her "beautiful cat like eyes and cool languor," Norma Shearer said Gloria "symbolized what every woman wanted to be—the modern seductress with the Mona Lisa smile." Clothed in some of the most fabulous furs, jewelry, and lace ever seen on the screen, she inspired the imaginations of females throughout America. Halfway through their six-film collaboration, Swanson's name began to be billed above De Mille's.

She bucked trends from the very beginning. Stardom was a new phenomenon, and many believed it hinged on having a singular persona à la Mary Pickford and her curls, but Gloria changed her hairstyle with every film. She was an anomaly who broke a variety of taboos. Movie magazines were beginning to cover the personal lives of actors, albeit in a sanitized fashion, and most were presented as unmarried and childless, whether they were or not. Her producer, Jesse Lasky, told Swanson, who had married film distributor Herbert Somborn, that having a child would ruin her career, but she was blissfully photographed with her baby daughter, Gloria Junior. Swanson immediately returned to the screen and was more successful than ever, but Lasky didn't have time to breathe a sigh of relief. Within months, she announced she and her husband were separating. Somborn, however, claimed he had been instrumental in escalating her salary to $2,500 a week, and requested a large chunk of that money as he filed for divorce on grounds of adultery. He named over a dozen men with whom he claimed Gloria had been unfaithful, including Zukor, Lasky, and De Mille. She protested the list was fabricated, but there was no denying her affair with the director Mickey Neilan, also named, as they had openly appeared together in Hollywood, New York, and Paris.

Nineteen twenty-three was not the time for anyone in Hollywood to flaunt questionable morals. The fear of scandal was still palpable follow-

Gloria Swanson

ing the Arbuckle trial and studio bosses seized the opportunity to inject a "morals clause" into actors' contracts. The little paragraph threatened to nullify the studio's obligations if the star was caught in a compromising position, defined in part as "adulterous conduct or immoral relations." Nothing had to be proven; it was guilt by column inches. If any "such charges . . . are published in the public press," the studio was free to void the contract. Gloria's natural bent was to fight, but the odds were too overwhelming. With financial help from the studio, she settled a hefty amount on Somborn and signed a new contract with the morals clause included. The only silver lining was that she was given permission to make her next film at their Astoria studios on Long Island, with the experienced Allan Dwan directing.

Gloria had already made three films that year when she arrived in New York in the summer of 1923. She took a decade-long lease on the roof of a Park Avenue apartment building and proceeded to spend over

$100,000 creating a penthouse. Her family now included an adopted son she named Joseph after her father but dubbed "Brother." She didn't want little Gloria raised as an only child, yet Swanson was rarely at home so the children were supervised by their governess, Miss Simonson. When they joined Gloria in New York, she bought a twenty-five-acre estate in Croton-on-Hudson and poured another small fortune into repairing the house and building the children their own cottage. Swanson worked hard and played hard and over the next year and a half, she made five more films at Astoria, four of them directed by Dwan. She blossomed in a creative arena where "everybody had their say," yet none of the films featured strong co-stars; Swanson was the one and only star of a Gloria Swanson film.

She enjoyed being away from the everyday constraints of Hollywood and her next stop was Paris to film *Madame Sans-Gêne,* the tale of a Napoleonic-era washerwoman who rises to royalty. Allan Dwan was scheduled to direct, but though the French authorities agreed to allow an American company to film in Fontainebleau, they insisted on a French director and Léonce Perret was agreed upon. Gloria was now making $7,000 a week and the cost of "traveling like a diva" with a large entourage, her housing, and most other accoutrements was all picked up by Paramount.

Among her needs was a translator; one arrived in the form of Henri, the Marquis de la Falaise de la Coudraye. He was five foot nine with light hair, an athletic build, and a distinguished mustache, and his looks reflected his aristocratic heritage, which traced back to the eleventh century. While there was no longer a fortune attached to the title, his mother was a Hennesey of the liquor family so he was hardly deprived. He had served as an officer in the French cavalry during the World War and was currently in the insurance business in Paris, living a very social life. Henri was the perfect aide-de-camp, easing the way for Gloria in the City of Light and soon he was at her side day and night. One of his attractions was that he claimed never to have seen a single one of her films.

Happiest when she was in the throes of a new affair, Swanson sailed through the filming of *Madame Sans-Gêne* and she and Henri made plans to marry. They were still waiting for her final divorce papers from Somborn when she realized she was pregnant. As much as she thought she wanted more children, no amount of hiding or hedging would fool the powers that be. With the morals clause hanging over her head, she married Henri on January 28, 1925, and the next morning checked herself in to a Paris hospital to have an abortion. She was back at their hotel that afternoon, but soon the headlines declaring her the first Hollywood star to become literal royalty were pushed to the side as newspapers covered a two-week-long life-and-death vigil. Infection had set in and her temperature spiked so high her head was shaved in an attempt to cool her down. She was reported suffering from food poisoning, but she couldn't speak for days and was so weak she couldn't walk for a month. When she finally recuperated, she was the most famous woman in the world. The international coverage of her marriage followed by her sudden, life-threatening illness had made the one name "Gloria" instantly recognizable.

Her return to America was triumphant. "Gloria Swanson" was spelled out in the biggest electric letters in theater history on the Rivoli's marquee and *Variety* reported "never has Broadway seen such a splash." Her cross-country train trip to Los Angeles with her marquis turned into a whistle-stop tour as thousands thronged the stations along the way and children were let out of school for a glimpse of "royalty." As overwhelming as the crowds were, they paled in comparison to the reception that greeted them in Hollywood. A brass band met the train and "Welcome Home Gloria" banners decorated the station. Tossing flowers and standing on their toes to catch sight of the couple, the fans stood so deep that the open limousine barely inched along in spite of the blaring sirens of their police escort. The premiere of *Madame Sans-Gêne* nearly caused a riot.

"Gloria's popularity has been sweeping the country like wildfire," Adela Rogers St. Johns explained in *Photoplay,* because of "her amazing marriage, quite the biggest marriage any motion picture star has ever made, her illness in Paris when for days we thought we might lose her, and her long absence from this country." The unprecedented response was an incredible affirmation of her popularity. She was thrilled, she was a little scared, and, most of all, at this pinnacle of success, she felt very much alone. Although she had sent Lasky a telegram instructing him to "Arrange ovation," she also felt very used.

Swanson had made millions, but the money ran through her fingers. Her personal expenses were astronomical and she spent a fortune on such retainers as maids, chauffeurs, secretaries, masseuses, managers, and attorneys. She blamed De Mille for her expensive tastes, claiming "he has made me wear gowns that are just simply gorgeous" and after that she couldn't "compromise" on her personal wardrobe. Her lingerie bill alone was $10,000 a year, with an additional $500 a month spent on perfume, owing to her habit of going through several bottles of Forbidden Fruit each week. "Even assuming exaggeration," *Photoplay* reported, "she was at all times the diva," but Swanson didn't see her compulsion with her appearance as self-absorption. She viewed it as the utmost in professionalism to always appear as the star, in public and private.

As she entered negotiations with Lasky to increase her salary and lengthen her commitment to Paramount, she envisioned Henri as the strong partner at her side. He certainly looked the part, dashing yet demure, and was quickly sought after by Hollywood society. Yet while he was a natural as a diplomat and a charmer, he was so polite and eager to please that he was out of his league in meetings with the likes of Jesse Lasky. As Gloria kindly but accurately put it, "Henri was too noble in every way for Hollywood."

Feeling more on her own than ever, she listened to Lasky's proposal to pay her $1 million a year for four films. No actress had ever received such a sum, but Paramount's astounding offer was based on more than just the profits they made on her films. They used the promise of the golden box office from a Swanson film to force theater owners to book dozens of other Paramount films sight unseen.

She was to be the highest paid woman in the world and yet she wanted more. She was resentful of what she saw as Lasky "exploiting the Swanson goldmine to the fullest" and convinced herself she had been manipulated into signing that morals clause and been "forced" into having an abortion. Lasky's daughter, Betty, maintains that because Jesse was one of the few moguls raised in a middle-class home, he "was hindered by his lack of street smarts," yet to Gloria he became the devil incarnate. She worked herself up to the point that she did not see the benefit of the huge salary or having a company behind her that was willing to finance her films and a substantial portion of her lifestyle. Instead, she thought of herself as a victim sacrificed on the altar of stardom and decided to look elsewhere.

Mary Pickford and Doug Fairbanks had first spoken to Swanson about joining them at United Artists when she was making *Madame Sans-Gêne.* They assured her that "if I could do what I had just done in Paris all by myself, I certainly didn't need Jesse Lasky anymore." While Gloria had hardly done it all by herself, Mary and Doug had planted the idea that there were options.

United Artists was essentially a cooperative, with each of the star members being responsible for producing their own movies, which the company then distributed. Joe Schenck, an experienced film entrepreneur, had signed on as chairman of the board in 1924 and his wife,

Norma Talmadge, joined as a star member. Schenck also established the Art Finance Corporation as a funding entity, separate from United Artists, so the stars wouldn't have to turn to outside financiers or use their own money.

Envisioning creative independence and personal liberation, Gloria signed her contract with United Artists on July 15, 1925, promising to produce six films over the next three years. The schedule was luxurious compared to what she was used to, and she would be her own boss and set her own salary. At UA, her films were to be sold and promoted individually, and so she assumed that meant more profit in her pocket. Of course, as producer she would be responsible for the budgeting, financing, story, crew, and casting, but that didn't seem like a problem. She was blinded by the upside.

United Artist historian Tino Balio believes that Swanson's decision was "the result of cold self appraisal. To sustain her career she would have to make fewer and better pictures and exploit them with care." Perhaps so. Gloria's career had steadily climbed upward over the last decade, while dozens of other stars had risen to the top only to pass from the public's awareness. Florence Lawrence, Pearl White, Cleo Madison, Clara Kimball Young, and Anita Stewart were just a few of a long list of actresses who had commanded their names above the title only to fall into oblivion by the mid-1920s. Even Mary Pickford's popularity was nothing like what it had been in the late teens. And reviews of Swanson's recent films noted that they had little but her presence to recommend them.

Swanson was smart and she was feisty. Even Cecil B. De Mille, a gentleman not prone to complimenting others, gave Gloria full credit for her intelligence and patience in handling her career. But she had also grown self-indulgent and was tired of being told what to do. She trusted her own judgment above anyone else's and who could argue with her? After all, "I was the golden girl and everyone said so."

Gloria rushed to complete the movies she needed to fulfill her Paramount contract and by April of 1926 she was finally free and ready to begin her own films for United Artists. Free maybe, but hardly ready; she needed an office, a staff, a budget, and, most of all, a script. Three months later, she chose *The Eyes of Youth,* a story told in four parts with the main character choosing her fate from several played-out futures. It had been a popular Broadway play and a successful 1919 film for Clara Kimball Young; with a familiar title and opportunities to showcase her trademark glamour in spectacular wardrobes, *The Eyes of Youth* seemed like an inspired, if none too original, choice.

Slowly, and in no particular order, Gloria put her company and crew together. She signed the director Al Parker to a two-picture contract and for her leading man hired the handsome stage actor John Boles, who had never made a film before. She thought that would save money since he worked for a relatively low salary, yet it actually was costly because he had to be trained on the set. That was just one of the many expensive results of Gloria's inexperience as a producer and every decision had a ripple effect. She rented studio space months before a script was ready and once the cameras were rolling, she ordered retakes upon retakes. When filming was finally completed in early December of 1926, she took a month off for the holidays. Bills continued to pour in. While she was supervising the editing and titling, she decided that to make the film truly her own, she had to change its name to *The Love of Sunya*. As a result, she threw out the benefits of having a known quantity as well as all the publicity materials that had been prepared heralding *The Eyes of Youth*. More printing was ordered, more expenses were charged. Joe Schenck was shaking his head over the way she was conducting her business. Her film had already cost over half a million dollars. When the initial advance on her next film arrived, she used it to finish *The Love of Sunya*.

*The Love of Sunya* premiered as the opening film at America's newest and finest movie palace yet, New York's $8 million Roxy theater. It was the most prestigious venue possible and the two-week run brought in $50,000. Reviews, however, were decidedly mixed and, after several months in release, it was clear *The Love of Sunya* would barely make back its costs. Gloria was to see profits only after paying back all her production loans and that was either a long way off or never. Pete Bedard, her Hollywood production manager, and her New York business manager, Tom Moore, urged her to start a new film as soon as possible.

Swanson had already spent over $10,000 on several stories she was no longer interested in when Schenck suggested she make *The Last of Mrs. Cheyney*, a Broadway play for which he owned the rights. The story of a jewel thief who falls for her intended victim was a perfect starring vehicle for her, but Gloria was hesitant to put her full trust in Schenck. To agree with him was to empower him, so she spent several more months vacillating.

If the obvious choice was to go with a proven formula that might get her bank balance back up to zero, Gloria went to the other extreme. She decided to take on the Hays Office and film Somerset Maugham's short story "Miss Thompson." The tale of a prostitute who enraptures and brings down a minister was a classic example of what Hays was supposed to be keeping off the screen, yet Gloria and her chosen director, Raoul Walsh, had a plan. They roped in Joe Schenck and developed a less than forthcoming course of action.

Schenck arranged for an anonymous broker to buy the rights to the play *Rain,* which was based on "Miss Thompson," to get it off the market and Swanson optioned the rights to the short story, on which they planned to base their film. Gloria then arranged a lunch with Will Hays and explained she had found a "powerful story about tolerance." She assured him she was changing the minister to "a reformer" so no one would be offended, but she needed Hays's support in approaching Maugham because she feared the author might resent the alteration. One can only imagine the homely little man with big ears leaning in and being verbally vamped by the beautiful movie queen, telling her he appreciated her respect for his rules and pledging his cooperation.

When the news broke that Swanson was planning on playing Sadie Thompson, Schenck received a scathing cable signed by fifteen members of the MPPA board, including one Joseph P. Kennedy. They demanded to know how UA dared to film a banned story. (After all, they all had assumed they couldn't produce it.) Hays was in Hollywood at the time and when he was notified of the board's action, he responded that he was "ascertaining exhaustively and authentically the facts" of the matter. It seems difficult to believe he didn't remember his lunch with Gloria, or perhaps he just wanted to claim ignorance for the moment, but either way, he promised to deal with the issue at their next meeting. By that time, Gloria had written to each of the signers informing them that Hays had "no objection" because "I am not using either a missionary or a clergyman in the picture" and Schenck promised that the film would be "very innocuous." It was in Hays's interest to have the entire incident settled as quietly as possible and Marcus Loew set the tone of the members' response when he apologized to Gloria for the "misunderstanding." The rest of the board fell in line and Schenck bathed Gloria with rare praise, calling her "brilliant" for masterminding the plan.

Swanson was patting herself on the back for her successful coup, yet all that time, energy, and money had been expended and the cameras had yet to roll. *Sadie Thompson* took almost three months to shoot and Swanson and Walsh, who co-scripted and co-starred in addition to directing, had their share of problems. The cameraman had to be replaced halfway through and the high cost of housing and feeding over a hundred actors and crew members on Catalina Island for a month combined to escalate the half-million-dollar budget to $650,000. And this was before the

Gloria Swanson as Sadie Thompson

costs of postproduction and publicity. *Sadie Thompson* would have to gross almost $1 million just for Swanson to break even.

By the time filming was completed and Gloria put her head up, her creditors were closing in. She owned a twenty-two-room mansion on four acres in Beverly Hills, a Manhattan penthouse, and an estate in upstate New York, and she was deeply in debt. Her *Sunya* director, Al Parker, was threatening to sue to collect the $60,000 she owed him for their two-picture deal. Gloria had no intention of working with him again, but they had a personal contract so she had no protection. To make matters worse, she had borrowed $20,000 from him. By October, she had paid Parker almost half of what she owed him and Tom Moore was trying to negotiate the remainder to be carried in a long-term promissory note, but Parker knew of Swanson's precarious financial situation and wanted collateral. A reasonable request perhaps, but there was little left to allocate.

For the past year, Tom Moore and Pete Bedard had made what they thought of as constant attempts to bring her finances under control. Bedard, a Harvard man who had been a bank executive before joining Gloria at UA, oversaw the day-to-day spending and was frantically trying to find cash wherever he could. The Croton-on-Hudson property was sold and her New York apartment was rented out for $1,000 a month. When Irving Thalberg, who had married Norma Shearer in September, wanted to rent Gloria's Beverly Hills home for six months at $1,200 a month, Pete assured Gloria he could find her another home nearby for half that amount and called the savings "a godsend."

From New York, Moore attempted to monitor what UA was adding to the production costs and keep the Internal Revenue Service at bay. Their latest missives claimed Gloria owed $100,000 in income taxes going back to 1921. Tax laws were in flux and several of Hollywood's luminaries, including Thalberg, had their returns questioned, but there was no way the IRS was going to agree that Swanson's off-screen wardrobe was a necessary and deductible business expense.

In desperation, Bedard announced he was cutting the costs of the New York office from $2,500 a week to $1,500. By November that was close to meaningless to Grace Crossman, Gloria's New York–based secretary. She had only enough money left to pay that week's rent and the telephone bill. Among the creditors putting pressure on her was Swanson's personal projectionist, who was owed for the last eight screenings. If he didn't get $40 "right away," he was threatening "to sell the chauffeur's fur coat."

For the most part, Gloria remained above the fray. If half her staff's energy went into trying to cut her expenditures, the other half was spent protecting her from the unsavory details. In the midst of one of her discussions with Tom Moore, she urged him to come to California where he might have better luck in getting United Artists to reduce their charges or put some of her staff on their payroll. However, she failed to mention that by the time he arrived, she would be heading east herself. Henri was in New York, having just returned from his semiannual trip to France to renew his visa as mandated by the immigration authorities, but when he came home to Beverly Hills, Gloria was packing.

She was off to New York to meet Joe Schenck, who was returning from a month in Europe; together they were to oversee the final editing of *Sadie Thompson* as well as discuss a new contract and much needed loans. Seeing no alternative, her staff confronted her about her desperate financial situation and while she urged them to deal with it, she did become somewhat involved. She owned leaseholds in Malibu and in looking for someone to take them off her hands, she turned to Allan Dwan, who had built a home there. He suggested that Robert Kane, the producer he was currently working with, might be interested in the property and have some ideas for fresh financing as well. Gloria approached Kane, who indeed wanted the Malibu leases; while it didn't bring in new money, it at least took an expense off the books. In search of a sympathetic ear, she told Kane of her problems. Tom Moore swore he was searching for alternate financing, but there were few bankers familiar with the picture business. That sparked an idea. Kane knew a man who understood both banks and moving pictures; she might want to meet him while she was in New York, and they agreed he would contact Joe Kennedy on her behalf.

As Swanson boarded the train on Monday, November 7, 1927, she was feeling optimistic. Encouraged by the audience's positive reaction to the sneak preview of *Sadie Thompson* in San Bernardino that past weekend, she carried the response cards to show Schenck. They wouldn't hurt with the Hays Office either, which still had to give its final stamp of approval to release the film. Yes, she was convinced she had a real hit on her hands.

# CHAPTER 11

# "Together We Could Make Millions"

## (NOVEMBER–DECEMBER 1927)

Gloria Swanson should have recognized Joe Kennedy's name when Bob Kane mentioned it to her. It had been on the list of signators objecting to *Sadie Thompson*; she had sent a cable to him in response and received one back telling her Mr. Kennedy was currently out of town. Yet for an actress as self-absorbed as Gloria, it was reasonable that she paid attention only when it could be of use to her. When Kane told her of Joe's background as a banker and his growing reputation as a financial wizard, her ears perked up. She was facing a debt of almost half a million dollars; a banker was just what she needed.

With a slight bow to frugality, Swanson refrained from staying at the Plaza and checked in to the Barclay on East 48th Street instead. Still, she didn't want to appear needy or indebted, so she suggested that Kennedy meet her in the hotel's dining room. There she could instruct the maître d' where to seat them, to have him call when Kennedy arrived so she wouldn't be the one waiting, and to have the tab put on her room bill.

Kennedy was seated at a corner table when Gloria entered, and he watched as the other patrons turned their heads to get a glimpse of the diminutive star. With those large blue eyes and full mouth that broke into a dazzling smile, Gloria radiated personal confidence. She wasn't classically beautiful like Barbara La Marr, she didn't tug at the heartstrings like Mary Pickford or radiate sex appeal like Clara Bow, yet Gloria Swanson, on screen and off, exuded an aura of pure glamour that personified the unattainable. A bit mysterious, very much self-contained, this clearly was a woman who was a challenge to impress.

If Kennedy let his mind wander, Gloria was focused on her purpose: advice and ultimately the refinancing of her company. She was used to charming by becoming the enraptured listener and soon he was telling her about his wife and seven children. As they spoke of their families, she was taken aback at the thought of so many children and he was surprised that Brother had never been baptized. He was also thrown by her insistence on eating only steamed vegetables, and while they found commonality in the fact they both suffered from ulcers, he flatly turned down her offer to put him in touch with her California nutritionist. If there was a moment when he didn't appear totally confident, it was when she pulled out a cigarette and he realized he didn't have a light. A waiter stepped in to alleviate his embarrassment.

They danced around each other, taking the other's measure. Gloria was unlike any woman Joe had ever been with and he certainly didn't look like any banker or studio mogul she had seen before. There was nothing sedate about him. When he laughed, it was loudly and he often slapped his leg to accentuate his pleasure. His apparent comfort with her made her comfortable with him. Finally, Swanson brought out the two proposals she had for financing her next film, one from Joe Schenck and the other she had just received from "Doc" Giannini.

Joe, always a quick study, immediately began showering her with questions about budgets, grosses, and distribution figures, most of which she couldn't answer. This led him into his mantra that people in Hollywood didn't know how to apply normal accounting practices, "to depreciate, to amortize, to capitalize." There was the cost of making the film and then it had to be printed, sold, promoted, and delivered to the theater's door, yet without an audience willing to pay to see the results, it was all just a list of numbers. "The central fact about a movie producing company is the unreality of its real assets."

He was clearly taken with her and Gloria knew it, so she was surprised when he didn't offer a financing plan of his own and instead suggested that she stay with Schenck. The door was left open with talk of gathering more figures, but as she left for more United Artists meetings, she wasn't sure the lunch hadn't been a waste of time.

Kennedy, however, returned to his office enthralled with this beauty. He was fully aware he had just dined alone with "the best known woman in the world," and his mind was racing as to how he would see her again. While he appreciated her frankness, he suspected she had already talked too much to too many other people. One of them was Robert Kane, who knew enough to think that Gloria's problems offered an opportunity for the three of them to work together. Joe wasn't sure what he was going to do with Gloria, but he knew his plans didn't include anyone else. He dictated a letter to Kane assuring him it had been a pleasant meeting, but that she "practically has her financing straightened out." He closed by saying, "As far as I know, I can do nothing further." With that, Joe began making arrangements to take Gloria to dinner.

Swanson wasn't surprised when the hotel desk clerk reported Kennedy had called several times while she was in her meetings. She called him back and agreed to his plan to continue their discussions over dinner. Lunch had been on her turf and now dinner was his opportunity to show her what being with Joe Kennedy meant. He arrived with an orchid corsage and escorted her to his chauffeur-driven Rolls-Royce. And the forty-five-minute drive to the Long Island restaurant gave her plenty of time to appreciate all the amenities, including the car's heater, a rarity much appreciated on a cold November night.

He entertained her with stories about "his" Harvard lecture series and presented her with a copy of *The Story of the Films* fresh from the printers. He reviewed the list of participants and they laughed together over the idea of Zukor with his heavy accent addressing an Ivy League classroom. Gloria shamed Joe for not having any women on the list, suggesting that there was no one who understood the industry better than Mary Pickford's mother, Charlotte, who was known to step into a theater and size up the box office in seconds. Joe agreed but suggested Gloria should have been the female representative. Gloria didn't need the compliment; she was already impressed with him. Everything he said made simple sense. He didn't try to mystify the business, and he paid attention to details. This time, when she brought out a cigarette after the meal, he was ready with a light.

On their ride back to Manhattan, Joe made his move. He wanted to do more than simply help finance her next film; he wanted to handle every aspect of her career. Together, they could make "important" films. "Together," he said with total conviction, "we could make millions." He was confident, he was enthusiastic, he had, professionally speaking, swept her off her feet. Before they said good night at the Barclay, she gave him carte blanche to go over all her records.

Early the next morning, Gloria's phone rang and she heard the very concerned voice of her secretary, Grace Crossman. Two men "who looked like gangsters" had just arrived at her office claiming they had authority to go through the files. Gloria laughed and assured her it was with her approval. "The man they work for is a Harvard graduate." Crossman wasn't so sure, but considering the financial situation they were in, any help was welcome.

Swanson's short trip to New York turned into weeks. A month after her first meeting with Kennedy, she was still at the Barclay and Henri was in Los Angeles, supervising the family move to the rented house. *Sadie Thompson* was supposed to have been completed in October, but it was now December. She had spent all her *Sadie* money and needed another advance to pay for the prints and advertising. She was personally responsible for her New York expenses, yet she stayed on and showed few signs of cutting costs, being driven around town by a full-time chauffeur, buying new gowns, taking a box at the opera, and hosting parties. She also continued to meet with Joe Kennedy. She proudly screened *Sadie Thompson* for him, and while he was impressed, he doubted it had the potential to wipe out her debts. Besides, now that he was going to be involved in her future, anything she had accomplished to date couldn't compare with what they would do together.

Kennedy reviewed her accounts in earnest, and he was shocked at their condition. The balance sheet for 1924, the year before she had become an independent producer, was a single handwritten page. It reported that she had personally gone through almost $300,000, but the level of detail went from minute to nonexistent. For instance, while $60 was noted for donations, with $469.19 for cigarettes and cigars, "Misc. expenses" were $4,415. "Paris office" was listed as costing $20,029, and "house bills" came to $3,044.07, without any delineation.

The numbers on the page told Kennedy far more than just what was going out. They revealed that her accounting was all reaction without any planning or responsibility and there was no improvement in the haphazard methods when her expenses ballooned by taking on all production costs.

The more at ease Gloria became with Joe, the more she railed against United Artists and Joe Schenck. She said they fought over every detail: Who was to pick up the cost of stamps for fan mail or the dishes in her studio dressing room? Was food eaten at the studio charged to the production or to Gloria personally? It was endless. She wanted UA to pay Tom Moore's salary because his time was spent monitoring their numbers, but while Schenck said that Moore was the "only real good man you have" and urged her to fire "all the rest," he wasn't about to hire him. She had thought joining United Artists would mean board meetings "over coffee on the terrace of Pickfair" and instead, it was these "long grueling business sessions in New York with Joe Schenck and a shrewd gang of lawyers, accountants and bankers."

Joe Schenck had been born in Russia and came to New York as a child with his brother, Nick. Together, they had risen to run Palisades Park in New Jersey before Joe branched into movie production with his

Norma Talmadge, Joe Schenck, and
Rudy Valentino, 1926

wife, Norma Talmadge. With a bulldog face and a fire hydrant body, Joe was as streetwise as they came, yet many in Hollywood found him to be a mensch. He had stood by Fatty Arbuckle during his trials and when the actor could not find a house he could afford, Schenck bought one and rented it to him for a nominal fee. In a town where late-night, high-stakes poker games could become treacherous, witnesses reported that Joe would "deliberately help whoever was deepest in the hole." Frances Marion and Anita Loos adored him, and Irene Mayer Selznick, the daughter of Louis B. Mayer and the wife of David Selznick, described Schenck as "worldly and likable, a smooth operator who wore an aura of power. He was big-time, generous, a sport."

Swanson, however, could not see anything larger than her own situation and just as she had done with Lasky, she cast Schenck in the role of evil overseer. He was frank with her, but she was afraid to listen to him, convinced he was looking out for himself first and the company second, with her interests coming in a distant third. With her debts mounting, she worried that he wanted to do to her what she thought he had done to Rudolph Valentino. When that popular star had found himself massively in arrears, Schenck stepped in, paid off Valentino's creditors, and put him on straight salary. Sight unseen, Schenck bought the rights to the book *The Sons of the Sheik,* and told his writer to throw out everything but the title and make that singular. Valentino reprising his most famous role was a surefire moneymaker and, when the star died in August 1926 shortly after the New York premiere of *The Son of the Sheik,* the box office went through the roof.

While many in Hollywood thought Schenck had rescued Valentino, Gloria was convinced that he wanted to bury her with debts in order to force her to do his bidding. The fact that she herself had run up these bills didn't seem to occur to her. Yet she knew she was in over her head and, as a result, more than a little scared. She had no one who could look her in the eyes and say "No." The closest she'd ever had to a mentor was Cecil B. De Mille; her father had been gone from her life since she was twelve. She had no family besides her mother that she was close to. Other major female stars such as Mary Pickford, Lillian and Dorothy Gish, and the Talmadge sisters all had strong, formidable mothers who kept an eagle eye on their daughters' affairs. Gloria's mother had hovered over her when she was very young, but after Gloria started working, Addie spread her own wings. She would marry two more times and while Gloria sent her money every week, she asked her not to put her name on the envelopes because, according to Gloria's daughter, "she didn't want the neighbors bothering her with questions about Gloria Swanson."

As she felt pressured and unsure, it was little wonder Gloria turned to Joe for support. Although he agreed with Schenck that she should make another film as soon as possible and get rid of most of her staff, he kept those thoughts to himself for the time being. Instead, he sympathized with her and encouraged her doubts about what "those people" were doing to her. "There is no question that one of the bonds between them that Joe exploited was that she had been taken advantage of by Jews," says William Dufty, Swanson's sixth and final husband and her companion for the last seventeen years of her life. Yet those bonds grew slowly; first Joe told her "it would be ridiculous" for the two of them to make a formal agreement until they figured out how to get her out of her current situation. Then he put the fear of God into her, explaining she had "so heavily mortgaged her future that very drastic steps must be taken." Only then did he provide the way out, promising to "work out her problems without any cost to her." There was a catch, of course. He was to have total control and represent her not only with Schenck, but with her current employees as well. It sounded great to Gloria and before she returned to Beverly Hills for the holidays, she told Joe to do whatever he needed to do on her behalf.

AS CHRISTMAS APPROACHED, things couldn't have been going better for Kennedy. It was the family's first in Riverdale and Rose was seven months pregnant with their eighth child. FBO sales had increased almost $1 million over the year before and they had made forty-three feature films and seventy-four shorts, another record. Best of all, his prominence was finally being recognized by the trades. He opened his

The Kennedy family Christmas card, 1927

December 23 issue of *Motion Picture News* to find their editorial page praising him as "sage and solid" and prophesying that "he will go far." And when *Film Daily* ran their annual column on what movie bigwigs wanted to find in their Christmas stocking, there was Joe Kennedy wishing "for another Harvard movie faculty" alongside Adolph Zukor asking for "a set of golf clubs that will break ninety," and D. W. Griffith longing "for the good old days."

For Kennedy, these were the good old days. He was in the habit of sending holiday gifts far and wide, but this year he ordered hundreds of copies of *The Story of the Films* with his name prominently displayed on the book's spine and cover page as editor, and sent them to an impressive list of players. Everyone who had participated or helped him organize the lecture series received one as well as almost anyone of stature he had done business with in the past such as John Hertz of the Yellow Cab Company, and Joseph Powell from his Fore River days. Not that he had to know, let alone have met, the recipients of his largesse. *The Story of the Films* was the perfect calling card to send to the likes of Douglas Fairbanks and Mary Pickford, simultaneously introducing himself and establishing himself as one of the privileged few.

With each package, Kennedy sent a note, claiming this was one of the first copies printed and that he "would esteem it a great honor and privilege to have you read this book." For many, he had their names embossed in gold on the cover. In addition to every studio head and the editors and publishers of the trades and major newspapers, he sent copies to more than a hundred theater owners and managers. Books went to the likes of Sid Grauman and Alexander Pantages as well as less famous names on what Joe labeled his "B list"—men with the power in Akron, Provo, and Wichita to book a film produced by Joseph P. Kennedy.

The response was immediate and notes of appreciation poured into his office. "Please don't think that I am trying to flatter you when I say that for the short time you have been in this industry you have done more to place it on a higher plane than any one individual," wrote Sam Dembow of the Publix theater chain in a sampling of the responses Kennedy received. Magazines such as *Motion Picture News* praised the book as "an exceedingly interesting volume . . . well worth the attention of everybody in the industry," and one New York reviewer noted that "it does seem strange that the best 'movie' story we ever read should come out of Harvard University."

As usual, Joe was planning on going to Palm Beach shortly after Christmas, but first there was much to be done and much to be delegated. Pat Scollard drew the assignment to go to Brookline and open their house in advance of Rose's arrival to await the birth of her child. It had been closed up since they moved to Riverdale, but she wanted to be near her Boston doctor so the children stayed in New York where their care was supervised by Mary Moore.

Kennedy spoke to Swanson on the phone almost daily. He promised he would deal with Joe Schenck, but there was an order to his plan. First, he checked in with A. H. Giannini regarding his financing proposal for her. Joe implied he was concerned that the bankruptcy of a star of Gloria's stature could damage the entire industry. Giannini agreed and pledged to give her a line of credit if Joe helped her reorganize.

Kennedy knew he was going to get rid of most of her staff, but how he revealed his cards was crucial, so he turned to the only man who had access to all the information yet did not depend upon Swanson for his income: her longtime attorney, Milton Cohen. Joe wrote him in the most pleasant and noncommittal tone possible, asking him, at Gloria's request, to prepare "a list of all her obligations and also the market value of her assets as you view them."

Kennedy then called in E. B. Derr and told him to pack for Hollywood. He briefed him on the Swanson situation, laid out who he was to talk to, in what order, and the overall goal: to free Gloria of all obligations so they could enter into an agreement without the burden of her debt. If that couldn't be done, he didn't want the deal—and he wanted the deal. Joe was counting on the gang to pull this off; he was to be kept informed but was delegating the details to them. Kennedy had the big vision and set the agenda; it was their job to accomplish it. How the team that Gloria came to call "The Four Horsemen" succeeded is a case study of their methods, their skills, their loyalty, and their united determination to accomplish whatever Kennedy wanted.

Derr arrived in Los Angeles in early January, checked in to the Ambassador, and went to see Milton Cohen, who had been Swanson's attorney. Cohen had represented her former husband Herbert Somborn in their divorce, and soon afterward, he told Gloria he regretted his role and offered his services to her at any time. She took him up on it and over the past five years he had been "invaluable" to her and rarely sent a bill. Cohen adored her and worried about her so he agreed to do what Kennedy asked without revealing who was behind the request. Within days of receiving Kennedy's letter, Cohen had Tom Moore's seven-page, single-spaced memo listing Gloria's immediate obligations and his recommendations for action, based on the assumption he would continue to be a part of her operation. Cohen then informed Moore, who was still in California at Gloria's request, that his services would no longer be needed and asked for a proposed separation agreement. By the time Derr met with Cohen, the settlement papers were on the lawyer's desk, asking for $50,000 in United Artists stock and payment to cover his return to New York.

With Tom Moore on his way out, the rest of Gloria's staff fell in line. Her secretary, Grace Crossman, had turned over all her files. She assured Derr, "If I don't know the whole story, I can usually hunt up the pieces and make a whole out of them." She had been the first to be in on Kennedy's involvement and had proven her loyalty by keeping it to herself. Because she was so friendly with everyone and seemed so inconsequential, she was a constant source of useful gossip. Now she sent copies of everything to Derr and Eddie Moore and occasionally Kennedy himself.

Pete Bedard was just as cooperative. Gloria promised he would always have a place with her and he was almost relieved not to be responsible for juggling the dwindling funds. He itemized outstanding debts and even joined in the intrigue, assisting Crossman in getting official copies of all her United Artists contracts without arousing suspicion that anything was in the works.

Charlie Sullivan had returned home for the holidays, but before he went back to Hollywood, he worked with Grace Crossman to pay off Gloria's former director Al Parker. Pat Scollard and Eddie Moore were in the loop now as well, compiling information as it came in and assembling a full list of Gloria's current staff, assets, and liabilities.

In Los Angeles, Derr had Cohen make an appointment to see Joe Schenck. It was 5:30 in the afternoon when they arrived at his office to find the Hollywood mogul getting a manicure. Clearly he was not expecting Derr, and he ordered everyone but Cohen and Derr out of his office. After Cohen's introductions, Derr opened the meeting with the explanation he and Kennedy had previously agreed upon: Bob Kane and Doc Giannini had told Gloria to consult Kennedy and therefore they were creating a plan to clean up her affairs. Swanson, Derr said, "has a bee in her bonnet to clear out" of United Artists by filing for bankruptcy, based "on the grounds of excessive interest and censorship." This none too veiled charge brought out a predictably defensive reaction from Schenck.

Why hadn't Gloria come to him directly? Where did anybody get the idea of "excessive interest"? He hadn't made "a cent" himself. Derr watched and listened as Schenck "ranted and blustered and puffed" his resentment.

Derr tried telling him that Kennedy's only interest was to keep Gloria out of bankruptcy because he saw that as threatening all film financing.

"That's bunk," replied Schenck. "It might if Lasky or Mayer went bankrupt, but who would have sympathy for a girl getting $6,500 a week going bankrupt? Besides, she has her house and stocks and enough assets to keep her solvent. She just needs quick cash."

So Derr switched his approach. Perhaps Schenck was offended because Joe hadn't come in person to discuss it and maybe Cohen should have mentioned the purpose of the meeting. Hopefully, he added, Schenck understood that this "was the more courteous and gentlemanly way to handle this."

"No," Schenck told him in no uncertain terms. "Kennedy should have written me and told me Gloria had approached him and seen if I had any objections." Getting that off his chest seemed to soften Schenck a bit, but he kept up his monologue. Derr should understand how upsetting it was to have a *Variety* reporter questioning him about Kennedy's involvement in Gloria's affairs before anyone had told him directly.

"What does Kennedy expect out of this?" was Schenck's next question. "What's he doing it for? Is Kennedy altruistic? Am I to believe that?" Then Schenck turned his wrath on Gloria.

"I've had more trouble with her and her pictures than all the others [United Artists stars] combined. She's too lazy and slow and spends too much. That last picture cost 200 thousand too much. She has nothing but bad advice, but no real help. Gloria always listens to the last guy she talked to and now it's Kennedy. If Kennedy wants to help out and that's his only object, why doesn't he just loan her the money? That's all she needs is money and Kennedy has plenty of that. Let her leave United Artists. Let Kennedy take over her loans. Let Kennedy have her. She's nothing but trouble."

"You've always been fair and honest," inserted Cohen, seeking to pacify Schenck. "There are no complaints about you." But Schenck didn't want to hear it because he wasn't finished with Derr. How was it that this perfect stranger was walking in on him to talk about Swanson? "What's the game? What does Kennedy want?"

Derr repeated his original lines about just wanting to help Gloria and when it was obvious Schenck wasn't going to get any other answer, the discussion turned to the business at hand. Cohen outlined Kennedy's plan: all rights to the first two pictures Swanson had made with UA, *The Love of Sunya* and *Sadie Thompson,* would be turned over to Schenck. She would forfeit all profits and percentages and he'd release her from what his books said she owed him. United Artists would distribute her next picture, whatever that was to be, but it would be financed independently with Schenck paying her $175,000, less the $50,000 he had already advanced. The goal was to have Gloria "free and clear after the third picture."

The atmosphere in the room had relaxed to the point that Schenck called for the manicurist to return and then he took the floor again, mulling over the proposal out loud. "The first picture is no good, but the second picture might be different." He needed time to think and suggested Cohen come back tomorrow at noon and perhaps they could settle something.

Derr drove home with Cohen and the lawyer was the picture of hand-wringing anxiety. Perhaps the meeting had ended with the glimmer of possibility for agreement, but he was concerned that Derr had not shown enough deference. "Schenck has to be handled with soft soap." As for Gloria, she had to stop this talk of bankruptcy. "You have no idea what I have been through with her. She signs her name to everything and then comes to me to pull her out of the fire." Every time he put her on the right path, she would agree and then, a minute later, she was resisting again. This time would be different, Cohen promised almost to himself, as if being with Derr had given him courage. This time he was really going to stand up to her.

Derr followed Cohen into his house to be at his side when he called Swanson. The lawyer started to tell her about the meeting, but he didn't get much in before she interrupted. "It's all so messy. Wouldn't bankruptcy be easier?" Instead of being firm as he had vowed just minutes before, Cohen verbally petted her and assured her they would work it out. She should meet with him and Derr at eleven the next day, before he went back to see Schenck.

Gloria had little respect for anyone she could roll over and while she appreciated all Cohen had done for her, if he didn't stand up to her, how could she believe he would stand up to Schenck? So Gloria went into FBO early that next morning to meet with Derr alone and once again she railed against Schenck, repeating her concern that he wanted to do to her what he had done to Valentino. Whatever Schenck was up to, she knew Derr was the man to handle him. Cohen could not go into that meeting alone. Derr was already tiring of her complaints as well as her new habit of coming to FBO as if she worked there. He suspected that was how the *Variety* reporter Schenck had mentioned had figured out she was doing something with Kennedy. She owned five cars including two Rolls-Royces and a Peugeot and any of her distinctive automobiles were bound to be noticed.

Derr wasn't going to let such obstacles deter him. The boss knew what he wanted and it was Derr's job to get it done. And Swanson was probably right about Cohen. To the attorney's relief, Derr went alone to the meeting, determined to hammer out an agreement. Schenck greeted him warmly, apologized for his attitude of the day before, and didn't comment on Cohen's absence. Schenck announced he would be "very glad to go through with this deal, if . . ." He then proceeded to suggest several ways that he could be protected by Gloria's next picture if the income from *Sunya* and *Sadie* failed to cover the remaining bills. Derr sat and listened and then asked Schenck, "Do you know any bankers who would be willing to finance a picture which carried not only its own obligations, but some other picture's as well?" Schenck had to say no and admitted if the conditions were reversed, he would never agree to it.

Schenck had given it a shot, and while he feigned otherwise, releasing Gloria was tempting for a variety of reasons. Things were looking up at United Artists; Sam Goldwyn had joined as a partner in October and Schenck had just signed Lillian Gish to a two-film deal with the idea of reuniting her with D. W. Griffith, an original UA partner who had been less than productive. They were opening two-thousand-seat theaters in Los Angeles, Chicago, and Detroit over the next few months. And under her contract, Gloria should have completed six films by now. Instead, they were just getting ready to release the second one. He found her "unreasonable and ridiculous" in her near constant negotiations and renegotiations. He was tired of her problems, her whining, and her attitude of entitlement.

Now it was Schenck's turn to make a proposal. Gloria still owed him $92,000 on the first two pictures and another $12,000 he had advanced her to make a payment to Al Parker. Schenck agreed that in exchange for total ownership and all rights to the first two films, he would write off the entire debt. She would continue as a member of United Artists and be given two years to pay for the preferred stock she had committed to purchase when she joined the company. She was welcome to produce her next film however she wanted and United Artists would distribute it. He even agreed to let her use her stock to pay off Tom Moore and Al Parker.

It was time to get it all down on paper and Schenck and Derr agreed to meet again the following Monday with their attorneys. By the time they were shaking hands goodbye, Schenck was a different man than he had been the day before. He was happy they had come to a settlement and reminded Derr that he had let Fred Thomson out of his agreement to join UA at Kennedy's request. "Joe Kennedy has always indicated a friendly attitude. I'll do anything to help somebody I like, and I like Joe Kennedy." In showing Derr out, Schenck said, "Give Joe my personal respects and tell him that I will personally cooperate in any way that Joe thinks is advisable to square up Gloria's affairs."

Derr left the meeting thinking, "He talks just like a slippery eel," but Derr had completed his mission: Gloria was about to be free of encumbrances and ready to be delivered to Joe on the proverbial silver platter.

IN NEW YORK and Los Angeles or from the road, Kennedy's men cabled or talked to each other almost daily. Like their boss, they used the phone frequently and put as little as possible in writing. In their missives to each other, Gloria was referred to as "the client" or simply "star." Schenck was "Big Boy" and Kennedy was occasionally "J.P." but most often "Boss." It wasn't just people who had code names. Each major film company was designated as a state: Paramount was Maine, Fox was Vermont, Pathé was Connecticut, and so on.

Derr, Scollard, Sullivan, and Moore assessed the progress they were making on the Swanson front. On Derr's instructions, Pete Bedard cleaned out her California bank accounts and turned the money over in two separate checks, one for $20,000 and the other for $14,150. Derr sent the checks to Eddie Moore in New York, asking him to use the first to open a new trustee account at Kennedy's Columbia Trust in Boston and the second to pay Gloria's outstanding New York bills. Moore looked over Grace Crossman's shoulder as she wrote out checks to pay off department stores (Bonwit Teller, B. Altman's, and Saks), beauty salons (Elizabeth Arden, Helena Rubenstein), and jewelry stores, along with the more mundane charges from cleaners, the telephone company, and Western Union. Moore then saw to it that each check was either delivered or put in the mail to the respective creditor and only then deposited the check. Out of that came Crossman's salary and a $100 payment to Gloria's New York auditor, Mr. Speidel, which Moore delivered in person. He insisted that the accountant first sign a prepared statement releasing Swanson from any future claims. That accomplished, Eddie handed him the check and informed him his services were no longer needed. After all the bills were paid, $100 remained in the account.

There was also the Internal Revenue Service to be dealt with. Through Kennedy's contacts, he learned the government was "inclined to be lenient" if they thought her cash-strapped condition was temporary. However, if she was selling off assets without paying the government, they were prepared to bring action against her. Kennedy put his lawyers on the case to negotiate "adjusting her obligations" while simultaneously quietly selling what available stock she held in her name.

Now it was Pat Scollard's turn to step to the fore. His charge was to replace the current Gloria Swanson Productions with a new entity they called Gloria Productions. As a template, Scollard used the incorporation papers of Fred Thomson Productions. He produced a similar corporate structure with bylaws that allowed for maximum flexibility while keeping all the power in-house. Derr was named president, Scollard vice president, and Pat arranged for all stock to be issued to himself to be allocated later as Joe instructed. However, Scollard ran into a brick wall when it came to filing the papers in Delaware; it was one of the rare instances when it became problematic that none of the Horsemen were attorneys. The Corporation Trust Company of Delaware required a lawyer to approve the papers before final filing and since secrecy was key, Scollard didn't want to show the papers to anyone outside the "family."

The Corporation Trust agreed to take the legal approval over the phone and Scollard went through his personal phone book looking for

Boston attorneys he could trust, but he found they "were all out of town or out to lunch." His reluctance to bring in FBO's counsel Benjamin DeWitt reveals how surreptitious he viewed his charge to be, but time was of the essence, so he simply told DeWitt, "We're forming a dummy corporation at the Coast." The lawyer made the phone call as instructed and Scollard made sure DeWitt didn't have anything in writing. While it was all technically legal, it skimmed the edges. "Five minutes later," Scollard told Derr, "I had a man in an automobile going over the road from Wilmington Delaware to Dover to file the charter and I want to tell you that there was never a corporation formed with the speed that this one was formed. If I don't go to jail on this deal, I never will."

By the middle of January, Kennedy was confident everything was going as planned and in his daily calls to Gloria, he began campaigning to have her join him in Palm Beach. She could rest, they could get business done, bring Henri. Lance Heath, Gloria's publicist, was begging her to come to San Francisco for the opening of *Sadie Thompson,* but that was history now as far as she was concerned. Joe was right. She deserved a vacation. Why not Palm Beach?

With her debts paid, agreed to be written off or isolated into separate dealings, and the new corporation in place, the final stage was set. Early in the morning of January 25, Derr saw Henri and Gloria off at the train station and assured her that everything was under control. While the corporation papers had yet to be printed and signing the agreement with Schenck would have to await his return from the East, Derr had prepared a five-page power of attorney giving him the authority to sign everything on her behalf. Right there on the platform, Pete Bedard signed as a witness, making it all the more official, as he served as secretary and assistant treasurer of Gloria Swanson Productions, Inc., the old corporation Derr was about to abolish. With her signature, Swanson gave Derr the power to buy, sell, receive, demand, sue, deliver, lease, mortgage, transact, endorse, negotiate, receive, vote, manage, settle, adjust, and generally to "execute and deliver any and all documents and contracts" as legal proxy and representative of Gloria Swanson, both personally and professionally.

Gloria and Henri boarded the train unaware that *Variety* and *Film Daily* were headlining the Swanson–Kennedy partnership. Pat Scollard couldn't help laughing with Derr that no one had known "anything about the deal at all until it broke this morning in the papers and now they are wondering what it is all about."

After leaving the station with Gloria's power of attorney in his pocket,

Derr's next order of business that morning was to inform Milton Cohen that his services were no longer needed. The attorney was shocked, yet instead of blaming Kennedy or Derr, he assumed Gloria was behind his dismissal. Finding that she had already left town, he cabled her at her next stop expressing his outrage: "Regret your attitude exceedingly. Wish always to be your friend but never your lawyer. Arrange immediately for other counsel."

Gloria didn't have any idea what Cohen was talking about, but she was already taking to heart her instructions to turn over everything to Kennedy's men, so instead of responding to Cohen, she cabled Derr. After repeating the contents of Cohen's communication, she wrote, "Can't see what I have done that is so terrible. Advise whether I am to cut my throat or not. Best Regards, GS." And with that, she continued on her way to Palm Beach and didn't look back.

# CHAPTER 12

# "Like a Roped Horse"

## (DECEMBER 1927–FEBRUARY 1928)

*J*oe Kennedy had masterminded the reorganization of Gloria Swanson's professional life during that New York winter of 1927, but he spent most of his actual time focusing on broad-range plans. He and Guy Currier incorporated their FBO holdings in a Delaware corporation they named the Gower Street Company. The incorporation gave them a structure in lieu of a partnership agreement, a place to roll their stock in and out of, all the while keeping their dealings as private as possible. Then Kennedy went back to Pat Powers and bought his remaining FBO stock for $400,000. Joe Schnitzer wanted to keep some of his stock, but his holdings were minor enough not to interfere with any of Kennedy's plans and he was still with the company, albeit downgraded from head of production to supervising distribution.

Before he expanded his interests, Kennedy needed to assure himself all was on solid ground at FBO. December was the time for year-end conferences and everyone of import within the company was called into his office. Bill LeBaron, along with the heads of marketing and sales, reviewed the upcoming season's production and publicity plans. Joe wanted every possible association maximized and no angle was overlooked. The local Chamber of Commerce was sought out to support *Coney Island,* and a clothing company's magazine ads featured pictures of Lois Wilson and other *Coney Island* stars wearing their bathing suits with copy promoting the film. *Hello Bill* was retitled *Moulders of Men* and, because it was based on a story by the editor of the Elks magazine, it was promoted in the country's 1,500 Elks lodges. In full-page ads, "The Master showman Joseph P. Kennedy" promised theater owners that *Moulders of Men* "dwarfs all tie-ups of the past and offers an entirely new merchandising angle."

Films were not made and then marketed; they were initiated with marketing in mind. For *Legionnaires in Paris,* a small crew was sent to the City of Light to film during the International Legionnaires convention,

Joe Schnitzer (center), Bill LeBaron, and E. B. Derr (on
his right) celebrating Kennedy's two years heading FBO

giving FBO an excuse to promote the film through every American
Legion Hall in the country. *Legionnaires in Paris* and *Chicago After Midnight* were to be released as "specials" in February under the umbrella of
a "Grand Jubilee commemorating the two year anniversary of Joseph P.
Kennedy's entrance into the picture business." Every piece of promotional material included Kennedy's name and often a picture of him as
well. If Joe could sell more movies and promote himself at the same
time, why not?

Kennedy trusted LeBaron when it came to production, but he needed
his own man on the ground in Hollywood on a full-time basis and Charlie Sullivan was chosen. He squeezed in a brief trip to Boston before
packing permanently for the coast. Sullivan's official title was assistant
treasurer of FBO, second to Derr, and he was made an FBO vice president as a reward for the move. Kennedy had faith in the quiet Sullivan to
monitor and report back on personnel, finances, and the nuances only an
inside man would notice.

With his FBO housekeeping completed and his personal promotion campaign underway, Kennedy looked to new realms to conquer within the ever changing business. When *Jesse James,* the first Fred Thomson "super western," was released by Paramount in the late fall of 1927, some accused it of glamorizing the outlaw, but reviewers praised the film as a new high-water mark in production values with its hundreds of extras and lush location shots. *Motion Picture World*'s review took up half a page with the other half devoted to a film almost clunky in comparison, predominantly silent yet with a few lines of dialogue and songs that appeared to come directly from the screen. It was destined to become one of the industry's historic benchmarks.

*The Jazz Singer* was hardly the first time sound had been synchronized with film; experiments had been conducted since the 1890s. Yet no less an authority than Thomas Edison, "the father of the motion picture," believed there was no future in sound films. He was always confident that "voices can be reproduced to fit in just the right place," but he considered it "a waste of time. I don't think the talking picture will ever be successful in the United States. Americans prefer silent drama . . . they will never get enthusiastic over any voices being mingled in. Yes, there will be a novelty to it for a little while, but the glitter will soon wear off and the movie fans will cry for silences or a little orchestra music."

Most studio chiefs took solace in that pronouncement, but in October of 1927, when Al Jolson ad-libbed from the screen "You ain't heard nothin' yet," at least two men besides the Warner brothers knew he was right: Joe Kennedy and David Sarnoff, the head of the Radio Corporation of America.

At first glance, David Sarnoff might have appeared to be another "pants presser," an immigrant Jew who got lucky, but luck was hardly the word to describe Sarnoff's early years. Kennedy had heard tales of ancestral oppression; Sarnoff had witnessed it with his own eyes. Born in poverty in Uzilian, a village in Russia's Minsk province, David was five when his father left for America. David was sent to live with his grand-uncle, a rabbi who ordered him to study the Talmud twelve hours every day, chanting the pages until the texts were chiseled into his memory.

Four long years later, when his father had earned enough to send for the family, David was reunited with his mother and two younger brothers. As they huddled together waiting for the train, they watched Cossacks on horseback whip a crowd of women and children. After over a month in steerage conditions, Leah Sarnoff and her three young sons arrived in New York in the summer of 1900.

Instead of a long delayed childhood, David found his sickly father in a fourth floor walk-up on New York's Lower East Side and the now ten-year-old boy barely squeezed in a bit of school before becoming the family breadwinner. A sister and brother were added to the family before Abraham Sarnoff died a few years later. David worked several jobs at a time, as a delivery boy, a newspaper hawker, a singer in the local synagogue, but it was when he was hired as a telegram delivery boy that he discovered his passion. Teaching himself Morse code and reading everything he could find about wireless technology, young David went to work on ships at sea as a wireless operator. Legend has it he was on duty at the new Marconi station at the top of a New York department store on the night of April 14, 1912, when he began decoding the incoming message that the *Titanic* had hit an iceberg and was sinking fast. After notifying the police and the press, Sarnoff stayed at his station for days, recording the action and disseminating the names of survivors as they came in.

It wasn't until 1919, when General Electric bought American Marconi and formed the Radio Corporation of America, that Sarnoff found support for an idea he had minted in a detailed memo several years before. His concept was to make and sell "radio music boxes" that he prophesied would be akin to phonographs and pianos in popularity. While his main purpose was to "bring music into the house by wireless," he added the alluring possibility of sending out lectures, concerts, and even baseball scores to the hinterlands up to fifty miles away. While a variety of others including Lee De Forest, Edwin Armstrong, and Reginald Fessenden had experimented with the idea, Sarnoff had a company with capital behind him. The first radios were small crystal sets and the number of listeners to the returns of the Harding-Cox election in the fall of 1920 was only in the thousands. It took the broadcast of the world championship boxing match between Jack Dempsey and Georges Carpentier to light the fuse of what was soon a national craze.

Over the next few years, Americans spent over $100 million on radios, crystals, and batteries, and Sarnoff rose in proportion to radio's success. He was in the forefront of the many patent battles, a key player in their settlement, and brought in Westinghouse as a 40 percent owner of RCA's manufacturing arm. By 1926 he was vice president and general manager of RCA and had established the National Broadcasting Company, the first nationwide broadcasting system, as a subsidiary of RCA.

Through it all, Sarnoff had learned to speak superbly articulate English and became an office politician par excellence. Instead of resenting the fact he had been deprived of a childhood, Sarnoff lived his profes-

David Sarnoff

sional life the same way he had once studied the Talmud, putting in superhuman hours with intense determination. Always looking forward, Sarnoff had been singing the praises of the potential of "talking" pictures since the early 1920s.

William Fox had purchased the rights to a variation of sound-on-film technology and he turned to Sarnoff for the other components he needed to make the system complete. Fox offered "to make him a very rich man" if they came to an agreement, but Sarnoff wasn't after short-term personal gain; he was an empire builder with long-range plans. Within the industry, Sarnoff was called "Napoleonic" and there was little doubt his ambition was "ultimate sovereignty" of RCA. Still, Fox's convictions intensified Sarnoff's belief that it was time to move into films and move quickly.

Sarnoff was talking with his friend Boston department store magnate Louis Kirstein when Kennedy's name came up. Kirstein was an investor whose dividends kept coming in every quarter so he highly recommended the one man he knew in the film business. While Kennedy later told the story that he and Sarnoff had cut a deal over lunch at Grand Central Station's Oyster Bar in early October of 1927, correspondence between the two men indicates that they didn't actually meet in person until December, after Kennedy had sent him a signed copy of *The Story of the Films.*

Sarnoff was two years younger and several inches shorter than Kennedy, but both men were supremely self-confident, prided themselves in dressing meticulously, and possessed sharp blue eyes capable of mercilessly sizing up the other. Their approach to business could not have been farther apart: Sarnoff was zealous about his medium and in building his company for the long haul, while to Kennedy films were a product to be sold at the maximum profit in the shortest time possible. Yet "persuasive," "dynamic," and "obstinate" were words used to describe both men and whatever else they thought after their initial meeting, they knew they needed each other. Kennedy had the studio and Sarnoff had the equipment. They put their heads together and started planning.

Within weeks, their association was made public with the announcement that RCA was buying twenty thousand shares of FBO for $24 a share, the same shares that had been valued at $6 only two years before. The deal made sense for both parties and to the trades: Kennedy was putting FBO in the forefront of talking pictures, and RCA, along with its partners, General Electric and Westinghouse, now had a base of operation to showcase their technology.

"A revolution in entertainment" is how their joint FBO/RCA release described their affiliation even though RCA's rival, Western Electric, clearly had the edge. They were working with the Warner brothers and had several other major studios under contract already. Fox too was advertising "a new era" with his Movietone sound on film. However, for almost all the talk, functionality was something else again. Other companies' equipment was not that far ahead of Sarnoff's, and RCA's relationship with FBO was unique because they were actually buying into the film company. Sarnoff and one of his bankers, Charles Stone, were added to the FBO board and, in return, Kennedy received half a million dollars in new capital and free access to sound equipment and "the services of the three greatest electrical companies in the world."

Kennedy visited Schenectady, where Sarnoff gave him a personal tour of the General Electric laboratories, demonstrating the sound-on-film recording equipment that was ready to go into large-scale production. Joe proclaimed their system "staggering in its possibilities" and couldn't resist adding the paternalistic claim that he was "happy indeed that FBO will be able to bring them to the industry." He was also shown another idea being developed, called "television," which Sarnoff saw as a way to take movies into private homes; however, the minimal press coverage predicted it was doubtful that "radio pictures" would "become practical for a considerable period of time, if ever."

With his relationship with Sarnoff out in the open, Kennedy next went behind closed doors to meet with the new head of Pathé, John "J.J." Murdock. Pathé was one of the original film companies, founded by Charles and Emile Pathé in France in 1896. While Lumière and Edison were working on their innovative machinery, the Pathé brothers focused on what could be created with the film. By the turn of the century they were in position to catch the wave of popularity of screening short movies at fairgrounds and music halls. Pathé flourished by creating the first weekly newsreels, and by 1914 it had five thousand employees in France and 1,500 more throughout the world.

Before Kennedy entered the picture, many financial interests had been in and out of Pathé, and since late 1926, Elisha Walker, president of the private banking and investment firm Blair and Company, had held the largest stake. Walker was an MIT graduate now in his mid-forties who was becoming well known (and very rich) on Wall Street, working with the Rockefellers and financing "a number of spectacular oil industry transactions." With the backing of J. P. Morgan and Company, Walker entered filmmaking by investing in Pathé, buying a portion of Producers Distributing and Cecil B. De Mille Productions and then merging the companies.

The moneyman behind Producers Distributing and De Mille was Jeremiah Milbank, a staunch Republican and a "deeply religious" man who had been swept into films by De Mille's enthusiasm for *The King of Kings.* Milbank agreed to become the director's partner and with the new infusion of money, De Mille bought what had been the Ince Studios in Culver City, reopening it with a ceremony that rivaled the pomp of Louis B. Mayer's christening of his nearby MGM the year before.

As Pathé expanded, part of the newly merged vaudeville theater company Keith-Albee-Orpheum came under the Walker-Milbank umbrella. It was another example of the prescient Kennedy's prediction of Darwinian consolidations and what had once been a voice in the wilderness was beginning to be common knowledge. "As the industry moves on," summarized a *Film Daily,* "the field narrows."

The newly enlarged Pathé brought together a combination of personalities and interests so diverse, they were a challenge to get in the same room, let alone to agree on how to proceed. There were now fifteen members of the Pathé board, including Edward Albee, Cecil B. De Mille, and Charles Pathé, as well as financiers such as Walker, Milbank, and Ed Lynch, and they were foundering in their attempts to find common ground. They may have merged on paper, but most of the players were still primarily looking after what they considered their own interests.

The two men with the most money on the line, Elisha Walker and Jeremiah Milbank, decided that John Murdock, the general manager of Keith-Albee, had the experience and wherewithal to head the new Pathé. Yet after several months, Walker was growing concerned. The sale of debentures they had floated in June had not been a success and their stock was slumping. Bankruptcy was a possibility "unless everything could be cut to the bone." They had not given up hope of turning the company around, but were hedging their bets with plans for a "gradual liquidation."

The trades had been predicting a merger of Pathé with First National, a consortium of theater circuits that also produced its own films, yet Walker and Milbank didn't think it was time to get bigger, which would take even more money, or to sell their company at fire sale rates. They needed someone capable of bringing the numbers into shape for making a real profit or, failing that, getting Pathé in a position to sell. And that's where Joe Kennedy came in. His turnaround of FBO was well publicized and he was the only man in Hollywood who was "a banker by profession" with hands-on experience in the film business. He was golden. Walker already had invested $6 million and he made it clear he was willing to put another much-needed $2 million into the company only if Kennedy came in. Walker instructed Murdock to meet with Kennedy as soon as possible and make it work.

For any ordinary film man, the thought of running one company while managing and expanding another was inconceivable, yet Pathé intrigued Kennedy for a number of reasons. His ego was stroked, of course, and there was no doubt in his mind that he was uniquely qualified to improve the company's bottom line. Pathé also opened up a variety of doors to him: new financing, new studio space, and, through the Keith-Albee-Orpheum connection, new theaters.

Murdock entered his meeting with Kennedy knowing he was being sent in to make a deal, no matter what the demands were, yet he was no easy mark himself. At sixty-eight, J. J. Murdock was a small, dapper man who sported a mustache and a shock of long white hair parted cleanly on the side. Born in Scotland, he had come to America at the age of twelve and was soon working as a stagehand. He moved on to Chicago where he managed theaters and, in 1909, formed the International Producing and Projecting Company to import European films. Murdock then joined the Keith vaudeville circuit and within a few short years rose to the position of general manager.

If Kennedy's way of insinuating himself was to feign self-deprecation, Murdock's was to profess ignorance and then proceed to milk the person's mind of the business details he was after. He figured that if the opponent thought you were smart, he would be intimidated and hold back, but those who assumed you really didn't know about the subject at hand would relax and pour their stories out. His dark, deep-set eyes rarely missed a trick, but this time it was Murdock who poured out the situation he was facing.

When Pathé and Producers Distributing had merged, they both had sales and distribution systems in place. It was assumed they could save over $1 million a year in reducing those duplications, yet many of the exchange offices had long leases and the high-priced executives had multiyear contracts. The only place to make real cuts was in the sales force. It did not take long to realize they had fired salesmen with solid personal relationships with exhibitors and accounts were lost as a result. Over half of their movies were two-reel westerns that should have sold themselves, but now they were looking at several million dollars' worth of films sitting on the shelf. There was a glut on the market everywhere. FBO was shutting down for January, Warner Bros. had done the same, and both United Artists and MGM were laying off staff, yet Pathé's unsold backlog was the largest in the business.

With all of Pathé's problems, Murdock knew he should be concentrating on what he knew best, and that was theaters. He was confident he could handle Ed Albee and the other executives inherited in the mergers. Murdock's biggest challenge was Cecil B. De Mille. When pressed to cut costs, De Mille informed Murdock "that would not be possible" and proceeded to increase the quality (and price) of his productions. Murdock might be president, but De Mille wasn't listening.

*King of Kings* was the latest grand spectacle from the man who had been dubbing himself "Director General" since directing his first feature. In the fifteen years since, De Mille had been with several companies and his current agreement with Milbank gave him the freedom to direct his own films while supervising a dozen others. No one was disputing his genius, but his habit of wearing a "uniform" of riding pants and puttees, carrying an omnipresent megaphone, and being followed by an entourage at the ready with anything he might need including a chair, set a new level of autocratic and egocentric behavior.

De Mille now wanted another $1 million for improvements at the studio. If his full slate of films for the next season was put into production, it would cost $5 million. The primary concern wasn't the one or two films a year De Mille himself made; although they were expensive, they eventually showed profits. It was the dozen other films he was currently supervising where the costs had to be slashed. If Pathé was going to continue to operate or be profitably sold, De Mille had to be dealt with. Milbank knew it, Walker knew it, and Murdock knew it. They just had to get De Mille to know it and they saw Kennedy as the man to convince him.

Rescuing a company spending more each week than it was bringing in was just the challenge Kennedy loved and to go mano a mano with the man who had given him such a hard time before deigning to come to Harvard would be a personal pleasure. And it was all at the request of Elisha Walker and Jeremiah Milbank, serious moneymen it couldn't hurt to please. Still, Joe didn't want to appear too eager and he had a few caveats. His staff was to have several weeks to go over all the numbers and during that time, this was all to stay just between the financiers, Murdock, and Kennedy. If they moved forward, he was to be publicly labeled an "adviser" to Pathé with no salary attached, with the private understanding that he would receive a fee for services of not less than $500,000, which would come in the form of 100,000 shares of the company's stock (at the moment valued at $10 a share). Pathé was to keep some money in the bank by not paying dividends for the next quarter with the explanation that "the company has decided to conserve its resources." Kennedy didn't want any public association with that or any announcement until he was back at his desk in late February. In the meantime, he was off on vacation.

With Rose in Boston, days away from giving birth, Joe bid goodbye to his seven children in New York and, along with Eddie Moore and Ted O'Leary, boarded the train for Palm Beach. The men were all installed at the Royal Poinciana Hotel by the time Gloria Swanson and her marquis pulled out of the Los Angeles train station. Kept informed of every detail of Derr's machinations by cable or by phone, Kennedy was feeling upbeat as he, Moore, and O'Leary, dressed in their straw hats, "tropical suits and white shoes," waited on the Palm Beach platform to meet his new star and her husband. The die was cast when Joe, after abruptly kissing Gloria as he greeted her on the train, ushered Henri, Ted, and Eddie into one of the waiting cars and Gloria into the other so they could be alone for the ride to the hotel.

Swanson's arrival was big news, even in a resort used to larger-than-life celebrities. Invitations and cards awaited her, but the most exclusive party in her honor had been arranged by Kennedy. Eddie Moore told her competition for inclusion was so great, "anybody who didn't get an invitation has just one week to commit suicide or leave town." Joe roared with laughter, revealing what Gloria saw as "an endearing, boyish pride in himself."

Pat Scollard came down for a few days to join the group for business sessions. Gloria was briefed on her new streamlined operation, in which Derr was the key man with Sullivan in charge of the finances. No longer was she carrying "a bunch of worthless passengers" on her payroll; if she had any qualms about anyone, including Milton Cohen, being let go, she kept them to herself. She was "so pleased and grateful" to no longer be making decisions; she thought only of the joys of what she considered to be a well-deserved vacation.

The partying was intense, with Joe showing off his Hollywood royalty "as if he was P.T. Barnum and we were Lavinia and Tom Thumb." Everywhere they went, Joe was beaming with pride. Financially, he had been able to afford Palm Beach for some time, but now he was trumping their social game in a way he had never even dreamed possible. He was royalty by association.

Still, Joe wanted more. He arranged for Eddie Moore to take Henri deep-sea fishing, then begged off at the last minute by claiming he had "business calls to make that won't keep." Gloria entertained herself shopping on Worth Avenue, but shortly after she returned to her hotel room, she looked up from her bed to see Kennedy standing at her door, "in his white flannels and his argyle sweater and his two-toned shoes."

In her 1980 memoir, Swanson told of Joe rushing at her as he moaned, " 'No longer, no longer. Now.' He was like a roped horse, rough, arduous, racing to be free." Within minutes, it was over with "a hasty climax" and "apart from his guilty, passionate mutterings, he had still said nothing cogent." Somehow, she "had known this would happen" and didn't even feign resistance. Instead, she concluded that "the strange man beside me, more than my husband, owned me."

The very attributes that had attracted her to the marquis—his gentleness, his adoration, and his superb manners—had slowly become a hindrance. In Paris, Henri had been indispensable, dealing with everything from the press, to the bureaucrats, to the travel arrangements with dispatch. In America, he had no real role to play. As James Quirk, editor of *Photoplay,* put it, "I can't imagine a more difficult position for a young man than to become the husband of the most talked about woman in the world."

Gloria needed a man who would forcibly stand up for her and to her; that was not Henri. Swanson paid for everything, set the social schedule, and ruled the roost at the studio and at home. She was, as he called her, "ma patronne." He had entered her life as an employee and an underling he would stay. After watching him in the meetings she had insisted he attend, Gloria concluded that Henri was "thoroughly unexceptional."

While she had no desire to divorce, she was on the rebound when it came to looking for a personal and professional partner and she was convinced she had found him in Joe Kennedy.

Joe stepped in to take care of Henri by arranging for him to become Pathé's man in Paris. It was a brilliant solution. The marquis saved face with a salary and position of his own and, with him out of the country, the path was clear for Joe. Of course, Henri needed to leave for his new post as soon as possible. Gloria departed Palm Beach feeling lighter than she had in years, knowing "Joe Kennedy had taken over my entire life."

J. J. Murdock telephoned Kennedy several times in Florida, but was always told he was "out on the links." When Joe finally took a call, Murdock tried to get him to cut his vacation short, but Kennedy told him he wasn't coming back for just more "hot air." However, he promised when he did return to New York, Pathé would be his first stop. After his three glorious weeks in Palm Beach, Kennedy entered into an intense week of meetings. In his absence, his men had collected and reviewed all the Pathé numbers and contract obligations; they were waiting for him topped by one-page summary memos.

There was no doubt that he was going ahead with the Pathé deal, no matter what the numbers said. In fact, the worse they were, the better it was because it just showed how much they needed their rescuer to ride in on the proverbial white horse. Pathé bonds were plunging; they had lost over 10 percent of their value just during the time he had been in Palm Beach. Their stock had dipped to a new low of $9 a share, down from $45 the previous August.

Under instructions from Elisha Walker, Murdock was ready to do whatever Joe wanted and what he wanted was more money and a formal connection with those Keith-Albee-Orpheum theaters. They decided that cash would be added by having KAO buy a minority interest in FBO.

Guy Currier had no reason to know about or question the depth of Kennedy's association with Pathé. Bringing theaters into their equation made simple business sense and so to set that in motion, the Gower Street Company held a board meeting to enlarge the number of FBO shares and then turned around and sold forty thousand of FBO common to Keith for $600,000. The FBO board of directors was expanded to include Murdock and the incorporation agreement was changed to give voting rights to shareholders of FBO common. Currier and Kennedy then took out over $100,000 each in profits. The money wasn't needed to run FBO; that's what Cinema Credits Corporation was for.

While the meetings were taking place, rumors were flying that FBO was about to merge with Pathé. Every day for a week, the trades ran front-page stories full of conjecture, but behind closed doors Walker, Murdock, and Kennedy knew the two studios would remain separate entities yet "under the same management." That management, of course, was Joe Kennedy. He demanded and received truly all-encompassing powers, verified by a letter signed by Murdock as president:

> I confirm your appointment to act on behalf of the company, with full authority to discharge any or all employees or officers of the company, and in the case of existing contracts to cancel and compromise the same in your full discretion. You are also empowered to engage such new agents and on such terms as you may consider in the best interest of the company.

With that letter in his pocket, Kennedy publicly called the merger rumors "absurd." He was joining Pathé as a "special advisor . . . purely on a desire to help Pathé out of a situation" because of "his close friendship and mutual admiration" with Murdock. There was "no remuneration" and no stock was changing hands. Technically, he was right. It wouldn't be until May that the Pathé board formally presented him with 100,000 shares of stock, $2,000 a week salary retroactive to February, and an agreement to pick up all his related expenses. If his pronouncements stretched credulity, it didn't matter to the financial press. They immediately proclaimed Pathé to be "in a stronger position" because of Kennedy's association.

While refusing to go into detail, Kennedy did announce he was "planning a trip to the coast to reorganize Pathé and meet with De Mille," but first he needed to make a quick trip to Boston, to see his wife and the two-week-old daughter she named Jean Ann. Joe presented Rose with a diamond bracelet and found her surrounded by dozens of floral bouquets, including one from Gloria Swanson, as well as literally hundreds of cards and cables, many from his Hollywood friends and associates. Rose's may have been reflected glory, but glory it was just the same. When Barbara Walters later asked her about her husband's serial absences, " 'No matter,' she said with a wink and a smile. 'A diamond bracelet makes up for the loss.' " And Rose stayed in Boston for yet another month to rest, while the other seven children remained at the house in Riverdale, New York, still under Mary Moore's care.

Eddie stopped in for a visit with his wife, but soon it was time to pack up again. As Joe explained to Rose, Gloria Swanson was in "a financial morass" that needed his immediate attention.

# CHAPTER 13

# "Industry Wide Influence and Respect"

## (MARCH–APRIL 1928)

When Kennedy returned to Los Angeles in mid-March of 1928, he once again checked in to the Ambassador Hotel, but his interests had expanded since his last trip. In addition to FBO, he now had Pathé and Gloria Swanson, so one of Eddie's first assignments was to find him a house.

In contrast to previous visits during which Joe's activities were concentrated around the Ambassador on Wilshire or at FBO in bustling Hollywood, his immediate task took him to the still isolated village southwest of Los Angeles, Culver City. A real estate developer, Harry Culver, had incorporated the area over a decade before and set his sights on it becoming "The Heart of Screenland." He persuaded Thomas Ince to build his studio there, but in spite of promotions claiming "All roads lead to Culver City," the area remained less than cosmopolitan. As a studio secretary described it at the time, "Culver City is such an ugly little town and outside of a lot of fast roadhouses, cafes and nightclubs, there is absolutely nothing else one can do here or go to." Nothing, that is, except go to work at the original Ince Studio, which was now Metro-Goldwyn-Mayer, or at his second creation, now housing Pathé. The rest of the town may have left much to be desired, but the studio edifices were magnificent.

Kennedy was driven down Washington Boulevard and into Pathé's long curved driveway. Ince had based the imposing colonial-style administration building on Mount Vernon and another antebellum touch was still very much in evidence: a black man dressed in full livery stood at attention at the entrance, ready to run down the steps, open the car door, and then run back up the stairs to bow as he held open the main door.

Kennedy's presence was the talk of the lot. Everyone suspected it meant serious changes were afoot and was anxious to hear what was to happen next, but it was Joe who was kept waiting. De Mille sent word

Downtown Culver City, 1928

he was busy filming, yet if he was going for a psychological advantage, he was underestimating a formidable opponent. Joe wasn't about to sit in an office cooling his heels and instead used his time to walk through the studio as if it were his own. Finally, the director left the set to go behind closed doors with him.

Walker had written De Mille that Kennedy was coming in as an advisor, but when Joe told him they needed to discuss the settlement of his contract and the liquidation of the company, De Mille became visibly upset.

Who was this banker to talk to him this way? Had he only made *The Ten Commandments* and *King of Kings* he would have been regarded as Hollywood's greatest director, if only for the business they did. With D. W. Griffith a spent force, De Mille was regarded as the towering genius of American film and arguably the man who had established Hollywood. In his own mind, he had no equal and while he knew Kennedy from the Harvard series and as a Hays sycophant, that certainly did not give him the status to dictate what was coming next. De Mille believed that "when banks came into pictures, trouble came in with them," but he knew the power behind Kennedy and so he held out a thread of hope that Joe was the exception: a banker who understood movies.

After his initial outburst, De Mille radiated cordial civility as he told Joe he "welcomed" the idea of him straightening out Pathé. Venting to Kennedy and warming to him in the process, De Mille was frank in his judgment that Murdock might be a capable administrator of vaudeville theaters, but he didn't know much about moviemaking. De Mille had approved the idea of merging the various companies, but had voiced concern that they were running the ship into the ground. Surely Joe appreciated the pressure and frustration he was feeling. Everyone had agreed on a production plan for the year and now, suddenly, he was summarily informed everything had changed. Walker and "the officers in the east," as the director disdainfully called them, had not been "forthcoming." He had done the best he could during this maelstrom and even praised Murdock in the press, and what had been his reward? He was being "treated as an employee, not as a partner."

Kennedy sought to pacify him, claiming that he too was "shocked" that the trades had somehow gotten wind of the company's condition. He adamantly denied responsibility for recent headlines that proclaimed "De Mille will have to make cheaper films, says Kennedy." With a straight face, the director said he was "confident that you have been misquoted" and presented himself as the model of decorum. Tempted as he was, he would refrain from going to the press to counter these "false reports" of his wasteful spending. He claimed his own production unit was the only "economical operation" on the lot, but his protestations have the ring of Louie being "shocked, shocked" to find that there is gambling in Rick's back room as he is handed his winnings in *Casablanca.* In addition to De Mille's own generous earnings, the salaries he was paying others were among the highest in the industry: his screenwriter Jeanie Macpherson was making $1,000 a week, his older brother, William, $2,000, and William's new wife, the screenwriter Clara Beranger, $1,000. In just two months, De Mille had gone through more than $1.2 million on *The Godless Girl* and the ten, supposedly much lower cost, films he was supervising. He argued that canceling any of those at this point would cost almost as much as going ahead, but Kennedy knew Walker was so anxious to get rid of De Mille, he would only agree to finish the movies already actively in production.

Clearly, this was a man suffering from wounded pride and Joe had an almost innate sense of knowing when to soothe and when to lunge. Now he sympathized as only a messenger could and claimed he was just there to prevent bankruptcy, which was to everyone's advantage. Maybe so, but before De Mille could even talk about a settlement of his contract, there had to be an agreement that the company would make an official public statement professing his budgetary responsibility. Besides, he didn't have time for any of this. He had *The Godless Girl* to direct and what he had heard to date was so insulting, he "preferred receivership to any such settlement."

Cecil B. De Mille with his screenwriter Jeanie Macpherson

The meeting was over and no others were scheduled. Yet there was no doubt about who was now in charge. Kennedy announced that all production departments were to notify their employees they were being discharged as soon as their current projects were completed. All contracts with independent producers were being canceled. Privately, Joe assured the likes of Mack Sennett that their exit arrangements would be negotiated, but the message was clear: De Mille could think all he wanted; his days at his studio were numbered.

At every turn, Kennedy conferred with Walker, usually on the phone, for, as Joe put it, "I prefer to clear up these items with a talk rather than a telegram." Pleased with what he considered his "progress," Joe reported that everything was "working along satisfactorily" and, with that, left town. His departure may have been a dramatic message to De Mille, but there was another purpose as well. Kennedy was off to Palm Springs because that was where Gloria Swanson was waiting for him.

Palm Springs was just remote enough for privacy. A travel writer at the time called it "an audacious little village" in the desert where until only a few years before, the biggest attraction had been a sanitarium for tuberculosis patients. Then came the Desert Inn, designed to welcome a clientele who wanted a "select, expensive and chic" resort experience, and its success led to the building of the recently opened El Mirador, where Gloria had ensconced herself.

El Mirador in Palm Springs, where Gloria and Joe went to escape for a week, 1928

Kennedy might have told his wife he had to be in California because of Swanson's "financial morass," but in reality, everything had been settled by the time Joe arrived in Los Angeles. His minions had a system in place to keep Gloria in line and her expenses monitored. Swanson's production manager, Pete Bedard, had spent over two months doing the gang's bidding while watching Tom Moore, Milton Cohen, and a series of others be shown the door. The dressmaker and seamstress were taken off their weekly retainers and the household staff was reduced. All through the process, Gloria assured Pete that he was a valued friend whose position "was secure," so it came as a shock when Derr informed him that he too was off the payroll. As Derr told Kennedy, while Bedard "is a peach of a fellow, I know lots of peaches I can't pay $250.00 weekly." When the cameras were rolling again, Pete could return, but not until then. Derr said he was being "ruthless" in his recommendations and was prepared to be the fall guy if Gloria objected, but she didn't. When Pete tried to reach her, she refused to respond to his cables or take his calls. Her new alliance was complete.

Derr had overseen the significant reduction in Swanson's expenses and established an intricate system of checks and balances. Grace Crossman remained as Swanson's New York secretary, but the Fifth Avenue office was closed and she was given a desk at Pathé on 45th Street. She took direction from Pat Scollard down the hall where he was responsible for overseeing Gloria's contracts, bonds, insurance policies, and other legal necessities. In Hollywood, Lance Heath was still on salary as her publicist and, even though Derr thought they could find someone to keep the books for less than $75 a week, Irving Wakoff was kept on as her accountant.

Wakoff was given an office at the FBO studio where he collected and recorded Gloria's income and documented all her bills, generating weekly account sheets. These were sent upstairs to Charlie Sullivan to be paid out of what was called the "Special Sullivan Account." Copies of the reports were also sent to Pat Scollard in New York where he double-checked the figures and, when needed and authorized, sent money into Sullivan's account. Ten cents off was not too small an amount to be caught and reconciled. With bank accounts established at Columbia Trust and A. P. Giannini's Bank of Italy (which would soon become Bank of America), Kennedy in many ways had simply replaced Schenck, but he also provided a new organizational structure and a firm hand to guide it.

If Kennedy delegated most tasks, one he handled himself was the assuaging of Gloria's husband. Joe took to writing Henri long letters, friendly but professional, with never a hint of a possibility that the two men might have differing goals. Joe funneled assignments to the Paris-based Henri such as following up on actresses who might be brought into the Pathé fold and meeting with Somerset Maugham about writing that discussed sequel to "Miss Thompson." When Henri had trouble with his passport, Kennedy stepped in and assigned his attorneys to follow up. Joe treated him with familiar respect, promising that upon his next visit to the States, Ted O'Leary would be in New York ready to "serve as a reception committee to you" and Joe himself would be "glad to see you back in California." Not too soon of course.

After two years of knowing she was in over her head, Gloria finally felt she could relax and she was doing just that in Palm Springs. For someone who had been so hesitant to put her faith in anyone, Gloria was grateful and relieved to put everything in Kennedy's hands. She genuinely liked him. She was impressed by his stories of having "withstood oppression and endured prejudice" and admired him for it. No one was better at playing the diva in public than Gloria, but she felt a kinship with Joe for what she considered their mutual rise from obscurity. He made her laugh and his confidence gave her solace.

Her abrupt experiences with him in Palm Beach had proven her latest conquest was hardly an impressive lover. "The idea that they were a great sexual match is a joke," said her last husband, William Dufty. "Gloria was very intrepid sexually, but in terms of her relationship with men, she was hobbled emotionally by the fact she had been raised more or less fatherless, she had no brothers or male cousins. She was very vulnerable."

Vulnerable in some ways to be sure, but the lack of physical satisfaction on Gloria's part gave her a control that she wouldn't have had otherwise. Not being swept up in physical passion herself, she was free to believe she was pleasing Joe; she was taking care of him in one way and he was taking care of her in another. She found herself completely trusting his "superior business sense" as well as his "promise of enduring security." To her mind, he adored her and would do anything for her. That was much more difficult to find than good sex.

Joe, on the other hand, must have found the sex incredible. Here was a woman willing to jump into bed for the sake of pleasure and in this and other ways, Gloria was the antithesis of Rose. The star was overtly sexual and flouted convention. She was funny, irreverent, and intimately involved in his work. As confident as Joe was, he must have been amazed he was actually waking up next to one of the world's most glamorous women.

After a week in seclusion with Gloria, Joe returned to Pathé to do battle with a somewhat calmed De Mille. Elisha Walker had sent him a conciliatory cable, but the director continued to object to the recent turn of events. His five-year contract had more than four years to run and it came with some impressive guarantees: his personal productions were to be financed up to $1.5 million a year; he could supervise the making of thirty films a year, and hire whom he wanted when he wanted. He needed board approval only for contracts lasting more than a year or paying more than $2,500 a week. De Mille was receiving $250,000 annually as a base salary as well as a percentage of the gross of both the films he directed and the ones he supervised. He was the star of the lot and had incredible freedom for someone who rarely had to think about financing. He even had his own radio station at the studio for the sole purpose of communicating with his yacht, the *Seaward.* He was protected if Pathé defaulted on any payments; if his current contract wasn't renewed for another five years, he had an automatic option to buy the studio.

Kennedy had studied and annotated his copy of De Mille's contract and, on paper, there was no question that the director was in the driver's seat. Still, De Mille was no one's fool and it was obvious that the power had shifted and the bankers were now in control. Independently, Walker and Kennedy told him that if Pathé was to be saved, they all had to act first and foremost as businessmen. After all, he was a stockholder himself, albeit a minority one. Walker rather patronizingly reminded him that because of "the unsatisfactory condition of the Company, we must all make some sacrifices." Kennedy stressed that it wasn't he who wanted to end the relationship, but "our banking associates" and his contract would be worthless if they weren't bluffing about filing for bankruptcy. If all that logic failed to move De Mille, there was also an implied threat: if he had any thoughts of suing, the defense would be "that the quality and cost of his pictures made it impossible for anybody to distribute profitably." The director agreed to sit down for some serious discussions.

Slowly, items on their to-be-negotiated list were checked off. First, it was agreed that De Mille was to be immediately relieved of his production duties on all films except for *The Godless Girl*. He was to remain on the Pathé board and if he wanted to take certain personnel with him wherever he went next, that could be arranged. Pathé was to retain the rights to most of the films he had made there, but he kept the rights to *King of Kings*.

That left the details surrounding *The Godless Girl* to be settled. The film was given its own designation as "David's special" for coded cables and was far and away their biggest of the season. Seven hundred thousand dollars had already been spent when filming wrapped at the end of March, but the editing process would be a challenge because De Mille had outdone himself by shooting forty-five feet of film for every one that would eventually be seen on the screen.

Joe began by offering him 25 percent of the gross of *The Godless Girl*, but De Mille responded by saying gross figures meant nothing if Pathé was releasing because they didn't know how to distribute films effectively. He thought it was better to let United Artists or Famous Players do it, but Joe wasn't budging. Nor would he agree to De Mille's demand that he be guaranteed $200,000 regardless of what the film brought in. Instead, Kennedy suggested a 40 percent gross against the first $500,000—still totaling $200,000, but the box office receipts had to be there first. Walker had already agreed to go as high as 50 percent, so everyone was pleased.

De Mille signed his separation papers on April 18, 1928, publicly claiming he was receiving $1 million, but only $250,000 changed hands. Another $200,000, to repay previous loans and investments he had made to the company, would come later with caveats attached.

Kennedy sent a positive, upbeat account to Walker. Now the director was at least under restricted control as he finished his work and his contract was no longer in effect. Yet Joe urged Walker to consider leaving open the possibility of bringing De Mille back to direct another picture or two. He was concerned that "with De Mille gone, the standard of pictures will be very cheap" and theater owners might rebel against Pathé. He understood that others on the board might say, "We got rid of him, let's stay rid of him," but if they could agree to one film a year, everyone would benefit. Kennedy suggested a budget limit of $1 million, most of it financed from outside the company, with De Mille receiving $200,000 for directing and then 5 percent of the gross. If the director went over budget, it came out of his own pocket. Kennedy assured Walker "we can get along without him and will," but he believed the De Mille name "has a great value" with exhibitors and the trades. This new proposal would not affect the separation agreement and might well add value to Pathé if they sold it. There was no doubting the director's talent; he just needed Joe to rein him in.

"I hold no brief with [De Mille] except from a business point of view," Kennedy told Walker, but he let the director think he revered him and was advocating on his behalf. United Artists had prepared a contract for De Mille and while he told Kennedy he wanted more time to think about it, Joe believed it was his "tremendous pride" that kept him from becoming one of many after being the one and only "Director General." At UA, De Mille would also have to arrange his own financing so Kennedy told him he was willing to step in personally, separate from Walker or anyone else, to finance his films.

The end result of Kennedy's machinations was that his stock had risen with both De Mille and the men in the East. Walker was relieved and more than pleased with Kennedy's settlement and De Mille left with a new respect for Joe and the door open to do business with him. There was still plenty to do at Pathé, but now Kennedy could shift his attention to the more traditional problems of cutting budgets and personnel.

No man had ever run two studios at the same time, but no one seems to have looked upon the situation with suspicion or trepidation. To the contrary, his relationship with Pathé was praised in the trades as "evidence of the widening influence of Mr. Joseph P. Kennedy," which "thus far has been wholesome and constructive." Never before had anyone moved so quickly to establish "industry wide influence and respect." The film business was "fortunate in having won the interest and association of Mr. Kennedy." In Hollywood, Kennedy meant Wall Street and any and all approval from that front was seen as a positive. Pathé was one of the few entertainment companies whose stock prices were up and *Variety* credited that to "the prestige of Joseph P. Kennedy."

Kennedy was a master delegator, on top of every detail of every contract and aware of where every penny was going. He spent some time at

Pathé in Culver City, some at FBO in Hollywood, and bragged "he had an army of employees at his beck and call, all on trial and therefore anxious to prove themselves."

Eddie Moore had found a house to lease, a two-story Craftsman at 801 Rodeo Drive in Beverly Hills, complete with a clay tennis court that ran parallel to the swimming pool. With five bedrooms, four fireplaces, and a polished teak staircase, it had a comfortable, informal feel in spite of its large size. Joe's master bedroom on the second floor looked out on the bridle path down Rodeo where riders on their horses could be as commonplace as cars, especially on Sunday mornings. Only Eddie would actually live in the house with him, but the other men were in and out and it soon took on the aura of a well-appointed clubhouse. It came fully staffed with a butler, maids, a cook, and a gardener and had the added advantage of being down the block and around the corner from Gloria's house on Crescent. With her finances under control, she didn't need to continue to rent out her estate to save a few hundred dollars a month and she, her children, and an albeit reduced retinue returned to her home that summer.

Kennedy made being in Hollywood work for him. As always, he spent up to an hour each morning reading "a prodigious amount of information" and then it was to the telephone. He was back on the phone again in the early evening and that was the time set aside for calls home, letting Rose know through the FBO office in New York when he would be available to talk. Still, Kennedy was so busy every day that Eddie Moore reported to Scollard, "We haven't had the golf sticks out of the bag since we arrived."

FBO was percolating with a variety of films, all made on low budgets. Where Sam Goldwyn opened his wallet to reach out to his "Eminent Authors," Kennedy went to the pages of *True Story Magazine* for *Sinners in Love.* Hearst had access to his own *Cosmopolitan* magazine for screen material, but Joe had *Barney Google* from Hearst's comic pages for two-reelers. The RCA technicians were beginning to arrive at Gower Street to install the components of their first sound unit and Bill LeBaron was hopeful they could put musical scores into some films by the summer.

More and more, Kennedy's name appeared on the screen and in print, on the films, in the ads, and on the lobby cards. "Joseph P. Kennedy presents" was even printed on the music cue sheets that accompanied the films for the theater's organ or orchestra. He took to addressing theater owners directly through bylined columns in the trades and with ads headlined "From one Showman to another." In a straight-shooting style that still aimed at Main Street rather than Broadway, he assured them he

Gloria Swanson's Beverly Hills estate, opposite the Beverly Hills Hotel

understood their needs: "Melodrama is our meat, but high class melo-drama. Concentrating on this type, we are able to give the exhibitor a superior type of production at a price that will enable him to make money and draw all classes of patrons."

FBO's publicity arm expanded to create a "Department of Showman-ship" to assist theater owners in all their "exploitation" plans. Kennedy used his salesmen as two-way streets, to sell the films that were already made as well as solicit the theater owners' opinions on what packed their houses. The exhibitors were courted and Joe made sure his men didn't arrive empty-handed. Faux leather notebooks with FBO imprinted on the cover laid out a yearly calendar for keeping track of bookings. A pho-tograph of a handsome "Joseph P. Kennedy, President" graced the open-ing page, with promises of a new film season that would "excel, by a wide margin" the previous year and expressing the "hope that FBO may be largely instrumental in your success."

Kennedy had positioned himself into a unique role in an expanding business and his star was shining. He was experiencing the joys of unprecedented public success, but then, for the first time, his eyes that had never wavered from the bottom line blinked and he went "creative."

WHEN THEY HAD BEEN in Florida together, the news was slowly leaked out that Gloria Swanson and Joe Kennedy had reached an agree-ment to make her next three films at FBO with Kennedy financing and

*Greater*
# FBO
### 1927-28
#### Film Booking Offices of America, Inc.

*Statement from*
**JOSEPH P. KENNEDY**
*President*

THE phenomenal growth of F.B.O. during the past year with its record of brilliant achievement may be attributed to the soundly human principle underlying our policy.

For the season of 1927-28 our program of pictures is full of great promise. Our production will be under the direction of masters of the art of entertainment and of the science of showmanship. Our stories both in theme and execution, our stars through their fame and their performance, are certain to earn the good will of the exhibitor and to hold the interest of the audience. The fact that we own no theatres, that the exhibitor is our customer and not our competitor, makes F. B. O. Pictures more attractive than ever.

The prime purpose of our policy is always to offer to the exhibitor, whether large or small, a program high in box-office value at a cost sufficiently low to allow him the fair margin of profit to which we recognize that he is justly entitled.

Joe talks straight to theater owners in this typical full-page ad in the trades.

United Artists distributing. So far, they had appeared together in print only professionally, but his pride in their association was starting to go to his head. Since the early days of his marriage, he had dallied with a variety of ingenues, indeed considered them one of the side benefits of the business, but Gloria Swanson was something else again.

"She was a huge star. She was the ultimate trophy mistress," reflects William Dufty. With Gloria at his side, Joe envisioned himself on the verge of greatness. She was "perfectly reconciled to go back to work," but what that work was to be remained undecided. She was intrigued by several possible stories, but Joe decided "none of them appeal very much to me." Once again, he told her, "Together, we could make millions" and he was looking for that "important" film, that "great story."

In order to prove to his "ultimate trophy mistress" he was the ultimate producer, Kennedy needed the ultimate director and he found him in Erich von Stroheim. Stroheim and "important" were synonymous. Almost as exalted as Griffith or De Mille, Stroheim was famous for his lavish epics that took the art form to a new level. Swanson had made fifty films, Stroheim had directed seven, yet to Kennedy it was a match made in heaven. And Gloria was thrilled when Eddie Moore called to tell her to prepare for a meeting because the "the boss has got von Stroheim."

Kennedy prided himself on not being easily impressed, but he was in awe of Stroheim, who presented himself as an aristocratic Austrian. The director was "immaculately groomed" and "steeped in Viennese culture" as the three met at Swanson's home. Stroheim fawned over Gloria, calling her "Madame la Marquise" as he praised her films. The actress and the director traded tales of studios "butchering" their work and bathed each other in sympathy for what they had endured. If Gloria was concerned that Joe was being slighted in the conversation, she was reassured when she saw him smiling "broadly enough to show his teeth, like a dog who had run up out of the garden and presented me with a choice bone he had uncovered, as if to say 'What do you think of that?' "

Erich von Stroheim

Joe continued to smile as Stroheim regaled them with the story he was planning to create "exclusively" for Gloria. Perhaps in deference to Joe, Stroheim's heroine was a Catholic girl with the Irish name of Kelly. Her chance meeting with the prince of a European kingdom leads to a fire at her convent and then a night at the castle where the lovers are discovered by the queen, who whips Kelly and orders the prince arrested. Kelly attempts suicide before returning to the convent where she learns she has inherited her aunt's brothel in Africa, so it is off to "the dark continent" where Kelly is eventually reunited with the prince after a gripping chase.

A brothel? A convent? Why weren't they raising questions about the film's settings or a storyline that called for Gloria to go from a sweet young novice to a madam to a queen? Swanson was swept away by the "richly cinematic" story with its drama, thrills, and romance as well as feeling flattered it was being designed just for her by this "major artist." Kennedy was just as intrigued and, still grinning, agreed that Stroheim should start writing the script immediately. After the three had shaken hands and the director had departed, Gloria shared in Joe's excitement, concluding that landing Stroheim was "one of the proudest accomplishments of his life."

The idea that Kennedy had scored a great coup in "getting" Stroheim was ludicrous; the director had been out of work for over a year. Today, his films such as *Greed* and *The Wedding March* are seen as glorious, but the efforts to get them to the screen were well-known horror stories at the time. And his pedigree was hardly what he claimed. He presented himself as the Catholic son of an Austrian count and a German baroness, schooled in war colleges before serving in the Austrian military and then immigrating to the United States at the age of twenty-four in 1909. In reality, Erich Oswald Stroheim had added the "von" along with a string of middle names when he arrived at Ellis Island, having left behind the other members of his relatively poor Jewish family and their failing millinery shop. Stroheim began in films working with D. W. Griffith, both behind the camera as an assistant and in front of the camera in small roles, billing himself as "Count Von Stroheim."

It was at Universal that Stroheim had found a home as a director, screenwriter, and actor. While gaining a reputation for his autocratic demeanor and expensive attention to detail, he was showing a profit at the box office. It wasn't until his third film, *Foolish Wives,* that he was confronted by Universal's new, twenty-year-old production chief, Irving Thalberg, who was already envisioning the tight production controls he would later institute at MGM. He found Stroheim "absolutely impossible," so he informed him if he wanted to make another picture at Universal, he either directed or acted, he couldn't do both. Stroheim chose to direct *Merry-Go-Round,* but he refused to live within Thalberg's budgetary restrictions and was fired after six weeks of shooting.

Stroheim moved to the Goldwyn Company where he was deep into the year he spent filming *Greed,* his 330-page script of Frank Norris's novel *McTeague,* when the company was merged into the newly created Metro-Goldwyn-Mayer. Stroheim's new boss was his old nemesis Irving Thalberg and almost inevitably they clashed again. Irene Mayer Selznick remembered going to the studio early one morning to see the director's cut of *Greed,* which Stroheim had "reduced to forty reels." He refused to cut it further and Irene arrived "prepared to do battle" on his behalf, but when she left the screening room the sun had set and she was having second thoughts. Parts of it were "riveting," but the idea that a masterpiece was devastated when MGM drastically edited *Greed* was a myth perpetuated by people who "never saw the original and who heard about it from others who also hadn't seen it."

Stroheim's contract with Goldwyn had been absorbed in the MGM merger and the rights had already been purchased for his next film, *The Merry Widow*. This time it was Louis B. Mayer who reportedly came to physical blows with the director, but there was a rapprochement between Stroheim and Thalberg, who brought him back to finish it after firing him again. *The Merry Widow* made many of the "best films of the year" lists and Stroheim was credited with getting the performance of a lifetime out of his star, Mae Murray.

Released in the summer of 1925, *The Merry Widow* was the most recent Stroheim film audiences had seen when Kennedy and Swanson met with the director in the early spring of 1928. He had made *The Wedding March* for Kennedy's former associate turned independent producer, Pat Powers, but after eight months of shooting 200,000 feet of film at a cost of over $1 million, production was stopped. Budd Schulberg remembers the last straw being Stroheim's purchase of one thousand pairs of silk underwear for the extras because it helped them "feel" the part. In frustration, Powers sold the unfinished film to Paramount where it was still awaiting its fate.

While Stroheim's crews were exceptionally loyal, actors who had worked with him reported mixed feelings and there was no debate among producers. Thalberg was the only one to have worked with Stroheim more than once and he had fired him twice.

Kennedy had to have heard at least some of the tales of Stroheim's loggerhead showdowns, his insistence on total control that resulted in the doubling and tripling of budgets, and "finished" films that were six to eight hours long. When Joe asked Louis B. Mayer as "a personal favor" to loan him an MGM cinematographer, the studio head refused because the cameraman was busy elsewhere. However, Mayer took the opportunity to tell Kennedy that "I hope your results with Von Stroheim will be all that you wish them to be—and I have no doubt they will. With your intelligent handling, I believe he can be an asset in the direction of this particular picture." When Mayer closed with the comment, "At least if you weather the storm you will have something worth talking about," Kennedy chose not to read between the lines.

The trades had long reported Stroheim's history of giving producers "plenty of grief" and Kennedy knew people who were only a phone call away if he wanted to know more. The obvious conclusion is that Joe thought he knew better. Despite the stories, or perhaps because of them, Kennedy envisioned himself as the one producer who could bring out the best in Stroheim. Like the general manager who signs a ballplayer who has disrupted every clubhouse in the league, Joe believed he was somehow superior to every other studio head who had contracted with the director. Swanson claimed she asked Joe if he knew Stroheim had "a growing reputation for being an undisciplined spendthrift, a hopeless egotist and a temperamental perfectionist," but he responded by saying "Yes I am, but I also know he's our man. I can handle him."

All the warning signs aside, Kennedy was not alone in being enchanted by the man who seemed bigger than life. Stroheim made the top ten list when the directors polled their own in 1928 even though he had not had a film released in over two years. When asked what would attract someone like Kennedy to Stroheim, Budd Schulberg says with a smile and a sigh, "Ahhh, it was the flame of genius in him."

Joe proudly finalized the arrangements and nothing was going to dampen his excitement. His confidence in his own and the gang's abilities was such that he had no doubt he could handle two studios as well as two such high-maintenance directors as De Mille and Stroheim. Besides, he was getting ready to drop one of his earlier investments, Fred Thomson.

What Joe had failed to mention to Fred when he made the deal with Paramount was that it was the best one for Kennedy. For guaranteeing $75,000 in financing, that amount plus $100,000 would be returned to Kennedy for each film. The fact that Paramount also had to pay Thomson $15,000 each week he was filming and then make a profit was not Joe's worry. However, the Paramount-Kennedy agreement was for only four films, three of which were now complete.

Kennedy, as he had promised, did all the talking with Paramount. He wanted it that way, but it also meant Thomson and his needs continued to take his time and attention. Joe didn't understand Fred's resistance to the all-out publicity that he deemed necessary. Kennedy reached out to Gene Tunney to help promote Fred with the large-city theater owners who had never booked Thomson's films and initially the boxer was willing to help. However, when he realized Joe wanted him to contact sportswriters such as Grantland Rice who would never be used as a blatant shill, Tunney backed away from Kennedy and his ideas.

The reviews for *Jesse James* found Thomson "splendid," but Fred's fans didn't want him to die at the end of the movie, no matter how historically accurate. While the film made a profit, the others that followed were not as successful. Pat Scollard in New York stayed in close contact with the Paramount executives and reported to Kennedy that when Sidney Kent, Paramount's general manager for distribution, saw Thomson's *The Sunset Legion,* he found it a "good picture," but not worthy of "a

Broadway run." Yet not having a Broadway theater screen for *The Sunset Legion* would give Thomson reason to complain and Joe was tired of that as well.

Thomson's attempts to "stretch" to larger theaters and wider audiences had not succeeded as he had hoped. His dedicated fans found themselves waiting in vain for Fred and Silver King because to cover the hefty expense of paying both Thomson and Kennedy, Paramount had increased the price of first runs. Fred's core audience in small-town theaters didn't get the films for months after their release, if they were available at all. For several years, fans had known which theater would be showing the next Fred and Silver King movie, but now they had to look around, maybe even go to another town, and they, along with the theater owners, became disgruntled. As one Iowa theater manager said in frustration, "We have played them all and they have made us a nice little sum and pleased our patrons. But if Paramount wants us to pay more than we are now paying, we will have to let them go by."

With all these forces coming together, it was clear to Kennedy that his Thomson bonanza was ending. The *Exhibitors Herald* had just released their annual "Top Stars of the Year" survey and Fred Thomson was listed as number two, with John Gilbert eighth and Douglas Fairbanks coming in at number ten. The one man who squeaked in above Thomson was Tom Mix, so it was no surprise that Joe perked up his ears when he heard that Mix might be available.

After ten years and seventy films, Tom Mix's contract with William Fox was ending. The venerable cowboy star was forty-seven years old and had been making movies since 1911, just solid cowboy movies where he rode his horse, Tony, caught the bad guys, and got the girl, yet that very dependability kept the cash coming into the box office. He was hardly the paragon of virtue Thomson was off-screen; Mix had been jailed and in the courts more than once and suffered through a nasty divorce or two as well. His personal lifestyle had not come cheap and Mix had run through much of the fortune he had accumulated. He was not in a position to be demanding and as long as he was well paid and could keep his crew together, he wasn't fussy about the stories or plot lines.

Mix had announced he was going to Argentina to make movies, but Kennedy wasn't about to have a company filming where they could not be watched. Suddenly headlines proclaimed Mix had changed his mind; he was staying in America and "joining the circus." Actually, he was making a series of public appearances because Kennedy saw an opportunity to bring his various assets together: Mix appearing in person at

Keith-Albee-Orpheum theaters and promoting FBO films. Best of all, K-A-O was there to pick up the tab for the unprecedented publicity. Joe Schnitzer quietly made arrangements for FBO to finance and distribute Mix's films and Colvin Brown was sent to Kansas City, where the cowboy was on tour, to get his signature on the contracts. The last thing Kennedy wanted at the moment, however, was for Fred Thomson to hear about the deal so when Joe was asked to make time to have photographs taken with Mix, he refused and told Schnitzer that for the time being, "no personal publicity of mine goes out in connection with Mix."

Fred Thomson and Frances Marion were happily oblivious and on their first prolonged vacation together in several years. They were in Florida where Fred was preparing to compete in boat races featuring engines he had designed, but soon rumors began to reach them. At first, they couldn't believe Joe would betray them by working with their only real competition. Something must be very wrong and so they decided Fred should make a quick trip to New York to meet directly with Paramount executives.

Thomson was graciously greeted at the Paramount offices where the facts were explained to him. It wasn't his salary of nearly $100,000 a film that was the problem, it was the $100,000 per film they had to turn over to Kennedy for his "services." They wanted to sign Fred directly, but only after he broke free of Joe. Paramount's contract was with Fred Thomson Productions, not Fred Thomson, who now realized for the first time that he had absolutely no control over his own future.

Kennedy had known exactly what he was doing; Thomson was Joe's "property" under their personal contract. He had told Fred the corporation was simply "for tax purposes as well as having a convenient medium for handling transactions," but the incorporation papers gave Kennedy license for much more than that. Four meticulous pages spelled out the possibility of involvement in every aspect of financing, producing, distributing, building, exporting, mortgaging, etc. etc., not just films, but "real and personal property of every class and description."

While one thousand shares of stock were authorized under the corporation, its initial corporate papers allotted only ten shares and they were divided among the three people listed as board members, all Delaware residents and presumably employees of the Wilmington-based Corporation Trust through which the company was created. The first board of directors meeting had been held three weeks after the incorporation in February of 1927 in Pat Scollard's New York office. For the momentous occasion, Pat and two secretaries "elected" Scollard president of the board and the women were named to share the roles of vice president, secretary, and treasurer. Kennedy's attorney, Benjamin DeWitt, was counsel for the corporation. All the corporate rules were followed: a seal was adopted and a stock certificate book procured, and then the newly "elected" officers proceeded to the real business of the afternoon, to issue the remaining 990 shares of stock to Joseph P. Kennedy in payment for assigning the Thomson contract to the corporation. At the time of the meeting, Kennedy himself was knee-deep in preparation for the Harvard series, but he was sent a copy of "a draft of the minutes" of the first board meeting, asking him to "return the draft with your approval or with such alterations as you wish to make." In spite of the pretense of corporate officers, Kennedy exercised total control.

Too late, Thomson consulted attorneys and learned that it was all tight as a drum. He had neither stock nor any role in the corporation that bore his name. When he had signed that personal contract, he had unwittingly given Kennedy unconditional power over his professional life.

After all the years of feigned friendship, Thomson was just a product to be sold. Fred had brought millions of dollars into FBO and Kennedy had personally profited to the tune of almost half a million dollars off the Paramount contract, but the gravy train was ending. There was a glut of westerns on the market anyway; every studio had come in with the low-cost Tylers and Steeles and the genre was simply not as popular anymore. Now that Joe had Tom Mix under contract, he could reduce his competition by keeping Fred off the screen.

Fred suggested they could tear up the contract and negotiate another that would split profits three ways between himself, Kennedy, and Paramount. Thomson was even willing to produce the films himself if Joe would release him. Kennedy refused and did not respond to Fred's continued attempts to reach him.

The Thomsons were stunned. For some time they had known they had outgrown their need for Kennedy, but their loyalty to him had been reinforced by his comforting affability and all the positive press. Fred returned to Los Angeles, went to work on *Kit Carson*, and, when it was completed, he was forced into idleness.

None of this was being reported while it was going on. Instead, Kennedy was being praised for Pathé's stock enjoying "a sharp rise." He had over $800,000 charged off the old books, stripping the overall value of the company to clear the way for him to be the one to claim credit for its future success. With the usual help from E. B. Derr and Charlie Sullivan, Kennedy created a new accounting system, instituting weekly production reports and individual budgets for each film. The exhibitors' pipeline was now being fed with low-cost features averaging under $100,000 each. De Mille's departure was the key to the cost cutting, but Joe told Walker that his settlement of Mack Sennett's contract alone saved the company over $800,000. Nothing was too small for Kennedy to notice; eliminating six people being paid a combined total of $195 a week meant an annual savings of $5,000. Dozens of actors and directors were released from their contracts.

It was assumed that William Sistrom, De Mille's head of production, would be replaced, but Kennedy and the gang watched him in action and liked what they saw. Joe overheard a conversation Sistrom was having with a director who wanted $125,000 for his next picture on the promise that the following one would cost only $60,000. Sistrom said that was fine, but he had to make the $60,000 film first. Clearly on the same wavelength, Sistrom stayed on when Kennedy returned east, taking E. B. Derr and Eddie Moore with him.

During his California visit that spring of 1928, Joe had reorganized Pathé, overseen the beginning of sound at FBO, formally staked his claim on Gloria Swanson, committed them to making an epic with a renowned director, negotiated a settlement with Cecil B. De Mille, dropped the second biggest star of the screen, and picked up the reigning King of Cowboys. Not bad for six weeks' work.

Once again, Joe left Los Angeles just as Henri was arriving in America to renew his visa and visit Gloria. And as Kennedy boarded the train, he knew he wasn't about to slow down. Elisha Walker had cabled him that he was so "enthusiastic about the job you are doing," he was ready to back him in yet another, much bigger venture.

# CHAPTER 14

# "I Have Gone into the Vaudeville Game"

## (MAY 1928)

*T*he "big deal" Walker had in mind was the total takeover of Keith-Albee-Orpheum. Keith-Albee was the famous vaudeville circuit company that, since the death of his partner, Benjamin Franklin Keith, in 1914, had been run single-handedly by Edward F. Albee. The two men had first met at the circus, the teenage Albee's destination after running away from his Maine home. Five years later, in 1883, Keith opened a "museum-cum-freak show" in Boston with Albee as his partner. Keith specialized in finding aberrations like huge pigs or "a chicken with a human face" and Albee added stage shows featuring comedians and portions of (usually pirated) plays. Together they grew with vaudeville and became real estate magnates in the process, buying up theaters throughout the East Coast. Refusing to be limited by the traditional two shows a day, they promoted "continuous vaudeville" beginning at 9:30 in the morning and running until after ten at night. It created new pressures and exhausted the performers, but quadrupled profits for Keith and Albee.

Their control became so tight they broke the back of the performers' union. Even while Keith was alive, Albee picked up the nicknames of "The Lord High Executioner" and "The Ol' Massa" because he fired anyone he thought had crossed him and treated his employees as if they were his slaves. It was common knowledge that Albee listened in on phone conversations, encouraged actors to turn stool pigeon and kept an active blacklist that *Variety* eventually called "the scourge of all vaudeville."

Albee ruled his empire from his office above Broadway's Palace Theatre. Publicly professing piety, he was "foul mouthed" in private and lived an imperious lifestyle. He had few friends and fewer sympathizers. Still, Kennedy paid Albee obsequious deference in late 1927 when he sent him a copy of *The Story of the Films* with a note saying, "From my earliest recollections of the amusement business, I have always connected

Edward Albee

the name of 'Albee' for [sic] the successful development of it, and I feel that the changes, due to take place in the industry in the next few years, must be guided greatly by your hand."

It was an interesting sentiment, especially since Albee had a history of forbidding his performers to appear in films. He vociferously maintained that "there will always be an audience for vaudeville," yet others around the company were beginning to believe they would be in receivership "within six months without altered direction."

Chief among the concerned was Elisha Walker. He had entered into a financial relationship with K-A-O for the theaters and for the real estate, but Albee was turning out to be more trouble than he was worth. Elevating John Murdock from being Albee's number two man to president of Pathé brought Murdock under Walker's wing, and his loyalties shifted as well. Within weeks of mailing off his letter to Albee, Joe was in his first meeting with Murdock and their discussions soon turned to how they could take K-A-O away from the "Czar of Vaudeville."

Murdock and Kennedy quickly established a genuine friendship. Joe picked up many of the nuances of the business as he listened to stories of how Murdock put a value on a vaudeville act and what he looked for in his theaters. While there were few as experienced or knowledgeable about vaudeville, Murdock was no sentimentalist. He knew the future was in films.

Theaters were manna to Kennedy. Not having his own screens made distribution time-consuming and expensive and it was becoming a real hindrance to competitive success. Paramount had methodically constructed an impressive theater chain, MGM had their Loew's theaters, and First National had originated as a consortium of theater circuits.

Keith-Albee had merged with the Orpheum theaters the year before, resulting in their full to partial ownership of almost seven hundred theaters throughout the United States and Canada. Between FBO and

Pathé, K-A-O would provide the last building block Joe needed for a completely integrated company with the making of films, their distribution, and their screening all under his aegis.

Kennedy also knew he could slash the cost of running K-A-O because vaudeville required much more personnel than movie theaters. He also saw the possibility of making some of the best-known stage performers into film stars. It had been ten years since he had signed Fred Stone for the movies, and with K-A-O, he would have access to hundreds of actors.

Once again, Elisha Walker and Joe Kennedy found themselves on a mutually beneficial path. Joe was to be the front man for the holding company financed by Walker, Jeremiah Milbank, and Lehman Brothers. For his role, he was to receive 12,500 K-A-O shares outright, the equivalent of over a quarter million dollars, and be allowed to purchase 25,000 shares. Their initial negotiations were so top secret that in sending papers to Pat Scollard to hand-deliver to Walker, Charlie Sullivan told him "this is the most confidential document that you ever handled. In fact, it is so confidential that even I have not read it and I know that you will appreciate from this the tantamount importance of it."

The holding company's first influx of stock came from John Murdock, who went behind Albee's back and sold them the options he had accumulated over the years. Then Walker put together the deal memo authorizing Kennedy to offer Albee, by far the majority stockholder, up to $21 a share for what was currently trading at a year's low of $16. (That was a $3 drop in only a few weeks so one can't help but wonder if Kennedy, with all his experience, didn't have a hand in the dip.) Yet even for $4.2 million, Albee needed to be assured he would remain president of K-A-O before agreeing to sell his 200,000 shares.

While it was Walker who was pulling the strings, reporters gave Kennedy full credit for masterminding the takeover, praising him for his staggering ability to raise more than $4 million cash in forty-eight hours. The trades covered the story as if Kennedy was acting alone and once again his biography was expanded impressively as it was run through the presses. Readers of *The New York Times* were reminded that he had been America's youngest bank president and the number of employees he had supervised at Fore River now doubled to more than fifty thousand.

As agreed, Albee signed the papers by May 15, 1928, the day a special meeting of the K-A-O board of directors was held at the Palace Theatre. Kennedy joined the dozen board members a little before noon to make everything official; "everything" being, first and foremost, Kennedy's role and his compensation. He was to be chairman of the board for five years, reelected at one-year intervals. He was also the chief executive officer and chair of the executive committee, consisting of himself, Murdock, Elisha Walker, and Blair and Company's Richard Hunt. The board was expanded to make room for Kennedy, Walker, and Hunt as well as two people Joe could name later. Walker, Hunt, and Kennedy, as well as his two future members, were exempted from the company requirement that they have no financial interests in other entertainment companies.

As with Pathé, Kennedy was to have no reported salary, but in addition to the 37,500 shares he was being given and purchasing, he received an option to buy up to 75,000 additional shares of K-A-O at the same price Walker had paid for them, the equivalent on the day he accepted their offer of over $1.5 million. He also had a new company to pay for his expenses and to pick up a portion of the gang's salaries.

With control over decision making in Joe's hands, Albee was allowed to stay on in the now titular role as president. Publicly it was made to sound that Kennedy's "important capacity" was all Albee's idea. "It was only natural that I should look to the picture industry for a new associate," Albee said for the press release. He called Kennedy "energetic, dynamic and a straight shooter" who had "shown, in a brief but colorful career in the picture business, such constructive and organization genius that we consider him a tremendous asset to our business."

Now it was three companies that Kennedy was heading and still there was nothing but praise. "He has shot FBO into the front ranks of the independent picture concerns and also restored Pathé to a substantial standing financially within 60 days from assuming its charge." Kennedy's "prestige" and proven track record turned the outlook for K-A-O from negative to positive. It was assumed that a "more liberal policy" toward performers and that their theaters would now emphasize films over vaudeville. While it was pointed out that K-A-O had "never handled" its own film booking with any success, "with Kennedy at the helm, it's different."

It was different because of what wasn't being reported; Kennedy was combining his various companies, his connections, and his ability to play the market to his advantage. K-A-O owned 150,000 shares of Pathé stock, and by running up the price of Pathé and then having K-A-O sell some of its shares, he saw K-A-O's balance sheet soar and the stock price increase accordingly. Within three weeks of his takeover, K-A-O was selling at $24, $3 a share more than what Walker et al. had paid for it and $8 more than its value days before the purchase.

There were questions about where Kennedy was taking his new consortium: Would Pathé and FBO become one large producing unit, would vaudeville performers flood the screens? Kennedy encouraged the perception that little would change. He wrote to Louis B. Mayer that "not feeling that there was enough excitement in the picture business, I have gone into the vaudeville game—God knows what will happen there." Joe knew exactly what was going to happen. K-A-O had been bought for the theaters.

Kennedy's leadership role at K-A-O marked another, much more private, shift in his life as Elisha Walker was replacing Guy Currier as his silent partner. Occupied with his own multiple interests, Currier had been relatively passive and gone along with RCA and K-A-O buying into FBO because investors took the pressure off and increased the potential profits. However, he was becoming concerned Joe was overextending himself. Guy's focus was on FBO and Cinema Credits, the two companies he had recommended as investments to his friends. As long as they were taken care of, he gave Kennedy a long rope, but now, Currier demanded he be kept better informed and Joe took the reprimand seriously enough to change his method of communication. Occasional phone calls and brief telegrams gave way to typed, single-spaced letters addressed "Dear Mr. Currier" containing detailed, if somewhat condescending, updates. Kennedy put out the word to the gang to include Currier when he asked to be and to be polite about it, but the men also knew they were free to make snide remarks about him to each other and to the boss as well. Until Currier left for an extended vacation in Italy that spring, Joe cabled him regularly on particulars of specific films and then asked him if, while he was abroad, he could follow up on a movie FBO was negotiating to produce on "the inspired leadership" of Italy's Benito Mussolini, written by the "Fascist and veteran" Gina Rocca. However contrite Joe appeared, he was just keeping Currier temporarily at bay. In Elisha Walker, he had a new mentor willing to open his purse strings and back him to new heights.

As Joe expanded his interests, he put members of his inner circle in various positions of power, but covering Swanson, FBO, and Pathé on a daily basis was already stretching Derr, Moore, Sullivan, and Scollard to their limit. So for K-A-O, Joe again reached back to his days at Fore River and called on Johnnie Ford, the accountant he had placed as William Gray's executive assistant at the Maine and New Hampshire Theatres Company. Since Gray's death in 1927, Kennedy had taken over the theater chain, named Ford manager, and moved the headquarters to Boston. Now Joe told Johnnie he needed him in New York to head the K-A-O office and he came running.

From the moment Kennedy put Ford in as his "assistant and personal representative," there was little question about what he was doing at K-A-O. Albee could talk all he wanted about the combination format of live performers and movies, but Kennedy was only interested in the theaters for their screens. He told Ford to "get busy at once" wiring the theaters for sound; he wanted a substantial number of them ready in time for "the fall openings."

The key to profits was to cut overhead, so Ford's next order of business was to strip the company of the now unnecessary booking agents. Even the head of scheduling who had been with Albee for over twenty years was forced to resign.

While the trades reported that the "Kennedy-Ford machine gun squadron has turned its attention to agents and bookers, executing many of each, with more to follow," there was still remarkably scant criticism of Kennedy. Now that Albee's wings were clipped, the long-held resentment, if not hatred, of him was allowed to vent and, as a result, he was blamed for his "failure to protect" his loyal lieutenants. Kennedy was still viewed as a savior and heralded as "bringing to an end the old feud between films and vaudeville." The feud was ending because vaudeville was dying. Joe was pulling the trigger that killed it because when the vaudeville stages were turned over to the movies, there were fewer and fewer venues for live performers. Yet Kennedy reached his goal: within three months, the K-A-O spreadsheets were projecting a $900,000 reduction in costs.

The truth was that Albee was impotent to protect anyone, including himself, from the new regime. While he was still president on paper, he was made to feel powerless in a multitude of ways. Along with everyone else in the New York office, he received a memo from Johnnie Ford telling him he was expected to be in the office no later than nine every morning. Kennedy instructed Ford to "find out just how far we are obliged to pay [Albee's] salary" and then "explain conditions" to him. Joe suggested cutting his salary from $100,000 to $25,000 a year. When Albee protested his treatment directly to Kennedy, Joe turned on him and said "Didn't you know, Ed? You're washed up, you're through."

As his empire expanded, Kennedy was becoming more abrupt and exhibiting little patience with those around him. Still, he took nothing for granted and sent letters of thanks to publications that mentioned him favorably and goading reminders to those that did not. He arranged for lavish, thoughtful gifts to editors and studio executives as well as the secretaries of powerful men. He also stepped in to offer assistance to *Photoplay*'s editor James Quirk when he needed to refinance his magazine.

Joe and the gang worked tirelessly to ensure public attention and private gratitude.

Kennedy hardly took time to bask in the glory of his latest acquisition. Within hours of being named chairman of K-A-O, he was off to the railroad station again, this time heading to Chicago where both FBO and Pathé were holding separate sales conventions within days of each other. Even the train was no place to rest and Joe, with Eddie Moore at his side, immediately began drafting cables to be sent from stops along the way.

From wherever he was, Joe kept tabs on Gloria Swanson. She had tried her hand at tennis, but the result was a week on crutches after twisting her ankle. Her tiny feet were so used to high heels that when she put on tennis shoes and swung her racket, she lost her balance and fell over. After a brief visit to America, Henri had returned to Paris where he was now spending ten months a year. Gloria held a few meetings on her own with Stroheim and she remained enamored with the idea he was writing a story "just for her." Feeling secure that she was on track to make a great film with Joe as her overseeing protector, she was able to relax and concentrate on her wardrobe and the lifestyle of being a star.

While Stroheim was working away on his script, the fact that he was still under contract to Pat Powers came to the fore. Powers had removed Stroheim from *The Wedding March* and sold the rough cut to Paramount, but the director remained obligated to him for another film. Stroheim claimed that the contract had been "breached" when he was fired, but Powers thought otherwise.

Joe was irked at the so-called confusion and demanded the situation be "cleaned up at once." He didn't want anyone, let alone Pat Powers, to be in a position to block his plans and cables raced back and forth across the country. Harry Edington, Stroheim's business manager who had been busy ingratiating himself with Joe, accompanied the director to New York to see what could be negotiated with Powers.

Keeping his options open, Kennedy cabled De Mille and, after assuring him he was "still confident you must be with us" at Pathé, asked him for "a great personal favor." Would he be willing to direct Gloria "in a picture to start as soon as possible," a film "similar to what you used to do with her?"

De Mille responded immediately, agreeing to "do anything in my power to assist in solving the Swanson situation." Writing in the third person, the director told Joe he was ready to develop "a big part for her in a personally directed Cecil B. De Mille film." The public would "expect to see a real De Mille picture with Swanson in it" and he suggested a million-dollar budget, but promised a million-dollar profit. He had it all figured out down to the release date: start filming mid-August and it could be delivered by Christmas.

Yet De Mille's quick reply had to give Kennedy pause. As the director himself had pointed out, the movie would first and foremost be a De Mille film, then a Swanson film, and coming in a distant third was the producer Joe Kennedy. The star and the director had a celebrated history so what was Kennedy bringing to the table? De Mille couldn't have known when he called attention to the tremendous "publicity angle" of a Swanson and De Mille reunion that that was exactly what Kennedy didn't want. Gloria and Cecil didn't need Joe to bring them together, but he had delivered Stroheim to her.

For the moment, Kennedy had two of the biggest (and most egotistical) directors in Hollywood planning films for "his star," but there really wasn't much debate over which way to go. Once Kennedy received word that Pat Powers was willing to "loan" him Stroheim, Joe thanked De Mille for his suggestions while vaguely dismissing him at the same time. "I am afraid it might be a little difficult to work out for the next picture, but after that, feel it can be arranged for the following one." Stroheim was relieved, but he also felt the pressure of Kennedy's displeasure and he was soon promising a twelve-week shooting schedule that was to begin in August.

Staying on top of every situation, the gang went into preproduction mode with Charlie Sullivan, officially vice president of Gloria Productions, acting as the hub of activity in Hollywood, and Pat Scollard, the corporation's treasurer, negotiating a half-million-dollar line of credit for the expenditures that were about to begin in earnest.

De Mille didn't seem to harbor any ill feelings, for his concern focused on whether Pathé was interested in "continuing our association." He was still in meetings with United Artists and had even suggested that if he directed a Swanson film, it would be distributed by UA and count as his first picture for them. Kennedy stood ready to assist to the point he had a draft press release written, beginning with the phrase, "Joseph P. Kennedy announces . . ." and spelling out an agreement for De Mille to make films "under the general supervision of Joseph P. Kennedy."

Joe encouraged De Mille to wait to sign with UA until he could plead his case at Pathé's Chicago board meeting. The director now sided with Kennedy to the point he was willing to give him his Pathé proxies, but the board formally decided to accept the Kennedy-negotiated separation agreement without having De Mille direct another picture for them. Joe

Welcoming Tom Mix to FBO, 1928

told Cecil that while he had sung his praises and "there was not one word of adverse criticism expressed," the board decided that "because of the conditions in the industry," they didn't dare commit the amount of money required to do such a film justice. Kennedy opined, "I regret more than I can tell you" that they wouldn't be working together, but at least De Mille had been reelected to the board and they would see each other soon. In less than two months, Kennedy had gone from being, in De Mille's view, an underling bearing bad tidings to a trusted advocate and confidant.

Kennedy's cables to De Mille might have had a solemn ring to them, but Joe's time in Chicago was yet another moment in the sun for the new mogul. At the FBO convention, they had "to reinforce the roof" when he made the official announcement that Tom Mix would be providing four of the sixty features in their upcoming slate of films. And at the Pathé sales meeting, Murdock proclaimed that, in contrast to "the loss sustained last year," the company "has now turned the corner" thanks to Joe Kennedy's reorganization. The gathered throngs were also reassured that he would continue with Pathé "for an indefinite period."

# CHAPTER 15

# "Another Big Deal in Prospect"

## (SPRING–EARLY SUMMER OF 1928)

Officially, Kennedy was in Chicago to make public appearances at the Pathé and FBO conventions, but he also made time to enter serious private negotiations to further increase his power. On the very day he was elected chairman of K-A-O, Kennedy had cabled De Mille that he had "another big deal in prospect." In fact, it had the potential to be a very big deal for he was being approached to run the giant First National.

First National had been founded out of an instinct for self-preservation. In the mid-teens, smaller theater owners throughout the country were growing disgruntled over Adolph Zukor's attempts to force them to buy his hundred-plus films a year en masse, sight unseen. This block booking allowed them to screen the latest Mary Pickford and Douglas Fairbanks films at reasonable prices, but they were also agreeing to buy all the other Famous Players-Lasky films as well, many of which were low-budget, no-star vehicles. In an attempt to combat Zukor's power over them, twenty-six theater owners united in 1917 to buy and distribute films themselves. Dividing the country into zones, they could pay competitive rates and not compete against each other. The idea was so successful that within a year, First National Exhibitors Inc., where "The Good Guys Get, by Getting Together," had over six hundred theaters in their cooperative. While they continued to buy movies from other producers, they formed First National Pictures and began signing actors to make films directly for them. The first star they put under contract was Zukor's own Mary Pickford. Lured by the assurance of creative control and $750,000 to make three films, "the girl with the curls" jumped to First National, and Charlie Chaplin, D. W. Griffith, and the Talmadge sisters soon followed.

Their utopia, however, was short-lived. Without a studio to work out of, stars leased their own space and essentially served as their own producers, which quickly ran up unexpected costs. When Chaplin asked the First National board for more money, the cold shoulder he received was a part of what drove him, Pickford, Griffith, and Fairbanks to form their own United Artists in 1919.

In the beginning, First National was just an irritation to Adolph Zukor, but with their expanding number of theaters followed by the stealing of his stars, it was becoming a real threat. In response, he began to buy controlling interests in several of the theater circuits represented on First National's board of directors, but his drive ran into a roadblock via a Federal Trade Commission investigation. Paramount was charged with attempting to "dominate and monopolize the motion picture industry," and Zukor backed away from his bulldozing tactics, content-ing himself with a mere interest in First National.

First National now represented almost a third of the nation's theaters, and to provide a temporary home for the stars, writers, and directors they were putting under contract, they leased United Studios on Melrose. What space they weren't using, they subleased to independent produc-ers. Planning ahead, they bought seventy acres in the farm area of Bur-bank and issued stock to build what the prospectus called "The Greatest Studio on Earth."

Zukor had been biding his time, but with the Coolidge administra-tion's hands-off approach to business, he went back to buying theater chains, including the large, Chicago-based Balaban and Katz. That raised concerns not only within First National, but with other studio heads such as William Fox who went on a buying spree to force a fight for control of First National. While some agreed to sell out to either Fox or Zukor, other companies wanted to remain independent and, to do that, they needed to keep First National independent as well.

Irving Rossheim, the thin, balding, and bespectacled president of the Philadelphia-based Stanley theater chain, was one of those who wanted to keep the company out of the clutches of Zukor and Fox. Rossheim proposed that if other like-minded companies pooled their stock, their unified strength could prevent a takeover. They found financing with Kennedy's old company, Hayden, Stone, but some board members believed they needed someone much stronger than their current general manager, Richard Rowland, to run the show.

A First National representative had approached Kennedy back in March of 1928 when he was just beginning to tackle Pathé. Now, two months later, Rossheim was firmly in charge and he wanted Joe to come in and reduce costs while maintaining the number of films they produced. As word of Kennedy's meetings with First National leaked out, many could not believe he was ready, willing, or able to take on a fourth company. *Variety* pointed out his current workload was already overwhelming: "Other than his own company, FBO, which is running smoothly, he has undertaken to readjust Pathé, not so easy, and also to rehabilitate the Keith circuit, the latter a stupendous job for anyone at this point." Still, the trades could see how it might work: "First National would devote its attention to Class A features; FBO to features for subsequent runs and smaller theatres, while Pathé would distribute short subjects exclusively."

For Kennedy, First National was a gift he was not about to pass up. It would allow him to put into effect the theories he had been advocating since the early 1920s. Finally that "period of consolidation" he had long predicted was about to move to the next stage and he was to be at the helm.

Joe agreed to start with First National before finalizing negotiations, assured that his demands for total control, $3,000 a week for five years, and an option to purchase 25 percent of the company's stock all would be approved. Irving Rossheim remained president on paper, but as Eddie Moore put it in his understated cable to Bill LeBaron in early June: "First National now under Joe's supervision. Nothing else new."

As the news of Kennedy's takeover spread throughout First National's studio, "everyone was excited" because it was assumed it meant the company was to remain independent and operations could continue unabated.

Unlike Pathé when he took it over, First National's recent profit reports had been positive, but Joe still needed to know exactly how the money was being spent. He assigned Arthur Poole, an accountant who had been at Pathé when Joe arrived and had impressed him with his attention to detail and follow-through, to oversee the review. Poole discovered that each of First National's branch offices had different accounting formats. Shaking his head in disbelief, Kennedy ordered the immediate changeover to systems that mirrored those used at Pathé and FBO so that any out-of-line spending could be caught at a glance.

To make First National his own, Kennedy began looking for a few serious picture men. As the head of what was soon to be Hollywood's largest studio, he needed films for both Broadway and Main Street. He reached out to directors such as Mickey Neilan to enter into five-picture deals. Before the goal of reducing costs could be reached, there was a pipeline to K-A-O and First National theaters to be filled. As soon as

each studio had been brought up
to speed, he would be in a position to merge his interests.

Harry Edington, having successfully released Stroheim from
his contract with Powers, continued to hover in the background
and now he went on a search for
new personnel. First on Edington's list was Barney Glazer,
whom he touted as someone who
"stands out head and shoulders
above them all." At the moment,
Glazer was Paramount's lead man
for sound experimentation, but
his contract only had another
month to run and he was being
courted by MGM. He sounded
great: a proven playwright with
over a dozen silent films to his
credit, including the Garbo-

Benjamin Glazer

Gilbert smash *Flesh and the Devil.* Glazer's *Seventh Heaven* had brought
Janet Gaynor to stardom and won him the first Academy Award for
screenwriting. He had proven his worth in other areas as well, earning a
law degree from the University of Pennsylvania. He combined technical
skills with the ability to produce, direct, and write, "saving the big cost
of buying published material." He also had collaborated with Stroheim
on *The Wedding March* and Kennedy looked ahead to the possibilities of
what Glazer could do for Swanson. As far as Joe was concerned, it didn't
hurt that he had been born in Belfast.

Kennedy gave Edington the go-ahead to get Glazer and then went
after Irving Thalberg's friend and MGM's resident "story expert," Paul
Bern. Trained at the American Academy of Dramatic Arts, Bern had
worked around the New York theater, acting and stage-managing for six
years before coming to Hollywood in the early 1920s. He had written
films for Paramount, United Artists, and MGM, and was now a rising
star as a production supervisor. While he was a small and physically
unassuming man, Bern was known around town for squiring beauties
such as Joan Crawford and Barbara La Marr. Harry Edington thought so
much of Bern that he told Kennedy, "I know if I were running a studio

Paul Bern

and wanted to make high class pictures at the most economical price, one of the first men I would reach for would be Bern. I am sure I could make a Thalberg out of him." And Kennedy certainly could use "a Thalberg" of his own at the studio he envisioned.

The picture Kennedy painted to Glazer and Bern was hard to resist: he was about to put together a new organization that would outshine any other in Hollywood. He had Pathé, FBO, Keith-Albee-Orpheum, and now First National just waiting to be combined into the greatest conglomerate yet. At other studios, men such as Bern and Glazer would be slotted as writers or supervisors under the thumb of others, but with Kennedy, they could rise as high as their abilities took them. Joe made no pretense of knowing about filmmaking; he knew budgets, he knew personnel, he knew administration. What he needed were a few key men who understood making movies and he was willing to pay them well.

In spite of the offers from the more established and secure MGM and Paramount, both Bern and Glazer signed with Kennedy. While they bided their time waiting for Joe's holdings to be brought together, there was plenty for everyone to do. Glazer was put "in sole control" of sound productions at both Pathé and First National and Bern was named chief of production at Pathé. His first assignment was to review all the movies currently in preproduction "in order to avoid delays and revamping of scripts" once filming began.

While the press continued to speculate on Kennedy's plans, his new status was never in doubt. Louella Parsons called him "the Napoleon of the movies" and he was hailed as "the new czar of the big time." It was becoming clear that Kennedy was a studio chief unlike any Hollywood had seen before.

The first obvious difference between Kennedy and the other moguls was in origin and background. Sam Goldwyn had been born Schmuel Gelbfisz in Warsaw and, as a teenager, had walked to Hamburg in the first lap of his long journey to America. Carl Laemmle was the tenth of his German family's thirteen children and had come to America alone at the age of sixteen. Louis B. Mayer had been born Lazar Meir in Russia and William Fox was born Wilhelm Fried into an Orthodox Jewish home in Hungary. None of them had had much formal schooling, let alone graduated from Harvard.

They had all begun in careers unconnected to entertainment. Goldwyn was a glove maker, Mayer had been in the junk business, and Marcus Loew was a furrier. All of the men were truly exceptional in their own way, disciplined, focused, and determined, but none had given signs in their original occupations that greatness lay ahead, unlike the man who had been labeled "America's youngest bank president."

For everyone but Kennedy, their companies were their identity. They had overcome incredible odds to build, "stone by stone," a business, a studio, an industry. The moguls were hardly paragons of virtue, but they did take their roles as leaders in the community seriously, and how they were perceived by that community was a vital part of their self-image. Kennedy alone was untethered by any sense of obligation to anything larger than himself and his family. As Neal Gabler, author of *An Empire of Their Own,* observes, "to everyone else, their studios were their life; to Kennedy it was a financial investment."

Another disparity between Kennedy and the other studio heads was how they spent their time. The others focused internally on their own company, in their office with their financiers, stars, directors, and producers. They visited the lots, watched the films their studios made, and went to the previews and the premieres. Kennedy looked outward, juggling his various companies, often on the run and always with an eye to what was next. Follow-through and communication with his employees was left to the gang.

It is difficult to overestimate the importance of having the likes of Eddie Moore, E. B. Derr, Pat Scollard, Charlie Sullivan, Johnnie Ford, as well as Ted O'Leary and a few select others in multiplying Kennedy's effectiveness. Each studio head had secretaries and assistants, but no one had a cadre that came close to the efficacy or single-mindedness of Kennedy's gang.

"Nothing deterred them, or even seriously challenged them, because they knew how to anticipate difficulties and avoid them," Swanson remembered. "They seemed to accomplish everything with dispatch."

Joe took care of all of them, to a point. Eddie Moore was on Joe's personal payroll in addition to payments from the various companies, but the others were well paid, though less than the going rate for studio executives. Bill LeBaron made twice what E. B. Derr did. All the men had bank accounts at Columbia Trust where Ethel Turner was available to access them. Those accounts were also used by Kennedy and, over the years, hundreds of thousands of dollars was transferred in and out of them. In addition to his own special bank accounts at Columbia Trust, Eddie Moore spread his money throughout the Northeast in a dozen bank accounts under his and his wife's names.

Kennedy had developed the habit of having "even his simplest casual questions" taken down in shorthand by secretaries always close at hand, leaving the gang to follow up. Yet when it came to commitments, it was almost innate for Joe to resist putting details in writing. More often, he sent a cable reading simply, "Will call tonight."

"Joe used a telephone the way Heifetz played a fiddle," echoed Morton Downey, who watched his friend's methods over the years. "He could do business on a telephone in a few minutes that took his supposed peers a day or a week to accomplish across a desk in an office or a conference room." Cross-country phone calls were placed through operators and cost around $2 a minute. At a time when the price of prime rib was 20 cents a pound, a half hour on the phone between New York and Los Angeles cost $60, yet Joe, so inured to the cost benefit analysis of every expense, still chose to use the telephone. Of course, Kennedy and the gang always made sure that one company or another absorbed every expense, including the phone calls.

It all took an extraordinary amount of energy, and his climb was reported matter-of-factly, but with a trace of awe. *The New York Times* opened their story with the simple sentence "Joseph P. Kennedy, the Boston banker, who is head of FBO pictures, Chairman of Keith-Albee-Orpheum vaudeville circuit and special advisor to Pathé, will sign a contract which places him in charge of First National Pictures for five years."

"A rather sorely tired young man packs his bags and hies himself to Hollywood," was the way *Film Daily* put it in their much more informal and picturesque story that July. "Mr. Joseph P. Kennedy is getting pretty tired. He's finding out there's nothing light-weight about running four organizations at one time. Yessir, four of 'em: First National, Pathé, FBO and Keith Albee Orpheum. That's a job, don't ever kid yourself otherwise. It would be a trying task if all of the outfits were hitting it off in grand style, but when several of them are holding on to Mr. Kennedy because they expect him to do the Moses and lead them out of Egypt, the going merely gets tougher. And, mind you, there is no reflection on Joe Kennedy. Joe is new to this business and for a newcomer, he sure has bitten off an awful tough bite."

Four companies were indeed an overwhelming number for anyone, yet suddenly everyone was a newcomer because of talking pictures.

# CHAPTER 16

# "You Ain't Heard Nothing Yet"

When the upcoming 1928 film year was heralded, no mention was made of sound films. By early summer, *The Jazz Singer*, which had received mixed critical reviews, had been in release for eight months. Calling it melodramatic does not begin to describe this sentimental yarn of generational alienation, mother love, assimilation, and good old show business. *Motion Picture News* pronounced it a "nice Jewish picture" of "no great caliber." *The Jazz Singer* unspooled with traditional title cards used in silent films, but, when audiences heard Al Jolson say "you ain't heard nothing yet" straight from the screen before he broke into song, they were not only ecstatic, they kept coming back for more. The film had been in and out and back again in cities such as St. Louis where Western Electric's Vitaphone equipment was installed, removed, and then reinstalled. With ticket prices at a dollar a pop, it was worth the effort.

Still, many in positions of power continued to dismiss "the current talking picture craze as nothing more than public curiosity." Joe Schenck prophesied that "they will not last more than four or five months" and announced that United Artists "was not going to make talking pictures." Even "the boy genius," Irving Thalberg, said that "talking pictures are just a passing fad."

The men who had been visionary trailblazers only a decade earlier had not totally lost their touch. Their resistance was based on the very real fear that sound meant a creative revolution and financial upheaval. As Cecil B. De Mille explained, "All this would be enormous waste if, after the novelty wore off, the public preferred their screens to be silent." And there were plenty of other arguments against sound.

Creatively, the earliest talkies were clunky at best in contrast to the sweeping silent epics such as *The Big Parade, The Winning of Barbara Worth,* or *The Wind.* The technical advancement in lighting, cinematography, and editing had reached the point that, as Mary Pickford put it,

"Adding sound to movies would be like putting lipstick on the Venus de Milo."

Many believed that silence was at the heart of what drew audiences to the theaters. People went to the movies to be taken away from the chattering that surrounded them every day. Yet their visceral response to sound films could not be denied. William de Mille, the older and less pompous brother of Cecil B., remembered his first experience hearing an actor speak from the screen. " 'Ladies and Gentlemen . . .' he said. He said! A thrill ran through the house . . . I felt a nervous quiver run through me [like] an explorer who suddenly finds that new land has been discovered. The nervous tension and sense of excitement which I felt on that night was to last all through the first two hectic years of 'sound.' "

Two years. That is at least how long it would take to make the transition that was shaking their world. When the Warner brothers premiered their first "all talking" picture, *The Lights of New York,* in the summer of 1928, *Photoplay* concluded "sound films will have to work out a better technique to advance." Yet audiences weren't as discerning. *The Lights of New York* opened at the Strand in New York during a particularly muggy July and the days were punctured with downpours, factors that usually kept the box office down. Not this time; every screening was standing room only. Suddenly, everyone was talking about talking pictures and, as the flailing toward sound began in earnest, fear set in.

Sound films meant seismic economic changes and each of the major studios was forced into its agonizing assessments. Before examining how they were going to do it, Jesse Lasky and Adolph Zukor announced that Paramount would release a sound film every other week. They weren't trying for "all talking" movies, just trying to stay in the running with "spoken sequences, songs, dance, instrumental numbers" somewhere in each picture. Paramount signed with Western Electric to provide the technical know-how, but only one small stage on their entire lot was conducive to recording. Costs soared as directors and actors were kept waiting for their turn on the single soundstage and crews were soon working around the clock. Lasky estimated it might take as much as $1.5 million to fulfill their initial sound program, but just like almost everyone else, he was underestimating the price tag.

Over at MGM, Irving Thalberg knew he didn't know what to do or whom to trust, so he turned to his brother-in-law, Douglas Shearer, a Canadian radio engineer. They soon realized sound meant major physical changes and several buildings were demolished, trees chopped down, and gardens overturned so a foundation could be laid on "vibrationless piles" for a stage surrounded by eight-inch-thick concrete

With Jesse Lasky of Paramount, 1926

walls. In the meantime, they leased a building on New York's Upper East Side and put workers on overtime to soundproof stages.

Almost everything needed to be replaced or updated. Because the arc lights that had been perfected for silent films emitted a slight hissing noise, all new incandescent lights were mounted in special reflectors. They were quiet, but the resulting heat was unbearable without a new ventilation system. And all this was before sound engineers installed a single microphone.

Then there were the cameras. Cinematographers had refined their art and developed cameras that could be moved easily on dollies or cranes. No more. Cameras too had to be silenced so they were anchored in padded soundproof boxes with a window for the actual filming. The cameramen sat inside the stifling booth wearing headphones to hear instructions from the director. Audio technicians were cramped into similar boxes nearby.

Once their collective mind-set had shifted to sound, it was assumed that everything and everyone associated with silent films might have to be replaced. Could scenarists write dialogue? Could their actors speak the lines, let alone memorize them? Soon "every train coming from the east brings someone who steps into a job," usually replacing a worker judged to be no longer relevant.

Playwrights were suddenly in demand. Kennedy's Harvard classmate Robert Benchley was a successful writer at *Vanity Fair* while he perfected his sideline of dry comic appearances on the stage and the party circuit. He, along with his routine entitled *The Treasurer's Report,* was nabbed by Fox and soon his fellow *Vanity Fair* refugees, Dorothy Parker and Robert Sherwood, joined him in the film capital. Their literary work might have proved more personally fulfilling, but there was no arguing with the paychecks.

Yet words alone did not a moving picture make. In fact, the static nature of plays was one of the worst things about the first talkies—they didn't move. The early results proved that it was a greater challenge to teach playwrights how to write movies than it was for screenwriters to adjust to dialogue. Many took the money and ran back to New York, but others such as Parker, Ben Hecht, Charles MacArthur, and Herman Mankiewicz stayed on for years.

While the westward flow of writers slowed to a trickle, one-way tickets to Los Angeles were handed out en masse to New York stage actors. When Walter Huston left Broadway for the movies, he was replaced in his role by Ralph Bellamy, who in turn was soon Hollywood-bound.

Even the greatest stars were vulnerable as the quality and tone of their voices entered into the equation. After being swept away watching the beautiful Brooklyn-born star Viola Dana play a deathbed scene, Sam Goldwyn's secretary was shocked when the cameras stopped rolling and the actress turned to her maid and yelled, "in a very tough" twang, "Hey Mame, gimme a cigarette." If a seasoned studio secretary was stunned, how would audiences respond?

No one needed to ask Norma or Constance Talmadge that question. Their "lower Bronx" accents had not hampered the fortune they had made in silents, and they tried a talkie or two but then gracefully retired from the screen. Marion Davies, however, cared passionately about her career and when she saw *The Jazz Singer,* she turned to a friend and announced, "I-I-I have a p-p-problem." She worked for months using a variety of physical and psychological programs, including speaking with marbles in her mouth, to cure her speech impediment at least when the cameras were running. Vilma Banky, Goldwyn's biggest female star, who had appeared opposite Rudy Valentino in *The Son of the Sheik,* could barely speak English through her heavy Hungarian accent. Vilma's most constant co-star, Ronald Colman, was a British stage-trained actor and therefore in the rare position of having a secure future. Few others were as lucky. Even if their voices sounded "normal," the fear of what the microphones would record was so intense everyone had to be tested.

Bebe Daniels was among those unceremoniously dropped by Paramount, but she found work with other studios and was a smash in *Rio Rita.* When Adolph Zukor asked production chief B. P. Schulberg why he had let Daniels go, Schulberg responded without a trace of irony, "She couldn't talk."

Studios were awash with voice coaches and, while most came from New York, MGM went all the way to Italy to import the world-renowned Dr. Marafioti. After their training, actors went before Lionel

Barrymore, who, with his years of stage experience, directed many of their sound tests.

Songwriters flooded Hollywood to meet the newly created demand for theme songs and mood music. Fox dropped $100,000 into George Gershwin's lap for a film score and another $50,000 for the use of *Rhapsody in Blue.* Several symphony orchestras and brass bands were needed for studio recording, but musicians who had played for actors on the lot to set the atmosphere were dropped. Then there were the more than fifty thousand musicians throughout the country being paid to accompany silent films. Their jobs were threatened with every theater that was wired for sound. References to "human orchestras" began to appear, in contrast with "recorded music." While the musicians and their unions resisted their expulsion from theaters, they were gradually pushed into the inevitable.

Sound films were seen as separate and distinct from silent ones. There was even much debate over what this new aberration was to be called. At first it was "talkies" but that hardly described it since most of the earliest attempts featured only synchronized music. One fan magazine ran a contest to gather ideas for an appellation. Gradually "sound pictures" became the phrase of choice, but exactly what that meant was still open for discussion. Sometimes it was just prerecorded music or perhaps a dialogue sequence stuck into the last reel that was so startlingly different in tone and style from the rest of the film, audiences left the theater shaking their heads. Attempts were made at inserting sound intermittently, but then the sequences ended abruptly, as a method to fade out sound had yet to be developed. While sound was becoming a mandate, no matter how awkward or disconcerting the results might be, the trades warned producers: "Don't misrepresent. The public wants to know the difference between pictures with synchronized scores and those that actually have spoken dialogue."

*Film Daily* created a column entitled "Sound Pictures" in late May of 1928, but it ran only twice a week. It took *Photoplay* until September to premiere a new section labeled "Department Devoted to Sound Film Reviews." Of the six films mentioned in that issue, the only one to rate "the wow of the talkies" was a single-reeler of George Bernard Shaw talking and walking. It was worthy of note because "you hear his footsteps—scrunch, scrunch—on the path."

By the late summer of 1928, only four hundred of the country's twenty thousand movie theaters were ready to run sound pictures so when a new one was about to open, it was big news. Weeks in advance, banners proclaiming "Vitaphone coming to town" were hung at train stations, hotels, and offices, building anticipation and giving the arrival a circuslike feel. The rate at which theaters were being wired increased by the fall, but the situation was exacerbated by the question of whose union the job fell under, electricians or theater workers. The studio heads had methodically kept unions out of Hollywood, but the American Federation of Labor was fairly strong in major cities and that brought further "complications."

RCA's Photophone, like Fox's Movietone, recorded the sound onto the film and the resulting negative looked like a train track, hence the term "sound track." Warner's Vitaphone was a sound-on-disk method, with the records synchronized to the films. All of the systems required projectionists to learn to use new or altered equipment. To the monikers Photophone, Phonofilm, Movietone, and Vitaphone were added Bristolphone, Kinographone, and others, but the race at the moment was between methods as much as brand names.

The trades reported that "Gloom hangs over the studios." Many closed for as long as two months while a total of seventeen sound studios were constructed throughout the Los Angeles area. Relatively speaking, Pathé and FBO should have been in great shape. Kennedy had been committed to sound films since late 1927, ahead of everyone but the brothers Warner and William Fox. It had been over six months since Joe had toured the RCA labs and over three months since their equipment arrived at FBO, but those days of effusive enthusiasm were fading. They were still struggling to synchronize music and sound effects and not a single K-A-O theater had been successfully wired, including their New York flagship, the Hippodrome.

Pathé and FBO were both scrambling for stories or plays they could turn into sound films and reading departments were established in New York. In the meantime, they went back over their current batch of silent films to see where sound could be inserted in at least a few scenes. A sound effect, music, an ending with a bit of dialogue; it didn't matter as long as they could advertise it as having "sound." At Pathé, it was natural to turn to their biggest film in line to be released, Cecil B. De Mille's *The Godless Girl*. It was laced with spectacular scenes made possible only because it was filmed as a silent. The camera, on a huge crane, had been free to move up three floors of activity and then capture a girl's fall through the multistory staircase.

Kennedy brought in Robert Kane, the experienced independent producer who had been the catalyst for his meeting Gloria Swanson, to try

Cecil B. De Mille directing *The Godless Girl*

to speed up the transition. When the delays continued, Joe sent him to RCA to get to the bottom of it.

In spite of the bumps in the road, Kennedy and David Sarnoff met to discuss expanding their empires by becoming partners in a holding company. RCA was to put in $4.2 million and Kennedy (with Walker's backing) was to put in 200,000 shares of K-A-O stock valued at $4.2 million. Each group would hold an equal amount of stock, giving them joint control as well as enough stock left over to pay themselves back when it was sold. The purpose of the company was to create, distribute, and screen sound films in theaters as well as homes, churches, and schools, a passion of Sarnoff's.

RCA brought funding and technical ability to the table while Kennedy and Walker agreed that K-A-O, FBO, and Pathé would use Photophone exclusively. Who would handle the actual distribution was not decided, but the last line of the draft agreement read "Consideration should be given to the question of acquiring further stock or all the assets of FBO and/or Pathé."

Within weeks of their meetings on their proposed joint venture, Kennedy's and Sarnoff's frustration with each other came to a head. Kennedy was irritated over what he saw as the lack of follow-through from RCA, while Sarnoff was tired of picking up the entire cost for the sound experiments at Pathé and FBO. In mid-July, Sarnoff put his foot down and demanded that their long discussed agreements to have the two studios use only Photophone be put in writing or he was going to pull out of the synchronization that was already in progress. Yes, RCA had an interest in both studios, but Photophone was not operating to subsidize those investments.

Elisha Walker stepped in to negotiate, bringing Sarnoff and his envoy with the studios, E. E. Bucher, and Kennedy's representative, Robert Kane, into his office at Blair and Company. Joe was still in California, but he joined the discussion by telephone and acknowledged that there seemed to be "some misunderstanding" about the finances. To Sarnoff, there was no misunderstanding. So far everything had been paid for by Photophone and there was not even a plan in place to give them a percentage of the profits once the films were released. "An orderly basis" had to be agreed upon.

According to Kane, Photophone had indeed spent at least $40,000 to record music for two films for Pathé and two for FBO. The real cost was much higher when transporting the equipment across country, the installation, and the engineers were all factored in. Yet after all that time and work, there was only one film ready for release and that was a reissue of De Mille's *King of Kings* with a synchronized musical score added. It had just opened at the Rivoli in New York and Sarnoff wanted a written agreement for a percentage of the profits. Walker and Kane agreed in principle to reimburse Photophone proportionately, but they were still at loggerheads over what came next. Kane claimed they needed better equipment so they could rerecord much of what had been done so far. If more equipment and engineers were needed, Sarnoff demanded the cost be borne by the studios. Sarnoff saw Kennedy as someone very free with other people's money, but unwilling to spend his own. He wanted written confirmation on Photophone licenses from Pathé and FBO and he expected the same royalty and copyright fees that the rival Vitaphone received.

No one was particularly happy. Kennedy knew that one of the reasons FBO and Pathé had shown an increase in profits was because RCA was paying the bills for the sound experiments. And Sarnoff knew that if Kennedy was successful in uniting all his companies into a giant combine, he wanted to be a key player in the alliance. Still, he wasn't willing to be used while he was waiting.

Never before had anyone in Hollywood had access to as many companies' assets as Kennedy did, yet he felt thwarted by his inability to make inroads as quickly as he wanted. He was moving ahead at First National, but there was nothing he could personally do at the moment to accelerate effective recording and no amount of coaxing seemed to prod Stroheim to speed up his writing.

As was his pattern when something was beyond his control, Joe turned to a subject he could manipulate, and this time it was his own image. His years of cultivating the press were paying off in the coverage he was receiving in the columns and the trades and now the national media began taking notice as well. Kennedy might have had an unprecedented number of companies to manage, but he still made time for interviews with carefully chosen journalists.

He opened his door to *Photoplay,* the influential fan magazine, and the result was a six-page spread featuring individual pictures of each of his children in addition to photos of Joe and Rose. Billed in the subheadings as "the screen's leading family man" who "brings Americanism and substantiality to the industry," Kennedy was painted as irresistibly affable, sharp as a tack, infused with joie de vivre, and devoted to his wife and children.

*Photoplay*'s "Intimate Visit" inspired an in-depth profile in *American Magazine,* a popular national monthly with a circulation of over two million. This time, Kennedy invited the reporter to spend a day with the family on Cape Cod where he could watch "the young man at his hearth with a robust and somewhat vociferous band of youngsters around him." The result was an extravagantly positive article in the May 1928 issue.

The *American Magazine* feature was followed within weeks by a *New York Times* personality piece headlined "Movie Chief's Rapid Rise," complete with a large and impressive photograph of the man himself. These

His first big spread in *Photoplay* as a "Famous Film Magnate," 1927

three major articles worked together to increase Kennedy's visibility and, in small ways and large, to rewrite his biography.

Kennedy's image was polished with a thick coat of Horatio Alger veneer. He had been born in near-poverty and pulled himself up by his bootstraps. He hadn't just graduated from Harvard, but gone on to Harvard Business School. His time as a state bank examiner was more than doubled and placed after his marriage to Rose, making it so "for three years he and a growing family were limited to an income of $125 a month." While each article referred to Kennedy as having been "America's youngest bank president," no one noticed that his father had been a founder of that bank or that having a father-in-law who had been the mayor of Boston might have come in handy along the way.

Familial devotion underscored everything. His marriage "was the best thing that could have happened to me," the news he had been brought into Pathé was "dwarfed" by his joy at the birth of baby Jean, and, at the juncture of every major decision, "Mrs. Kennedy and I discussed it." Joe said his wife was the reason he entered films because she insisted he take on a business "that was not my idea of a sound and progressive career." And with his family as "my first board of review," he was committed to "produce only clean pictures."

None of the articles had him involved in any aspect of filmmaking before he purchased FBO nor did anyone mention any other investors, silent or otherwise. Kennedy actually went so far as to claim he had turned down all requests from motion picture companies prior to 1926. It was as if he had tripped over FBO and somersaulted into owning it. "It had not been his intention to enter the business," claimed *The New York Times,* but then he "found himself at the head of the Film Booking Offices." *Photoplay* had him buying it when a fortuitous phone call came in and the serendipity intensified in the version he told the reporter from *American Magazine*: "Lord Inverforth walked into my Boston office, where I was busy doing nothing . . . and before he left Boston I had control of one of the largest and most unprofitable motion picture concerns in the world."

Joe was portrayed as handsome, enthusiastic, and energetic. He was a man of the people with a passion for candy and baseball. Self-deprecation was another recurring theme, but always with the twist that he came out ahead. He set it up so that if his bubble popped, he could claim he never cared about the business anyway. He had risen from close to nowhere to the very top in banking, shipbuilding, the stock market, and now films. As *Photoplay* put it, "He carries the authority of pre-proved success." He was a good-looking, red-hot executive with a knack for handling people, finances, and any task he took on.

One of his biographers has compared Kennedy's "folk hero" status to that of Lindbergh and Babe Ruth, yet Joe's reputation resulted much less from achievements that generated a mass following and much more from press coverage that was sought after and contrived. Yet the comparison is interesting, because it exemplifies the aura emanating from the stories. If the executive suites of Hollywood could have a folk hero, Kennedy was it. No other studio head received anywhere near the amount of column inches that he did.

The articles would serve as the basis for future stories and biographies that repeated many of Joe's tales without further investigation or correction. At the time, for those who didn't know Kennedy or had only heard his name, they combined to portray a charismatic business genius and committed family man, firmly established and going nowhere but up. However, those few who did know Kennedy well or had partnered with him in any of his ventures must have been shocked by some of the statements presented as fact. David Sarnoff could not have been happy to read in *The New York Times* that it was Kennedy who had single-handedly united RCA, GE, and Westinghouse with FBO and was credited as the man who "brought together the two industries—film and radio." And Guy Currier must have raised an eyebrow when the only time his name was mentioned in any of the three articles was as the attorney who, searching for "striking executive ability," suggested Kennedy for the job at Fore River.

Joe, however, couldn't have been more pleased. He decided it was time to invest in a clipping service to send him copies of all articles in which his name appeared. And he hired the *Photoplay* reporter who had started it all, Terry Ramsaye, to come to work for him in the publicity department at Pathé.

# CHAPTER 17

# "Swinging the Axe"

## (JULY–AUGUST 1928)

*I*n early July of 1928, Kennedy returned to California where Gloria awaited him. So did Pathé, FBO, and K-A-O, but the source of his greatest excitement at the moment was his scheduled "tour of observation" of his latest takeover, First National. He was clearly the new king of the realm as he walked through the sixty-two glorious acres in Burbank, four times larger than FBO and twice the size of Pathé. Joe's stride radiated power; in many ways, this was a very different man than the one who had made his first trip to Hollywood just two years before. In that short amount of time he had become one of the most influential men in the business. He knew it and he reveled in it.

Kennedy was all business at First National, where the workforce, from executives to secretaries, quickly learned to speak only when spoken to. One of his inherited employees was Alexander Korda, who would later be knighted as a British film tycoon, but in 1928 was a recent arrival, brought along with his wife, Maria, who had been signed as First National's answer to Garbo. When Korda recognized Kennedy taking his constitutional through the lot, the director silently bowed to the new studio chief. Joe ignored him and said to a nearby supplicant, loudly enough for everyone including Korda to hear, "Who does that guy think he is, some kind of fucking baron or something?" Joe was soon being avoided for more than his verbal abuse. In a matter of days, twenty-five executives and producers were fired and more writers, directors, and actors were dismissed soon after.

When Kennedy took over First National, thirty-four actors were under long-term contract, but he reduced that number to seventeen. Colleen Moore and Loretta Young survived, but Mary Astor, Lewis Stone, and Maria Corda were among those let go. Joe was convinced it was cheaper to hire actors for single films than to keep them on payroll week to week. It also reduced the line on the balance sheet for salaries and, in turn, made the profits look higher.

First National Administration Building

He examined their production methods and made more changes. First National had gone from depending upon independent producers to making their own fifty-plus films a year under a unit system, each with their own groups of talent. A small administrative office served the entire studio, but each unit was free to operate more or less as they saw fit with their own budgets and schedules. That was anathema to Kennedy, who ordered the studio reorganized under the same system as his other companies, with all talent open to assignment on any given film.

While claiming he had "no intention of turning First National into a five and dime proposition," Kennedy was, as *Variety* put it, busy "swinging the axe." Richard Rowland, who had risen to general manager of First National after being in the business for almost thirty years, resigned suddenly, claiming that he "planned a long rest." Most of Rowland's underlings, including his assistant manager, the head of the accounting department, the studio manager, and the chief story editor, were all let go. Sam Spring, the company's treasurer and secretary, was also removed, making way for the gang to institute their own accounting methods.

It was announced that Al Rockett, one of First National's more successful unit producers, was now in charge of production, but Barney Glazer was brought in as production advisor and, most importantly, E. B. Derr was there to actually oversee the operation. While Kennedy's "broom continued to sweep" the old employees out the door, members of his "Irish stock company" began appearing on the studio's payroll. Even Henri got in on the deal as First National was added to the list of companies for which he served as "foreign representative."

One of Kennedy's colleagues, however, didn't share in the First National wealth and he wasn't happy about it. David Sarnoff had been willing to "split" Kennedy with First National because he wanted their "so called talkies" to be recorded by Photophone. He even agreed to put $25,000 into synchronizing the sound effects and music for First National's *Lilac Time,* yet when the aviation epic starring Colleen Moore and Gary Cooper opened in New York, it was with a live orchestra because the theater had not been wired in time. The Los Angeles premiere at the Carthay Circle was disappointing as well. The theater was ready, but the sound was uneven and the "deafening roar" of several sequences jolted the audience out of their seats. This time the blame was put on unions, but at the moment, Vitaphone was a proven method and Photophone was struggling at best. Kennedy told Sarnoff he had tried, but he couldn't deliver First National to RCA after all. It didn't help when Joe told reporters that if Photophone continued to drag their feet installing equipment in theaters, their future was far from assured. To add insult to Sarnoff's injury, *Lilac Time* was "remade" using Vitaphone.

If that wasn't enough to push Sarnoff to the edge, another Kennedy move that summer did. Joe came to the conclusion that their plan to remodel an old New York studio for their joint venture, Sound Studios, wasn't sufficient; he wanted to create a brand-new, million-dollar studio instead. Sarnoff saw no reason to invest in a new building when they were still negotiating over license fees and had more immediate problems to deal with, but Kennedy didn't take his no as an answer. He went over his head to the chiefs at General Electric, confident they would be convinced by his enthusiasm. To his surprise, they reiterated that Sarnoff was in charge and sent Joe back to him. Sarnoff won the battle and was given one more reason not to trust him.

The entire industry was rife with rumors about Kennedy, "the industry's big mystery man." What was he planning behind his "stony silence"? Was Pathé to move their production to First National in Burbank and the Culver City studio to be "disposed of"? Were all of FBO's sound pictures to be made at Pathé? Kennedy churned up the interest in the press and then refused to commit to specifics.

While the press's attention was riveted on First National, Kennedy made visits to FBO and Pathé for meetings and declarations that all was running smoothly. He also spent time with Gloria at his house on Rodeo and met with her and Stroheim, who was still writing his script. Joe had put the task of watching the director "every minute" into the combined hands of Bill LeBaron and Barney Glazer. He had such confidence in them that when Jesse Lasky warned that Stroheim's "chief talent was his genius for spending large sums of money," Joe replied, "Nothing can go wrong. I've got two good men to police the Kraut."

Appearing as self-possessed as ever, Kennedy bypassed reporters on Monday, August 6, and boarded the train east to formalize his agreement with First National. He told a few people he had been walking around with the contract in his pocket for a month, as if he was still making up his mind, but he hoped to sweeten an already incredible deal.

With his entourage of Moore and Derr, Kennedy arrived in New York to be greeted by half a dozen men, all wanting a piece of his time. There was Bob Kane, Ned Depinet of First National, as well as Joe Schnitzer and Lee Marcus of FBO. There was no question of the importance of the man being escorted through the station and into the waiting car. Their first stop was the Palace Theatre on Broadway for a special K-A-O board meeting where Kennedy's chairmanship was affirmed, as was the exemption that allowed him to have financial interests in other entertainment companies. Then it was on to the First National office where he spent the rest of the day and the next in meetings and on the phone, supervising the preparation of reports for their board of directors meeting.

In between, Kennedy and Derr were fielding cables from Charlie Sullivan in Culver City, and amongst the updates was the warning that the Swanson-Stroheim epic would not begin filming within the next two weeks as planned. Four weeks was more like it. After receiving the "tentative script," Sullivan thought that it was "impractical" at best. At the moment, Kennedy had other issues to deal with, but he proceeded on the assumption that it was a normal preproduction problem. He informed Al Lichtman at United Artists that while he didn't have time to meet with him at the moment, he was looking forward to sitting down soon to "outline the campaign" to promote Gloria's upcoming film.

On Friday morning, the First National board meeting was opened by President Irving Rossheim, the man who had been the lead negotiator with Kennedy and who now introduced him to the other board members. For all intents and purposes, Joe had been running First National for two months and if he was verging on arrogance, he had the numbers to back it up. He took the podium and spent the next several hours going over the details of his plan. He proudly informed them that he had already reduced overhead by $20,000 a week and, if the Pathé operation was moved to the First National studio, more savings would result. Joe was dangling some very large numbers. He had often repeated his goal of a 40 percent cost reduction, but now he suggested the savings could be even greater. The current combined operational costs of FBO, Pathé, and First National totaled $8 million a year; with Joe in "supreme command," he suggested he could achieve a reduction of $4 million at "no sacrifice in quality."

Between Rossheim's enthusiasm and Kennedy's charismatic presentation, any reservations the board might have had were kept to themselves. They went on meeting right through lunch, but in the middle of the afternoon, Rossheim took a break to announce to the waiting press that Kennedy had officially signed with First National. His title was to remain "special advisor," but make no mistake, he was to have "absolute power" to "run the whole shebang." He had signed a five-year contract at $3,000 a week with options to purchase 25 percent of the company. And, as Joe had hoped, they increased his compensation by agreeing that after three years, he would receive 10 percent of all profits.

As the meeting continued, E. B. Derr was brought to the fore and introduced as the man who would oversee the studio on a day-to-day basis. Kennedy told them there was "no better soul alive on office operation and management" and confidently left Derr behind to work out any remaining details. Flushed with his latest and biggest victory to date, Joe headed to the Cape to see his family for the first time in two months.

Kennedy's intent was to stay in Hyannisport through most of the week and then return to New York before boarding the *Ile de France* with Rose for a long-planned voyage to Europe. Now that he was in the unprecedented position of simultaneously running four major companies, it might seem a bizarre time to take off for six weeks, but it made perfect sense to Joe. He had raised the concept of delegation to a true art form, the supervisor whose ultimate goal was to have nothing left for himself to do except focus on the big picture. Kennedy was convinced that by putting the right people in the right roles, reporting in the right way, the machine was in place to function smoothly. John Murdock was joining him on the ship, allowing them time to look to the future together. And there was always foreign business to conduct.

From his summer home, Kennedy sent cables to his European contacts, telling them that in addition to his already scheduled appointments for Pathé and FBO, he had "just taken over complete charge of First National" and was eager to discuss production and distribution for that company as well. He also answered his routine correspondence, thanking Pat Powers for suggesting Mae West as a potential film star and then writing Bob Kane to ask him to "see how we could use her."

To Joe, sitting on his sunporch surrounded by secretaries and his stock ticker as he watched his children playing in the ocean only yards away, it looked like smooth sailing ahead. Yet behind closed doors in New York, Boston, and Burbank, three separate, but powerful, forces were initiating discussions that would roil his world.

The first was David Sarnoff in New York. He saw himself as the one with the technological ability to merge radio, film, and nascent television; it was Kennedy's job to make the production and distribution a reality. As far as Sarnoff was concerned, Joe had not lived up to his part of the bargain. When Sarnoff called in his underlings at Photophone to explain their failure to progress, they put the blame squarely on Kennedy and his promises "to deliver each and every one of the worthwhile film companies."

It had been almost three months since Sarnoff had sat down with Elisha Walker and Robert Kane and straightened out—he thought—the arrangements between the studios and Photophone. During that time Sarnoff's suspicions of Joe and his motives had continued to grow, for FBO had yet to pay the money he thought he was owed nor sign the license agreements. He was infuriated when he received a bill for the musicians used for recording and synchronizing the film *Gang War*. As he explained one more time, "I do not want Photophone to act as a financier for picture companies. There is no good reason I can see why we should lay out the money for the cost of synchronizing pictures. This is the responsibility of the picture company itself."

Sarnoff concluded that he and Kennedy were on divergent paths and he became determined "to get started on a sound policy as he saw fit." Sarnoff began buying up Pathé stock and working behind the scenes to increase RCA's influence. He also muted Kennedy's threat to go with Vitaphone instead of Photophone by announcing that the two sound processes were now interchangeable. It was Photophone that had to make the slight technical changes, but by this point it was almost inevitable that all systems would eventually work together.

Kennedy responded to the news of Sarnoff's stock buying as "a lot of baloney," but he knew he had dragged out RCA paying for his studios' sound experiments for as long as he could. When Joe returned to New York from the Cape on Thursday, the day before he was to board the ship, he met with Bill LeBaron and Joe Schnitzer and then finally and formally signed the license agreements to use RCA's Photophone for both Pathé and FBO, putting his companies on the same paying basis that every other studio had with their sound companies. Kennedy also attempted to ingratiate himself with Sarnoff by reiterating his praise for Photophone and announcing that he would use it for Swanson's upcoming film. Sarnoff had played hardball and won.

In Boston, Guy Currier had also reached his limit. For some time, his frustration with Joe had been building and the accumulating slights, feigned innocence, and subterfuge had taken their toll. Too many outside deals too quickly had left Currier certain that his interests and those of his investor friends were no longer in the forefront of Kennedy's concerns. Joining First National was the last straw. He no longer cared what gains Joe might claim were around the next corner; Currier was ready to end their relationship.

Currier told Kennedy in no uncertain terms he "wanted to get out" and the letter was waiting for Joe when he arrived in New York that Thursday. It was the last thing he needed at the moment and he waited until the next morning to reply, professing he had tried to phone him but there was no answer. He claimed he asked Elisha Walker if he would be willing to buy out Currier's interests, but Walker wasn't about to make "any further commitment" at the moment. Joe said he was sorry that Guy felt the way he did and told him, "I am perfectly willing to get out myself if and when we can find a buyer for the company." There was no way Kennedy wanted to sell FBO; it was part of the package he was delivering to First National. Yet for a decade he had been able to cajole Currier into seeing things his way. He just needed some time and so he promised "to take it up again" upon his return from Europe.

Now the only thing standing between Kennedy and the *Ile de France* was one last meeting. He had received a cable from Irving Rossheim, in Maine for his own well-deserved vacation, saying that he had been hearing from dissatisfied board members. Given time to talk to each other, they were beginning to raise questions about Kennedy and his plans. Rossheim had not been able to calm the waters and he asked Joe to please make time to meet with two of the directors, Barney Balaban and Spyros Skouras, and the Stanley Company's attorney, Morris Wolf, before leaving the country. Rossheim regretted he could not be there personally, but assumed all they needed was reassuring. He was comfortable with Wolf serving as his representative and "any agreement you reach with the group will have my full approval."

Since the official announcement of Kennedy's signing with First National, board members' telephones had been ringing with calls from directors and producers at the Burbank studio, unhappy with the conditions Joe's "reforms" had created. It was impossible to believe that he could slash costs by 50 percent with "no sacrifice in quality." With so many cuts already made and more reportedly in the offing, they were without the support system that had attracted them to First National in the first place. They were troubled by the number of heads that had rolled; reducing overhead was one thing, all-out slaughter was something else again. Fear was omnipresent, with Alexander Korda coming straight out and calling Kennedy's leadership a "reign of terror."

Resistance to Kennedy was percolating. It was as if the board members suddenly realized that they were declaring themselves null and void by turning over so much power to one man. Joe had been brought in as a "super administrator," but he had removed so many employees so quickly that it scared them into wondering what was next. First National was both a film studio and a consortium of theater owners who had come together to meet a mutual need. Whose needs would Kennedy be meeting? There had been potential conflicts from the beginning, particularly over the fact that Kennedy also headed K-A-O with their several hundred theaters. What if he decided to merge his theaters with Rossheim's Stanley theaters into a giant combine? Where would that leave the likes of Balaban and Skouras?

Spyros Skouras was a Greek émigré who had arrived in America in his early teens and worked as a bellboy by day while taking accounting and law classes at night. He and his two brothers had begun with nickelodeons in 1914 and Skouras was now the head of their St. Louis–based company with more than forty theaters.

Barney Balaban was the eldest of ten children of Russian immigrants. Home was Chicago's Jewish ghetto where the family lived in two rooms above the market their mother managed. Working from the age of nine, Barney had left school entirely by fourteen. His mother was the family entrepreneur and, with her encour-

Spyros Skouras

Barney Balaban

agement, Barney and his siblings opened a movie theater. Barney used his experience working in cold storage to build the first air-conditioned theater in the country and now he headed Balaban and Katz, Chicago's largest theater circuit with over one hundred opulent theaters specializing in first runs throughout the Midwest.

Balaban, a year older than Kennedy, and Skouras, four years younger, had a combined forty years of experience as theater owners; tough, proven professionals who were not about to be bluffed by someone they considered, at best, a newcomer. They had worked their way up, believed they knew the theater business as well as anyone and, for the life of them, couldn't see why they needed to give so much power to a banker, let alone one with so many other interests.

On Friday, literally hours before he was scheduled to board the ship, Kennedy met with Balaban, Skouras, and Wolf. The two board members told Joe they were willing to welcome him to First National, but insisted on creating an executive committee to monitor all major activity. Surely he could understand that self-preservation demanded they have a place in the decision making process? No, he couldn't. Since childhood, one of Joe's axioms had been "If you can't be captain, don't play," and to his thinking, he had already compromised by not being on the board and not being made president. He had the power, the purse strings, and the option to purchase a quarter of the company, the rest would follow as it always had. But these grumblings, to say nothing of this new restraint of an executive committee, were an attempt to tie his hands and he wouldn't hear of it. To their faces, Joe told them he refused to work under such a constraint. It was "complete and absolute control" or nothing. They could go ahead and form their executive committee, but he gave them an ultimatum: "If you do, it's without me."

On that note, Kennedy left the meeting. He would later tell his youngest son, "Coming down the last stages of the lap, a good runner doesn't quit at the finish—that's the time he puts on the speed." Yet this time, there was nowhere else to run, except to the ship that would take him to Europe and away from all this. With Sarnoff's reproaches, Currier's rebukes, and the First National axe falling, the *Ile de France* had suddenly become a desperately needed refuge.

Avoiding reporters on the way up the gangplank, Joe embarked on that Friday evening and was on the high seas before the news of his split with First National began to spread. If Kennedy had hoped that Balaban and Skouras would cave in, he was wrong. As far as they were concerned, when Joe left their meeting, he had left First National. Nothing had appeared to be amiss so the industry was shocked when the announcement was made the following Monday: due to "differences over policy" the relationship between Kennedy and First National had been "ended by mutual consent."

Scrambling for a rationale, some faulted Kennedy's demand for complete authority that "made the company appear as if it had reached that state where artificial respiration was necessary." Clearly there had been a few reservations during the board meeting itself—why the title "special advisor" instead of president or chairman? And he was on the board of every other company he ran—why was he not elected to a seat this time?

Yet another story put the blame on Kennedy's libido, having him dining with a beautiful woman while the board meeting was going on and telling her he was about to become "the new ruler of one of the largest motion picture companies, having wrested control from a dumb and ignorant Jew." But the woman in question turned out to be Rossheim's mistress and when she repeated the tale to the company president, Kennedy was out.

It's a great yarn, but the reality was much more mundane. Kennedy had moved too fast too quickly. Had he started to believe his own press clippings praising his brilliance to the point he considered himself invincible? Or had he simply run head-first into two men willing to stand up to him? The combination of forces resulted in the first chinks in the armor of the industry's "white knight" after two and half years of soaring influence and effusive promotion.

Through cables from the ship, Kennedy dismissed the debacle as a minor annoyance and referred reporters to First National for any further comment. He was "the big topic of conversation" but the trades didn't know what to make of it and *Motion Picture News* didn't even try to explain it. Instead they concluded, "In this business of surprises . . . you never can tell what'll happen next. That's what makes it so interesting."

Rose, John Murdock and his wife, as well as Murdock's longtime friend and colleague, Pat Casey, were all on board. Kennedy was more than ready to relax so he could not have been pleased to see that among his fellow passengers was Fred Thomson's wife, Frances Marion. Since completing his final Paramount film, *Kit Carson,* two months before, Fred had sat at home, swimming with his young sons and spending hours in his lab developing camera lenses or in the garage building new boat engines.

The press kept reporting that Fred would have "no trouble" finding another company to work with because they knew nothing of his personal contract with Kennedy. Thomson had spent a lifetime solving problems by tackling them head-on; there was always a logical solution to a mathematical challenge, a stunt to be performed, or a race to be won. While he thrived on those types of victories, this legal morass was beyond his ability to cope with. Fred continued to meet with lawyers in search of a solution, but they could not get around the fact that by signing that contract with Joe, he had signed away his right to make films without Kennedy's approval.

With the hope of restoring Fred's love of life, or at least diverting his attention, Frances planned a trip to Europe. She spoke French and Fred, who knew Spanish and Italian, always loved to travel. She arranged for a long vacation when she renewed her MGM contract and then Joe Schenck approached her about stopping in Salzburg; he wanted her opinion on a film Lillian Gish was planning to make with her new mentor, Max Reinhardt. The side trip would pay for the Thomsons' entire vacation and they renewed their passports with anticipation. Then, only days before their planned departure, Fred told Frances he couldn't go after all; his attorneys were hopeful of a breakthrough and he thought he should stay close at hand. Frances didn't share his optimism, but knew there was no budging her stubborn husband. She had committed to the trip, but not wanting to leave Fred for long, she shortened it to a few weeks. For company, she called her friend, the actress Hedda Hopper, to go with her.

Frances and Hedda boarded the *Ile de France,* where they too were surprised to find Joe Kennedy in the crowd of passengers. Steeling herself, Frances approached Joe, but he made it clear he had nothing new to add to his vague assurances that something would work out. Rose, whom Frances had hosted and respected, was even more taciturn. Frances's innate diplomacy made her hold her tongue and while she clung to the hope that Fred really could make something happen from California, she spent most of the voyage in her cabin while Hedda socialized with the other passengers and had them sign a ship's menu to send to her good friend, Louella Parsons, who would go unchallenged for another decade as moviedom's premier columnist.

Kennedy and Murdock had much to discuss as they huddled in their deck chairs and that didn't include the problems of a cowboy star. Glad to be out of range of reporters' questions, they began planning their way out of their current situation. Together, they had Pathé and K-A-O and Kennedy had FBO. He was determined to regroup without First National.

Their sea voyage was almost over by the time the First National board of directors met again on August 22 and announced that everything was running smoothly without Kennedy. They reviewed the appointments and dismissals that had been made over the past two months and affirmed that Al Rockett was "in complete charge of production." For the most part, those who had survived Kennedy's slashings remained and those who had been cut stayed gone. The most immediate result of Kennedy's departure was a dramatic rise in studio morale.

There were reports that First National had been strengthened by Kennedy's "hasty departure" and that the company was once again running efficiently "under the direction of the men who built it up." Then the real digs at Kennedy began with stories that his efficiency system was actually costing money because it now took "twice as long to turn out the required quota of work." Many of those who had been fired were needed after all, but by the time that was realized, "it was impossible to regain their services for less than twice their salaries or to replace them with other people at the original salaries." The implication was that while his "principles of efficiency" might be applicable in other industries, anyone who really understood filmmaking would never have made the mistakes Kennedy had.

While the men at the studio might have thought all was well, the financiers behind the scenes were not as sanguine. They exerted more authority than any single board member and because of the stock pooling that had taken place to fight off Zukor and Fox before Kennedy was brought in, it was Goldman Sachs who held the purse strings at First National. They were also the primary bankers for Rossheim's Stanley Theatres as well as Warner Bros. Within weeks of Kennedy's departure, it was announced that Warners was buying Stanley and, by putting

Aerial view of First National, soon to be Warner Bros., studio

down $2.5 million, they bought enough shares of First National stock to gain control of the studio and their theaters.

And so it was Warner Bros., not Pathé or FBO, who moved onto the First National lot. While there was much talk of maintaining separate identities and for a period of time films were released with each company's name on the screen, it was Warners that eventually prevailed, investing millions in what became a state-of-the-art sound studio. And to this day, it is that same Burbank lot that the camera surveys under the credits of Warner Bros.' films.

## CHAPTER 18

# "Now He's Back and Almost Anything May Happen"

## (SEPTEMBER—OCTOBER 1928)

*K*ennedy's European sojourn wasn't all meetings with Murdock and international distributors. He knew he needed a serious stretch of vacation and be it Palm Beach, Cape Cod, or France, he always found the ocean refueled him. His fortieth birthday was hardly a time of self-reflection, however, as he spent it in the splendor of the Hôtel du Palais in Biarritz where he swam in the Atlantic and entertained visitors, including Gloria's husband, Henri.

As usual, Joe stayed in near-constant touch with the gang, and there were days his cables cost more than his hotel suite. The news grew disquieting, for in addition to the evolving situation at First National, Sarnoff and others were quoted making derogatory remarks about Kennedy, including the charge that his "headcutting tactics" at K-A-O were resulting in a new low in "efficiency and morale." There were reports that Ed Albee was trying to retake K-A-O and that Kennedy was out if he didn't turn things around, even though his role as chairman had been ratified only two months earlier. Joe had planned to stay abroad longer, but while Murdock and Casey remained in Europe, Kennedy returned home to "personally take charge of the Keith matters."

On Friday morning, September 28, *Film Daily* headlined "Kennedy Returns" and the man himself smiled widely as he walked down the gangplank of the *Aquitania* later that day. Once again, he was greeted by reporters, this time wanting his response to rumors of the sale of K-A-O. He was not about to say something specific, but his irritation that anyone would even think of doing anything without him was clear. "The industry is watching with interest," was the best the press could report, adding the caveat, "Now he's back and almost anything may happen."

Outwardly, Joe was as confident as ever, even appearing on Sunday

Kennedy and the Marquis de la Falaise vacationing in France
for Joe's fortieth birthday, September 1928

night as a guest on *Collier's Radio Hour*. Billed as an important leader of
the entertainment industry, he had risen to the role of philosopher and
prognosticator king of the film business, which he now proclaimed to be
in a state of "flux and experimentation." He used the opportunity to
praise his fellow studio chiefs and review film's historic achievements,
and he predicted that "the time will come when television will carry the
best of entertainment into the home." While acknowledging movies had
"crippled legitimate drama and even invaded vaudeville," he defended
the art form as providing the world with "amusement and instruction at
a cost within the reach of everybody." He closed his address with the

claim that "A country finally gets the quality of government it deserves. It receives only the type and grade of entertainment it wants."

To the reporters who gathered at the radio studio, he was still the "mystery man." They wanted a comment on his plans and rumors that Warners, Fox, and RCA had offers on the table for K-A-O, but all they got was a silent smile as Kennedy walked past them.

For almost a decade, he had been forecasting the consolidation of companies for survival and profit. He was right, but with his failure to keep First National, his plans to personally lead the charge had floundered. For once, he wasn't sure what was going to happen and the next morning, the first Monday after his return, he went behind closed doors with Elisha Walker to assess the situation.

Kennedy still controlled FBO and, along with Walker and the other financiers, Pathé and K-A-O. He was chairman of the board and the holder of 37,500 shares of K-A-O with options on another 75,000, so it would be difficult for anyone to take over without Joe's consent. He, along with the members of Walker's holding company, held firm control, but under their purchase agreement of the previous May, they were only obliged to stay together as a bloc for a few more months. They needed to make their move soon and, for Joe especially, the war drums were beating. Currier wanted out of FBO and while Walker was still willing to back Kennedy, he planned to reduce his film-related holdings.

Joe was intensely realistic when it came to recognizing the difference between what he could control and what he could not. He knew he was a builder and a promoter, not a long-term administrator. Over the past few months, profits from sound films had zoomed upward and there was no question that their popularity was here to stay, yet fewer than 5 percent of the country's theaters were wired for sound. The entire process was going to take a lot longer than originally anticipated and much more time, money, and work would be required. Let someone else take the risks and deal with FBO where, in spite of all the public pronouncements, the sound equipment was still not totally functional. Always the pragmatist, he decided it was time to maximize his profits.

"One of the sure ways of making money in pictures," Kennedy quipped, "is to sell at a time when some one wants to buy," and David Sarnoff was ready to do just that. Paramount, MGM, Universal, United Artists, and First National had all signed with Western Electric's Vitaphone and many believed they "had mopped up all the gravy," but Sarnoff was convinced there was plenty of business left on the plate. He believed Vitaphone's sound-on-disk system would soon be obsolete and that he had the superior products for the long run. He had diffused his focus by spending his time trying to put films into schools, churches, and homes as well as theaters, but when First National was taken over by Warner Bros., the linchpin company for Western Electric, he had to move quickly and "without being hampered by individual organizational problems." In other words, without Joe Kennedy.

Sarnoff's immediate concern was the rumor that Warner Bros. was seeking to buy K-A-O. With Warners (and their bankers Goldman Sachs) already controlling their own and now First National's theaters, adding K-A-O would give them an overwhelming advantage. Keith-Albee-Orpheum was the last large, "first class" independent chain in the country and Sarnoff needed those theaters for Photophone. Further complicating the situation, Ed Albee's talk of returning to power increased the possibility of a bidding war.

The leaks started spinning out of control to the point it was reported that the sale of K-A-O to Warners had "progressed to a stage where only the details are to be straightened out." Yet the ace up Sarnoff's sleeve was that he already had a working relationship with Elisha Walker, whose investments in K-A-O were on the line, and Sarnoff brought in Walker's Blair and Company along with Lehman Brothers to finance his moves.

Walker's cooperation was needed for more than K-A-O, since Sarnoff's plan was to buy FBO as well and establish the first studio created to make sound films exclusively. With K-A-O's theaters, FBO's studio and distribution arm, Photophone's sound systems, RCA's radio patents and recording abilities as well as the National Broadcasting Company, it would be the fully integrated company Kennedy had been envisioning for years.

If Joe felt a sense of defeat, he was clear about his decision and his priorities: "I entered the amusement business with the viewpoint of a banker. If, after the organization of a new corporation is running smoothly, I look around and get a good offer for my holdings, I will make a trade." Yet everything wasn't running smoothly and he wasn't getting out entirely. He still had Gloria, the "important" film they were making together, and he still had Pathé. He (along with Walker and Murdock) would keep that company, which was in no position to be sold at the moment anyway. Pathé stock had fluctuated wildly that summer, in part because of the merger rumors. Standing alone, Pathé was judged to be in "a stubborn fight" for survival. The independent *Standard Trade and Securities Service* declared Pathé in "the weakest position" of all the film companies and announced stock "purchases are not advised at this time."

In selling FBO and K-A-O, Kennedy was looking at an opportunity to triple or quadruple his fortune, but in order to maximize his profit, serious negotiations lay ahead. Still, he found himself unable to focus exclusively on them as Gloria Swanson was weighing heavily on his mind.

Preproduction on their Stroheim film had consumed the summer and early fall and the accumulated costs had mounted to almost half a million dollars. It was a staggering amount, and while Kennedy could rightly question Stroheim's "relentless perfectionism," much was also wasted because of Gloria's and Joe's inexperience as producers. At Kennedy's direction, the gang had moved ahead and hired personnel long before they were actually needed. Stroheim's hand-chosen first assistant director as well as his personal publicist and his script girl had all been under contract for five months.

The leading cast members had been collecting pay checks since early August. Walter Byron, an English actor Sam Goldwyn had hired to star opposite Vilma Banky in *The Awakening*, was to play the "wild and roistering" Prince. Seena Owen, a dependable feature actress in her early thirties who had been making films for fifteen years, was waiting to portray the evil Queen Regina, and Tully Marshall rounded out the featured roles as Jan, the "brutal, lustful" villain.

In addition to the salaries, the studio, offices, carpentry, props, and stages all had to be paid for. According to the terms of agreement signed on August 1, Gloria Productions was to pay FBO $5,000 for the use of the studio's equipment, stages, and projection room. Swanson was also to reimburse FBO for utilities and any of the personnel she used. The almost incestuous nature of the arrangement was apparent in the contract signed by Bill LeBaron for FBO and Charlie Sullivan for Gloria Productions. At the moment of signing, both men's salaries were being paid by FBO. Kennedy took from one pocket and filled the other, keeping everything on paper aboveboard.

Over at the United Artists publicity department, concern centered on a title "guaranteed to keep audiences away in droves." Since early summer, the phrase "Gloria Swanson in *The Swamp*" had been headlining ads promoting their upcoming season. All the while, the UA publicists bombarded Gloria with requests that she "secure a more attractive title." However, Stroheim resented anyone attempting to change anything of his and Joe didn't seem worried about it.

For a man who had been renaming films to maximize audience drawing power for years, Joe should have been the first to suggest another title. *The Swamp,* described in Stroheim's earliest drafts as "a waterfront dive" and "an establishment of rather ill repute," was not only an unappealing title, but it put the emphasis on a place, not on the star. If Gloria was consciously aware of that or not, she did agree a change was needed and when Joe came around to the same conclusion, he brought Stroheim with him.

A variety of names were subjected to a thorough legal vetting. *The Scarlet Saint?* No, because that had been "a very poor" First National film a few years before. *The Saint in Scarlet* was available, but it was too similar. There was already a play entitled *The Orchid Lady*, and *The Orchid Woman* was a magazine article that was being made into a film. By process of elimination, they decided on *Queen Kelly.*

Shooting had been scheduled to begin in early September and everything appeared ready—everything that is but Erich von Stroheim. The director argued that if he was to meet the now ten-week shooting schedule he had agreed to, he needed more time to perfect his script. Two and a half months in front of the camera might be more than twice the time taken to make most films, but to Stroheim it was a "quickie." He had spent between twenty-six and one hundred weeks to complete his previous creations. The trades were doubtful that Stroheim could be controlled, with *Variety* asking if "the Gower Street thrift bug will bore into hitherto impenetrable surfaces," none too subtly referring to the director's skull.

A Stroheim film was big news so every nugget of information was monitored and the latest delay was blamed on various uncontrollable forces: installation of sound equipment at the studio, sets that had to be built instead of borrowed, and then there were those hundreds of costumes to create.

Upon Kennedy's return from Europe, Bill LeBaron reported to him that he was going into a "final, all night session" to cut down Stroheim's "finished" script, currently consisting of 735 scenes. LeBaron tried to soothe Joe's ire, telling him he knew "it has been hard for you to understand why so much time has been necessary to get the story straightened out and the script finished," but the bottom line was "the work could not be done any faster by Stroheim, and there was nothing else that could be done until his work was finished."

If there wasn't anything Kennedy could do to get the cameras rolling, he could at least do something about Gloria. There she was on the cover of the September *Photoplay,* staring out at him from every newsstand, yet he hadn't seen her for over two months and it would be at least another month until he was free to return to California. If he didn't speak to her every day on the phone, he cabled her, sometimes in code or by sending every other word in two different telegrams. Their machinations heightened his excitement over their relationship and now, from New York, he told her how much he missed her and urged her to come for a visit.

In Kennedy's absence, Swanson had been entertaining herself. With time on her hands, she even agreed to take part in a stunt, dressing in a frumpy disguise of a blond wig and less than fashionable clothes and then making the rounds of casting offices looking for work as an extra. When she was turned down flat by three different studios, Gloria got a big laugh and young women who were trying to break into the business had their confidence boosted.

Gloria Swanson on the cover of *Photoplay,*
September 1928

Bored with being asked about working with Stroheim when they hadn't even started yet, Gloria declined most requests for public appearances, but she did attend a few parties and her friends Lois Wilson and Virginia Bowker both came for visits. By the end of September, it was clear the director wasn't going to be ready for at least several more weeks, but before she agreed to come to New York, she wanted some money. Her agreement with what she considered her own company was that she was to be paid a total of $50,000 for her appearance in *Queen Kelly,* but she needed cash now for "reasonable expenses and pressing debts." Between Kennedy and the lines of credit he had established, the money was there and the funds were "advanced" against her eventual salary.

Feeling flush, Gloria gave in to Joe's pleadings to put herself and the children on the train. If she thought about it, and she did occasionally, Gloria believed she was being the mother she was supposed to be by bringing the children with her. Miss Simonson, the governess who had been with them since shortly after little Gloria's birth, accompanied them as well, but for eight-year-old Gloria and Brother, now six, spending two weeks in a New York hotel suite was hardly their idea of fun. Yet at home they were sheltered as well, enrolled at the private Curtis School with various tutors and music teachers coming to the house for lessons. They made sporadic appearances at the birthday parties of other stars' children, but Gloria didn't allow them to go to the movies with friends. She considered sending them to a Swiss boarding school, but even when they were with her, she was rarely hindered by motherhood. In New York, that meant being an active participant in the city's social life and going out with Joe almost every night.

Swanson insisted other friends be with them when they made their public appearances, but she claimed that Joe didn't see why a beard was necessary. He had always maintained a separate life away from home and even if that was now in Riverdale, only half an hour away from Manhattan, separate was separate. Part of their continued attraction was their willingness to stand up to the other but when Joe saw how adamant Gloria was, he went along with her mandate. Even if they were in a group, Joe loved walking into a room with her and watching everyone's heads turn in her direction and therefore in his direction as well.

Yet being in New York with Gloria on a nightly basis still wasn't enough; he wanted to show her off to the home crowd as well and announced he had "promised" his family that he would bring her to their house for a visit. While she refused to meet the wife of the man she was sleeping with, she compromised by allowing the children to go to Riverdale. Eddie Moore, who knew Gloria Junior and Brother well from being with them in Beverly Hills, was assigned to drive them to the Kennedy home for the day and they returned to their hotel suite with stories of more children under one roof than they had dreamed possible. To the two lonely and protected siblings, it looked like Nirvana.

Fueled by Gloria's visit, Joe spent most of his October days and nights in Manhattan. While Arthur Poole and other accountants pulled together the numbers, E. B. Derr and Colvin Brown reviewed the multiple agreements that would have to be untwined or altered before any companies changed hands. John Murdock returned from Europe on Friday, October 12, and much of that weekend was spent conferring with Kennedy about the stance they would take come Monday morning and their first official meetings with RCA about selling K-A-O.

RCA was offering $30 a share for K-A-O stock, $9 more than the Kennedy-Walker group had paid in May, but $2 less than its current high on the surge of all the buyout talk. Joe was convinced they could get even more. They had been in and out of meetings with RCA for two full days when he produced a letter from Goldman Sachs, Warner Bros.' bankers, with a direct offer to buy his options on 75,000 shares for $36 a share. Kennedy had already done enough backpedaling in his relationship with Sarnoff and the last thing he wanted to do was complicate things with Walker, yet the Goldman offer, his K-A-O chairmanship, and his stock options combined to give Joe the power to "hold the whip" in the negotiations. When they finally emerged from several days of intense discussions, it was with an offer of $36 a share and an extra $150,000 in Kennedy's pocket for "facilitating" the deal.

Before, during, and after the K-A-O meetings, Kennedy was pulling together everything necessary to sell FBO. As part of the process, he needed to submit the company's balance sheet and he listed its value at a little over $7.2 million, a 600 percent increase in the price he and Currier had paid for it two and a half years before. RCA not only accepted that value, they overpaid, offering almost $7.5 million in a stock swap deal.

FBO's 208,796 shares of stock were owned by a total of twenty-three individuals or companies. Stockholders included RCA with 27,000 shares and Keith Orpheum with 11,715 shares. Many of the men Currier had brought in to help purchase the company in the first place, such as Louis Kirstein, Frederick Prince, and Joseph Powell, still held their stock, with Currier's friends combining to own a little over fifty thousand shares. Another 15,000 shares had been distributed to FBO employees or retainers: E. B. Derr held five thousand, Kennedy's attorney, Benjamin DeWitt (who was on the FBO payroll at $2,000 a month), had two thousand, and Bill LeBaron 1,500. Joe Schnitzer still owned seven thousand shares from when he and Pat Powers had invested in the company in 1923.

With almost 100,000 shares, the largest single owner of FBO stock was the Gower Street Company, otherwise known as Joe Kennedy and Guy Currier. There had been no meetings of the Gower Street board since June, but two meetings were held in October, in addition to the perfunctory annual meeting in Delaware. The board still consisted of only Kennedy, Currier, and Ted Streibert. They met to "sell" themselves 37,500 shares of FBO each at "cost first acquired," presumably the $6 a share established when they created the company. With that, the stock was placed in escrow at the National City Bank to wait for the official issuing of the new company's stock at $36 a share, or $30 of clear profit on each share of FBO.

Finally it was time to go public with the plan and on October 18,

1928, Kennedy released a letter to all FBO stockholders announcing the agreement between RCA and FBO to create "a new company to be known as Radio-Keith-Orpheum Corporation." Shareholders had six weeks to exchange their FBO stock for that of the new company, quickly dubbed "RKO."

The following Monday, Joe's name was on another announcement, this one from K-A-O. Their board had agreed to sell the company to RCA and since the board and executives in the meeting represented 40 percent of the shareholders, only 11 percent more was needed to finalize the arrangement. The remaining shareholders were put on notice they had until November 15 to ensure "the full benefits" of the stock swap. At a value of $36 a share, it was an impressive profit for the Walker group, who had bought at $21 only five months and three days earlier.

After two weeks together in New York, Joe ushered Gloria and her family onto the train and assured her he would join them in California soon. He then spent the last week of October in New York in and out of Pathé meetings and hosting his regional directors at a lunch at the Roosevelt Hotel. To publicly put to rest any remaining rumors of dissatisfaction between him and Sarnoff, Kennedy organized a tour of the RCA studios for the Pathé men where they screened portions of upcoming sound releases.

There was one more piece of official business to be taken care of before going west and for that Kennedy went to Boston to appear with his wife, Cardinal O'Connell, the president of Harvard, and other local luminaries at the opening of the new Keith Memorial Theatre. It had been in the works for three years, but Joe was there to play host and claim credit for the "magnificent theater" with its black and gold carpet, a ceiling painted in gold leaf, and a backstage area complete with gymnasium, nursery, and private rooms and baths. It would be one of the last of the great palaces built with the intention of presenting vaudeville acts along with feature films. For Kennedy, it was another opportunity to be seen by his former hometown crowd and he took center stage, praising Keith and Albee as "one of the finest partnerships in theatrical history."

While Kennedy was providing Keith with a revisionist biography as a "progressive," the trades speculated over Joe's role in the new RKO. At first it had been assumed that the sale meant his "complete withdrawal," but stories to the contrary kept swirling. Kennedy and Sarnoff appeared to be sharing authority when they both signed a statement to all K-A-O employees telling them there should be "no concern about being replaced" and to "pay no attention to any rumors there may be in circulation as to changes contemplated in the Company." Of course, these very words were familiar to employees of Pathé and First National who had received similar missives before Kennedy's "reorganizations," as well as to the K-A-O workforce who had heard the same phrases only months earlier, just before the "Kennedy-Ford machine gun squadron" took aim on that company.

Kennedy positioned himself so whatever happened, it would appear to be his call. While continuing to refuse to be pinned down, he made clear he was making "a tidy sum of money for himself and plenty for those associated" with him. He claimed "when I originally came into this industry, it was supposed to have been for only six months." It had been over two years since then and while he remained "intrigued" by the movies, the only thing he ruled out was that he would retire. For the moment, he was going to California to supervise Swanson's film, continue running Pathé, and, along with Sarnoff, RKO.

# CHAPTER 19

# "The Dollar Sign Implanted in His Heart"

## (OCTOBER–DECEMBER 1928)

*T*his time it was Eddie Moore and Ted O'Leary who accompanied Kennedy to Los Angeles, and once he was home on Rodeo Drive, he faced some serious personnel decisions. Losing First National meant losing slots for his employees and during his three months away, some of the men he had left behind had literally tripped over each other trying to establish their own power bases.

After Joe's abrupt departure, E. B. Derr never returned to the First National lot. Instead, he stayed on in New York, visiting with his wife and daughter for several weeks. In spite of his initial resistance, Derr was spending more and more time in California and soon he was off again, stopping in Chicago where he and Joe Schnitzer spoke to the FBO sales meeting. They announced plans for over fifty films, almost all of which would have "talking sequences." They were as upbeat as possible, but it was increasingly obvious that if any of these rumored mergers went through, there would be major changes at FBO.

Barney Glazer had lasted only a few weeks as First National's "director general for sound" and then returned to Pathé, "pending further instructions from Kennedy." Yet instead of a welcome reception, Glazer found that Paul Bern was adamant he was in charge of all production at the Culver City studio. Bern had failed to live up to Harry Edington's prediction that he was "equal to or better than Thalberg." Aside from his obvious talent and ability, Thalberg was known for keeping his own name off the screen and out of the trades while Bern seemed almost incapable of not promoting himself. As soon as Kennedy's ship had sailed, Bern put out a release announcing he was "in complete charge" at Pathé. Le Baron, Derr, and Sullivan all met with Bern at various times, encouraging him to work collaboratively, but he produced his contract, which indeed stated he was to be in charge of production. The other men thought it was best just to "let things ride" until Joe's return, but they continued to be irked that Bern spent most of his time worrying about "what kind of office he had and how much personal publicity he can get." Now Kennedy was back, and he declared both Bern and Glazer "unit producers"; in spite of the grand plans of only three months ago, this was the new reality.

Joe had been in California for a week when it was clear he was out of the new RKO, whether he wanted to be or not. On November 15, the date established as the deadline to complete the K-A-O–RKO transition, Kennedy received a polite but firm request for his resignation as chairman of the board of K-A-O. The final paragraph assured him that this "does not necessarily mean you are to be replaced," but his resignation was needed in order to "make such changes as they may deem necessary and advisable." Yet the writing was on the wall when Sarnoff took his key personnel along with a few moneymen on a retreat to White Sulphur Springs and Joe was not included.

Kennedy had been pushed, but he had never been one for power sharing and he appeared gracious as he switched gears to play the only role available, that of transition advisor. He lost some men in the process; Bill LeBaron was to be RKO's head of production and Joe Schnitzer was staying in their New York office. Of course neither man had to change addresses, but for Schnitzer, waiting, defering, and keeping his nose to the grindstone had finally paid off as he moved back into the office suite he had lost to Kennedy almost three years before. Privately, Joe praised both men to Sarnoff and then offered to be on call to help if needed.

On a corporate level, the merging of FBO and K-A-O into RKO was a relatively smooth one. General Electric, Westinghouse, and RCA were all represented on the new board of directors as was Lehman Brothers and Blair and Company. Sarnoff's friend Louis Kirstein, the man who had first introduced him to Kennedy, was added and Elisha Walker and Jeremiah Milbank continued to serve.

Sarnoff surprised everyone by anointing Hiram Brown, president of the U.S. Leather Company, as the new president of RKO. Brown was forty-six years old and had started as a teenage office boy before working himself into the executive ranks in a variety of businesses. Sarnoff made the point that RKO was already heavy with men experienced in entertainment and therefore he was looking for "an administrator whose capacity has been so thoroughly proven in other fields."

RKO initially kept FBO and K-A-O as separate secondary divisions. Ed Albee continued in his role as president of K-A-O, hoping in vain that the veil of administrative oblivion was to be lifted. He could not have been encouraged by the fact that Johnnie Ford was staying on as vice president and general manager. Joe Schnitzer was elevated to head of FBO and one of his first announcements was that he was spearheading a "radical reversal in production policy"; under his management "Cheap product is completely out." He proved it by paying Flo Ziegfeld $85,000, more than the average cost for an entire FBO film, for the rights to make a talkie out of his stage hit, *Rio Rita.*

For a man whose company commitments had been reduced by 75 percent over the past three months, Joe Kennedy still had his hands full. He had to breathe life into Pathé and then there was his passion, Gloria Swanson and the long-awaited *Queen Kelly.* Before the cameras started to roll, Stroheim's *The Wedding March* was finally released, almost two years after he had filmed it. He had "cut" it down to six hours and, after Pat Powers sold the film to Paramount, they had taken the first half and reduced it to two hours. Even as Stroheim bemoaned the "butchering," there was no debate regarding "the possessory credit"—there on the screen was the pronouncement "In its entirety an Erich von Stroheim Production."

Kennedy must have been given pause when he watched *The Wedding March,* a cynical, almost contemptuous tale. Stroheim starred as a hedonistic young prince, the only son of spiteful, moneygrubbing royal parents whose hatred of each other is made clear in the opening scene. Fay Wray is the young innocent from the countryside who falls in love with the uniformed prince and believes his promises of love as he literally deflowers her in a rain of apple blossoms. The analogy appears again when, in a brothel, the prince announces that he "craves apple blossoms" as a euphemism for wanting a virgin. He marries the innocent, rich, and deformed ZaSu Pitts, who carries apple blossoms instead of a bouquet. Subtle it was not; twice skeleton hands are seen playing the church organ and crucifixes abound.

According to Fay Wray, over a month had been spent filming the brothel scenes that occupy fifteen minutes on the screen. The cinematographer Hal Mohr confirmed that they "were played with an exactitude that would have caused apoplexy at the Hays office [and] involved prostitutes from Madame Lea Frances's bordello and gallons of bootleg gin." The attention to detail, the ornately decorated uniforms, the crowd scenes, and over thirty different sumptuous sets gave the epic a lush, authentic aura, but *The Wedding March* should have set off warning bells.

Kennedy had to see the similarities between *The Wedding March* and *Queen Kelly* that verged on repetition. Orchids replaced apple blossoms as the recurring floral theme, but both were Cinderella stories with an odious twist. If one heroine was a poor Viennese girl and the other a virgin at a Catholic convent, each met her prince as he paraded on horseback and both were the subjects of lecherous desire.

Right there in *The Wedding March* program was an article by Stroheim's "collaborator" Barney Glazer telling of the director's refusal to take shortcuts and how, during the writing process, "heaps upon heaps of manuscripts accumulated" and "scenes multiplied into thousands." The initial box office was respectable, but *The Wedding March* was pulled from the Rivoli in New York after only two weeks and sent to smaller, less prestigious theaters to be screened as part of a double bill where it might run for a week or less.

Yet with all this information right in front of him, Kennedy was not about to second-guess himself. He continued to assume that the combined creative vitae of Stroheim and Swanson was beyond question, and his rationale for the less than stellar returns for *The Wedding March* was that audiences had more alternatives than ever. It had been a year since the release of *The Jazz Singer* and big-city moviegoers could now choose among several different sound films. In contrast, *The Wedding March,* even with synchronized music, seemed "instantly dated and old fashioned." Joe told Stroheim that "the lousiest sound film will be better than the best silent film" and, as early as the summer of 1928, plans were being made to incorporate sound into *Queen Kelly.* The entire film would be made as a silent, then the last two reels reshot with dialogue and music, perhaps including a song sung by Gloria. Kennedy was given full credit in the trades for this "smart idea" and he had visions of the best of both worlds—a lavish epic redolent of the finest silent films and then a dialogue and musical extravaganza for audiences in the large cities.

While the press made the assumption that someone besides Stroheim would direct the sound portions, Kennedy was careful to include a clause in the director's contract to cover dialogue. To make those twenty minutes of sound happen, four Photophone engineers were assigned to bring an entire baggage car full of the latest equipment from New York to Los Angeles. Duplicate sets were built to be installed in a soundproof stage. A musical director was hired to arrange for a forty-piece orchestra. A new position was created on the production roster whose sole responsibility was to be Gloria's "voice director," and that was separate from her voice coach, signed in New York at $100 a week and on his way to the coast to begin her daily lessons. More sound equipment was ordered and installed in the projection room in Gloria's home. The investment was massive, but it wasn't questioned. Warner Bros. had just reported $3 million in earnings for the last three months, more than they had made in any previous year.

Finally, on Thursday, November 1, after months of postponement, the cameras started churning on *Queen Kelly*'s fabulously elaborate palace set. Joe arrived in Los Angeles a few days later and while he scheduled meetings at Pathé, he happily spent most of his time at FBO where the actors and crew were on the set an average of fourteen hours a day. On the second day of filming they were dismissed at 6:30 in the morning. Stroheim was soon holding up the entire company for hours while he acted out scenes or rehearsed an actor for a close-up. Then he stopped production to demand the smallest change on a backdrop. Kennedy stepped in, declared the schedule "inhumane," and told the director he had to change his ways, but they still were getting along famously.

Kennedy joined Swanson, Stroheim, and one of the cinematographers, Paul Ivano, in the projection room to screen the results of the first week's shooting. Together they watched as the Prince was introduced, returning to the palace in the early morning hours, surrounded by a half dozen half-dressed women of the night. (Once again, Stroheim had turned to Madame Frances's Hollywood brothel to provide him with his hand-picked cast.) Then came Seena Owen as the Queen with "her nakedness covered with nothing but a big pure white Persian cat," most delicately placed. They all agreed the film looked absolutely magnificent and Gloria remembered finding the rushes "breath taking. Every scene was alive with glowing light play and palpable texture."

The only apprehension anyone expressed was over Swanson's first appearance on the screen. A portion of Griffith Park had been turned into a Germanic countryside where the Prince, out riding with his entourage, encounters the young convent girls walking through the fields. His head is turned by sweet, innocent Gloria and, as they are exchanging meaningful glances, her underwear falls to her feet. When the Prince starts to laugh, she throws the panties at him and he waves them under his nose before pushing them into his pocket.

While Gloria would later claim to have been off the set when the Prince's close-up with the underwear was filmed, Paul Ivano remembers watching the rushes with her, Stroheim, and Kennedy. When Ivano volunteered that he didn't know how the scene would get past the censors, he received quick kicks from both Swanson and the director. They were pleased with the results and hoped Joe wouldn't notice, but he had seen it all and just laughed, saying, "Oh I guess we'll get away with it."

For a man who only months before had been fearful that romanticizing Jesse James might run afoul of the morality watchers, Kennedy seems to have been swept away in the unique camaraderie of working alongside the woman he loved. He rarely saw the movies his companies produced and he had certainly spent precious little time on the lot while they were being made and so he found a new excitement in being in on every aspect of the creation. At long last, after a year of talking about it, he and Gloria were embarking on their "important" picture. Yet as much as he was enjoying himself, he had other concerns that demanded his attention.

Gloria's character in *Queen Kelly* meets her Prince for the first time

Except for his regular visits with Gloria, Joe stayed away from social Hollywood and made few public appearances. He had successfully quashed any rumors that he was leaving Pathé and he was now visibly involved in lining up plans for the next season. If he wasn't on the *Queen Kelly* set, he was in meetings, actively participating in day-to-day decision making alongside executives and directors.

After much ballyhoo and full-page ads, Pathé's "Sound News" debuted in late November. Pathé had invented newsreels in 1910 and audiences had come to depend upon them as the only real supplement to newspapers in the years before radio. Pathé needed to add sound to stay competitive, but the production costs doubled. The premiere edition opened with their trademark rooster audibly crowing for the first time followed by a loud blast from a gun and the sound of shattering glass as a bullet headed directly for the camera. Then came the deafening noise of riveting from bridge builders over the Hudson River and the final segment consisted of highlights of the previous eighteen years of Pathé newsreels.

The sound for newsreels had been accomplished with relative ease, but it had taken six months from the time the first equipment had been delivered to Culver City to put it to use at what was dubbed "Sound Unit #1." Pathé's first feature film made exclusively for sound was just going before the cameras, a mystery melodrama titled *The Missing Man,* but in terms of both time and money, Pathé could not afford to make "all dialogue" films from scratch. Technology might have changed, but the goal remained the same: maximize the distribution potential with "bring 'em in" titles at a minimum investment.

Recently completed silent films were screened for spots where sound effects or bits of dialogue could be inserted. *Show Folks, Sal of Singapore, The Shady Lady, Square Shoulders, Noisy Neighbors,* and *Office Scandal* were all run through Sound Unit #1. They had already recorded the sequences for *Gang War,* starring Mary's younger brother, Jack Pickford, and Olive Borden, but sound remained a challenge. The unit secretary reported that "everything is more or less experimental," but LeBaron, in one of his last glass-half-full memos, said he thought the sound work on *Gang War* was "the best I have heard anywhere."

WITH PATHÉ as his lone corporate base, Kennedy felt new pressures from financial circles. When he had taken over the newly recapitalized company eight months earlier, it had been assumed that he was preparing Pathé to be sold or merged into a larger entity and the stock price had risen accordingly. Once Pathé wasn't included in the deal that created RKO, Joe had to scramble to make the company look good standing on its own.

His "economy programs" reached into every area of studio life and no amount was too small to save. Low-level crew members and secretaries who were paid $35 a week had always stayed on the payroll no matter how few films were being made, but now they all were let go and then a few hired back on a week-to-week basis. Even the remnants of Cecil B. De Mille's personal radio station were sold for $100.

Kennedy jumped into expanding Pathé in Europe, assigning Bob Kane the task of laying the groundwork to make sound films there. Foreign markets had been bringing in as much as 40 percent of a film's gross and now that was threatened with the coming of sound. When Lillian Gish called silent films "the international language," she was speaking of the art form of pantomime that transcended words, but it also underscored the fact that to send them around the world, the only change that needed to be made was the language of the title cards. It was all very cost-effective. Dialogue films, however, required "language doubles" or the even more expensive proposition of multiple filmings in multiple languages. And acceptance of American sound films was not even guaranteed in other English-speaking countries: the British threatened to "laugh off the screen" actors speaking "in the nasal twang of the Yankee." The French were even more vociferous, with one Parisian paper warning that "Americans should not imagine that in addition to having to swallow their films, we will have to put up with their language."

European theaters were even slower than their American counterparts to be wired for sound, but Kennedy foresaw that making movies in France and Spain would give them immediate access to native-speaking actors, while tariffs, which took a chunk out of overseas profits, would be muted. England and France had recently tightened their rules concerning how many American films could enter their countries so production abroad would get around that issue and, if money was kept in the country where the films were made, taxes could be saved as well.

Since his Hayden, Stone days, Kennedy realized that the attractiveness of a stock was "a phenomenon often unrelated to the strength of the company itself." Even if Pathé was on shaky ground, its stock continued to rise and while some observers called that "unexplainable," it wasn't unexplainable at all. Letters were sent to current Pathé shareholders and others claiming that the stock was soon to move upward because of "important information" about to be released. Customers were urged to buy immediately to take advantage of the moment. Under the guise of being from a "stock tip firm," these letters were sent from offices in Los Angeles and Chicago, but Boston was the city of origin and from an office on Milk Street at that. The method was shady, but still legal, and there can be little question that Kennedy was the source of the addresses of the Pathé stockholders as well as the content of the letters; running up a stock's price was almost second nature to him.

Instead of investigating the story behind the "mysterious" rise in Pathé's stock price, the trades headlined "Pathé shows a profit under new management" and gave Kennedy the credit for turning the company around. The price of the stock had doubled since he had taken over and it was simply assumed that reflected the strength of the company.

Kennedy knew better. While encouraging others to buy Pathé, he was selling his first installment of 25,000 shares in small batches of one hundred to two hundred shares at a time through his brokers in Boston and New York. Some was sold under Kennedy's name, some went into accounts in the names of Ted O'Leary and Eddie Moore, but the vast majority was listed under Pat Scollard. It was Scollard who handled the paperwork, passed on the stock certificates, and collected and double-checked the account receipts as they came in almost daily.

There were few questions being asked about anything concerning the stock market, in spite of what, in retrospect, was cause for concern. More and more people were buying in and ticker machines were everywhere, in workplaces, ocean liners, and, as Joe had, in private homes. Signs were hung in Hollywood offices warning "Don't talk to your broker on studio time." Over at Warner Bros., employees caught buying or selling during office hours were "shown the gate." Stock market fever was so intense that *Motion Picture News* claimed "the principal cause for production delays, lack of concentration, resulting in poorer pictures, is simply too much stock market gambling within the studio walls."

The underlying assumption was that prices could only continue to climb and therefore everything was salable at a profit on a moment's notice. Stimulating the increase in buying was the propensity to purchase on margin, the practice of putting down only a small portion of the actual price and borrowing the rest from the seemingly endless pool of money flowing into Wall Street. There were precious few voices of caution. The amount of money being loaned for buying on margin had soared from $1 million in the early 1920s to almost $6 million by the time Herbert Hoover celebrated his landslide victory over Al Smith in November of 1928.

The first viable Catholic candidate for president had gone without Kennedy's support and he implied to friends he had voted for the Republican Hoover. Yet while Wall Street was celebrating, Joe knew that Pathé was not alone in having a stock price that wasn't tied to the actual value of the company. To the old bank examiner in him, the massive amount of loans translated into a dangerous rise in speculation driven in large part by a mystique that Kennedy himself had fueled and profited from, but never bought into. Taking advantage of the fever that boosted prices was one thing, holding out for the last dollar was another. Joe began to slowly sell almost all of his holdings.

On November 21, Kennedy signed off on the agreement to exchange his K-A-O stock options for RKO stock. A week later, RKO was up and running on the New York Stock Exchange and on the opening day, he sold three thousand shares in a dozen small increments, netting himself $150,000 in profits. Over the next few weeks and months, using several different brokerage firms and accounts, Kennedy methodically sold off his RKO shares. Paying $21 to exercise his options on the 75,000 former

K-A-O shares he earned from his five months as chairman of that company, he sold them for between $35 and $52 a share. He sold his 37,500 former FBO shares, for which he had paid a maximum of $6 a share, for the same amounts. Then there were the 12,500 shares of K-A-O he had received outright for fronting the purchase of the company, the 25,000 shares he committed to buying, and the four thousand he received from Blair and Company as a participant in their block of stock; those sales brought in another quarter million dollars.

At a time when a brand-new Ford cost $460 and the per capita income for Americans was $681 a year, Kennedy cleared a profit of at least $4,250,000 on the RKO deal alone.

WHILE HIS BROKERS WERE BUSY on Wall Street, Joe was still in California on the first of December 1928. Every FBO film that had been in production when the studio became RKO had been completed and nothing new was scheduled to begin. As a result, *Queen Kelly* was the only movie being shot on the Gower Street lot and, in their isolation, they were running even more behind schedule. Yet there was still an upbeat and positive feeling surrounding the epic and Paul Bern was sent to the United Artists sales convention in Chicago to report in person on *Queen Kelly*'s glorious progress. Derr scurried to prepare a trailer to highlight "important scenes" and Swanson and Stroheim sent off laudatory telegrams, praising each other and the "excellent progress" they were making. Evidently feeling the need to please the boss, Stroheim also spent an extravagant $75 on Christmas flowers for Rose Kennedy.

Henri returned from Europe for the holidays, stopping in New York before moving on to Beverly Hills just as Kennedy was packing up at his house on Rodeo Drive. At a stop in Albuquerque, New Mexico, Joe received a cable informing him of the results of "the new FBO" board meeting, operating under the RKO umbrella. Hiram Brown was chairman and board members included David Sarnoff and Guy Currier. Joe Schnitzer was president and Charlie Sullivan was vice president, with Pat Scollard treasurer and Tom Delehanty secretary. Even if it was likely they would not stay on for long, Scollard told Kennedy that he and Delehanty had been "disappointed" that their resignations were not accepted on the spot.

Kennedy arrived in New York just as the news of his resignation from all his various roles at FBO and K-A-O was appearing in the press. Joe claimed that it was his own choice not to be an active participant in RKO and, once again, instead of questioning why, the press used the

Gloria with her husband, the Marquis de la Falaise, on the set of *Queen Kelly*

opportunity to hail his genius at managing vulnerable companies. They heralded the splendid new offices being prepared for him and his "personal executive staff" at Pathé's New York headquarters. Kennedy took advantage of the attention to release new numbers for Pathé that claimed a net profit of $65,000 for the latest quarter, in contrast to the almost half a million dollars they had lost the quarter before he was in charge. That brought forth even more praise, with *Film Daily* calling his "perseverance, hard work and dogged determination" proof that "the apparently impossible can be overcome."

At the same time, RKO was looking at just what they had purchased in FBO and K-A-O and they were not pleased. They ordered a new audit and, after paying K-A-O dividends and putting the costs of the transition in the mix, they found that the two companies combined to lose over a million dollars for the first half of the year. It was a far cry from the balance sheets Kennedy had presented, but the public release of the numbers did little to tarnish his still glowing reputation.

Still, he wasn't the major mogul he had been only months before. When fifty-four "important executives" of the film industry were polled for their opinions on the upcoming year, there was room for David Sarnoff, but not for Joseph P. Kennedy. Yet he was lauded in *Variety* as a "money maker for himself and others" and the proof was in the fact he was one of the only twenty thousand millionaires in America. While there were rumors that he was on "the fence for the future," it was assumed he would stay with Pathé and perhaps be elected president of the company. Undoubtedly, more success lay ahead because he was unique in having a "duplex mind that runs equally smart in the show business as it does to banking."

That "duplex mind" had indeed served to quadruple his personal bank account, but the ripple effect of his actions was now taking its toll on others. Frances Marion had returned home from her shortened trip to Europe in the early fall of 1928 to find her husband still in limbo. She brought him an English bulldog to add to their already large menagerie, but nothing seemed to energize Fred. If their hopes were raised by the creation of RKO, there were no cowboys on their roster and K-A-O had already announced that because of low box office receipts, they "were off westerns." Thomson, however, continued to believe in the genre so deeply he took to writing syndicated newspaper articles on their power to teach clean living and he reached out to Gene Tunney about the possibility of him becoming his producer. There were even some conversations with MGM; if there was one man in Hollywood willing to take on Kennedy it was Louis B. Mayer. Still, it would mean legal wrangling and publicly airing their differences, so Thomson remained in a twilight zone of inactivity, vacillating between grandiose plans and despair, sitting at home, "looking very depressed, holding his head in his hands," Fred's nephew Carson remembers. "This was a Fred none of us had ever seen before."

Fred Thomson died on Christmas Day 1928 at the age of thirty-eight. The death certificate listed the cause of death as tetanus, but his wife would tell family members that she was convinced Fred had lost his will to live. Headlines throughout the country expressed the shock over his unexpected death and accolades and condolences poured in. "Fred Thomson was the finest influence who has ever touched the industry of motion pictures," wrote Harry Carr in the *Los Angeles Times. Photoplay* devoted an editorial to "the idol of millions," claiming that "none of the heroic figures he portrayed on the screen were ever cleaner or finer or more courageous than Fred Thomson in his own life and work." Nowhere in all the coverage was a mention of his association with Kennedy or the fact that he hadn't made a film in more than six months.

The tumult around Thomson's funeral was compared to Valentino's. Thousands of fans converged outside the Beverly Hills Community Pres-

Fred Thomson and his sons, Richard and Fred Junior

byterian Church where Harold Lloyd, Cecil B. De Mille, Sam Goldwyn, and Louis B. Mayer were among the mourners. Doug Fairbanks, Tom Mix, and Buster Keaton all sobbed openly. Even William Randolph Hearst, who detested funerals, came to show his respect, yet Joe Kennedy was not in attendance.

To Kennedy, this was no time for sentiment. Fred's death meant a new source of income: life insurance. The corporation had taken out a $150,000 policy on their star and within days of Fred's funeral, Charlie Sullivan and Pat Scollard, the on-paper president of Fred Thomson Productions, set about collecting it. Always on top of the calendar, they wanted to move quickly before another premium was due. Then Fred's childhood friend, David Faries, a lawyer who had been named executor in Thomson's deathbed will, wrote to Kennedy seeking information about the insurance and the money he assumed the family had coming to them. Scollard asked the Los Angeles–based Sullivan to inform Faries that the corporation was the beneficiary, Thomson had no stake in that corporation, and that the only way he was to see a dime over his salary was if and when a film cleared over $100,000 in net profits. With Kennedy's approval, Sullivan gave Fred's attorney copies of financial statements showing that, with the exception of *Jesse James,* Thomson's Paramount westerns were "hopelessly in the red." Scollard and Sullivan decided in advance that if pushed, they would contend that the

$150,000 in insurance would "just about cover the anticipated loss" on Fred's films. They also agreed to omit the insurance money from the corporation's financial statements because if the estate asked for an audit, they concluded in an understatement, "it might give rise to controversy."

Without the rights to his films or the corporation bearing his name, Thomson left an estate valued at $25,000. Yet even when Fred's "estate" was sued by Jesse James's granddaughter for breach of contract because she thought she had money coming from that film, Frances never asked for an audit. Fred had signed the incredibly one-sided contract and even if there had been grounds to fight it, she was still too deep in mourning and too private a person to publicly air her grievances. Besides, Kennedy's name in Hollywood was still golden; it would be years before it was acknowledged, as Jesse Lasky's daughter Betty put it, that Joe "always wore a wide grin on his face to camouflage the dollar sign implanted in his heart."

Frances took several months off from MGM and spent her days inside the walls of her hilltop home with her children. It was not until the spring of 1929 that she made the decision to sell Enchanted Hill, move into Hollywood, and get on with her life and work. The forty-year-old Frances was left to raise their one- and two-year-old sons alone and go on to win two Oscars for writing *The Big House* and *The Champ*. She lived another forty-five years. "Frances was so generous," recalled her daughter-in-law Joan Thomson. "She rarely said anything negative about anyone, but she hated Joe Kennedy with a passion." Frances's son Richard confirmed, "If there was someone she didn't like, she said nothing at all. Except for Joe Kennedy."

Charlie Sullivan was still at his Gower Street office, but now on the RKO payroll and Pat Scollard was at Pathé in New York. Whatever their titles or, for that matter, whoever was paying their salaries, their first and foremost loyalty was to Kennedy. For months following Fred Thomson's death, both men made time to collect Thomson's insurance as well as press Paramount for a full accounting of the films still in distribution.

Scollard and Sullivan exchanged dozens of letters and, as necessary, sent updates to Kennedy. In the process, Sullivan discovered over one hundred cans of Thomson's FBO movies in what were now the RKO vaults. "We are shortly going to need all of our vault space," so he asked Scollard what Kennedy wanted done with the films. Trained over the years to look at the next quarter's balance sheet, Scollard instructed Sullivan that "unless there are some shots there that you could sell and get some money for, I think it would be the best plan to junk it all and send me a check for the scrap film." After all, that could bring as much as a penny per foot. In doing so, they destroyed 2,200 pounds of "scrap film" or, in other words, Fred Thomson's life work.

# CHAPTER 20

# "Gilding the Manure Pile"

## (SPRING–SUMMER 1929)

While the gang stayed busy on his behalf, Kennedy headed for Palm Beach and by the end of the first week in January of 1929, he was back at the Oasis Club. Eddie Moore and Ted O'Leary had accompanied him, but soon Joe was enjoying the company of other old friends as well, playing basketball with Herbert Bayard Swope, poker with New York columnist Heywood Broun, and golf on an almost daily basis. He swam in the ocean at the Breakers' Beach where he was tossed by such a strong wave he was afraid his nose was broken, but the next day he was back on the links without any bandages. He was feeling better than he had in months.

By the middle of January, J. John Murdock and Pat Casey joined the group and the third week brought the arrival of Rose as well as Gloria's husband, Henri. He had left Beverly Hills after a brief visit claiming Paris "business affairs demanded his attention," but he took the long way back and spent several weeks in Palm Beach. Yet just as the full roster of guests had unpacked, others began to leave. Ted O'Leary, along with Pathé cohorts Ambrose Dowling and Tom Gorman, cut their vacation short to arrange for the New York premiere of Pathé's new "sound added" *Godless Girl.*

It had been only a year since Murdock was chasing Kennedy by phone to persuade him to join Pathé and now they were confidants who had been through the wars together. They had emerged from the RKO negotiations a bit scathed, but much, much richer. Pathé was operating in the black, but without K-A-O, they had lost their instant access to theaters. RKO was looking to expand their theater holdings and William Fox was on a spending spree, "rapidly accumulating the largest theater chain in the world." If Murdock and Kennedy wanted Pathé to be a serious player, they needed theaters of their own.

Murdock still held an interest in a few theaters, and with those as a base, he and Kennedy decided to investigate putting together their own circuit. There were pockets of smaller chains unaffiliated with K-A-O, First National, or the major studios and they were undergoing their own crisis. Audiences were demanding sound films and that required an outlay of money many smaller owners simply didn't have. Even when they were able to invest, their order went on a six-month waiting list. All these factors combined to put the pressure on them to sell so when the rumor went out that Kennedy and Murdock were ready to buy, they didn't have to go looking. Theater owners in Texas, the Midwest, Michigan, and Illinois all came to them. Then there were the large theater palaces owned by Alexander Pantages that were reportedly on the block.

With Elisha Walker's money, Kennedy planned to purchase one hundred to two hundred theaters throughout the country, up to $60 million worth of real estate. Pat Casey was to run the circuit. Murdock, Casey, and Kennedy were deep into their discussions, but Joe kept being pulled away to take calls from Gloria Swanson in California and the tone of her daily reports was taking a turn for the worse.

Problems with *Queen Kelly* had been escalating since Joe had departed Los Angeles in early December. His protests against "inhumane" hours were quickly forgotten and the daily schedules habitually ignored. Six workdays a week was the norm for studios, yet on *Queen Kelly,* the cast and crew were routinely still on the set after midnight. Stroheim "began keeping the company until 2:00, 3:00, and even 6:00" in the morning and then starting again only a few hours later. It didn't take long for exhaustion to plague the entire company and several of the crew fell sick. "Everyone was tired," Paul Ivano remembered, "awful tired. Everyone, that is, but Erich von Stroheim. He alone seemed to be enjoying it."

Stroheim's "Teutonic tendencies" frequently emerged; the cast was summoned to the set with a bugle call, and the crew informed the director all was ready by telling him the "Officer's attention" was needed. He belittled almost anyone who questioned him and yet considered himself the one who was put upon. He was appalled when he first saw the soldiers' helmets, screaming, "I ask for silver gilt and you give me gold. Must I be a painter, too?" His confidence was such that with a straight face he said, "I am the best director in the business," and while executives such as Thalberg and Powers had come to the conclusion that "vanity had sealed his fate," Gloria still trusted him. Slowly, however, doubt seeped in as she watched him "photograph a tea cup this way, then that way, with a spoon and without a spoon, with lipstick, without lipstick." While she preferred to concentrate on "being the star," she could step in when she needed to. She was more than his leading lady, she was also his producer and it fell to her to keep the peace as he repeatedly, sometimes several times a day, sacked one of his cameramen and Swanson rehired him. "Peace" was hardly the word for it when the epithets flew, but then, an hour later, a rapprochement would be reached and filming resumed, at least for a scene or two.

Swanson continued to keep Kennedy informed, but he found it difficult to believe things were as problematic as she painted them. He had left the studio confident in LeBaron's and Glazer's ability to monitor Stroheim "with an eagle eye" and "hold him down." Yet LeBaron's attention quickly turned to his transition to RKO. He left for New York and appointed his assistant, Louis Sarecky, to "supervise" *Queen Kelly* in his stead, which in reality meant that Glazer was left alone to watch the director "every minute." Glazer might have been a very competent writer, but he had worked with Stroheim before in a subservient position and he found it difficult if not impossible to stand up to him. To make matters worse, Gloria disdained weakness in others and she had come to the conclusion she "hated, loathed, and despised" Glazer.

If LeBaron had been unable to rein in the director, his assistant didn't have a prayer and Glazer didn't know which way to turn. By default, it fell to E. B. Derr and Charlie Sullivan to step in, but they quickly found themselves feeling like boys at the dike, blocking one leak only to have three more break forth.

There was no stopping the hemorrhaging of funds. Because of "the huge quantity of statuary" Stroheim demanded, a special plaster plant was built to create columns, cupids, and statues "under the supervision of experts who insisted on faithful copies of original pieces." Not only had tens of thousands of dollars been spent on costumes, but it turned out that duplicates had been made and, in spite of Sullivan's best efforts, Western Costume Company had the order sheets to prove they weren't in the wrong.

Stroheim was adamant that he was not responsible for the spiraling costs and began sending memos to Derr documenting the inadequacies he had to endure. Dozens of people, most of whom he had personally hired, were at his beck and call and yet Stroheim managed to find fault with almost all of them. The slow pace was due to the mistakes of everyone but himself, and he put the blame for the budget overrun on "Swanson's salary and her personal publicity." It was true that there were now over fifty people on the payroll, but many of them were being kept waiting for hours on end. Charlie Sullivan declared that "a magician or a crystal gazer" was needed to foretell what Stroheim would complain about next and placed the responsibility for the delays on the director's search for absolute perfection that was "beyond any stretch of imagination."

While Sullivan negotiated with vendors over the ever increasing costs, Derr tried to reduce the number of scenes in the script. Filming had been allowed to begin on a script with 502 scenes—two hundred fewer than LeBaron had grappled with in September, but still ludicrously over-length. Derr might not have been an experienced producer, but he was learning and, most importantly, he could do the math: the film had to be kept to ten reels and it was already "a picture and a half."

On the night of December 5, he met Stroheim and proposed various cuts. For instance, the plan to film the African scenes on Catalina Island meant higher and unpredictable expenses and the director agreed to look for ways to shoot those scenes at the studio using a trick water background. Derr then pointed out that the story called for two separate suicide attempts by Gloria's character. The first had her wandering to a turreted bridge and jumping in the river before a policeman came to her rescue and returned her to the convent. It had yet to be shot and required an elaborate set that wasn't to be used again. Couldn't the policeman simply pick her up outside the castle, a change that would save time and money as well as make the later suicide attempt more dramatic? Stroheim said he would think about it, then decided that Kelly's jump from the bridge was "a milestone" that needed to be shot. In exchange, he agreed to abandon his plan to film the Queen lying in state surrounded by hundreds of extras.

These were small victories and they didn't make a dent. While the details of the film's ending were still being "slowly worked out in von's mind," Derr met privately with Glazer in an attempt to present a united front. Glazer was enthusiastic until the director walked in; then he melted in the face of Stroheim's insistence on his "milestone" scenes. Only a grand coronation was a fitting conclusion for his epic. It was a "milestone." The banquet scene was "a milestone." The suicide attempt was "a milestone." There were so many "milestones," Derr couldn't resist concluding, "I wish he had one around his neck." Derr saw the script becoming increasingly convoluted and in his frustration suggested that the only logical conclusion to the film was for Gloria's character to "go into an insane asylum instead of being made Queen."

Believing he had done all he could on the first half of the film, Derr looked ahead to the African portion of the story, desperate to make cuts before the set decorators and the costumers ran up more bills. Glazer was working on a draft dialogue treatment for the sound version of *Queen Kelly* and Derr asked him to simultaneously look for scenes to cut from the silent version. Together they reviewed the section of Stroheim's story where Kelly first arrives in Africa and found eight separate scenes that included "bawdy details of drinking, gambling, dancing and fighting" just between the time Kelly disembarks and when she arrives at the brothel. Glazer pointed out the obvious: "special precaution should be taken here with censorable mixture of whites and blacks. The blonde dancing with the buck nigger is certainly out. The fight between the United States Marine and a colored soldier over a harlot is unnecessary, as is also the homosexual inference of the two German soldiers dancing cheek to cheek." In a burst of logic, Glazer suggested that "Instead of shooting these eight scenes and then throwing away the film, let us cut the scenes out now." Once again, Stroheim would only agree to think about it.

Kennedy was being kept generally apprised and he occasionally jumped in with his own ideas. When he read that the Prince of Wales was traveling to Africa, Joe asked Derr to check out the possibility of getting some shots that could be used in *Queen Kelly.* Derr immediately followed up with Pathé's newsreel division, but the Prince had already departed and no cameramen had accompanied him. How about something of the ship from the coastline? No, there was nothing that would meet their needs. Not willing to give up entirely, Derr asked them to search for any general newsreel footage of Africa. While they were at it, they should also look for file footage of fires, preferably "German fire department film."

Everyone was getting into the act. Paul Bern suggested cuts that echoed Glazers, but he could not resist adding a suggestion to "make the characters more believable." Bern proposed there be a time lapse after Kelly's arrival in Africa and "we find Kelly not the resplendent, gorgeous madame, but that liquor and atmosphere have pulled her down. We must get over here, of course, that she has allowed no man to touch her. . . . I would take it for granted that she has been drinking all along and that when the Prince arrives unexpectedly, he finds her a drunken sot. To me, that has infinitely more pathos. I think it is a mistake for the Prince, who is supposed to have made a great sacrifice to come resplendent with guards and uniform on the warship. I think he should be a very simple, distraught figure in a plain ordinary uniform. Then I will believe that he has made a sacrifice for her."

After six weeks of exhausting filming, Derr was not about to engage in a debate over the characters' motivations. Realizing he was on his own, Derr decided he needed to see *The Merry Widow.* It was the last film of Stroheim's to make a profit and Derr wanted to know the total footage and the exact number of title cards that appeared in each reel, as well as how many long shots, medium shots, and close-ups were used. When he couldn't find a copy of the film in Los Angeles, he wired FBO's New York office to search for a print, have an expert cutter view it, and send him the information he "very urgently" needed. It was a good idea, but after "every effort" was made, they couldn't find a print anywhere.

In between his frustrating conferences with the director, Derr reviewed the contracts and found that it had been so long since Pat Powers had released Stroheim, an extension was needed. He also discovered that everyone's agreements covered sound and dialogue except for Walter Byron's and for that they had to go to Sam Goldwyn, from whom they were borrowing the actor. They might as well ask for an extension at the same time since their current arrangement ran only until the first of the year. Derr was comfortable approaching Goldwyn directly, but he wanted Kennedy to sign off on it. He also warned Joe that if they didn't get Byron's contract straightened out quickly, they would be forced to complete all the Prince's silent scenes out of order and then try to film his speaking parts in a vacuum separate from the other actors.

While he was handling these challenges at the studio, Derr was being questioned by Pat Scollard, who was sitting at his desk in New York trying to make sense of the accounts. Why wasn't the word "FINAL" appearing after any of the expenditures on the budget sheets? And then came pressure from the United Artists sales department. Did they have permission to start selling the film overseas? That was the only way to begin to recoup the money so there was no choice but to give them the go-ahead. So far only seven hundred theaters in the United States had signed contracts to screen *Queen Kelly,* adding up to less than $200,000 in potential income. That left a long way to go to break even.

The situation might have come to a head sooner if filming had continued at FBO, but because of the RKO takeover, production was stopped and everything moved to Pathé. The convent set, the palace's marble floors, and all the accoutrements, from fifty gold crowns to a dozen candelabras, were packed into thousands of crates for the trip from Hollywood to Culver City. The change also meant new contracts with Pathé and this time the cost jumped from the $5,000 Gloria Productions was paying FBO to $10,000. (Kennedy might be in charge of both companies, but business was business.) Then there was the expense of reconstructing the sets for which Gloria Productions reimbursed the Pathé crew's salary plus 10 percent. Meanwhile, new sets continued to be built. The move did not provide much of a breather; retakes were filmed on Christmas Eve, and on December 26 yet another conference was held from eight at night until 2:30 in the morning.

Initially, Gloria couldn't have been more pleased with the move to Pathé, in large part because Joe had surprised her with "the most elaborate bungalow in Hollywood." It was even more luxurious than Marion Davies's stand-alone abode at MGM, which was nicknamed "the Trianon." Gloria's featured a private entrance and garage, as well as a living room large enough for a grand piano. The full kitchen and bedroom ensured her solace twenty-four hours a day. (There is no indication that she was aware of the bugging system Betty Lasky says was discovered in the dressing room several years later, presumably installed during the construction.)

At the moment, solace was what Swanson needed as she watched the move from FBO put *Queen Kelly* even more behind schedule. The original agreed-upon ten weeks was almost over and they had yet to tackle a single scene from the second half of the story. Finally, on January 2, 1929, at nine in the morning, the cast and crew gathered at Pathé to begin filming the African sequences on a huge, two-story set with a bar downstairs and a long hallway and bedrooms upstairs. Ten hours later, they had filmed one scene in the upstairs hallway.

After four more full days of shooting, averaging eleven hours each, they had moved only from the upstairs hallway of the "notorious resort" into the aunt's bedroom. If this pace continued, they had four more months of filming in front of them. Decisions had to be made. On the first Sunday after they moved to Pathé, Derr called a meeting with Swanson and Stroheim to announce there was no more time "to think about it."

It was a clear case of conflicting goals—the director wanted a great, lush, extravagantly detailed epic, Gloria wanted a triumphant starring vehicle, and Derr, on Kennedy's behalf, wanted both, but with a tighter story on a reduced budget. According to the original storyline, they still had Kelly becoming "Queen" of the bordello, her forced marriage to Jan and their trip through the jungle, the Prince's arrival in Africa, his attempted rescue of Kelly, the two of them being tied together on an orchid-laden tree over a swamp filled with crocodiles, Jan's plunging to his death in the same swamp, the Queen's death that elevates the Prince to King, and of course the "milestone" coronation of "His Majesty" and "Queen Kelly." Well, all that had changed. Derr told the director the boss had ordered him to cut the coronation and all the other "excessive sequences to get it down to ten reels."

Stroheim refused. After all, his entire outline had been accepted and approved months before. He was passionate that his characters' motivations be realistic and he needed time on the screen to play them out or their actions would be reduced to pure melodrama. Stroheim's agony was real and it must have been intensified by the awareness that he was personally pulling off a virtuoso acting job in his own daily life: twenty-four hours a day he was a Jew pretending to be Catholic, a humble private pretending to be an aristocratic officer, torn between despising that class and yearning to be a part of it. The complexity and duplicity inherent in each of his waking hours is almost impossible to comprehend; he was also a brilliant artist unable to fathom why others failed to appreciate his compulsion for perfection.

To escape the pressure of the studio, Stroheim went to Glazer's house to work. Even Glazer was adamant that the script was "much over length" and should be cut to "the barest essentials." Finally Stroheim agreed, but only if the rights to everything they took out from the story reverted back to him because "someday, this will make a great picture." Glazer knew enough to jump at the chance and went to the telephone to place a call to Kennedy. Joe was at the dinner table, surrounded by guests including a Catholic priest, but he had the phone brought to him and he listened to Stroheim's proposition. By this point, Joe didn't care what it took; he just wanted the film wrapped as quickly as possible. He told the director he could have his swamp and his crocodiles and his coronations back as long as he "satisfactorily completed" the current film. Just finish the damn movie.

Feeling confident he could have his own "great picture" as his next project, Stroheim promised to rewrite the end and prepare a rough cut of what had been filmed so far. Derr turned his attention to the dialogue portions that Glazer had written, but now Swanson didn't like his script any more than she liked Glazer. In search of a second opinion, she reached out to Edmund Goulding, a multitalented bon vivant, and asked him to write his own version or at least a new ending.

The English-born Goulding had been in and out of America for the past decade, making a living as a singer, film editor, playwright, novelist, screenwriter, and director. Mentored by the likes of Frances Marion and the vaudeville star Elsie Janis, who were enthralled by Eddie's humor, attitude, and genuine talent, he had risen to direct Greta Garbo and Joan Crawford by the time he met with Swanson. Goulding lore includes tales of his brilliantly telling a story off the top of his head, being paid for it, going out to celebrate his good fortune, and awaking the next day not remembering a word. Budd Schulberg remembers him with a smile of admiration: "In a land of magical bullshitters, he was the best." Eddie thrived on not being tied down and danced between Select, Famous Players-Lasky, Fox, Warner Bros., and MGM, where he had most recently written the script for their first all talking and singing smash, *The Broadway Melody.* If he was known to be mercurial and someone who played as hard as he worked, he was also earning a reputation for bringing films in on time and under budget.

Kennedy had put Goulding on Pathé's payroll back in December to write an original story for Gloria, presumably to put some pressure on Stroheim, but Goulding had turned out a treatment within a week so he began directing screen and voice tests. He was so fast and so confident he was completing an average of twenty-five tests a week and soon was consulting with Derr and Bill Sistrom on the next year's production schedule. Sistrom found Goulding's input so valuable he credited him with helping to mold over half the films on the schedule.

When Derr received Goulding's dialogue script he did not want to be the one to choose between it and Glazer's version. To remove himself from the role of arbitrator, Derr brought in Eugene Walter, a prolific Broadway playwright who had caught the early talkie wave from New York to Hollywood where several of his plays had been turned into movies. Gloria found Walter to be a "very blasphemous character," but she agreed his help was needed. His assignment was to screen the rough cut, review both scripts, and then assess, "without prejudice," where dialogue should be inserted.

Two weeks after the Swanson, Derr, Stroheim showdown over the script, they gathered again on Sunday, January 20, to screen the assembled film. As they watched it unfold, it became obvious that while the title was *Queen Kelly,* Gloria's character was far from being the focus. In the midst of the scene-chewing histrionics of the Queen and the Prince, Kelly paled in comparison and Gloria saw the picture slipping away from her. She had risen to fame as a glamorous clothes horse, draped in jewels, furs, and designer gowns and now she found herself in a wardrobe that consisted of "a novice's habit and a nightie."

Sitting in the dark, Gloria sank into depression, realizing that the work of the past few weeks was "utterly unrelated to the European

Tully Marshall dressed as
*Queen Kelly*'s "brutal,
lustful" Jan

scenes. They were rank, sordid and ugly. Mr. von Stroheim's apocalyptic vision of hell on earth [was] full of material that would never pass the censors." She was worried for her image as well as her financial commitment as a producer. "Something was terribly, terribly wrong." LeBaron was gone, Glazer was useless, and the only one around at the moment she still had any respect for was E. B. Derr. And she was growing ever more resentful of the fact Joe wasn't there with her.

The next morning, Monday, January 21, Gloria was filled with trepidation for the entire film as shooting began on her character's wedding scene. Surrounded by men and women of various colors in various stages of undress, Tully Marshall took Swanson's hand to begin the ceremony and tobacco juice drooled from his mouth and onto her fingers. That did it. Gloria, "nauseated and furious at the same time," screamed at Marshall, demanding to know how he dare do such a thing. When he calmly explained he was only doing what Stroheim had told him to do, Gloria pulled herself up to her full five feet, turned, and walked off the set. She went straight to the telephone and found Joe still basking in the Palm Beach sun.

"Joseph, you'd better get out here fast," she furiously informed him. "Our director is a madman."

Kennedy had cajoled Swanson before, but this time she was unappeasable. She detailed the most recent traumas and reminded him that he had tried to stop her from making *Sadie Thompson,* but that film "was *Rebecca of Sunnybrook Farm* compared with what *Queen Kelly* was turning into." She concluded with a question that was also an ultimatum: "Are you coming out here and starting to make decisions or aren't you?"

He promised to come as soon as possible, but Gloria demanded immediate action and she got it. Only twenty minutes after she had left the set, Stroheim was called to the phone: it was Kennedy informing him he was off the picture.

Joe put out a brief statement that Stroheim had been removed because of "a controversy over production costs," but he remained in Palm Beach, hoping against hope that Gloria was wrong. He checked in with Derr, who concurred that it had reached the point where Kennedy alone could decide what to do next. To help formulate their course of action, Derr asked Eugene Walter to shift from reviewing the dialogue scripts and write an "objective opinion" of the current film instead. Swanson peeked into the screening room and saw Walter "walking among the seats, pacing up and down and saying, 'Jesus Christ! Son of a bitch! He's a paranoid.' " Two days later, Kennedy received a cable summarizing Walter's response to those first thirty reels. It was devastating.

"The director has been vulgar, gross and fantastically impossible in the conception and execution of situations, character, incidents of narrative and their relationships," Walter wrote, "and more than that, he has utterly lost every element of human, natural characterizations." When it came to the African scenes, "here language fails me . . . I have never been so shocked and revolted." He pronounced the film lacking in the "fundamental rudiments of story construction" and "not coherent, believable, in good taste, human or acceptable from any possible angle. The production is magnificent and the composition may be noteworthy and commanding, but in my humble opinion it is mostly gilding the manure pile."

Walter's memo detailing the fiasco was six pages long, but what had to be the most distressing in terms of salvaging the film was his observation that during the entire thirty reels, Gloria "never is given one situation for herself . . . she is either the most exasperating sap or a potential prostitute. . . . Any third class leading woman could play the part."

Derr tried to soften the blow by telling Kennedy they were working on rewrites that might be ready to go before the camera as early as the next week. He also assured him it was the right decision to release Stroheim; if they had continued they would have been "criminally negligent" in killing off Gloria as a star. Derr also warned Joe to be careful not to say anything publicly about problems with the film itself because their only legal grounds for termination were the budget and the schedule they had agreed upon. It was his strong suggestion that Kennedy not pay the remaining $20,000 that Stroheim would be demanding. After all, he had already received $15,000 on signing his contract, $10,000 for the story, and over $40,000 for directing.

Harry Edington, still Stroheim's manager, cabled Kennedy directly to try to collect more money. Edington was "quite belligerent" over the fact that Derr had not personally informed him of Stroheim's firing. Joe sent him back to Derr, who was shocked by how petty Edington was being, but that was nothing compared to his reaction when the two men conferred in person to finalize the director's departure. Derr offered Edington the choice of saying that the decision was "mutual" or he could receive "a legal notice of termination due to violation of contract."

Edington answered by asking a question: "Which way do I get the most money?"

Kennedy knew he had to get to Culver City as soon as possible. Publicly, it was announced *Queen Kelly* was "finishing," but questions remained. How much had been completed? Who would take over? How much had it cost so far? Speculation ran rampant and articles appeared claiming that Stroheim had walked off the set after a "quite heated" argument with Derr, leaving the crew and dozens of actors in the lurch.

To draw attention away from *Queen Kelly* and onto his other various activities, Kennedy helped fan some rumors, both new and old. Was he coming to Los Angeles to meet with Alexander Pantages about purchasing his theaters? Was he buying a large interest in Universal? Was he investing in his own sound production company? Was Pathé merging with RKO after all? Denials from the other parties eventually appeared, but it was more than enough to keep everyone guessing. Kennedy added intrigue by refusing to talk to the press on the record for the moment, but promised them "front page stuff" in the near future.

As soon as Joe and Eddie Moore arrived at the studio, they went straight to the projection room where, sitting alongside Derr, they watched the film Stroheim had "edited." Joe's worst fears were confirmed. He had been so enthusiastic about the rushes he had seen two months before, but the results on the screen in front of him forced him to confront a new reality. What had appeared as brilliant in snippets was now a perverse fairy tale, complete with the Wicked Queen, a handsome Prince, and Tully Marshall's Ogre. The real "star" of the film was the sets and the costumes.

There was Seena Owen as the Queen, awakening to guzzle champagne in a huge round bed encircled on the base and on the canopy above with dozens of sculptured cherubs. (In spite of Prohibition, Stroheim had insisted on real champagne on this and every scene where it was poured to ensure "the proper spirit.") When Owen wasn't walking around naked with the precariously placed white cat, she was in fabulous furs. Catching the Prince and Kelly together, the Queen grabs one of the half dozen whips that just happen to be hanging near the door, orders the Prince arrested, and lashes out at Kelly, chasing her down the ornate staircase and out the marble foyer, yelling (via title cards) "He's mine, mine, mine." As Walter concluded, the Queen, "with soap bubbles at her mouth indicating rage, can do nothing more than cause gales of laughter

Seena Owen as the wicked Queen in *Queen Kelly*

from any normal audience providing the censors didn't remove her from the picture first."

Stroheim had built up the characters of the Queen and the Prince to the point that Swanson was in fewer than half the scenes. The twenty-nine-year-old Gloria was supposed to be a radiant teenage virgin, yet her penciled eyebrows and false eyelashes belied that and she looked down-right dowdy in her nightgown under a bulky overcoat. This was the film that Stroheim had claimed would give Gloria "a range of characterizations unprecedented in her screen careers"?

Swanson was in her bungalow when Kennedy rushed in, "cursing Stroheim and LeBaron and Glazer. Stopping abruptly, he slumped into a deep chair. He turned away from me, struggling to control himself. He held his head in his hands and little, high pitched sounds escaped from his rigid body, like those of a wounded animal whimpering in a trap." Finally, Joe composed himself to the point he could talk, but all he said was, "I've never had a failure in my life." When he stood up again, "he was ashen and went into another searing rage at the people who had let this happen." Then he "yanked me into his arms and soon my face was wet with his tears."

Kennedy had experienced failures, but nothing this public or personal. He had been able to veil his loss of First National as a point of principle over his control, but what was he to do with this fiasco that the press had been following unabated for a year?

According to Joe, it was Gloria who was prostrate in anger and anxiety. He wrote Henri that when he arrived in Los Angeles, he "found Gloria in very bad shape in the hospital as the result of practically a nervous collapse. She was down to 108 in weight and her attitude towards the picture, and everybody connected with it, was quite hostile."

While Kennedy's report was from that moment and Gloria's was in retrospect, they both had other agendas when they wrote their accounts and there is little doubt each exaggerated the situation. Yet in neither version is there even a hint of self-reflection. Joe only questioned the people he had trusted to execute his orders, was furious at LeBaron and Glazer for deceiving him, and "didn't want to see any of them again." The thought that any of this was his own fault doesn't seem to have occurred to him. He had simply been betrayed.

Both Gloria and Joe were also partially right as well. Individually, they were frustrated, furious, and, of course, scared. Then, to add insult to Kennedy's injury, Swanson received a letter from the Academy of Motion Picture Arts and Sciences informing her that *Sadie Thompson* had earned her a nomination as "Best Actress" under their new awards program. Two weeks later, *Film Daily* named *Sadie Thompson* one of the ten best films of the year. The movie to which Kennedy had sold the rights, based on his unquestionable assumption that he and Gloria would create something much greater and more "important," was now being hailed all over again.

Any mutual support gave way to bitter accusations. Joe reminded

Gloria how much money had been spent, who had loaned most of that money, and who owed it to him one way or another. In a fury, she looked around for someone else to turn to and, since she couldn't very well run to Joe Schenck, she turned to the producer she had once viewed as evil personified, Jesse Lasky. He wasn't about to cross Kennedy or touch any of Gloria's financial woes; he had been burned once and since she had left him over four years before, she had completed only two films. It is difficult to imagine why Gloria would think Lasky would want to work with her again given their history and when Joe learned of their meeting, he exploded. They had a "drastic showdown," but when the smoke cleared, they were still in it together. They knew that they risked losing not only money, but the prestigious reputations they had both worked so hard to attain. It was in their best interest to put a positive public face on the situation while privately looking for a new solution.

That same winter, Douglas Fairbanks was grappling with a similar situation, having just spent almost a million dollars on the swashbuckling epic *The Iron Mask*. In order to take advantage of both theaters that were wired for sound and those that weren't, Fairbanks recorded a talking prologue to introduce each act, leaving the picture itself essentially a silent film. It was a compromise to say the least, but *The Iron Mask* did manage to bring in $1.5 million at the box office.

Kennedy couldn't decide what to do. As all this drama was being played out behind closed doors, United Artists was in its seventh month of promising that "millions will be charmed" by *Queen Kelly* and urging theater owners to book it immediately. Unaware anything serious was amiss, UA kept asking for more pictures from the set to inspire their publicity department. Kennedy was careful to continue a dialogue with Joe Schenck and even helped him with financial reorganizing at United Artists, but he wasn't about to share his problems with anyone.

When they moved from FBO, expenditures had already exceeded $700,000. Only $50,000 of that had gone to pay Gloria, $15,000 less than had been paid to Stroheim for his story and direction. The sets and costumes alone had cost over a quarter of a million dollars, yet Kennedy had to admit that the money was there on the screen in the gowns, uniforms, and incredibly detailed sets. He had to find a way to save at least part of this film.

With all his experience, Kennedy had never made a film or dealt directly with "talent" before and a multitude of decisions lay ahead. For instance, much care had been given to Stroheim's contract to ensure that bonus payments were made only if he stayed on schedule, but the actors had been signed to "run of filming" contracts and they remained on salary even though they hadn't been working for weeks. After almost six months of being paid for the "services" of Walter Byron, Sam Goldwyn decided he needed the actor back "pronto." There was one small bit of good news. MGM wanted to borrow Tully Marshall and were willing to pay $1,000 a day for three days of work.

Derr, along with Walter and Glazer, had been in intensive script meetings seeking a story with characters who had more than one dimension, in which Gloria was no longer a whimpering sap, and the Prince had motivations "beyond his desire to conquer a virgin." They now proposed that instead of inserting dialogue in the middle of the African sequence, they open the film in Africa, where Kelly's aunt runs a bar with dance girls and gambling "but not prostitutes." Kelly would then be sent to a convent in Germany, which would allow them to lace in the old scenes with the Prince and film new ones to establish their characters and "palliate" her eventual seduction. It was decided that if Jan, the "repulsive cripple on crutches with slimy mouth spitting tobacco juice," survived as a character, Kelly would not marry him. The entire film was to be "rewritten and disinfected."

Before they could move ahead, they had to find a new director. While Kennedy tended to keep everything as private as possible, Swanson was just the opposite. Before she had met Joe and was facing her potentially disastrous financial crisis, she had sought advice indiscriminately and now she repeated that pattern in seeking a solution to *Queen Kelly*. She reached out to half a dozen directors, including her old friends Mickey Neilan, Raoul Walsh, and Allan Dwan, but she hung her highest hopes on Eddie Goulding. She wanted him to pick up where Stroheim had left off, but after Eddie screened the accumulated reels of *Queen Kelly* and read through all the scripts again, he pronounced the film hopeless. His advice was to "shelve it," but whatever they decided, he told them in no uncertain terms that he didn't want anything to do with it.

Unable by nature to kowtow, Goulding didn't even try to say nice things about the movie, but Kennedy and Swanson had no time to be offended because he immediately suggested that he write and direct something totally different for Gloria, a lighthearted talkie that could be finished by the end of the summer. The way Eddie presented it, everyone would win: Gloria would be back on the big screen, United Artists would have a film to distribute, and Kennedy would be given time to decide what to do with *Queen Kelly*.

Desperate for a solution, they agreed that Goulding should get to work on a new script as soon as possible. Eddie envisioned a three-way partnership, but his attorney, Fanny Holtzmann, was in London. No problem, Joe assured him. Eddie would stay on his Pathé contract for now and the rest could be worked out later.

Kennedy went to work putting a wedge between *Queen Kelly* and Stroheim. Joe's heavy hand was apparent in the negative pieces about the director that began appearing in the trades alongside positive mentions of Kennedy's tolerance. One of the more blatant was *Film Weekly*'s summation: "It is so sad about Erich von Stroheim. The kind hearted producers have done everything they could to help him turn over a new leaf. When by all rights, they could have spanked him and sent him home to mother in disgust, they have found it in their hearts, time and again, to forgive." The article doubled the number of reels filmed and gave details that practically repeated the Eugene Walter memo verbatim.

Stroheim had his defenders. The actress Louise Brooks was adamant that Stroheim was "the one pure visual genius of film" and it was "those two vulgarians, Kennedy and Swanson, who really destroyed Erich." The director Clarence Brown thought highly of his talent, but acknowledged Stroheim thought of "every scene as a five reeler."

In the end, Stroheim went quietly, but when he eventually recorded his own defense, he painted himself as the victim and almost as constitutionally incapable of self-reflection as Kennedy or Swanson. The director claimed any stories of friction on the set were "entirely fictitious" and he placed the blame for "invented stories of internal strife" on the "scandalmongers." He said "there was no other reason" for stopping the film than the advent of sound. In his version, he had finished "the first part" when Kennedy and Swanson saw *The Jazz Singer.* On the spot, they decided it "was the death nail for silent films" and therefore "reasoned it was better to stop the film then and there." Stroheim was right when he described the producers as "panic stricken" over sound, but his protestations ring hollow since *The Jazz Singer* opened in October of 1927, over a year before the cameras had started to roll on *Queen Kelly.*

Kennedy faced other pressures besides *Queen Kelly,* the most immediate being personnel issues. He could always find slots for the gang for whom his own interests were their raison d'être: Derr, Scollard, Sullivan, and Moore. Ted O'Leary and Ted Streibert were still in New York covering Kennedy's other bases. Steve Fitzgibbon had been with Kennedy since the earliest days of RCNE and Columbia Advertising, and while he had never made it to the innermost circle, he was on Pathé's payroll as a production manager. Johnnie Ford had continued as general manager of

K-A-O after the RKO purchase, but he left in the spring of 1929. Joe was more than willing to find a place for him at Pathé, but Ford wanted to return home to Boston to run the enlarged Maine New Hampshire Theatre circuit. Ford based himself in the Metropolitan Theatre on Tremont Street; there he was also available to look after Kennedy's other New England interests.

It was time to make decisions about the other executives who had come into his employ such as Colvin Brown, Paul Bern, Harry Edington, Arthur Poole, and Barney Glazer. The LeBaron/Bern/Glazer fight for power had been alleviated somewhat by LeBaron's decision to go with RKO as their head of production. Bern and Glazer continued to butt heads, but after several months of back and forth, Bern resigned, publicly complaining that "he was supposed to be production chief, but several other executives appear to have similar authority."

Barney Glazer was shifted to writing dialogue for sound films and out of Gloria's way. Harry Edington's rising star had crashed with Stroheim's firing. Joe didn't think he was "whole heartedly on our team," so Edington promised to retire as a "business administrator" and devote himself exclusively to Pathé. However, Derr didn't want anything to do with him so Edington decided to take a "long vacation" to think about his future. Arthur Poole, on the other hand, had proved his loyalty and was promoted to the role of Pathé's comptroller. Kennedy sent Colvin Brown to Europe, to assess sound films' progress there and to "corral" Pathé stock that was "in foreign hands."

Other studios were facing other challenges. FBO/RKO was still struggling after over a year of delivering and installing sound equipment. They had loudly proclaimed themselves the first all sound studio, but successfully recording on location remained a challenge. With no westerns on their upcoming schedule, Tom Tyler's horses Flashlight and King, Bob Steele's Black Beauty and Babe, as well as Buzz Barton's Rags were all put up for sale. Any films featuring animals were complicated because trainers could no longer give voice commands so most of the dogs who had been so dependable at the box office were "retired to their kennels"; Flash, Ranger, Strongheart, and others were all off the screen and only Warner Bros.' Rin Tin Tin stayed in front of the camera and the microphone.

There were tribulations of a different sort over at MGM where Irving Thalberg and Louis B. Mayer were shocked to learn that their company was being sold out from under them. Nick Schenck, Joe's brother who had taken over for Marcus Loew when the corporate chief passed away the year before, had gone behind their backs to sell his and the Loew family's shares to William Fox. Thalberg had been appalled by how much time Mayer had been spending away from the studio campaigning for Herbert Hoover for president, yet Mayer was able to raise the specter of monopoly with Hoover's Justice Department and stave off the Fox purchase of MGM.

In comparison, Pathé was looking relatively calm and Kennedy was convinced they had "an excellent program" lined up for the next year. He announced he was proceeding with a dialogue version of *Queen Kelly,* "adapted from Erich von Stroheim's original story" and confirmed that Gloria was not only to talk, but to sing as well. Paul Stein, an Austrian who had written plays with Max Reinhardt and was already under contract at Pathé, was named the new director with the explanation that since he was European, he was uniquely qualified to film a story with a German setting. Camerawork was "scheduled to begin in the immediate future" and the picture was to be in theaters by late summer.

Between his plans for *Queen Kelly* and Goulding working on his story for Gloria, Kennedy finally felt he was on track with a plan of action. He had been in California for five weeks and he had not seen his children for almost three months so when he received word that his seventy-one-year-old father was in the hospital in Boston, Gloria could hardly blame Joe for leaving. She was gaining back some of the weight she had lost during the height of her Stroheim crisis and her normal, more cheerful mood had returned.

By the time Kennedy, along with Eddie Moore and E. B. Derr, boarded the train on March 7, 1929, Joe and Gloria were feeling much better about their relationship—both personally and professionally. Once again, it looked like blue skies ahead.

# CHAPTER 21

# "Give Our Love to Gloria"

## (SUMMER 1929)

*P*athé was suddenly a blaze of activity. The skeleton staff of the previous month was supplemented by dozens of new personnel, busy with preproduction on a variety of films. Contract players who had passed the first round of sound tests were in and out of vocal classes and having Gloria Swanson at the studio added a prestige that had been missing since Cecil B. De Mille's departure.

On the back lot, the *Queen Kelly* convent chapel and dormitory, music room, library, and hallway sets were all being reconstructed. The latest scenario called for merging the most elaborate scenes into a story that took place entirely in the German kingdom. Tully Marshall's tobacco-drooling Jan was eliminated. A choir director from Kelly's convent was the Prince's rival for her affections and a local police commissioner her bête noire. While dialogue was used intermittently, music was to be laced throughout and the film opened with Swanson singing in the convent choir and soloing on "Ave Maria."

Optimism reigned. The new opening wouldn't take more than a week to shoot and the plan was to have both a silent and a sound version ready in six weeks. It would cost another $200,000, but at the moment that seemed reasonable.

Under the direction of Paul Stein, the cameras began to roll on April 1 with Gloria and two dozen young women as the convent choir. Nine days later, however, it was apparent that the new film was too drastically different from the earlier version to merge into anything close to acceptable. To further complicate matters, Gloria had decided she didn't like the new ending. It called for her to fade out with tears in her eyes, pulled between her love for the Prince and her devotion to the convent and its choir director. Between the inadequate sound portion and Gloria's dissatisfaction, it was decided once again to put *Queen Kelly* on hiatus. New writers were assigned and Glazer was given the task of supervising the cutting of sixteen crates of film down to five reels—about an hour-long movie—for Kennedy to view before deciding on the next step: build it up into a full-length silent film, add dialogue, or "scrap the misfit" entirely. From the East Coast, all Joe could do was hope that Glazer had a magic wand and that Goulding was writing one fabulous script.

Once given the go-ahead, Goulding took off as only he could. He was effusive in his excitement over the "new dramatic value" dialogue and sound effects brought to his storytelling and he included Gloria in everything. He said his secret of working with strong actresses was to "make them partners. Consult with them, ask their opinions, learn their tastes and preferences. Lead them . . . but lead them as partners, not dependents." Gloria certainly responded to his style and their relationship became one of those rare collaborations where each person brought something unique and necessary to the table, in this case, literally to Gloria's kitchen table where Eddie, Gloria, and Laura Hope Crews sat pounding out the story. Laura was an actress and an old friend of Goulding's and he claimed there was "no one in the world with a better ear for the spoken word."

Swanson decided that Goulding was akin to Charlie Chaplin in his ability to master any subject or skill in record time. "There was nothing he couldn't do in the creative world, but the problem was to get him to put it on paper. He needed somebody to regulate the flow of his ideas." And that's where Gloria and Laura came in; Swanson was there to mold her character and highlight her own abilities while Crews worked on the segues between Eddie's gems of ideas for individual scenes. A secretary was added to their ménage and within days, Laura moved into one of Gloria's guest rooms for "the duration."

"One minute the three of us praised each other, the next we fought like savages, and the demure stenographer took it all down—script dialogue, gossip, arguments and sandwich orders," was how Swanson summed up their marathon sessions. When she and Laura became too much for Eddie, he would hide himself in the bathroom until Gloria went around through the backyard and knocked on the window to force him to come out. Yet if it was a bit chaotic, they made excellent progress and Gloria was having a wonderful time. She and Goulding shared a dry sense of humor and he managed to dote on her while poking fun at the same time. For her thirtieth birthday, which could have been traumatic to say the least, Eddie regaled her with over a dozen, separately delivered telegrams, some within minutes of each other. "Isn't she popular. What a lot of telegrams," one of them read, and his exuberance blended with adoration was appreciated by Swanson.

Their script was ready within a month and Eddie came up with the title, *The Trespasser.* Gloria was to play a poor, honest secretary to a big Chicago lawyer who is swept off her feet by a rich man's son. Cut to a married and secretly pregnant Gloria singing "I Love You Truly" before walking out when her new husband keels to his father's wishes to have the marriage annulled. She tries to raise the child on her own, and then her old employer steps in to help. When he dies, he leaves her a fortune, fanning the flames of gossip. Tragedy looms at every turn and multiple heartstrings are pulled over a threatened custody battle, but there is the proverbial happy ending. In between, Gloria's character was to sing several songs and leave those dreaded convent clothes behind; in *The Trespasser* she showed off no fewer than ten evening gowns, stunning jewelry, and luxurious furred capes.

In casting the film, they looked at a young actor who had been on the Broadway stage and already been tested at MGM where the casting director said that his large ears reminded him of "a giant sugar bowl." Though Swanson was impressed with Clark Gable, she thought he "looked like a truck driver and spoke like a private eye" and she needed someone "at home in a white tie and tails." Instead, they cast Connecticut-born and -bred Robert Ames, who had already made a talkie and Gable would have to wait a little longer before landing featured roles in *The Secret Six* and *Dance, Fools, Dance* to catch movie audiences' collective eye.

The men of United Artists were not at all pleased with the title, *The Trespasser.* In his first letter of complaint, Al Lichtman called it *The Transgressor* by mistake and when he was corrected, he said he thought they were both equally bad. UA was "unanimous" that it was "not easy to pronounce or easy to remember" and it had nothing to do with the story. Kennedy said he was happy to hear new suggestions, but *The Trespasser* it stayed.

Back in New York, Kennedy read *The Trespasser* script out loud to Ted O'Leary and "we both cried" tears of relief. Joe needed something to feel positive about. His confidence was further boosted when he consolidated his power at Pathé by being elected chairman of the board of directors. His salary of $2,000 a week was to continue and he was given an option on another 100,000 shares at $7.50 a share. Twenty thousand shares were to be bought shortly after signing the agreement, but the remaining eighty thousand could be purchased at any time over the two years. Once

After the plain costumes of *Queen Kelly,* Gloria was back
in satin and lace for *The Trespasser.*

his new Pathé agreement was signed, Joe began chafing to return to California, but his father was still hospitalized with a degenerative liver disease and so Kennedy was in and out of Boston, assuming the end was near.

Another death was looming, one of a friendship. Guy Currier had had it. It had been less than four years since he had agreed to back Kennedy in his pursuit of FBO and as Joe's name appeared with increasing regularity in the trades and in the national press, Currier had remained in the background. Yet the public coverage that Kennedy coveted was one of the sources of Currier's suspicions. Guy had continued to defend Joe to his friends whose concerns were deeper than their anti-Catholic bigotry; they questioned the stories that whirled concerning how Kennedy had made his money and the conduct of his private life. When pushed, Currier would say "Joe's all right until he gets to believing his own publicity" and Kennedy had clearly been believing it for some time.

It had been six months since Guy had told him he wanted out and four months since they sold FBO. However, the Gower Street Company still had over half a million dollars' worth of holdings and Cinema Credits remained an ongoing concern. Currier wanted to continue with some of his film-related activities; he was on the new FBO board of directors as a part of RKO and he was working on labor relations with Will Hays and Joe Schenck. He also looked forward to pursuing other interests such as expanding his library and spending time with his family at his villa in Italy and his summer home in New Hampshire.

Currier's patience was at an end. Kennedy kept hedging, so Guy turned the tables and offered to buy him out. Again, Joe asked for more time, but Currier had an answer for that too. He sent over an agreement to be signed immediately for a sale to take place in nine months, stating he would buy Joe's remaining 155 shares of Gower Street common stock for a minimum of $298,505.29. It even stipulated that any profits from Joe's separate deal for *Moon of Israel,* which had been placed in the Gower Street Company, would continue to flow to him.

Kennedy knew he was up against the wall. Until now, Currier had kept his own counsel regarding his concerns about Kennedy, but how long could that last? Still, Joe rebuked Guy for his proposal and accused him of "calling his note" as if he were a debtor no longer to be trusted.

Currier's response was that of a man exhausted with playing games. Fine, he said, don't sign the agreement. Sign this letter instead. Currier replaced the impeccably legal five pages with a one-page letter effectively saying the same thing: "On January 2, 1930, I will buy and you will sell your half of the stock in The Gower Street Company at its actual liquidating value." This time there was no minimum amount listed, but if there was a difference in opinion, an accounting firm was named to arbitrate. In the meantime, neither of them would sell their stock "without consent of the other." Currier closed the letter with the gentlemanly agreement that "my representatives on the Board of Directors shall act as if charged with a trust for the benefit of all the stockholders." The letter was hand-delivered to Joe, who, seeing no other alternative, signed it on May 6, 1929.

Now, more than ever, Kennedy wanted to head west but, as he told Henri, his father's illness was "dragging on." P.J. appeared to rally during the second week of May and Joe was confident he had plenty of time for a trip to the coast. Yet within hours of disembarking in Los Angeles, he received the call telling him his father had died. According to Rose, Joe was in "a sea of despair," racked with guilt over leaving his father's bedside, and it was "a source of painful regret all his life." Yet instead of returning for the funeral, Joe stayed in Hollywood.

More than a thousand other people, however, filled the Church of St. John the Evangelist in Winthrop to overflowing. P.J. had left public life long ago, but he was still widely beloved and one of the reasons was epitomized by his request to his daughters during his final hospital stay. Over the years he had loaned or simply given money from his own pocket when he saw it was needed and he asked them to burn the papers he kept in his desk at home. Allan Goodrich, the historian at the John F. Kennedy Library, assumes that it was because P.J. didn't want anyone, most likely his son, finding records of unpaid loans and trying to collect on them.

Notes of sympathy poured in from acquaintances and film industry colleagues and Joe responded with cables of appreciation, often including a variation on the line "the burden is lighter because of friends like you." The cables were all billed to Pathé.

There is no question about the depth of Joe's respect for his father or his regret at his inability to be two places at the same time. "I was terribly disappointed not to be there myself," Kennedy wrote Joe Junior, now thirteen, after hearing "lovely reports" of his conduct at the funeral. "I was more than proud to have you there as my own representative." He told his family he hoped to return soon, after "I have finished the job I came out to do."

Yet in contrast to his other Los Angeles arrivals, when he had to invigorate a studio, confront De Mille, or deal with an out-of-control production, Joe found a smoothly functioning Pathé and a film about to go before the cameras. While it was reported that he was in town to "make a final decision on *Queen Kelly*," his initial attention turned to *The Trespasser* and his star.

The difference between a Stroheim set and a Goulding set was night and day. After two weeks of tests and rehearsals, shooting began on June 3 at the time called. Their workdays averaged nine hours, but they usually didn't start until eleven in the morning and regularly broke for tea at four in the afternoon. In his "uniform" of silk scarf, blue blazer, and light pants, Goulding was dapper, yet casual, and always bubbling with ideas. When friends such as Noël Coward dropped by, they were welcomed and if Goulding drank and partied excessively after hours, and he did, he was the picture of professionalism at the studio.

Sound might have intimidated others, but it was made for Eddie Goulding. His stage experience, musical talents, and general faith in himself all came together to blossom under the challenges of talking and singing pictures. *The Trespasser* was written with the use of sound at the very core of the story, not as a silent film with sound added as an afterthought.

Goulding was allowed free rein and his quick if manic decision making process was exemplified by his search for music for Gloria to sing. Songs were used to set a tone and move the story along, not just to be inserted to buy time or show off talent. He wired his friend, the Welsh composer and performer Ivor Novello, asking for "world rights" to his song "Bless You." But the scene was to be shot two days later and not hearing back, Eddie decided to compose his own song. The only problem was he couldn't write music. So when Goulding whistled an original tune Gloria and Laura loved, several frantic phone calls were made before a musician was found to come to the house and put the notes down on

Eddie Goulding directing Swanson in *The Trespasser*

paper. His old friend Elsie Janis wrote the lyrics and the song, "Love, Your Spell Is Everywhere," was created.

One day on the set while Goulding was busy filming, Eddie Moore showed up with a sheath of papers under his arm. "Joe wants these signed," he said as he handed Goulding a pen and held the papers out in front of him.

"What is it?" Eddie asked, still focusing on the actors and the cameras.

"We're publishing the song," replied Moore, and Goulding, visualizing the money pouring into his pocket, happily signed the documents without reading them. When Scollard reviewed the "world rights" contract for "Love," he noticed that William Sistrom had signed as the seller and Goulding had signed as the purchaser. Scollard asked Sullivan to have both men initial the contract to acknowledge the mistake. So much for Goulding's concentration when it came to legal papers.

Charlie Sullivan had been the last of the gang to leave RKO where he had been a vice president and studio manager. All along he had continued, in his "spare time," to serve Kennedy and Gloria Productions, and now after a brief trip to Boston, he was given a new office at Pathé in Culver City. He was put in charge of the business end of all production and while he kept tabs on every film, *The Trespasser* quickly became his focus. He and Derr had learned the painful day-to-day realities of producing on *Queen Kelly* and now they put that knowledge to work. Along with Pat Scollard, they handled everything from making sure the continuity and dialogue sheets corresponded to the film to negotiating the payment schedules and overseeing distribution plans. With Kennedy's approval, they later arranged private screenings for influential friends such as James Quirk, publisher of *Photoplay,* as well as Marion Davies and William Randolph Hearst.

Sullivan also took the brunt of the requests for studio visits from friends of Kennedy's or friends of friends and, frequently, friends of Mayor Fitzgerald's. Honey Fitz had talked so much about being an owner of a studio that it seemed everyone he knew who was visiting California wanted a personal tour. Sullivan was amazed at how many "personal friends of Mr. Kennedy" there were whom he had never heard of before, but he handled most of the intrusions with an easy grace. While he knew to draw the line when they started inquiring about employment, it was all part of the job.

From New York, Pat Scollard oversaw the making of the trailer, learning as he went from the men at the lab who compiled it and the UA publicity people who picked their favorite scenes.

E. B. Derr became the key man on publicity for *The Trespasser*, working with Gloria's publicist, Lance Heath, reviewing still photographs, poster ideas, and the press book. While Kennedy signed off on the final posters, it was Derr who was responsible for seeing that everything was of the proper caliber and moved along efficiently. He was also the liaison with United Artists, ensuring they had everything they needed to promote the film, and he supervised plans to syndicate the story in newspapers when the time came.

Derr was becoming so detail-oriented that he even personally measured the back windows of various town cars to see which would be best for superimposing images. For the outdoor and panoramic scenes, he once again turned to Pathé's newsreel division. He sent the relevant portions of the script to the head man in Chicago and then talked to him on the phone to fine-tune exactly what was needed.

The silent scenes were relatively easy, but another sound truck had to be sent to Chicago since the two they had been using were "out of service." The new truck arrived with flat tires and after they were replaced, engineering problems developed. Permits were required, but the truck was ready and the police had been dealt with in time for a Saturday morning attempt to film the lakefront. However, weekend visitors made the shore too crowded so they had to wait until early Monday morning. Most of the remaining background material was simply shot mute and still it took another week to complete the long and medium shots of Lake Shore Drive apartments, Michigan Boulevard, and a "bird's eye view" of the city from the thirty-sixth floor of the Tribune Building.

The newsreel photographers and soundmen had it a little easier in New York because all they needed were shots in front of the Plaza. The hotel was cooperative, but the police were not about to block off the street, so the sound trucks were ready just as the sun rose to record the doorman blowing his whistle, a taxi with squeaking brakes, and "general traffic and noises" before the real traffic took over. The newsreel division was instructed to bill the studio only for "extraordinary" expenses and absorb the rest.

Derr reviewed every inch of film and was pleased with everything except the background shots to be superimposed in those car windows. They had been taken from a rooftop and so didn't align to the viewpoint of a passenger in the car. He ordered them redone.

All this support helped Goulding turn out the film quickly, but a large part of the credit went to the innovations he created as he went along. His sets "walked" into each other so the actors could move from room to room while the cameras, sometimes over a dozen operating simultaneously, recorded every move from every direction. Microphones were stationary, but everywhere. The setup allowed Goulding and his cinematographers, George Barnes and Gregg Toland, to shoot scenes lasting up to ten minutes each. Because of the intricate planning, what normally would have taken three days was completed in one afternoon. More film was used, but it tightened the editing process. *The Trespasser* finished ahead of schedule and under budget, wrapping on July 5, after only twenty-one days, and setting a new record for sound films.

As writer and director, Goulding collected $45,000, Gloria received $50,000, and even with the padded costs from Pathé for the crew, set construction, and recording facilities as well as adding $25,000 in "executive overhead" for Kennedy and Eddie Moore, *The Trespasser* price tag came to $725,000 for both a silent and sound version. (Joe also received his $2,000-a-week salary from Pathé as well as billing them for his expenses when he was in Los Angeles, which averaged $1,000 a week.)

Kennedy might have been down to one company, but he was going to let the world know about it as he oversaw a massive promotion of Pathé's twenty-fifth anniversary. Full-page ads in the trades and major sections in both *Variety* and *Exhibitors Herald World* featured Kennedy's name in bold print. Reiterating Pathé's history of "firsts" (first newsreel, first use of color, first serials, first *Our Gang* comedies, and so on), Kennedy promised that the company was and would continue to be "as virile and aggressive as its trademark rooster."

Feeling "virile and aggressive" himself, Joe appeared more solicitous than ever toward Gloria. He was proud of her luxurious star bungalow, an outward and visible sign of her unparalleled rank, and was more than comfortable making himself at home there.

For all the restrictions the gang had put on Swanson's spending, she was hardly being deprived. She even had her own personal masseuse. Sylvia Ulbeck was Hollywood's "masseuse to the stars" and her client list included Marie Dressler, Ronald Colman, and Norma Shearer. Massage was all the rage for fitting into a specific costume, general health, and relaxation. It was so popular that many of the most successful in the film business had designated massage rooms in their homes. When Gloria expressed an interest in signing Sylvia to an exclusive contract, the masseuse was tempted, but declined because she had rebuilt her clientele after an unhappy exclusive experience with the petulant Mae Murray several years before. But it was Sylvia whom Gloria wanted so Joe stepped in. He was impressed when she spotted his flat feet within min-

Constance Bennett

utes of meeting him and he cut a compromise deal. Sylvia would have her own bungalow at Pathé to service the more important personnel, including executives, in order of priority. Gloria, needless to say, was first on the list; if she called, anyone else was to be left on the slab. Sylvia was free to see other clients during her off-hours. For this, she was to receive $750 a week, more than most of the featured players and certainly more than many executives including E. B. Derr.

The proven stage actresses Ina Claire and Ann Harding signed Pathé contracts that spring to great acclaim, yet it wouldn't have occurred to anyone to contest Gloria's standing as the undisputed star of the lot, that is until Constance Bennett arrived in Culver City. Gloria later said she was the one who suggested to Joe that he consider signing the "beautiful slim blonde" who "showed up everywhere with Hollywood's fast set." That at least had been the case back in the early 1920s when Bennett was making films for Sam Goldwyn and MGM, but she had left Hollywood abruptly in 1925 after marrying Philip Plant, the heir to a railroad and shipping fortune. The couple moved to Europe and appeared in all the finest watering holes, but by early 1929, they had separated and Constance let it be known she was ready to go back to work. Since she was in Paris, Joe sent Henri to investigate her interest in Pathé.

It was apparent that Constance wanted more than a contract, she wanted the Marquis as well. If Henri knew about his wife's affair with Kennedy at this point, he wasn't saying anything. In their letters, Joe and Henri continued to treat each other with affable respect. Kennedy asked his opinion on various business questions and kept him abreast of Pathé's and Gloria's work. Joe implied Rose was with him when she wasn't, but if Henri knew he was being cuckolded, he chose the civilized reaction of turning his head the other way while holding it high. Yet he was not about to resist the beguiling Bennett; he signed her and bedded her and then sent her off to Hollywood in the middle of April 1929.

Gloria might have known nothing about Constance's relationship with Henri, but her general suspicions had to have been aroused when she first ran into her, not at the studio, but at Kennedy's house on Rodeo Drive. Gloria walked in to find Constance leaning against the banister, smoking a cigarette, and while Gloria made small talk, she found her "laconic answers meant either that she was embarrassed to be seen there or that I had put her off by being so much at home. She reminded me of Frances Marion's great line about typical Hollywood females: 'I don't know why she doesn't like me. I never did anything for her.' "

Gloria asked her if she was staying for dinner and when she said no, Gloria went into the library, leaving Constance in the foyer. By the time Joe came bouncing down the stairs, Constance had left, but Gloria noted that Kennedy was in a particularly "chipper mood." Trying to be non-chalant, Gloria asked him what Constance was doing at the house and Joe told her, "Going out with one of the boys." He then volunteered with a wink and a laugh, "She couldn't hook the boss, so she settled for one of the boys." With that, they went in to dinner.

According to William Dufty, Gloria always assumed that at some point Kennedy slept with Constance, but it wouldn't be until later that she discovered that "one of the boys" Joe was referring to was her own husband.

Constance Bennett's first film for Pathé, *Rich People,* had to be post-poned for several weeks because, in contrast to most stars who had spent time traveling, Constance needed to put on some weight before she went before the cameras. Since their initial meeting at Joe's house, she and Gloria behaved cordially to each other in public and when they were brought together again at Joe's home for a dinner he hosted where the other guests included Laura Hope Crews and Sylvia, the masseuse who would be needed to help get Constance in shape. Yet to keep peace on the lot, Kennedy had Sylvia go to Constance's apartment for her treatments.

If others noticed the chill between the two stars that summer, and they did, Gloria's preeminence was not about to be seriously challenged. Constance might have quietly had the Marquis on a string, but Gloria had the head of the studio and, at least until the end of June, he was in residence in California. Keeping it from Gloria, Joe posed for a portrait of himself that he proudly presented to her, assuming she would hang it in her home. More appropriate for the hall of a men's club, "It pictured him as he wanted to see himself," she told her daughter, the strong, powerful film mogul capable of handling whatever came his way.

She wasn't about to display the portrait over her mantel, but Joe and Gloria's affair had been going on for well over a year and had reached the level of Hollywood common knowledge. She could talk about how discreet she was, but too many people from that time have tales to tell to believe it was much of a secret. In letters and cables, friends and colleagues told Joe to "give our love to Gloria" or "remember me kindly to Miss Swanson," further evidence of their renown as a couple.

Joe was proud of his relationship with her and wanted others to know about it. He immersed himself in Gloria's life and was particularly conspicuous strutting around the party he hosted at her house following her son's baptism. Since their first meeting, Kennedy had been bothered by the fact that the boy, now seven, had never been christened and Gloria agreed to go through with a ceremony. Joe made all the arrangements, which included his own role as godfather. Brother, as the child continued to be called at home, had been named Joseph after Gloria's father at the time of his adoption. Now, at Joe's urging, he was given the middle name of Patrick, mimicking Kennedy's own first and middle names. Though the child was clearly too old to have been his biological son, Joe made sure the many Hollywood people, including Allan Dwan, Winfield Sheehan, and Lois Wilson, who were all at the party, knew of the boy's new name. It underscored his importance to Gloria and fanned rumors, still repeated today, that Kennedy and Swanson had a child.

One of the friends who accompanied Gloria and Joe on their nights on the town was Sport Ward, and during a quiet moment, he leaned over to Gloria and said, "You have to take your hex off this poor man." Joe was clearly proud of being with her, but at the same time Ward felt the "constant tension between the two of them. You had to be an idiot not to know they were together as a couple."

Joe and Gloria were frequent guests at other people's homes as well, including J. J. Murdock's. He had purchased a large estate on Foothill Boulevard only a few blocks from their homes on Rodeo and Crescent. Murdock's mansion was a resplendent example of the intersection of an abundance of money and exquisite taste. The three-story house featured arched entryways and a plethora of beautifully wallpapered bedrooms and sitting rooms. The pièce de résistance however was below the ground; one third of what in other homes would be a large basement was

The portrait Joe had painted for over Gloria's mantel, 1929

a spa and exercise area including a steam room with walls, ceiling, and floors all tiled in a soft yellow. There was also a ballroom that featured a stage and built-in projector. To the left of the stairs was a billiard room and a full-size bar area, complete with a private still. Outwardly, Murdock was the antithesis of a party guy, but the house also came with a steel door that could close off the bar area with a flip of a switch from upstairs, just in case the authorities made an unexpected appearance.

Merian Cooper, a popular personality who had traveled the world before directing hits like *The Four Feathers* and *King Kong,* told Kevin Brownlow in a 1971 interview that he had been a guest at a most unusual dinner party at Kennedy's house on Rodeo. The large rectangular dining room jutted out from the rest of the house with windows on three sides looking out on the corner streets and the landscaped backyard with its pool and tennis court. Twenty people could easily be seated at the long dinner table, but since the downstairs rooms opened up into each other, many more guests could be comfortably accommodated. Company for dinner was commonplace, but this particular evening, Joe decided to appear inspired instead of jealous when news reached him that Gloria might be seeing someone else. He "got a picture of every man that was known to have slept with her. He had life sized blown up photographs all around the dining room. He invited everybody that was 'in' in Hollywood to the dinner. In sweeps Gloria and she looked around at these pictures and said, 'Joe, I'm glad you remembered my former life.' She wasn't fazed at all. She wouldn't give a damn, you know." Everyone thought it was hilarious and Cooper remembered it as "the funniest joke I ever saw."

If Joe hoped the fact they were known as a couple would affect the way people saw him, it didn't help with the likes of Cooper. In his opinion, Joe was "a mean old, tough son of a bitch" and Gloria was "a wonderful person. I love her."

Others viewed Kennedy differently. Paramount's production chief B. P. Schulberg considered Joe one of the most intelligent men in the business and "always a gentleman." Josef von Sternberg, the director who "discovered" Marlene Dietrich and was known for his discernment if not outright arrogance, found Kennedy to be "a brilliant and charming man."

Hollywood society could have their disparate opinions about Joe and Gloria, individually or as a couple, but they would always be amateurs compared to the community's most prominent unmarried couple, William Randolph Hearst and Marion Davies. Their mutual activities were monitored by the fan magazines and some newspapers, if not Hearst's own. There Marion alone was trumpeted, but photos appeared in *Photoplay* and *Silver Screen* of the two of them together. The press walked a tightrope, treating the Davies-Hearst relationship as a professional, if very close, one. Gloria's twenty-two-room Beverly Hills mansion on several acres, while elegant and well staffed, was half the size of Marion's fifty-plus-room beach house, and Kennedy's leased house was just one of many while Hearst played host at the incomparable San Simeon.

It was Joe who was the welcome guest at "the ranch," as Hearst called his massive estate on the coast halfway between Los Angeles and San Francisco. Hearst found him interesting and intelligent and Marion thought he was charming and full of "Irish self assurance." While Joe was occasionally with Gloria, Marion was not impressed. Davies had little patience with what she considered Swanson's "hauteur and pretensions" and even parodied Gloria in *Show People*. Marion's favorite foil was anyone she thought took themselves too seriously and Gloria fell loudly into that category. The guest list for those San Simeon weekends was always impressive; over a few short years, Albert Einstein, George Bernard Shaw, Presidents Hoover and Coolidge, even the King of Siam, were among their houseguests and Kennedy fueled his sense of belonging in such surroundings.

Joe lived fully and comfortably in his new world in California, but it must have nagged at him that his family remained in what he would have considered an unsettled state at a rented home in Riverdale. Once again, it was Eddie Moore who was sent house hunting and he found a six-acre estate in a plush New York suburb suitable for the Kennedy tribe. The large brick Georgian-style home, which *The New York Times* called "one of the most imposing in Bronxville," boasted a tennis court, beautiful grounds, and a purchase price of $250,000. A quarter mile up the hill from the village, the house came with everything except a father. Now even more staff was needed; there were gardeners and chauffeurs, a cook, laundresses, and housemaids along with nurses for the younger children and governesses for the older. Six of the staff lived in and as Rose began to supervise the children's annual summer pilgrimage to the Cape, private physical education teachers and tutors supplemented the retinue.

After almost two months in California, Joe returned east, bringing E. B. Derr with him. Their first stop was Pathé's annual sales convention in Atlantic City where, now almost by rote, Joe took the stage and announced plans to release thirty "all dialogue" films over the next year, in addition to their newsreels and dozens of short comedies. The numbers were never sacrosanct; it was the hoopla that mattered. His role was to electrify the men of Pathé with enthusiasm to go out and sell, sell, sell.

# CHAPTER 22

# "Having Tea with His Wife and My Husband and the Vicar"

## (SUMMER AND FALL 1929)

K ennedy watched the rough cut of *The Trespasser* in the privacy of his own screening room and he was thrilled. He told Gloria, "if this isn't the greatest motion picture that anyone ever shot, I want to go back to stock manipulation." He was genuinely pleased for her because he knew it had been a painfully protracted two years for her between films. For Joe himself, the best part had to be that, finally, up there on the big screen was the phrase: "Joseph P. Kennedy presents Gloria Swanson."

When *The Trespasser* was previewed at New York's Rialto Theatre at the end of July, they knew they had a hit on their hands. Joe wanted a grand and lavish premiere, but because the film had been completed so quickly, theater availability became an issue. Both of the United Artists New York theaters were booked through the fall and while Joe Schenck personally stepped in to give *The Trespasser* preferred treatment, there was little he could do. No one wanted to wait for the revenue stream to begin, so when it was suggested there be a European premiere with an American opening to follow, Joe enthusiastically embraced the idea.

He jumped into the planning with UA's foreign representatives and publicists. Which London theater attracted patrons to both evening screenings and matinees? How many showings could be scheduled each day? Henri was asked to select "the most worthy" theater in Paris. Since that premiere would attract Americans, should the English talking version be used for the first night only and the silent version shown for the remainder of the run? What about Berlin or Brussels?

Kennedy's zeal for his European plans made him more daring on the personal front; he would take both Rose and Gloria and meet up with Henri. All would be well with the world. Needless to say, Gloria balked.

"Joe," she firmly stated, "you and I cannot travel on the same boat going over even if we're going to meet my husband." Kennedy countered with the plea that Rose had "never been to Europe and I've promised her this trip."

Rose had been to Europe half a dozen times by then, but Gloria wouldn't necessarily have known that. She had yet to meet the woman. All she could think of was that Joe was asking her to "throw a shawl over my scarlet letter and have tea with his wife and my husband and the vicar, doubtless, not to mention the press." She thought she resisted, but soon gave in because "when his mind was made up, there was not a big enough lever in the world to move him."

Leaving the children at home, Gloria boarded the train in Los Angeles on July 17. Her publicist, Lance Heath, finally had something to promote so he arranged for interviews at stops along the way. In Chicago, she picked up her friend Virginia Bowker, who had agreed to come along as a traveling companion, but was soon aware of her dual role as a beard. Once in New York, Gloria recorded her *Trespasser* songs for release on RCA's Victor label, the music and record company Sarnoff had purchased earlier in the year, further expanding his entertainment reach. She also made appearances on his NBC radio. Gloria was one of the few pieces of gold Joe still held that could be of use to Sarnoff.

The original plan was for Gloria and Virginia to leave for Europe on the second of August, but Joe pressed them into making a weekend visit to the Cape where he could show them off to both family and friends. Gloria had refused to go to Riverdale, but if she was going to travel with Rose, she might as well meet her now. Ted O'Leary and Eddie Moore met Gloria and Virginia in Manhattan and they headed to the Hudson River where they all boarded an amphibious airplane for a flight to Hyannisport. Joe, his family, and even his father-in-law were all there to give the appearance of propriety to their dramatic arrival. The glamorous star visiting the home of their own movie mogul at the height of the summer season was big news. Gloria's appearance at the Beach Club made a sensation worthy of front page coverage in the local press.

Gloria and Virginia were to board the *Olympic* for Le Havre. Kennedy had booked a deluxe suite on the *Ile de France* the following week. The cost of the one-way voyage was $1,175, billed to Gloria Productions.

Lance Heath arrived in France two days before Gloria, giving him time to arrange for hordes of photographers to be on hand when Henri greeted her at the pier. Off they went to the Plaza Athénée Hotel in Paris, where Virginia could make herself scarce while Gloria and Henri became reacquainted. They had not seen each other since the previous Christmas and Gloria later wrote that there was awkwardness between them. Her rationale for why neither of them said what they really felt was because of their separate relationships with Kennedy. Henri had gone from being Gloria's employee to being Joe's and was hardly in a position to rock that boat, personally or professionally. The genteel and politic thing to do was nothing and soon enough they were off to England.

The Kennedy party reached London on Saturday, August 31, and three days later Gloria and her entourage joined them at Claridges. The coterie must have been something to behold: Gloria with Henri and Virginia, Rose and Joe and his sister Margaret, who had come along to keep Rose company while Joe was occupied elsewhere. In addition to Gloria's publicist, other Pathé and UA employees were in and out helping with arrangements.

Never before had a major American film been shown in the capitals of Europe before making "a home appearance" and that piqued the press's interest. Everywhere the "First World Premiere" was billed as a Kennedy-Swanson production. Joe was the impresario presenting his wares and to promote Gloria's first talking—and singing—film, he wanted to showcase her voice. He scheduled her for radio appearances and even a short singing performance during a concert at Queen's Hall where he walked on stage to introduce her to the crowd. He subjected her to various promotional stunts such as having her host "a tea party" for several hundred waitresses. During the event, and almost everywhere they went, she was called on to sing "Love," proving over and over again it was her "real voice" in the film. American-style publicity had backfired in the past in England, but this time Gloria could do no wrong, except with the drivers caught in the hours of traffic jams caused by her public outings.

*The Trespasser* premiere at London's New Gallery Cinema on Monday night, September 9, 1929, was, according to *Variety,* "a sensational smash." Uniformed police linked arms for over two blocks along Regent Street to hold back "the near riot" of over five thousand fans. The hordes were primarily female and the image of sedate English matrons was called into question when eight "burly" policemen were literally swept off their feet by the throngs. As Gloria put it to a reporter that night, "I thought this kind of thing only happened in America."

Swanson was cheered for over fifteen minutes as she entered the theater, and when she went on stage after the screening, again escorted by

Joe, the applause lasted at least as long. Looking out at the packed audience, bathed in adulation, Kennedy couldn't have been more pleased. Swanson described him as being "so proud and happy that his mouth was perpetually half open in an ecstatic smile." And the long-term box office prognosis was fabulous. Reviewers raved that *The Trespasser* was "the best talker seen here yet" and "as natural and fluid" as the best silent film.

At that moment in London, Clara Bow was "talking" in *Dangerous Curves* and Norma Shearer was doing the same in *The Last of Mrs. Cheyney.* While both were doing "enormous business," the *London Chronicle* proclaimed "Gloria Swanson has taught them all how to do it." The combination of Gloria singing "like a prima" and Goulding's direction and technical wizardry were hailed as showcasing the true possibilities of sound. With articles trumpeting Gloria's "personal triumph" and declaring her "even more accomplished" in talkies than in her silent films, the group left London feeling elated. They went en masse to Deauville for a few days before hitting Paris where Kennedy made time for meetings to have Pathé become a 50 percent partner in a limited corporation to make foreign versions of American films. He had been discussing the plan with Bob Kane for almost a year and now he committed Pathé sound equipment and cameras to be shipped to France and Spain to begin production as soon as possible. While Joe was in conferences, Gloria introduced Rose and Margaret to the joys of haute couture. Rose had shopped in Paris before, but now she took to the pleasure of having gowns made exclusively for her and maintained the practice for the rest of her life.

Everything seemed to be going along smoothly when there was a sudden explosion; the fuse was a cable Gloria opened by mistake because of an "e" added to the title of Marquis. It was a love letter to Henri from Constance Bennett, still in Culver City but preparing to leave for France in a few weeks to finalize her divorce.

"Cold, royal rage" surged through Swanson, according to Rose, who came running along with Joe when he was summoned. Gloria announced she was suing for divorce on the spot and there was absolutely no way she was going to be seen in public with Henri again. Farce or high drama, it must have been quite a scene with Gloria claiming outrage that her husband was sleeping with another woman when the man she was cuckolding him with was sitting opposite them. Henri could hardly call her on it with Rose there as well, so he simply withdrew to another room while Joe went into action, calming Gloria by reminding her how much was at stake for both of them. She was a great actress; surely she could get through the next few days pretending they were the "devoted, happy and glamorous couple" the public expected. And, after much coaxing, that is what Gloria agreed to do, calling Henri back in and negotiating the arrangements for the remainder of their time together.

Finally, after what had to be an exhausting three weeks of roller-coaster emotions, Gloria, Joe and Rose, Virginia, and Margaret boarded the *Ile de France* on September 18, leaving Henri on the pier waving goodbye for his farewell performance for the photographers.

If they had kept up pretenses by taking separate boats to Europe, there were no such restraints on the return crossing. However, Rose, Joe, and Gloria all gave very different versions of the voyage. Joe claimed in a letter to Henri that Gloria "remained in bed on the boat the whole trip, with the exception of one night." Rose, on the other hand, said that she was the one who was "tired from the emotion of the trip, so I stayed in my stateroom." And in her memoir, Gloria recalled that when they were all on board together, "Joe Kennedy behaved in an alarmingly possessive or over solicitous fashion toward me." She was bemused by Rose, who was also overly attentive and almost maternal. Even though she was less than a decade older, Rose treated Gloria and Virginia "like a pair of debutantes it was [her] bounden duty to chaperon."

Rose took on a condescending air over Gloria's apparent need to be constantly attended to. The recurring adjective Rose used to describe Swanson was "poor" as in "poor little Gloria." William Dufty said that it was Rose's appellation of "poor Gloria" and painting her as an empty-headed star in her book, *Times to Remember,* that was the catalyst for Gloria writing her own memoir after years of vowing she never would.

Still, Rose never publicly wavered from her deep-seated belief that Joe's relationship with Gloria was purely professional. "Obviously the best advisor-manager-financier in Hollywood was Joe Kennedy," so it was natural that "poor Gloria" turned to him. "Everyone seemed to have a fully trustworthy adviser, but she had none and really needed someone like Joe." Rose told Doris Kearns Goodwin that "reporters mistakenly decided that something was going on between the two of them and, from that moment on, all sorts of rumors began to fly. But I knew I never had a thing to worry about and I only felt sorry for poor little Gloria."

Goodwin was incredulous about Rose's "strange solicitude" and concluded that "it is impossible to believe that Rose did not know," yet she had "willed" that knowledge out of her consciousness. It was "better perhaps to follow the pattern set by her mother long ago: to suffer in silence rather than take the enormous risk of shattering the entire family and bringing public disgrace upon herself and her husband."

Many others have speculated over Rose's state of mind. Hedda Hopper, who had great respect for Joe and believed he possessed "one of the best sets of brains in the country," said she "often wondered how [Rose] weathered" the affair, which she simply refused to acknowledge.

Gloria too was shocked at Rose's failure to see anything untoward in her relationship with Joe. "If she suspected me of having relations not quite proper with her husband, or resented me for it, she never once gave any indication of it." Was Rose "a fool, I asked myself as I listened with disbelief, or a saint? Or just a better actress than I was."

Swanson's autobiography is exceedingly well written (thanks in part to ghostwriters, including Wayne Lawson and William Dufty) and it has been taken verbatim by many biographers ever since. Yet when her accounts are compared with newspapers of the day, other witnesses, or most convincingly her own papers, events are occasionally out of order and her actions are slanted to position herself as an otherwise intelligent person overwhelmed by Kennedy's strength and sincerity. However, she doesn't create events out of whole cloth and that is what makes her account of what happened shortly after their return to the States so intriguing.

After disembarking, Rose returned to Bronxville and Gloria was installed at the Plaza where Ted O'Leary called her to say there was "an important person" she needed to meet. There was nothing unusual about that; names were rarely used and she just assumed Joe had given Ted his instructions until she was escorted into a hotel suite and found herself face-to-face with Cardinal O'Connell of Boston in full clerical garb. He wasted no time with small talk. "I am here to ask you to stop seeing Joe Kennedy." Swanson suggested he take it up with him, but the cardinal informed her that Joe had sought permission from the Church to separate from Rose after being told he could never have the marriage annulled. Gloria's silent fury built to a fever pitch as the prelate continued to entreat her to make the break, saying, "Each time you see him, you become an occasion of sin for him."

"I repeat," Gloria responded, "it's Mr. Kennedy you should be talking to," and with that, she rose to leave. When the cardinal blocked her way, she stood her ground without saying another word until he finally stepped aside and she left the room, taking the stairs down to the lobby, where she confronted a nervous O'Leary.

Ted apologized profusely. She pushed him to tell her who had instigated the meeting, but all he would confirm was that Joe knew nothing about it; the cardinal had approached Ted personally and directly.

The thought of O'Leary, who at this point had been with Kennedy for almost a decade, doing anything not previously approved by a boss who demanded total loyalty is difficult to believe, yet the cardinal may well have been the lone higher authority in the Catholic O'Leary's personal hierarchy.

Whether or not they knew it at the time, an incredible level of hypocrisy was added to the equation by the fact that the cardinal's nephew was a Boston priest living a double life as a married man in New York. According to his biographer, O'Connell allowed his nephew to continue his charade because he "threatened to expose evidence of financial chicanery with the church funds and proofs of the Cardinal's sexual affection for men." Cardinal O'Connell had been in Joe's life for several decades, had married him and Rose, and was a source of information as well as the spiritual leader of Boston Catholics. Yet around this time, Joe switched his private allegiances from the cardinal to Bishop Spellman. Kennedy was living in New York, but in the Boston bishop, "he found a churchman who met him on his own terms." Spellman's biographer believed that "neither man minded being used by the other, as long as they both benefited." Whether Kennedy's shift of focus from O'Connell to Spellman was precipitated by the cardinal's visit with Gloria, it certainly didn't help cement the relationship.

Doris Kearns Goodwin doubts Gloria's story of meeting the cardinal because he was known to hold "himself aloof from the everyday problems of his parishioners." She also wondered if Joe was seriously thinking of leaving Rose since he had just purchased the home in Bronxville. Yet Kennedy was hardly a typical parishioner; he was one of the richest and most public Catholic figures in the country and buying the estate could have been seen as a settlement just as easily as a commitment.

Gloria's detailed recounting of the cardinal's appearance, down to his "beautifully manicured hands," the setting, and the extensive dialogue all add veracity to her story. While she never publicly recounted whether she discussed it with Kennedy directly, she did tell several friends that Joe wanted not only to marry her, but to have children with her as well. "What he wanted more than anything was for us to have a child." In a burst of devotion, Kennedy proclaimed he had been "faithful" throughout their relationship, but the very concept "stunned" Gloria. After all, they were both married to other people and she had certainly continued to have relations with Henri. Joe, however, was indignant and pointed to the fact that he and Rose had not had a child since February of 1928, shortly after he and Gloria had begun sleeping together. That was Joe's definition of "faithful."

Another witness corroborates Kennedy's discussing leaving his wife for the star. Rose's niece, Geraldine Hannon, said she overheard Joe arguing with his father-in-law, who threatened to tell Rose everything if Joe did not stop seeing Gloria. Hannon said that Joe's response was to call Fitzgerald on his bluff, telling him to go ahead because then he would "simply marry Gloria." Various other, less immediate sources told similar stories, such as Hedda Hopper, who always believed that it was Honey Fitz who "ordered" Joe to drop Gloria "or certain secrets would burst out into the open."

It makes sense that it was John Fitzgerald who asked the cardinal to intervene. While Allan Goodrich of the Kennedy Library says Fitzgerald was "not one of the Cardinal's favorites," Honey Fitz was used to going to the source to get things done and he would have done anything to protect his eldest daughter if indeed he thought her future was in jeopardy. This was the daughter he had ordered to return to her husband almost a decade earlier and he was not about to sit by and let her be divorced. To be married and carry on an active and separate life was one thing, to divorce was out of the question.

During that late fall of 1929, Joe appeared more enamored of Gloria than ever and part of his joy stemmed from the success of their film. Five weeks after the London opening, *The Trespasser* was still "going strong" and the critical response was as overwhelming; "Brilliant," "Swanson gives better performance than *Sadie Thompson*," and "She transcends perfection" were just a few of the quotes pulled from reviews.

Both Kennedy and United Artists wanted her at *The Trespasser* New York premiere, but that was scheduled for a month after their return from Europe. The film was being released throughout the country as theaters became available; it opened in Detroit and then a dozen other cities before it opened in New York. The children and their governess came east to join Gloria as did Laura Hope Crews, who along with Virginia Bowker helped with the various activities, such as the series of afternoons when Gloria opened her hotel suite to reporters. Even though she wasn't feeling well and both the children had sore throats, Swanson charmed her audiences as she made radio appearances and fielded dozens of phone calls from writers in the towns and cities where *The Trespasser* was about to open. Gloria fell comfortably into answering the same old questions as if hearing them for the first time and never giving a hint that her personal life was in turmoil.

IF KENNEDY WAS NEAR EUPHORIC that October, almost everyone else who had anything to do with Wall Street was becoming gravely concerned. Joe would later tell self-deprecating tales of getting out of the stock market on a hunch, saying if shoeshine boys were giving him tips, clearly everyone was an expert and he should give up. While Joe had sold most of his film stocks, he still held a wide-ranging portfolio.

Yet Kennedy listened carefully to the few people he respected. He had tried to see J. P. Morgan, Jr., earlier in the year, but was rebuffed by the great man's secretary, because, according to Morgan's biographer, Ron Chernow, Kennedy "bore the double stigma of being a Catholic and a stock market operator." Guy Currier, however, was still speaking to him and in the spring of 1929, he was predicting "a business depression" and warned "it is not an attractive time to go into new matters." Currier, along with Frederick Prince, were among the few to counsel that stocks were too explosive to be dependable much longer. Joe also appreciated the concentrated effort stock profiteering required and with his attention distracted by Hollywood, he knew it was the wisest course to remove himself from the market. He made his decision and stuck to it, but it could not have been easy when stock prices continued to rise over the summer and word of his moves spread among his former colleagues. It made him even more of an outsider on the Street, yet he reassured himself with his doctrine, "Only a fool holds out for top dollar."

On October 2, 1929, Kennedy exercised the remaining portion of his K-A-O/RKO options, cashing in the final 15,000 shares he had purchased at $21 and clearing almost half a million dollars in the process. He kept most in cash, but put some into bonds. At the same time, he finished divesting himself of the 100,000 shares of Pathé he had received in quarterly segments over the past year in payment for running that company. Blair and Company had bought some of them, passing the profits back to him, but the remainder was sold in dozens of transactions, usually in increments of five hundred or one thousand shares at a time. Only a few thousand shares were sold under the name of Joseph P. Kennedy; all the rest initially went into accounts of "E. E. Moore" and "C. J. Scollard." When the columns were all added up that fall, between K-A-O and Pathé, Kennedy had made a pure profit of more than a million dollars.

Only a few weeks later, after several months of roller-coaster prices, came the crisis days of late October 1929. As *Variety* headlined it, "Wall Street Lays an Egg." Over $10 billion of value vanished in a single day from just the New York Stock Exchange. Yet the next week Kennedy was able to tell the lawyer handling his father's probate, "The crash in the stock market left me untouched; I was more fortunate this time than usual." "Fortunate" was an understatement. Any remnant of hope that the much heralded organized support by bankers could prop up the market had disintegrated. Newsboys waved their papers, shouting, "Read 'em and weep!"

While men who had been millionaires the week before were now facing the unthinkable, Kennedy's attention was riveted on the New York opening of *The Trespasser,* scheduled for Friday, November 1. Working with the publicity director for the Rialto Theatre, he arranged with the Irving Berlin company, which was publishing the sheet music, to have banners plastering the city's music stores. Copies of the score of "Love, Your Spell Is Everywhere" were sent to local orchestras and played on national radio. Swanson singing the song along with dialogue from the film were used for promotion on the radio as well.

While the European premieres had been exhilarating, this was Kennedy's opportunity to regale his old friends and former colleagues with his greatest success to date. He sent letters with tickets to key people in his life, back to Vera Murray, the producer C. B. Dillingham's secretary who had taken him in hand during the teens when he was just learning the joys of Broadway and chorus girls. Then there were those still in important positions to help such as Doc Giannini and a contingent from Blair and Company as well as the editors and publishers of the major newspapers and magazines. David Sarnoff and Joe Schnitzer, Bill LeBaron and Lee Marcus, all now with RKO, were not forgotten. Altogether, Kennedy and Swanson had over one hundred special invited guests for the New York premiere.

The crowds began gathering on the corner of 42nd Street and Seventh Avenue in the afternoon and by the time Gloria and Joe arrived, the throngs broke through the police barricades and pushed Gloria to the point she had to be picked up and carried into the theater. When the film finally unspooled, the sound was uneven and occasionally muffled, but the opening night crowd didn't seem to mind. She was greeted with a standing ovation at her curtain appearance.

The film had been screened for critics several days before and the sound had been perfect for them so they could vouch for Swanson's "clear as a bell" speaking voice and her "most pleasing" singing. New York's premier reviewer, Mordaunt Hall of the *Times,* gave it a rave, proclaiming the film "gifted with originality from beginning to end." Positive comments continued to flood in and they were highlighted in full page ads in the trades and newspapers throughout the country.

Gloria left New York for Chicago to attend that city's *Trespasser* opening, but Joe stayed behind and made several impromptu visits to the Rialto, checking on the ticket sales and the crowd's reaction. When the first week set a theater box office record, he made sure everyone knew it.

Kennedy didn't sit back and count the money, he shook the bushes for more. He sent cables to salesmen in areas yet to be booked, reporting the Rialto take and telling each one "this picture is entitled to the best terms a house can pay and you are the boy to get it." He wrote letters to the owners of the smaller theater circuits who had bought the film and told them that he had "a lot of money tied up in the Swanson picture" and "I will appreciate it if you would see that it gets a pretty good break." An advertising push and prime scheduling could make them both more money. He then wrote notes of thanks to theater managers who "really got behind this picture."

Everywhere the crowds were turning out in droves and the film was proving to be a huge financial success. After her protracted absence from the screen, Gloria had to be tremendously relieved. And Joe couldn't have been prouder, even if *The Trespasser,* while billed as a "personal production of Joseph Kennedy," had come to life only as an afterthought while deciding what to do with *Queen Kelly.* And so it was back to Culver City with a vengeance, for Joe was all the more determined to finish that film in a blaze of glory.

*The Trespasser* broke box-office records in November 1929.

Rumors of "a rift" in the Swanson-Falaise marriage began appearing in the trades shortly after Gloria's return from Europe. While no sources were given for the stories, Kennedy privately cautioned Henri that with Constance Bennett in Paris, he should "behave yourself and keep out of trouble and don't gallivant around too much." Whether or not Henri appreciated the irony of Joe giving him advice on how to conduct his affair, he did not heed it; he and Constance were "constantly seen together" in Paris. Soon they were telling friends they planned to marry as soon as they both secured divorces.

Gloria was hardly in a position to be shocked, but what had to gall her was the press lumping her with Pola Negri because she too had married European nobility as part of "the short vogue of silent film stars of Hollywood to annex a title." It was none too kindly pointed out that Pola was now losing her prince "by the same route."

While Swanson was not ready to face divorce court at the moment, all these questions about the state of her marriage put her more on edge than usual. Instead of dealing with her personal life, she joined Joe in trying to salvage *Queen Kelly* and, once again, she turned to Eddie Goulding for help. Eddie genuinely liked Gloria, but he reiterated that he thought the film was beyond repair. She should just forget *Queen Kelly* and make another film with him from a script he had just finished about a manicurist who marries into wealth and has to prove her worth. This was not what Gloria wanted to hear and, according to Goulding, she became "peevish" and "generally hotey-totey."

Goulding might have been surprised by Swanson's attitude, but others weren't. Her contemporary, the actress Louise Brooks, later claimed, "I watched Queen Swanson abuse Allan Dwan, her director, on the set, abuse Hank de la Falaise, her husband, at the dinner table, and abuse her secretary in her drawing room, so I was particularly anxious to learn what kind of abuse she would fire at Edmund Goulding."

Eddie tried to be sympathetic and wondered if Gloria wasn't suffering from an underlying insecurity, questioning whether it was her talent or his that was responsible for the success of *The Trespasser.* Joe and Gloria had been the ones in the spotlight with the film; Goulding had not gone with them to Europe and Joe had insisted he not even go to the Chicago premiere because "of the work piling up" at Pathé. Eddie had done what he was told. He stayed at the studio writing and producing the musical *The Grand Parade,* a film the New York distributors called "excellent" and just what "the territories are demanding."

Goulding was disappointed over Gloria's reaction, but he had been putting up with her airs for months and at times just considered them part of her charm. But what happened next truly shocked him into a new reality. He had remained under contract with Pathé at $2,500 a week and signed over the rights to *The Trespasser* and his other stories as was the practice of writers on salary. He considered it a clever way to save money. He was a notorious spendthrift and assumed he had a big payout coming from his "partnership" with Kennedy.

Both Kennedy and Fanny Holtzmann, Goulding's lawyer and confidante, traveled frequently, but even when they were in the same city, Joe found reasons to postpone their meetings. Holtzmann had heard enough whispers about Kennedy from her Wall Street friends that she had cautioned Eddie from the beginning that Joe was "a personal promoter, glib and dangerous." Goulding had dismissed her warnings and assured her that the film was fabulous.

"It's the contract I want to see, Eddie," Holtzmann told him, "not the picture!"

Yet she had no reason to doubt the director's story that Kennedy had promised a partnership, so when she and Joe finally met over lunch to discuss Goulding's deal, she was astonished when he announced he didn't owe him another penny beyond his Pathé salary.

"But that was just expense money, Joe!" Fanny protested. "Something to tide him over. After all, Eddie provided you with a great story. And he put the whole project together. Why, he gets more money than that for—"

Joe interrupted her mid-sentence. "Listen, I did the bum a favor. He was on the skids in Hollywood. . . . No other studio would touch him. I gave him a chance to get back on the screen."

"I can't believe my ears, Joe. Eddie had a deal with you, a clear verbal contract. You were partners."

"What contract?" Kennedy asked with a steely smile. Lunch was clearly over.

When Holtzmann broke the news of the betrayal to Goulding, it was slow to sink in. Eddie had thought of Joe as "his savior," allowing him the creative freedom to produce innovative films they would all benefit from. He couldn't fathom that Joe would so blatantly lie to him and decided to approach him directly. Kennedy repeated that he didn't owe the director "one penny," and Goulding, now desperate and realizing that what he considered his life savings wasn't there after all, told Joe he would see him in court.

An icy-cold Kennedy Eddie had never seen before turned on him and said, "You have that Jew girl go after me and I guarantee you'll never be on a screen again. I'll tell a federal jury about some of those wild Goulding weekends and you'll be deported for moral turpitude."

Goulding was stunned into silence. He knew he wasn't about to subject Fanny Holtzmann or himself to public slurs and while deportation seemed an unlikely possibility, he wasn't going to risk having his bisexual ways discussed in open court. Eddie decided Kennedy's duplicity was "beyond my earthly powers" to comprehend and determined the best thing to do was to dismiss the incident as "one of those things in which shrewd business had triumphed over my credulity" and move on.

Swanson wasn't much comfort. She was wrapped up in her own world and Goulding had little patience for temperament in others or idleness in himself. It was obvious he couldn't continue at Pathé and when the studio announced that he wouldn't direct *Queen Kelly* because he didn't want "his individuality impaired," he privately told Gloria, "To hell with it." He took himself and his script to Paramount.

Within a matter of weeks, both her husband and her director had publicly left her. Gloria was more dependent than ever on Joe Kennedy.

# CHAPTER 23

# "Things Are Bad Enough Here"

## (LATE 1929–EARLY 1930)

*A*t home on Rodeo Drive, Kennedy received daily cables from Ted O'Leary reporting *The Trespasser*'s box office take. After a month and a half at the Rialto, the film had grossed more than $250,000 and it was Al Lichtman, the United Artists executive who had predicted disaster with that title, who reported that *The Trespasser* had broken all UA records. The New York totals were spurred by the fact that screenings began at 10:15 and played continuously through 1:30 in the morning with an extra show on Saturdays. Still, at 50 cents for most tickets, a quarter of a million dollars was an incredible achievement.

Kennedy had put the word out that *Queen Kelly* required only "a couple of dialogue sequences" to be finished, but priority was being given to releasing and promoting *The Trespasser.* Now he had Charlie Sullivan review the *Queen Kelly* books to reduce the amount of money allocated to the film; the last thing they wanted was for it to publicly go over a million dollars. With a little shifting, Sullivan decided that almost $100,000 could be allocated as advances on *The Trespasser* and he came up with an "actual cost" of $648,611 for *Queen Kelly* to date. Charlie was also assigned to finalize the agreement with Stroheim to give him back the African portion of the story. Derr suggested the negotiations include the right to use his name on the credits of *Queen Kelly,* whatever version they ended up releasing. And once again, requests were sent to the Pathé newsreel division to find shots of Africa.

Efforts were underway to reunite the cast. Swanson was right there, ready and waiting, and she signed another release to her own company stating that the $50,000 she had received for the first version was all she was going to get. Seena Owen was put on half salary until filming began. Walter Byron remained under contract to Sam Goldwyn until November 10, but gave Charlie Sullivan his assurance he would be available then.

The contracts were testimony to the gang's omnipresent control. Seena Owen's was signed by Sullivan as vice president of Gloria Productions and then when it was time to renew their agreement to lease studio space at Pathé, Sullivan signed as a vice president of Pathé, and Gloria Productions was represented by its new, on-paper president, Kennedy's old friend Chris Dunphy, who had left hotel management and was now working on Wall Street.

The script for *Queen Kelly* had been revised yet again, this time by Laura Hope Crews. The film's sets, which had been struck, re-created, and then dismantled again, had since been altered for use in other films. Now they were reconstructed as best as possible, with the studio charging Gloria Productions for all the work. Pathé had been dark for a month when the *Queen Kelly* cast and crew came back together on the otherwise empty lot on December 9, this time under the direction of Richard Boleslawsky.

The Polish-born Boleslawsky had spent fifteen years with the Moscow Art Theater before coming to New York in 1920. He had only just arrived in Hollywood, yet another stage director experienced with actors who spoke their lines, but who had never made a movie before.

On the second day of filming, Kennedy was optimistic that the end was in sight when he received a call informing him of a catastrophic fire at Pathé's Manhattan studio.

Still struggling to bring efficiency to their sound operation in Culver City, they were leasing a studio at the corner of Park Avenue and 134th Street to produce short sound films. Pathé had bought the building in 1915, converting it from a saloon and dance hall into a movie studio, a relatively easy transition since there were already dressing rooms upstairs and a large stage below. Pearl White filmed some of her serials there, but the studio had been sold and used by many others since then and, at times, stood dormant. New York had emerged as a hub of sound film activity in part because it provided easy access to performers who could appear before the cameras during the day and on stage at night. Pathé had been operating there for over a month and were just beginning to turn out a film a week.

At 9:30 on the morning of Tuesday, December 10, a full panoply of cast and crew gathered to film a musical number for *The Black and White Revue* under the direction of Harry Delmar. Upstairs, the studio manager, Henry Lalley, and John Flinn, a Pathé vice president inherited in the merger with Producers Distributing and now in charge of all short sound films, were in their offices. Costumed chorus girls were readying in their dressing rooms or sitting in small groups at the top of the stairs, waiting for their call. Musicians were warming up as electricians, cinematographers, and the lighting men completed their checks.

From his perch on the upstairs railing, an electrician thought he saw one of the large arc lights, located above the cameras and surrounded by reflectors, "spit a glowing crumb of carbon" and land on the stage below. Just the day before, one of the dancers' feather headdresses had caught on fire as it grazed a scorching incandescent light, but a quick-thinking crew member had pulled it off her head and stamped out the fire. This time, however, the thick black velvet drapes that served as a sound-muffling backdrop touched the lights and in a few seconds were in flames. Two crew members tugged at the drapes in a futile attempt to limit the fire, but it quickly spread to the props and crates stockpiled behind them and to the stage itself. Calls of "everyone downstairs" were mistaken to mean it was time to go before the cameras so a few of the young women were in no hurry until they smelled the fire. Then there was a rush for the flight of stairs, with everyone being pushed by those behind them.

The wardrobe mistress escaped by jumping from a rear window and into the alley below. The janitor in the basement climbed up and out of the coal chute to scramble to safety. On the phone at his desk, John Flinn smelled the smoke and started to leave the office when his secretary, Frances Walsh, stood up and then collapsed. Flinn picked her up in his arms and headed to the stairs; seeing the flames, he returned to his office and scrambled out the window to the second-story ledge, where they were rescued by the firemen who were arriving in droves. Henry Lalley escaped the same way, but four chorus girls and six assorted electricians, makeup men, and crew members didn't make it out of the building in time. Most of the bodies were found piled on top of each other at the bottom of the stairs, just yards from the main doorway. A dozen others were injured and several were hospitalized with burns and broken bones.

Front-page stories the next day featured pictures of scared, scantily costumed young women huddled outside the burning building. As questions and accusations began to swirl, Flinn and Lalley were arrested on the charge of "technical manslaughter in the second degree," held, and then released on $15,000 bail. Flinn spent "a sleepless week," for after going through the booking process, he joined Pat Scollard criss-crossing the city, to attend the funerals of the victims.

From Culver City, Kennedy and Derr were in "constant touch" with New York and arrangements were immediately made to move production to RCA's Gramercy studios. From his desk at Pathé's main office, Terry Ramsaye told Denn that both Flinn and Lalley "conspicuously kept their heads and maintained their poise" and Scollard's "sober judgment and firm hand have been very much in evidence." They had shown "decided discretion in handling as painful and complex a situation as I have ever seen arise."

"Discretion" was an understatement for they needed to remove hundreds of thousands of feet of film from a studio where the law required a permit for storing over five thousand feet. While the notoriously flammable film did not play a part in the fire, the 45th Street headquarters might well be checked next so Ramsaye reported "with respect to incendiary activities, this building is sweet and pure," as he had supervised the removal of "approximately 1,000,000 feet of film."

New York newspapers were soon clamoring for new fire safety regulations. Hearst's papers were in the forefront of a "savage campaign against Pathé" as they accused the company of "spiriting away" thousands of feet of film on the night of the fire. Will Hays stepped in and tried to quiet the furor, but by the end of the week everyone from Mayor Jimmy Walker, the district attorney, the fire commissioner, and on down was falling over one another to claim the mantle of outraged reformer.

The studio had been served with notices to install a sprinkler system in 1919 and again in May of 1929, but the order had been appealed. Kennedy's own man, Steve Fitzgibbon, had paid $500 to the Croker Fire Prevention Engineering Company to grease the wheels with the promise of another $500 when the appeal was granted. Edward Croker was the city's former fire chief who had set himself up in a business that sounds very much like a protection racket, yet he was the tip of the iceberg in the corruption-riddled New York of the late 1920s.

In spite of the fact that Kennedy was chairman of the board of Pathé, his name rarely appeared in connection with the fire or the company in the literally hundreds of articles on the disaster and its repercussions. He remained in California where by the third day of Boleslawsky's attempt at filming Queen Kelly, it was all too obvious that the film could not be rescued with a combination of retakes and inserts. Stroheim's version was so lush and detailed, so intricately lit that as enthusiastic as the handsome, blond Boleslawsky was, his results were blatantly amateur in contrast. Once again, production was suspended. The only beneficiary of the aborted attempt was Pathé because the studio billed Gloria Productions for the sound and electrical equipment and prop construction as well as the salaries of those such as Boleslawsky they had under contract.

Kennedy could no longer hide the delays from United Artists. In mid-December, after a year of advertising and selling, UA formally notified exhibitors that "because of the failure of the producer to deliver" *Queen Kelly,* they were canceling their contracts. Instead of giving Joe pause, the announcement reinvigorated his determination to finish the film, and everyone seemed to have ideas on what to do next.

Even Ted O'Leary put in his two cents, suggesting "some 'slap-stick' comedy be written into the story." While Kennedy had come to the conclusion that the film had "a gypsy curse" on it, he now decided to turn it into a "musical operetta." He sent Henri to Vienna to sign Franz Lehár, the composer of *The Merry Widow,* to write a "great waltz as the big feature" of the film. The exclusive contract for the "Queen Kelly Waltz" cost Gloria Productions another $60,000, but Joe made the most of the announcement, giving the impression he was moving forward.

On December 19, 1929, Boleslawsky handed Kennedy "a little Christmas present," a new four-page treatment for yet another version of *Queen Kelly.* This one took place entirely in the German kingdom and opened with the Queen entering the city with bands playing as Kelly, a small child, is being deposited by her father at what is now a "convent Academy." Cut to fifteen years later when Kelly, still at the convent and now the beautiful Gloria Swanson, is teaching the other girls to sing songs "of love and future happiness," instead of the dull songs they learn in school. This time the Prince meets Kelly because he is inspired by her glorious singing to look over the academy wall. Stroheim's scenes of the Queen in the palace discovering Kelly and the Prince and the whipping sequence that followed would still be used, but when the Queen announces that she will marry the Prince it is proclaimed throughout town on placards, which Kelly histrionically tears down. The Prince sneaks out of the palace, takes Kelly from the convent, and they have a love scene in the forest before the Prince is arrested. Here the story took a dramatic shift with the cruel Queen revealed to be an impostor and, on Kelly's father's deathbed, it is discovered that Kelly is the rightful heir to the throne. The crowds rush the prison, free the Prince, and the Queen escapes "like a beaten dog." As the people sing their national anthem, the Prince and Kelly reunite.

As "Boley" put it, "it was a conventional story," yet it was "the cheapest solution" and "saves all that can be saved" from the original production. It actually was the first treatment that gave Gloria a three-dimensional character with both a backbone and a backstory. Its structure also provided the basis for a full-fledged musical.

Boleslawsky was excited and "feeling in a fighting spirit" with his new storyline, but what he didn't realize was that at that moment Joe was trying to replace him with MGM's Sam Wood. Laura Crews had already supplied Wood with the various scripts. Joe and Gloria agreed that he was their new savior and the director was willing to take it on if they made the necessary arrangements with his studio. That set the wheels in motion and, learning that Irving Thalberg was in New York, Pat Scollard called him at the Sherry-Netherland. Missing him, he sent a telegram, dictated by Sullivan and signed with Kennedy's name, pleading for Wood as "a personal favor" because "I have to finish Queen Kelly period." It included the promise that the director's work would be completed within the next six weeks. To underscore the seriousness of the request, Swanson left a message for Thalberg as well.

When at last Scollard reached him by phone, Thalberg said he couldn't make a decision before knowing what plans "the coast" had for Wood, but promised to get back to him soon. Yet almost a month passed and E. B. Derr was still sitting by his phone to confirm an appointment. The production chief, long back in California, always seemed to be "in conference."

The call finally came on January 8 and Derr went over to MGM to meet with Thalberg. The two men expanded these negotiations to include the possibility of loaning Gloria to MGM; Derr wanted $300,000 for that, but Thalberg thought that was too high. And he claimed he couldn't commit because "the director has complete authority on everything" including casting. Derr knew better, but admired the way Thalberg "played poker." The production chief agreed to loan Sam Wood "at cost," but not until April 15 and Kennedy wanted to start shooting within the next week or two. In the end, they agreed to talk again the next day.

Derr had to report to Kennedy that he had tried, but to keep the Queen Kelly cast on salary for three more months while waiting for Wood to be available was ridiculous. He told him that "if it were my money and my picture," he would trust the directing to Russell Mack, who was already on Pathé's payroll. And whatever Joe decided, he shouldn't reduce his price on loaning Swanson to under $250,000.

Nothing more was heard from Thalberg so Gloria stayed put and Joe reached out to her old friend Allan Dwan to salvage Queen Kelly. The three of them spent several hours reviewing the most recent versions, but in the end Dwan candidly told Kennedy, "I can't quite get the story line. It's either the story of a nun who turned whore or a whore who turned nun and I can't figure out which it is. But it's one or the other and in any case, it stinks."

In addition to the stress surrounding Queen Kelly, Gloria's emotions were strained by her son's illness that December. Both children had contracted strep throat, potentially life-threatening in those pre-penicillin days, but in the end only Brother was hospitalized to have his swollen glands removed. Yet Gloria had everything else taken care of for her, including her Christmas shopping. Her secretary bolted from toy store to toy store looking in vain for the billiards game she wanted to send to the Kennedy children; she eventually settled on a "large horse game, quite expensive, but suitable for all six children." For the youngest, she sent Bobby a toy ambulance and a doll for baby Jean.

Ted O'Leary was in charge of Swanson's professional gifts and arranged to send gold pencils to all the United Artists branch managers and other employees, engraved with their initials followed by "from Gloria Swanson." He then sent a sample to Gloria so when she received letters of thanks, she would know why.

It was typical of the gang to take care of each other. They had become so close-knit that while they kidded each other mercilessly, they were always there for each other, be it to recommend insurance brokers or bankers, to loan each other money or take care of gift giving. Scollard, on the East Coast, took responsibility for getting holiday flowers and candy to the families of the other men and handled their Christmas presents for the office personnel.

Joe turned to Scollard and Ted O'Leary to arrange for presents for Rose and the family, but Derr was in charge of purchasing the "personal gifts" given out under Kennedy's name to the West Coast press and studio employees and he was allocated $5,000 for the largesse.

It was time to put an eye to Pathé's end-of-the-year books and so more cuts were made. Reaching for a positive spin, they announced that Pathé "reduces to enlarge," with plans to "make fewer, but more elaborate productions." Contracts were reviewed and a few actors, such as Ann Harding and Helen Twelvetrees, had theirs extended—but a half dozen others were released. Among them were Goulding protégée Carole Lombard and Alan Hale, who chose not to have his weekly guarantee cut from fifty-two to forty weeks a year.

Kennedy was back east in time for Christmas with the family, but this year it was Rose who went to Palm Beach. Joe stayed in New York and was there on January 6 for the Pathé board meeting held in Walker's office. They "discussed at some length the business outlook," but no mention was made in the minutes of the fire the month before. On the same day, prosecutors were gathering a few blocks away to begin giving evidence into the "technical homicide allegations" against John Flinn and Lalley.

There was a cloak of solemnity if not outright depression in Kennedy's end-of-the-year communications. While he told Henri that in spite of *Queen Kelly,* the Pathé fire, and "various and sundry other items, it is still a great life," Joe's frustration was growing over things, large and small, not going at all smoothly. As he put it to Bob Kane in Paris, "Things are bad enough here now without having trouble over there."

But there was "trouble over there" and the plans to make films in Europe had become yet another black hole draining funds. Kane blamed everyone else, but after reading the balance sheets, Pat Scollard decided that "the whole thing is a bust and the sooner we close it up the better." Yet that was just one of the panoply of questions Kennedy was facing. It was time for some serious thinking, so in sharp contrast to his usual annual schedule, Kennedy headed to the Ritz-Carlton in Boston for a few days before spending a week alone in the middle of January at Hyannisport.

The film business wasn't fun anymore. It had been exciting when he was layering company upon company and cutting deals left and right. *The Trespasser*'s premieres had been invigorating; he loved being a show-man. But since then, *Queen Kelly* had stopped and started and stopped again and the Pathé fire was devastating. The cost of transitioning to sound combined with their lack of theaters made it a struggle to keep Pathé above water. Other smaller studios were laboring as well, but what was he doing spending time just buying time? Looking ahead had always been his forte and what he saw was not encouraging.

The industry had changed dramatically over the past year. The upheaval caused by the conversion to sound and the spate of mergers needed time to shake out. He had been the leading advocate of those changes, but since selling FBO and K-A-O, he had been on a path of steadily reduced influence.

Joe knew that for his talent to prosper, opportunities had to be there. That simply wasn't true anymore. There had been more than a hundred film companies operating when he had entered the business and now, a decade later, there were only a handful of successful studios. If he wasn't willing to wait around as a second-rate player, the only alternative was to lay the groundwork to leave the business entirely. He had already made a small fortune, but he was determined to make even more on his way out.

Once that decision was made, the only major question left was what to do about Gloria. Living his divided personal life had been one thing when they were both married to others, but their relationship was bound to change now that Gloria's marriage was headed to the divorce court.

The names of Swanson and Kennedy entwined on marquees was heady stuff. Marrying the mayor's daughter was good by Boston standards, but the queen of the movies was fuel for international acclaim. There were the children to consider, but he was used to seeing them only intermittently and staying on top of their activities from afar. His two oldest sons were already at boarding schools. As his son John described it later in life when asked why the Kennedy children "had turned out so well" compared with those of the Roosevelts and the Churchills, "Well, no one can say that it was due to my mother. It was due to my father. He wasn't around as much as some fathers, but when he was around, he made his children feel that they were the most important things in the world."

That impact could continue to be felt whether Joe lived in the same house with Rose or not, but his role as patriarch was a crucial part of his own identity. And then there was the tremendous importance of the family in the abstract. His image as a family man had been an inestimable boost to his public persona.

As much as he loved the spotlight, he knew that if he was at Gloria's side, he would always be in her shadow. Hollywood was her world, not his. No matter how many companies he ran or how powerful he became, it was Swanson whose every move was followed by local reporters. For all he had accomplished, for all the column inches his stories took up in the trades, Joe Kennedy was never mentioned in the society columns. In Hollywood, Joe was still the outsider and Gloria was one of them. If he became her fourth husband, the balance of power in their partnership would shift to her. That he could never tolerate.

Physically he had paid a heavy price for the way he had been living for the past several years. The first time he had been out with Gloria, he had fumbled to find a light for her cigarette. He had picked up not only a lighter but a smoking habit as well. He was more than twenty pounds underweight and the ulcers that intermittently plagued him were back again. Yet there was no way he was going to see the Glendale nutritionist Swanson swore by. She had even gone so far as to suggest Dr. Henry Bieler might help his daughter Rosemary's slowness and that resulted in one of the few times she saw the full force of Kennedy's temper directed at her. He was quick to return to his usual solicitous self and Gloria never knew if he had been upset at her suggestion or at his frustration over Rosemary. It didn't matter. She still believed he adored her and would do anything for her.

BY EARLY FEBRUARY OF 1930, Joe was back in Los Angeles in time to see four Pathé films going into production. He was planning on staying for two months, but he turned over almost all decisions to E. B. Derr. More than ever Kennedy was delegating authority to the gang, but he did step in when Constance Bennett returned to Hollywood from her Paris fling with Henri. Joe thought it best just to keep her off the Pathé lot and arrangements were made to loan her to Warner Bros. at $5,000 a week and follow that with a film at Fox. He could keep the peace and make a profit at the same time.

Elisha Walker came to San Francisco in early March to meet with A. P. Giannini, who offered him the presidency of his Transamerica, now a billion-dollar company that included Bank of America and Bankamerica-Blair, created when Walker's company became the securities affiliate of Bank of America the year before. Giannini was turning sixty and planned to remain on the board but he wanted Walker to take over active management of the company. Walker grabbed the opportunity and headed to Los Angeles where Kennedy hosted dinners for him, and the two men went behind closed doors for one-on-one meetings. It had been over two years since Walker had brought Kennedy into Pathé, and since then Joe had not made any major moves without Walker's support and counsel.

To Walker's mind, between Pathé and RKO, he still had too much money tied up in movies. Back in early 1928 they had talked of getting Pathé in position to be sold, and at best, it had been treading water since then. Others had told Walker they believed Pathé was in a tenuous state because Kennedy had essentially been "absent" from the company and "always given Swanson pictures precedence over Pathe's interests." Walker knew it was much more complicated than that. He had no illusions about Kennedy, but he thought he had a brilliant business mind. While others found Walker to be "a cold fish," he and Joe spoke the same language. He assured Kennedy that he wanted them to continue to work together, but it was time to get out of the film business.

John Murdock agreed. He was looking at his seventieth birthday and the idea of running around to create a new theater chain had lost its luster. Leave that to the young and the hungry. His fortune was secure with the sale of his K-A-O/RKO shares and he had a beautiful house in Beverly Hills along with a wife, a son, and a daughter he wanted to spend more time with.

One of the reasons Kennedy and Murdock had cooled on the idea of their own theater chain was that even with Walker's backing, the prices were proving prohibitive. They could pick up smaller theaters in less populous regions, but almost all the movie palaces in the big cities were already claimed by other studios. One of the last of the major independent theater owners was Alexander Pantages, a vaudeville magnate with all the self-righteousness of Ed Albee, but without his pious veneer. A Greek émigré who claimed never to have learned to read or write English and yet built a multimillion-dollar fortune over twenty years in vaudeville, Pantages had earned a reputation for double dealing, taking kickbacks, pennypinching, and breaking contracts. More complaints were filed against him than any other circuit owner. His shows, however, continued to do blockbuster business in part because he showed "a decided preference for cheap girl flash acts."

Pantages had switched from live performers to a preponderance of films in his theaters in the summer of 1927, so Kennedy did not have to convince him of the power of the movies when they first met in early 1928. Yet the impresario proved to be contrary at best, appearing amicable one minute and then claiming he already had an offer of $3 million just for his Los Angeles theater. Even his theater in small-town Fresno had cost over a million to build. Once Kennedy took over K-A-O he discontinued their discussions, but he was back a year later when he and Murdock were looking to buy.

There had been spates of interest in Pantages's holdings from Fox and others, but he had yet to sell. He owned or had leaseholds on twenty-six theaters in "practically every key city in the West." Joe found him an obstinate customer, holding meetings and then claiming, via the trades, that "the circuit is not for sale." Back and forth they went during the early months of 1929, arguing over a price tag estimated between $15 and $20 million.

Alexander Pantages

By the time Kennedy decided against moving ahead with his own chain, RKO was interested in the Pantages houses and they soon shared Joe's frustration. From March through August, there were half a dozen different offers on the table, which Pantages would then pull; in between, he was in talks with other potential buyers. When he finally signed on the bottom line, it was for RKO to buy six of his largest theaters, with Warner Bros. purchasing the San Francisco and Fresno houses. Pantages's plan was to keep the rest for his sons to manage when he ran into "a very nasty mess" that would haunt him for the rest of his life and tie his name to Joe Kennedy's until this day.

A month after the sales had been finalized, Pantages was arrested in his Los Angeles office on Friday, August 9, 1929, by policemen "responding to the screams" of Eunice Pringle, a seventeen-year-old dancer reportedly in his office seeking work. Pantages was charged with "criminal assault," spent the night in jail, and then was released after posting $25,000 bail. Headlines were soon reporting every possible scenario from a violent rape to a total frame-up.

Eunice Pringle, age seventeen

Los Angeles District Attorney Buron Fitts personally argued the case and over twenty-five witnesses testified, including an emotionally distraught Pringle. In the process, several of Pantages's witnesses were charged with perjury, with one admitting that the impresario had promised "no financial worries" for life if he lied for him. The sixty-two-year-old Pantages was convicted and sentenced to up to fifty years in San Quentin. After trying and failing to gain a release on medical grounds, Pantages hired the attorney Jerry Giesler who arranged for a new trial and, after dragging Pringle's reputation through the dirt, an acquittal.

Kennedy's off-and-on meetings with Pantages had been reported throughout 1928 and into early 1929, but several decades passed before the men's names were bound together in *Hollywood Babylon II*. Kenneth Anger reported that Kennedy had bribed Pringle to frame Pantages in

Eunice Pringle, age eighty

order to destroy the man and then buy his theaters for a song. The plot had been revealed, the story went, in Pringle's "deathbed confession" as she lay suffering from a "suspicious illness" in 1933.

A series of books and articles followed Anger's opus, each embroidering the tale: Kennedy had paid Pringle $10,000 and promised her a movie career, District Attorney Fitts was also in on the scheme, and poison was suspected in her death. One book went so far as to simply state "It had all been Joe Kennedy's idea." By the time Ronald Kessler wrote *The Sins of the Father* in 1996, he had Pringle as "violently ill and red in color, a sign of cyanide poisoning" on the night she died in 1933. Kessler asked, "did Joe have Pringle poisoned to silence her?"

He answered by saying the charge "rings true" because "no autopsy was conducted."

No autopsy was conducted for the same reason there was neither cyanide nor a deathbed confession: Eunice Pringle did not die in 1933. After the trial, she became an executive secretary, moved to San Diego, married, and gave birth to a daughter. Pringle died in 1996 of natural causes at the age of eighty-four. Joe Kennedy may have done some despicable things in his life, but bribing and murdering Eunice Pringle was not one of them.

ALL THIS WAS FAR into the future and Kennedy's reputation was still sterling as he continued to search for stories for Swanson to film. He asked Derr to look into the possibility of "a golf story" for her, evidently forgetting her mishaps when she tried to play tennis. He bought "the world sound motion picture rights" to the book *Purple and Linen* and then presented Gloria, fait accompli, with a bound script he had commissioned "just for her" entitled *What a Widow.* The only problem was, according to Swanson, "it was absolutely terrible." Allan Dwan had agreed to direct her next film and together they ran the script past several writers including James Seymour. The former publicity man from Harvard whom Joe had brought out to Hollywood after his lecture series was now under contract as a Pathé writer at $350 a week.

Kennedy continued to be nothing but optimistic about *What a Widow* and "assumed personal charge" of the production, approving the cast and monitoring the changes Gloria, Allan Dwan, and the writers were making in the script. Joe called in the press to announce they had filmed a dress rehearsal as a unique and experimental method for working out problems before going into production. The film did undergo changes as a result; Lew Cody replaced Ian Keith in one of the key roles and the plot and dialogue were modified as well. But the flurry of attention on *What a Widow* was also a guise for Kennedy to quietly release a statement saying that work on *Queen Kelly* "will not be resumed." After all the column inches that had been devoted to the saga over the course of two years, a short item in *Variety* reported it had been "scrapped" in spite of the estimated $800,000 spent to date. Settlements were made with the actors who remained under contract, and when pushed, Joe implied that the problem was that his plan to make it into an operetta was just "too much music, too soon" for Gloria.

It was to be the last contact Kennedy had with the press during his California stay. He had made his arrangements with Walker, finally bitten the bullet on *Queen Kelly,* and prepared to leave town. After charging Pathé almost $10,000 in expenses for their recent stay, Joe and Eddie Moore boarded the train on the morning of April 11, 1930. Only a few people knew that this time they were leaving for good. The Rodeo house lease was allowed to lapse and Moore cabled Derr from Arizona requesting that the two suitcases and anything else they had left behind be sent to them in New York.

# CHAPTER 24

# "A Good Trick If You Can Do It"

## (SPRING 1930)

*K*ennedy had been back in New York for several weeks when a one-page, three-paragraph press release with no headline went out on Pathé's rooster stationery.

"The Pathe Exchange, Inc. announces the retirement of Mr. Joseph P. Kennedy from active management of the company," the first sentence read. "Mr. Kennedy will, however, remain as Chairman of the Board of Directors." It went on to claim that the "marked improvement" of Pathé under Kennedy allowed him to turn the "active management" over to E. B. Derr on the West Coast and Pat Scollard in New York. Keeping his future vague, the release concluded by noting that Kennedy had come to Pathé "at the request of Elisha Walker" and, "after a brief vacation," would continue his association with Mr. Walker.

For over a year, there had been inklings in the press that Kennedy might leave "show business" for banking. As early as January of 1929, it was rumored he had been offered the presidency of a new bank as well as receiving "invitations" to join Blair and Company or rejoin Hayden, Stone. However, there was really no question where he would go next. Being with Walker gave Kennedy a proven financial backer and put an honorable and admirable face on his departure from Hollywood.

As if on cue, a variety of newspapers and the trades ran summations of Kennedy's "miraculous" accomplishments. Several gave his business acumen an aura of philanthropy by claiming he had never billed Pathé for his expenses. Rumors of a possible sale to RKO, Warner Bros., or Fox were bandied about, but it was reiterated that Pathé was not planning any mergers or changes in policies or personnel. No one believed that Kennedy's "retirement" meant the end of his activities. As one report put it, "Lon Chaney, 'the man of many faces,' is a piker compared with Joseph Kennedy, the man of many plans."

As always, Joe took the time to send personal letters of appreciation to reporters and editors who were particularly admiring such as Sime Silverman of *Variety,* thanking him for being a "loyal friend and confidant" as well as his "many, many kindnesses during my stay in the business."

As soon as the release went out, Kennedy headed for White Sulphur Springs in West Virginia to spend several weeks putting on some weight and regaining the strength he now believed Hollywood had sapped out of him. His secretary informed anyone trying to find out more that Mr. Kennedy was on "an extended vacation" and she didn't know when he would return. Soon, however, Elisha Walker joined him in West Virginia and together they went over their plans for Transamerica and, most immediately, the Pathé board meeting the first week of June.

Just before Kennedy had joined Pathé in early 1928, the company had raised $800,000 by selling what was called "8 percent stock" because it was supposed to pay dividends at the rate of 8 percent a year. However, to hold on to all available cash, they had not paid dividends for two years, the entire time Joe had been in charge, and that opened the board to a new vulnerability. The stockholders had no standing unless they failed to receive dividends for eight quarters in a row; that now being the case, disgruntled shareholders went into action.

Leading the charge against Kennedy was Richard Rowland, the former head of First National Studios who had "retired" when Kennedy took over. Rowland, who did not own any Pathé stock himself, was fronting for a group of bankers, stockbrokers, and shareholders concerned they would never see their investment returned. Rowland's dethroning was remembered and he was billed as an experienced film man ready to "bound back into the picture business."

Rowland was listed as "Chairman of the Pathé Preferred Stockholders Protective Committee" in the newspaper ads urging shareholders to join in their right to elect a new board. However, they stumbled from the beginning, claiming in their first letter that Kennedy had resigned as president and Murdock had resigned as chairman of the board, offices neither of them held in the first place. When the trades and many newspapers, including *The New York Times,* simply reprinted their release in quotation marks, including the errors, it gave Kennedy an opportunity to demand retractions and set the record, as he saw it, straight. Since neither Rowland nor the other three names listed in the leadership were stockholders and they were not ready to name the slate of officers they were proposing, it was easy to cast doubts upon their plans. The Protective Committee quickly became "the alleged committee" and the "so-called committee" and the press dismissed them as "disgruntled" and "antagonistic." *The Wall Street Journal* reiterated its confidence in Kennedy.

While the Protective Committee were spinning their wheels explaining themselves, Kennedy and his group were buying up available stock and gathering proxies. They were soon confident they would go into the board meeting holding control of at least 70 percent of the stock. Joe wasn't overtly worried, but the Protective Committee was a public thorn in his side.

Over 250 people poured into the Pathé offices on 45th Street in the early afternoon of Monday, June 9, 1930. Pat Scollard stepped forward with the gavel to call the meeting to order at 2:30 and, after the reading of the minutes of the last two board meetings, the business of the day was addressed. Two different slates of directors were put forward, one by the Rowland faction, the other by the current board. In spite of the impressive number of stockholders who were present in the room and the public attempts to rally support, the Protective Committee's slate received only 991 votes to 5,960 for Kennedy's. Once it was clear how the numbers fell, there was a call for a vote of confidence in the current management. This brought forth long speeches from the opposition, but to no avail. Not only did the vote of confidence pass, but it was followed by a motion "that all of the acts of the directors and officers for the past year be approved and ratified." That too was carried. The meeting would last until almost seven that night, but in the end, Kennedy not only survived, he triumphed.

The Protective Committee's "sorry showing" was reported so as to discourage anyone else from questioning the powers that be. Kennedy's "big majority" brought more public praise for his handling of the situation and letters of congratulation poured in, including one from Irving Rossheim, Richard Rowland's old boss at First National.

On Wednesday, less than forty-eight hours after the stockholders meeting, the new Pathé board quietly met in Walker's office at 44 Wall Street and elected officers: Kennedy was reelected chairman, Derr replaced Murdock as president, Pat Scollard was vice president, and longtime Pathé attorney Lewis Innerarity was elected secretary. Arthur Poole was treasurer, and Tom Delehanty, who had been with Kennedy longer than anyone but Eddie Moore, was elected assistant treasurer and assistant secretary. With Joe's financial allies Elisha Walker and Jeremiah Milbank among the remaining dozen board members, his control of Pathé was tighter than ever.

As was his habit, Guy Currier had spent part of the winter at his villa in Fiesole, Italy, and returned to Boston assuming he would be able to finalize the agreement, made the previous spring, to buy Joe out of the Gower Street Company. Contact between the men had dropped to a bare minimum. The mandated annual corporate meeting had been held in October and the three board members, Guy Currier, Joe Kennedy, and Ted Streibert, were reelected, but that could be done in absentia. Whether or not Currier knew it, Kennedy had made their sale agreement moot by having his attorney Benjamin DeWitt prepare an agreement between Joe and RKO that half of all the moneys still owed to Gower Street would go directly to Kennedy as of January 10, 1930. What Currier did learn when he returned from Italy was that Cinema Credits Corporation had been stripped of its assets.

While there were still several hundred thousand dollars' worth of stocks and bonds held under Gower Street, Cinema Credits housed the original $500,000 and another $100,000-plus that had accumulated through interest and investments. Cinema Credits had been created to finance FBO films and that need had dissolved with the sale of FBO. The investors had continued to receive their quarterly dividend checks through March of 1929 and now Currier thought it was time to return the investments. According to his family, Currier was furious and mortified when he discovered the money was no longer there because his primary concern was for the friends who had invested with his assurances. He had trusted his own instincts and taken a chance on Kennedy when no one else of his stature was willing to and he had put his own money and reputation on the line for him. The genuine shock Currier suffered and his desperate attempts to repay his friends out of his own money took a physical toll. He was literally made ill from what he saw as blatant treachery. Exhausted and weak, Currier suffered a heart attack, and at his doctor's insistence, went to his summer home in Peterborough, New Hampshire. It was there on the morning of June 21, 1930, he suffered a fatal heart attack at the age of sixty-two.

A dozen prominent Bostonians were honorary pallbearers including Currier's close friends and fellow investors Louis Kirstein, Colonel Tarafa, and Frederick Prince. Currier was praised for his intelligence, dignity, and contributions to his community in the lengthy and laudatory obituaries. Nowhere was Joe Kennedy's name mentioned.

He was on the East Coast and available to attend Currier's funeral if he had wanted to or been welcome, but for the Currier family, his five children, and their children, Kennedy's name became synonymous with

Guy Currier months before his death in 1930

betrayal. To them, Kennedy's actions were the cause of the illness that had felled their father and grandfather, just as Fred Thomson's descendants always believed that Kennedy had been responsible for Fred losing his will to live. Two very different families on opposite coasts, but both kept their burning hatred of Kennedy within their family circle for years.

KENNEDY TOLD REPORTERS who were still following his activities that he planned to spend his summer in Hyannisport with his family, but he shuttled in and out of New York, occasionally flying in to the Cape for a day or two. He rarely attended Pathé board meetings, but the minutes came to him for his approval and he handled other investments for Transamerica, including notes held on Fox Film Corporation.

The May press release that had announced Kennedy's departure from "active management" of Pathé also contained a one-sentence middle paragraph reading "Gloria Productions, Inc., also announces Mr. Kennedy's retirement from the active management of that company."

If others had been suspecting that Joe was ready to make a move, Gloria later claimed it came as a complete surprise to her. The version she told in her autobiography was that she caught him using Gloria Productions money for his own aggrandizement and when she called him on it, he got furious and left town. Once again, her facts were right, but the timing was off. She would be shocked to learn how much the relationship had cost her, but that would come later. Initially, the transition of the finances was relatively seamless. Her accountant, Irving Wakoff, rose to be both treasurer and vice president of Gloria Productions and although the communications between Sullivan, Scollard, and Wakoff were less frequent, they continued to flow. Kennedy maintained his control and it was reinforced by the fact that if there were papers to sign, they were passed to Chris Dunphy as president of Gloria Productions.

Swanson was immersed in filming *What a Widow* at Pathé where the Kennedy-Swanson split was the talk of the lot. Who had left whom? Had Kennedy given her special breaks to Pathé's detriment? "Gossip and hearsay" were rampant, reported Ed Tambert of the studio accounting office, "and some of the remarks overheard were to the effect that concessions were being allowed to Gloria at the expense of Pathe." Because of it, Tambert, "on my own initiative," reviewed all the Gloria Productions invoices. He obviously didn't know that the studio manager, William Sistrom, had already gone over all of the bills and removed duplications, corrected errors, and reduced some of the more outlandish charges.

Now Tambert reversed all of those credits and put together a bill that included everything ever charged to Swanson, whether accurate or not. Going to work on his project just after Joe's "retirement" was announced, Tambert was clearly trying to ingratiate himself with the company even though, as he stated to Sullivan in passing the invoices to him, he was "not familiar with the exact services rendered" and was not "in a position to pass on the merits" of the charges.

Sullivan, however, was in a position to judge the "merits" of the invoices; he had to know how much Pathé had already made off of Swanson. Still, the pressure was on to show a profit and Sullivan figured billing Tambert's invoices to Gloria would be "a good trick if you can do it." Using some discretion, Sullivan instructed Tambert to remove the expenses of "Mr. Kennedy and his staff" for half a dozen California stays since those were "entirely in the interest of Pathé." (Sullivan didn't mention that Pathé had already reimbursed Kennedy for all those expenses or that Gloria Productions had paid him an additional $25,000 for "executive overhead.") With that one caveat, Sullivan gave his approval to send the invoices to Wakoff for payment.

Swanson and her company had hardly been given a free ride. As Bill Sistrom put it, "the studio always gets the best of it" when outside producers work out of a studio and Gloria Productions had been a "life saver" to Pathé, providing a cash flow when no one else was working. He estimated that Pathé had made a clear profit of $150,000 from Gloria Productions before Tambert's billing of an additional $150,000.

The contract between Gloria Productions and Pathé called for a payment of $10,000 per film, but that was just the tip of the iceberg. During the time Swanson had been working on *Queen Kelly, The Trespasser,* and now *What a Widow,* at least $650,000 had gone through her books and into the studio's accounts. Directors, editors, and crew members under contract to Pathé had been "loaned," often with a 10 percent overhead added to their salary. For instance, Eddie Goulding's entire Pathé salary for five months had been reimbursed by Gloria even though he was working on many other Pathé films besides *The Trespasser* during that time. She had paid over $200,000 for construction of sets that Pathé would strike and use again.

Where the padded costs really added up was in the rental fees for the recording studios. Gloria Productions was billed $700 a day and $400 a night for using facilities that actually cost Pathé $200 every twenty-four hours to run. These figures were particularly onerous for *The Trespasser* since Goulding's practice of working from eleven until seven or eight in the evening allowed the studio to charge $1,100 for a "day" of recording. Over the course of a year and a half, Gloria Productions had paid over $40,000 for recording, enough to purchase two complete recording studios. Other charges might not have been as discreditable, but nothing was overlooked. Every time Pathé arranged a screening of *The Trespasser* for the press or influential visitors, Gloria Productions was billed $20.

Having been trained over the past two years to do what Sullivan and Scollard instructed, Irving Wakoff had paid all those invoices without a question, but not this time. He sent the Tambert invoices back, along with a formal complaint to Pathé's in-house auditor, Barney Fox. The new charges were a hodgepodge. Thousands were listed as compensation for the salaries of Barney Glazer and Laura Hope Crews, but without stating what they were working on or when. Gloria had already paid the outrageous recording facilities charges, yet Tambert added charges for days when the equipment was broken and for the repair of that equipment in spite of the fact Gloria's contract with Pathé made it clear that was all the studio's responsibility. He even billed $130 to tune the studio organ. Yet the most audacious item had to be the $19,000 for the building and furnishing of Gloria's bungalow. It was, after all, studio property, and their contract called for Pathé to provide suitable housing for their stars. The fact they had to build it underscored the increase in status Gloria's presence brought to the studio.

Barney Fox went back over the Gloria Productions contract with Pathé, compared it to the invoices in question, and agreed with every one of Wakoff's contentions. In his letter to Sullivan, Fox concluded, "we made a very substantial profit" off Swanson before these new invoices, most of which were inappropriate "attempts to be reimbursed for general overhead." Fox practically warned him that if Swanson hired outside auditors, they would likely find even more charges that she should not have been responsible for.

"We attempted to get as much as we possibly could get out" of Swanson, Sullivan told Derr after reading Fox's report, but "it seems to have failed to work all the way." They knew Fox was right about what an audit would find so Sullivan recommended they cancel the invoices "without any hesitation." Wakoff agreed to give Pathé all the sets free and clear in exchange for erasing the contested charges. Fox estimated that the value of the sets was at least $75,000 and if those could be official studio property, it would boost the bottom line of Pathé's value. Within two days, Sullivan turned around a "final agreement" to "cancel all additional charges" for Wakoff's signature.

But the damage had been done as far as Gloria was concerned. The extra invoices were the catalyst for her to look at her books for the first time in years and now she realized that Gloria Productions had been a sieve through which Pathé paid its personnel and covered its overhead when they had no productions of their own. Kennedy had loaned her money and then used it to pay expenses at his own studio, leaving Gloria responsible for paying back those loans.

Besides the $700,000 borrowed from Kennedy, a $500,000 line of credit at 6 percent interest had been established with Bank of America. Minimum payments had been made and the loan had continued to be renewed, but they held Swanson's UA contract as collateral.

While she had hardly been deprived, Swanson had personally been paid only $50,000 for each of the three films she had made under Kennedy's tutelage. It was a far cry from the million dollars a year Jesse Lasky had offered her. That "independence" she had so desperately wanted when she left Paramount had carried a heavy price tag. Now she was a million and a half dollars in debt, triple the amount of when she first sought Kennedy's help almost three years earlier.

Gloria was outraged seeing all the figures in one place. It was unprecedented to have the head of the studio also being in charge of the outside production company yet in spite of the rumors to the contrary, it was Pathé that had benefited at the expense of Gloria Swanson.

Later in life, Gloria said "Joe Kennedy operated just like Joe Stalin. Their system was to write a letter to the files and then order the exact reverse on the phone." Clearly her harsh judgment reflects her bitterness, but she was not alone in her assessment. Doris Kearns Goodwin sums up Kennedy's approach by saying, "He saw the world as a never ending battleground and he could plot and make use of people without compunction." Including the woman he professed to love.

What really infuriated Swanson was finding herself being treated like any other business investment, a property to be profited from. She had given Kennedy total control with total trust. She had watched as he had cut off a series of her previously close associates and witnessed him betraying his own colleagues, but now that it was happening to her, she was truly stunned. She had been blinded by their personal relationship. After all, hadn't they spoken of love and even marriage and children? At a minimum, she had assumed they were in it together. They weren't. He had arranged to loan the money and it was incumbent upon her to pay it back. By this time, the profits from *The Trespasser* were flowing in, yet they did not replenish Gloria's bank account. They went to pay back her financier. She would never fully recover.

There was a silver lining to her experience, William Dufty says. "You should have seen that woman read a contract. She made sure she understood every single word."

# CHAPTER 25

# "I Am Now Definitely Out of the Motion Picture Industry"

## (MID-1930—EARLY 1931)

Gloria Swanson was not the only one left on her own when Kennedy departed California that April. Joe and his gang had worked together for years like a tight-knit family, but that relationship was about to undergo a seismic shift. In a cable from the train, Eddie Moore told E. B. Derr, "Up and at em kid—do the best you can without me—I'll do same by you." That might have been taken as a typical farewell, but the response Derr received the next week when he ran questions past Kennedy was different from anything he had heard before. Joe wasn't even available to talk to him and it was Eddie who relayed the message. "He told me to tell you and to tell you in no uncertain terms that you two were running things there and this was one of the problems that you would have to straighten out yourselves for he would not talk with anybody any more about it. Best and good luck."

Derr and Charlie Sullivan had served long apprenticeships and when Derr was elected president of Pathé in June, he had no choice but to step out of the shadow. It didn't take long for him to be comfortable in his new role and he was soon making major changes. He began "personally supervising" all productions, increasing budgets on films he deemed worthy, and reorganizing the writing department under Eugene Walter. For almost four years, Derr had been commuting between coasts, but now his wife and daughter, Betty, finally made the move to Los Angeles.

The biggest shock Derr gave to the industry was his decision that Pathé would no longer sell films sight unseen. Since losing their access to most K-A-O theaters, they had to sell to exhibitors again and Derr was convinced they were getting so little for their films because of their history of second-rate features. He knew the only way to convince buyers he was serious about improvement was to let them see the films first and then, hopefully, pay top dollar.

He announced a 200 percent increase in production costs and was soon credited with "revolutionizing Pathé's production and sales." He dropped several actors' long-term contracts, concentrating on only a few stars and then filling in with single-film deals for character actors such as Hedda Hopper and ZaSu Pitts. The first big hit under his reign was the Philip Barry play *Holiday,* starring Ann Harding and Mary Astor. While Derr obviously had faith in the film, but even he was surprised when it grossed $1 million. His second success was *Her Man* starring Helen Twelvetrees, which brought in $800,000 at the box office.

The gang were now the front men to the point that photographs of Derr, Sullivan, and Scollard appeared in ads in the trades promoting Pathé's films. Yet it was "Derr the Doer" who was receiving the concentrated, positive press. He was labeled "solid, silent and sensible" and a proper heir to De Mille and Ince, who had previously overseen the same lot. Derr was credited with "knocking them over with distressing regularity" and keeping "his tight little organization on its collective toes." According to the trades, he was bringing glory days to his studio, which had been "on the skids a few months back." When *Holiday* premiered in early August, Derr was on the red carpet alongside "every celebrity in Hollywood" and he was there at the microphone being interviewed as the "president of Pathé and producer of the picture." It was heady coverage for a man used to operating behind closed doors and while Kennedy had been the one to push him out front, it had to give Joe pause.

While Derr handled the creative side, Pat Scollard monitored the minutiae of the finances and learned an appreciation of the nuances that made a difference on the bottom line. Too much blank film left at the end of a reel was a waste of money. So were too many copies of a film in distribution, but too few cut into profits. It was a delicate balance to say the least and it was Scollard who stayed on top of it all. Arthur Poole stepped up to help keep the records and he knew the per print earnings of every film, including the shorts and the newsreels, but it was Scollard who questioned the costs down to a one hundredth of a penny on a foot of film. He even factored in the cost of transportation in choosing where to develop film. Invoices had to be matched, credits given, and charges allocated. It wasn't unusual for a dozen letters to go back and forth over only a few dollars. At a moment's notice, Pat could tell Joe how many prints were out and exactly where they were, in America and throughout the world.

It had been almost three years since Kennedy had sat in Cecil B. De

Mille's office and threatened to sell the company, but now that he was really under pressure to sell, the stock price was becoming an issue. The sharp rise earlier in the year had been caused by manipulation and merger rumors, but there was little left in Joe's bag of tricks. The "insurgents" could be blamed for only part of the beating the stock took after the June meeting. Joe had everyone looking for income anywhere they could find it, selling stories to other studios and loaning out contract players. They even made a deal with an accounting firm to review their past tax returns to see if there was any chance they had overpaid the government. There was no initial fee, but they would split any refund.

While reporting a profit, Pathé's published financial statements were as vague as possible. Kennedy and his minions had used every bookkeeping device to put a rosy sheen on the company. He pushed much of the loss into the period before he had become chairman of the board in mid-1929, but it was getting increasingly difficult to blame the previous administration or sing the praises of a turnaround. Film properties were moved between Pathé Sound Pictures Inc. and Pathé Exchange Inc. and money was shifted among Bank of America, Bancamerica-Blair, and Jeremiah Milbank so that it was close to impossible for an outsider to get a real picture. Categories were adjusted so one balance sheet was not easily compared to another and a "special reserve fund" was created to absorb costs that had been underestimated. Between set-asides, transfers, and special reserves, even Price Waterhouse had to keep coming back for clarifications in order to do their in-house audit. The trades had given up trying to analyze Pathé's finances and reported their accounts "shed little light on the company's condition." In spite of or because of the lack of transparency, Bank of America gave Pathé "an adverse report."

The fact was that Pathé had no cash reserves, nothing to mortgage, and a negative earnings record. On top of that, the mortgage on the studio was due to be paid in full in a few months and they either had to extend it once again or come up with over $400,000. Only Joe, Arthur Poole, and a few others knew they were in the red by $1 million for the first three quarters of 1930.

It would have been possible, if challenging, to save Pathé and there were a few encouraging signs. Under Derr, the image of their feature films was improving, yet that would take time to make a real difference in the income flow. Turning the company around would also require a desire to make that happen, investors willing to stay in for the long haul, and an administration dedicated to building up the company. None of that existed anymore. While Derr was putting in long hours in Culver

City, Kennedy made only token appearances at the New York office that summer and fall. He wasn't even in attendance at the special meeting of the board in August when Derr flew in from Los Angeles to act as chair and give a several-hour presentation on where the company was production-wise and what could be expected through the end of the year.

Pathé had over one thousand employees throughout the world and over 13,000 stockholders, but Joe Kennedy was no longer one of them. Few if anyone outside of the gang knew of the tremendous personal profit he had made from selling his Pathé stock. He did not brag about his wealth or of dodging the stock market bullet of 1929. Instead, he downplayed his fortune and talked about trying to "hang on to what money I have." His tack also made it easier to dismiss the innumerable letters he received asking about employment. He had already made his killing so now Kennedy's focus was on his reputation and the holdings of Walker, Milbank, and Murdock. They were the ones with the most money remaining on the line and they wanted out.

Howard Hughes expressed an interest in buying Pathé and he spent some time around the studio. He also met with Joe Schenck about the possibility of joining UA and then bringing Pathé (and their stars) with him, but Schenck didn't believe the value was there and he was particularly concerned at the moment about theaters. United Artists had managed to put together a small chain of their own, but the last thing he would advocate was buying a studio without a theater circuit attached.

If there was a company with a compelling reason to purchase Pathé it was RKO. They were already intertwined through agreements that caused "much annoyance" to both companies: RKO was obligated to distribute films over which they had no control while not paying Pathé enough to warrant higher production values. Buying Pathé would nullify that contract as well as increase RKO's studio holdings and their star rosters, but even with that logic and a price tag *Variety* assumed to be "something of a bargain," Pathé was not an easy sale to make. RKO already had their collective hands full with reorganizations and cutbacks while having over $2 million riding on big budget films such as *Cimarron* with its six thousand extras.

In early June, Kennedy and Walker sat down with RKO's president Hiram Brown, who told them in no uncertain terms he wasn't interested in most of Pathé's assets, but he was willing to offer $1 million for the studio and the stars' contracts. That was assuming they first paid off the studio's $400,000 mortgage. Even then, Brown said he was willing "to bail them out entirely on account of his friendship with Mr. Walker."

"Bail them out?" Kennedy wasn't about to admit they needed that and he didn't want to sell Pathé piecemeal. The exception might be their newsreels, which both Paramount and Fox had expressed an interest in. As Derr was busy promoting the twenty-fifth anniversary of "the oldest trademark" in newsreels, Kennedy was debating whether he could get more for it as a separate entity or as part of a larger package.

Hiram Brown might have been hesitant, but David Sarnoff was serious about buying Pathé and Walker was serious about selling it, so Kennedy, along with Sarnoff and Walker, met with Brown in his office in late September to see if they could all get to the same page. They agreed that Joe would present a proposal listing all of Pathé's assets, and within days Brown had the financials on his desk. Kennedy put a total value of $12,714,000 on the company, almost half of which came from their 49 percent ownership of the DuPont-Pathé Film Manufacturing Company stock. DuPont-Pathé was paying dividends of $40 a share or around a 3 percent return on their investment. Brown wanted nothing to do with DuPont-Pathé; Kennedy could put a $6 million value on it, but the fact was that it was bringing in less than $200,000 a year. Brown was looking to grow RKO, but he wasn't interested in long-term investments, let alone any white elephants.

His balance sheet also included $1 million of "goodwill" attached to Pathé News and the contracts of Pathé's stars and directors. Their completed but unreleased films were valued at $1,750,000 and the same amount was given for the land, the studio, and all the equipment housed there.

Brown quickly went to work making his own notations on Kennedy's calculations. The half million Kennedy estimated for the "equipment at the home office and branches" was easily scratched because "many if not all of the branch offices would be valueless to RKO." Nor did they need Pathé's laboratories in Jersey City and Bound Brook or their British exchanges, because they had just opened their own foreign distribution unit.

Kennedy's other values weren't questioned as they could easily be confirmed or reduced through an outside audit. He didn't even put up much of a fight over the $1 million for "goodwill" as long as it covered the entire company. He was ready to move ahead with the caveats that they "could arrive at a fair price" for the assets that remained on his list and Pathé would accept payment in RKO stock because "all the working capital is necessary for continued operations."

Kennedy, on the other hand, wanted cash. What was Brown worrying about? After all, Lehman Brothers was there to back the purchase. But he refused to budge and just as Kennedy had taken off for Palm Springs during his negotiations with De Mille, Brown now left on a hunting trip to the Adirondacks where he would be out of reach for at least a week. This time it was Joe's turn to cool down.

Time was of the essence. Production-wise, Pathé was hedging its bets. They continued producing short films and made new deals for serials such as one with Knute Rockne to collaborate on one-reel football shorts; otherwise, the studio was now "featureless" with nothing new planned to go before the cameras. The major players such as Constance Bennett and Ann Harding were on loan to other studios, keeping the cash coming in, but leaving the lot empty. Derr was playing the good soldier, walking a tightrope as all decisions were now put through the filter of the potential sale. Almost anything he did impacted areas they might not be controlling for long, including his own salary. Derr had ascended to the presidency of Pathé without a raise from the $700 a week he had been receiving for years. That was way below that of other studio heads, yet knowing of the need to keep the costs low, Derr now asked Kennedy to increase him to $2,000 a week on paper until the sale went through. That way, once he was with the new company, his remuneration would be more in keeping with the Hollywood norm. Joe, however, took it to Hiram Brown, who was in no mood for hearing about any new expenses.

The parties gathered again at the end of October and by the first of December, the boards of both Pathé and RKO had approved the deal at a price of $4,500,000. They settled on half a million in cash and the rest in 6 percent notes to be paid in five equal installments. At 6:45 on the evening of December 4, 1930, Kennedy signed the contract to sell the agreed-upon portion of Pathé to RKO. Later that night, Joe cabled Elisha Walker that he thought the deal was a "magnificent one for us. I am happiest because I know you will like it." Within days letters went out to various interested parties, including Pathé stockholders, giving them twenty days' notice before they met to ratify the sale. Another letter was sent to Pathé's employees and it had a familiar ring to it, assuring everyone that RKO planned to keep "our entire present staff" and promised that "you need have no concerns." Kennedy also wrote to John Murdock, at home in Beverly Hills, "I can't tell you what a relief it is to me to get this cleaned up. It was so loaded with dynamite over the past three or four years that anything could have happened." Murdock had been riding the Pathé roller coaster with Kennedy and so he understood when Joe, uncharacteristically and dramatically, proclaimed, "I believe this has probably taken another five years off my life."

Kennedy was relieved and exhausted, but he needed to stay in New York for another month for the stockholders meeting in early January. Joe could call the deal "magnificent" because it was for the financiers such as Walker whose loans to the company were about to be repaid. The thousands of shareholders, on the other hand, were being asked to approve the liquidation of the company and therefore their chance at future profits.

Two thirds approval was needed so the push was on to gather proxies. Obviously Walker, Milbank, and Murdock were among the largest shareholders, but others came through as well, such as Cecil B. De Mille, who still held 26,000 shares. In the meantime, lawyers and accountants were going over everything with a fine-tooth comb.

The Protective Association, which had sought to replace Pathé's leadership six months earlier, came out in force once again. It had been a little over a year since the crash and the stock market had continued to slide. People were desperate to find something of worth in their portfolios, and for many their Pathé stock was their last hope. This time there was no stock swap. Pathé shareholders would be left with an investment that consisted of little more than DuPont-Pathé stock.

Kennedy spent the first two weeks of December in and out of meetings with disgruntled stockholders, but his patience with calls for audits and company records was running out. He found such demands "perfectly ridiculous," but he told the Pathé attorneys to "tell me what to do and I will do it." The lawyers drafted a letter for Kennedy's signature claiming that any outside audits at this time "would seriously hamper the officers of the Company in the performance of their duties." The best they were going to get was a meeting with Arthur Poole and perhaps a representative of Price Waterhouse.

Scollard took some of the heat, fielding calls and holding meetings, such as one with a Mr. Wickham, who worked for $100 a week in the escrow department of Citizens National Bank in Los Angeles and had used most of his savings to buy $16,000 worth of Pathé stock. Even after spending two hours with Scollard, Wickham was not placated and vowed to use his last $2,000 suing to stop the sale. He joined others who refused to be mollified and filed a suit against RKO, Pathé, and a dozen individuals including Kennedy, Walker, Derr, and Scollard, to stop the sale. The New York federal court gave the defendants twenty days to respond, a date coinciding with the Pathé board meeting of January 5.

Those "dissidents" seeking relief in court were only a small portion of those questioning the sale. Some who wrote Kennedy expressed their concerns very politely such as Dan Sullivan, who had worked with him at Columbia Trust. Sullivan had put $1,000 into Pathé stock, buying when it was near a high point, but believing Kennedy's "business ability" meant "the speculation would prove profitable." Sullivan still had enough faith to include his proxy and Joe responded by saying while he "made a firm practice" never to prophesy, he hoped that the liquidation of the company would result in the stock being worth more than he had paid for it. How that could be possible, he didn't explain. He assured other shareholders who wrote him personally that he would "never urge any of my friends to buy securities" in any of his own companies, but "I honestly believe that this proposed trade will be of great benefit to the corporation and I urge you to send your own proxies with those of your friends." He never actually said it would benefit the shareholders, but he made it sound as if it was his idea not to include the DuPont-Pathé stock as part of the sale. He claimed that RKO was buying only "losing assets for a substantial amount of money" and that keeping DuPont-Pathé gave them equity interest in "a company that is very prosperous."

Other letters were pleading and desperate, but a handwritten and unsigned letter he received bears reprinting in full and unedited:

> Mr. Kennedy,
> We are going to put you on the spot. You have fair warning. We are not going to be like you, sell Pathe Inc out on the stock holders and then push them out with nothing.
> We are not going to plug you or we are not going to stick you in the back, but we are going to cut your throut from ear to ear as a warning to others what pulls the same deal. Now you can go to Europe or any other place but we will get you anyway when you least expect it. You know Kennedy the stock holders of Pathe are all poor people and nothing else, and you ruined them to make yourself more richer than what you are. You have Roals Royce cars a house full of servants, all with your crooked work but you are the end of you roap. This is one time you made a mistake, we were very careful and went and found out who sold out the stock holders and pushed them out with only a piece of paper to hold and we found out that you are the one that pulled the deal. Well so long till we see you the sooner the better.

You will have a note pinned on your cloth to tell why you
passed out.

The letter obviously had an impact on Kennedy because he kept it in
his permanent files. Perhaps he took the threat seriously enough that in
case something did happen to him, evidence would be there. Yet it
didn't dampen his determination to go through with the sale and it certainly didn't make him more empathetic.

It had been over a year since the fire at New York Pathé's studio had
claimed ten lives and injured dozens. Insurance settlements averaging
$15,000 each had been negotiated with most of the families of the
deceased.

John Flinn and Henry Lalley would persevere through over two years
of trials and multiple grand jury hearings before finally being cleared by
the New York Court of Appeals in the spring of 1932. If Flinn thought
he would have support from Pathé, he was mistaken. Initially he had
been reassigned to Culver City, with trips back and forth between the
coasts for court appearances, but the board decided that when his contract came up for renewal, it should be "allowed to lapse." The Flinn
children and grandchildren grew up knowing how his need for years of
legal counsel had drained his savings and aware of his belief he had been
betrayed by the company. John Flinn III, still in the family business as an
Emmy-nominated cinematographer, remembers that at just the mention
of the name Kennedy, the look his grandfather gave "told the entire
story."

For Joe Kennedy, it was back to the Pathé offices on 45th Street on
January 5, 1931, for the stockholders meeting to approve the sale of the
company to RKO. This time, there was plenty of warning of possible
trouble so when he entered the room, he was surrounded on both sides
by private detectives with their uniform jackets pulled back to reveal
belts "laden with cartridges and big revolvers." Joe was greeted with
jeers that could be heard throughout the building, and the detectives
stood near him and the ballot box throughout the meeting.

The armed men didn't intimidate Joseph Conn, a Rhode Island theater owner and Pathé investor, who committed on the spot to buy Pathé
for $1 million more than RKO was paying. He even waved a certified
check for $25,000 to seal the deal and claimed he had moneymen wait-
ing at the Astor Hotel for word of his success. However, when Conn
refused to name his backers, he lost the momentum of the gathered
throng. Still others yelled out that Pathé was worth three and four times

the selling price, as much as $25 million. The hordes were obviously going to continue to be rowdy as long as Kennedy was there, so he left the room. The New York independent theater owner Sidney Cohen then announced that after "careful examination," he was supporting Kennedy and the sale. The crowd booed louder than ever and accused Cohen of being paid off. Another voice charged that it was an inside deal since some men were on both the RKO and Pathé boards.

In spite of the vocal and at times menacing howls, when the ballots were counted the insurgents found themselves with fewer than ten thousand votes compared with 668,000 for the Kennedy regime. Joe went home to pack for Palm Beach, but just as it looked like nothing could jeopardize the sale, Constance Bennett made headlines that did exactly that.

For almost a year, the actress had been threatening to cause trouble. Since spending the holidays in France with Henri, Constance had been encouraging rumors of their impending marriage. Yet Gloria had not filed for divorce and Constance was not happy about being tied to the studio where her lover's wife ruled the roost. After being loaned to Warner Bros., Bennett found that studio more to her liking. When she went directly to Kennedy with her complaints, he called Henri in Paris to discuss the situation. Henri was still in Pathé's employ, but he was hardly crucial to their operation. Bob Kane told Joe he found Henri "absolutely useless. He would like to give the impression he is a big guy, and when he does not succeed in giving this impression, he runs away and sulks." Kane assured Kennedy that many others in Paris shared his opinion, but Joe knew exactly what Henri brought to the table. He had been hired originally to get him out of Gloria's bed and while that was no longer necessary, he required tending. His affair with Bennett was part of the problem, but so far he had been the proverbial "perfect gentleman" waiting for Gloria to make a move. No one needed to say out loud whom he could name as co-respondent if he was the one to file the divorce papers.

Now Henri advised Joe that it would be best for all concerned if Pathé released Constance immediately because "she wouldn't be happy otherwise." It was, as he none too subtly put it, "the only way to quiet everything and avoid unpleasantness." There was little doubt that Constance could make matters much worse. Her own sister, the actress Joan Bennett, called her "quixotic, turbulent, stubborn and aggressive." Yet Constance had become one of Pathé's biggest moneymakers and Joe wasn't about to release her. If that was the case, she demanded changes in her contract. It fell to E. B. Derr to handle the negotiations and after much discussion, it was decided Bennett would remain under contract to Pathé through 1934 at the increased rate of $2,750 a week for forty-two weeks a year. She was also given a $10,000 bonus and the rare right to share in the profits made by loaning her to other studios. Derr signed off on the new contract in early September of 1930, but it is impossible to believe he and Kennedy did not discuss it, let alone that Kennedy wasn't the one who urged him to placate her in the first place.

Derr had always done everything Kennedy had asked him to do and for years, Joe's had been the only opinion that mattered. Derr's loyalty was proven yet again that year when he cleaned up another loose end for the boss by sending Gloria Swanson a legally laced letter claiming that he had never had her power of attorney, but if he ever had, he had done only what "Miss Swanson, or the Gloria Productions, Inc., authorized me to do" and he had not used it during the year 1930.

With her contract changes in the offing, Bennett was back on the Pathé lot and her film, *Sin Takes a Holiday,* gave Derr a third solid smash hit. Shooting had begun in July, just as Swanson was wrapping *What a Widow.* Gloria threw herself into promotion plans for her film, posing for pictures to promote a contest for trips to Paris, where the lucky two dozen winners could follow the route taken by Gloria's character in the film. Then the release date was postponed a month in order to shoot a new ending featuring her flying home on a Dornier airplane to coordinate the film's release with the airline's first transatlantic passenger flight. Even Swanson's costumes were packed up to be displayed in a tour of department store windows as *What a Widow* was screened in various cities. If the picture wasn't all she had hoped for, the attendant publicity was the biggest and most unabashed yet.

When Gloria stopped her whirl of activity, it was hard not to notice that Henri had returned to Los Angeles, moved into a hotel, and was frequently out and about with Constance, even occasionally attending the same parties as Gloria. Finally in October, Swanson filed for divorce on the grounds of "abandonment." She set the date of Henri's "desertion" as September 18, 1929, the day she and the Kennedys had sailed from Europe after the explosion in the Paris hotel room. Her attorney was none other than Milton Cohen, the lawyer so abruptly dropped several years before.

Constance Bennett was now able to enjoy her stardom and her new contract alongside her now formally announced fiancé. Still that wasn't enough for her. She saw her opportunity to publicly declare her bankability when Warner Bros. offered to pay her $300,000 for those ten weeks a year she wasn't working for Pathé. That price tag resulted in the

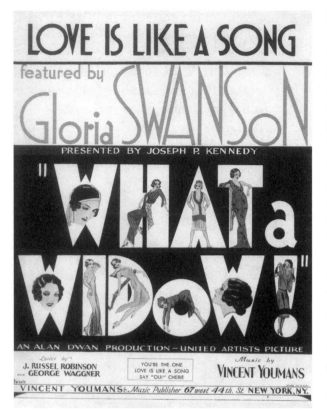

Kennedy even put his name on the music
that accompanied his films.

headlines that January of 1931 that threatened to throw a wrench into the Pathé sale. Bennett was considered a Pathé asset and her value raised new questions about Pathé's actual worth. That $300,000 worked out to be over $1 million a year, more than RKO had paid for all of Pathé's contracts with actors and directors with the newsreel division thrown in. Had Kennedy devalued the company just to pay back Pathé's biggest investors?

Some dropped their jaws at a salary that was the equivalent of $800 for each working hour, but Pathé's board of directors was not amused. As the members turned apoplectic, Kennedy knew he had covered himself at a "special" behind-closed-doors meeting the month before where he suggested that perhaps "the making and modifying of contracts" needed to be "more clearly defined." In the past, contracts had simply been reported under "Miscellaneous business" without being ratified, but Joe proposed that no officer of the company had the power to alter contracts without "the express authority of this Board." The motion passed unanimously and, to seal the potential blame on Derr, Kennedy added a line declaring that this did not constitute approval of "any such action heretofore taken by any such officer."

Pat Scollard was assigned to "investigate" Bennett's Warner Bros. contract, and a week later, the board held another special meeting. For the first time since Kennedy had taken over the company, neither he nor Scollard was present. However, Scollard's report was there and it put the responsibility for the changes in Bennett's contract directly in the lap of E. B. Derr and, to a lesser degree, Charlie Sullivan. The board voted to send letters to both Bennett and Warner Bros. informing them that "a secret attempt" to establish "an alleged supplement agreement" to her original Pathé contract was "totally void." If they moved forward, Pathé would file a complaint with the Hays Office. The board also voted to inform Derr that his "attempted modification" of Bennett's contract was invalid because he "totally lacked authority to enter any such agreement." They needed a fall guy and Derr was it. Kennedy had provided the rope, Scollard tied the noose, and the board pulled it.

Frantic that the contract dispute not derail the sale of Pathé, the board decided it was best to "fully explain" the situation to RKO and then follow their wishes. Hiram Brown said he did not think that the revelations should hinder the agreement, but he put Pathé on notice that if Derr and Sullivan remained employed beyond their next board meeting, "any unauthorized acts . . . would have to rest upon the company."

Brown certainly had no love lost for Derr after he had taken his best films out of RKO's distribution channels and sold them to the highest bidders. Brown was not that enamored with the entire Pathé deal, but he wasn't about to go against Sarnoff, Walker, or even Kennedy. Yet if Derr thought anyone, including Kennedy or Scollard, was going to stand up for him, he was sadly mistaken. Kennedy and Scollard became silent and unavailable and were absent again at the next board meeting two weeks later where it was affirmed that an officer of the company could be removed "with or without cause" by a majority of the board. It was "resolved that Mr. E. B. Derr be and hereby is removed from the Office of President of the Corporation and his employment forthwith discontinued," effective immediately. Pat Scollard was put in "full charge of all the Corporation's business and property in California" and was assigned to notify Derr of the board's action. It was also left to Scollard to inform the banks that "Mr. Derr no longer has the power to sign checks." Charlie Sullivan was not an officer of the company, but his firing was implied and that too was left for Scollard to handle.

Derr had witnessed Kennedy turning against and cutting off close associates before, exercising his sanguinary actions without a qualm. He had seen the shock and pain inflicted on the likes of Fred Thomson and Guy Currier. Derr had helped Joe to strip Gloria Swanson of her employees and watched as she became totally dependent upon him, only to be dropped herself. Yet the gang had seemed sacrosanct and the thought that the boss might betray one of them had never entered the equation.

For years, they had served Kennedy without question, whenever and wherever he needed them. But without Pathé, let alone the rest of his companies, he didn't need all of them anymore. While none of the specifics of the Derr situation were not made public, it was reported that he and Kennedy were no longer on "friendly terms."

Scollard, who had spoken with Derr and Sullivan on an almost daily basis for five years, had to make a choice and he chose Kennedy. Pat had remained in New York and therefore was physically closer to Joe and less susceptible to hearing the criticism or seeing the impact of Kennedy's actions. Not that outside opinion had ever seriously influenced the gang. The fact was that Derr and Sullivan had served their purpose and were now disposable.

Just as he had shoved the baseball into his pocket and walked off the field at Harvard leaving behind the shocked players who had thought they were a team, Kennedy had turned and walked away from those who believed they were his partners, Fred Thomson, Guy Currier, Eddie Goulding, Gloria Swanson, and now E. B. Derr and Charlie Sullivan. It was as if a steel curtain went down and they all ceased to exist. Without emotion or introspection, Joe had become a man capable of insulating himself in self-justification. After all, they had all let themselves be put in a situation where they could be taken. If there was any fault to be found, it was with them for being naive.

Kennedy kept those he needed. Eddie Moore and John Ford were still on the payroll and Arthur Poole stayed with Pathé where he could monitor the financials and keep Joe apprised of information before anyone else. From the beginning it was obvious Poole had a grasp on more than just numbers and Kennedy had grown to depend upon him for analyses of people as well as accounts. Scollard's responsibilities shifted as he fronted property holdings and stock sales for the boss as well as serving as the overseer of Kennedy's diverse investments. Pat's loyalty was rewarded by being elected treasurer of Pathé and he picked up an extra $200 a week with the title. He was also elected to the board of directors of Columbia Trust, where Ethel Turner was still serving as the hub of activity for various bank accounts, including Scollard's. Both Poole and Scollard continued to operate out of the Pathé office at 35 West 45th Street, but the company went from filling nine floors of the building to a total of nine employees.

Hiram Brown moved quickly to announce that the "resignations" of E. B. Derr and Charlie Sullivan "have already been accepted" and that RKO was challenging Constance Bennett's contract with Warners. What remained of Pathé was now referred to in the trades as "the other Pathé," the shell of the former company that held the DuPont stock and

RKO-Pathé Studios

minor miscellany such as the New Jersey film laboratory they hadn't been able to sell to RKO. The Pathé name continued to appear on the screen and operate separately as "Pathé-RKO" until October of 1931 when David O. Selznick was brought in to supervise the merger of all RKO's production units.

Kennedy had left for the Oasis Club in Palm Beach shortly after the stockholders meeting in early January. For the rest of the month, opponents continued to challenge the sale, taking out ads and requesting support from shareholders to "press our fight more vigorously" through lawsuits and at the annual meeting. They were of little enough concern to be left to Arthur Poole to monitor and he dismissed their attempts as "unimportant" and "too vague to induce anyone to part with hard cash." When the sale to RKO was official on January 30, 1931, Poole told Joe they celebrated by drinking "a toast to the old Pathé."

Joe was ready for some serious relaxation and, in his correspondence, it was clear a weight had been lifted. As he put it to B. P. Schulberg in declining his invitation to become a member of the Academy of Motion Picture Arts and Sciences, "I am now definitely out of the motion picture industry."

Kennedy always said "the only real place for a vacation is Palm Beach" and he wasn't so exhausted that he cut down on his socializing. Gloria's old friend Sport Ward reported to her that he had seen Joe out and about with a woman he thought at first glance was Gloria, but upon closer inspection it turned out to be the actress Nancy Carroll on Joe's arm. "Of course," Sport told Gloria, "Joe and I had a good laugh over it afterwards."

# CHAPTER 26

# "The Richest Irish American in the World"

## (1931–1935)

*J*oe Kennedy was one of the few people laughing in early 1931. With the sale of Pathé, he had completed his mission: taking care of himself, his family, and the few other men who mattered to him at the time. He was not only an isolationist politically, but personally as well. He had become a man who had friends and cronies, but none he considered an equal. There was no one he respected who could look him in the eye and say "no."

He was forty-two years old and the basis of his fortune was firmly established. As the rest of world sank into the Depression, he was worth at least $15 million and was declared "the richest Irish American in the world." *The Boston Globe* calculated he had made as much as $12 million from the film business. *Fortune* magazine "conservatively estimated" that "Kennedy profited personally some four million dollars by his FBO dealings, three million from Pathé and K-A-O, one million with RKO and, very probably, half a million from sidelines—a total of $8,500,000." And that was "profited personally." A *New York Times* reporter later concluded that when Joe left Hollywood, "He already had so much money that making the rest of it, which must have been many many millions, was almost a routine affair."

Kennedy's departure was perfectly timed. Initially, the Depression did not affect the movie business for films were the one cheap form of entertainment people could afford and needed more than ever. And the moguls seemed impervious to the world's reality; while breadlines were forming across the nation, Louis B. Mayer's daughter Edie was receiving gold demitasse spoons from Tiffany's as a wedding present.

Yet once the Depression circled the globe, it hit Hollywood with a wallop and box office receipts dropped by almost 50 percent. Over 12 million people were unemployed, with little money for food, let alone movies. The glamour films that Swanson had perfected were no longer in vogue; now it was the broad comedy of the matronly sixty-year-old Marie Dressler that packed the theaters. MGM, with the help of *Min and Bill, Tugboat Annie,* and *Emma,* was the only major studio operating in the black; Paramount, RKO, and Fox were either in receivership or on the verge of bankruptcy. Universal shut down citing "national emergency." No one was safe and even bosses such as Joe Schenck suffered "tremendous losses."

When Kennedy finally submitted his letter of resignation as chairman of Pathé in May of 1931, due to "the condition of his health," it was accepted by the board "with deep regret." By then he was back at the Cape, enjoying his first real summer at the beach in years and Rose welcomed him back with open arms. Photographs from the time are witnesses to Joe's presence and Rose's radiating smile of relief. Her stoic perseverance during his long affair with Gloria Swanson had paid off, at least in her mind. Joe's return to the family hearth was further testified to by the arrival in early 1932 of their ninth and final child, Edward Moore Kennedy, four long years after the birth of Jean.

As he sat back and assessed the world around him, Kennedy was more concerned than ever about the state of the world's economy. He saw the growing international Depression as genuinely threatening capitalism; the haves were fewer than ever and millions of have-nots were mired in poverty. He believed "there cannot simultaneously and successfully exist in the same nation a political democracy and an economic oligarchy" and therefore came to what he considered the practical conclusion that he preferred to hand over half his fortune to taxes rather than to lose all of it to a socialist revolution. He also understood that with the crash and the Depression, power was moving from the financial centers to Washington.

Kennedy joined the presidential campaign of Franklin Roosevelt, contributing his own money and soliciting others with such fervor that he was soon labeled one of its key "financial fathers." Joe and Eddie Moore flew to Warm Springs, Georgia, for a weekend of meetings with Roosevelt and then Kennedy made a trip to San Simeon. While he couldn't resist placing calls to a variety of former colleagues to drop the fact he was in residence, Joe was there to talk to Hearst about supporting Roosevelt. The publisher continued to hedge his bets for the moment, but it was Kennedy's phone call to him from the Chicago convention that many credited with swinging Hearst, and the California delegation, Roosevelt's way.

Joe and Eddie spent several weeks that fall campaigning by train with

Roosevelt. Just as he had stood out in a room of studio moguls, the "remarkably handsome and charming" Kennedy was noticed among the politicians and top advisors as an affable raconteur. He worked his magic to bring in old acquaintances such as the banking Giannini brothers into Roosevelt's sphere and was also appreciated for his generosity when he provided buses for the group to visit the Grand Canyon and tickets to the World Series so his fellow travelers could witness the New York Yankees defeat the Chicago Cubs.

Kennedy's involvement in the campaign was so well publicized that when Roosevelt won in a landslide that November, Joe was inundated with letters of congratulation. Will Hays simply referred to him as "Mr. Secretary," assuming he would receive a cabinet post. Joe responded by saying that returning to the picture business would "give me much more pleasure" than anything in government. He continued his practice of sending Christmas presents to his film contacts.

In spite of his protestations, there was nothing Kennedy wanted more than to be secretary of the treasury. Yet he was hardly the typical New Dealer, the phrase Roosevelt had first used in his nomination acceptance speech and was soon applied to his supporters. Other Roosevelt insiders were suspicious of Joe, but the president-elect loved a good give-and-take and was hardly above setting his advisors against each other. While he valued Joe's broad reach and insights, Roosevelt didn't know what to do with him.

So Kennedy simmered as he sat in his leased Palm Beach home from January through April of 1933 and, as his disgruntlement grew, he used his time to continue to profit in the stock market. After mild fluctuations, prices had dropped even more severely over the two years since the crash, but he managed to benefit just the same. Using Eddie Moore's name for some accounts and working out of various brokerage houses, Joe entered a few well-chosen stock pools and perfected the practice of selling short, borrowing stock at the going price, selling it when the price dropped, then returning the stock and pocketing the difference. Any company he thought was vulnerable was fair game; one of his prime targets (and personal profit makers) was Paramount, which continued to fall.

While he hadn't heard from the president directly, Joe continued his friendship with the Roosevelts' son Jimmy. James Roosevelt had graduated from Harvard, married the beautiful Boston socialite Betsey Cushing, and started in the insurance business in Massachusetts, where his success had grown in direct proportion to his father's importance.

Kennedy had befriended the twenty-six-year-old Jimmy during the campaign and soon Joe was being billed as "one of the first and biggest discoverers of Jimmy." Kennedy underwrote some of his travels and put money directly into young Roosevelt's account at Columbia Trust.

Now Jimmy acted as his father's conduit, asking Joe if he would be interested in being a trade minister to Uruguay or ambassador to Ireland. Kennedy was insulted and more determined than ever to profit from his campaign support.

If Roosevelt was not going to take advantage of him, Joe would take advantage of Roosevelt. Communicating through the president's son and his secretary, Missy LeHand, Joe was soon the proud possessor of "two enormous permits" allowing him to import alcohol for "medicinal" purposes. Providing the alcohol for doctor's prescriptions was a huge market by itself, but there was tremendous potential profit in having liquor at the ready when Prohibition was repealed.

Joe and Rose took the young Roosevelts with them to London, where Jimmy was seen as the American equivalent to the Prince of Wales. His star power opened the doors to Haig & Haig and Dewar's, where Kennedy locked up most of the whiskey output of the British Isles. He returned to New York just before Utah became the thirty-sixth and final state necessary to ratify the twenty-first amendment ending Prohibition. He formally incorporated his liquor importing company, calling it Somerset, presumably taking the name from Boston's preeminent and exclusively Protestant social club. Ted O'Leary and Tom Delehanty were still in Joe's good graces and they were given the job of running Somerset Liquors. By the time Prohibition was officially lifted, a significant amount of Kennedy's liquor had already crossed the ocean and been distributed throughout the country, ready to supply a thirsty nation.

Christmas of 1933 found Joe back in Palm Beach where he finally bought a home of his own. Once again, his timing was perfect. Having resisted jumping into the Florida land boom of the 1920s, he now picked up a seven-bedroom, Addison Mizner–designed oceanfront estate with a pool on two acres on Millionaires Row at the Depression-induced price of only $100,000.

Kennedy was becoming convinced that any governmental appointment of merit was going to elude him and told friends he was "seriously considering going back into the picture business." Yet when others reached out and tried to get him (or at least his cash) involved again, he claimed, "When I retired from Pathé and the Swanson thing, I really washed up my entire interest in the picture business and conditions, to me, look so unsettled today that I am still of the opinion that I want to remain on the side lines."

Then, once again, Jimmy Roosevelt stepped in, facilitating an invitation for Joe and Rose to visit the White House. Kennedy joined the president at the Gridiron dinner and Rose began her practice of writing each of her children individually on White House stationery. Their scrapbooks would reflect the tangible evidence of their parents' importance.

After a year in office, Roosevelt was deep into revamping the economy through regulations, creating federal programs to put people to work and rebuild the country's infrastructure. The Securities and Exchange Commission was still in the process of being created, but its purpose was to reform Wall Street and "to eliminate fraud, to eliminate misrepresentation, to eliminate concealment of information and to make members of the exchange, members of the market, accountable for what they did." Would Kennedy be interested in heading up the commission to abolish the market's most blatant abuses that he had so handsomely profited from?

The president was under attack by the business community for "trying to overturn this society in a fundamental sense" and certainly no one could question Kennedy's knowledge of the stock market. He was a capitalist to the core, knew where the loopholes were, and as Joe himself put it in classic understatement, "I had a technical training and I had some years of experience which gave me knowledge of a very intricate business." Roosevelt was said to have told intimates with a smile that "it takes a thief to catch a thief."

In a private meeting, Kennedy swore to Roosevelt that "the bulk of my money had been made by business acumen rather than Wall Street operation" and promised he would "be a credit to the country, the President, himself, and his family—clear down to the ninth child." The president might have been convinced, but he still waited until the night before he left for a month-long vacation cruise to announce Kennedy's appointment.

Wall Streeters saw Joe as a traitor and New Dealers saw the appointment as a sellout. Once again, he was the outsider on the inside, but this time he was on the national stage and he knew what he had to do. In Hollywood, he had studied how people became personalities and now he applied that art to himself. He had been working the Washington press since being on the campaign trail and now he turned to the likes of Herbert Swope and the financier Bernard Baruch to solicit their support in reaching out to reporters willing "to give him a good start in his new job." One of the most important was Arthur Krock, the Washington-based correspondent for *The New York Times*. Krock was "charmed from the start" and believed Kennedy was a man who "had so much money" that his only concern was repaying "the debt he owed the country where he and his family had thrived so extraordinarily well."

Krock began trumpeting both Kennedy the man and his appointment, further refining the biography Joe had so carefully cultivated. Now *The New York Times* was giving its imprimatur to the story that he had been a star on the baseball field at Harvard, had turned down offers from professional teams to enter banking, and that it had been only because of his "ability so extraordinary" that he was "invited" to become president of Columbia Trust. His time as a "business administrator" of various film companies had earned him "the admiration of both Hollywood and Wall Street," but he retired from the movies because his "health [was] impaired." Still, Krock's claim that most strained credulity was that Kennedy had "never been in a bear pool in his life or participated in any inside move to trim the lambs. His Wall Street operations have been with his own money, in the interest of his own holdings."

After a tumultuous first meeting behind closed doors with Roosevelt's other commission members, Kennedy emerged as chairman of the SEC. He beamed as he met with reporters and announced that "the days of stock manipulation are in the past." In answering the barrage of questions, Joe assured his new public that "any success I ever achieved was in administrative work and not in market operations." His next step to elevate his persona was to give his first major speech as SEC chairman to the National Press Association, complete with a nationwide radio hook-up. His message was one of hope for economic recovery going hand in hand with market reform, assuring investors that "no honest man need fear the regulations."

At work at his $12,000-a-year job in an office that he personally paid to have air-conditioned, Kennedy reestablished his relationship with the president. It wasn't unusual for Joe to be at the White House several times a week. He took to his role as the market's regulator with a vengeance and set about hiring a staff that was young, smart, and unaffiliated with Wall Street. He reached out to future Supreme Court Justice William O. Douglas, then a professor at Yale, who in turn brought in his prize student, another future Supreme Court Justice, Abe Fortas. Eddie Moore was there as well, as "confidential assistant." He stayed on Kennedy's private payroll, but was also made a government employee at one dollar a year to allow him access to all government documents.

There was some talk of the family moving to Washington, but they remained in Bronxville while Joe leased a thirty-three-room Maryland estate known as Marwood overlooking the Potomac River. Several miles northeast of Washington, Marwood stood on over one hundred acres and featured a dozen master bedrooms, a pool, and a basement made over into a one-hundred-seat movie theater. The three-story mansion came completely furnished and with a full complement of household staff. With only Joe and Eddie in permanent residence, it quickly became a party house, or as the frequent visitor Arthur Krock called it, "an amazing chateau."

Joe regularly entertained press lords and reporters, senators and congressmen, and even the president and Missy LeHand. Dinners on the terrace for twenty or more were common several nights a week and while Joe would occasionally go north to visit the family for the weekend, more often he stayed at Marwood. He made full use of the theater, arranging to show films before or just as they were being released, keeping up the impression that as his power grew in Washington, his connections to Hollywood were as strong as ever. Joe was in touch with someone near or at the top of almost every studio and they were "perfectly willing to cooperate" with him, but instead he went directly to Will Hays to ask him to arrange with "all the companies to make available pictures for showing at my home." It was a micro-example of Kennedy's methods of operation in which little was not calculated. If he asked the studios for films, they would be doing him a favor. If Hays made the "gentle suggestion," providing Kennedy with films became the fulfillment of a request from the MPPA. The result was that his position of power was reinforced without any chits accumulating in his column.

Hays was suffering some slings and arrows, primarily from Catholic and other "reform" groups leading a renewed charge for censorship. Crime movies such as *Public Enemy* and "fallen woman" films such as *Red Headed Woman* and *Blonde Venus* had provoked their wrath to the point that Hays asked Kennedy to talk to Boston's Cardinal O'Connell about toning down his protests. Yet after years of assuaging the zealots with lists of "don'ts" and "be carefuls" for film content, a full-fledged, unwavering Production Code was now to be enforced. Hays tried to put a positive face on it, claiming that "at last, we had a police department," and its new chief was the very Catholic Joseph Breen, a former public relations man who had transformed his push for the Code's enforcement into a well-paying job. Questions were raised whether Hays had negotiated himself into a position where he was a "mere Hindenburg" with Breen as the new "Hitler of Hollywood," but Hays held on.

Kennedy kept up with all the latest by corresponding regularly with his old friend Arthur Houghton, now at the Hollywood office of the MPPA. Joe stayed in touch with Nick Schenck, Sidney Kent, and other studio executives, lunching with them when he was in New York. One of Eddie Moore's tasks was to ensure that Kennedy's lifetime subscription to *Variety* was changed with each move, from Cape Cod to Washington to Palm Beach, and back again. Joe almost couldn't help himself from looking at possible ways to reenter the film business. He made sure he had prints of the films he had produced and had not been scrapped. He double-checked that he retained the rights as well, just in case he wanted to remake them. Yet no one was clamoring for his services at the moment and, as he wrote to Houghton in early 1934, while there were plenty of companies needing a steady hand, "I still see no signs of any sanity in the picture business."

The members of the gang who remained were now part of a more decentralized operation, yet they were still the traffic cops, making sure everything ran like clockwork—Pat Scollard oversaw Joe's remaining Wall Street investments and various Delaware corporations while Johnnie Ford was in Boston, supervising Maine and New Hampshire as well as Kennedy's other New England properties and investments. Arthur Poole had remained at RKO, but available for special assignments, and Isidor Kresel had replaced Benjamin DeWitt as the primary attorney. Ted O'Leary and Tom Delehanty were at Somerset Liquors, headquartered at 230 Park Avenue, where business was booming for the "exclusive importers of Dewar's and Haig & Haig."

Eddie and Mary Moore took an apartment at the Park Chambers on West 58th Street. Joe had his suite at the Waldorf, but he needed a New York base and someone to oversee that operation. To fill that role, he promoted Paul Murphy, who had been taking care of small details for him since the late 1920s and would be depended upon for decades to come. Murphy continued to work out of Pathé on 45th Street until Joe took a suite of offices at the newly opened Rockefeller Center in late 1934.

Loyalty was still key to survival and the overall purpose was the same—to keep everything running smoothly and profitably with a minimum of Joe's involvement. Travel arrangements and the coordination of the various Kennedy homes fell to Murphy, down to keeping the inventory of the liquor at each abode, but it was Johnnie Ford who made several trips to Bronxville to check on how their electric bills could be lowered and what trees needed to be removed. Murphy and Ford also handled the hiring of the household staffs down to the chauffeurs.

The giving of gifts to family and friends continued to be delegated. Some employees and extended family members were simply sent cash from the New York office where a holiday gift list was maintained. Rose relayed her wishes to the office and then Paul Murphy sought Joe's approval for her requests. Rose also used Murphy to communicate with her children's schools and doctors and the older boys grew dependent on "Sir Paul," as Jack called him, to meet their personal needs.

The Kennedys' twentieth wedding anniversary was celebrated by sending each other loving cables as Joe stayed home and Rose went to Paris. Roosevelt appreciated the image Kennedy projected photographed with his wife and nine children, yet the president knew full well of his philandering. In private, he advised him to be more discreet, but Joe wasn't about to change his ways.

Kennedy continued to work hard and play hard, averaging twelve hours a day at the office when in town and chalking up 65,000 air miles over the course of a year. Still, he rarely missed his morning horseback ride, a swim in his pool, or an outing that would serve his interests such as the White House Correspondents Dinner. In addition to his relationship with Arthur Krock, which showed its presence regularly in the pages of *The New York Times,* Joe befriended the columnists Walter Winchell and Drew Pearson and publishers such as Colonel McCormick of the *Chicago Tribune* and Cissy Patterson of the *Washington Times Herald.* Joe also made frequent appearances in newsreels that showed him in shirtsleeves behind his desk at the SEC.

Kennedy made time to socialize with a few like-minded men within the administration such as Gene Vidal, Roosevelt's director of air regulation over at the Commerce Department. Gore Vidal remembers his father speaking fondly of Kennedy and the days when they were, unencumbered by their marriage vows, "two young guys on the make, both chasing girls."

After fourteen months as chairman of the SEC, Kennedy resigned in September of 1935 and reporters and cameras packed his office to review his accomplishments. The number of stock exchanges had been reduced; they all operated under the same rules and stocks had to be registered before they could be sold. The response to his departure was just as vocal as the one that had greeted his appointment, but this time it was overwhelmingly positive. He made the cover of *Time* and Kennedy's SEC was "generally conceded to be the New Deal's most successful reform." What had not even existed a little more than a year before was now a "going concern" on a "firm foundation."

As was his practice, Joe sent several dozen letters to reporters, editors, and publishers from *The New York Times* on down, graciously thanking them for their coverage. The letters were slightly personalized, but each began with the phrase "I am leaving public life for good" and then went on to express his appreciation and best wishes. Words like "fairness," "most helpful," and "deeply grateful" were sprinkled throughout. He knew how to leave them smiling.

Certainly there had been bigger and more famous Wall Street wolves, but none made a more dramatic turnaround. Kennedy had done what he did best, go into a new territory with his figurative guns blazing

His first cover of *Time* magazine as he turned forty-seven, September 1935

and make an impact in record time. Years before, he had told a fellow broker they had to make their killing before someone passed a law against it and now Kennedy was the public face of those changes. It was emblematic of his perfect timing—he had been in there with the best of them when the going was good, but hadn't spent an ounce of energy resisting what he knew was inevitable. Instead, he embraced the shift and claimed it as his own.

# CHAPTER 27

# "Wall Street Awaits Kennedy's Findings"

## (1936–1937)

*A*fter leaving the Securities and Exchange Commission, Kennedy took off for a European vacation, but by November of 1935 he was back in New York, profiting from a bear market, catching up with old associates, and looking for new opportunities. His Hollywood experience came back full force in an unwanted way when he was called to testify before Congressman Adolph Sabath's committee. They were investigating real estate transactions in corporate reorganizations, and since theaters were deemed to be real estate, several film company executives were subpoenaed.

Johnnie Ford had been called before the committee in October and his testimony was a primer on how to answer without saying anything. He responded "yes" or "no" or "I don't know" to questions that were often based on misconceptions that Ford did not correct. He could honestly say that Kennedy didn't own any film company stocks because if he did, they were held under the names of Delaware corporations.

Kennedy had already had several run-ins with Congressman Sabath over the SEC and testifying in private at the New York field office, he put the committee on notice that "the whole transaction savored of persecution." Then, just days before Christmas, he was recalled from Palm Beach to testify again and this time he didn't wait to voice his complaints. He opened by informing the committee that any questions about Pathé were outside their "proper scope" because it had not been in receivership nor reorganized prior to its sale to RKO. Technically he was correct. Pathé stockholders may have been severely shortchanged if not downright defrauded, but they never had been bondholders of real estate subject to bankruptcy. And the last thing Kennedy wanted was a microscope put on that sale.

It had been almost five years since RKO had bought Pathé and the changes in Hollywood since then had been substantial. The tremendous cost of transitioning to sound was just beginning to be recouped when the bank closures of early 1933 strapped the studios for cash. The studio heads responded by slashing salaries up to 50 percent and that became the catalyst for the formation of unions, so long successfully doused by Louis B. Mayer and his fellow moguls.

David Sarnoff, still president of RCA, had faced a variety of crises of his own, but the company had grown to be a behemoth with subsidiaries larger than many corporations. RCA was a leader in almost every area of communication and before the crash the stock was over $500 a share, but the company had been hit hard since then. Antitrust action forced General Electric and Westinghouse out of RCA and in spite of Hiram Brown's confidence that selling movies was "just the same as selling anything else," he was proven to be in over his head when RKO went into receivership. By 1935, RCA was millions of dollars in debt and in desperate need of reorganization.

Sarnoff may have parted with Kennedy under strained circumstances, but he had always respected Joe's abilities and now he needed him again. RCA had solicited three different recapitalization plans, but there were conflicting interests. Each favored one of the three types of RCA stock and Sarnoff wanted an impartial viewpoint that emphasized the long-term health of the company. Kennedy had just left the SEC; who better to ensure that its revised structure was on proper legal and fiscal grounds? Would Joe consider coming in for a month or so to study the plans and make his own recommendations for recapitalizing? For his time and trouble, he would be paid $125,000.

It was the type of assignment that was perfect for Kennedy. He had a clear task he was uniquely qualified to carry out with complete access to all the books. He agreed to Sarnoff's proposal and by early December 1935, Joe was in residence in Palm Beach, quietly going over the company's accounts.

He made a quick trip to New York, interviewed a few key people, and took the promoters of the various plans to lunch. In less than a month he submitted his twenty-three-page report recommending that all three of the proposals be rejected in favor of his own "Kennedy Plan." Joe told David—and it was once again Joe and David—it was equitable and, most important to Sarnoff, "management retains the good will of its stockholders and the confidence of the investment and speculative public."

Kennedy personally reviewed the printer's proofs of his proposal, which was accepted by both the board and the shareholders. He spent the rest of the season in Palm Beach, basking in the praise generated in the press over the RCA recapitalization. Sarnoff announced earnings were projected to be over $1 million for the next quarter and all three levels of RCA stock saw an increase in value.

Did this foreshadow Joe's reentry into the film business? *Variety* reported that "various approaches had been made" to him, but predicted that if Roosevelt was reelected, Kennedy would be named secretary of the treasury. No announcements "should be expected until after the election." The source for the speculation was obviously Joe himself as he seems to be the only one who consistently put his name forward for that cabinet post, but as he looked around in early 1936, there were several studios temptingly ripe for a takeover.

At the top of the list was Paramount. It had everything Kennedy had tried to put together elsewhere: a bustling studio, a dynamic distribution unit, and thousands of theaters. And, best of all, it was in a chaotic mess just begging to be saved from itself.

Adolph Zukor had withstood previous assaults and was no slacker when it came to a fight. He had taken on William Hodkinson back in the teens and First National in the early 1920s and, in the process, accumulated one of the largest theater circuits in the country. Paramount was still operating in the black when 1931 dawned, claiming $300 million in assets and almost $20 million in annual profits. However, Zukor's personal wealth of $50 million was in Paramount stock and he used it to buy more theaters, guaranteeing the stock value at $80 a share. When the price fell to below $50 and those purchase agreements were called, Zukor lost his fortune and the company fell into a complicated bankruptcy.

"A railroad receivership is child's play compared to this vast multiheaded company," the attorney Elihu Root said in justifying his firm's $1 million legal bill. The morass eventually involved over fifty law firms in bitter, lengthy court fights. The maelstrom of lawsuits—even the lawyers were sued—left the company close to anarchy. Zukor's longtime partner, Jesse Lasky, left in 1932 to join RKO; Sidney Kent, who had headed distribution, moved to the presidency of the new 20th Century Fox, and Sam Katz, after attempting to dethrone Zukor, had jumped to MGM.

Paramount emerged from these battles with "a clean new corporate structure," but with fewer than a thousand theaters and a board of directors made up of "ill-assorted bankers and real estate men" representing the largest claimants against the company. As *Fortune* reported tongue-in-cheek, "all that remained was for the new management to learn the movie business." The now sixty-two-year-old Zukor was moved to what was commonly acknowledged to be "the harmless office of Board Chairman."

After almost a year of floundering, the new Paramount regime was facing the public release of their annual financial statement and there was no hiding the fact their stock price had sunk to $8 a share. The board needed to do something dramatic to assure their shareholders they took their situation seriously and several members suggested that Joe Kennedy had the combination of skills and experience to make a powerful statement: a man who had run more studios than any other executive yet who also spoke Wall Street's language.

The last week of April of 1936 found Kennedy in New York negotiating to be Paramount's "Special Advisor" with "full and complete authority" to conduct "a survey of the affairs of the corporation." In other words, everyone in the company was mandated to cooperate with him and provide any information he needed to turn the company around. Joe could hire whomever he wanted with all his expenses covered, but the amount of his salary was left to be determined at a later date. That was just how he had started with Pathé and he ended up chairman of the board, so he agreed, but with a few demands of his own.

Kennedy was most adamant that he was to be free of any interference and warned he wouldn't be reporting back to the board until his findings were complete. In the meantime, they weren't to fill any of their current vacancies. Ready to do whatever he wanted, a special board meeting was called for Friday morning, May 1, to ratify the agreement and that very afternoon Joe was in Paramount's New York office beginning his latest challenge. One of his first moves was to bring in Johnnie Ford to handle the theater end of the investigation. Paramount's theater holdings may have been slashed by two thirds, but that real estate was still a major portion of the total value of the company.

Leaving Ford in Manhattan, Joe, along with Pat Scollard and Arthur Poole, headed for the airport to fly to Los Angeles. Poole had stayed on at RKO as treasurer through the fall of 1935 when he decided "I can always get a job, but I can't always get the kind of job that is most worth while." He took Joe up on his long-standing offer to rejoin him and moved into the Rockefeller Plaza office. As a show of trust, Kennedy put Poole on the board of his Cinema Credits Corporation, kept active as a shell to house his stock holdings.

By Monday, the trades were headlining the news that Kennedy had been "unanimously invited" by Paramount to spearhead "a survey of the situation, to report and make recommendations." In a quote that echoed the Pathé appointment of eight years before, it was stated that "in his role as adviser he is assuming no direct authority."

On Tuesday morning, Kennedy, Poole and Scollard were at the Paramount Studio on Melrose, which dwarfed the abutting RKO (formerly Joe's FBO). Paramount was bigger all the way around. They had more than eighty actors under contract including Gary Cooper, Carole Lombard, Fred MacMurray, Claudette Colbert, and Charles Boyer. They also boasted sixty writers such as Preston Sturges, Charles Brackett, Clifford Odets, S. J. Perelman, and Dorothy Parker.

The boys were back in business. Kennedy spent his first day in meetings with Adolph Zukor, whom the board had authorized to have a voice in production. A series of production chiefs, including B. P. Schulberg, Walter Wanger, and the director Ernst Lubitsch, had been shown the door, and Kennedy's former employee, William LeBaron, was now holding that position. It had been over seven years since he had left Kennedy and *Queen Kelly,* which he was supposedly supervising, to go with RKO, but that was water long under the bridge. There were other familiar faces as well such as Barney Glazer and Cecil B. De Mille.

From the outset, Kennedy broadened his scope. A master of sending messages while actually saying very little, he praised the company and then asked, "How that potentiality can be most fully realized: what line it should take, what changes in major policies? These are the questions I shall try to answer in my role which is equivalent to a Committee of Survey and Policy." He emphasized his assignment was open-ended and claimed he had "no preconceptions" about what he was going to advise.

The word was out that the "slate is to be wiped clean" and "New York" was no longer making the decisions. When Joe moved into the office suite of the current president, John Otterson, there was no question of who was in charge. Underscoring Kennedy's power, Scollard settled into the second-largest office.

Kennedy had come up in the world in more ways than one; this time he took up residence in the Beverly Hills home of the Countess di Frasso, a jet-setter before there were jets. Rich in her own right through family money, she had picked up a title by way of a second marriage and was famous in the movie capital for taking Gary Cooper to Europe and teaching him the finer things in life. She gave headline-grabbing parties when she was in town, but just as often she was at her villa in Italy or her apartment in Manhattan. Joe reported he "couldn't have been more pleased" with the Bedford Drive home and the full staff that kept it "running like a top."

Joe didn't have to let people know he was in Los Angeles; the trades took care of that for him. He was soon inundated with letters from old associates, some wanting just to catch up, others looking for work. To most, he reiterated that he was "not mixing in any question of personnel whatsoever."

Being unattached in Hollywood gave Joe a new social freedom and he became friendly with the town's preeminent agent, Charlie Feldman. Having an agent as a close friend was anathema to most studio heads, even former ones, but Charlie and Joe both considered themselves the best at what they did and they gravitated to success in others. They were also both charming if notorious womanizers known for their self-deprecating sense of humor. Charlie, like Joe, never let a little thing like marriage get in the way of a good time.

Orphaned at a young age, Feldman had worked his way through USC Law School and practiced for several years before he handled his first Hollywood contract. It didn't take a genius to figure out that a $5,000 paycheck for negotiating a million-dollar deal for Edward G. Robinson would have been $100,000 if Feldman had been his agent instead of his lawyer so he changed shingles. By the mid-1930s, Charlie was firmly established, but he ran head-on into Louis B. Mayer's wrath when he married the gorgeous MGM ingenue Jean Howard. Mayer had it in his head he was going to marry her, in spite of still being married himself, and when Jean wed Charlie, Mayer swore he would not allow the agent on the lot or hire any of his clients. Hollywood being Hollywood, Mayer had to break down eventually, but not before disparaging him all over town. Everyone knew that to help Charlie Feldman was to cross Mayer, but Kennedy couldn't have cared less. In spite of the fact Joe was supposedly only advising, he upped the Paramount contract for one of Charlie's biggest clients of the moment, Claudette Colbert.

From behind his big desk at Paramount, Kennedy interviewed executives and reviewed production records. He had the perfect excuse to question everyone about everything: the methods behind their operation, the way they organized production, and the efficacy of outside contractors. It was a refresher course on how to—or how not to—run a fully integrated film company.

Their costs were out of control, but Kennedy was most shocked by the board's blatant mismanagement. He had been among the first to bring financiers onto boards of directors, but the complexities of Paramount's receivership had allowed creditors and bankers to dominate decision making to the point there was no one who understood filmmaking. Not that Kennedy was going to go after all the board members. Instead he set the stage to play some against others and he cultivated those who could be of long-term interest. John Hertz, whose Yellow Cab company Joe had "saved" over a decade before, had been on and off the Paramount board over the past several years, and Henry Luce was currently on the board. Kennedy had socialized with Luce in Washington, reaching out to the man a decade younger who had created *Time* magazine shortly after graduating from Yale. Luce was still in the process of building his own publishing empire when he and his new beautiful blond second wife, Clare Boothe, came west and asked Joe to dine with them. Luce was fleshing out ideas for his latest creation, *Life* magazine, and Clare was working on a play entitled *The Women.* They may have been the power couple of the moment, but Clare dubbed Joe "the destiny shaper of the West Coast."

After almost a month in Hollywood, Joe flew back to New York to meet with the Paramount board. He was as vague as possible and told them his report would not be ready for several more weeks, just in time for their scheduled annual stockholders meeting on June 16, 1936. At the moment, the board was more concerned about Adolph Sabath's congressional investigation, which had expanded to include lawyers and others who had profited from receiverships. Paramount, with its tortuous and complicated legal history, was a prime target. With their annual meeting only weeks away, the last thing they needed was a public airing of their failures. Joe took on the challenge, and though he had rebuffed the committee the previous winter, he now cabled Sabath that he was "deeply appreciative of the constructive work" he was doing, but was concerned about "the ultimate good of the security holders." A hearing at this time would only "confuse matters." Couldn't they at least postpone the hearings until after Paramount's stockholders meeting? Kennedy was enough of a Paramount outsider and a Washington insider to pull it off; Sabath agreed to defer calling Paramount indefinitely.

Kennedy's swift and effective action was a tremendous relief to the board and as he returned to Hollywood, *Variety* fanned the flames of anticipation by headlining "Wall Street Awaits Kennedy's Findings." Joe wasn't talking. Instead, he went into seclusion, along with Scollard and Poole, to write a devastating fifty-page report on Paramount's condition.

What had gone wrong at Paramount? According to Joe, just about everything. He claimed the company's recent financial report showed only a "bookkeeping profit" and in reality they were $7 million over budget and lying to their stockholders. The opening pages of his report were a course in basic film economics. While acknowledging business in general had been bad, he pointed out that since 1934 every studio but Paramount had been recovering.

No one was left unscathed. Talent was now "unfortunately unionized," which strengthened their "salary grabbing methods." Then there were the agents, who were strangling producers with their "death hand clutch." Producers habitually overspent, but he found De Mille the worst offender. The "shooting schedules were being disregarded," expensive stories "junked," and, as *Fortune* later summed up his charges, "costly stars were being alienated, writers were loafing, truck drivers were sulking and things generally were in one hell of a mess."

Kennedy saved his harshest shots for the men at the top. He practically charged the board with fraud and ineptitude and suggested that executives should have "fixed nominal salaries with bonus payments when and if net earnings" justify them.

His report was cloaked in secrecy because his plan was to deliver it personally at the stockholders meeting where he could "sway the convention" into believing he was the only one who could save the company from itself. The trades speculated that Kennedy "had too many outside interests to confine his future activities to Paramount," but if it was necessary for him to take over after submitting his report, he would oblige. *Variety,* among others, got wind that Kennedy was planning to call on the entire board to resign and name an "outside proxy committee." Joe didn't comment directly, but he did allow that he "did not know of any movie man competent and willing to take charge of Paramount."

The rumors were enough to convince Adolph Zukor that Joe was planning a coup. Zukor wrote Rose a "thank you note" for "letting" Joe come to Hollywood and told her "we all feel it would be a great loss if he did not remain with us," but that was the last thing he wanted. If Kennedy ran Paramount, Zukor knew he had no chance at a continuing, viable role and therefore he had to find an alternative leader. So while Joe returned to New York by plane, Zukor boarded the train with Barney Balaban, who had continued to run Balaban and Katz theaters since their merger with Paramount, and "talked his ear off all the way." According to Balaban's son, Leonard, Zukor believed Kennedy would take over the company unless something drastic was done. He was confident the one man the troops would rally around was Balaban, who was "blunt, uncomplicated," and respected within the company.

If Balaban was on the fence, the idea of Kennedy taking over Paramount had to move him. He had "distrusted and actively disliked" Joe since their run-in over First National almost a decade earlier and Balaban had come to think of him as a man interested in films only because "he craved recognition and loved the reflected glory."

Zukor might have been a man out of favor within his own company, but according to Balaban's son, he still had the clout to arrange for Kennedy to be met at the boardroom door, be paid off on the spot, and barred from entering the meeting. The story of the payoff may be apocryphal, but the results were the same. Instead of the stockholders hearing Joe's conclusions, his report was accepted without being read. The board didn't want Kennedy's criticisms to be publicly aired and, as Zukor had hoped, Balaban was elected president, in part because he was a known quantity with unassailable experience and in part because he stopped Kennedy.

Joe went home and waited and, after two weeks, he had his attorney draft a letter telling the Paramount board that "Since I have had no word from you that you desire me to press the investigation further, I assume that my services are at an end. I would thank you, therefore, to fix my compensation as provided in said resolution and cause the same to be paid to me."

When he finally heard back in early July, it was to thank him profusely for his report and claim they had "given a great deal of time and thought to the solutions of its management problems." After several pages of resolutions stating their appreciation and "due consideration," they concluded that the prompt action Kennedy had called for had been dealt with by electing Balaban president. Joe would have to wait for a decision on his remuneration.

As Balaban moved to New York to take over Paramount and Zukor returned to Hollywood to supervise production, Kennedy seethed in Hyannisport. He had been the horse at the gate, chafing at the bit to take over, and now they had dismissed his work, used his chits with Congressman Sabath, and had yet to establish his fee. Several more weeks would pass before a letter arrived telling him that the executive committee had set his stipend at $50,000, less than half of what he had received for the much less time-consuming RCA restructuring. Kennedy was livid, but what could he do? He had agreed to keep his compensation open under the assumption it would lead to greater things. He curtly informed them he was willing to accept that amount "without further discussion," only because "of the condition of the company." He couldn't resist one final jab and, addressing the full board of directors, asked that copies of his report be sent to all stockholders since "my recommendations have not been followed."

His three-month-long mission to skyrocket to the top of the business had misfired. To minimize any public damage and make it look like his choice, Joe sent a blanket missive to *The New York Times, The Wall Street Journal, Variety,* and a dozen other press outlets stating, "I have concluded my work as special advisor with the filing of my final report and am not now associated with the company in any capacity." Privately he told individual reporters that Paramount was "still in a mess" and he was "not at all impressed with their idea of working it out."

The irony was that, with all he had learned and experienced, Kennedy may well have been an excellent studio head. He appreciated aspects and nuances of the business that only a man seasoned by both success and failure could, but he had named names and taken no prisoners. To have elevated him to president would have emasculated the board and most of Paramount's executives as well as called all the studio's operations into question.

FRANKLIN ROOSEVELT turned to Kennedy to help raise campaign funds for his reelection, but Joe suggested something else he could do that would promote both the president and himself: author a book entitled *I'm for Roosevelt.* Joe claimed he wanted to "take a crack at the people who should be down on their knees thanking Roosevelt" because he "had saved the capitalistic system." As supportive as his verbiage was, he didn't actually write the book. While still in Hollywood with Paramount, he arranged for John Burns, who had worked with him at the SEC, to write a comprehensive outline and then Kennedy offered Arthur Krock $1,000 a week for five weeks to "help put it in shape."

*I'm for Roosevelt* was released in August of 1936 and almost immediately went into extra printings. Full of facts and figures, it was a detailed and credible review of conditions in the country when Roosevelt came into office and the success of his programs to date. The book was syndicated in newspapers, thousands of copies were distributed to local Democratic organizations, and it was a catalyst for profiles and articles on Kennedy in national newspapers and magazines. In the process, he was promoted as "a financier of national reputation" and "a father of nine children," both taglines being crucial to the image that was being massaged into celebrity status. Just as *The Story of the Films* had increased his credibility within the film community, *I'm for Roosevelt* set Joe apart from other New Dealers and added a patina of power and prestige.

In spite of this new burst of publicity, Kennedy was without a specific job or assignment. Friends noticed a change in Joe as "he was given to long silences, deep distractions." By late 1936, Pat Scollard had served his purpose. He was removed from his various positions including as the on-paper president and treasurer of the ubiquitous Fred Thomson Productions. The corporation had been kept alive to house stocks Kennedy had owned for years but didn't want his name attached to, as well as recent acquisitions that were turned around quickly such as Paramount. To further distance himself, Kennedy had Thomson Productions placed under the trust he created for his children.

Eddie Moore shepherded seven of the Kennedy offspring through Roosevelt's second inauguration in early 1937: the speech, the parade, and a White House reception. Joe stayed close to home as Rose was suffering a deep depression and had not left the house since the unexpected death of her sister Agnes the previous September. Rose was "not well by any means," Kennedy wrote Missy LeHand in declining Roosevelt's invitation to dine at the White House.

Instead of waiting for a phone call that didn't come about a cabinet appointment, Kennedy began working with William Randolph Hearst. They had now known each other for fifteen years and their friendship continued even though W.R. had broken with Roosevelt, taken to calling the New Deal the "Raw Deal," and thrown his support to Alf Landon in the 1936 election.

Marion Davies was completing what would be her last film, *Ever Since Eve*. In spite of the speech impediment that still plagued her in private, she had tenaciously conquered her stuttering when the cameras were rolling and turned into a delightful romantic comedienne. Yet Hearst had wanted more for her, dramatic roles such as Marie Antoinette and Elizabeth Barrett Browning. At MGM, those parts went to Irving Thalberg's wife, Norma Shearer, and as important as Hearst and Davies were to Louis B. Mayer, the studio head was not alone in being unable to see Davies successfully portraying those characters. Hearst took it as a personal affront, and in 1934, they dramatically left MGM for Warner Bros., dismantling Marion's famous fourteen-room "bungalow" into three sections for its move from Culver City to Burbank. Marion was pushing forty and still looked great, but it was a challenge to play the ingenue, and after only four Warner Bros. films she decided it was time to get out. Hearst was more than thirty years her senior and although he loved watching her on the screen, he also wanted her at his side as they traveled the world.

Davies was also aware that Hearst had reached the point he needed tending, not so much physically, but in facing a looming financial crisis. After years of borrowing and hedging his properties to pay for his massive buying sprees, the Depression, increased taxes, and his extravagant spending were catching up with him. With circulation of some of his newspapers and magazines at new lows, he asked Kennedy to come up with a "corporate reorganization" for his empire. The old bank examiner could never resist unrestrained access to someone else's books, especially for a man as rich and powerful as Hearst. Kennedy took the balance sheets and, along with Arthur Poole, evaluated the situation. Joe's suggestion was to sell new bonds attached to Hearst's property, but the reforms instituted by his own SEC mandated real numbers be appended to the prospectus and so it was out there in black and white how tenuous Hearst's position was.

Marion Davies and William Randolph Hearst in the mid-1930s

Canadian banks began demanding that their notes be paid before newsprint was released. Without paper, his publications would halt and Hearst was urged to sell some of his floundering newspapers, but he couldn't bring himself to part with any of them. At the point of desperation, Hearst and Davies were at their apartment at the Ritz Towers in New York when Kennedy arrived with an offer: $14 million for all of the Hearst magazines. If Joe's proposal was considered, it wasn't for long. Even in the depths of the Depression, the magazines were bringing in that much each year.

Yet dire action of some sort was needed and Marion, who had been making $10,000 a week as an actress, had access to much more cash than Hearst at the moment. She sold $1 million of her assets and handed it over to him. One can only imagine how difficult it was for the proud Hearst to accept, but that million, along with loans from two other women, Cissy Patterson and Abby Rockefeller, bought him the time to turn his situation around. (Marion later could not resist pointing out that Hearst's wife, Millicent, who was more than taken care of as she raised their four sons in New York, didn't lift a finger to help.)

If Hearst was "shocked" by Kennedy's low-ball offer for the magazines, as his son later claimed, it doesn't seem to have made a dent in their relationship. There is no doubt that Hearst ran hot and cold in his feelings about Kennedy, but he considered him "a trusted friend and a gentleman." Joe was on the short list of contenders to be named the trustee for Hearst's holdings, a step considered necessary to restore investor confidence. Kennedy also continued to advise W.R., and was one of the five hundred people invited to one of their biggest parties yet, a circus-themed celebration of Hearst's seventy-fourth birthday in April of 1937 at the Santa Monica beach house featuring a full-sized merry-go-round. Joe thanked Marion for the invitation, assuring her "there is nothing in the world I would like better than to attend the circus," but his work "on matters in connection with Mr. Hearst's interests" and his new assignment from Roosevelt forced him to stay in Washington.

After losing out on Paramount, Kennedy claimed he was "going to take up 'the bum's life,' " but then, as he explained to a friend, Roosevelt had been so persuasive he convinced Joe to "give up my business, give up my leisure to take up the most unworkable bill I ever read in my life, but you know that man's winning ways." Joe's latest mission took him to the fourth floor of the Commerce Department building as chair of the Maritime Commission, recently created by Congress to "see if a respectable merchant marine could be created out of the high cost, low efficiency, strike plagued shipping industry." The Maritime Commission was similar to the SEC in that it was a new agency designed to rein in an important slice of the private sector. There was no denying it was a second-tier appointment, yet in explaining his hesitancy to take the job, Joe implied it meant turning down "very profitable" enterprises such as Paramount or the Hearst Corporation, neither of which were actually available to him.

Kennedy returned to Washington and his Marwood estate determined to make the Maritime Commission a showplace for his abilities. With Eddie Moore at his side, he worked long hours "hanging on to the telephone," negotiating, bullying, and charming the agency into effectiveness. Within three months of taking over, Kennedy settled millions of dollars' worth of claims by a dozen shipping companies for pennies on the dollar. Since he was simultaneously negotiating with them for new operating subsidies, they had more than enough reason to cooperate, yet it was a tremendous coup and his dramatic accomplishments created a new chapter in the Kennedy book of legends.

Harvey Klemmer was hired to handle publicity, but he soon realized his boss "was a genius in public relations. He had the whole country waiting for the economic survey. He built up the suspense like it was the second coming of Christ." Just as if he were preparing to premiere an epic film, Joe released his "monumental study" surrounded by reporters and banks of cameras. The innately isolationist Kennedy touched a national nerve and played on fears that suggested the country was unprotected without him. Newsreels proclaimed Roosevelt's "hard boiled troubleshooter" as the savior who had once again solved a national crisis that had eluded lesser men. Joe was heaped with adulatory praise as "straight talking, extremely able and highly picturesque."

Almost every print medium carried stories on Kennedy and a full-page photograph of him in *Life* magazine was headlined "Chairman Kennedy calls for a new Merchant Marine built for war." Joe was diligent in his courting of the press, but his primary focus was *Fortune* magazine and the cover story they had been working on since shortly after the creation of the Maritime Commission. Kennedy agreed to make himself and his associates available for interviews on the condition that he be allowed to review the article prior to printing and *Fortune*'s managing editor, Russell Davenport, approved the terms. For years, Joe had managed to play most reporters like violins, promoting the version of his life

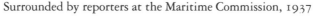

Surrounded by reporters at the Maritime Commission, 1937

he wanted projected and serving as the editor of his own biography. However, the *Fortune* reporter, Harry Looker, began doing his own investigating and when Joe read the draft of the article, he fumed that it was "permeated with distrust of my character, dislike of my occupations and social prejudice against my origin." He told Davenport it contained more than fifty "inaccuracies" and was so "cheap and tawdry," reading it made him ill. It was "the brain child of a psycho-pathetic case" with "an ingrained hatred of the Irish."

There were indeed some cheap shots and the overall tone was flippant. Kennedy's sisters' voices were "shrill," Winthrop, Massachusetts, was "dismal," and Joe had made "a shambles" of K-A-O. Stereotypical innuendoes of his heritage, such as "he could bellow like an Irish cop," laced the piece. Kennedy questioned the "taste and justice" of such comments, but he didn't argue other ethnic clichés, such as calling an Italian "swart." There were a few blatant inaccuracies: *Queen Kelly* had been "suppressed" because it might have offended "the Church" and that at the time of his takeover, FBO was one of Hollywood's "largest producers and heaviest losers." Joe couldn't have been pleased when the reporter alleged that few in the press had heard of Kennedy before he was named to the SEC. Some of Joe's points were totally legitimate, but his biggest concern had to be that this was the first article to raise real questions about his character. Looker stated that Joe was "a cold blooded bear of exceptional shrewdness" with "dirty money-changing hands" and a history of being "dictatorial." He summed up Joe's professional life as "twenty two years of quick profit taking [and] fourteen months of public service."

Kennedy wasn't about to allow the piece to see the light of day, but even he had to be surprised when Davenport practically gave him carte blanche to make changes. Another writer was immediately assigned and in mid-July, Kennedy was sent a new draft with a note from the editor, who assumed "it's a big improvement" with its major changes in "style, pace and content." Still, if anything "stirs your ire," Joe was "to holler." To be sure all was to Kennedy's liking, Davenport asked to set up a meeting to go over it in person and promised him that "we are open to discussion" on everything, "because you have in me your very sincere admirer."

The cover story that eventually ran in *Fortune*'s September issue led by describing Kennedy as "a legendary man of action." The content and tone had been altered substantially and the handsome full-page photograph of his smiling face and sparkling eyes, his slightly receding hairline, and the freckles he had retained since childhood verified the image he presented of himself—a straight-talking common man who just happened to be a multimillionaire.

Kennedy could still find some fault, but there was much less to argue with. *Fortune* credited his film companies as a major source of his personal fortune and found that "tracing his path from Boston to Hollywood leads you into the ruins of vanished corporations . . . from which there arise whiffs of an atmosphere distinctly gamey."

That was the biggest question the article raised and the remaining pages piled praise upon praise. Kennedy had fought hard for this picture of himself, using a combination of charm, fury, and influence to have his way, and for good reason. The *Fortune* article, along with the pieces written by Krock in *The New York Times* and those that had previously appeared in *Photoplay* and the *American Magazine,* would be used as underpinnings of almost everything written about him from then on.

He had taken the lessons of Hollywood, fashioned his own image, and then marketed it. Once again, Joe was promoted as having pulled himself up by his proverbial bootstraps from a poor childhood, graduating from Harvard as a star of the baseball field, finding economic success through disciplined diligence, and then this fabulous, large family that he was so devoted to; in other words, the quintessential success story. As he would tell his sons, "It is not what you are, but what people think you are that is important."

# CHAPTER 28

# "The Embers of Terror, Isolationism, and Racism"

## (1938–1940)

Kennedy's public relations blitz gave Roosevelt new reasons for both pride and concern, yet to Joe's mind, the president still owed him for taking two less than stellar appointments and turning them into administration triumphs. Arthur Krock was dining with Joe at Marwood when Jimmy Roosevelt came calling to see if Kennedy was interested in serving as secretary of commerce. After half an hour, Joe returned to Arthur and reported, "FDR promised me London, and I told Jimmy to tell his father that's the job and the only one I'll accept." He was determined to be "the first Irishman to be Ambassador from the United States to the Court of Saint James."

History has provided a variety of answers to why Roosevelt agreed to appoint Kennedy to the prestigious, but potentially perilous, post. After all, Kennedy's previous international experience had been limited to a few trips to Europe and foreign box office receipts. Henry Morgenthau, the man who received the coveted post of secretary of the treasury, claimed that the president told him that "Kennedy was a very dangerous man and that he was going to send him to England with the distinct understanding that the appointment was only for six months and that furthermore, by giving him the appointment, any obligation that he had to Kennedy was paid for." Joe himself repeated the idea of a short tenure when he told his aide Harvey Klemmer not to pack too many bags. "We are only going to get the family in the Social Register. When that is done, we come on back and go out to Hollywood to make some movies and some money."

Kennedy's appointment as ambassador was big news, especially in Boston. Even though his "home" there for the past decade had been the Ritz-Carlton Hotel, Kennedy was treated like a conquering hero by the local press. He couldn't resist claiming he had accepted the post only at "the President's insistence," but no one was more pleased than Joe himself when he wrote in his diary on February 18, 1938, "Today I resigned as chairman of the Maritime Commission and was sworn in as ambassador to Great Britain."

England was in American headlines for more reasons than Kennedy's appointment. With the death of King George V in January of 1936, his eldest son, the thirty-nine-year-old Edward, assumed the throne. Soon, however, his affair with the twice married Wallis Warfield Spencer Simpson was the subject of international gossip and political concern. While she was seeking her second divorce, Edward was busy negotiating with the Church and Parliament for a special dispensation to marry her. Newspapers throughout the world updated

The new ambassador arrives at the White House.

the soap opera daily and passions were fanned: it was blasphemous, it was an unprecedented crisis for the monarchy, it was the greatest love story of the century. Finally, on December 11, 1936, King Edward VIII went on the radio to announce that it was impossible for him to remain king "without the help and support of the woman I love." The story was whipped into such an intense frenzy, Wallis Simpson became the first woman to be named *Time* magazine's "Man of the Year." Edward's younger brother, George, was crowned, but by the end of his first year as monarch the world had much more pressing concerns than his brother's love life.

Since Adolf Hitler's rise to chancellor in early 1933, the world had been given innumerable reasons for concern. That first year alone, there were book burnings, anti-Jewish boycotts, and the establishment of Dachau. Yet the "Jews Not Wanted" signs had been removed in Berlin for the Olympics of 1936 and many international visitors left with feelings similar to those expressed by Joe Junior during a visit to Germany in 1934. "Hitler is building a spirit in his men that would be envied in any country." He did acknowledge that "it is a remarkable spirit which can do tremendous good or harm, whose fate rests with one man alone."

Generalissimo Francisco Franco had ignited the Spanish Civil War, Benito Mussolini's Italy had conquered Ethiopia, and under the guise of anti-communism, Germany and Japan formed an alliance. While Kennedy joked with a fellow American diplomat that "you and I will be able to settle the affairs of the world either on horseback or the golf course," he had to be aware of the dark and complex clouds hovering over Europe. Still, Joe's immediate focus was on his triumphant send-off. Cameras lined the dock to capture his family waving goodbye and a week later, even more cameras greeted his arrival. His first official act as ambassador on March 16, 1938, was to present his credentials to the king at Buckingham Palace, followed by lunch at the Savoy hosted by London-based American correspondents.

Kennedy was now a star on the international stage and he meant to make the most of it. He was once again alongside banks of cameras several weeks later to meet Rose and the first "installment" of five of his children. The media attention given to him and his family was phenomenal. Their arrival was covered as if it was a Hollywood premiere and the publicity that followed was cultivated to ensure a long run.

Rose and five of the children waving from the pier, 1938

Eddie Moore was on staff and Kennedy added a *New York Times* State Department reporter as his embassy press secretary, but his job description was "tantamount to those of a press agent," promoting Joe as much as American interests. Even with a phalanx of staff, Joe was hands-on when it came to dealing with the media. He paid particular attention to the newsreels that were to be shown in America and the results were sensational. "The press went absolutely ape over the entire family," remembered Page Wilson, an embassy secretary. "I don't think there was a day in a month that there wasn't a photograph of the Kennedy family" in the newspapers. When Joe hit a hole in one, there was "extensive coverage" in both Britain and the United States, twelve-year-old Bobby was photographed laying the cornerstone of a children's hospital, and six-year-old Teddy was "starred" cutting the ribbon that opened a children's zoo.

Within less than two months of Kennedy's arrival in London, Franco claimed victory in Spain and Hitler expanded his power by absorbing Austria into the German "union." Joe filed regular briefings to the president and Secretary of State Cordell Hull, but to those Joe saw as his allies, such as William Randolph Hearst, Walter Lippmann, Arthur Krock, *Fortune*'s Russell Davenport, and a dozen others, he took to sending weekly "Private and Confidential" reports on issues of the day. The criteria for inclusion seemed to be what the receiver could do for Kennedy rather than whether they supported Roosevelt. In fact, the contents were not reviewed by anyone in the administration and the president was not on the list of recipients.

Kennedy's diary entries highlighted his socializing, meetings with various British leaders, and the resulting press coverage. Rose, Kathleen (known as Kick), and Rosemary were presented at court and they all, particularly eighteen-year-old Kick, dove into "the London Season," that sizzling period from May through July when formal dances were held four nights a week and then continued through the weekend at country estates. The choicest of these, the Astors' Cliveden, became almost a second home to the Kennedys.

Finally, Joe had the status he felt was his due. As ambassador, memberships in a variety of exclusive clubs were his without applications or fear of snubs. People wrote him simply to ask for his autograph. The appreciation of what the position brought them and the children was the first thing in years Rose could truly share with her husband. The marriage she had fought to save was what she had always dreamed it would be. Sitting at the king's right at dinner, lunching at Lady Astor's, and dining with the prime minister at 10 Downing Street was suddenly the norm. For the

Rose and Joe with King George VI and Queen Elizabeth, 1939

rest of her 104 years, Rose would reflect on her time as the wife of the ambassador at the Court of St. James as "the happiest of my life."

Kennedy claimed that before coming to London, they hadn't given twenty dinner parties during the entire twenty-five years of married life, but now they were entertaining several times a week. The fact his salary of $22,000 a year plus $5,000 for expenses required him to pour his own money in to cover the level of servants and entertaining he expected was the least of his concerns. Screening new American films quickly became a hallmark of dinner at the ambassador's and while a few of their guests commented that the movies were "not ones that we would have paid ten pence to see on our own," to question the appropriateness of the custom doesn't seem to have occurred to the Kennedys. To Joe, access to films before they were released was a visible sign of his continued importance in Hollywood and he simply assumed they were a special treat he was in the unique position to provide. When *Test Pilot,* starring Clark Gable and Myrna Loy, was screened following their dinner for Lord and Lady Halifax, Charles and Anne Lindbergh were among the guests and Rose proudly noted that the famous pilot found "the aeronautical display was very authentic and well worth seeing."

When King George and Queen Elizabeth were the honored guests, fresh flowers and strawberries were brought in from France and Virginia ham, two Disney cartoons, and *Goodbye, Mr. Chips* were flown in from the States. Rose remembered that the Robert Donat and Greer Garson film was "long, as it had not been cut—to use moving picture parlance—but excellent and marvelously acted. It was quite sad, and after it was finished, it was very plain to see that the Queen had had a little weep."

In the royal presence on a regular basis, Kennedy fell into interacting with the monarchs the same way he had treated the stars in Hollywood. He was particularly comfortable with the queen and reported to his diary that she blushed one evening when he told her "she looked particularly beautiful." The historian Michael Beschloss surmises that Joe was the first American ambassador "to have told the queen that she was 'a cute trick.'" He was even more informal with the young princesses and made a habit of talking movies with them, asking what they had seen and what their favorites were. When Princess Elizabeth told him she enjoyed the recently released *Snow White and the Seven Dwarfs,* Kennedy arranged to give her an original color drawing of Snow White signed by Walt Disney for her thirteenth birthday.

Joe was often at his desk until six or seven, occasionally much later, but he didn't limit his work to his ambassadorial duties. He rode his horse almost every morning and, weather permitting, golfed every Saturday with Eddie Moore. Letters and cables to Paul Murphy monitored his investments and he frequently checked in with Ted O'Leary at Somerset Liquors. Johnnie Ford was left with "a million and one responsibilities" running Maine and New Hampshire as well as minutiae such as furniture appraisals for the Palm Beach house, weather damage at Hyannisport, a termite infestation in Bronxville, and various requests from Rose including dealing with her parents.

Almost daily, some time was devoted to cultivating the press. No longer dealing with *Variety* and *Film Daily,* Kennedy now mingled with the publishers and editors of the major newspapers and magazines in America and Europe. He put his name on an article for *The Saturday Evening Post,* this time to praise Roosevelt's domestic programs and none too presciently tell the business community that "Not soon again, if ever, will we establish in office the philosophy that the welfare of the nation is advanced if we guarantee prosperity for the few." *Woman's Day* told of the "Nine Kennedys and How they Grew," crediting Rose as the ever vigilant "general manager" of the photogenic family. The ambassador agreed to cooperate with *The Ladies' Home Journal* as long as they showed him the piece first "so he might correct factual errors." Joe's ace in the hole was

Clare Boothe Luce

the same as it had been at *Fortune*; he knew the publisher and was not above demanding changes to the point that the journalist didn't recognize it and "it almost seemed as if the Ambassador had written it himself."

Kennedy's scrapbook was beginning to bulge as he received more press than any member of the administration besides the president. Joe enjoyed the company of reporters and publishers for there was always interesting information to swap and his zest for their camaraderie went beyond their immediate usefulness to him. The embassy guest lists often included visiting press barons such as Arthur Sulzberger, publisher of *The New York Times,* and Henry Luce, who, by the time he visited London in the spring of 1938, had already proved himself more than generous to Kennedy, putting him on the cover of *Time* and giving him two major articles in *Fortune* as well as frequent, positive mentions.

Yet it was Luce's wife, the beautiful Clare, who had just celebrated her thirty-fifth birthday, that piqued Kennedy's interest this time around. The play she had been working on when they had dined together in California two years before, *The Women,* was now a hit, but being the darling of Broadway was not enough for her. As her friend Irene Selznick summed her up, "Clare's ambition was so great she never stood a chance of satisfaction." Clare herself proclaimed her determination "not to live for anybody but myself" and she rarely missed an opportunity to bed someone of power and influence; her lovers included the sixty-plus-year-old financier Bernard Baruch and Randolph Churchill, the just-twenty-year-old son of the future prime minister.

Now Clare turned her eye on the ambassador and to ensure his notice, she had her mail sent to his attention at the embassy. Notice he did. Kennedy valued Luce as an influential contact, but that did not deter "his libidinous interest" in her. The following month, when he made his first ambassadorial return to the States, the Luces were his fellow passengers and Clare, according to her biographer Sylvia Morris, "made no secret in reveling in 'Joe's' company."

If Kennedy enjoyed the crossing, he was even more pleased when the *Queen Mary* entered New York harbor and "the press literally stormed me" at the dock. Only a few weeks before, *Liberty* magazine had run an article entitled "Will Kennedy Run for President?" with the subheading "A candid close-up of a prospect that looms arrestingly large on the political horizon." *Liberty* proceeded to bat down every possible objection to his candidacy, practically crediting him with single-handedly ensuring Roosevelt's 1932 nomination and praising him as the president's "bluntest advisor." If the country was ready to "demand a man who can make business and progressive reform pull together toward sound prosperity," then Kennedy was their candidate. The article further refined Joe's biography: "of course" he had withdrawn from all stock market activity since joining the administration, he had taken "most of the campaign trips with Roosevelt," and their close friendship stretched over twenty years.

Roosevelt was serving his second term as president, no one had ever been elected to a third, and the *Liberty* article set up Kennedy as his heir apparent. The New York *Daily News* pronounced Kennedy "the Crown Prince of the Roosevelt regime" and his "personal selection as his successor" so when Joe met with Roosevelt at both Hyde Park and the White House, the tension of Kennedy's potential candidacy had to permeate their discussions. Joe had unequivocally said, "I have no political ambitions for myself or for my children" during the 1936 campaign, but it was a different story now.

The coverage ignited by Kennedy's potential candidacy clearly had his full cooperation. "He thought he was about the most qualified individual on earth to be President," concluded his aide Harvey Klemmer. Arthur Krock was convinced that "without any question" Kennedy wanted to be president. "Yes, he did. Very definitely." And Joe assumed he had the wherewithal and the support to pull it off. He viewed himself as a popular personality, hailed in newspapers, magazines, and newsreels. "He thought his services had so impressed the country, and there was money behind it for a gigantic propaganda machine." With cameras and reporters hanging on his every word becoming a common occurrence, Joe was now viewing the idea of his running as an "inevitable question" and his diary entries reflect his seriousness at the prospect. Like so many others before and since, Kennedy began believing his own press clips.

As more newspapers picked up on the story of Kennedy's candidacy, Roosevelt had had enough. Besides the disloyalty, it must have seemed outrageous that this man who had never run for, let alone held, elective office seriously thought he should be president. Was there no limit to the hubris? Roosevelt instructed his press secretary to find an appropriate publication to report his displeasure of Kennedy's self-promotion as well as his awareness of the existence and contents of all those "Private and Confidential" missives. When the *Chicago Tribune* reported that there was a "chilling shadow" over their relationship, Joe was blindsided, hearing about the article just after what he had considered a pleasant dinner with Roosevelt. Kennedy had been serving as ambassador for almost six months, the time limit he and the president had separately voiced as sufficient, yet for different reasons, both men decided he should carry on. If he genuinely saw Kennedy as a potential rival, Roosevelt had to think that he was better served by having Joe thousands of miles away and in a position where he, at least publicly, had to remain loyal.

Only a few weeks after Kennedy had been greeted at the dock with such interest and acclaim, reporters now asked about the "chill" between him and the president as well as the latest issue of *The Saturday Evening Post.* It carried an article asserting that it was Jimmy Roosevelt who had "helped Kennedy to reach the two real positions which he now holds— that of Ambassador to London and that of premier Scotch whiskey salesman in America."

Joe attempted to keep things light as he boarded the *Normandie* to return to London, along with his two eldest sons and Arthur Krock, who was traveling at Joe's expense. Krock noted that Kennedy was "a very

Joe with Joe Junior and Jack on their way to London, 1938

imperious man and it must have been difficult for him to smile and be friendly when he was under strain." Yet Joe was also attuned to turning his focus to the next step, in this case entrenching his popularity as ambassador and paving the way for Joe Junior, who had just graduated from Harvard and was to become his secretary at the embassy, just as the sons of John Adams and others had done before him.

The family was all together for the first time in quite a while, and as had been his pattern since he could afford it, Joe took time for serious relaxation in a sumptuous location. In Europe, that meant the French Riviera and so that August he leased a villa several miles east of Cannes, abutting the Hôtel du Cap, already one of the world's great luxury hotels. Enshrined on twenty landscaped acres on the tip of a peninsula, the du Cap featured an exquisite expanse of grounds that included a huge saltwater pool built into the rocks at the edge of the Mediterranean. A series of private cabanas ribboned the cliffs and a sign soon graced the largest one, reading "J. P. Kennedy's Family." The exclusivity of the Hôtel du Cap assured fellow guests that they were all members of rarefied society and so the Kennedys quickly found themselves mingling with other guests, including the ménage of Marlene Dietrich.

Rose may have been feeling a new security in her marriage with her husband close at hand, yet proximity seemed to have little impact on Joe's behavior. A high-profile beauty always turned his head and his eye was caught by the international film star. Dietrich had appeared in several films in her native Germany before stunning American audiences in Josef von Sternberg's *Morocco* in 1930. Yet seven years and ten films later, she joined Katharine Hepburn and Greta Garbo in being declared "box office poison" by a theater owners' organization. Marlene flatly turned down Hitler's offer to return to be "Queen of UFA [the German film studio] where she could name her price, her script and her director" and instead applied for American citizenship and exiled herself to the South of France with her extended family: her thirteen-year-old daughter, Maria, her husband, Rudi, Rudi's longtime lover, Tami, and Marlene's current amour, the author Erich Maria Remarque. Marlene, now thirty-six and as gorgeous as ever, had always set her own standards and lived by her own code. If her style of group travel bothered others, it didn't concern her. More eyebrows had to be raised when Sternberg arrived at the du Cap while Remarque busied himself beginning the novel that would become *Arc de Triomphe.*

Kennedy kept in touch with London and Washington and hired "a beautiful French girl" to take his dictation. Rose and the children had their own, separate routines and as each day passed, Dietrich's young

Marlene Dietrich, in Hollywood, in the mid-1930s

daughter became more and more infatuated with the Kennedys, particularly the twenty-one-year-old Jack. Maria felt "gawky" around the children with their "smiles that never ended" and she longed to be their friend. Because the older Kennedy children were permitted to join their parents at Elsa Maxwell's summer ball, Maria was allowed to go as well. Jack would remember that evening too, but for a very different reason. He danced with Marlene to "Begin the Beguine" and she was "holding me so tight and then she slipped her hand down my trousers." Later he would wonder if his father "put her up to it," but smiled when he remembered her "terrific perfume."

As the Kennedys were becoming important to her, Maria noticed the ambassador becoming a frequent visitor to her mother's cabana. She was embarrassed and feared her new friends would ostracize her as a result, but Rose continued to show Maria kindnesses, invite her to join the family for lunch, and in general act as if everything could not have been more normal. Maria concluded that the Kennedys must be "as used to their father disappearing as I was my mother."

Even if Maria didn't observe a change in her, Rose's pattern of taking off by herself resumed as soon as their holiday ended. Instead of staying in London and overseeing her children's return to school, Rose went to Paris and then Scotland. It was in Glasgow that Joe reached her with the news that she needed to return to London as soon as possible for war was at hand. Still, she stayed in Scotland for several more days, taking golf lessons and buying what she feared was to be "the last for tweeds."

Hitler's army was gathering along Czechoslovakia's border and tin hats and gas masks were distributed throughout the embassy. "In feverish haste," Londoners were digging trenches in public parks for shelter from the bombs they assumed were coming. Then came the announcement that "Peace is at hand." Prime Minister Neville Chamberlain was cheered in the streets of Berlin and he, France's Édouard Daladier, and Hitler all shook hands in late September to a collective, if short-lived, sigh of relief.

There was no question in Kennedy's mind that the ultimate goal was to keep America out of this "European conflict." He was passionate that America's future, and his family's, depended upon his country staying out of the war. Yet the more he publicly pronounced American neutrality, the more questions were raised about his appropriateness as ambassador. As the glow over "peace in our time" gave way, insecurity grew. When Kennedy advocated "trying to work out something with the totalitarian States," a new round of criticism followed. He was chafing under the restriction of having his public words approved in advance and his private thoughts second-guessed. Used to being his own boss and pleasing only the few he cared about at any given moment, Joe was far from a natural as a diplomat.

In his worldview, it was "economic maladjustment" that was at the

With Bobby, Teddy, and Jean at the Hôtel du Cap

heart of "the world's unrest." He saw Hitler as a CEO of an adversarial corporation and maintained his faith in the power of negotiation. There had to be something "England can do to satisfy Hitler." Kennedy was so sure he was right and others were wrong, he decided. "The papers have made up a pile of lies about him," Joe Junior reported to his diary in early December 1938. "He also doesn't like the idea of sitting back and letting the Jewish columnists in America kick his head off." Kennedy vented to his eldest son that "he would give it up in a minute if it wasn't for the benefits that Jack and I are getting out of it and the things Eunice will get when she comes out next Spring."

Joe did see his position giving tremendous advantages to his children; the older girls received the ultimate in social acceptance by being presented in court and Joe Junior and Jack had front row seats to the events of a lifetime. Yet if the family was uppermost in his mind, Kennedy had a strange way of showing it. Christmas found him once again separated from them, with Rose, Joe Junior, and the younger children spending the holidays in St. Moritz while Joe and young Jack headed to Washington and Palm Beach. Joe met with Roosevelt several times during his two months stateside and he noted in his diary that during the final meeting he had asked for and received the president's assurance that he had his full confidence.

Kennedy returned to London just as the Nazis were entering Prague and he talked to Roosevelt on the phone almost every day (in the early evening London time, around ten in the morning for the president). Jimmy Roosevelt, now a vaguely defined "vice president" of Samuel Goldwyn Productions, came to London to promote *Wuthering Heights* and Joe arranged for them to spend a weekend at Windsor Palace and screen the film for the king and queen.

Jimmy was also at the palace as the son of the president and he confirmed his father's invitation for the royals to come to America. Joe saw that as evidence the administration was going around him and he was unhappy not to be included in the king and queen's visit that summer. Yet while they were at the president's side at the World's Fair in New York, Kennedy was busy entertaining Clare Boothe Luce. She had signed her latest cable to him "Love, Clare" and he immediately responded by offering to meet her ship at the dock and personally escort her to London. In town for the West End production of *The Women,* she cut a social swath through town seeing the likes of Lord Beaverbrook and George Bernard Shaw. Most conveniently, Rose was spending several weeks in the States and Clare's biographer notes that "Kennedy's name appears more frequently than any other" in her diary that month.

No diplomatic complications were going to keep at least part of the Kennedy family from returning to the Riviera in August of 1939 and, once again, the entire Dietrich famille was there as well. This time Joe had competition for Marlene's affections, not only from Erich Remarque, but from Jo Carstairs, the cross-dressing oil heiress. Carstairs held the world record as the fastest female speedboat racer, but she dramatically arrived at the Hôtel du Cap on her three-masted schooner. Nothing prevented Joe and Marlene from picking up where they had left off the year before and the Kennedy and Dietrich clans swam and dined together often.

Rose returning alone to the States for a visit, 1939

Marlene, who let her normally pale skin go bronze, took to calling the ambassador "Papa Joe" to delineate him from all the other "Joes" in her life: his eldest son, Jo Carstairs, and Josef von Sternberg.

Marlene had been off the screen for two years when the producer Joseph Pasternak called her at the du Cap to offer her a job. She thought the role of a dancing girl in a western sounded "ridiculous," but she turned to Papa Joe for advice and he quickly jumped into the negotiations. As if he had never left the business, Kennedy placed transatlantic calls to Universal where Pasternak assured him he wanted Marlene so much there were also job offers for both Rudi and Remarque. Later that evening, Joe announced "the money is too good to refuse," and so Marlene accepted the offer to play opposite Jimmy Stewart in *Destry Rides Again*.

Before she was willing to leave, however, Dietrich needed one more assurance. She had become an American citizen, worked actively on behalf of refugees fleeing her homeland, and even tried to sway Kennedy from his adamant neutrality. She was worried about Germany's next move and said "I can't be away making a stupid film if anything happens." Kennedy promised that "her family would be given the same protection as his." Marlene left for Hollywood and Joe returned to England sooner than planned. After meeting with the prime minister, Kennedy announced that it was "advisable for American travelers to leave England."

Within the week, Maria, Rudi, Tami, and Erich were on their way to Cherbourg in time for the *Queen Mary*'s departure for New York on September 2, 1939, just as German troops marched into Poland.

Rose, along with Kathleen, nineteen, Eunice, eighteen, and Bobby, thirteen, returned to the States on board the visibly armed SS *Washington* to find Joe's picture, once again, on the cover of *Time*. The inside article gushed that "from one point of view, Joe Kennedy is a common denominator of the U.S. businessman: sage, middle of the road, a horse trader at heart, with one sharp eye on the market and one fond eye on his children. But he is a super common denominator, uncommonly common sensible, stiletto shrewd, practical as only a former president of a small bank can be." With references to his unprecedented close and friendly relations with the palace and members of the British government as well as his efficient if unconventional approach to problem solving, it was clear Kennedy himself had been the chief source of information for the article.

In the midst of the breaking war, Kennedy still made time for the movies, but one in particular struck him as "nothing short of criminal." *Mr. Smith Goes to Washington*'s depiction of a corrupt United States Senate was so offensive to him that he wired Will Hays that it was "one of the most disgraceful things I have ever seen done to our country" and sent a copy of his cable to the president. Joe genuinely believed that "in foreign countries this film must inevitably strengthen the mistaken impression that the United States is full of graft, corruption and lawlessness."

Kennedy had calmed down somewhat five days later when he responded to cables from Harry Cohn of Columbia and the film's director, Frank Capra. Joe acknowledged they were "looking at the picture though different eyes," but stood his ground and reminded them that American films "are the greatest influence on foreign public opinion." He thought Capra's "fine work makes the indictment of Government all the more damning" and will "do inestimable harm to American prestige all over the world."

From the Hays Office, Arthur Houghton tried to soothe Kennedy by assuring him there were no violations of the Production Code and that was all they had the power to enforce. Joe's opposition to the film was a voice in the wilderness. Louella Parsons called it a "smash patriotic hit" and most critics echoed her sentiments, finding that audiences left the

When the rest of the family returned to the States, Joe kept Rosemary in England along with Eddie and Mary Moore.

theaters with "an enthusiasm for democracy" and "in a glow of patriotism." *Mr. Smith Goes to Washington* went on to be nominated for eleven Academy Awards, but lose almost all of them to *Gone With the Wind.* Joe continued to grumble about the film however, reminding Arthur Krock that "the danger doesn't always come from Communists."

Kennedy's Hollywood days reentered his life serendipitously when he flew home for the holidays on a Pan Am "Dixie Clipper." Also on board was Erich von Stroheim, on his way to California to accept an offer from Fox to act in *I Was an Adventuress.* Stroheim had appeared in over a dozen films in the ten years since *Queen Kelly,* but had directed only one, a low-budget Fox film called *Walking Down Broadway* in 1933.

In America, the *Time* cover story fanned Kennedy's presidential prospects and he did little to discourage it. With only months to go before the Democratic National Convention, Roosevelt had yet to announce his plans. Names such as Secretary of State Cordell Hull and Postmaster General James Farley had been raised as possible successors, yet time and again, Kennedy was mentioned as one of the most prominent half dozen possible candidates. Those men, however, had to walk a very thin line between rousing support for themselves and appearing to remain loyal to the unusually coy president. While Joe publicly claimed not to be interested, the *Boston Post* headlined "Kennedy May Be Candidate."

During his three months at home, Kennedy made enough speeches saying, in various ways, that "The United States must not permit itself to be drawn into this conflict, either directly or indirectly" to firmly establish him as the isolationist alternative. Joe spent some time in Palm Beach, where Rose's parents and Johnnie Ford and his wife came for visits. Ford was taken aback by "the madhouse" created with Joe constantly on the phone and juggling "all the different visitors who wanted to see him." Kennedy, however, appeared to be having a great time entertaining himself while polishing his image, spending an afternoon with Walter Winchell and Damon Runyon at a Miami beach club.

When Joe returned to London in late February of 1940, "his physical condition was a great deal better than when he first landed" and who else should be on board the ship but Clare Boothe Luce. Now even more famous because *The Women* had been turned into a hit film by MGM, Clare left her husband at home and came to Europe to work on a book, yet she made time to spend several days with Kennedy at his country home. When she headed to Paris in April, he followed and spent "all morning" in Clare's Ritz Hotel bedroom.

In May, the prime minister that Kennedy had championed, Neville Chamberlain, was replaced by a man for whom he had little respect, Winston Churchill. As Joe became more vociferous in his differences

Joe relaxing with Damon Runyon and Walter Winchell in Miami, 1939

with the president's policies, the king and queen told Roosevelt they were "terribly disturbed" by his ambassador and alternative lines of communication with the British government were established.

If grumblings about Kennedy were growing louder in Washington and London, there were no complaints from Hollywood. The trades praised the ambassador for giving "every request immediate action, resulting in a much better relationship in London than our business ever had before." The war was curtailing British film production and the demand for American movies was greater than ever. Kennedy facilitated meetings between Will Hays and Lord Halifax, who told them England needed "to have pictures—a lot of them—to keep up the people's morale." Payment for those films, however, went from slow to slower and Hays appealed to Kennedy to help. Hays kept Joe "constantly briefed" and his "telephone calls to London were many and long."

Kennedy always made time to stay in touch with his old colleagues from Hollywood, even when they simply dropped by. Jack Warner was in London when he decided to stop in at the embassy without an appointment and the studio head was thrilled that when his name was announced, Joe "rushed out, pulled me into the study and was exactly the same friendly, forceful, down to earth warm Joe Kennedy I had always known."

In June of 1940, France fell to the Germans and the Nazis began bombing London. After the first night, Joe walked with his aide Harvey Klemmer around Piccadilly and said, shaking his head, "I'll bet you five to one, any sum, that Hitler will be in Buckingham Palace in two weeks." On paper, Kennedy's opinion that Britain would lose was difficult to argue with. As Henry Luce said after listening to his conclusions, "I told him I could not match him argument for argument, I could only tell him I did not believe they would be [defeated], and so I prayed." Or, as Pamela Harriman put it, Joe "didn't understand the British steel."

In the midst of the chaos and his dire predictions, Kennedy made moves to secure his own financial position. With the Nazis in the streets of Paris, the French ambassador closed his embassy and Joe took the wines in his cellar and shipped them to Ted O'Leary at Somerset Liquors. Kennedy had ensured their stock by shipping hundreds of cases before the war began, but as the oceans became more vulnerable and cargo space more valuable, he used his ambassadorial status to "preempt shipping space" for 200,000 cases of Haig & Haig. With other companies unable to ship their goods, he was quietly informed questions might be raised in Parliament, and so, according to Klemmer, "we tapered off a little after that."

Roosevelt's decision to seek an unprecedented third term was not made official until he was nominated by the Democratic National Convention in Chicago in July. By then, his relationships with those considering running in his stead had suffered, but the breach between the president and Kennedy was more complex. Yet Joe concluded that the failure of his presidential "boomlet," as he called it in his drafted memoir, was due to the fact that "the time was not propitious" and not to what others saw as blatant self-promotion, disloyalty, or lack of experience.

Kennedy began lashing out with less discretion than ever, including to his "friends" in the press. Finally, he told Secretary of State Hull that he was welcome to announce that he was being recalled, but one way or another, he was coming home. Joe privately threatened to endorse Roosevelt's opponent, Wendell Willkie, and arrangements were made for him to immediately go to the Luces upon landing and publicly make that announcement. However, Joe and Rose, who strongly believed he should remain loyal to the president because he had opened such important doors for their children, were whisked to the White House. Over dinner with Roosevelt, Kennedy vented his frustrations and complained of what he considered his maltreatment, but within days Joe was endorsing his reelection in a national radio broadcast. While Kennedy used the forum to underline his own belief "there is no valid argument for putting America into war," he was not his usual smiling self as he gave his speech. This time it was all seriousness, and his eyes did not make their habitual contact with the newsreel cameras. It was almost as if he had a gun to his back and his words were being spit out instead of spoken. The next night, Roosevelt was in Boston where he called Kennedy "my Ambassador" and assured his audience, "Our boys are not going to be sent into any foreign wars."

Roosevelt was reelected with over 60 percent of the vote and three days later, Kennedy offered him his formal resignation. If there was any doubt it would be accepted, Joe sealed his own fate when he proceeded to give an interview to several reporters including Louis Lyons of *The Boston Globe.* Kennedy would later say he thought the conversation was off the record, but he never denied his words that resulted in headlines quoting him as declaring "Democracy is finished in England." He had gone on to say that it wasn't Hitler as much as "national socialism" that was going to finish democracy; to the ultimate capitalist, socialism was just as dangerous, if not more so, than losing to Germany. Kennedy had said similar things before, but not to reporters outside the inner circle.

All the years of saying one thing in private and another in public were finally catching up with him, but before that played out, on the very day he had given the interview, Joe flew to San Francisco where he was met by his son Jack, who had been auditing graduate classes at Stanford University. Together father and son flew north to Wyntoon to visit William Randolph Hearst at his Northern California estate where the two friends could console each other with their mutual "America first" sympathies. Joe and Jack then headed for Los Angeles to stay at Marion Davies's huge Santa Monica beach house where the staff "couldn't have been nicer."

Under duress, Joe endorses Roosevelt days before the 1940 election.

The centerpiece of Joe's Southern California visit was a lunch at Warner Bros. where four dozen of Hollywood's almost all Jewish moguls gathered to hear the ambassador speak about the "European situation." He was to debrief them on the renewal of the British Film Exchange Agreement, but during the three-hour meeting, Joe reiterated the themes he had stressed about *Mr. Smith Goes to Washington:* that "American films are the greatest influence on foreign public opinion" and producers "must assume their responsibilities much more earnestly than they have to date. . . . We must be more careful."

It was another "off the record" session and Joe forcefully repeated "there was no reason for our ever becoming involved in any war." Charles Lindbergh and groups such as the Legion of Decency and America First were "not so far off the mark when they suggest this country can reconcile itself to whomever wins the war and adjust our trade and lives accordingly." Going beyond his isolationist position, Joe sounded as if he were speaking of the world after Hitler's victory. He appealed to what he saw as the studio heads' basic economic interest: Hitler liked and appreciated films, but in order for him to allow them to be shown, "You're going to have to get those Jewish names off the screen." Charlie Chaplin had just released *The Great Dictator* and Kennedy warned the assembly that they had to "stop making anti-Nazi pictures or using the film medium to promote or show sympathy to the cause of 'democracies' versus 'the dictators.' "

He came close to accusing the Jews of fanning the war's flames. "Jews are on the spot" because in England, "the Jews were being blamed for the war." If the studio bosses used their power "to influence the public dangerously then we all, and the Jews in particular, would be in jeopardy, if they continued to abuse that power." If they complained about Hitler, the more people would think "a 'Jewish war' was going on." In other words, their only hope was silence and shame.

Kennedy had "thrown the fear of God" into them, and certainly riddled them with enough doubts that, for the most part, they remained publicly silent. A precious few objected. Douglas Fairbanks, Jr., whose father was half Jewish, protested to Roosevelt that Kennedy was stirring "the embers of terror, isolationism, and racism." There was no doubt in Fairbanks's mind that "his Excellency" had "made a very definite impression and there were many who were susceptible to Joe's undoubted powers of persuasion." Ben Hecht agreed, reporting that the result of Kennedy's tirade was that most "influential Jews . . . espoused the Kennedy hide-your-Jewish-head psychology."

Joe returned east as confident as ever that his judgments were right, and his letters and diary were laced with anger. If he considered the resignation he had tendered in early November as perfunctory, the president did not. After receiving reports from Fairbanks and others that mirrored and magnified those of the reporters in Boston, Roosevelt was convinced that Kennedy's "repudiation" of the newspaper accounts was without merit.

When Kennedy met with Roosevelt at the White House on the first of December, the president told him point-blank, "I don't want to send you back." Joe reported to his diary, without a hint of irony, that he added "you've done enough." Kennedy thought it was an amicable wide-ranging discussion, but shortly after the meeting, Roosevelt wrote his son-in-law that "the truth of the matter is that Joe is and always has been a temperamental Irish boy, terrifically spoiled at an early age by huge financial success; thoroughly patriotic, thoroughly selfish and thoroughly obsessed with the idea that he must leave each of his nine children with a million dollars." He concluded with his belief that subconsciously Kennedy thought "the future of a small capitalistic class is safer under a Hitler than under a Churchill."

With every other venture Kennedy had taken on—the stock market, the movies, the SEC, and the Maritime Commission—he had left as soon as he could declare success. Yet his ambassadorship was beyond his power to turn into a positive to almost anyone beyond himself and his family. He became wrapped in self-justifications. He still had his fortune and he had his children. As he slowly realized his own retirement from public life was permanent, he turned his innate need to succeed into a dynastic imperative.

# "The First and Only Outsider
# to Fleece Hollywood"

## (1941–1969)

While Kennedy continued to protest that America's entry into the war "would be the biggest piece of foolishness the world has ever seen," nothing kept him from staying on top of the news from Hollywood. He lunched regularly with old colleagues such as Will Hays and continued to see films in the privacy of his homes before they were released. Without much passion, he frequently commented on movies, but he was outraged by Orson Welles's *Citizen Kane*. Not since *Mr. Smith Goes to Washington* had a film so disturbed him. While he found it "one of the greatest pictures I ever saw," he told Arthur Houghton it was also "the most cruel job I have ever seen done on anybody. I am against it, first because I don't think the industry should portray living people without their consent, and secondly, because of my personal regard for W.R. and Marion. I regard this as a hateful piece of propaganda by an avowed communist." Still, Kennedy couldn't help but be impressed that the film had been made "by a man who never did one before, by actors who never acted in one before, by musicians who never scored one, and by a sound man who never worked on one."

From his post at the Hays Office, Houghton passed on the news that Gloria Swanson had signed a three-year, three-picture deal with RKO and was spending the next three months in "vocal study." Joe clearly was not in direct contact with her because he responded, "I am delighted to know that Swanie had a comeback. If you run across her or find a way of talking with her, tell her that you wrote me the news and I sent back word that it's the only good news I have heard from the pictures in years."

Kennedy often expressed interest in reentering the industry and then just as quickly justified staying out. The movie business was in "a terrible mess," domestic box office was down by over 20 percent and there were "no prospects of foreign business." He was convinced Fox was in so much trouble that they "are liable to do nothing more in the next two or three years but answer stockholders' suits." He entered into meetings in late 1941 to take over RKO, but then he decided "there is nothing to work for and I don't want to take on responsibility at this time."

He continued to live on the road, vacationing in Virginia for several weeks with Ted O'Leary, back to New York where he kept a suite at the Waldorf, then on to the Ritz-Carlton in Boston or the Drake in Chicago. With Palm Beach for winter, Hyannisport for summer, and his various temporary residences, Joe decided to sell the house in Bronxville and become a legal resident of Florida where there was no state income or estate tax. That was fine for Rose and Joe with their separate, but equally peripatetic, lifestyles, but at the age of nine young Teddy was sent off to what would be a series of boarding schools and all the children lost the one real home they had known. When they arrived in Palm Beach from their various schools and travels, their first question was to ask which room to use this time.

As Kennedy adjusted to being a multimillionaire untethered to any specific business, he turned his attention to his daughter Rosemary. According to Eunice Kennedy, it had been Rose who "had carried the main responsibility for Rosemary, taking her to doctors, educators, and psychologists," but now Rosemary occasionally experienced unpre-

With his daughter Rosemary

dictable rages and ran off from her school at night. The danger that she might be kidnapped or become pregnant loomed in their fears. Joe's relationship with his eldest daughter was loving and supportive, "but he was much more emotional, and was easily upset by Rosemary's lack of progress." Joe decided she was better off separated from her siblings so she would not be as aware of her difference and pronounced, "She must never be at home for her sake as well as everyone's [*sic*] else."

Kennedy heard of the newly heralded prefrontal lobotomy, which was reported to bring "back to useful life" those suffering with "troubled minds." What happened next is so clouded that even Joe's granddaughter Amanda Smith, with familial access to all information, was unable to piece together the exact details for "no mention of Rosemary survives among her father's papers after 1940." Evidently telling no one, including his wife, Joe arranged for Rosemary to be operated on. The twenty-one-year-old Rosemary awoke with the mind of a small child, not even knowing who she was. As devastated as Joe must have been, he kept the results a secret from the family, either to protect them or in fear of Rose's wrath. He sent Rosemary to St. Coletta in Wisconsin, a highly respected residence for the developmentally disabled. Joe announced that she was "teaching in the Midwest" and Doris Kearns Goodwin says Rose did not see her daughter again until the early 1960s. Rosemary's brothers and sisters were used to visiting and writing her; now, suddenly, nothing. If the veil of secrecy surrounding the reality of their parents' marriage had gradually seeped into their consciousness as they matured, what must they have thought when their sister literally disappeared from the family? The message of ultimate loyalty to the family was clear, but even within that tight circle, there were subjects that were to be simply accepted and not discussed.

Joe now had two failures to cope with, one very public, the other very private. According to Amanda Smith, Kennedy was "ostracized, increasingly embittered and isolated," and he put the full force of his energy into his sons, particularly his namesake. At Joe Junior's birth, Honey Fitz had declared that his grandson would be the first Catholic president of the United States and as early as 1932, both Joe Kennedy and Eddie Moore were quoted as saying the same thing. Having grown up with that familial understanding, Joe Junior was at Harvard Law School when he wrote his father in late 1940 that he had decided to enlist in the Navy Air Corps. They had discussed his joining the Naval Reserve, which would have allowed him to continue school relatively uninterrupted, but he assumed Jack's poor health would prevent him from serving and therefore, "with your stand on the war, people will wonder what the devil I am doing back at school with everyone else working for national defense." And then he reached out, with almost heartbreaking dutifulness, to reassure his father regarding what he saw as Joe Senior's ultimate concern: "It seems that Jack is perfectly capable to do everything, if by chance something happened to me."

Kennedy was in Palm Beach in December of 1941 when the Japanese bombed Pearl Harbor and America finally entered the war he had dreaded for so long. He cabled Roosevelt his willingness to serve in any capacity, but he heard nothing in return. He decided the president wanted some kind of apology before taking him back to the fold, and that was out of the question. "Well I'm not sorry so to hell with it."

A sense of ennui and bitterness enveloped Joe, almost as if the war was all about him. In spite of his own beliefs, he had helped pull strings for Jack to enlist, but instead of staying behind a desk, Jack "wants to get out on a destroyer in the Atlantic. It makes me sick to think of it." His eldest was stationed in England, and Joe sardonically told a friend, "Kathleen has enlisted as a Staff Assistant to the Red Cross and Bobby is getting ready to go this year, so all in all, this war is great."

"I can't interest myself in private business," Joe wrote to David Sarnoff in February of 1942, or anything else besides his two oldest sons. "My energy from now on will be tied up in their careers rather than my own." Presuming they "are eventually going to make their homes in Massachusetts, if they get through this war successfully," he asked Sarnoff to keep his eyes open for a radio station there he could buy for them.

Kennedy didn't buy a radio station, but he did invest in Miami's Hialeah Racetrack and used his Somerset Liquors as the avenue to stay in touch with Hollywood. He sent cases of liquor to studio executives and others such as the Production Code's Joe Breen. Though Joe believed Eddie Mannix of MGM would never agree to a formal product placement agreement, he sent him two cases of scotch with the suggestion that if the studio used Pinch or Gordon's or his other labels in their films, more would be forthcoming. Even in "retirement," Kennedy couldn't pass up an angle.

If there wasn't a movie he wanted to make, he did find a play and so Joe became a Broadway producer. Frederick Lonsdale, who had written *The Last of Mrs. Cheyney* and Douglas Fairbanks's *The Private Life of Don Juan,* had a new light comedy entitled *Another Love Story.* Joe took pity on "Freddie" because he had opposed the war and "had a very hard time with the Jewish boys" in Hollywood. Kennedy decided he "needed something to keep my mind active" and hoped the play might be turned into a film after a Broadway run, even though it was essentially a sex comedy dependent upon divorce and adultery as plot points.

To direct it, Joe reached out to Eddie Goulding without regard for their disagreements of a decade before. To Joe, Goulding had the "magic touch" and was "easily the best we could get with this kind of story because he can help with the writing as well as the directing." Eddie was also willing to forget and, pronouncing *Another Love Story* "sure fire," jumped on board. Kennedy left the Cape for a week of meetings at the Waldorf and then headed to Wilmington for the play's preview in mid-September. By that point, however, Goulding and Lonsdale were locking horns and when *Another Love Story* opened in Washington, Goulding had washed his hands of it. Kennedy was there, but when he suggested that "Clare Luce might make some cuts," Freddie haughtily announced that he had a contract. Frustrated because he thought the play "could be a smash success if that thick headed Lonsdale let anyone work on it," Joe packed his bags and "left him cold."

Kennedy was in New York for *Another Love Story*'s opening at the Fulton Theater on October 12 where Lonsdale was credited as both writer and director. The play ran through January, giving over one hundred performances and allowing Joe to recoup his money, but his enthusiasm had waned and after opening night, he spent his time attending another New York attraction, the World Series.

Eunice went to Stanford in 1942 (with help from a letter of recommendation from Will Hays) and she stayed with Arthur Poole and his wife, who had moved to Palo Alto. While in California, Eunice visited Hollywood where Arthur Houghton took charge and treated her to studio tours and meetings with various stars including Greer Garson. The next summer, Patricia took a trip to Hollywood and this time it was Will Hays who not only arranged her schedule but also gave her the use of his Los Angeles apartment. Joe believed his daughter to be so "stunning looking" she might have a career in pictures, but even if producers were interested, Pat wasn't; she wanted to get back to the Cape and spend the rest of her summer on the beach.

After graduating from Finch and serving a stint as a reporter for a Washington newspaper, Kathleen had returned to England, officially to work with the Red Cross, unofficially to continue her relationship with William Cavendish, the Marquess of Hartington, heir to the Duke of Devonshire, known as Billy. As eldest son of one of the richest families in

England, he was considered an appropriate match for Princess Elizabeth, but that didn't matter to Rose Kennedy. A marriage to anyone outside the faith would condemn her daughter to hell. Kathleen spent a year trying to wangle a dispensation, but after much agonizing, she married Billy in London with her eldest brother the only family witness. The cables her parents separately sent to her on her wedding day summarize their relationships with their daughter: Joe's message ended with "You are and still and always will be always tops with me" and Rose limited herself to one word: "Heartbroken."

Jack had managed to talk his way into being sent to the Pacific to command one of the newly instituted PT boats that patrolled the Solomon Islands. Then, in early August of 1943, Joe received word Jack was missing in action. His boat, with thirteen men on board, had not returned from patrol and a funeral service was held on the islands. Joe kept the news from Rose and the rest of the family and Arthur Krock remembered thinking Joe's reaction "was perfectly extraordinary. He took it with remarkable stoicism." Yet his relief was palpable when he learned a week later that Jack had survived.

Two of Jack's men had died when a Japanese destroyer cut their boat in half and, from all accounts, more lives would have been lost were it not for Jack's leadership and his fortitude in swimming for hours (and doing considerable damage to his already vulnerable back) while pulling one of his injured men. There were many stories of heroism that were not celebrated, but Joe made sure this was. John Hersey wrote of Jack's experiences for *The New Yorker* and then the article was condensed to reach a much larger audience in *Reader's Digest*.

The fate of his boys had hung heavily on Kennedy every day they were gone, but in early June of 1944 he could, at last, breathe a sigh of relief. Jack was recovering at the Chelsea naval hospital in Massachusetts and Joe Junior wrote from the base in England where he was stationed as a bomber pilot that "it looks like I am going to be on my way home in about ten days." He could have been released before June 6—D-Day—but, as he said, "I am delighted I stayed for the invasion."

Back in Hyannisport, Kennedy waited through the rest of June and July "expecting to hear the telephone ring and to hear you were in Norfolk," where troops disembarked from Europe, but it wasn't until early August he received a letter from his eldest saying he was staying on for just one more mission, "something different" with "practically no danger." Upon reading the letter on August 9, 1944, Joe immediately responded, "I quite understand how you feel about staying there, but don't force your

Joe Junior, in September 1939

luck too much." But Joe Junior did force his luck. He had been in harm's way for over a year, had flown thirty-five missions, and could have returned home with honor. Yet he volunteered to pilot an experimental plane, gutted of everything but room for pilot, co-pilot, and the ten tons of TNT that would literally turn the plane into a bomb. His mission was to lock on to a German target and bail out, but the plane exploded in midair before reaching its destination.

On Sunday afternoon, August 13, Joe was napping when two priests arrived asking to see him. Rose went upstairs to wake him and she was the one to put on the brave face for the children; Joe stayed in his room, listening to somber music hour after hour, going days without talking to anyone and eating so little his wife feared for his health.

Jack was still in the hospital when he heard the news of his brother's death. As he tried to cope with the devastating loss, one thing was clear: as he told his friend Red Fay, "the burden falls to me." Kathleen returned stateside to be with her family, for after being married for only a month, Billy had been sent back to join his regiment. She had been home a few weeks when she was notified that Billy too had been killed. A widow at twenty-four, she returned to England to stay.

Joe's mourning turned to a deep bitterness. He was only fifty-six, but he told friends "all my plans for my own future were all tied up with young Joe, and that has gone smash." When Harry Truman, Roosevelt's choice for vice president for his extraordinary fourth term, came for a visit, Kennedy asked him, "Harry, what the hell are you doing campaigning for that crippled son of a bitch that killed my son Joe?"

Almost a year after Joe Junior's death, Arthur Houghton's son was killed in the Pacific and Joe wrote him, "I won't offer you that hocus pocus—that he died for a great cause—I don't believe he did. I believe he died like young Joe as a result of the stupidity of our generation. The one thing he did die a martyr to was his own conscience. He wanted to do the right thing because it was his idea of the thing to do and for that and that alone he died. That is the satisfaction which you and I will always have."

Joe did not even want to leave the house, but he knew "I probably have to interest myself in something." He met with the producer Mike Todd to discuss going into business together, but Kennedy claimed "I looked at his balance sheet and that was enough." Joe Schenck approached him about going into "private production," but again, he couldn't get excited at the prospect. He continued to screen films several times a week and kept his friends apprised of his opinions, particularly about female stars. After watching *Dragon Seed*, he said he thought "Katharine Hepburn borrowed those slacks from somebody in Long Island and any minute she was going to take off her wig, shake out her hair and say, 'Let's take the car over to Southampton.' "

His libido was back however as he prodded both Eddie Goulding and Arthur Houghton to introduce him to a young actress who had caught his fancy, Joan Fontaine. Goulding told Joe he would have to "put her on ice" because she was busy filming, but then Houghton was sent in to find out the details of her schedule.

After over a year of inaction, Kennedy entered into a flurry of real estate deals, including the purchase of the Merchandise Mart in Chicago. It was the largest privately owned office building in the country, and he paid a fraction of the $30 million it had cost to build fifteen years earlier. He also created the Joseph P. Kennedy Jr. Foundation, which would go on to finance a variety of humanitarian efforts with emphasis on retarded children. Then Joe turned his attention to Jack's future.

During his first seventeen years, Jack had spent over a year in hospitals with various ailments. Joe had been supportive and hands-on when it came to finding medical experts, and it was assumed his second son would be an observer and a writer. If Jack was to step in to take on his brother's proactive role, he first needed to regain his health. He went to Arizona for what he thought might be as long as a year. Every morning he received the *Boston Post* by mail and every night at five o'clock he received a call from his father. "You could set your clock by it," remembers a friend who was with him.

After only three months of recuperation, Jack was feeling well enough to head to Hollywood where he partied at Gary Cooper's and had his head turned by Joan Fontaine's sister, Olivia de Havilland. He found more success with starlets, signing his letters to a friend, "the extra's delight." Then, on a visit to a film set, he met the actress Gene Tierney. She was only twenty-five, but had already been nominated for an Academy Award and iconized as the haunting *Laura*. While she was still married to Oleg Cassini and the mother of an institutionalized daughter, she became so smitten with Jack, she began divorce proceedings. For Jack, it was up to San Francisco where his father had arranged for him to report on the United Nations Charter meeting in May of 1945 for the Hearst newspapers.

With the decision that Jack would run for what had been a part of Honey Fitz's congressional seat, they had to reestablish Boston and Massachusetts as the family base. What better way than to have the governor announce that Joe Kennedy was investing $500,000 in small companies in the state? He was actually selling what remained of Columbia Trust to Shawmut Bank and transferring the money from one company to another, but the aura created around the announcement was that the family cared about the state and considered it worthy of investment. It also helped Joe, who had been out of the public eye for half a dozen years so he needed to publicly rehabilitate himself, give his biography a fresh face, and clean up loose ends. He became chairman of a commission to establish a Massachusetts Department of Commerce and took out ads picturing his smiling self promoting the state's economy.

The last item on his to-do list was to sell Somerset Liquors, the company he had established with an investment of around $100,000. There was no reason to give the opposition ammunition to attack Kennedy's association with liquor and while the company had served as a great source of profit and prolific gift giving over the years, he picked a perfect time to sell; Somerset went for $8 million cash. Kennedy had used the still active Fred Thomson Productions to hold his liquor company and with the sale, the corporation, which had served so many purposes and channeled so much profit, was finally and formally dissolved in the summer of 1946.

Ted O'Leary and Tom Delehanty had been in Kennedy's service since the early 1920s, but as Joe pocketed his $8 million, he gave the two men bonuses of $25,000 each and let them go. From the old days, only Eddie Moore and Johnnie Ford remained on the payroll.

Joe continued to express an interest in returning to Hollywood and he checked in with Arthur Houghton and Charlie Feldman to see "if there is anything of interest out there in pictures." Yet he continued to balk because "I don't know any industry in the world that is as vulnerable for pay raises as the motion picture business. The topside people get so much that the little fellow down below feels he is getting a bad deal and I don't think you will ever change it." He was also concerned with the growing strength of unions; "I have always been against putting money into anything that had a big labor quotient."

Wherever Joe was, a buzz of activity surrounded him. Sunday morning in Palm Beach meant Mass followed by loading everyone into cars for the trip to Hialeah Racetrack. "The first car was old Joe" with men friends who might include "two ex Senators," remembered Pamela Harriman. Then there were several cars of young people, the Kennedy children and friends who were staying at the house, and bringing up "the rear was Mrs. Kennedy and two priests."

When Rose was out of town and even sometimes when she was in residence, Joe became quite blatant in parading a series of secretaries, chorus girls, or various choices of the day upstairs to his bedroom right past anyone who happened to be gathered in the house. "It never bothered me at all," explained Arthur Krock, "because Rose acted as if they didn't exist and that was her business, not mine."

The Kennedy children had become inured over the years to their parents' unique relationship. As they grew older, Joe regaled them with stories that implied his conquests and it wasn't just the boys; the girls' friends and future daughters-in-law were included in the conversations about his serial infidelities. Kathleen was still at Sacred Heart in Connecticut when her friend Charlotte McDonnell walked into Joe's suite at the Waldorf where they were to meet. She called out and Joe yelled from the shower that Jack and Kick were across the hall. A few minutes later, Joe joined them, wrapped only in a towel and laughingly told Charlotte, who had left her bag and coat in his room, that "Will Hays came in and saw your coat and turned around, thinking I had a girl in the bedroom." The three Kennedys all thought this was hilarious, but Charlotte was left shaking her head in confusion. When Kathleen and Eunice were working in Washington and their father came to visit, friends were solicited for ideas of women he could dine with. As one of Jack's girlfriend's sons later recounted, "she thought old Joe was awfully hard—a really mean man. He could be very charming when she and Jack were with him, but if Jack left the room, he'd try to hop in the sack with her. She thought it was a totally amoral situation, that there was something incestuous about the whole family."

While friends were welcomed at Palm Beach and the Cape, they were also warned. When they joined in watching films in the basement screening room, female friends "became reluctant" to accept Joe's invitations to sit next to him because he would "pinch them during the feature. He kissed all female overnight guests on the lips—including girl friends of his sons."

Any pretty young woman who came into Joe's purview was fair game. He seems to have treated them just as he did his business conquests: if they allowed themselves to get caught, it was their own fault and if they somehow eluded him, no umbrage was held, but there was always the hope of another day.

"The Ambassador likes to prowl at night," is how Jack cautioned one young woman staying at the family compound. Actually, it was early in the morning when "the old bugger" slipped into Pamela Harriman's room, she told her friend Truman Capote. Harriman, then Pamela Churchill, was in her mid-twenties and just divorcing her husband Randolph, the son of the prime minister, when she was Kathleen's guest at Palm Beach the winter after war's end. Capote went on to fictionalize the story in his novella *Answered Prayers,* and wrote from the point of view of his female character that Joe "was already between the sheets with one hand over my mouth and the other all over the place. The sheer ballsy gall of it—right there in his own house with the whole family sleeping all around us. But all those Kennedy men are the same: they're like dogs, they have to pee on every fire hydrant." That is Capote talking, not Pamela, but Truman's biographer Gerald Clarke claimed that "Pamela had actually experienced everything" described in the story.

Why all the women? Kennedy "regarded women as a kind of food—to be consumed," remembered Harvey Klemmer. Gore Vidal uses another analogy for what he considered Joe's "super-alpha-male" approach to women; they were "like collecting stamps."

Joe proudly told Joan Fontaine that he had instructed his children not to "fool around at home, but do what you like when it doesn't throw a shadow on the family." Yet as he aged, he failed to follow his own advice and became more blatant in his flaunting of women in front of family and friends.

After finally meeting the star he had lusted after, Joe made his move fairly quickly. They shared a few lunches in New York, and then he called Fontaine to say he was coming to Los Angeles and would like to take her to dinner. She was already planning a party for that night and so invited him to come. Joan thought all was going well as the dinner plates were being cleared when Joe got up from his place on her right and "beckoned me into the living room. 'I like it. I like your guests, your children, your house. Tell you what I'll do. I'll live here whenever I come to California. I'll invest your money for you.'" He assured her, "You can do what you like when I'm not here, but there's only one thing, I can't marry you." In recounting that night decades later, Fontaine still laughs in bemusement over his assumptions, but at that moment she was "stunned. Joe had never even held my hand." Or, as she put it to Liz Smith, "Can you imagine that old man coming on to me?" That night at dinner she just smiled and returned to her guests and they never spoke of it again.

Fontaine says she knew one other man for whom women "were just a possession," and that was Howard Hughes. Still, she continued to see Joe occasionally when she was in New York and he became a sort of "father confessor." What attracted her to him? "He was so powerful that he was very relaxed about it," adding he made you feel like "you were the only one in the world" who mattered. Although he insisted that he would do anything for her and invited her to visit Palm Beach, the one time she did call, she was with her daughter and "there was no room at the inn."

Other women, however, did not have the confidence or experience Fontaine possessed and there seemed to be a never-ending number willing to serve him. He expected friends, from Igor Cassini to Frank Sinatra, to procure for him. Occasionally their efforts were thwarted such as the time Caroline Graham, a lovely nineteen-year-old who was working for Liz Smith, then a writer for Cassini's column published under the moniker of Cholly Knickerbocker, returned to the office with the news that Igor "had been so kind as to arrange for her to have dinner with

Ambassador Kennedy." Liz informed the naive girl, "You are not going to dinner with him and if you do I am calling your mother and sending you back to England." Smith is convinced that while Caroline might have escaped Joe's grasp, there were plenty of others lined up to take her place.

Kennedy, in turn, took care of his powerful friends. When Bernard Baruch was heading to Hollywood, Joe assured him that "everything [would be] done to his heart's content" and then wired Arthur Houghton to take care of Baruch, who was "still partial to beautiful blondes."

AS JACK'S CAMPAIGN for Congress began in earnest, he grew from a gawky greeter of potential constituents to a confident campaigner. He was often up and out at six in the morning, shaking hands and attending events on through the night. Behind the scenes, Jack's friend John Galvin recalled, "Joe Kennedy could get almost anything done that he wanted to get done. He could reach almost anyone he wanted to reach." While he helped finance the campaign, there was no "extra money floating around. They wanted accountability for everything they bought." Joe's contacts with the media were legion and now he called in favors to the point that two of Boston's daily papers literally left "space every day for a two column picture and some story about Jack Kennedy."

Jack's election that November of 1946 bucked a national trend as Republicans swept into control of both the House and the Senate for the first time in almost twenty years. That translated into powerful committee assignments and among them was the new chairman of the House Un-American Activities Committee, J. Parnell Thomas of New Jersey. One of his first announcements was that hearings to investigate subversion in the film industry would take place the next summer, but they had to be postponed because there was so little to base the investigation on until Thomas went hat in hand to the FBI. Director J. Edgar Hoover instructed his agents to "extend every assistance to the committee" and soon Thomas was in possession of blind memos and lists of organizations, "fronts," and individuals deemed subversive as well as those who were potential "friendly witnesses."

One of the thirty-two names on Hoover's list of "cooperative or friendly witnesses" was Ronald Reagan and another "informant" (Hoover insisted on using that term instead of "informer" because it "sounds more admirable") was Joseph P. Kennedy. Knowing the FBI director held files on both himself and Jack, Joe let it be known he would be happy to "assist the Bureau in any way possible." Joe was designated a "Special Service Contact" and in multiple conversations with agents, he expressed concern about "the threat of Communism to our domestic institutions" and "pinkos" in the film business. He specifically volunteered that he had "many Jewish friends who would furnish him, upon request, with any information in their possession pertaining to Communist infiltration."

Hoover and his close personal friend and assistant Clyde Tolson visited Joe at his Palm Beach home, and shortly afterward, the FBI director told agents they should feel free to ask Kennedy about people and use anything he offered, but to keep Hoover informed. Joe kept up a steady stream of correspondence with Hoover over the years, praising some action or speech. Joe told him that he was his candidate for president, whatever year, whatever party. On their own, they are friendly, often innocuous, notes, but taken together, they read almost like love letters, similar to the ones Kennedy wrote Will Hays, showering him with admiration, telling him he wasn't appreciated enough and that the world or a portion of it would fall apart if something happened to him.

Left-leaning Hollywood was just one of many of Joe's concerns that his son did not share. Jack had an intense curiosity, sought knowledge for knowledge's sake, and had an empathy for others his father never had. Joe McCarthy was Joe Kennedy's friend, not his son's. While Bobby would work for McCarthy and Jack walked a thin line in his relationship with the senator, Jack and Bobby very publicly crossed American Legion picket lines to see *Spartacus,* starring Kirk Douglas and commonly known to have been written by one of the most celebrated of the Hollywood Ten, Dalton Trumbo.

Jack's interest in the film business continued to center on Gene Tierney and she even spent a week at the Cape. Although her family and her now ex-husband, Oleg Cassini, warned her that a Kennedy would never marry a divorced Episcopalian mother, she hung on to the hope for over a year. Tierney went to Washington to watch Jack working the floor of Congress and then, finally, one afternoon he quietly informed her, "You know, Gene, I can never marry you." With that, she did not see him again, but later in life she remembered she "wore her heart on her sleeve for a long time."

Breaking with Tierney hardly curbed Jack's appetite for Hollywood and he fell into the habit of visiting regularly. He usually stayed at the Coldwater Canyon home of his father's friend, the agent Charlie Feldman, who was now also producing, buying the rights to stories and then packaging the actors, directors, and writers he had under contract and presenting them fait accompli to the studios. Charlie often set Jack up with beautiful young actresses, but Joe was growing concerned that his son's promiscuity was becoming too public.

On a trip of his own to Hollywood in 1947, Joe took it upon himself to find an appropriate woman for Jack and discussed the situation on the golf course with Feldman and RKO executive Phil Reisman. Charlie's eye for the ladies had not dimmed in the slightest and he was always cultivating new talent so he told Joe about his latest find, a young woman who was not only a real beauty, but a virgin besides. The just twenty-year-old Arlene Dahl was in Hollywood because Jack Warner had seen her in a New York musical and signed her to a contract. She had passed her screen test and was waiting to start her first film when she received a phone call inviting her to join the three men at Romanoff's. "It was an interesting lunch and, as it was ending, Joe said to me, 'I like the way you think and I would like to talk to you. Can I come by your apartment later this afternoon?' "

Looking back, the actress laughs at her own naïveté for agreeing to see him, but she did and once he arrived, even she was surprised by his mission. " 'I have a son I would like you to meet,' and assured me, 'He's a very nice young man.' He went on to tell me a little about him and then asked me who was handling my business affairs and offered to advise me." And shortly thereafter, a call came from Boston; Jack was coming to Hollywood and would she go out with him?

It was the night of a black-tie affair at the home of Charles and Elsie Mendle and "Jack arrived straight from the airport in a rumpled brown suit, brown shoes and when he sat down, I noticed one sock was black and the other was brown. Well, I didn't have a black suit in my closet, so I asked him if I could press his suit for him. If it made me happy, that was all that mattered. So he was sitting there in my hot pink chiffon robe when my roommate walked in. He didn't care; we all just laughed and he thought it was very amusing. He even let me comb down his cowlick, but he drew the line at hairspray."

The evening was a great success and Jack returned regularly to Hollywood, usually staying at Charlie's and seeing Arlene. "He never had his own car or a driver or carried any money. So it was always my car and I made the reservations, but when we went out it was mostly to private parties. I loved dancing and because of his back, he couldn't dance. He always had that bad back. He never complained about it, but occasionally he might say 'If I am a little strange tonight it's because I took one or two more pills than I should have. I just don't want to think about it.' "

Dahl's screen career was taking off and she moved to MGM where she remembers introducing Jack's sister Patricia, whom Arlene worked with on Catholic Charities, to the Metro star Peter Lawford. In between her dates with Jack, Joe would check in with Arlene to see how things were going and eventually it was he who asked Arlene if she would marry Jack. "I think he was in awe of my virginity" and, knowing of her charity work with Pat, simply assumed she was Catholic. When he discovered she was a Midwestern Lutheran, he asked her to convert. But in the end, while Arlene found Jack to be "so handsome and interesting . . . I admired him on almost every level," they both insisted on deciding for themselves whom they would marry.

Asked if she heard from Joe again after her break with Jack, Dahl says, "Oh, no. Once he knew I wasn't going to marry his son, I was off the list. He was on to Plan B." Looking back over those years, she concludes, "I think I was the only Hollywood star NOT to have slept with Jack Kennedy."

Joe gave up on guiding his son's love life and added the South of France to his list of annual pilgrimages. The children were almost all grown and out on their own. Eunice, now twenty-seven, was working as the executive secretary at the Justice Department's Juvenile Delinquency Committee. Bobby, twenty-three, was out of the Navy without seeing action and back at Harvard, while Jean, twenty, was a student at Manhattanville College in New York where her roommate was Eunice Skakel (soon to become Mrs. Robert Kennedy). At sixteen, Teddy had already attended almost a dozen schools in his short life and was now at the Milton Academy.

Kathleen had remained in England since the death of her husband, but after several years of widowhood, had fallen in love with the married Lord Peter Fitzwilliams, whom friends described as "quite the rogue male" with a charm and bravado that reminded them of Joe Kennedy. Rose would never approve, but Kathleen hoped her father would give them his blessing. She and Peter were flying to France to meet with him when their plane crashed into a mountain during a storm. Joe was in his George V hotel room on May 14, 1948, when he received the phone call from a Boston reporter. Kennedy flew to Lyon, drove to the crash site, and identified the body of the daughter he adored. He called home, told the family how peaceful she had looked, and then holed up in his hotel, not knowing what to do next. It was Kick's former mother-in-law who came to the rescue, suggesting that Kathleen be buried in their family plot. Joe agreed and went to England to attend her burial a week later, surrounded by the friends who had loved Kathleen, but disliked him for what they thought he had done, or not done, as ambassador.

Joe continued to travel and have enough stature to meet with leaders such as President Truman and Generals Douglas MacArthur and Dwight Eisenhower. He stayed in touch with a few of his remaining Hollywood friends such as Morton Downey, Will Hays, and Arthur Houghton as well as those in the press such as Arthur Krock. Yet with less reason to be pleasant to get ahead, he became more presumptuous and quicker to condemn. He grew more conservative and claimed that "the Democratic party that considers nominating LaGuardia for United States Senate certainly isn't the Democratic party in which my father was interested." When he was asked to come to California to speak at a Democratic dinner organized by Joe Schenck, he declined the "honor," privately telling friends the schedule clashed with a more important commitment, the World Series.

While both Kennedy and Gloria Swanson continued to make dismissive remarks about each other to friends, they saw each other off and on over the years in Los Angeles and New York. Gloria and Rose occasionally ran into each other in foreign ports and the two women carried on a sporadic correspondence, recommending doctors, sharing family news as well as flowers and notes of sympathy when Joe Junior and Kathleen died.

Joe Schenck eventually bought back Swanson's UA stock and severed the relationship. Gloria would make several films in the 1930s, but neither her screen career nor her bank account ever recovered from *Queen Kelly.* The Internal Revenue Service continued to haunt her. To her fury, Joe consistently claimed to have no records, yet his files hold substantial accounts regarding her films as well as his profits from Eddie Goulding's song "Love."

Swanson would marry three more times, each ending in divorce, and gave birth to another daughter, Michelle, during her brief marriage to Michael Farmer, a British playboy friend of Eddie Goulding's and Noël Coward's. Gloria was introduced to a new generation of filmgoers in Billy Wilder's *Sunset Boulevard* in 1950. She was in her early fifties, but Norma Desmond would become her signature role and she reveled in it. Unlike her character, however, Gloria lived very much in the present, involved in a wide variety of projects. She moved to New York where she developed a clothing line, was a spokeswoman for Jergens and other products, and took up sculpture. She hosted a television show and went into the cosmetics business where she was her own chemist. She became a vocal advocate of organic farming and nutrition. She was always determined to be as self-sufficient as possible and never had another mentor. "The only person she ever really loved and respected was her mother," says her daughter Michelle, who went through her own private hell growing up in boarding schools. One of the positives Michelle remembers is her mother repeatedly telling her, "If you don't discipline yourself, life will."

Swanson's children, particularly Joseph, continued to look upon Kennedy as an authority figure. Gloria sent Michelle to see Joe when she was balking at following through on an acting contract, and Joseph consulted with him when he faced major personal decisions.

Kennedy's and Swanson's mutual willfulness came out in both public and private conversations. Kennedy often regaled friends with stories of Gloria and claimed she had "wrecked my business, wrecked my health and damn near wrecked my life." She in turn would dismiss him in interviews and when pushed to explain their relationship, she waved her hand and said, "What did I know, my job was to look good and show up."

Gloria tried to salvage *Queen Kelly* with the help of Stroheim in 1956 and went so far as to round up Seena Owen and Walter Byron, who were both amenable to reprising their roles almost twenty years later. Yet when she approached Kennedy for help with the financing, he refused. She was forced to give up on the film and another thirty years would pass before preservationists combined the remaining footage with stills to produce as complete a version as possible.

IN 1952, Joe was invigorated by Jack's run for the Senate against Henry Cabot Lodge. Eddie Moore, who would pass away the next year, was too ill to participate to any great degree, but Johnnie Ford was still based in Boston and helpful in ways large and small. Once Jack became the junior senator from Massachusetts, Joe was more concerned than ever about his son's love life, at least the possible publication of it, so he was relieved and genuinely pleased when, in the summer of 1953, it was announced that Jack was engaged to the Newport socialite cum Washington photographer Jacqueline Bouvier. His sons' escapades had been a source of pride to Joe and he had even gone so far as to reimburse Jack's friend Lem Billings when he took young Bobby to the same Harlem whorehouse where Jack had lost his virginity. However, now there was an image to protect and Joe wrote to Jack's friend Torb Macdonald, "I am a bit concerned that [Jack] might get restless about the prospect of getting married. Most people do and he is more likely to do so than others. . . . I am hoping that he will take a rest and not jump from place to place and be especially mindful of whom he sees." Joe never showed any remorse for his own infidelities, let alone curtailed them for any length of time, but now that Jack was a public figure, monogamy was "a price he should be willing to pay and gladly."

A Newport society wedding was the perfect backdrop to stage a massive publicity campaign and Joe wanted a separate tent for the press with an open bar. However, he met his match in Jackie's mother, Janet Auchincloss, who insisted that a few friends who happened to be with the press could be invited as guests, but there would be no separate facilities at her daughter's wedding. She won the battle of the tent, but enough reporters and photographers were given access to have the September 12, 1953, wedding covered prolifically in national magazines.

Joe's portion of the guest list ranged from J. Edgar Hoover and Clyde Tolson to his old friend Marion Davies and Horace Brown, the man she had married less than three months after Hearst's death two years before. Davies and Brown stayed in the East so Jack and Jackie could spend a week of their honeymoon at Marion's Beverly Hills estate, secluded yet with every whim met by the dozen-plus household staff.

Kennedy had stayed close to Marion. He had inserted himself into discussions with Hearst over her future, saying, "I hope I'm not being too forward," but "it seems to me that things . . . should be earmarked for her right away so any disputes might be avoided." He added that "you might tell her if she needs advice on anything else to call me. I would like nothing better than to see that she had whatever protection I could give her against that hungry hoarde [sic]," referring to the Hearst Corporation.

Hollywood came back full force into Kennedy's life a few months after Jack's wedding when Patricia brought the actor Peter Lawford to Palm Beach for the holidays. The Lawford family had a title, but little money. Peter's parents, Sir Sidney and Lady May Lawford, had been married to others when May's pregnancy by Sidney moved them to divorce their respective spouses and wed. They created quite a scandal in the process and most of Peter's youth was spent traveling the globe. Sir Sidney was unable to get money out of England, but May insisted on keeping up their globe-trotting ways. Almost twenty years older than his wife, Sidney was nearing seventy and so Peter became the primary breadwinner, working at gas stations and parking cars. When the family moved to Los Angeles, he quickly went from theater usher to movie actor and was in half a dozen films including *Mrs. Miniver* and *A Yank at Eton* before signing a contract at the age of nineteen with MGM.

When it became clear that his daughter was serious about the now thirty-year-old Lawford, Joe began investigating him. He heard rumors that Peter was bisexual and had several gay friends so Kennedy called Lawford's old boss, Louis B. Mayer, who had been out of MGM since 1951, but he was willing to tell Joe what he knew. Mayer was proud that he had cultivated young talent and considered Peter one of his finds, along with Jackie Cooper, Elizabeth Taylor, Judy Garland, and Mickey Rooney. Mayer told Joe that the gay rumors had been started by Peter's own mother, who had come to him with her "concerns" about her son's sexuality. At the time, Lawford was in the middle of a torrid affair with Lana Turner and Mayer assured Kennedy that the rumors were just that; Peter was heterosexual through and through.

To double-check, Kennedy placed a call to J. Edgar Hoover and within days Joe was reading through Lawford's FBI file. The pages included the fact that Peter had turned over the name of a Hollywood figure to the FBI as "Oh, so Red," but most of the documents dealt with the repeated times that Peter's name had been found during the bureau's investigations of prostitution rings. As one of Lawford's biographers notes, "Such information would have turned most fathers against a prospective son-in-law, but not Joe Kennedy." He concluded that Peter was not only a proven anti-communist, but "a normal, red blooded American male," and that, plus the almost $100,000 in the actor's bank account, convinced Kennedy that Lawford would do just fine.

Still, Joe put Peter through his paces when he called on Kennedy in his New York office to officially ask for his daughter's hand in marriage. Joe greeted him with "If there's anything I'd hate more for a son in law than an actor, it's a British actor," and asked him about his finances. Joe had a lengthy prenuptial agreement prepared for Lawford to sign, but he pulled it when the actor consented to the idea. To prove both his sincerity and his net worth, Peter gave Pat an eight-carat diamond engagement ring.

Even Rose did not object too strenuously to Peter. Although he was an Episcopalian, he agreed to raise the children as Catholics and the major upheaval that had greeted Kathleen's marriage was not repeated. This time the outrage came from Peter's mother, who called the Kennedys "barefoot Irish peasants." She was a thorn in Joe's side, but it was Peter who was scornful of her, fed up with her pretenses and the way she treated just about anyone who wasn't obsequious to her.

The April 24, 1954, wedding was a relatively small one at St. Thomas More Roman Catholic Church on New York's Upper East Side, but the glamour of a Kennedy-Lawford wedding took on the look of a Hollywood premiere and captured the imagination of the media. More than three thousand curious spectators congregated outside for a glimpse of the newlyweds, requiring police cordons. Joe stoked the publicity machine and Igor Cassini used his column to hail the marriage as "one of the great romances of the year."

Joe actively coordinated, solicited, and monitored the press coverage of his family in general and Jack in particular. W. R Hearst was gone, but Joe stayed in touch with his son, W.R. Jr., who had taken over the Hearst enterprises, and Hearst's national editor, Frank Conniff. When W. R. Hearst III was born, Joe sent the infant several shares of stock in blue-chip companies.

Kennedy maintained efficient offices in each of his homes and in Palm Beach he had his one-hundred-square-foot walled, open-air "sun box" with padded benches and chairs where he could sunbathe while having the privacy he needed as he "worked the phone." Decades before the term "telecommuting" was coined, Joe was running his kingdom poolside.

He was looking at a fortune of around $400 million (or the equivalent of $2 billion today) as he prepared to stay behind the scenes, but still actively participate in his son's campaign for president. As Jim Landis, who had stayed friendly with Joe since their New Deal days, described it, "The Kennedy fortune is different from most others. It isn't paper; it's real. Joe could write a check for nine million dollars just like that." He owned more real estate than any other individual American and he was ready to spend what it took to see his vicarious dream come true.

Kennedy was painfully aware that his public appearances would not help the campaign. In spite of his years of playing the press and desperately trying to create a sterling biography for himself, questions raised over the years had careered like a game of telephone into the "common knowledge" that the family fortune was the result of bootlegging and stock market manipulation.

Joe may have lain low, but he stage-managed. He declined an offer from *The Ladies' Home Journal* for Rose to write an article "extolling her children," but cooperated with *Redbook* for an article on Jack's life and scheduled his children's summer visits to coincide with the arrival of a reporter from *Collier's*. Throughout the 1950s, multiple articles appeared under Jack's name in venues as diverse as *Look, Vogue, TV Guide, McCall's, Life,* and *The New York Times Magazine.*

Kennedy also made time to keep his proverbial eye on his other children and their families. Peter Lawford had found some success in television, but after his run as Nick Charles in *The Thin Man* series was off the air, he went behind the camera as a producer. Carl Reiner was looking for backing for a new situation comedy he had written and planned to star in called *Head of the Family* about a television writer named Rob Petrie who worked in New York and lived with his wife and son in New Rochelle. Both Reiner and Lawford were represented by William Morris and their agents put the men together. Reiner remembers going to the Sherry-Netherland hotel in Manhattan for their first meeting where he found Lawford "wearing velvet slippers with gold embossing and no socks—that's important—no socks, that's what stood out." Lawford agreed to back the pilot. And then a few weeks before shooting began Reiner received a request: "Could you please send a copy of the script to Florida?" Reiner slowly realized that meant it needed to pass muster with Joe Kennedy for the ultimate green light. According to friends, Lawford was "terrified" of Joe and the Kennedy wealth "hovered over the Lawfords like an enormous carnivorous bird," and so with some trepidation, Reiner sent the script off to Palm Beach. The filming went ahead as scheduled so he assumed that since there was nothing "anti-Irish or pro–Gloria Swanson" in the story, Joe had given his approval. *Head of the Family* was not picked up, but less than a year later, Sheldon Leonard, along with his partner Danny Thomas, convinced Reiner his scripts were great, but they needed someone else to star and so *The Dick Van Dyke Show* was born. Lawford's role as producer ended with the pilot and he went on to his next project, a film based on a story he had optioned, *Ocean's Eleven.*

As Jack Kennedy's campaign for president picked up steam, Joe was rarely seen in public, but from Antibes, Palm Beach, and Hyannis Port, he made it his business to keep in contact with friends in the press and other influential players, soliciting their ideas and promoting Jack. He also called in favors. There are variations of the story of assistance from the mob and one of those willing to talk on the record is Tina Sinatra, who says her father told her that Joe called him to come to his Waldorf suite early in 1959. He arrived assuming he would be asked to fundraise, but instead Joe told him they needed help in West Virginia in the primaries and Illinois in the general election. "You and I know the same people and you know the people I mean," Joe told Frank. " 'Sure,' my father said. He didn't need to have the dots connected. 'I can't go to those people,' the old man went on. 'It might come back at Jack. But you can. The best thing you can do for Jack is to ask for their help as a personal favor, to you. Keep us out of it.' "

Tina says that "Dad had never done anything like this before," for no one was more aware "it was not a good idea to be in their debt," but he took Chicago Boss Sam Giancana out on the golf course. After Frank relayed the request and assured him he was getting nothing out of it himself, Giancana told Sinatra, "It's a couple of phone calls. And tell the old man I said hello."

During the primaries, Joe spent time at the Cal Neva Lodge on the California-Nevada border and visited Sinatra at his Palm Springs home. Sinatra's valet claimed that "the abuse [Joe] heaped on all of us" was "cruder and meaner" than that of any other visitor in the fifteen years he worked for Frank.

Joe bought a plane so Jack could fly more comfortably and expeditiously around the country, saying he "had risked a million dollars before on an adventure much less worthwhile." In July of 1960, the Democratic National Convention was held in Los Angeles and Joe set up residence at Marion Davies's Beverly Hills estate. It had been Hearst's home for the last four years of his life and was fully equipped, not only with the obligatory pool and tennis court, but with a switchboard and a dozen phone lines in addition to a full phalanx of staff. It was a perfect arrangement for a man who wanted to be invisible yet in constant contact.

The delegate voting was to begin on Wednesday night and that day Jack managed to get away unnoticed to spend several hours alone with his father at the Davies home. With all that was going on and all that needed to be done, father and son shared the ability to remove themselves for a few hours of rest and relaxation. Two nights later, the rest of the family was at the convention to hear Jack's acceptance speech, but Joe had left that morning to fly to New York to watch his son's speech at the home of Henry Luce, "in the company of the single most powerful influence on the minds and opinions of America."

Once Jack's nomination was assured and the campaign against Richard Nixon went into high gear, Joe physically removed himself from the country, spending the rest of the summer on the French Riviera, where he was photographed walking the golf course with his beautiful young "caddy" who also happened to be in residence at his villa. While Joe stayed in constant touch with the campaign by phone, he had been laying the groundwork for years. The "crucial difference" between Nixon and Kennedy, concludes Seymour Hersh, "as had been foreseen and carefully orchestrated by Jack's father, was Kennedy's celebrity status, and his confidence and ease in front of the camera."

AS THE VOTES were being tallied on election night, Jack, the family, and their friends including Ben Bradlee and his wife gathered at what was now the family compound of houses on the Cape. They went down to the basement theater to watch a John Wayne movie, and when that failed to hold their interest, *Butterfield 8,* starring Elizabeth Taylor, and released in theaters just days before, was put into the projector instead.

Early the next morning, Jack awoke as president-elect and when his family accompanied him to the local armory for his press conference, Joe was photographed with his son for the first time in many months.

Joe Kennedy was seventy-two years old that January of 1961 and proud to claim that the tuxedo he wore as ambassador still fit him for his son's inauguration. The festivities were star-studded with Frank Sinatra, who had provided the campaign with its theme song, a variation on "High Hopes," literally producing the inaugural ball. Yet the planning turned rancorous as Sinatra resented what he considered the shabby treatment of Sammy Davis Jr., whom Joe insisted be disinvited after he married the very white Mae Britt. Peter Lawford was the bearer of that news and he took the brunt of Sinatra's anger.

Nothing was to spoil the triumphant day for Joe, who saluted his son, now the president of the United States, as Jack passed the reviewing stand and tipped his hat to his father. It was the ultimate culmination of fifty years of telling the rest of the world they could go to hell.

Alongside the multitude of family members sat Marion Davies and her husband, Horace. Joe had made arrangements for them to stay in the Presidential Suite of the Sheridan Park Hotel and be treated as very special guests throughout the festivities. Marion was wearing silk scarves to cover the results of an operation to remove cancer of the jaw and when Joe realized what was happening, he made it his business to talk to her doctors and then have two New York specialists sent to examine her. He took several of his grandchildren along with a nurse to visit her for a week in Palm Springs. He added a doctor from Illinois to her retinue and they operated on Marion early that summer. She believed she was getting better, but in trying to walk, she broke her leg and was bedridden for the two months before she died on September 22,

A young Marion Davies

1961. Mary Pickford helped Horace choose the casket, but few friends from those glory days of the teens and 1920s were left. Joe was an honorary pallbearer.

While photographs decorated many walls in the Hyannis Port house, Joe's bedroom featured only one and that was on his night table: a smiling picture of a young Marion Davies. "She was a wonderful woman. She was a great friend," Joe told his chauffeur, Frank Saunders, when they heard the news of Marion's death. "She was a woman who understood men. She understood men who wanted great things. She understood me."

SHORTLY AFTER HIS ELECTION in 1960, Jack Kennedy was relaxing in Hyannis Port, playing backgammon with his friend and distant in-law Gore Vidal. "You know," Jack said, "I am getting a little tired of reading how my father bought me the election. I think of the things I did—I was the one out there."

"Well," Vidal responded, "he certainly made a big contribution. What do you think drove him?"

Jack paused, looked out to the sea for a moment, and then said with finality, "Vanity."

It was vanity and, of course, much more. Joe Kennedy was a very complicated man who could be harsh and brutal in his business dealings, able to cut off formerly close friends without a blink. There was nothing unconditional in his life except his love for his children. Joe had always been the center of the familial universe and a major player in the world at large, but now the second son, who had spent his first twenty-five years in the shadow of his elder brother, had emerged as the one in the floodlights.

Friends such as John Kenneth Galbraith, who had known Jack since Harvard and went on to become his ambassador to India, believed that Joe Kennedy had "a diminishing influence" on his son. "Certainly by the time he was president, Jack Kennedy was very much in control himself. He was kind to his father. He admired his father, but he did not feel it necessary, perhaps even wise, to be guided by his father." Many people commented on how Joe must have had to restrain himself from calling Jack on a regular basis; instead he waited to be called. He was there for him when he needed to talk such as in April when Joe reported to Rose he spent most of the day on the phone with Jack and Bobby, venting their frustration over the Bay of Pigs.

In Hyannis Port, Joe had the outdoor field turned into a helicopter pad for presidential visits and he laid the groundwork for his youngest son, Teddy, to run for Jack's former Senate seat in the fall of 1962. Joe also helped negotiate the movie rights for Bob Donovan's book, *PT 109*, for $150,000 with $2,500 for each of the crewmembers or their widows and the remaining $120,000 to Donovan.

Bobby Kennedy, as Jack's attorney general, had tried to learn to live with J. Edgar Hoover, who overtly disdained the man who was technically his boss. There was little Hoover enjoyed more than turning the screws so he must have smiled as he passed a memo to his "superior" on December 11, 1961, that wiretaps on the phone of Sam Giancana had revealed that the Chicago mob chief had "made a donation to the campaign of President Kennedy but was not getting his money's worth." Bobby, of course, would have told Jack and the next weekend, the president stopped in Palm Beach after a brief trip to South America, arriving in Florida on December 18.

Jack spent the evening with his father and it's hard to believe they didn't discuss the Hoover memo. The next morning they drove together to the airport for Jack's return to the White House. Joe returned to the house and then went golfing with his niece Ann Gargan, the now-grown daughter of Rose's sister Agnes. Several hours later, Ann returned with Joe to the Ocean Front house reporting that he had felt faint on the course and wanted to rest.

Later that evening, an ambulance was finally called to take him to the hospital where he was put on life support. Joe had suffered a severe stroke and over the next year attempts at physical therapy and rehabilitation were made, but they were aborted on several occasions. Ann Gargan became his caregiver and "given complete authority" over him.

The right side of his body was paralyzed and, according to his private

Joe with Rose's niece Ann Gargan, 1960

nurse, Rita Dallas, "he did not know what the words were that he was saying. He knew the words he wanted to use, but the directive mechanism, the portion of the brain that directs this ability, was not operating." He lay there with a functioning brain unable to communicate, except for the word "No." There were variations in tone and length, but still the only thing that came out was "No."

Efforts were made to promote the idea that little was wrong. He was taken in a wheelchair to his New York office where subordinates were brought in to report to him in a one-way conversation. Yet privately it must have been agonizing for Joe knowing what he wanted to say and being unable to say it, embarrassing for his employees, and emotionally draining for the family. He was brought to the White House and his children all visited regularly, carrying on as if all was normal, giving him accounts of their activities yet without the familiar response and counsel.

For decades, all activity had revolved around him and he had been able to pick up the phone and reach into almost any area of power. That man was gone. Rose agonized over "my poor son. So much responsibility and

President Kennedy with his ailing father, 1962

there is no way for his father to help him now." It is possible, even probable, that neither Jack nor Bobby knew all the details of Joe's various relationships, including those with the mob, and only a few months after the stroke, that pivotal role was sorely missed.

Frank Sinatra was making very public plans for the president to stay at his Palm Springs compound where both Jack and Joe had been guests before. Now Frank added a helicopter landing pad and multiple phone lines with visions of his estate becoming "the western White House." Only two days before the long planned presidential arrival, Peter Lawford informed him that the Secret Service thought the house was "too open and unsafe, too big a security risk." Sinatra didn't believe it for a minute and the ultimate insult immediately followed when he was informed the president would be staying at the Palm Springs home of Republican Bing Crosby instead. "Had the Kennedys sought deliberately to humiliate my father, they couldn't have done a better job," says Frank's daughter Tina. Sinatra cut off his relationship with Peter Lawford and he never trusted Bobby, but "Dad couldn't bring himself to blame Jack."

Bobby clearly wanted to distance Jack from any friends of Sam Giancana no matter how helpful they had been in the past, and when the attorney general went after the mob and Giancana particularly, Tina says "Dad was stunned when the administration began to prosecute the very people it had enlisted for help just the year before. He had gone to Giancana out of friendship for Jack Kennedy and expected nothing back. What he did not expect was to be set up like a fool." The rebuff of Sinatra sent reverberations deep into the mob, who had to wonder what was next.

IF THERE WAS ONE AREA in which friends saw the pattern of Joe's life repeated in Jack, it was in his eye for actresses and his congenital, emotionless womanizing. Jack's attitude toward his father's conduct seems to have evolved from acceptance to almost respect if not awe. When Joan Fontaine dined at the White House in 1962, she told the president the story of Joe "offering" to move in with her and Jack's response was, "Let's see . . . how old would he have been then? Sixty-five? Hope I'm the same when I'm his age."

Just as he had when he was a congressman, Jack continued to squeeze in a trip to California whenever possible. The Santa Monica beach was turned into an impromptu helicopter pad as the president landed and ran escorted into the oceanfront house of Pat and Peter Lawford. "There were always a lot of women around," one of their neighbors remembers, "but Angie Dickinson was the perennial." Another regular visitor was Marilyn Monroe, whose relationships with Jack and Bobby have been discussed elsewhere.

The president's escapades with movie stars weren't limited to his time away from Washington. Marlene Dietrich, whom Jack remembered as the glamorous woman in the South of France who had massaged him seductively when she wasn't off in her bungalow with his father, was past sixty when she brought her sold-out, one-woman show to Washington in September of 1963. Both she and her daughter had campaigned for Kennedy and Dietrich was "flattered" by his phone call inviting her to the White House with directions for arrival at the South Entrance. She later told several friends including Gore Vidal that she was shown upstairs and found the president alone and expecting her. The tour consisted of the West Sitting Room and the bedroom where he made a "clumsy pass." Her initial protest of "You know, Mr. President, I am not very young" soon gave way to "Don't muss my hair. I'm performing." After an "ecstatic three to six minutes," Jack was quickly asleep. Marlene "pulled herself together" and, already running late and not wanting to just wander the halls, woke Jack. He apologized and rang for his valet, who was clearly "used to this sort of thing." The president asked for Miss Dietrich's car to be readied and then, with a towel around his waist, he led her to the small elevator across the hall from the bedroom. He "shook her hand as if she were the mayor of San Antonio," but something else was on his mind.

"If I ask you a question, will you tell me the truth?" Marlene "did not guarantee" anything, but said, "Fire ahead."

"Did you ever go to bed with my old man?"

Knowing exactly what he wanted to hear, Marlene demurred. "He tried," she responded after a brief pause, "but I never did."

Jack was "triumphant. 'I always knew the son of a bitch was lying.' "

Marlene couldn't resist a little bragging of her own. She returned to her New York apartment where she was greeted by her son-in-law, who was staying there. Before even saying hello, Marlene smiled, opened her bag, and pulled out a pair of pink panties and waved them at his nose. "Smell! It is him! The President of the United States! He . . . was . . . wonderful!" As Marlene's daughter recounts the story, she is quick to note that her husband immediately moved to a hotel.

IT WAS ONLY TWO MONTHS LATER that Jack and Jackie took off on a pre-reelection campaign trip to Dallas. Joe and Rose and their retinue were still in Hyannis Port, with the staff readying to make the annual move to Palm Beach in time for Thanksgiving. Joe and Rose were napping in their separate bedrooms when Frank Saunders, the family chauffeur, heard the news on the radio and Joe's nurse went into his room to make sure he was still sleeping. It wasn't long before the Secret Service entered the house and informed the staff the president was dead, but Rose heard it from the television. She emerged from her room to instruct the help to keep the news from her husband. "I just talked with my children. They're coming right up. I want them to be with him. I want them to tell him."

The normal schedule was that after his nap, Joe watched a movie so Frank pulled himself together and went into the room a bit too cheerfully announcing "Hey Chief, it's movie time." Looking anywhere but at him, Frank put Joe into his wheelchair and rolled him into the elevator that took them to the basement screening room. A distraught Ann Gargan joined them and Frank went into the projection booth, dimmed the lights, and, with a quick focusing, *Kid Galahad* starring Elvis Presley illuminated the screen. *Kid Galahad* was Elvis's tenth film in six years and Joe usually had the patience to sit through all kinds of movies, but this day, not even co-stars Charles Bronson and Gig Young with an Irish backstory could hold his interest. The film was not halfway through when Joe started fidgeting and waving dismissively at the screen so Ann called to Frank to turn it off. Joe silently nodded when asked if he wanted to go back upstairs and while the staff expected an explosion when they told him his television was broken, they were relieved when he just gestured toward a magazine and settled for that.

Joe was in his bed when Eunice and Ted arrived, red-eyed and exhausted. They broke the news of Jack's death to their father and Joe sobbed as the reality sank in. After the unthinkable had happened to Joe Junior, his second son had accomplished the familial imperative of catching the gold ring and Joe had convinced himself, after thinking he was standing at Jack's deathbed on four different occasions, "I know nothing can happen to him." But it had, and while Rose joined the rest of the family in Washington for the state funeral, Joe stayed behind his closed bedroom door. This time there was the continuous coverage on television, which, now that it was "fixed," he watched off and on with Father Cavanaugh of Notre Dame, who had arrived to be at his side.

Five years later, no one tried to interrupt the television coverage as Joe lay watching and waiting during the twenty-four hours between the time Bobby was shot and when he died. This time it was Teddy's turn to give the eloquent and emotional eulogy as the last surviving son. Joe's agony is almost unimaginable, not only for the tremendous loss, but also his total inability to do anything about any of it.

When former President Eisenhower's funeral was televised in early 1969, Joe became visibly upset. His caregivers finally realized his grief was way beyond anything they had seen except for his sons' funerals and it wasn't until Teddy was called from Washington to come to his father's bedside that "the old man" was convinced he hadn't outlived his only remaining son.

While there had been several near-death scares, Joe's health severely faded over the summer and fall of 1969. The family, his two dozen grandchildren, and his widowed daughter-in-law Jackie, now married to Aristotle Onassis, made the pilgrimage to the Cape to say their goodbyes. Finally, on the morning of Tuesday, November 18, 1969, at the age of eighty-one and after eight years of being unable to speak, Joe Kennedy passed away.

The obituaries that headlined the country's newspapers and national magazines paid homage to the great patriarch, the father of a president, and a man who lived to watch four of his children die before him. There were references to his earlier life on Wall Street and as ambassador, but precious little was mentioned about his time in Hollywood, let alone his unique impact on the film business.

He had shifted the gears of an entire industry from one that took the creative long view to one whose guiding doctrine was the next quarter's balance sheet, unheard of then but taken for granted in today's multinational corporate Hollywood. The years had blurred his extraordinary influence and the fact that, as Betty Lasky, daughter of fellow mogul Jesse Lasky, put it, in the over one hundred years of the business of film, "Joe Kennedy was the first and only outsider to fleece Hollywood."

It was my friend Polly Platt, an incredibly strong and talented woman, who was the first to say out loud what I had suspected. After she read *Without Lying Down,* my book on Frances Marion and the powerful women of early Hollywood, she informed me in her inimitable way, "The real story is Joe Kennedy." Kennedy was a minor yet pivotal player in that book and it all came back in a rush. While I had been turning the pages of *Motion Picture World* and other trades at the Museum of Modern Art, I often found myself diverted by the name of Joseph P. Kennedy. At first I told myself to ignore the articles because he was not my focus and nothing makes research take even longer than fascinating tidbits not pertinent to the task at hand. Soon I stopped resisting and started copying. By the time I had completed my research on Frances Marion, I had a substantial file on Kennedy as well.

When I initially contacted the John F. Kennedy Library, which houses Joe Kennedy's papers, in the mid-1990s to inquire how I could see documents, they reacted as if they were guarding Fort Knox and I had asked for a few bricks of gold. By the time I came back five years later, a process was in place for scholars to apply, but recommendations were necessary and both Kennedy's granddaughter Amanda Smith and Arthur Schlesinger, Jr., were kind enough to put in a good word for me. Over the years since then, John Shattuck, Allan Goodrich, Megan Floyd Desnoyers, Sharon Kelly, Jennifer Quan, Maryrose Goodman, and the other staff members have time and again shown they run one of the finest archives in the country with knowledge and professionalism.

The first time I entered their still restricted premises, I was taking Polly's words to heart and was there to write an article for *Vanity Fair* on Kennedy's years as a film mogul. The library's collection is almost overwhelming and while there are a few papers that continue to be withheld, there is a tremendous amount that is now open. I tried to put my historian's blinders on and look only at material I needed, but it was soon obvious there was much more information than could fit into a five-thousand-word article. After spending seven years researching and writing *Without Lying Down,* I vowed not to live like that again, yet the fires were being kindled to take on another book-length project.

Working on Joe Kennedy was the flip side of my effort to excavate Frances Marion. It seems ironic that it took as long to write about a woman hardly anyone had heard of as it did to write about a man almost everyone thinks they know. Kennedy stories had been repeated so often, the challenge became to wipe the slate clean and reconstruct his actions based on his papers, the letters and papers of his associates, the newspapers and trades of the day, and interviews. In spite of the volumes written on the family, no one had written in depth about Joe's time in the film business. It may have been tempting to concentrate on other more familiar areas and the history of the studios is complicated. Yet I found that Kennedy and his time in the business fascinated me and it became my obsession to discover how he managed to become, as Betty Lasky told me early on, "the first and only outsider to fleece Hollywood." It was also clear that so much of what he did throughout his life was with an eye to public perception and that he must have learned his lessons in the apex of celebrity. It was a missing chapter in his legacy.

I read through scores of books with the name Kennedy in the title and then put all but half a dozen aside. Of those, the one I found myself turning to the most was Amanda Smith's groundbreaking book, *Hostage to Fortune: The Letters of Joseph P. Kennedy.* I am afraid because Amanda is a relative, the daughter of Joe's eighth child, Jean, and her husband, Steve Smith, she has not been given her due as the true scholar she is. Her annotated sections are some of the best researched and most fair of any written on Joe Kennedy and her footnotes alone are a treasure trove of information. I hope she continues to write and on a subject outside her own family because she has talent and a passion for history, all too rare traits.

Another important book was Doris Kearns Goodwin's *The Fitzgeralds and the Kennedys.* She was the first to have access to Kennedy's papers as well as to interview Rose Kennedy and other family members at length. She immersed herself in the family and their history and the book is an incredible accomplishment. Others might not notice, but she has single paragraphs that I know took weeks to research.

There have been several biographies of Joe Kennedy and the two best are *Joseph P. Kennedy: A Life and Times* by David Koskoff (whose papers are also at the Kennedy Library) and Richard Whalen's *The Founding Father.*

Initial support and encouragement for this book came unsolicited. Late one Sunday afternoon over ten years ago, I picked up the phone and found myself talking with William Dufty. I knew he had been Swanson's last husband, that they had shared a zeal for healthy diets, and he had written the book *Sugar Blues,* so I was initially intimidated because at that moment I had a mojito in one hand and a cigarette in the other. Bill had read *Without Lying Down* and he was calling to ask me to write Gloria Swanson's biography. Yes, she had written her autobiography and he had helped with it, but he believed there was much more to tell. I was flattered of course, but I was also very aware that such a venture required a deep connection with the subject. While I promised to think about it, too many of Frances Marion's friends had told me of Gloria's haughtiness and self-centeredness to allow me to enjoy spending years of my life with her. However, Bill's call was the beginning of a five-year friendship that lasted until his death in 2002. Our discussions were wide ranging and in the process he provided great information and insights, always with humor and intelligence.

One of the greatest joys of writing a book such as this one is gaining an extended family. Bill's friendship led me to Ray Daum, another great character who not only wrote one of the best books on Greta Garbo, but had become close to Swanson and curated her papers. His intimate knowledge of her life and attitudes was invaluable. Together, Bill and Ray introduced me to Michelle Farmer Amon, Gloria Swanson's only living child. Michelle had not talked to historians before, but she was my hostess in France and spent several days sharing memories of her mother. Michelle is a quiet, almost shy, and very gentle woman and I was surprised by her brutal honesty. Her humor and clarity have turned her into an inspirational survivor. Her tales of her own upbringing, her father, and being on the set of *Sunset Boulevard* don't belong in this volume, but I hope she is willing to tell them in print someday. She also assisted in giving me access to Swanson's papers housed at the Harry Ransome Center at the University of Texas in Austin where Steve Wilson made himself indispensable.

On one of my trips to Boston, I detoured to Dublin, New Hampshire, where Anne Anable is carrying on in the tradition of her grandfather Guy Currier as a "selectman." She welcomed me early one November morning into her home packed with family memorabilia and together we went through boxes she hadn't opened in years. We devoured all the notations in the family Bible, letters over a hundred years old still in their envelopes, photographs, and Currier's personal and professional records. By the time the sun set and we headed out for dinner, we were exhilarated by our finds.

When the British Film Institute was kind enough to invite me to London, I visited Kevin Brownlow, who screened films for me and shared his wisdom as well as the interviews he had conducted with Gloria Swanson, Fay Wray, Lillian Gish, Merian C. Cooper, and Clarence Brown. I am in awe of his generosity, witnessed once again by his willingness to edit this book as only he could. Kevin also introduced me to Phillip Whitehead, who had served in Parliament, had been a documentary filmmaker for several decades, and was writer, director, and producer of *The Kennedys* for Thames and PBS's *American Experience.* Whitehead and his wife, Christine, invited me to their house for dinner and after I watched the unedited version of his Kennedy documentary, he asked me to meet him the next day at his office where he gave me access to the transcripts for all the interviews he had conducted in the late 1980s. This was a gold mine of material from dozens of people who knew and worked with Kennedy, many completed just before their passing.

Catherine Wyler asked me to participate in her fabulous High Falls Film Festival in Rochester, New York, and arranged a screening of *The Trespasser* for me at the George Eastman House, the only archive in America with a preserved copy of the film. The women of the festival staff were wonderful and Patrick Loughney and Anthony L'Abbate of Eastman House gave me a tour of their archive and their photograph collection.

Other archives in Boston such as the Old South Meeting House and the Kennedy home on Beals Street provided some vital details as did the Bronxville public library and the historical societies of Palm Beach and Santa Monica. Gail Stein in the Historical Collections of the Beverly Hills Library was particularly helpful.

Back in Los Angeles, the UCLA archives house a variety of films and the papers of Benjamin Glazer. I spent days at the University of Southern California reading through the microfilmed copies of Will Hays's papers courtesy of Indiana University, and Noelle Carter guided me through USC's Warner Bros. collection. The wonderful Ned Comstock shared production files at USC's Library of Cinema and Television and also introduced me to Peter Sindell, the owner of a collection of Pathé Corporation minutes. Peter willingly made the arrangements for me to read through them at UCLA's William Andrew Clark Library with the help of Bruce Whilman. Sindell's collection, when combined with the Board minutes in the Pathé Collection at the Academy of Motion Picture Arts and Sciences, provided me with a complete corporate history. (It is my hope that the Academy or another archive will acquire Sindell's collection and provide this resource to future researchers.)

For several months, Rebecca Fenning and I spent four days a week at the Margaret Herrick Library of the Academy of Motion Picture Arts and Sciences. With our dueling laptops, we made notes in the microfilm room going through years of *Variety, Motion Picture Herald,* and *Film Daily.* It is easy to get distracted and blurry-eyed by the tiny black print on the screen, but Becky kept me on keel and spotted items I know I would have missed. Linda Mehr, Barbara Hall, Jenny Romero, Jonathon Wahl, Faye Thompson, Andrea Battiste, and all the staff of the library were always friendly, helpful, and resourceful, opening their fabulous collections such as those of the Hays Office, Paramount, Erich von Stroheim, and Pathé.

The Academy honored me with their film history scholarship in 2004. It came at a crucial time, just after I had suffered a major computer crash and I shall always be grateful to Steve Ross, Buffy Shutt, her committee, and their staff, Shawn Guthrie and Greg Beal.

In other parts of the country, Roger Falcon was busy in Boston and New York seeking out arcane newspaper articles. Mairi McCloud in Provo, Utah, researched the Cecil B. De Mille papers, and Liz MacGillicuddy Lucas, the spitting image of her grandmother, the screenwriter Bess Meredyth, volunteered to cull Cape Cod newspapers. Liz's brother John Lucas also helped with photographs. Mary Lea Bandy, Charles Silver, and Larry Kardish at the Museum of Modern Art and Madeline Matz at the Library of Congress were the dependable stalwarts I have counted on for years.

At Paramount, Sherry Lansing, Lynda Obst, Earl Lestz, A. C. Lyles, and Robert Perry all aided in various ways, and Paula Wagner graciously provided details of her office, which had been Kennedy's when it was FBO. Marc Wanamaker, an always amazing source of incredible photographs and historical knowledge, accompanied me on a lengthy walk through of Paramount and the old FBO lot.

Many witnesses, historians, and scholars also assisted me. Each time I contacted someone I hoped would be willing to share their ideas and information I had a moment of questioning why they would talk to me, let alone take the time and energy to help. I was consistently amazed by their generosity and patience: Leonard Balaban and Judy Balaban Quine on their father, Barney Balaban, Tino Balio on United Artists, Bob Birchard on Tom Mix and Cecil B. De Mille, Peter Biskind on Charlie Feldman, Margaret Burk on the Ambassador Hotel, Allan Ellenberger on

First National, Neal Gabler on the moguls, Paul Gierucki on Roscoe Arbuckle, Seymour Hersh on the Kennedy family, Rick Jewell on RKO, Richard Koszarski and Rick Schmidlin on Erich von Stroheim, Sylvia Jukes Morris on Clare Boothe Luce, David Nasaw on William Randolph Hearst, Michael Nesbitt on his grandfather Michael J. Meehan, Thomas O'Connor on Boston history, Dana Polan on film studies, Peter Riva and Maria Riva on Marlene Dietrich, Gus Russo on the mob, Tina Sinatra on her father, Emily Thompson on sound, Mark Vierra on Irving Thalberg, and Marcy Worthington on her mother, Eunice Pringle.

Others who generously shared their memories, time, and knowledge include A. Scott Berg, Deborah Blum, Arlene Dahl, Dominick Dunne, Milt Ebbins, the late Douglas Fairbanks, Jr., John C. Flinn III, Joan Fontaine, Erika Glazer, Abban Gray, Randy Habercamp, William Randolph Hearst III, Arthur Houghton's granddaughter Carol, the late Jean Howard, Jill Jackson, Fay Kanin, Gavin Lambert, Betty Lasky, Christopher Lawford, Nancy Olson Livingston, Mary Anita Loos, Mike Mashon, Victor Navasky, Jack Newfield, Joe Newman, John Quincy, Jr., Carl Reiner, Budd Schulberg, Amanda Smith, Liz Smith, the Thomson family (Carson, Mary, Joan, Barbara, and Richard), and Gore Vidal.

Friends who gave their time, support, and direction at crucial points along the way include Jimmy Bangley, Margery Baragona, Marybell Batjer, Ian Birnie, Kristen Borella, Terry Christensen, Judy Coburn, Jarred Cooper and Marta Aliberti, Virginia Dean, Jennifer Fodor, Michelle Fuetsch, Calla Bacharach Ganz, Phyllis Guss, Judy Hartnett, T. Gene Hatcher, Ellen Hume, Barbara Isenberg, Arnold Johnson, Karen Johnson, Peter Jones, Susan King, Brooke Kroeger, Julie La'Bassiere, Martha Lauzen, Sandra Levinson, Irene Mecchi, Maggie Mosher, Carol Moss, Gabriella Ozurovich, Carol Neil, Marvin Paige, Peggy Rajski, Maggie Renzi, Connie Rosenblum, Carole Sergy, Susy Smith, Terry Smith, Michelle Sullivan, Rita Taggert, Rick Tait, Bridget Terry, Patricia Elliot Tobias, Kalyn Tran, Tara Veneruso, Jamie Wolfe, and Marina Zenovich. And special thanks to those who provided me with an oasis, Rosa Gonzales, Lisa Brisse, and Gigi Sutila. I hope each of you know the special place you have in my heart.

I am so fortunate to have come under Bruce Handy's wing at *Vanity Fair.* He is that rare editor who is a true partner. I am also grateful for the assistance of Walter Donohue and Peter Morgan in reviewing many of these chapters, with special thanks to Peter for finding the title. My beloved Martha Lorah, who served Frances Marion as her secretary and companion for many years, read the entire manuscript while giving me her love and unconditional support.

Gail Slamon volunteered for active duty and, as she has for over several decades, exhibited tolerance and patience when I imposed upon her. And when I couldn't see the forest for the trees, two of the busiest women I know, Carrie Rickey and Mona Onstead, made time to help me clear the way and I am forever in their debt.

Charlotte Sheedy has extended a steady hand at every turn and I have come to depend upon her as both an unerring agent and a kind and caring friend. Victoria Wilson at Knopf saw the possibilities of the story from the start and her knowledge and appreciation of Hollywood have been invaluable. I am also indebted to her assistant, Carmen Johnson, a most patient and professional champion juggler.

And of course my thanks to my immediate family, Nancy, Catherine, Blake, Tom, Teo, and Jake, who know how much I love them and depend upon them. I know it hasn't always been easy for them, but I so deeply appreciate and value their respect for the joy I find in my alternative world.

# NOTES

ABBREVIATIONS USED IN NOTES

*(See also Magazines, Trade Publications, and Newspapers on pp. 480–482)*

AMPAS: Academy of Motion Picture Arts and Sciences
AS: Amanda Smith, *Hostage to Fortune: The Letters of Joseph P. Kennedy*
CBL: Clare Booth Luce
DDC: Delaware Department of Corporations
DKG: Doris Kearns Goodwin, *The Fitzgeralds and the Kennedys*
DMC: Cecil B. De Mille Collection
FDR: Franklin Delano Roosevelt
GSA: Gloria Swanson Archives
GWC: Guy W. Currier
JFKL: John F. Kennedy Library
JPKP: Joseph P. Kennedy Papers at the JFKL
JPK: Joseph P. Kennedy
MOMA: Museum of Modern Art
REFK: Rose Kennedy
WRH: William Randolph Heartst
Note: Interviews are indicated by the name of the interviewee, a slash, and the name of the interviewer (e.g., Fontaine/CB is a Cari Beauchamp interview of Joan Fontaine).

PREFACE

xv   "wickedly handsome," Thomas and Witts, p. 55; "the most," DKG, p. 124; "seduction," Looker draft, 5/37, JPKP; "his warm," Marion Off, p. 90; "not just," Fontaine/CB.

xv   "the most" and "personality who," *NYHT*, 9/16/28; "blonde Moses," *FD*, 6/17/28; "the coming," Oakland Tribune 6/17/28; "small" and "Kennedy," *Fortune*, 9/37; "He already," Arthur Krock oral history, JFKL; "richest," *Independent*, 10/11/92, *BG*, 9/25/32.

CHAPTER I: "AMERICA'S YOUNGEST BANK PRESIDENT"

3   "coffin ships" and "married well," Allan Goodrich/CB; 1860 census and other primary documents at JPKL; Whalen, pp. 14–18; DKG, pp. 226–27; half of Boston Irish, Koskoff, p. 3.

4   Pat, Allan Goodrich/CB. Although P.J. was in the legislature, he listed his occupation as "liquor dealer" on his son's birth certificate, JPKP.

4   Columbia Trust corporation documents, JPKP; "running," Whalen p. 15. In addition to his duties as a representative, P.J. also served on the Boston Elec-

tion Commission, Wire Commission, and Fire Commission, Looker draft, 5/37.

4  "the sweetest," Looker draft, 5/37; "worshipped," Allan Goodrich/CB; "all," DKG, p. 229; "Joe decided," DKG, pp. 227–28, 269.

5  various jobs, *BH,* 1/8/38; E. M. Kennedy, p. 3; Whalen, p. 21; *American Mercury,* 5/28.

6  Boston Latin, *NYT,* 4/28/35; ferry and batting average, *Fortune,* 9/37; "will make," 1908 Class Prophecy, JPKP.

7  "adequate," E. M. Kennedy, p. 5; tour bus, *PP,* 9/27; "a choice," Collier and Horowitz, p. 36; DKG, p. 233.

7  "wanted" and "here," E. M. Kennedy, p. 14.

7  "Democrats," E. M. Kennedy, 18; "he looked," DKG/Whitehead; "We tire," John Quincy/CB; "these," Milton Katz/Whitehead.

8  "Joe Kennedy saw," Whalen, p. 34; "You can," Harvey Klemmer/Whitehead.

8  "If he," Whalen, p. 27.

8  "very," DKG/Whitehead; house and habits, E. M. Kennedy, pp. 3, 10–11, 18; Collier and Horowitz, p. 25; Allan Goodrich/CB; unidentified clips circa 5/23, JPKP.

9  "sociable Irish," DKG, 123; Fitzgerald, DKG, pp. 66, 70, 107–10; Fitzgerald's parents died within a few years of each other, Rose Kennedy, p. 8.

10  "intelligent," Cameron, p. 54; "kept himself," Whalen, p. 20.

10  names linked, Boston Latin Class Prophecy of 1908, JPKP; "two dinners," quoted from papers of the day by Cameron, p. 49.

10  Cameron, pp. 57–59; Collier and Horowitz, pp. 29–30; Rose said they were taught the "arts of housewifery," and while there was discussion of her and Agnes staying on, they returned after one year at the convent. REFK, p. 32.

10  DKG, p. 198; Cameron, p. 65.

11  "the only," Klemmer/Whitehead. "Sooner," *AM,* 5/28; "If you," Cutler, p. 248; 60 percent, Rudnick, p. 60. The "Bread and Roses" strike began when textile mill owners increased the speed of factory looms, and then lowered wages for thousands of women and child workers. The Massachusetts National Guard and private and city police countered 23,000 strikers for two months, resulting in numerous deaths and mass arrests. When police and militia assaulted a group of women and children, the public outcry forced the mill owners to capitulate.

11  Neither the customers nor the board members of Columbia Trust were exclusively Irish Catholic; Protestants, Jews, and Italians were all represented in the working-class neighborhood of East Boston. *BH,* 1/21/14, says $100,000; *Newsweek,* 9/12/60, says $200,000. Brahmins are considered to be the highest Indian caste, the purest of the pure destined to teach mankind and, since at least the mid-1850s, the term was used to refer to the monied, WASP leaders of Boston.

11  Wellington background, DKG, p. 237; on seeing the mayor, DKG, p. 240. Kennedy would later tell a reporter that "Mr. Fitzgerald may think and hope he secured this position, but it was really secured by Alfred P. Wellington," JPK to Davenport, 5/24/37, JPKP.

12  "we make," *AM,* 5/28; "there was," Whalen, pp. 35–36.

12  "born," DKG, p. 124; "leader," DKG, p. 203; "dapper," Cameron, p. 30.

13  DKG, pp. 248–49; Hamilton, pp. 20–21; "well known," *BH,* 12/29/13.

14  *BH,* 1/21/14; DKG, p. 253. At the same board of directors meeting, Alfred Wellington was elected both VP and treasurer. J. E. O'Connell and Lewis K. Southard were chosen directors.

13 "Things don't," AS, p. 12; photo captions, Underwood & Underwood, Corbis; smallest bank, "The youngest," Ramsaye, *PP*, 9/27, and AS, p. xxi; never paying relatives back, Leamer, p. 55, quoting Joe's niece Mary Lou McCarthy.

14 "hostess," DKG, p. 198; coming out party, Cameron, p. 66; *BH*, 10/8/14; AS, p. 14.

15 Rose's wedding log, reprinted in AS, pp. 14–15; the Braves had gone from last place in mid-July to sweep the Athletics in four games to win the 1914 World Series.

15 "overwhelmingly," DKG, p. 260; "common" and "a gay," Rose Kennedy's own writing reprinted in AS, p. 14; "His voice," E. M. Kennedy, p. 22; Hoover, Chernow, p. 314; weekends, E. M. Kennedy, pp. 15, 17. Real estate, agreement between JPK and Hub Real Estate, 7/23/15, JPKP; Old Colony Real Estate, Whalen, pp. 36–37; JPK initially invested $1,000 in Old Colony Real Estate and it had grown to over $25,000 when the company dissolved during the war, Whalen, p. 37.

16 economy, Leuchtenburg, p. 17; "the truth is," DKG, p. 283.

16 "resulted in," AS, p. 4; Nigel Hamilton/Whitehead. Wilson signed the Selective Service Act requiring America's 10 million men between eighteen and thirty to register for the draft on May 18, 1917. Daniel, p. 218. John Kennedy was born on May 29, 1917.

17 JPK to District Draft Board No. 5, 2/18/18, AS, pp. 15–18; Currier family Bible, family papers, courtesy of Anne Anable; *BH*, 6/23/30; *Stage and Screen*, 1920; Guy Currier was born and raised in Lawrence and the family money came from generations of trading and supplying the growing state. Guy's head was turned by a beautiful blond actress, Marie Buress, whom he soon discovered was a debutante and chaperoned everywhere she went. Undeterred, he married Marie in 1894 and she continued to act occasionally while becoming an important supporter of Boston theater and cultural events. Guy served as a trustee of the Boston Library and various other community institutions. Anne Anable/CB.

18 "an excellent brain," Anne Anable/CB; *BH*, 6/23/30; DKG, pp. 274–75; "one of the," *BP*, 5/29/17.

18 AS, pp. 15–16; Allan Goodrich/CB. Shipbuilding increased tenfold between 1916 and 1918. Shortly after Kennedy arrived, a week-long strike by three thousand Fore River machinists was brought to an end by "an appeal to their patriotism by Assistant Secretary of the Navy Franklin D. Roosevelt," *NYT*, 11/6/17. Seymour Hersh says that Fitzgerald tried to join his son-in-law in profiting off a "large federal housing project" adjacent to the shipyards, Hersh, p. 46.

19 "worried," JPK to J. Larkin, 9/16/18, JPKP; "this amateur," Powell to JPK, 5/14/18, JPKP.

19 Powell to Draft Board, 2/17/18, 3/27/18, JPKP; "in Class 1," AS, p. 5.

19 "from nervous," AS, p. 6.

19 "resembled," DKG, p. 274. One of the stories that Kennedy told was that he had met and hustled a job offer from Stone by finagling a seat next to him on a train, but the two men had known each other for several years.

20 "his sense," *Fortune*, 9/37.

CHAPTER 2: "THIS IS ANOTHER TELEPHONE"

21 Fred Stone had literally run away to join the circus as a child in Colorado, *V*, 3/11/59; meeting Houghton in 1917, E. M. Kennedy, p. 105; contract,

signed May 2, 1919, JPKP; AS, pp. 15, 30, 31; letters to and from Herman Robbins of Fox and JPK, 10/8/19, 10/10/19, JPKP; "Joe Kennedy knew," Swanson/Brownlow.

22 Summerhouse lease, 2/20/19, JPKP. Born in Kansas, Bill Gray left his Denver home when he was twelve. He left a wife and daughter in New York when he moved to Maine. *V,* 12/14/27, 12/21/27, *MPN,* 12/23/27.

22 "What's this" and other quotes, Conway to JFK, 8/12/54, JPKP; Gross and value, Lyne to JPK, 3/3/20, JPKP.

23 "Look at," Whalen, p. 75.

23 "chasers," Besas, p. 77; Zukor, pp. 61–62, 69–71; "History," Ramsaye, p. 607; de Mille, p. 232. Box office estimates for *The Birth of a Nation* run as high as 15 million dollars (Ramsaye, p. 644) and was "by far the greatest financial success of the silent era," Koszarski, *Entertainment,* p. 320. While theater owners throughout the country made a fortune on the film, Griffith was shortchanged. One exhibitor said to have underreported his take to the point he accumulated enough money to enter film production himself was one Louis B. Mayer, the New England distributor for *The Birth of Nation.*

24 Beauchamp, *WLD,* p. 83; "The movies," Brownlow, *Hollywood,* p. 81.

25 Lewis Jacobs, pp. 160–61; one hundred companies, Los Angeles Directory.

25 cash business, Balio, pp. 35–36; flu epidemic, *FD,* 5/24/28.

25 AS, p. 13.

25 Rogers and Houdini, *MPW,* 9/6/19; Creamer, p. 207; Ruth to Taylor, 9/4/19; Lyne to JPK, 10/1/19; undated memo on Hayden, Stone paper signed by JPK and Ruth; Robbins to JPK, 10/8/19; Ruth to JPK, 10/31/19; all JPKP. *NYT,* 2/23/04; At the time, Ruth's pitching was more impressive than his hitting. Frazee's agreement to sell Ruth's contract was signed on December 26, 1919, and announced on January 5, 1920. As a Yankee, Ruth went on to star in two films, *Heading Home,* a five-reeler produced by Kessel and Bauman in late 1920, and *Babe Comes Home,* a feature-length film made in 1927 by First National. He also had a cameo in Harold Lloyd's *Speedy.*

26 "altogether," JPK to Treman, 1/2/20, and JPK to Selisberg, 1/16/20; "tangle," McNally to JPK, 1/20/20; history and purpose of NE exchange, 10/8/19; "disposition" and price, R. H. Cochrane to Daniel Lyne, 12/17/19, all JPKP.

27 Columbia Trust involvement, multiple letters in JPKP, 1919–20; "It's the," E. M. Kennedy, p. 37; various examples including multiple notes to Missy LeHand, Roosevelt Papers, Hyde Park, and letters to Vera Murray, JPKP.

27 Moore correspondence files, JPKP; Peters to Moore, 5/5/20, JPKP. In spite of Moore's presence, Kennedy's restaurant contract was canceled in 1920, AS, p. 6.

28 "count on," undated handwritten letter from JPK to Houghton on Columbia Trust paper; "I hope," JPK to Houghton, 9/19/20; Barrymore, etc., AJH to JPK, 7/9/43, all in JPKP.

29 summer home leases, JPKP; "Even," DKG, p. 303; music and novels, REFK at Beals Street house.

29 "diamonds," and "promiscuity," Higham, pp. 77–78.

29 "simply couldn't," Hamilton/Whitehead.

30 "a mini," DKG/Whitehead; "Go back," DKG, p. 307.

30 "You have" and "my enterprise," DKG, p. 313.

30 "Rosie," DKG/Whitehead.

31 Hayden, Stone memo, 6/28/20, JPKP; Peters's letters re Jack, 2/25/20, JPKP;

letter re dinner, Peters to JPK, 4/7/20, JPKP; JPK to Houghton, 11/25/21, JPKP; dinner rituals, DKG/Whitehead; "made me feel," DKG, p. 313.

31 Hamilton, p. 814; DKG, p. 313, Whalen, p. 57. The Abbotsford house was bought for $16,000 in the name of Columbia Trust with a loan signed by P. J. Kennedy and Alfred Wellington. JPKP; Moores at Beals Street. While Mayor Peters and other luminaries endorsed Kennedy's appointment, it appears that Secretary David Houston already had someone else in mind to replace Assistant Secretary R. C. Leffingwell, who had resigned, Houston to Peters, 4/26/20, JPKP.

32 accounts at Columbia Trust, E. M. Kennedy, p. 47.

CHAPTER 3: "I HAVE JUST REORGANIZED THE COMPANY"

33 "There is," AS/CB.

33 AS, p. 8; memos and letters, JPKP; "better," MPW, 9/6/19.

33 "that would," and "entirely," JPK to Hayden, 12/4/19, JPKP.

34 stock delivery to JPK, Hall to JPK, 12/17/19, JPKP; "special features," MPW, 9/6/19; JPK to Hayden, 12/4/19, JPKP; "very much" and details of financing arm, Hall to JPK, 12/19/19, JPKP; Willard-Dempsey, contract between Hallmark and JPK, 5/1920, JPKP. The May contract calls for $30,000 from JPK but other money had clearly changed hands before then. AS, p. 9. Kennedy continued to be in and out of New York and was walking up Wall Street on September 16, 1920, when he was "hurled to the ground" by the bomb blast that killed thirty-eight people and injured three hundred, Chernow, p. 212.

34 Court records, Los Angeles Superior Court; "ignorance," JPK to Cole, 9/24/20; DeWitt to JPK, 8/16/20, JPKP.

35 Hall to JPK re Cole, 12/19/19, JPKP; fifty-two films a year, MPW, 9/13/19; studio report, 6/29/21. Cole had begun his career at Graham's & Co., AS, p. 25. R-C's major American backer, the New York brokers Wagman and Company, was going bankrupt and their English financiers, Cox and Company, was teetering on the brink.

35 JPK to Cole, 11/19/20; Cole to JPK, 11/24/20; "My experience," JPK to Cole, 8/30/20; "unplayed business," Cole to JPK, 12/2/20, all JPKP; King, p. 37.

36 "My dear," AS, pp. 26–27. Ethel Turner was a dedicated and loyal employee who would stay with Columbia Trust for over thirty years but fortunately for historians, she did not follow the last sentence of his instructions.

36 Conway to JFK, 8/12/54, JPKP; JPK to Turner, 1/21/21, JPKP.

37 JPK to Schnitzer, 8/15/22; JPK to Gray, 1/18/21; JPK to Gray, 1/20/21, all JPKP; hiring Ford, DKG, p. 345, V, 12/21/27; "drop in," JPK to Fitzgerald, 1/21/21, JPKP; Lyne to Kennedy, 2/7/21, JPKP.

37 "Every wish," Cole to JPK, 2/21/21; "magnificent," Gray to JPK, 2/21/21; JPK to Houghton, 4/25/21; JPK to DeWitt, 9/27/21, all JPKP.

38 Cole to JPK, 12/27/20, JPKP. Cole wanted Kennedy to find men willing to put in a total of $500,000 a month until $3 million was raised and for this the investors would own up to 40 percent of the common stock.

38 JPK to Cole, 3/9/21; "not nearly," JPK to Cole, 12/28/20; "very good," JPK to O'Leary, 7/16/35, all JPKP. In 1935, Cole was a car salesman in Chicago and wrote to Kennedy for help finding a job. JPK wrote to Ted O'Leary recommending him for the Chicago office of their Somerset Liquors, but nothing seems to have come of it.

38 Graham's and Cox, AS, p. 25; JPK to Crum at Plaza in NY, 3/29/21; JPK to

Crum, 4/5/21; JPK to Stone, 4/6/21, JPKP. Films were often financed by individuals who wanted a percentage of the gross, and short-term loans were charged up to 18 percent, Lasky, p. 15; Crum to JPK, 4/14/21; Goodwin, p. 342; excessive rates causing failures, *The Story of Films*, p. 86; JPKP Crum to JPK, 4/14/21; sixty days, JPK to Stone, 4/6/21; JPK to Crum 4/9/21; "in excellent," JPK to Thayer, 3/28/21, "desire to," JPK to Crum, 3/29/21; JPKP. Crum to JPK, 7/22/21; complaints, JPK to Crum 6/24/21; Cole to Crum, 4/30/21; JPK to Thayer, 3/28/21, JPKP.

Whether they knew it or not, the R-C Studio in Hollywood was nurturing some interesting talent. The actors Milton Sills and Seena Owen were there, as was the director Henry King. Lewis Milestone was a film "patcher" before rising to editor and director.

39 Hodkinson was born in Independence, Kansas, on 8/16/81 and died in Los Angeles, 6/2/71. He resigned from Paramount shortly after Lasky and Zukor bought 50 percent of the company stock in May of 1916. The following month, Zukor and Lasky created Famous Players-Lasky Corporation, but kept the name Paramount for distribution and later for production. Hodkinson left the film business in 1927 and went on to become pioneer in aviation, opening an airplane manufacturing company in Glendale to build his own design for a six-passenger, tri-motor airplane called, of course, The Hodkinson. Hodkinson oral history, AMPAS; Slide, pp. 256, 334.

40 "foresight," Hodkinson oral history, AMPAS; "practically," Hodkinson to JPK, 7/22/21, JPKP; Slide, p. 397. "Not much" and "it would give," JPK to Cole, 7/25/21; "strikes me," JPK to Crum, 7/23/21, Hodkinson to JPK, 8/16/21; JPK to Hodkinson, 8/17/21, 8/24/21.

40 Bankruptcy discussed in undated and unsigned diary in 1921 papers, JPKP. "we should," JPK to Crum, 10/21/21; RC to Thomson, 8/26/21; JPK to Cole re Tom Moore, 11/18/21; Report on stories, 6/29/21; Minutes of the Board, all JPKP.

41 "all these" and "I have just" and get hold of," JPK to Godsol, 6/27/21, JPKP. JPK to MacFarland, 6/18/21, JPKP; JPK to Cosmopolitan, 7/11/21 and 7/12/21, JPKP; "He recognized," David Nasaw/CB.

CHAPTER 4: "FIGHT LIKE HELL TO WIN"

43 RCNE balance sheet, 9/3/21, JPKP; selling RCNE, Lyne to JPK, 10/26/21; "unceasingly" and "was worth," JPK to Thomson, 11/18/21; Crum to JPK, 12/12/21, all JPKP.

43 JPK to Crum, 12/23/21, JPKP.

43 JPK to Gray, 4/24/22, JPKP; Murray to JPK, 8/21/22, JPKP.

44 Rolls and chauffeur, Cutler, p. 249; donations file and club file. JPKP. "The oldest," Coolidge to JPK, 10/11/20; "Irish Catholics," JPK to Coolidge, 11/26/20, JPKP.

44 Whalen, p. 58; "his cut," Bancroft to Dean, 6/8/22, Dean to Luce, 6/2/22; "application," Bancroft to Dean, 8/14/22, all JPKP.

45 Speculation, e.g., Whalen, p. 59; "an Irish," Chernow, p. 439; "fight," AS, p. 272.

45 "the House," Hersh, p. 37; Fitzgerald campaigns, Whalen, p. 57; JPK to Toma, 11/1922, JPKP. A comic included the line "I'm singing Sweet Adeline here, but John Fitzgerald will sing it at the State House" and "it receives a round of applause at every performance," Henry Taylor to JPK, 10/12/22, JPKP; Fitzgerald and grandsons, Dallek, p. 27.

45 The National Board of Review had been created in 1909 to put the stamp of approval on films, and censorship was more or less a constant issue for discussion in the trades, Leuchtenburg, p. 78.

46 "more than," Allen, vol. 1, p. 129.

46 There had been scandals before, such as the "champagne orgies and cocaine" alleged in the death of Olive Thomas, but she was associated with the *Ziegfeld Follies* more than the movies and, since she died in Paris, distance defused the scandal. *NYT,* 9/11/20; "The idea," Brownlow, *Hollywood,* p. 110.

46 "deepening," Thackrey, p. 17; Leuchtenburg, p. 169; Hays, p. 294. While other producers desperately tried to quiet the rumors, William Randolph Hearst, who made more money from his newspapers and magazines than from his films, further provoked the situation with accusatory headlines and editorials.

46 Douglas Gomery, introduction to the Will Hays Papers; Page Smith, p. 626. William Henry Harrison was a Whig, which would later emerge as the Republican Party, and his grandson was the Republican president Benjamin Harrison.

47 Hays, pp. 323–30; *NYT,* 1/17/22; "Acquittal is not enough," *NYT* 4/13/22; Brownlow, *Hollywood,* p. 110. Paul Gierucki/CB. Arbuckle was acquitted on April 12, 1922, and the ban was announced on April 18. Rumors still fly about the trial and one must wonder how such a verdict could be reached and a statement written so quickly unless it had been prepared for or by the jurors in advance.

47 "A Real Leader," *PP,* 5/22; "the unsavory," Hays, p. 324; *V,* 2/10/22.

48 Hays decision and current law, Hays, p. 331; "salacious," Cole to JPK, 9/29/21, JPKP.

48 Hays, pp. 324–33; "prominent," Hays, p. 455; "the people's," Hays, p. 333. Hays not only served on the board of Sinclair Oil, but had been Sinclair's attorney and was a bag man for collecting more than $1 million from Sinclair for the Republican National Committee. Hays was called before the congressional committees investigating the oil swindles, but managed not to taint his own reputation. McCartney, pp. 185, 223–27, 276.

49 Stone resigned January 1, 1923, DKG, p. 329; "never," JPK to Davenport, 5/24/37, JPKP.

49 Specific agreements, names withheld, JPKP.

50 Multiple letters and cables, JPKP; "auxiliary memory," Swanson, p. 344; "infinite," DKG, p. 434, quoting Raymond Moley; "served," *SEP,* 1/18/36.

50 "the intangible," E. M. Kennedy, p. 31.

51 "Accustomed," Marion, "Hollywood," p. 133.

51 "clean" and "kneel," Marion, "Hollywood," p. 134; other financing, Marion, *Off,* p. 107; "Joe, please," Marion, *Off,* pp. 90–91.

52 Beauchamp, *WLD,* 87–88, 120–21, 128–31.

52 "This will" and "I was," Marion, *Off,* pp. 90–91.

CHAPTER 5: "WE HAVE VALUED YOUR ADVICE AND ASSISTANCE"

54 "whole," *Fortune,* 9/37; friends, *FD,* 5/4/27; housing arrangements, Mansion House to JPK, 12/2/22, JPKP; REFK diary, quoted in AS, p. 36.

54 Various cables, Dunphy file, JPKP; Spencer, pp. 21–25. The Breakers opened the same year as the Oasis. While WASPs predominated, Catholics such as Edward Bradley, owner of the largest gambling club in Palm Beach, was accepted in part because he owned so much property in town. He also donated the majority of the funds to build St. Edward's Catholic Church.

55 "Hopper" "at a," and "I gave up," Mary Moore to Gloria Swanson, 1/14/30, GSA.

55 "You're a great," Rose Kennedy, p. 93; photo files, JPKP; JPK to REFK, 4/8/23, 4/16/23, 4/23/23, 5/9/23, JPKP; AS, pp. 37–38. The strains of learning these lessons would take their toll. Jackie Kennedy, seeking to explain her husband to journalist Teddy White, told him that Jack's mother hadn't hugged him, even as a small child. "This lonely sick boy and his mother didn't love him." Rose tried in her own way, but she was withdrawing more and more into herself, her church, and her travels; White's handwritten notes, JPKP. When both Joe Junior and Jack started school at the public elementary a few blocks from their home, it was usually a maid who picked them up from school. Honey Fitz was the family member most often bearing witness at their ball games or school activities. Searls, pp. 39, 41, 45.

56 "never," BG, 5/23/23. Rose lost her sister Eunice that September to tuberculosis, which she was reported to have contracted doing war work on the Boston Common, AS, p. 39.

57 Lahey to JPK, 6/5/23; JPK to Dr. Lahey, 6/11/23, 6/14/23; JPK to Turner, 7/25/23; JPK to PJK, 7/22/24; all JPKP. Neither of Joe's sisters had married yet so P.J. lived with them in Winthrop.

57 "amicable," Cole to JPK, 7/28/22, JPKP.

57 "I am," Cole to JPK, 5/1/22; "the treatment," memo to directors from Cole, 5/1/22; RC board minutes, 2/17/22, all JPKP. Cole went back into the automobile business, becoming a Stephens Motor Car distributor.

57 V, 8/4/48; Gabler, p. 64; Slide, p. 365. Pat Powers had briefly been a policeman in Buffalo and in between his departure from Universal and joining up with R-C, he had formed the Powers-Cameron Company, Slide, p. 268.

58 "one of the most," Ramsaye, p. 497; Harry Berman also invested along with Powers and Schnitzer. Schnitzer: FD, 5/24/28, 12/5/28; MPH, 7/29/44; MPW, 9/6/19. In 1920, Schnitzer became president of Equity Pictures and left that perch to join R-C.

59 JPK to Williams, 7/24/22, 7/25/22; board meeting of 11/28/22; exploitation and income, JPK to Schnitzer, 8/15/22; JPK to Schnitzer, 7/13/22; "I am all through," JPK to Schnitzer 11/9/22, all JPKP.

59 "knowing no one," Crum to JPK, 2/8/22; "hands" and "absolutely," Thomson to JPK, 4/29/23; settlement, JPK to Thomson, 7/13/22; "at a substantial profit," Conway to JFK, 8/12/54; "we have" and "regrettably," Crum to JPK, 7/10/23, all JPKP.

59 Columbia Films board minutes, 11/20/23; "without," MPFC incorporation papers, 11/26/23, JPKP; DeWitt and clauses, contract between Renco and JPK, 11/22/23; letter to DeWitt, 5/14/25, all JPKP.

60 Board members, waiver motion, 2/3/24; office, Fitzgibbon to JPK, 8/3/23; sales, Slattery to JPK, 8/7/23; Chicago, etc., Fitzgibbon to JPK, 3/13/24, and Slattery to JPK, 3/4/24, all JPKP. Columbia Advertising Company corporation papers were filed in Massachusetts 11/15/23 although they began operating the previous August, JPKP; "Kennedy was," Amanda Smith/CB.

60 AS, p. 20; FD, 5/24/28; EHMPW, 5/19/28; V, 7/23/30; Pathé release, 6/16/30; JPK to Fitzgibbon, 8/18/24. JPK trusted Scollard to the point that when the land between Columbia Trust and property owned by the East Boston Bank became available, Joe arranged for a loan for Scollard to purchase the property in his name. Property deeds signed on January 22, 1925; Scollard borrows $20,000 from Columbia Trust on 1/22/25, JPKP; CA board

meeting ballots, 1925, 1926, board minutes, 2/7/27, Columbia Advertising files, JPKP.

61 *BH,* 6/23/30.

61 "completely," Leuchtenburg, p. 103; JPK memo to Brush, 12/14/23, JPK to Brush, 12/14/23, JPKP.

61 "bankers," Leuchtenburg, p. 113; "by all accounts," Hersh, p. 45.

61 AS, pp. 10, 41; "carried," Chernow, p. 307. Howey would spend most of his career in Chicago where he worked with Charles MacArthur and Ben Hecht, who would use Howey as their inspiration for Walter Burns in their play *The Front Page.* Howey was also the uncle of the actress Colleen Moore.

62 "Kennedy saves," Looker draft, 5/37, JPKP.

62 *BP,* 2/8/26; Boston College, JPK to Wellington, 6/30/21, JPKP; loan lists 1924, JPKP; notes on forms for annual meeting of Columbia Trust, 1/20/25, JPKP; JPK to PJK, 1/16/22, JPK to Turner, 5/29/24; "the collateral," JPK to PJK, 1/21/21; "make all" and "yours for," JPK to Thayer, 2/14/21, all JPKP.

63 "It is all," Russo, pp. 359–60.

63 E. M. Kennedy, p. 23; DKG, p. 442; Rose's youngest brother, Fred, would later die as a result of acute alcoholism at the age of thirty-one, DKG, p. 496. John Murray threw in the towel and left the beer business to open a Boston candy and ice cream parlor.

63 Year and ruling, Behr, pp. 70, 46, 80–81; moving to basement, DKG, p. 443; "to," Adams, *March,* p. 260. The final passage of the Eighteenth Amendment was spurred in part by the anti-immigrant and anti-German sentiment fanned by the war years and by the fact that a large number of America's brewers were of German ancestry.

64 "served," Repetto, p. 109; Beauchamp, *WLD,* p. 167; Beauchamp, *Adventures,* p. 56; Joe Newman/CB; Daniel, pp. 262, 267.

64 New York's, Repetto, p. 105.

64 "his hand," Vidal/CB.

64 "bought," Russo, p. 360, Katz, pp. 64, 67; of the many men who claimed close ties, the one acknowledged to have been an actual friend of Kennedy's was Frank Costello. As one of his biographers points out, Costello was different from other mobsters in that "there was nothing menacing about Costello. He was soft spoken, quiet and friendly. Respectable businessmen didn't feel threatened in his company." That didn't mean he was any less dangerous, for his mentor was the dapper Arnold Rothstein, who "had shown him how to make money out of business, instead of bullets," most famously by having a hand in fixing the World Series of 1919 in the Black Sox baseball scandal before he was gunned down in a New York hotel in 1928, Wolf, p. 51. Kennedy may have also met Rothstein, as one of the gangster's best friends was the journalist Herbert Bayard Swope, a fellow Harvard alum whom Kennedy saw in New York and Palm Beach, *VF,* 5/2005.

64 PJK's papers, DKG, p. 410; JPK to Robert Potter, 8/17/20, JPKP. Potter was a fellow Harvard grad and Joe wrote him "I finally got some figures today from my father's head man" and he owes $212. Amanda Smith says that sherry and port had been ordered and set aside before Prohibition went into effect; JPK to Albert Garceau, 5/8/21, long list of wines he received, bill is $163.45, JPKP; one page listed as "Accounts Receivable/Whiskey" dated 1/11/22 in closed files; example re Buffalo: JPK to PJK, 1/21/25, "went to Buffalo last week and will settle that matter," all JPKP. Canadian government tax records from that time repeatedly list the name "Joe Kennedy" as a

buyer from Hiram Walker, but the name was the equivalent of John Smith and there were many people going by that name, Russo, p. 360.

65 "hundreds," Hersh, p. 47; "it is harder," DKG, 442–43; "I've never," Hamilton/Whitehead.

CHAPTER 6: "I'M BEGINNING TO THINK I'M A PICTURE MAN"

66 Jewell, p. 8; AS, p. 25.

66 JPK personal worth, DKG, p. 339. Frederick Prince was a unique character of his era, known as "an outspoken capitalist" and speculator who opposed government intervention in business, yet supported expanded government social programs, NYT, 2/3/53; FBO stockholders list, 8/17/28, JPKP.

67 Prince of Wales, PP, 9/27. From his papers and letters to Rose during the trip, he says "we" but never identifies the people he is traveling with, JPKP; suits in London, JPK to Rose, 8/23/25, JPKP; Paris bills, Kennedy correspondence 1925, JPKP; "extensive palaver," AS, p. 10; Schnitzer to JPK, 2/16/26, JPKP.

67 Whalen, p. 71; Lasky, p. 13; DKG, p. 342. "plenty," JPK to Pat Powers, 2/5/26, JPKP; Thomson, MPW, 2/20/26; Gray to JPK, 2/4/26, JPKP; Inverforth, EH, 2/20/26; notes and cash, V, 2/10/26; $200,000 down and $9 million in losses, V, 10/20/26; JPK to Inverforth, 2/5/26, JPKP; the actual agreement was between "Joseph P. Kennedy, Reserved Assets Company and Graham's Trading Company Limited," Scollard to DeWitt, 2/16/32, JPKP. The remainder of the asking price was to be paid over the next three years. Kennedy was actually purchasing four companies: R-C Pictures Corporation, Film Booking Offices of America, Inc., Film Booking Offices of Canada, Ltd., and FBO Studios, Inc.

68 "Boston Financier," MPW, 2/20/26; "Boston Banker," NYT, 2/8/26; EH, 2/20/26; V, 2/10/26.

68 Surprise, Schnitzer to JPK, 2/26, JPKP; B pictures, FD, 1/10/27; "A banker" and "home and," PP, 9/27.

69 "proved," EHMPW, 5/19/28; "lofty," PP, 9/27.

69 "under resident control," NYT, 2/8/26 V, 4/28/26; "actively interested" and "since the day," BP, 2/8/26.

69 "You'll have," PP, 9/27.

69 "I hope," JPK to Gray, 2/5/26, JPKP.

70 "General," multiple letters, JPKP; "a real honest," JPK to Hays, 2/11/26, Hays Papers; "it is going," Hays to JPK, 2/9/26, Hays Papers. To join the MPPDA meant the studio agreed to follow Hays's "voluntary" restrictions on what could appear on the screen and they paid a fractional percentage of profits as a membership fee. It was the equivalent of full membership in the filmmaking community.

70 "one of the," and "much," EH, 2/6/26; projection room, V, 1/20/26.

70 Derr, Pathé biography, circa 1930, Pathé collection, AMPAS; "could work out," Swanson, p. 344.

71 V, 7/23/30; "never," Swanson, p. 344.

71 AS, p. 20; FD, 5/24/28; EHMPW, 5/19/28; V, 7/23/30; "they looked," Swanson, p. 341; "take the," Derr to Scollard, Pathé collection, AMPAS.

72 contract, V, 3/24/26; "greatest confidence" and "I'm beginning," JPK to Schnitzer, 2/11/26, JPKP.

72 Cole to JPK, 2/9/26, JPKP; "be glad" JPK to Powers, 2/5/26, JPKP. V, 5/14/26. Powers was by then in independent production in Los Angeles.

73 CCC files, JPKP; CCC incorporation papers, Delaware; BG, 6/22/30.

73 Accounting sheets, JPKP; "All you," Schulberg/CB.

74 Cole to JPK, 2/9/26, JPKP; *EH,* 3/13/26.

74 400 features, *PP,* July 1926; 90 percent, *The Story of the Films,* p. 40.

CHAPTER 7: "I NEVER NEEDED A VACATION LESS"

75 Before the Ambassador opened in 1921, visitors' choices were limited to the likes of the Hollywood Hotel, which Charlie Chaplin called "a fifth rate, rambling, barnlike establishment." Chaplin, p. 202. The Beverly Hills Hotel was considered too far west on Sunset for anything but a vacation and the Ambassador was only a few miles south of the FBO studios, Burk, p. 24; Starr, *Material Dreams,* p. 97; Margaret Burk/CB and tour of the Ambassador. The Ambassador Hotel is also where Robert Kennedy was killed in June of 1968. It has since been demolished.

76 Parrish, p. 33; *Film Daily Year Book,* 1926, p. 701; *PP,* 2/26, 3/26, 6/26, 7/26; "find of the year," *V,* 2/24/26. According to Cecilla De Mille, Cecil B. capitalized the D in their family last name and there was always a space between the De and the Mille. Cecil's older brother William continued to use the small "d" in de Mille, Brownlow/CB.

76 Leuchtenburg, p. 225; population, Hart, p. 172; Los Angeles Directory, 1920.

76 "Report on Studios," 6/20/21, JPKP; Jewell, p. 8.

77 "Fred Beetson" and "drink and," Schulberg, pp. 315–16; Schulberg/CB; "while you" and "FBO should," Beetson to Hays, 3/20/26, Hays Papers; *EH,* 4/6/26. Kennedy applied to the MPPDA within days of his takeover and the spring meeting formalized the acceptance.

78 "I can," *PP,* 9/27

79 *V,* 3/26/26 and 4/7/26; "ocean," *FD,* 10/2/26; Stage 3, *LAT,* 4/3/31; Thomson reception, *LAT,* 3/31/26.

79 "new" *MPW,* 5/12/23, *MPW,* 8/25/23.

80 Contract, Superior Court, Los Angeles; FBO pickup, *EH,* 2/2/24; Wyatt, p. 128; "skyrocketed," *MPW,* 5/16/25.

80 "box office," *MPW,* 4/16/25; $75,000, *V,* 4/7/26; gross, *V,* 10/24/26; "biggest," *V,* 1/6/26.

80 *PP,* 7/26; 20,000, *The Story of the Films.*

80 Wyatt, p. 68; theater statistics, *PP,* 7/26; "Thomson Pictures," *EH,* 3/13/26; letters and envelopes, Carson and Mary Thomson.

81 "very modest," Rice, p. 210; "humble" and "he would smoke," *PI,* 1/29/91; *LAT,* 1/29/91; costume ball, *PP,* 4/26; "three years," *V,* 9/1/26.

82 *LAT,* 1/21/91; *V,* 6/23/26. Grange's manager was C. C. Pyle.

82 "Super Specials" and "star," *EH,* 3/13/26; "In other words," *BG,* 8/4/26, quoted in DKG, p. 347.

82 *V,* 4/14/26; *V,* 8/3/27.

82 DeMarco, pp. 17, 33; salaries and production costs, *V,* 4/21/26; tennis, *V,* 9/8/26, 9/15/26. Ranger, through his trainer Fred Bennett, reached a salary high of $110 a week in 1928, RKO agreement addendum, 10/18/28, JPKP.

83 *V,* 5/5/26.

83 King, *V,* 3/24/26; films and units, *V,* 4/7/26.

83 "weekly" and "will show," Derr to Sistrom, 6/7/28, JPKP.

84 "grave," "can," Looker draft, 5/37.

84 *V,* 6/1/26, 6/4/26, 7/21/26. Alberta Vaughan was brought in to play *The Adorable Deceiver* and Phil Rosen agreed to direct.

84 "I didn't," *V,* 6/1/26; O'Neill, *V,* 6/16/26.

85 *V,* 8/4/26.
85 Title changes, *V,* 8/18/26; *V,* 7/28/26; ad with letter from BSA, *V,* 11/9/26; serialization, *V,* 1/29/27.
85 Krazy Kat cartoons, JPK to JPK Jr., 7/28/26; "worthy" and "well balanced," AS, p. 11; lunch, *BG,* 8/4/26, quoted in DKG, p. 347; Ringling Brothers, *V,* 8/4/26.
86 "unusual," undated REFK scrapbook clipping, JPKP.
86 On Brown: JPK to JPK Jr., 7/13/26, AS, p. 47; EH, 2/26, *V,* 2/10/26; *V,* 8/4/26; *V,* 8/11/28; "we do," Currier to Prince, 8/13/26, JPKP.
87 "I never," JPK to Moore, JPKP; hotels and schedule, REFK receipts, JPKP.
87 "a great," Quigley to JPF, JPKP, *V,* 8/18/26; "You'll like," *PP,* 10/26.
87 "fed up" and "kissed," *V,* 8/4/26; cables, JPKP.
87 Derr, *V,* 8/25/26.
88 "asinine," Tunney, pp. 199, 286; Beauchamp, *WLD,* 188–89.
89 *NYT,* 9/21/26, 9/22/26, 9/23/26, 9/24/26. Entire pages of newspapers were devoted to the fight, and ringside seats, defined as the first sixty rows, cost $27.50.
88 Lunch held on 10/8/26, quotes from *MPW,* 10/16/26.
89 *FD,* 10/3/26; Grange back, *V,* 8/4/26. Frances Marion had written the script for *Don Mike* under her pseudonym, Frank M. Clifton, Clifton being Fred's middle name and Frank M. for Frances Marion.
89 Thomson budgets, *V,* 4/7/26; Marion, *Off,* p. 166.
90 UA signing, Derr to JPK, 1/28 memo, GSA; Paramount offer, *V,* 8/4/26; JPK Thomson contract signed 10/29/26, "for tax purposes," JPK to Thomson, 1/22/27, JPKP; Minutes of Fred Thomson Productions, 3/11/27, JPKP; contract Superior Court of Los Angeles; consent for corporation signed 10/29/26, Scollard to Sullivan 2/26/29, JPKP.
91 "period of consolidation," *LAE* 10/15/26; *V,* 8/4/26; *V,* 10/19/26.
91 *PP,* 9/27; Eddie and Mary, JPK to Moore, 11/18/26, JPKP; "pleasant" and "an artist," *SEP,* 1/18/36.
91 "making," *V,* 1/5/27; "leaders," *FD,* 1/3/27; gross, *V,* 1/24/26; *FD,* 2/10/27.

CHAPTER 8: "THE INNER CABINET OF THE FILM INDUSTRY"

93 "The inner," 1/29/27, Hays Papers; DKG, pp. 370–71; Donham may have been influenced by the fact he had worked at Old Colony Trust, where Kennedy kept a major portion of his Cinema Credits Corporation funds and whose chairman, Gordon Abbott, was an FBO investor. A film class had been discussed at Yale, and Columbia offered an extension course on scenario writing. Dana Polan/CB. JPK's commitment was for $10,000 a year for three years. Multiple letters, JPKP.
93 "completed," JPK to Hays, 1/13/27, JPKP. Dana Polan/CB; "too many," Hays to Milliken, 1/14/27, JPKP.
94 *MPN,* 3/25/27; Lasky, pp. 17–18. The MPPDA had dropped the word "Distributors" from the organization's name and they were now simply Motion Picture Producers Association or MPPA.
94 Beatty to Hays, 1/17/27, Hays Papers; 1/29/27 press release, Hays Papers; *V,* 1/26/27, 2/22/27; *FD,* 1/28/27.
94 "Dr. Kennedy," Edward R. Forbes to Hays, 1/21/27 and Harvard release, AMPAS.
95 Minutes of meetings, 1/16/27 and 1/20/27, Hays Papers; "harmony," goals of Academy, 6/20/27, AMPAS.

95   "Youngest" and "the cultural," Hays Papers.
95   "supervision," *The Story of the Films,* pp. 3–53.
96   "spent most," JPK to De Mille, 3/18/27, JPKP.
96   *The Story of the Films,* p. 285; "I cannot begin," Lasky, p. 18. Loew would pass away in September of 1927 at the age of fifty-seven, *V,* 9/5/28.
96   "the opportunity," Dana Polan/CB; "in a matter," Lasky, p. 19.
97   *WP,* 4/3/27; "the date," *NYMPN,* 4/15/27; *NYW,* 1/24/27; Seymour, *V,* 6/29/27; letters to Seymour, 3/28/27, AMPAS.
97   Joseph P. Kennedy, editor, *The Story of the Films,* A. W. Shaw Company, Chicago and New York, 1927, republished by Jerome S. Ozer in 1971; "would be," letter, 7/11/27, JPKP; Arch Shaw, who had been working with the Harvard Business School for fifteen years and had published other tomes resulting from work at the school, published the book under his imprint. William Leahy of Boston helped prepare the lectures for printing, but the sheer volume of pages in Kennedy's file reveal his hands-on involvement with the series and the publication, JPKP.
97   JPK to Sullivan, 5/24/28, JPKP; Sullivan to Derr, 5/26/28, JPKP. Sullivan later settled with King, agreeing to pay him $52,000, exactly half of what he would have been owed under his contract.
98   *FD,* 12/23/26, 3/6/27; *LAE,* 2/10/58.
98   LeBaron, 20th Century Fox Biography, undated, AMPAS; *FD,* 4/24/27; martinis and popular, Swanson/Brownlow.
99   convention and films, *V,* 3/2/27, 4/13/27, 4/27/27, 5/4/27. The fact that Fanny Brice was tested for *Kosher Kitty Kelly,* but that she turned FBO down in favor of United Artists, was left out of the speeches.
99   *FD,* 4/26/27; *V,* 5/4/27.

CHAPTER 9: "ALL RECORDS HAVE BEEN BROKEN"

100   DKG, 358–60; "blow torch," Independent, 11/10/92.
100   Joe Junior to REFK, 5/15/27, AS, p. 50.
101   *FD,* 5/17/27.
101   Paramount agreement, Kent to JPK, 1/5/27, JPKP: deal and salary, *FD,* 4/6/27; "establish a new," *V,* 4/25/27; "break," JPK to Thomson, 1/22/27, JPKP; "a bit," JPK to Thomson, 2/15/27, JPKP; Carson and Mary Thomson/CB. The Thomsons' twenty-plus-acre estate had been designed by the architect Wallace Neff, with Frances working closely with him at every turn. It was generally conceded to be one of the finest examples of Neff's works, and I was privileged to spend many hours at the magnificent estate on multiple occasions. Then it was purchased in the late 1990s by Paul Allen, the billionaire co-founder of Microsoft, and he tore it down.
103   "the house," *VF,* 1/27; "would never," Marion, *Off,* p. 166.
103   "poise" and "magnificent," Marion, "Hollywood," pp. 309–10; "lousy haircut," Hopper, *Whole Truth,* p. 299.
103   "peers," Loos, p. 121.
104   *V,* 5/12/26; Hamilton, p. 61; Wyatt, p. 185. *Silver Comes Through* was released on May 29, the same day as the party, and was Fred's next-to-last FBO western before moving on to his Paramount deal.
104   *FD,* 5/24/27, 6/14/27; Berg, *Lindbergh,* pp. 141, 144; "I have grave," letter dated 7/22/27, JPKP; "There is," *FD,* 6/14/27. Lindbergh agreed to a print exclusive of his story through *The New York Times,* but he declined the film offers.

104 Grange, *V,* 1/26/27; "terrible actor," Derr to Sullivan, 8/10/28, JPKP; Nareau, pp. 1–9; FBO cowboys, *V,* 8/3/27. Bob Custer left FBO after turning out two dozen westerns.

105 *V,* 5/11/27, 12/7/27, 7/6/27.

105 *V,* 6/15/27; *V,* 6/29/27. Michael Curtiz is the name Mahala Kurtez adopted. The star of *Moon of Israel* was the actress Maria Corda, the wife of Alexander Korda. JPK purchase agreement, JPKP. When Joel turned the rights over to the Gower Street Company, he received an additional three hundred shares of stock. Gower Street minutes, 12/12/27.

105 *FD,* 5/27/27; "all records," *FD,* 6/10/27.

106 *V,* 7/6/27; *FD,* 7/24/27; Hamilton, pp. 61, 816; Saunders, p. 6; Los Angeles to New York, *V,* 6/1/27; ticker, *Fortune,* 9/37. While today the accepted use is to separate Hyannis and Port, through the 1940s, residents made a point of identifying outsiders as those who didn't write it Hyannisport.

106 "grandly," Whalen, p. 74.

CHAPTER 10: "THE REIGNING QUEEN OF THE MOVIES"

107 *FD,* 3/27/27, 9/20/27; *V,* 4/20/27, 8/31/27, 1/16/57. Kane also helped boost the early careers of Barbara Stanwyck, Frank Capra, and Ben Hecht.

107 "the reigning," Ramsaye, p. 824; "the most," *PP,* 4/25.

107 "dazzling" and "She was," Coffee, p. 50; "Nordic," Marion, "Hollywood," p. 168.

108 *PP,* 9/23; Charles J. McGuirk, *PP,* 3/25; Swanson, pp. 43–82.

109 De Mille, p. 223; "sex a la mode," William de Mille, p. 241; Swanson, p. 83; Mashon, p. 22; "beautiful," "Arrouge" p. 321.

109 Marion, "Hollywood," p. 169; Gloria Junior was born October 7, 1920, *PP,* 4/25. According to Michelle Amon and Ray Daum, Somborn took a large portion of his divorce settlement money and put it into the creation of the Brown Derby on Wilshire Boulevard. Gloria Junior would always defend Somborn as a caring father and he willed her the proceeds of the Brown Derby property.

110 "such charges," Swanson, p. 232; Ray Daum/CB.

110 Swanson, p. 196; *PP,* 10/24; New York apartment and Croton, Crossman to Wakoff, 3/6/28, GSA. Swanson's son was occasionally referred to as "Buddy" in the press, *NYT,* 8/18/29; Miss Simonson, Michelle Farmer Amon/CB; "everybody," Kobal, p. 12.

111 Ramsaye, p. 825; "traveling like," Swanson, p. 221.

112 *PP,* 6/25; Swanson, p. 228.

112 While *Variety* raved about the "frantic mob" of fans at the theater, they panned *Madame Sans-Gêne,* saying without Gloria "it would stand mighty little chance at the box office," but with her, "it's going to make money," *V,* 4/22/25; Dufty/CB; Swanson, pp. 225–43.

112 "Gloria's popularity," *PP,* 4/25, 7/25; "Arrange ovation," Ray Daum/CB.

112 "he has," *Theatre Magazine,* vol. 29, no. 5; "Even," *PP,* 3/23, 10/24.

113 "Henri was," Swanson, p. 270.

113 Balio, p. 57; "exploiting," Swanson, p. 7; salary, Birchard, p. 138; Lasky, Ray Daum/CB; abortion, Mashon, p. 27. Jesse Lasky was born and raised in San Jose, California, where his father was a shoe salesman, Betty Lasky/CB.

113 "if I," Swanson, p. 219.

114 Contract, Swanson/Derr power of attorney, 1/31/28, and other agreements in GSA; Balio, pp. 52–55; Swanson, p. 265.

114 "the result," Balio, p. 58; reviews, e.g., *Madame, V,* 4/22/25.

114 De Mille, p. 220; "I was," Swanson, p. 4.

115 Mashon, pp. 35–44; GSA files. Parker had worked with Swanson at Triangle before he went on to shepherd Young's *The Eyes of Youth* and then direct John Barrymore in *Sherlock Holmes* and Douglas Fairbanks in *The Black Pirate.*

116 "powerful," etc., Swanson, p. 302. When Swanson approached Maugham, he acquiesced to the changes and offered to write a sequel.

116 "ascertaining," Hays to JPK, 6/14/27, JPKP; "no objection," GS to JPK, 6/13/39, JPKP; "very innocuous," Schenck to JPK, 6/11/27, JPKP; "brilliant," Swanson, p. 304; *V,* 8/10/27; GSA correspondence and production files.

116 *FD,* 7/3/27; *V,* 8/10/27.

117 Al Parker had a personal contract with Swanson. If it had been between him and UA or her corporation, she would have had a buffer. "a godsend," Bedard, 11/30/27, GSA. In the summer of 1927, Thalberg rented a home on the beach at Santa Monica and a few months later, he rented a home at 9401 Sunset from the actress Pauline Frederick. It was there he was married to Norma Shearer on September 29, 1927. After their wedding, Irving and Norma continued to live with his parents and his mother ruled the domestic front. It was she who pronounced that Irving would have the bedroom at one end of the house, Norma a bedroom at the other end. According to Shearer's unpublished autobiography, by the time they rented Swanson's home, Thalberg's sister Sylvia and her husband, MGM producer Larry Weingarten, were living with them as well. The agreement shows Thalberg rented Crescent from December through June at $1,200 a month. Swanson rented 1735 Angelo for $700 a month for the same period. Rental agreements, GSA. Thomas, *Thalberg,* pp. 115, 119; Flamini, pp. 48, 92, 100; Lambert/CB; Swanson had bought 904 Crescent, built by King Gillette, from Jesse Speidel for $105,000 plus $45,000 for furnishings. Swanson's final payment was made on October 19, 1925, cables, GSA.

118 IRS, Moore to Bedard, 9/7/27, GSA; rental starting 10/27, Crossman to Wakoff, 3/6/28, GSA; taxes owed, Moore to Cohen, 12/29/27, GSA. Thalberg and taxes, Marx, p. 115.

118 Bedard, *V,* 2/29/28; expenses, Bedard to Moore, 8/27/27, GSA; "right away" and "to sell," Crossman cables, 11/1/27, 11/21/27, GSA.

118 *V,* 10/12/27; multiple cables, GSA.

119 Moore to GS, 9/14/27, 9/29/27, GSA. What was soon known as the Malibu Colony was originally part of a land grant bought by a man named Rindge who refused to allow any development. It took twenty years of court cases before a road was even built up the coast. Rindge had passed away by then, but his widow decided she still couldn't sell any coast property. Finally, in the late 1920s, she allowed sections of the land to be leased at ten-year intervals. Gloria bought a two-parcel leasehold and Allan Dwan was among the first to build a house on his leasehold. Woon, pp. 82–83. While there was an increasing number of banks and financiers willing to back proven filmmakers, Tom Moore had failed to find anyone willing to loan Gloria more money based on her production record.

119 *V,* 11/16/27; *FD,* 7/31/27; Mashon, p. 5; Swanson, pp. 324–26.

CHAPTER 11: "TOGETHER WE COULD MAKE MILLIONS"

120 Cables, GSA; St. Johns, p. 155.

121 Cables to Barclay, GSA; "He seemed" and "to depreciate," Swanson, p. 328; "The central," *Fortune* 3/36.

121 "the best" *PP,* 7/27; "practically," JPK to Kane, 11/15/27, JPKP.

122 "Together," "who looked," "The man," Swanson, pp. 340–41.

123 Financing maxed, Moore to Swanson, 12/5/27, GSA; on spending, Crossman to Moore, 11/26/27, GSA; Bedard to Swanson, 12/16/27, GSA.

123 Accounts, GSA. While the battles with the Internal Revenue Service continued, interest accrued.

123 Contract squabbles, Bedard to Loeb, 10/6/27, GSA; Moore on salary and "only real," Schenck to Swanson, 9/16/27, GSA.

124 Beauchamp, *WLD*, p. 191; "deliberately," Selznick, p. 168; "worldly," Selznick, pp. 61–62; Paul Gierucki/CB.

124 Derr notes, GSA.

124 Swanson, p. 281; Dufty/CB; disbursement reports, GSA; "she didn't," Michelle Amon/CB.

125 "those people," Ray Daum/CB; "There is," Dufty/CB; "so heavily," JPK to Cohen, 12/20/27, JPKP; cables to and from Barclay, GSA.

125 $1 million, *V,* 12/28/27; "sage," *MPN,* 12/23/27; "for another," *FD,* 12/23/27.

126 M. R. Lewis to JPK, 1/10/28, JPKP; "would," JPK to Edward Albee, 11/27/27, JPKP; AS, p. 68; *MPN,* 12/9/27; Swanson to Kennedy, 1/4/28, GSA; letters and lists of names and addresses, JPKP.

127 "Please," Dembow to JPK, 1/12/27, JPKP; "an exceedingly," *MPN,* 12/2/27; "it does," *NYHT,* 12/18/27. The book is still valuable today as a window on that moment in the business and as monologues from those intimately involved in different aspects of the business, how they saw the industry, and how they saw themselves.

127 Scollard memo, undated JPKP; *V,* 1/25/28.

127 Derr notes, GSA; "a list," JPK to Cohen, 12/20/27, AS, pp. 68–69.

127 Scollard to Derr, 1/20/28, GSA; Derr to coast, *FD,* 1/6/28; "Four," Swanson, p. 342.

128 "invaluable," Swanson, p. 303. While Swanson says he never charged her, there are several thousand dollars' worth of bills from Cohen on the list of debts in 1928 in her files, GSA; Moore memos, 12/29/27 and 1/3/28, GSA.

128 "If I," Crossman to Derr, 1/19/28, GSA; Crossman to JPK, 1/11/28, GSA.

128 Series of letters from Bedard during January and February 1928, GSA; Bedard to Swanson, 2/28/28, JPKP; *MPN,* 12/30/27.

129 All conversations verbatim from ten-page handwritten memo by Derr, GSA; cars, Crossman to Bedard, 2/23/28, GSA; Schenck advance of $12,000, Scollard to Derr, 1/17/28, GSA; Goldwyn, *MPN,* 10/28/27; Gish deal, *MPN,* 12/16/27; UA theaters, *MPN,* 11/25/27; "unreasonable," Joe Schenck to GS, 6/23/26, GSA; all other quotes taken from four-page single-spaced FBO internal memo, GSA. Swanson signed over all rights to *The Love of Sunya* and *Sadie Thompson* to Schenk's Art Cinema in an all-inclusive agreement dated 3/2/28, GSA.

132 Multiple cables, JPKP; states and companies spelled out, Sullivan to Derr, 6/30/28, JPKP.

133 Derr to Moore, 1/12/28, GSA; Scollard to Derr, 1/23/28, GSA.

133 Undated internal memo, GSA. The IRS claimed Swanson owed $80,000 from the years 1921, 1922, and 1923 and that didn't include her unpaid 1927 taxes. Kennedy's men tried to get her loans settled with stocks instead of cash, but her creditors were "disinclined" to settle for anything but cash.

134 "were all," "We're forming," and "Five minutes," Scollard to Derr, 1/25/28, GSA. In Swanson's book she says Sullivan was nicknamed Pat and he was the one who arranged the corporation papers, but the papers in her archives clearly show that it was Pat Scollard who handled it.

134 Heath cables, GSA; power of attorney, 1/25/28, naming Edward B. Derr of Forest Hills, New York, "our, and each of our, true and lawful attorney," GSA; Moore to GS, 9/29/27, GSA. Tom Moore, the former vice president and treasurer of the production company, had resigned the month before and those positions had remained vacant.

134 Swanson–Kennedy Deal, *FD,* 1/25/28, *V,* 1/25/28; "anything," Scollard to Derr, 6/25/27, GSA.

135 JPK to Derr, 1/18/28, GSA; "Regret," Cohen to GS, delivered at 1:15 at Indio, California, 1/25/28, GSA.

135 Swanson, p. 351; Cohen cable, 1/25/28, GSA. There is a letter from a law firm in Swanson's files alluding to a libel and slander suit filed by Cohen against Swanson that was settled in March of 1928 for $1,600.

CHAPTER 12: "LIKE A ROPED HORSE"

136 Kennedy later claimed it was Currier's idea to have the holding company. Petitioner's brief, *Old Colony Trust v. Commissioner of Internal Revenue,* 10/33, JPKP; Powers stock, *V,* 12/14/27. The purchase was financed by Gower Street and the Powers stock was placed in that holding company. Schnitzer shares, FBO shareholders list, 10/28, JPKP.

136 "The Master" and "Grand," *Moulders of Men, FD,* 2/16/27, undated *FD,* JPKP. Sullivan, *V,* 12/21/27; LeBaron, *V,* 12/28/27.

137 Sullivan, *V,* 12/21/27.

138 *Jesse James, The Jazz Singer, MPW,* 10/22/27.

138 Schatz, p. 63. The four Warner brothers had come to America from Poland several years after their father had been working in Baltimore. They eventually settled in Ohio where the boys joined forces to buy their first movie projector. It was Sam Warner who vociferously argued sound would be their salvation. The 1926 release of the Warner Bros.' *Don Juan,* with music and sound effects added, had been dramatically promoted with special advance sales (and prices), yet it failed to ignite the public interest.

138 "voices," *FD,* 3/4/27.

138 Lyons, pp. 24–25; *Collier's,* 10/12/56.

139 "bring," Lyons, pp. 71–72; Dreher, pp. 40–46.

139 Sarnoff's goals were not limited to financial success. In fact, his first idea for a broadcasting company was to make it a public service and he had to be convinced that advertising was needed to finance the venture. Lyons, p. 94; *Collier's,* 10/12/56; *LAT,* 10/25/99.

140 "to make," Lyons, p. 142; "Napoleonic" and "ultimate," Lyons, p. 130.

140 Sarnoff to JPK, 12/12/27, JPKP.

140 Lyons, pp. 137, 138.

141 *FD,* 1/20/28, 1/24/28; "A revolution" and "the services," draft release of RCA-FBO deal, JPKP; tour, *V,* 1/11/28; "staggering" and happy," *FD,* 1/5/28; "become practical," *FD,* 1/9/28; *FD,* 8/15/28; "a new era" ad, *V,* 1/22/28. Sarnoff was not alone in believing in the potential of television. Irving Thalberg thought the time might come when films were made exclusively for television, Thackrey, p. 193.

142 *EHW,* 7/6/29. Pathé opened an American studio in Jersey City and became known for serials such as *The Perils of Pauline,* but by the end of the World War, they were concentrating on distributing pictures made by other companies.

142 "a number," A.S., p. 71; Walker/Morgan, *V,* 3/9/27; *NYT,* 2/1/32, 11/10/50; Walker bought a controlling interest in Pathé from Merrill Lynch in 10/26,

*EHW*, 7/6/29. Walker was on the board of directors of several major corporations, including Chase National Bank and Sinclair Oil, and owned magnificent homes on East Sixty-ninth Street in New York City and in Syosset, Long Island.

142 Producers Distributing had begun life as William Hodkinson's distribution company, which Milbank had renamed after purchasing the company. Birchard, p. 200; Walker bought half of Milbank's interest, *FD*, 10/11/26.

142 *FD*, 10/22/26. Keith-Albee had an interest in Producers Distributing and also had a separate agreement with Pathé, *V*, 11/3/26; "As the," *FD*, 10/4/26.

142 *FD*, 10/4/26; *V*, 6/5/27; *FD*, 6/19/27.

142 Murdock was operating as chief during the consolidation process but didn't officially become president until May, *V*, 11/3/26; *FD*, 4/21/27, 5/13/27; debentures, *FD*, 6/8/27; stocks slumping, *V*, 9/28/27; *MPN*, 12/30/27; "unless" and "gradual," Armsby to Walker, 3/16/28, JPKL; Milbank reducing role, *FD*, 10/11/26; Milbank wanting out, *V*, 3/9/27.

143 Walker to Armsby, 3/16/28, JPKL; *V*, 2/8/28; multiple *V* and *FD* reports, April–December 1927; Pathé, *V*, 11/30/27; JPK to Krock, 7/16/34, JPKP.

143 *V*, 2/10/48, 6/8/27.

144 Cutting staff, studio shutdowns, Belletti to Prima, 1/16/28, AMPAS; of eighty-six pictures, fifty-two were two-reel westerns, *V*, 12/28/27.

144 *FD*, 11/28/26; *V*, 12/15/26; executress, *FD*, 5/13/27.

144 De Mille's budget, *FD*, 11/8/27; studio improvements, *FD*, 1/17/28; $5 million, *V*, 2/8/28; the dozen De Mille "specials" each cost an average of $260,000.

145 *V*, 2/27/28; Walker to Armsby, 3/16/28, JPKP; arrangement, JPK to Krock, 7/16/34, JPKP; 100,000 shares, Looker draft, 5/37; "expected," *FD*, 1/22/28.

145 JPK to Derr, undated, JPKP; "tropical," Swanson, p. 351; at the Poinciana, January 16–February 4, Moore to Kresel, 2/15/33, JPKP; Murdock to JPK, 1/31/28, JPKP.

145 "anybody," "endearing," and other quotes, Swanson, pp. 351–52.

146 Parties, *V*, 2/8/28; "as if," Swanson, p. 353, "business calls" and other quotes, Swanson, pp. 356–57.

146 "I can't imagine," *PP*, 6/25; "patronne," Swanson, p. 228; "thoroughly," Swanson, p. 357.

147 Swanson, pp. 357, 401; JPK to Marquis, 3/3/28, JPKP.

147 "out on," Murdock to JPK, 2/1/28, JPKP; various Pathé memos, JPKP.

147 Stock price, *V*, 2/8/28.

147 For the first Gower Street meeting, all three of the company's directors, Kennedy, Currier, and Ted Streibert, were present, for the second, only Kennedy and Streibert. Agreement between Gower Street Company, B. F. Keith Corporation, JPK and GWC, 2/15/28; Gower Street minutes, 2/14/28 and 2/15/28, JPKP; "under the same," *FD*, 4/28/28. After an initial payment of $50,000, the agreement prorated the delivery of stock with monthly payments of $25,000 each until March 1, 1929, when the $275,000 final payment was due.

148 "I confirm," Murdock to JPK, 2/15/28, agreement, JPKP.

148 "absurd," *FD*, 4/24/28; *FD*, 2/12/28; *V*, 2/8/28; Murdock to JPK, 2/1/28, JPKP; "special advisor," *V*, 2/13/28; "close friendship," *EHMPW*, 2/14/28; *FD*, 2/12/28; *FD*, 2/13/28; "in a stronger," *FD*, 2/15/28.

148 "planning," *FD*, 2/15/28; flowers and cards, DKG, p. 396; "No matter," Walters, p. 157; trip to Boston, *V*, 2/21/28; "a financial," DKG, p. 395. Derr also went west at the same time, JPK to Marquis, 3/3/28, JPK.

CHAPTER 13: "INDUSTRY WIDE INFLUENCE AND RESPECT"

149 "Culver City is" and "full livery," Beletti to Prina, 3/31/26, AMPAS. The mansion/office building would later be made famous by David Selznick, who used it as his trademark at the beginning of films such as *Gone With the Wind* and *Rebecca.*

150 "when" and "welcomed," De Mille, pp. 288–89; *EDR,* 2/14/28. De Mille had participated in the conferences that merged the companies and agreed to everything at that time, *V,* 12/15/26. De Mille praise for Murdock, *V,* 6/8/27; "treated," De Mille to Murdock, 3/7/28, JPKP.

151 "confident," De Mille to JPK, 2/18/28, DMC; "false reports," De Mille to JPK, 3/14/15, JPKP; De Mille spending, *FD,* 11/8/27; salaries, budget for the last two months of 1927, story files, Pathé Collection, AMPAS. De Mille's cutter, Anne Bauchens, was making $125 a week, the same salary as her male assistant. Over $50,000 had been invested in stories that might or might not be made. Macpherson was also De Mille's mistress and while that was well known, he would have many mistresses and few writers so it was never believed she continued as his writer for any reason other than her talent.

151 "preferred," Armsby to Walker, 3/15/28, JPKP.

152 Sennett and "I prefer," JPK to Walker, 4/4/28, JPKP; discharge following completion, *FD,* 3/14/28; contracts canceled, *V,* 3/16/28; "working," Armsby to Walker 3/15/28, JPKP.

152 "an audacious" and "select," Woon, pp. 150–55; Swanson was at the El Mirador in Palm Springs March 14–27, 1928, and it cost $501.65, GSA; JPK in Palm Springs, *V,* 3/28/28.

153 "was secure," Bedard to Swanson, 2/28/28, GSA; "peach" and "ruthless," Derr to JPK, 1/25/28, JPKP.

154 Multiple letters between Sullivan, Scollard, Derr, and Wakoff, GSA; correcting a ten cent error, Scollard to Sullivan, 2/29/28, GSA; bank accounts, Derr to Moore, 1/12/28, and Scollard to Sullivan, 4/24/28, GSA; Mashon, p. 89.

154 "serve," JPK to Marquis, 3/3/28, JPKP.

154 "withstood," Swanson, p. 353.

154 "The idea," Dufty/CB; "superior," Swanson, p. 389.

155 De Mille contract dated 4/11/27, JPKP; yacht and radio station, Pathé Collection, AMPAS.

155 Joe's copy of De Mille's contract, JPKP; "the unsatisfactory," Walker to De Mille, 3/16/28, JPKP; "our banking," Armsby to Walker, 3/16/28, JPKP; Walker to Kennedy, 3/15/28, JPKP.

156 *V,* 4/18/28; loans, De Mille to JPK, 3/14/28, JPKP. While *King of Kings* had already premiered in New York and had special road show screenings, it had yet to be put into general release and Pathé's cash flow would benefit by distributing. It would be in release for several years in both a silent and sound-added version, cut from its original eighteen reels down to twelve. Birchard, p. 218.

156 "David's special," Derr to Sullivan, 5/1/28, JPKP; "insisted," Birchard, pp. 232, 227.

156 Walker to JPK, 3/15/28, JPKP; Walker to JPK, 4/5/28, JPKP; Armsby to Walker 3/26/28, JPKP; JPK financing memo, 4/29/28, JPKP; *V,* 4/18/28; JPK's copy of De Mille's 2/27 contract, JPKP; loans, De Mille to JPK, 3/14/28, JPKP. De Mille took Jeanne Macpherson; the actress Julia Faye; his editor, Anne Bauchens; and his "right hand," Gladys Rosson, with him. He later arranged to buy the contract of his set designer, Mitch Leisen, who went

on to become a respected director. Kennedy also approved De Mille taking his various insurance policies, including a $1 million life insurance policy, which the company had been paying for. JPK to McCarthy, 6/8/28, JPKP; Edwards, p. 110; Leisen agreement, 10/12/28, De Mille Collection.

156 Malone to JPK, 11/28/35, JPKP; "with De Mille gone" and following quotes, JPK to Walker, 3/27/28, JPKP.

157 "I hold," JPK to Walker, 3/27/28, JPKP; De Mille to JPK, 3/14/28, JPKP.

157 *EHMPW,* 2/1/28; "evidence of," editorial, *EHMPW,* 3/3/28; "the prestige," *V,* 2/29/28.

157 details, multiple cables and letters, e.g., JPK to McCarthy, 6/8/28, JPKP; "he had," Swanson, p. 342; *FD,* 2/15/28; *EHMPW,* 2/7/28.

158 Swanson, p. 342; *V,* 4/11/28; staff, JPK to Sullivan, 5/24/28, JPKP; O'Leary to JPK, cables, JPKP; Sullivan to Derr, 8/9/29, JPKP. House tour and interview with current owner. The house was built in 1913, owned by a Mrs. Locke, and was just down the block from the Beverly Hills Hotel, which was opposite Gloria's home.

158 "a prodigious," Thomas and Witts, p. 117; calling instructions, JPK to Scollard, 3/21/28, JPKP; "We haven't," Moore to Scollard, 4/9/28, JPKP.

158 *Sinners in Love,* etc., *EHMPW,* 5/19/28; sheet music, author's collection; "From one Showman," *EHMPW,* 5/19/28; "Melodrama," *V,* 5/30/28.

159 "Department," *FD,* 3/14/28; *FD,* 2/7/28; *MPN,* 12/9/27; calendar, author's collection.

160 "She was," Dufty/CB; "perfectly" and "none," JPK to Marquis, 3/3/28, AS, p. 70; "Together," Swanson, p. 339.

160 "the boss," Swanson, pp. 339, 344. Swanson recalled the meeting taking place in December of 1927, but the March 1928 trip was Joe's first to California since he and Gloria had met.

160 "immaculately" and other quotes, Swanson, pp. 345–46.

161 Stories and scripts, JPKP and GSA; "richly" and "one of the," Swanson, p. 347.

161 Universal press release, AMPAS; Koszarski, *Von,* pp. 3–4, 25; Brownlow/CB.

162 "absolutely impossible" and "the ugliest," Stroheim Collection, AMPAS; "prepared," Selznick, p. 56.

163 blows, Marx, p. 72, Bob Thomas, p. 80. *The Merry Widow* cost $600,000 to make, more than any other MGM film during their first three years of existence with the exception of *Ben-Hur,* but it brought in over half a million dollars in profits.

163 Schulberg/CB.

163 "a personal favor," JPK to Mayer, 5/25/28, AS, pp. 741–75; "I hope," Mayer to JPK, 6/5/28, JPKP; Mayer and Stroheim, Bob Thomas, p. 82.

163 "plenty," *V,* 5/5/26; "a growing," Swanson, p. 347; directors poll, *FD,* 7/1/28; "Ahhh," Schulberg/CB. At the end of May, Kennedy was assuming filming would begin in nine weeks.

164 Letters, Tunney/JPK, JPKP; "splendid," *FD,* 10/23/27; "good picture," cables from Scollard to JPK, 3/27/28 and 3/28/28, JPKP; *LAT,* 5/14/28.

165 "We have," *EHMPW,* 2/4/28.

165 *EH,* 12/31/27. This was also the final issue of *EH* as it became *Exhibitors Herald and Motion Picture World* for a year and then *Exhibitors Herald World* in 1929.

165 *MPW,* undated clip, 3/28; Schnitzer to JPK, 3/30/28, JPKP; "no personal," JPK to Schnitzer, 4/4/28, JPKP; Brown in Kansas City for Mix, *FD,* 4/24/28; FBO to distribute, *FD,* 2/26/28; "joining the circus," 4/18/28,

4/19/28, uncited clips, AMPAS; Mix tour, *EHMPW,* 1/28/28; Ringling Bros., *FD,* 9/2/27; UA, *FD,* 10/27/27.

165 *V,* 4/25/28; "for tax," JPK to *FT,* 1/22/27; "real and," certificate of incorporation, Fred Thomson Productions, 2/18/27, DDC.

166 The first ten shares were divided among the three people listed as board members: T. L. Croteau, eight shares, A. L. Miller, one share, and Alfred Jarvis, one share. All were listed as residents of Wilmington without an address given. Board minutes, 3/11/27, JPKP; "a draft" and "return," DeWitt to JPK, 3/18/27, JPKP.

167 *V,* 4/25/28; corporation structuring, Fred Thomson Productions minutes, 3/11/27, JPKP; glut of westerns, *V,* 10/3/28; Joan Thomson/CB; Carson Thomson/CB.

167 "a sharp rise," *V,* 5/9/28; Pathé financing memo, 4/29/28, JPKP; actors and directors let go, *V,* 4/25/28; Derr to Sistrom, 6/7/28, JPKP; Brown, *V,* 4/25/28; Moore and Derr, *EHMPW,* 5/1/28; Walker to JPK, 5/5/28, JPKP; Henri, O'Leary to Moore, undated, JPKP; JPK to East, *EHMPW,* 5/1/28; Derr, Moore, and JPK left 4/22/28, Sullivan to Scollard, 4/23/28, JPKP.

CHAPTER 14: "I HAVE GONE INTO THE VAUDEVILLE GAME"

169 "museum" and "a chicken," Gussow, p. 23; "continuous vaudeville," Besas, p. 67; "The Lord High" and "The Ol' Mass," Gussow p. 23; stool pigeon, *V,* 8/8/28; "the scourge," *V,* 12/19/28.

169 Palace Theatre, *MPN,* 11/18/27; the Palace was located at 1564 Broadway, *FDYB,* 1928, p. 693; "foul mouthed," Besas, p. 91; "from my," JPK to Albee, 11/27/27, JPKP.

170 "there will," *MPN,* 11/18/27; "within," *V,* 3/19/30.

170 Murdock, *V,* 12/10/48; Pathé was making over 450 films a year counting their newsreels and serials, *FD,* 6/7/27; working agreement, *FD,* 2/27/28; for 1928 FBO had sixty features and more than seventy short films, *FD,* 3/25/28. Keith-Albee had merged with Orpheum in mid-1927 and the company owned outright or held over 50 percent ownership in 110 theaters and the remainder were affiliated with a percentage of ownership. K-A-O also operated the booking systems for the performers. Theater ownership breakdown, *FDYB,* 1928, p. 693; merger of Keith-Albee and Orpheum, *V,* 10/26/27; seven hundred theaters, *FD,* 2/27/28, *NYT,* 1/27/28.

171 *V,* 4/27/27; *MPN,* 11/11/27; "this is," Sullivan to Scollard, 4/15/28, JPKP; options, Koskoff, p. 31; agreement, Walker to JPK, 5/9/28, JPKP; $21 was the high point of the past year and $16 the lowest, *NYT,* 5/4/28; JPK's 12,500 shares, Blair and Company to JPK, 5/15/28, JPKP; 25,000 shares, Walker to JPK, 5/9/28, JPKP; holding company and purchase price, Lasky, pp. 25–26.

171 *V,* 5/9/28; biography revisions, *NYT,* 2/27/28. Since January, Lehman Brothers held options on fifty thousand shares and those were brought into the Walker fold.

172 Option on additional 75,000 shares, JPK to Blair and Company, 5/10/28, JPKP; agreement between Kennedy and K-A-O, 5/15/28, JPKP, spells out that the options are to be his compensation and that he is entitled to reimbursement for all expenses.

172 "important" and "It was," K-A-O press release, 5/26/28, JPKP; "energetic," *NYT,* 5/17/28.

172   "He has shot" and "more liberal," *V,* 5/23/28; "never handled," *V,* 2/29/28; stock prices, *NYT,* 5/4/28, 6/5/28; *V,* 12/5/28.

173   "not feeling," JPK to Mayer, 5/25/28, JPKP.

173   Currier, JPK Keith agreement, 2/15/28; JPK to Currier, 4/7/28; JPK to Currier, 4/3/28; multiple cables, 4/11/28; Italian film, 4/13/28; "the inspired," Mussolini letters and Brown memos concerning film, 2/14/28; "Fascist," Brown to JPK, 3/8/28, all JPKP.

173   Currier to JPK, 9/26, JPKP; Scollard to JPK, 9/26; JPKP.

173   *FD,* 12/27/27; *V,* 3/28/28; Derr moved to Pathé, Poole to Derr, 5/22/28, JPKP. Gray left an estate of over $500,000, with $3,750 a year going to his daughter and almost all of the rest of it to local charities, *V,* 5/30/28. Boston move, *Fitchburg Sentinel,* 6/2/28.

173   "assistant," *Fitchburg Sentinel,* 6/2/28; "get busy," JPK to Ford, 7/2/28, JPKP.

174   "Kennedy-Ford," *V,* 6/27/28; "failure," *V,* 7/25/28; "bringing," *Syracuse Herald,* 9/16/28; $900,000, Looker draft, 5/37.

174   *V,* 3/19/30; employee memo, *V,* 8/1/28; "find out," JPK to Ford, 7/2/28, JPKP; "Didn't you," AS, p. 76.

174   Quirk to JPK, 4/14/28, JPKP; multiple letters and cables, JPKP.

175   Henri to Paris, *V,* 5/2/28; *FD,* 4/12/28; Amon/CB; Dufty/CB.

175   "breached," Stroheim to Powers, 5/2/28, GSA; *FD,* 5/16/28.

175   Multiple cables, JPKP; "cleaned up," JPK to Sullivan, 5/1/28, JPKP; Edington billed Kennedy almost $2,000 for the trip, Edington to Sullivan, 6/1/28, GSA. Harry Edington, 1887–1949, was a physically small man with a taste for cashmere who often has his name misspelled as Eddington, but his imprinted personal stationery uses only one "d." He began in film as controller for Goldwyn and stayed on when it became MGM, going to Rome as a production executive on *Ben-Hur.* He was at MGM when Greta Garbo arrived and soon she was under his wing. He reportedly was the one who counseled her not to talk to the press as her candid comments could only get her and everyone else in trouble. He soon switched his loyalties from the studio to individual clients, who included Garbo, John Gilbert, and Stroheim under the shingle of Edington's own Business Administration agency, *V,* 3/16/49.

175   "still confident," JPK to De Mille, 5/15/28, DMC; "do anything" and "publicity," De Mille to JPK, 5/16/28, DMC.

176   "loan," twelve-week schedule, August start, *FD,* 5/16/28, and JPK to Mayer, 5/25/28, AS, pp. 74–75. Powers agreed to release the director with the caveat that Stroheim film a closing scene for *The Wedding March* with "yourself and Cecilia in carriage following church ceremony" and to complete whatever else might be required "without additional compensation." Stroheim contract and release all in place on 5/23/28, Sterry to Sullivan, GSA; Powers to Stroheim, undated, GSA; Bank of America line of credit, 6/22/28, JPKP. Swanson's contract with UA was used as collateral.

176   "I am," JPK to De Mille, 5/17/28, DMC.

176   "continuing," De Mille to JPK, 5/16/28, DMC; draft release, undated, DMC; JPK to De Mille, 5/17/28, DMC.

176   De Mille to JPK, 5/18/28, De Mille Collection; De Mille to JPKP, 5/22/28, DMC; "there was not" and following quotes, JPK to De Mille, 5/25/28, DMC. Finally, in August, De Mille signed with MGM for a three-picture deal where he would not need outside funding; Birchard, p. 234. According to Sam Marx, De Mille's MGM films *Dynamite* and *Madam Satan* "were big losers," while the remake of *The Squaw Man* barely retrieved its cost. Marx, p. 146.

177   "to reinforce," *FD,* 5/14/28; "the loss" and "for an indefinite," *FD,* 5/28/28.

Colvin Brown moved over from FBO to serve as the new executive vice president of Pathé.

178 "another," JPK to De Mille, 5/15/28, DMC.

179 *V,* 4/21/26; "dominate," *FGA,* 1998.

179 In addition to signing talent, First National absorbed Associated Producers; *FD,* 4/19/27; a third, *Fortune,* 3/37.

179 Zukor buying two thirds interest in Balaban and Katz, *Fortune,* 3/37. The interlocking relationships between the companies belied any real independence, both in terms of ownership and financing. For instance, K-A-O owned part of the Stanley chain and bankers were involved with multiple companies, e.g., Hayden, Stone financed both First National and Fox. *V,* 5/5/26; *V,* 28/28.

179 Rossheim had to agree to put a Hayden, Stone representative, Richard Hoyt, on their board as the price of financing. *V,* 5/5/26; *V,* 11/16/28. First National profits, *FD,* 4/19/27; rumors of a merger between the two companies had been alive for almost two years, *V,* 5/12/26.

179 March approach, Rogers to Kennedy, 3/19/28, JPKP. There was also talk that Rossheim was interested in talking to Kennedy about merging K-A-O with Stanley, *V,* 10/24/28; "Other than," *V,* 6/13/28; "First national," *MPN,* 6/16/28; *FD,* 6/18/28.

180 "period of consolidation," *LAE,* 10/15/26.

180 Moore to LeBaron, 6/13/28, JPKP.

180 "everyone," *FD,* 6/10/28.

180 First National profits, *FD,* 8/27/28, 3/25/28; Poole memos of 7/19/28, 7/23/28, Warner Bros. Collection, USC.

180 Powers to JPK, 6/8/28, JPKP.

181 "stands out" and "saving," Edington to JPK, 6/4/28, JPKP; Glazer Collection, UCLA. Glazer's first name was Benjamin, but everyone called him Barney. While most of the studio heads were Jewish, there was a sizable contingent of producers of Irish descent such as Hal Roach, Mack Sennett, Sam Rork, Winfield Sheehan, and Eddie Mannix.

181 "story expert," *V,* 5/9/28; "I know," Edington to JPK, 6/11/28, JPKP; Golden, pp. 92–94; Bob Thomas, p. 95. Bern was born Paul Levy in Germany in 1889 and was one of eighteen children. He came to New York at the age of nine and changed his name when he took to the stage. Thalberg considered him an intellectual; Anita Loos called him "a German psycho." Bern was reported to be the father of Don Gallery, the son of Barbara La Marr. Gallery himself believes that to be true, but he was only three when La Marr died at the age of twenty-nine in 1926. He was then adopted by his mother's good friend ZaSu Pitts and her husband, Tom Gallery. Beauchamp, *Without,* p. 221; Don Gallery/CB.

182 "in sole," Glazer, *V,* 8/8/28; salaries, Glazer $3,000 a week and Bern $1,250 a week, financial files, Pathé Collection, AMPAS; Glazer was born in 1888 and died in 1956, *V,* 3/21/56; Bern and "in order," *V,* 8/15/28.

182 "the Napoleon" and "the new Czar," *Oakland Tribune,* 6/17/28.

183 Sinclair, pp. 14, 17; *V,* 9/5/28; "stone by stone," Selznick, p. 96; "to everyone," Gabler/CB.

183 "Nothing," Swanson, p. 343; gang accounts, e.g., Sullivan to Derr re $52,000 to Scollard account, 2/15/28, JPKP; Eddie Moore correspondence

files, JPKP. Contrast the way Kennedy operated with someone like Louis B. Mayer at MGM. First and foremost, Mayer had to deal with "New York," in the form of Marcus Loew and then Nick Schenck, to approve major expenditures. Kennedy might consult with others such as Guy Currier or Elisha Walker, but he was not limited by financial restraints or a need for prior approval. Mayer had Irving Thalberg as his number two and head of production and while they shared overlapping interests, they were also competitive with each other. Less love was lost between them with every passing year and that sapped Mayer's time and energy.

184 "even his," Looker draft, 5/37; "Will call," undated cable, JPKP.

184 "Joe used," E. M. Kennedy, p. 34; cost of calls, Ritz-Carlton to JPK, 6/26/30; various cables including one sent to the Whitehall Hotel in Palm Beach re Mrs. Kennedy's reservation are billed to Pathé, 2/24/30, JPKP.

184 *NYT*, 8/11/28; "A rather," *FD*, 8/12/28.

CHAPTER 16: "YOU AIN'T HEARD NOTHING YET"

186 Film year, *FD*, 1/3/28; "nice," *MPN*, 10/23/27; St. Louis, *FD*, 12/2/27; other cities, *FD*, 2/16/28. Al Jolson had been a last-minute replacement for George Jessel, who had "balked when he learned he was expected to sing, pointing out his contract called only for his appearance," *FD*, 5/26/27. Sam Warner, the brother credited with being the biggest advocate for sound, died at the age of forty the week *The Jazz Singer* opened, *V*, 10/6/27.

186 "the current" and "they will not," *MPN*, 8/11/28; "talking pictures," Marx, pp. 100, 105. When MGM first announced their plans for 1928, all fifty films were to be silent. "All this," Edwards, p. 109.

187 "Adding," Berg, *Goldwyn*, p. 173; "Ladies and," *L'Eredità DeMille*, p. 166.

187 "sound films," *PP*, 9/28; weather and standing room only, *FD*, 7/16/28. Sixteen films with portions of sound inserted had been released before the seven-reel, all talking *The Lights of New York*. Twelve were released by Warner Bros., four by Fox, *FD*, 7/1/28.

187 "spoken sequences," Lasky to Zukor, 7/18/28, AMPAS; Paramount sound films, *FD*, 6/25/28. In June of 1928, Lasky thought that it would take five years for the transition to all-sound films to occur, *FD*, 6/25/28. Day and night, *FD*, 8/30/28; cost of filming in Los Angeles, Starr, p. 98. To build one new soundproof building with four stages cost over half a million dollars, *MPN*, 10/6/28.

187 Shearer, Marx, p. 99; "vibrationless," *FD*, 7/22/28; MGM's New York sound studio at 127th Street and Second Avenue, *FD*, 7/24/28. Douglas Shearer's name would appear in the credits of almost every film the studio produced for the next thirty years.

188 *FD*, 10/14/28; Emily Thompson/CB.

188 "every train," *V*, 9/24/29; Dorothy Parker signed by MGM, *FD*, 11/16/28.

189 Playwrights returning east, *V*, 11/7/28; Huston, Beauchamp, *WLD*, p. 271. Robert Montgomery was spotted in New York as well, but Fredric March was signed by Paramount while his touring company was appearing in Los Angeles. *FD*, 11/16/28.

189 "in a very tough," Beauchamp, *Adventures*, p. 47; "lower Bronx," Thackrey, p. 148; *V*, 2/19/30; "I-I-I," Marx, p. 106. When Vilma Banky's latest, *Two Lovers*, was announced as "available in silent and sound" versions, it meant there were sound effects and synchronized music added. Goldwyn extended her contract for five years and tried to move her to talkies, but her heavy

accent proved close to impenetrable, *FD,* 9/14/28; contract, *V,* 7/7/29. Banky retired in the early 1930s while her husband, the Chicago-born Rod La Rocque, continued making films for another decade.

189 Marx, p. 106; "She couldn't," Lasky, pp. 47–48. The strength of Daniel's voice is underscored by the fact she also became a star of radio.

189 Some were victims of poor equipment. It is generally acknowledged that Jack Gilbert was hoist on the petard of faulty recording. Others such as Walter Pidgeon, who had been working in silents at $100 a week, passed his voice test to such acclaim his weekly salary jumped to $1,200. *V,* 10/24/28; Marx, pp. 106, 111; songwriters, *MPN,* 9/29/28; Gershwin, *V,* 8/15/28; brass bands, *MPN,* undated, 11/28; over fifty thousand, *FD,* 7/22/28; "human orchestras" and musicians losing jobs, *FD,* 8/15/28.

190 Naming contest, *PP,* 3/29; "sound pictures," *V,* 6/13/28; ending abruptly, *FD,* 7/29/28; "Don't," *FD,* 10/14/28; *FD,* 10/18/28.

190 "Sound Pictures," *FD,* 7/22/28; "the wow," *PP,* 9/28.

191 *FD,* 7/22/28; *FD,* 12/30/26; "Vitaphone coming," *FD,* 9/9/28; labor issues, *FD,* 8/5/28.

191 *FD,* 8/8/28, 1/9/28.

191 "Gloom," *FD,* 11/16/28; *V,* 9/24/29; Hippodrome, *V,* 8/8/28.

191 LeBaron to JPK, 9/25/28, JPKP.

191 Kane at FBO, *V,* 6/13/28; Photophone/RCA memo, 6/7/28, JPKP. The new company would also become a producing partner in sound films up to one fifth of the cost and left open the possibility of increasing that percentage.

192 Memo on conference, 7/24/28, on Photophone stationery, JPKP.

194 *PP,* 9/27; *AM,* 5/28; *NYT,* 6/3/28.

195 Harvard Business School and "for three," *NYT,* 6/3/28.

195 "was the best," etc., *AM,* 5/28.

196 "It had not been," *NYT,* 6/3/28; "Lord Inverforth," *AM,* 5/28; "He carries," *PP,* 9/27; "folk hero," Koskoff, pp. 36–37. JPK used his studios' publicity departments and depended on friends such as Chris Dunphy to suggest stories about him to various editors and to be available to reporters to verify his bonhomie; president of Crowell Publishing to Dunphy, 10/3/27, JPKP.

197 "brought together," *NYT,* 6/3/28; "striking," *AM,* 5/28; clipping service, *AS,* p. 12; Ramsaye memos, Pathé Collection, AMPAS. Terry Ramsaye was also the author of one of the first histories of the film business, *A Million and One Nights.* John B. Kennedy, the author of the *American Magazine* piece, would go on to become the RKO representative in England, ghost-write an article for Kennedy in *The Saturday Evening Post* in 1936, serve as editor at *Collier's,* and have his own radio program on NBC. Joe would ask his help in getting articles by Joe Junior published and having Joe Junior as a guest on his radio program; *AS,* pp. 173, 359, 381.

CHAPTER 17: "SWINGING THE AXE"

198 "tour," *FD,* 7/12/28; "Who does," Korda, pp. 78, 81; firings, *EHMPW,* 8/4/28.

198 *V,* 8/8/28. Maria spelled her last name with a "C," her husband was Korda.

199 Unit productions, *V,* 6/9/26; *FD,* 2/10/27; "no intention" and "swinging the axe," *V,* 8/1/28; "planned," *FD,* 8/3/28; other exits, *V,* 8/1/28; Sam Spring, *FD,* 8/17/28.

199 Glazer and reorganization, *V,* 8/8/28; Rockett ousts executives, *EH,* 8/4/28; twenty-five more resign and "broom," *FD,* 7/31/28; payroll matters, e.g. Sul-

livan to Derr, 8/10/28, Derr to Sullivan 8/10/28, JPKP; Henri, V, 8/15/28; V, 8/4/28.

200 "so called" and *Lilac Time* remade with Vitaphone, *Zanesville Signal*, 8/1/28; *Lilac Time* cost, undated, Walker memo, JPKP; *Lilac Time* with orchestra, V, 8/5/28; "deafening roar," FD, 7/29/28; FD, 7/31/28; unions blamed, MPN, 8/11/28; "there was no doubt," MPN, undated, early 10/28.

200 FD, 8/15/28; V, 8/15/28.

200 "the industry's," FD, 8/5/28; "disposed of," FD, 8/13/28; FBO to Pathé, V, 8/22/28.

200 "every minute," Swanson, p. 364; "chief talent," Lasky, p. 32.

201 Contract in pocket, V, 8/8/29.

201 notice of special meeting, JPKP; FD, 8/12/28.

201 "impractical," Sullivan to Derr, 8/16/28, JPKP; "outline," JPK to Lichtman, 8/17/28, JPKP.

202 "supreme" and "no sacrifice," FD, 8/10/28; $4 million, V, 8/15/28.

202 Contract, V, 8/8/29; agreement memo, 8/9/28, JPKP; NYT, 8/11/28; "special," "absolute," and "to run," FD, 8/12/28; 10 percent, JPK, First National files, undated memo, JPKP.

202 V, 8/15/28; "no better," FD, 8/12/28; MPN, 8/18/28.

202 "just taken," JPK to Weininger, 8/13/28, JPKP; JPK to Powers, 8/15/28, JPKP; "see how," JPK to Kane, 8/15/28, JPKP.

203 "to deliver," V, 12/26/28; NYT, 6/3/28; "I do not," Sarnoff to Webb, 9/4/28, JPKP.

203 "to get started," FD, 8/12/28. Even if the race for a monopoly could be won, it was the financial overseers who called the shots. RCA's partner was General Electric and Western Electric's parent was American Telephone and Telegraph. These major corporations had many overlapping interests and so "an open rupture over what is after all only one phase of their widespread business activities" served no one's benefit in the long run, FD, 8/13/28. Western Electric dragged its feet in agreeing with interchangeability, but finally acknowledged it in October; FD, 10/24/28.

203 "a lot of baloney," FD, 8/10/28; V, 8/8/28; FD, 8/28/28; meetings with LeBaron and Schnitzer, MPN, 8/11/28; signing, V, 8/22/28; Swanson and Photophone, FD, 8/28/28. Joe's hedging might have saved him a tidy sum over the past few months, but it had also delayed recording the sound additions to *The Godless Girl*, postponing that much-needed box office revenue.

204 "wanted" and "I am," JPK to Currier, 8/17/28, JPKP.

204 "any agreement," Rossheim to JPK, 8/15/28, JPKP.

204 LAT, 9/2/28; "no sacrifice," FD, 8/10/28; "reign," Korda, p. 84.

205 *Buffalo Courier-Express*, 8/19/28; Skouras, V, 8/18/71.

205 LAT, 8/18/71; V, 3/10/71; Quine, p. 47; Judy Balaban Quine/CB.

206 "If you can't," Collier and Horowitz, p. 24, "If you do," FD, 8/21/28.

207 "Coming," JPK to EMK, 5/8/45, in AS, p. 618; JPK to Currier, 8/17/28, JPKP.

207 statement from First National, V, 8/22/28; "differences over," MPN, 8/25/28.

207 "complete authority," "made the company," V, 8/29/28; "the new ruler," DKG, p. 379.

207 "big topic," *Daily Film Renter*, 8/22/28; "In this," MPN, 8/25/28.

208 Murdock, Casey, V, 8/8/28; Carson Thomson/CB.

208 "no trouble," *Seattle Post*, 5/7/28.

208 Beauchamp, WLD, p. 231; V, 8/8/28; Joan Thomson/CB.

209 V, 8/22/28; "in complete," FD, 8/28/28.

209  "hasty" and "under," *FD,* 8/28/28; "twice as long" and "it was," V, 8/29/28.

209  Goldman Sachs, Boston News Bureau, 6/15/28; *FD,* 9/5/28; *FD,* 9/13/28; FGA, Winter 1998; $2.5 million for 19,000 shares with the company valued at around $15 million, *MPN,* 9/29/28. It was also reported that Spyros Skouras would head the new theater division.

CHAPTER 18: "NOW HE'S BACK AND ALMOST ANYTHING
MAY HAPPEN"

211  REFK receipts, JPKP; "headcutting," *FD,* 9/4/28; V, 10/10/28; *FD,* 10/15/28; original trip plans, V, 8/8/28. K-A-O, *FD,* 9/16/28. *FD,* 9/30/28; "personally," V, 9/26/28.

211  "Kennedy Returns," *FD,* 9/28/28; smiling photo, *BG,* 10/1/28; "the industry," *LAT,* 9/2/28; "Now he's back," *FD,* 9/30/28.

212  *Collier's* transcript, 9/30/28, JPKP; *MPN,* 10/6/28.

213  V, 10/3/28; Walker's memo purchasing K-A-O, JPK agreeing not to sell before 1/1/29, JPKP.

213  profits and theaters, *Standard Trade and Securities Service,* 8/31/28; V, 9/5/28.

213  "One of the," *Film Mercury,* 10/19/28; First National and Western Electric, *FD,* 4/22/28; Western Electric contracts, *FD,* 6/20/28; "mopped," V, 10/3/28; homes, churches, etc., *FD,* 4/23/28; "without," *FD,* 8/10/28.

214  K-A-O-Warners, *FD,* 9/18/28; RCA decisions, *FD,* 10/7/28; Albee returning, V, 10/3/28; "progressed," *FD,* 9/16/28.

214  "I entered," Looker draft, 5/37; "a stubborn," *LAT,* 9/2/28, *Standard Trade and Securities Service,* 8/31/28.

215  Contracts for Stroheim's people, Edington to Sullivan, 5/29/28, GSA. Stroheim's brother-in-law, Louis Germonprez, was the assistant director, Ben Westland the publicity director, and Betty Mason the script girl.

215  "wild and roistering," Heath to Shapiro, 8/1/29, GSA; other character descriptions and casting notes, undated in JPKP; Owen, V, 8/24/66; Marshall, V, 3/17/43. Although Stroheim originally described the character of Jan as "a huge bulk of flesh" and had other actors in mind, he decided on Marshall, a thin but experienced stage actor who had been appearing in movies for over a decade. Marshall was now in his mid-sixties and had played a similar role of a degenerate in *The Merry Widow.* Stroheim had worked with both Seena Owen and Tully Marshall on Griffith's *Intolerance.*

215  LeBaron, Sullivan agreement, 8/1/28, GSA, suggests they might not begin filming until sometime between November 1 and December 1.

215  "guaranteed" and "secure," Derr to Heath, 8/22/28, GSA; sample ads, *FD,* 7/3/28.

215  "a waterfront" and "an establishment," scripts, JPKP; Derr to Heath, 8/22/28, GSA; "a very poor," Schnitzer to Derr, 6/20/28, JPKP; other various names, DeWitt to Lane, 6/20/28, JPKP. Exactly when filming was supposed to start and when the title changed varied from memo to memo. As early as August 1, 1928, William LeBaron stated it was to be called *Queen Kelly* and filming was to begin November 1, but on the same date, Lance Heath was telling United Artists it was still *The Swamp* and cameras would roll on the 1st of September.

216  ten weeks, V, 10/24/28; "quickie," V, 11/14/28; previous films, V, 5/16/28; "the Gower Street," V, 11/7/28; V, 9/5/28, 10/24/28.

216  "final," etc., LeBaron to JPK, 9/25/28, JPKP.

216  *PP,* 9/28; Dufty/CB; stunt, *FD,* 9/5/28.

217 "reasonable" and "advanced," Derr to Sullivan, 10/1/28, JPKP.
218 Dufty/CB; Amon/CB; parties, GSA records; Swanson, pp. 366–67; *FD,* 10/11/28; Curtis school, various financial records, GSA; movies, Swiss boarding schools, and tutors, *NYT,* 8/18/29.
218 Swanson, pp. 367–68; Michelle Amon/CB; Dufty/CB.
218 For instance, K-A-O's agreement to screen most Pathé films was reduced but not entirely erased and was not to go into effect until August 1929. K-A-O legal to Pathé, 10/22/28, JPKP; Poole to JPK, 1/1/31, JPKP; Murdock return, meetings, *V,* 10/17/28.
218 K-A-O stock prices, *FD,* 9/13/28; Goldman Sachs offered Kennedy $18 plus one sixth of a share of Warners stock for each share of K-A-O. The day before the offer was tendered, Warners was selling at $109 (having wavered over the past year between $80 and $132), making the value of the offer approximately $36 a share. Goldman Sachs to JPK, 10/17/28, JPKP. In their letter to Kennedy, Goldman Sachs stated they were interested in purchasing 556,000 shares, making theirs a $20 million offer. The K-A-O board accepted responsibility for getting back to Goldman and released Kennedy from any responsibility. "hold the whip" and meetings, *V,* 10/17/28.
219 The balance sheet listing $7,210,162.76 included the Hollywood studio valued at a little over $1 million, $4 million in accounts receivable, unplayed films, and publicity materials, as well as $1 million in "goodwill—exchanges," 7/28/28 FBO balance sheet, JPKP. The end-of-the-year balance sheet for FBO for 1927 listed FBO's value at $6,343,680.65, Kennedy, Currier et al., 2/15/28, JPKP.
219 FBO list of stockholders, 8/17/28, JPKP; DeWitt retainer, RCA memo of agreement, 10/28/28, JPKP. Schnitzer's stock was held in his wife's name. Keith and Orpheum were listed separately as stockholders with 5,858 and 5,857 respectively. Cinema Credits Corporation held 4,320 shares and Kennedy's father-in-law owned two thousand shares.
219 Meeting held in Currier's office, with Currier and Streibert present, 10/4/28, Gower Street minutes, JPKP; board members elected, minutes of 10/24/28, Currier and JPK present, JPKP; escrow, Gravath to Currier, 10/23/28, JPKP. Annual board meeting held on 10/17, DDC. At their meeting on October 4, they gave Sidney Kent five thousand shares of FBO "in payment for his services" in the sale of stock to Keith back in February and five thousand shares were to be delivered to David Sarnoff for $15 a share, "in accordance to the terms of an option given to him by Mr. Currier with the approval of Mr. Kennedy."
220 The two-page K-A-O document was signed by Kennedy, Murdock, Albee, and four other current board members. The same group of seven men had been named to the transition committee responsible for overseeing the exchange of K-A-O and FBO stock, Notice to Stockholders, 10/22/28, JPKP.
220 Gloria's departure, *V,* 10/11/28; schedule, *MPN,* 11/3/28.
220 JPK to O'Connell, 10/23/28, JPKP; JPK speech, JPKP. Jim Seymour, who handled the publicity around JPK's Harvard lecture series, coordinated the guests for the Keith Theatre opening as well. Notes, JPKP; theater details, *MPN,* 11/3/28.
220 "no concern," 10/28 memo to K-A-O employees, JPKP; "Kennedy-Ford," *V,* 6/27/28.
221 "a tidy sum," *FD,* 10/8/28; "when I" and "intrigued," *Film Mercury,* 10/19/28; both will run company, *V,* 10/24/28; *V,* 10/31/28; *FD,* 10/24/28.

CHAPTER 19: "THE DOLLAR SIGN IMPLANTED IN HIS HEART"

222   JPK departure, October 31, *MPN*, 11/3/28; Moore and O'Leary, *V*, 11/7/28;
       *V*, 10/31/28; Chicago, *FD*, 11/5/28; Derr in Chicago, *V*, 9/9/28.
222   "director" and "pending," *V*, 9/5/28; *V*, 9/12/28; "equal," Edington to JPK,
       6/11/28, JPKP; "in complete," *V*, 8/15/28; "let things ride" and "what kind,"
       LeBaron to JPK, 9/25/28, JPKP; Brown to New York, *V*, 9/28; "unit produc-
       ers," *MPN*, 12/1/28. Even after the meeting, Bern went to the *L.A. Times* and
       confirmed his position as head of production and announced the next season's
       films before Kennedy did.
223   "does not," Kahane to JPK, 11/15/28, JPKP. Kennedy had previously sent a
       letter to the K-A-O board claiming he was "ready to resign" as chairman and
       as a board member, but that was "conditioned upon the fact that it shall not
       be construed as a cessation on my volition to act as Chairman, but merely a
       resignation necessary in the proposed transaction"; JPK to K-A-O, 10/27/28,
       JPKP; Sarnoff meetings, *FD*, 11/16/28.
223   Schnitzer office, *V*, 12/12/28; JPK to Sarnoff, undated, JPKP.
223   *FDYB*, 1929, p. 542; *Syracuse Herald*, 12/6/28.
223   *V*, 1/12/28; "an administrator," *MPN*, 12/1/28.
224   "radical," *Syracuse Herald*, 12/06/28; *Rio Rita*, *V*, 12/12/28; *FD*, 12/6/28;
       Ford as general manager, *V*, 10/24/28. Elisha Walker also continued on the
       board of K-A-O, *NYT*, 12/6/28. Albee passed away in March of 1930 at the
       age of seventy-two leaving an estate estimated at $25 million, *V*, 3/19/30.
224   *The Wedding March* was premiered at New York's Rivoli Theater in October.
       Film viewing; Fay Wray/Kevin Brownlow; "were played," *The Wedding
       March* program notes, AMPAS. The incomplete second half of *The Wedding
       March* was dubbed *The Honeymoon* and released only in Europe and South
       America.
225   "heaps," *The Wedding March* program notes, AMPAS.
225   "instantly," Noble, p. 75; "the lousiest," "Corrected Index of the Work of
       Erich von Stroheim," MOMA; "smart idea," *V*, 12/29/28.
225   Sound, *V*, 7/12/28; *V*, 9/15/28: songs and talk, "voice director," *V*, 12/19/28;
       Derr to Heath, 8/22/28, GSA; voice coach, Scollard to Markoff, 1/8/29, GSA;
       Warner Bros. profits, *FD*, 12/4/28.
226   filming starts, *V*, 11/7/28; crew dismissed, *V*, 11/7/28. JPK Los Angeles, *V*,
       11/7/28; Pathé, *MPW*, 11/17/28; *V*, 11/14/28; Koszarski, *Von*, pp. 240, 248.
       Ironically, the production delays had allowed the cinematographer Gordon
       Pollock, whom L. B. Mayer could not loan Kennedy back in June, to join the
       team, Mayer to JPK, 6/5/28, JPKP. AS, p. 74; copyright, Derr to Sullivan,
       10/1/28, JPKP; Stroheim's story was officially accepted in early October in
       part because after all these months of talking about it, it had yet to be copy-
       righted. On the page, his characters were one-dimensional, almost to the
       point of farce. In his early, lengthy descriptions, written before the parts were
       cast, the Prince is a man "with the devil in his eyes"; an "all around Don Juan,
       Casanova and Jack Gilbert, all three in one." Jan has a "bloated mush face,
       little squinting pig eyes, smooth shave, of Hollandish parentage, coarse,
       boisterous . . . nigger rich thru vast possessions"; character descriptions,
       JPKP.
226   Madame Frances, Koszarski, *Von*, p. 248; "her nakedness" and "breath tak-
       ing," Swanson, pp. 368–69. Yet another delay had been caused when the cat
       started to scratch the naked Owen and "white mittens" to cover its paws were
       constructed. Koszarski, *Von*, p. 249.

226 Swanson, p. 370; Ivano and "Oh I guess," quoted from the documentary *Man You Love to Hate.*

227 *V,* 10/31/28; "Sound News," *FD,* 11/18/28; *MPN,* 11/17/28; *V,* 11/21/28.

228 Sound Unit #1, *Gang War* and "everything," Beauchamp, *Adventures,* p. 197; "the best," LeBaron to JPK, 9/25/28, JPKP.

228 Barney Glazer, along with a small staff, was charged with writing the dialogue to be inserted, but he was "far too expensive a man" to be delegated to such tasks for long. There was no longer the grand studio to produce for, but his talent was in writing "big scripts" for "prima donnas." Glazer was put to work outlining a treatment for Swanson's next film. LeBaron to JPK, 9/25/28, JPKP. Beauchamp, *Adventures,* p. 199. There are references to plans for Gloria to make a film entitled *Clothes* and at one point it was announced that Stroheim was to direct it after *Queen Kelly* was completed; *BHC,* 10/25/28.

228 Beauchamp, *Adventures,* pp. 199–201; "economy programs," *FD,* 11/12/28; *MPW,* 11/17/28; *V,* 11/21/28; radio station, Leavitt to Sistrom, 11/2/28, Pathé Collection, AMPAS.

228 *LAT,* 9/2/28; "the international," Lillian Gish/Kevin Brownlow; "language doubles," *MPN,* undated, 11/28; "laugh" and "Americans," *FD,* 6/25/28.

229 Foreign profits, *FD,* 5/24/28; French quotas, *MPN,* 8/18/28.

229 "the strength," DKG, p. 295; "due to" and "Pathé shows," *FD,* 11/21/28; *V,* 12/19/28.

230 "Don't talk" and "shown," *V,* 9/19/28; "the principal," *MPN,* 10/6/28.

230 $6 million, Galbraith, pp. 20–21, 81; Crash, p. 73; Hoover, JPK to C. F. Adams, 4/13/29, JPKP.

230 RKO listed on exchange, *NYT,* 11/29/28; *FD,* 12/2/28; agreement between RKO and JPK, 11/21/28, signed by JPK and Maurice Goodman, vice president of RKO, JPKP; pages of sales records from E. F. Hutton and Gurnett and Company, JPKP. RKO at $50, *NYT,* 1/25/29; four thousand shares, Blair to JPK, 2/7/29, JPKP; JPK to Bradford Ellsworth, 11/23/28; Ellsworth to JPK, 11/26/28, 11/30/28; memo from Blair to JPK, 11/26/28, all JPKP. Per capita income, Leuchtenburg, p. 178. There is no evidence that Kennedy actually put in the $6 a share in the first place, in which case his profit would have increased by another quarter million dollars. Others quadrupled their money as well. Joe Schnitzer had held 14,000 shares, which he put in his wife's name, and in May 1928, she sold seven thousand to Gower Street for $52,000, and when she sold the remaining seven thousand shares in December it was for $245,000; Schnitzer to JPK, 7/10/45, JPKP. At the November 27 meeting of Gower Street only Currier and Streibert were there to confirm the swapping of the stock. They traded the remaining 10,679 shares of FBO for an equal number of RKO stock, ten thousand shares of which were to be held and 679 of which were to be sold for cash "at not less than $35 a share," Gower Street 11/27/28 minutes, JPKP. Currier sold his 37,500 shares at $35 that November, making the profit of almost $1 million on his initial investment of a little under $400,000, U.S. Circuit Court of Appeals, First Circuit, October 1933.

231 *V,* 11/28/28; *FD,* 12/14/28; trailer and 12/14/28 sales convention, Derr to JPK, 12/11/24, JPKP; "excellent progress," Swanson, p. 371; flowers, Sullivan to Scollard, 12/24/28, JPKP.

231 "disappointed," Scollard to JPK, 12/3/28, JPKP.

231 JPK "retires," *NYT,* 12/6/28. "personal," *MPN,* 12/1/28; office, *V,* 12/12/28; *V,* 12/5/28; *V,* 12/19/28; *FD,* 12/9/28; "perseverance," numbers, and president, *FD,* 12/7/28. Pathé headquarters was located at 35 West 45th Street.

232 Loss, *FD*, 12/3/28.ss

232 *V*, 1/2/29; "important executives, *FD*, 12/31/28; "money maker," *V*, 12/5/28; millionaires, *V*, 1/23/29; "the fence" and "duplex," *V*, 1/2/29.

233 "were off," *FD*, 10/3/28; *Dallas News*, 6/13/28; Tunney, *FD*, 8/12/28; Mayer, *FD*, 12/15/28; "looking," Carson Thomson/CB.

233 death certificate, Los Angeles County records; Richard Thomson/CB; Joan Thomson/CB; "Fred Thomson," *LAT*, 12/27/28; *LAH*, 12/27/28; *FD*, 12/27/28; "idol of," *PP*, 3/29.

233 Valentino comparison, *EHMPW*, 12/31/28; funeral details, *LAT*, 12/29/28; *Herald World*, 1/5/29.

234 Beauchamp, *Without*, p. 237; Sullivan to Scollard, 1/2/29; "hopelessly" and "just about" Scollard to Sullivan, 3/5/29; contract, Scollard to Sullivan, 2/25/29; "it might," Sullivan to Scollard, 3/11/30, all JPKP.

235 Estate value, *LAT*, 1/16/29; lawsuit, *V*, 10/9/29; "always," Lasky, p. 12; "Frances was" Joan Thomson/CB; "If there," Richard Thomson/CB; Enchanted Hill had always been under Marion's name.

235 "We are," Sullivan to Scollard, 4/20/29, JPKP; "unless," Scollard to Sullivan, 4/24/29, JPKP; a penny per foot, Futter to Scollard, 9/26/29, JPKP; 2,200 pounds, Scollard to Sullivan, 5/9/29, JPKP. There were still some copies of Thomson's films in distribution in rural America and overseas, bringing in a small but steady cash flow. Today only one full film and portions of several others are known to exist. *Jesse James* and the other three Paramount films are all "lost."

## CHAPTER 20: "GILDING THE MANURE PILE"

237 JPK to Palm beach, *V*, 1/9/29; Oasis, *V*, 1/16/29; Broun and Swope, Henri, *V*, 1/23/29; Rose, *V*, 2/6/29; Breakers, arrival of Murdock and Casey, Dowling and Gorman, *V*, 1/16/29; "business affairs," *BHC*, 1/3/29.

237 Pathé in black, *V*, 1/9/29; "rapidly," *V*, 11/7/28.

238 Theaters and plans, *V*, 1/9/29; waiting list, *FD*, 8/5/28.

238 *V*, 1/9/29, 1/16/29, 1/23/29.

238 "inhumane," *V*, 11/14/28; "began" and "Everyone," Ivano, *MPM*, 4/29.

238 "Officer's" and bugle, *BCH*, 12/6/28; "I ask," *MPM*, 4/29; "I am" and "vanity," Beauchamp, *Without*, p. 172; firing cameraman, Koszarski, *Von*, pp. 241, 251; "photograph," Swanson/Kevin Brownlow.

239 "with" and "hold," Kobal, p. 16; LeBaron's assistant, *V*, 8/15/28; departure and assignment, *V*, 11/28/28; "hated," JPK to Henri, 3/13/29. Sarecky was hired as a production manager August 1, 1930, beginning at $400 a week. RKO agreement addendum, 10/18/28, JPKP.

239 "huge" and "under," *BHC*, 11/15/28; Western Costume Company to Sullivan, 12/7/28, GSA.

239 "Swanson's," Koszarski, p. 246; "imperfections" and "magician," memos re Stroheim 11/13/28, 11/14/28, GSA; "beyond," undated memo, GSA. For example, Stroheim insisted on calling in a chemist to check on the tar paper and smoke pots being used to create the convent "fire," causing hours of delay.

240 "a picture," Derr to JPK, 12/6/28, JPKP.

240 "slowly," "milestone," and "I wish," etc., Derr to JPK, 12/7/28.

241 Koszarski, p. 251; "special" and other quotes, Glazer to Derr, 12/10/28, GSA. Derr was impressed with the "gorgeous" work of the cinematographers Pollock and Ivano and, with Kennedy's approval, assigned Sullivan to put them both under contract for Pathé after the completion of *Queen Kelly*. He

wanted to move as quickly as possible to get Ivano signed at $225 a week because he had his own camera and because the "Cameraman's Organization" was close to imposing a $250-a-week minimum, Derr to JPK, 12/7/28, JPKP.

241 Derr to Brown, 12/4/28, JPKP; Brown to Derr, 12/6/28, JPKP; "German fire," Ramsaye to Derr, 12/4/28, JPKP.

241 "make the" and "we find," Bern to Derr, cc Goulding, 12/7/28, JPKP.

242 "very," Derr to Webb, 12/6/28, JPKP; "every," Kane to Derr, 12/8/28, JPKP.

242 Powers extension, Scollard to Derr, 11/22/28; Stroheim sound, Sullivan to Derr, 8/13/28; Byron situation, Derr to Moore, 12/3/28, all JPKP.

242 "FINAL," Scollard to Derr, 11/22/28; Derr to Scollard, 11/26/28; Scollard to Derr, 10/23/28, all JPKP.

242 Details of move, unsigned four-page memo dated 3/14/29, GSA. Swanson-Pathé agreement, undated annual report, GSA; retakes, Koszarski, *Man You Love to Hate,* p. 319.

243 "the most," Swanson, p. 372; Lasky, p. 57. The man who discovered the "primitive bugging device" was Russell Birdwell, the publicist for *Gone With the Wind,* who had spearheaded the nationwide search for Scarlett O'Hara. Ten weeks, *V,* 10/24/28; assistant director's reports, JPKP.

243 meeting, Koszarski, *Von,* p. 251; Swanson, p. 372.

243 Various script portions and story summary, dated 9/23/28, JPKP; copyrighted *Queen Kelly* treatment, 11/23/28.

244 "much over" and "the barest essentials," Glazer to Derr, 12/10/28, GSA; "someday" and "satisfactorily," Derr to Sullivan, 10/8/29, JPKP; Glazer to Stroheim, 1/3/30. This letter is a confirmation of their conversation with Glazer promising to back up the director if Kennedy fails to follow through on his promise, Stroheim Collection, AMPAS. Derr remembered that the cuts included the repulsive Jan, as an owner of mines and "a power in the jungle," teaching Kelly to shoot after they moved to their house on stilts in the swamp. He leaves her alone to visit his mines and "the black natives, having seen this beautiful white girl, 'rushed' the house and started to climb in all windows and Kelly started to drop them with bullets." The Prince rescues her, Jan returns and jumps to the conclusion they are lovers. When they try to escape, Jan "tied them both to a pole in the swamp and hung a lantern to attract the tsetse flies that would bite and poison them to death. Just then it seems that the Prince's adjunct missed the Prince and came on the scene just in time to save their lives and kill Jan or something like that." Derr to Sullivan, 10/8/29, JPKP.

In Stroheim's personal papers, there is a thirty-page treatment for a separate silent film using some of those rejected elements. This version opens at the African brothel bar run by a beautiful but mercenary virgin known as "Kitty Cold Cash Lady Kelly." She accepts the proposal of marriage from Jann (this time with two n's), the richest man in the area, and he takes her to his hundred-acre swamp so that no one else will even be able to look at his wife. Upon their arrival, he is bitten by a tsetse fly that results in a lingering sleeping sickness making him "helpless from the waist down," ensuring his wife's continued virginity. Once again, there are the "sailors of all nations" and "nigger servants," but when two years have passed and "Count Wolfram" arrives on the scene, having been "banished to darkest Africa," he and Kelly have never met before. Sparks fly and soon Kelly and her Count are planning their escape. They are caught in the monsoon and assume they will meet their deaths tied together on a tree stump, once again regaled with orchids and surrounded by crocodiles and once again they are miraculously rescued. However, in this version, Jann dies peacefully in his wheelchair instead of being swallowed by the swamp and instead of a grand coronation, Kelly and her Count end the film by departing Africa on "a German gun boat which brings them to safety and the promise of marriage and happiness." Stroheim Collection, AMPAS.

244　Beauchamp, *Without,* pp. 109, 216; Marx, p. 112.

245　Story done and twenty-five tests a week, *V,* 12/12/28; production schedule, Price Waterhouse report, 2/21/31, JPKP; molding half the films, Wycoff response to Price Waterhouse, undated, 1931, JPKP. One of Goulding's discoveries from the sound tests was Carole Lombard, *FD,* 12/17/28.

245　Goulding script, *V,* 1/23/29, *FD,* 1/25/29; Eugene Walter, *V,* 10/1/41; "very blasphemous," Swanson/Brownlow; "without prejudice," Walter memo, 1/23/29, GSA; "novice's," Swanson, p. 347.

245　"utterly" and "Something," Swanson, p. 372.

246　"nauseated," and "was *Rebecca,*" Swanson, p. 373. Paul Ivano confirms Gloria's version of the story. Swanson's words eerily echoed Mae Murray's to Irving Thalberg several years before from the set of *The Merry Widow*: "That madman is making a filthy picture." Bob Thomas, p. 81. A much more sedate Tully Marshall can be seen as one of the professors in the Gary Cooper–Barbara Stanwyck film *Ball of Fire.*

246　"a controversy," *FD,* 1/25/29; "objective" and first thirty reels, Walter memo, 1/23/29, JPKP and GSA; "walking," Swanson/Kevin Brownlow.

247　"The director," Walter memo, 1/23/29, JPKP and GSA; Derr to Moore, 1/25/29, JPKP.

247　"criminally," Derr to Moore, 1/25/29, JPKP; *Queen Kelly* production cost sheet, 12/28/28, GSA; Sullivan to Derr, 9/12/28, JPKP.

247　"quite belligerent," Derr to Moore, 1/25/29, JPKP.

248　"finishing," *V,* 2/6/29; "quite heated," *V,* 1/30/29.

248　JPK arrives in LA, *FD,* 2/7/29; Pantages, *FD,* 2/7/29; sound company, *FD,* 2/4/29; *FD,* 2/8/29, 2/10/29, 2/15/29, 2/18/29; "front page," *FD,* 2/21/29.

248　"the proper," *V,* 7/26/50; "with soap," Walter memo, 1/23/29, JPKP and GSA.

250　"a range," *BHC,* 9/9/28; "cursing" and other quotes, Swanson, pp. 373–74.

250　"found Gloria," JPK to Marquis, 3/13/29, JPKP.

250　"didn't want," Swanson, p. 374; nomination, Frank Woods to Swanson, 2/19/29, GSA; ten best, *FD,* 2/1/29.

251　Lasky meeting and "drastic," JPK to Marquis, 3/13/29, JPKP. In her autobiography, Gloria presents herself as sympathetic to Kennedy's plight, but letters of the day in both her and Kennedy's papers show otherwise.

251　*Iron Mask,* Brownlow/CB.

251　"millions," ad, *FD,* 2/28/29; UA promotion, Scollard to Derr, 2/1/29, JPKP; reorganization, JPK to Marquis, 3/13/29, JPKP.

251　Cost of *Queen Kelly* to date at "better than $850,000," *V,* 3/6/29; production account summary, 12/28/29, GSA.

251　Swanson, p. 374; "pronto," *V,* 1/23/29; Marshall's salary from Gloria Productions was $1,000 a week, Gloria Productions to MGM, 1/24/29, GSA.

252　"beyond," Walter memo, 4/23/29, JPKP and GSA; "repulsive," "but not," and storyline, Derr to Moore, 1/25/29, JPKP.

252　Other directors, Matthew Kennedy, p. 78.

252　Goulding assigned to write story, 2/25/29, Sistrom memo, 3/8/29, JPKP; writing new story, *V,* 3/6/29.

253 "It is so," *Film Weekly,* 2/25/29, quoted in Noble, p. 77.

253 "the one pure," Paris, p. 375; "every scene," Kevin Brownlow/CB; "entirely," etc., Noble, pp. 75, 79. At different points, Stroheim defined "the first part" of the film as either a third or a quarter of what he envisioned.

253 Fitzgibbon, *V,* 8/28/29; Ford, *V,* 2/27/29; all staying, *V,* 12/5/28; Glazer head, *FD,* 12/14/28; Bern for sound, *FD,* 12/30/28; "he was supposed," *V,* 3/13/29; *FD,* 3/8/29; Edington, "whole heartedly," LeBaron to JPK, 9/25/28; "long vacation," *FD,* 2/19/29; Derr was not alone in his opinion of Edington. According to Kevin Brownlow, the director Clarence Brown said "Harry Edington was the biggest crook in the business," a rather remarkable claim given the competition for the title. Poole, *V,* 2/27/29; Brown to Europe and "corral," *V,* 2/27/29. Bern returned to MGM and went on to mentor and marry Jean Harlow. Bern's death, a reported suicide, is one of the great Hollywood mysteries and the subject of several books. Colvin Brown would leave Pathé in August of 1929 and was soon head of production for Fine Arts Productions, filming grand operas, *V,* 8/14/29, 10/2/29.

254 Sound postponed at RKO, *V,* 3/6/29; horses, *V,* 1/9/29; voice commands, *BHC,* 5/15/30; "retired," *V,* 1/16/29. Fred Thomson's Silver King and all of their other horses were sold when Frances sold Enchanted Hill in March 1929. Silver King appeared on screen again in 1934 in independently produced westerns starring Wally Wales; Wyatt, p. 110.

254 MGM buyout, *FD,* 2/28/29; Justice Department, *FD,* 2/3/29; Mayer at White House, Marx, p. 113. Thalberg and Mayer held only a minority interest in MGM.

255 "an excellent," yearly summary of Pathé activity, undated, GSA; "adapted" and "scheduled," Lance Heath cable, 3/6/29, GSA.

255 weight and mood, JPK to Marquis, 3/13/29, JPKP; March 7 departure, *V,* 3/13/29, Sullivan to Derr, 3/11/29, JPKP.

CHAPTER 21: "GIVE OUR LOVE TO GLORIA"

256 Vocal lessons, *V,* 3/20/29; new script, Glazer collection, UCLA; $200,000 and schedule, Sistrom to Derr, 3/29/29, JPKP.

256 JPK to Henri, 4/15/29, JPKP; end-of-the-year summary of Pathé activity, undated, GSA; sixteen crates, Scollard to Sullivan, 11/4/29 and 11/5/29, JPK; "scrap," *V,* 4/24/29.

257 Goulding, *V,* 1/23/29; "new," *FD,* 7/1/28; *V,* 3/6/29, 3/13/29; "make them," Matthew Kennedy, p. 92; *V,* 2/6/29; "no one," Swanson, p. 381. Laura Hope Crews was a prominent character actress, remembered today primarily for her roles in Garbo's *Camille* and as Aunt Pittypat in *Gone With the Wind.* For over six months, plans had been in the works for Gloria's next film to be *Clothes.* Glazer, along with other writers including Goulding, had been working on the script, but now Swanson wanted nothing to do with it; LeBaron to JPK, 9/25/28. They sold the rights to *Clothes* the next year, Sullivan to Scollard, 6/26/29, GSA.

257 "There was," Kobal, p. 11; Swanson/Kevin Brownlow; "the duration," Swanson, p. 381.

257 "One minute," Swanson, p. 381; telegrams, Goulding papers, AFI; Matthew Kennedy, p. 79. Movie magazine pieces on Goulding reported that he had single-handedly created the 188-page scenario; *The Picturegoer,* 10/29, vol 18, no 106. Gloria, on the other hand, would later say it was because of Eddie's "funny kind of pride" that she allowed him to receive sole story credit. This was while she was claiming she had directed scenes and handled all the edit-

ing of *Sadie Thompson,* Kobal, p. 12; Swanson/Kevin Brownlow. The script was also massaged by the writer Ernest Pascal who would go on to serve as president of the Screen Writers Guild from 1935 through 1937; *V,* 11/9/66.

258 *V,* 9/18/29, 8/18/29. The credits of *The Trespasser* read "Costumes executed by Judge Johnson." Film viewed at Eastman House, November 2005.

258 "a giant," Beauchamp, *Without,* p. 271; "Mr. Gable," Swanson, p. 384.

258 "unanimous" and "not easy," Lichtman to JPK, 6/15/29, JPKP; JPK handwritten response, undated, JPKP.

258 "we both," JPK to Swanson, 5/17/29, Pathé Collection, AMPAS; Pathé contract, 4/1/29, JPKP.

260 Anable/CB; "Joe's all right," Whalen, p. 99.

260 *FD,* 12/5/28. Anable/CB.

260 Currier's work and contacts, Derr to JPK, 1/18/30, JPKP; "calling" and "On January," agreements, assignments dated April, and letter of agreement, 5/6/29, all JPKP.

261 P.J. hospitalized, *V,* 4/10/29; "dragging on," JPK to Henri, 4/15/29, JPKP; "a sea," DKG, p. 411; "a source," Rose Kennedy, p. 191.

261 *BG,* 5/21/29; undated articles from *Boston Globe* and *Boston Post,* JPKP; Allan Goodrich/CB. Aside from life insurance, P. J. Kennedy's estate was reportedly valued at $55,000, Whalen, p. 104. JPK paid the $450 funeral home bill, JPKP.

261 Multiple cables, e.g., JPK to Schenck, 5/23/29, JPKP.

261 "I was," JPK to JPK Jr., 6/3/29, JPKP.

261 "make a," *V,* 5/22/29.

261 Berkman, pp. 101–2; assistant director's daily reports, JPKP; Coward, photos, GSA.

262 Goulding to Novello, 6/18/29, GSA. Novello is portrayed by Jeremy Northam in Robert Altman's *Gosford Park*; whistling tune, Swanson/Kevin Brownlow.

263 "Joe wants," etc., Goulding to JPK, 9/12/51, GSA; Scollard to Sullivan, 8/8/29, JPKP.

263 Sullivan return, *V,* 6/26/29; back to coast, Scollard to Wakoff, 7/29/29; business head, *V,* 7/31/29; Quirk, Sullivan to Scollard, 9/4/29; "preferred," Derr to Sistrom, 7/29/29; Hearst, Scollard to Sullivan, 9/5/29, all JPKP.

263 Multiple cables, e.g., Scollard to Sullivan, 6/7/28, 6/11/29, JPKP.

263 Heath to Derr, 6/7/29, and multiple other cables through August, JPKP; trailer, Scollard to Chanier, 9/10/29, JPKP.

264 Measuring, Derr to Moore, 6/24/29, JPKP; Cour to Poppe, undated, JPKP.

264 Cour to Poppe, undated; "out of service," Cour to Ramsaye, 6/11/29; engineer problems, Cour to Derr, 6/22/29, all JPKP.

264 Ramsaye to Derr, 6/24/29; "extraordinary," Cour to Ramsaye, 6/11/29; Derr to Sistrom 7/2/29, all JPKP. It was also Derr, who was in New York in late June and July double-checking the final reels, who noticed that Gloria's name in the credits was several feet shorter than other names and had that corrected, Derr to Sistrom, 8/16/29, JPKP.

265 Swanson, p. 384; sets record, *V,* 6/26/29; $725,000, Sullivan to Scollard, 8/29/29, JPKP; July 5 wrap, Lalley to Malone, 4/11/31, JPKP; "executive," Scollard to Sullivan, 10/10/29, GSA. Sullivan and Scollard were careful in preparing the final cost statements knowing they "will be audited." As per UA's distribution deal, 27.5 percent was added to the cost. Kennedy's expenses, multiple cables, i.e., five weeks in early 1929 came to $5,347.89. Tambert to Sullivan, 3/25/29, Pathé Collection, AMPAS.

265 *V,* 7/3/29; "as virile," *EHW,* 7/6/29.

265 Sylvia, pp. 121–23. Invoices, Wycoff to Fox, 8/16/30, show that massages were billed to respective departments and films. Over the course of a year, Gloria was billed $6,190.80 for massages, Pathé Collection, AMPAS.

266 Claire and Harding, *EHW,* 7/6/29; "beautiful" and "showed up," Swanson, p. 381. When Constance arrived back in the States in the early summer of 1929, she brought with her a five-month-old son, Peter Bennett Plant. According to her sister, Joan Bennett, Constance identified the child to the press as her niece, Joan's daughter, who was a year and a half at that time. Many accounts say Peter was adopted, others claim he was the birth child of Constance and Plant, Bennett, p. 205.

266 JPK to Marquis, 3/13/29 and 4/15/29, JPKP; Bennett contract signed 4/5/29, Pathé board minutes, 1/13/31, Sindell Collection. Bennett was initially signed for $1,000 a week for forty weeks a year. Pathé Collection, AMPAS.

267 "laconic," Swanson, p. 401; Dufty/CB.

267 Sylvia, pp. 136–37.

268 "It pictured," Amon/CB; multiple cables, "give," Ward to JPK, 4/4/30, JPKP; "remember," Rothschild to JPK, 3/12/30, Pathé Collection, AMPAS.

268 Dufty/CB; Swanson, pp. 359–60; child known as Joseph Swanson, *BHC,* 2/16/28, 8/08/29; Wakoff to JPK, 7/22/29, GSA.

268 "You have to," Dufty/CB; Murdock home tour courtesy of the current owners. At the time, Murdock's address was 714 Foothill, but the numbers changed later as more homes were added to the block, JPK to Murdock, 12/9/30, JPKP.

270 "got a picture," Merian C. Cooper/Kevin Brownlow; tour courtesy of current owner.

270 "always a gentleman," Schulberg/CB; "a brilliant," Sternberg, p. 37.

270 Guiles, pp. 189–90.

271 "one of," *NYT,* 6/6/29. Six staff, Ellenberger, p. 139.

271 Two months, *V,* 6/12/29; *EHW,* 7/6/29; "all dialogue," *FD,* 3/15/29. Almost all the features would be released in a silent version to fulfill the needs of smaller theaters still waiting to be wired for sound.

CHAPTER 22: "HAVING TEA WITH HIS WIFE AND MY HUSBAND AND THE VICAR"

272 "if this," JPK to Swanson, 5/17/29, GSA.

272 JPK to Sistrom, 7/19/29; Rialto, *Picturegoer,* 10/29; Schenk, JPK to Schenck, 7/19/29, JPKP. Exhibition was one of the major problems UA was facing; where major studios owned or had access to hundreds of theaters, UA was largely dependent on "a hodgepodge of independent theater owners," Mashon, p. 3.

272 "the most," 7/9/29, unsigned dictation of meetings, JPKP.

273 "Joe," etc., Swanson, pp. 385–86. Goulding not going to Europe for the premiere, Scollard to Sullivan, 8/8/29, JPKP.

273 Scollard's initial requests were to just run some of the soundtrack from the film over the radio, but he was turned down. E. E. Bucher, RCA's executive vice president, refused to put in writing why he wanted nothing to do with a Kennedy film, but Gloria in person on the radio was too good to pass up. Scollard to RCA, 8/7/29, JPKP; Bucher to Scollard, 8/8/29, JPKP; RCA recording on Victor records, *V,* 7/17/29; RCA/Victor, *FD,* 1/6/29.

273 *NYT,* 8/18/29; *Hyannis Patriot,* 8/8/29.

273 *Olympic,* August 10, *V,* 7/17/29; *V,* 7/31/29; "deluxe," Wakoff to JPK, 7/22/29, GSA; *V,* 10/2/29; various cables, GSA.

274 Swanson, p. 389; various cables, GSA; Gloria to arrive on August 15, JPK to Kelly, 8/14/29, JPKP.

274 "a home appearance" *V,* 7/24/29; "First World Premiere," *V,* 9/4/29; JPK to GS, 8/16/29, GSA; according to JPK to Kelly, 8/14/29, JPK to arrive on 26th, cable, JPKP; traffic and singing, *V,* 9/25/29; "tea party," *NYT,* 9/14/29.

274 "a sensational" and "the near riot," *V,* 9/11/29; *V,* 9/12/29, 9/25/29; "the best," *V,* 10/2/29; "I thought," *NYT,* 9/13/29; "so proud," Swanson, p. 388. *Variety* noted that *"The Trespasser* shows definite swing away from filmed stage play and develops motion picture techniques in sound film presentation to a point not previously put on the screen," 10/2/29.

275 "enormous," *NYT,* 9/13/29; "Gloria Swanson has," quoted in *NYT* and cable, Nolan to Goulding, 9/11/29, GSA; "personal" and "even," *NYT,* 9/13/29; "like a prima," *V,* 9/18/29; REFK bills, JPKP; Derr to JPK, 8/31/29, JPKP; Kane to JPK, 9/25/29, JPKP; *V,* 3/26/30. They had originally hoped to open in Paris and Berlin as well, but only one synchronized print was able to make it across the ocean so they opened in London and promoted it elsewhere during their trip, JPK to Swanson, 8/16/29, GSA.

275 Cable, *V,* 10/2/29; Bennett's plans, *V,* 9/18/29; "Cold" and "devoted," Rose Kennedy, pp. 188–89; travel plans, *V,* 9/25/29.

276 Sailing, *V,* 9/18/29; "remained," JPK to Marquis, 10/2/29, JPKP; "tired" DKG, p. 416; "Joe," Swanson, p. 387; "like," Swanson, p. 386; "poor," DKG, p. 416. Dufty/CB. *Swanson on Swanson* was published in 1980.

276 "Obviously," Rose Kennedy, p. 186; "reporters," DKG, p. 416.

276 "strange," DKG/Whitehead; "It is," DKG, p. 395; "better perhaps," DKG, p. 396; "one of," AJH to JPK, 12/13/44; "often wondered," Hopper, *From Under,* p. 168.

277 "If she," Swanson, p. 387.

277 Schedule, *V,* 9/25/29; "an important," etc., Swanson, pp. 393–95.

278 "threatened," Maier, p. 101; "he found," Maier, p. 104.

278 "himself," DKG, p. 417.

278 "What," Swanson, p. 366; Dufty/CB.

279 "simply marry," DKG, p. 396; "ordered," Hopper, *From Under,* p. 168.

279 "not one," Goodrich/CB; "going strong," unsigned handwritten letter to JPK from London, 10/4/29; a Heath cable quotes reviews, Swanson, p. 391.

279 Release plans, *V,* 9/18/29; *V,* 9/25/29; *NYT,* 9/29/1929; JPK to Marquis, 10/2/29, JPKP.

280 Thomas and Witts, pp. 220–23; "bore," Chernow, p. 259; "Only," Whalen, p. 104; Morgan and Currier, DKG, p. 420. "a business," Currier to Kirstein, 4/1/29, Kirstein Papers/Baker Library. Prince was later credited with forecasting the crash and he survived with over $250 million intact, going on to pick up even more companies at rock-bottom prices in the early 1930s; *NYT,* 2/3/53.

280 bonds, DKG, p. 420; Pathé sales summary, JPKP, and multiple files, JPKP. The accounts show at least a $579,000 profit just from his Pathé stock.

280 $10 billion, Thomas and Witts, p. 399; *V,* 10/31/29; "The crash" JPK to Keating, 11/1/29, JPKP; Furman to JPK, 11/8/29, JPKP; "Read 'em," Chernow, p. 318; radio, *V,* 10/2/29. Kennedy being untouched by the crash was verified by his son Jack, who told the reporter Hugh Sidey, "We lived better than ever. We had bigger houses, more servants. I learned about the Depression at Harvard—from reading," Hersh, p. 33.

281   Invitations and letters, JPKP; "even" and "gifted," *NYT,* 11/2/29; *V,*
      10/2/29; JPK to Barutio, 11/4/29, JPKP; Chicago opening, JPK to Burke,
      11/4/29, JPKP. Chicago-based friends were invited, including Eugene
      Thayer, who was now with Central Trust of Illinois. The film grossed
      $70,000 its first week at New York's Rialto, besting previous record by
      $12,000, cables sent to twenty-five branch managers, 11/9/29, JPKP.
282   "this picture," sample cables, JPKP; "a lot," e.g., JPK to Richards, 11/4/29,
      JPKP; "really," JPK to Brennan, 10/22/20, JPKP.
282   JPK to Keating, 11/1/29, JPKP. *The Trespasser* had easily passed through
      most states' censorship boards; Ohio and Massachusetts were notoriously
      picky and the film sailed through both states and only one scene had to be
      changed for Pennsylvania; various letters, *Trespasser* files, JPKP; Scollard to
      Chanier, 10/8/29.
283   "a rift," *V,* 10/2/29; "behave," JFK to Henri, 10/2/29, JPKP; "constantly," *V,*
      12/4/29.
283   "the short," *V,* 12/4/29.
283   *V,* 11/6/29; "peevish" and "generally," Goulding to JPK, 9/12/51, Goulding
      Papers, AFI.
283   "I watched," Matthew Kennedy, p. 90; "of the work," JPK to Burke,
      11/4/29, JPKP; "excellent," Delehanty to Derr, 12/20/29, Pathé Collection,
      AMPAS. *The Grand Parade* was based on "the original minstrel play" by
      Howard Emmett Rogers and was directed by Fred Newmeyer, *EHW,* 7/6/29.
      Martha Lorah, Frances Marion's secretary, remembers a train trip to New
      York with Gloria and her secretary and being made to feel terribly uncom-
      fortable by the way Gloria treated her employee, especially when compared
      with the way Frances treated Martha, as a friend and a secretary. Lorah/CB.
284   Pathé cost sheets, JPKP; *Trespasser* agreement, 7/20/29, to Gloria Produc-
      tions, which was then billed by Pathé for reimbursement for Goulding's
      salary, JPKP; "It's the," "a personal," and other quotes, Berkman, pp. 101–3.
284   "his savior," Matthew Kennedy, p. 78; Still, Goulding's feelings about Joe
      had always been mixed. While Goulding told Kennedy to his face that he
      was inspired by the "overall picture of family and strength" Joe presented and
      that he was "stimulated and fascinated" by him, behind his back he later
      called Kennedy a "chicken hawk" who went after any young female who
      crossed his path. "Overall," Goulding to JPK, 9/12/51, Goulding Papers,
      AFI; "chicken hawk," *Blondie of the Follies* production files, USC. "You have,"
      Berkman, p. 103.
285   "beyond," Goulding to JPK, 9/12/51, Goulding Papers, AFI.
285   *V,* 10/2/29; "his individuality," *V,* 12/4/29; "To hell," Goulding to JPK,
      9/12/51, Goulding Papers, AFI; Goulding walks, *V,* 12/4/29. It wasn't until
      much later that Goulding realized neither he nor Elsie Janis had collected a
      penny from the music they had written for *The Trespasser.* When he investi-
      gated, he found that the rights were owned by Gloria Productions; he
      assumed that meant Gloria. Kennedy denied knowing that Goulding and
      Janis had not profited and Goulding believed him, again assuming that
      meant Gloria had benefited. But Gloria's own papers verify that she had not
      collected from the song either while JPK's records show he continued to col-
      lect royalties on the song for years. Jesse Lasky wouldn't take Goulding on
      until he received Kennedy's assurance that he had been released, but said "we
      need him pretty badly," Derr to JPK, 12/19/29, JPKP. The script Eddie
      Goulding had written for Gloria, *The Devil's Holiday,* might have sounded
      parochial and a bit similar to *The Trespasser,* but Nancy Carroll played the role
      and earned an Academy Award nomination for her efforts.

CHAPTER 23: "THINGS ARE BAD ENOUGH HERE"

286 O'Leary to JPK, multiple cables, JPKP; Wilkerson to JPK, 12/13/29; ads and hours of screenings, *NYT,* 11/1/29.

286 "a couple," *V,* 7/24/29; Scollard to Sullivan, 11/4/29, 11/5/29; new actual cost, Sullivan to JPK, 8/8/29; dealing with Stroheim, Derr to Sullivan, 10/8/29; African shots, Scollard to Sullivan, 9/25/29, all JPKP.

286 Byron available, Sullivan to Scollard, 10/5/29, JPKP. Byron's salary was to increase from $300 a week to $800; undated summary memo of Pathé/Gloria Productions for 1929, GSA; *V,* 12/4/29; Sullivan to Owen, 12/12/29, GSA; Sullivan to Dunphy, 2/17/30, GSA.

287 *V,* 10/30/29; sets, Tambert to Scollard, 11/1/29, JPKP; *V,* 12/11/29; *V,* 1/20/37; *EHW,* 7/6/29. Boleslawsky had "staged ensemble scenes" for Max Reinhardt on *The Miracle* and would later direct Garbo in *The Painted Veil* and Dietrich in *The Garden of Allah.* Dietrich was quoted as telling Joshua Logan that Boleslawsky was "a terrible man. He's Wussian. No sensitivity. He can't diwect women." Bach, p. 215. Thackrey, in her book, *Member of the Crew,* paints a very different picture. Boleslawsky died suddenly at the age of forty-seven, leaving his wife, the pianist Norma Drury, who can be seen in films such as *Stage Door,* and a two-year-old son. He died while in the middle of directing *The Last of Mrs. Cheyney* starring Joan Crawford, the film Schenck had wanted Gloria to make before she bolted to join Kennedy. His name also appeared as Boleslavsky in some credits and his reported birth name was Boleslaw Ryszard Szrednicki.

287 $60,000 more had been allocated for sound equipment for the Culver City studio at the May 28, 1929, board meeting, Pathé minutes, Sindell Collection; history of building, *NYT,* 12/11/29; the lease was for $1,100 a month, Pathé board minutes, 8/15/29, Sindell Collection; film a week, *V,* 11/20/29.

287 Delmar, Flinn, *NYT,* 12/18/29; *The Black and White Revue* would later be refilmed and released as *Sixteen Sweeties.*

288 "spit a glowing," *NYT,* 12/11/29; day before, *NYT,* 3/21/30.

288 "technical," *NYT,* 12/11/29; "a sleepless week" *V,* 12/18/29.

288 "constant touch," *V,* 12/18/29; "conspicuously" and "with respect," Ramsaye to Derr, 12/14/29, Pathé Collection, AMPAS; *NYT,* 12/11/30.

289 Hearst and Hays, *V,* 12/11/29; "savage," *V,* 12/18/29; Fitzgibbon, *NYT,* 3/14/30; Croker, *NYT,* 3/13/30. At the time of the fire, the current owner of the building was Stephen H. Jackson of 106 Lexington Avenue, *NYT,* 3/12/20, Pathé documents, JPKP.

290 "because of," Mashon, p. 97; "some 'slap-stick,'" O'Leary to Swanson, 12/23/29, GSA; "a gypsy curse" and "musical," JPK to Henri, 12/14/29, JPKP; "Queen Kelly Waltz," Lehár contract, 12/27/29, GSA. Lehár was sent a copy of the current script and was to receive half the money on signing, the other half when the waltz was delivered on or before March 1, 1930. Gloria Productions and Lehár were to split any profits from the music.

290 "a little" and "it was," Boleslawsky to JPK, 12/19/29, Glazer Collection, UCLA.

290 "feeling," Boleslawsky to JPK, 12/19/29, Glazer Collection, UCLA; Crews to Wood, Scollard to Sullivan, 10/9/29, JPKP; "a personal," JPK to Thalberg in cable text, Sullivan to Scollard, 12/18/29, JPKP; "the coast," Scollard to Sullivan, 12/18/29, Derr to JPK, 1/8/30, Pathé Collection, AMPAS; Derr to JPK 1/30/30, JPKP.

291 "I can't," Koszarski, *Von,* p. 256.

291 Little Gloria's strep, JPK to Henri, 10/2/29; Joseph at Good Samaritan,

*BHC,* 12/19/29; "a large," Crossman to Swanson, 12/26/29, GSA; JPK to O'Leary 12/11/29, JPKP; O'Leary to Swanson, 12/23/29, GSA.

291 Scollard to Sullivan, 5/5/29, 12/27/29, JPKP; Sullivan to Scollard, 12/31/28; gifts to Rose, e.g., JPK to O'Leary, 12/11/29, JPKP; Scollard to Moore, 4/4/28, JPKP.

292 Lombard/Goulding, *V,* 11/21/28; "reduces" and "make fewer," *V,* 12/4/29; Rose to Palm Beach housing memo, 2/15/33, JPKP; "discussed," Pathé board minutes, 1/6/30, Sindell Collection; "technical," *V,* 12/18/29. The Pathé board eventually set aside a $50,000 fund assuming the need to cover personal property damage claims and legal fees, Pathé minutes, 4/8/30, AMPAS.

293 "various," JPK to Marquis, 12/14/29; "Things," JPK to Kane, 12/30/29, JPKP. Kane reported that RCA, whose equipment was sent at Pathé expense to France, "absolutely refuses to help" with the inevitable engineering and equipment problems. The demand for pictures in foreign languages was "even greater than anticipated," they just kept running into trouble producing them, Kane to JPK, 11/23/29, JPKP.

293 "trouble," JPK to Kane, 12/30/29, JPKP; "the whole," Scollard to Derr, 2/3/30, AMPAS. Barney Fox, Pathé's auditor, had been sent to Paris to join Bob Kane and Steve Fitzgibbon and was busy sending sycophantic reports to Scollard and others. Fox to Scollard, undated early 1930, AMPAS; Ritz-Carlton, JPK letter, 1/8/30, JPKP; Hyannisport, JPK cable, 1/18/30, JPKP.

293 Looker draft, 5/37.

294 "Well, no one," Schlesinger, *Journals,* p. 150.

294 Smoking, Whalen, p. 99; Swanson, pp. 379–80.

294 Derr, *V,* 2/5/30, 2/12/30; Bennett, *FD,* 2/12/30.

295 Walker and Giannini, *NYT,* 5/30/29, 1/21/30, 5/6/30; Walker's visit, *V,* 3/5/30. Bankamerica-Blair was now the securities affiliate of Bank America James and James, p. 297. "always given," Brooks to Brown, 9/26/30, JPKP; Murdock, *V,* 12/10/48. Murdock would live another nineteen years and became an active philanthropist, establishing the Murdock Research Laboratories and Clinics in New York to promote cancer research, *MPH,* 12/18/48. During Walker's California visit, Ed Albee died at the Breakers in Palm Beach. *V,* 3/11/30.

296 Pantages reputation, *V,* 11/20/29, "a decided," *V,* 2/19/36.

296 Films, *FD,* 7/28/27; JPK to Casey, 4/18/28, JPKP.

296 "practically," *FD,* 3/25/29; and "the circuit," *FD,* 2/18/29; price tag, *FD,* 3/31/29.

296 Offers, *FD,* 3/25/29; *V,* 4/3/29, 4/17/29, 5/8/29, 5/15/29, 5/29/29; *NYT,* 6/7/29; "a very nasty mess," *V,* 8/14/29.

297 *V,* 8/14/29. Pantages's wife was at that very moment in court herself, charged with manslaughter after causing an accident where she was driving and a man in another car had died. She was found guilty and received ten years' probation and was not to "touch intoxicating liquor or drive her car" during that time; *V,* 11/13/29.

297 "no financial," *V,* 10/9/29, 10/16/29, 10/23/29; sentence, *V,* 11/13/29; medical, *V,* 1/1/30; acquitted, *LAT,* 6/16/02. Pantages would live until 1936.

298 "deathbed," "suspicious," and "It had," *LAT,* 6/16/2002; "violently" and "did," Kessler, p. 59.

298 Marcy Worthington/CB. Pringle's daughter grew up not knowing of her mother's past. She remembers when she was a young teenager and interested in singing, her father told her that her mother had once been raped by a pro-

ducer, but Marcy always assumed he was just trying to keep her off the stage. It wasn't until a few years ago that Marcy learned her mother had been featured in headlines, at times garnering more coverage than the stock market collapse, and is now working on a book to tell the full story.

298 "a golf story," JPK to Derr, 11/2/29, Pathé Collection, AMPAS; *Purple and Linen, V,* 4/2/30; purchased from May Edginton for $5,500, Pathé minutes, 5/27/30, AMPAS. *Purple and Linen* is credited as the source of *Adventure in Manhattan,* Columbia, 1936; "it was," Swanson, pp. 399-400; Seymour contract, *V,* 2/5/30. Seymour would go to Warner Bros. the next year and was eventually credited as a writer on dozens of films including *42nd Street* and *Gold Diggers of 1933.*

299 "assumed," *FD,* 2/12/30; "will not be resumed" and "scrapped," *V,* 3/12/30; "too much," *FD,* 3/12/30; *V,* 3/12/30, 3/19/30, 3/26/30. *What a Widow* payroll began on January 4, 1930.

299 Departure, *V,* 4/16/30; suitcase, Moore to Derr, 4/11/30, Pathé Collection, AMPAS. The Rodeo Drive house lease expired in June.

CHAPTER 24: "A GOOD TRICK IF YOU CAN DO IT"

300 The Pathé release is dated May 12, 1930, but reports reading verbatim were printed as early as 5/5/30, JPKP, Pathé collection, AMPAS, e.g., *NYT,* 5/8/30.

300 "show" and "invitations," *V,* 1/2/29; "miraculous," *V,* 5/7/30; expenses, *V,* 5/7/30, and *BP,* undated, and *Boston Traveler,* 5/9/30, "Lon Chaney," 1930 article, JPKP; *V,* 4/30/30; "loyal," JPK to Silverman, 5/7/30, JPKP.

301 "an extended," JPK office to Simmons, 5/14/30, JPKP; *V,* 6/2/30.

301 *V,* 5/28/30, 6/11/30.

301 "bound back," *EDR,* 5/27/30. The Pathé board had sought an extension on the DuPont stock options held by one E. I. DuPont DeNemoure. The request dragged out for several months and when their note was called, they formed the Pathé Investment Company, buying the shares with money borrowed from Pathé Sound Company and repayable at 6 percent interest. Board minutes of 6/3/30, 7/23/30, 7/30/30, 7/31/30, Pathé Collection, AMPAS. Another name prominently mentioned with the dissidents was Charles Rogers, an independent film producer who had first approached Kennedy about taking over First National.

301 Ads, e.g., *New York Evening Post,* 5/26/30; Rowland et al., 70 percent, *V,* 6/4/30; The official Pathé request for proxies went out under the names of Kennedy, Pat Scollard, and Lewis Innerarity, the company secretary, board minutes, 3/31/30, AMPAS; Protective Committee to Stockholders, 5/23/30, AMPAS; *NYT,* 5/27/30; Innerarity to Stockholders, 5/26/39, AMPAS; "alleged," Scollard to Strombaugh, 5/27/30, all Pathé Collection, AMPAS; "disgruntled," *V,* 6/11/30; *WSJ,* 6/7/30.

302 Armsby to De Mille, 6/6/30, De Mille to Armsby 6/6/30, DMC. Kennedy retains hold of Pathé, *V,* 6/4/30, *V,* 5/28/30, 6/11/30; Pathé minutes, 6/9/30, Sindell Collection. There were actually three slates of officers elected. The one in question was to represent the 8 percent preferred stockholders and the others were the Class A Stock and then the Common Stock.

302 "sorry," *V,* 6/11/30; Rossheim to JPK, 6/10/30, JPKP.

302 Pathé minutes, 6/11/30; untitled clip at AMPAS dated 6/30; news release, 6/16/30, all Pathé Collection, AMPAS. Delehanty was listed as general manager of Pathé.

303 The regular meetings of the Gower Street Company board of directors, which had been held as often as every few weeks since they formed it in 1927, had ended in November 1928 shortly after the sale of FBO. There is no record of Gower Street correspondence, open or closed, in the Kennedy files for all of 1929 except for one polite exchange of letters between the two men, JPKP. Assignment from Gower Street Company to JPK, April 1929, JPKP; undated DeWitt agreement, JPKP. According to the 1929 annual report in the state of Delaware records, Currier's secretary, Dorothy McKissick, was the treasurer, but that did not give her a vote.

303 *BG,* 6/22/30; *Boston Transcript,* 6/21/30; *BH,* 6/23/30; *NYT,* 6/23/30; Anable/CB. On November 28, 1930, papers were filed in Delaware amending the Gower Street original incorporation papers to expand the number of shares from 5,000 to 5,890, "all of which shares are to be without nominal or par value." Then a few weeks later, on December 17, 1930, the "unanimous consent to Dissolution of the Gower Street Company" was filed. The directors listed were the same for both filings: Lester Sweet of Dedham, Massachusetts, Warwick Harris of South Lincoln, and Dorothy McKissick of Cambridge. The company was the source of contention between the IRS and Currier's executors, the Old Colony Trust Company, in 1933. Several different hearings and court appeals were held to determine the rate of applicable tax. While at various times Kennedy had issues with the Internal Revenue Service, there are no records listed, open or closed, mentioning Gower Street as a tax problem for Kennedy. Certificate of Incorporation, 10/19/27, amendment certificate filed 11/28/30, and dissolution certificate, 12/17/30, DDC; U.S. Circuit Court of Appeals, 1st Circuit, 10/33.

304 Flights to Cape, *V,* 8/13/30; multiple correspondence re Fox, e.g., JPK from Blair, 8/29/30, JPKP; Pathé minutes, Pathé Collection, AMPAS.

304 *V,* 5/14/30; Dufty/CB; various memos, GSA, JPKP; e.g., Sullivan to Scollard, 2/27/30. Pat Scollard was still writing checks on Gloria Productions in November of 1930 when he sent $300 for an ad from Swanson in the *Variety* anniversary issue, Scollard to Silverman, 11/5/30, JPKP. Wakoff was listed as treasurer as early as May 5, 1930, and as vice president on August 16, 1930, JPKP. Gloria later claimed that one of the outrageous charges was for the car Kennedy reportedly gave Sidney Howard for coming up with the title *What a Widow.* There is no car on the extra invoices; however it may have been previously paid for and not disputed. Wakoff letter, Fox report, Wakoff response, JPKP, GSA, Swanson, p. 403.

305 "Gossip" and "not familiar," Tambert to Sullivan, 6/21/30, JPKP. *What a Widow* wrapped on 6/22/30, Kalley to Malone, 4/11/31, JPKP.

305 "good trick," Sullivan to Derr, 9/6/30, JPKP; "entirely," Sullivan to Tambert, 6/24/30, JPKP; "executive overhead," Scollard to Sullivan, 10/10/29, Pathé Collection, AMPAS.

305 "the studio" and "life saver," Sistrom/Price Waterhouse interview, 2/21/31, JPKP.

305 Scollard and Sullivan had looked at adding Ted O'Leary to the Gloria Productions payroll, but decided that since he was in Pathé's sales department, that should be covered under distribution.

306 Wakoff to Fox, 8/16/29, GSA; $40,000 and cost of facilities, Wakoff to Pathé, 3/31, JPKP; studio, Sistrom/Price Waterhouse interview, February 1931, JPKP. The initial contract had sound charges at $800 a day from eight in the morning until 6:00 P.M. and then $400 from 6:00 P.M. until eight in the morning, Pathé/Swanson agreement, 1/2/30; amended to $700, Sullivan

to Dunphy, 2/27/30; billings for screenings, Scollard to Drumm, 1/9/30, all JPKP.

306 Wakoff to Fox, 8/16/29, GSA; "we made," Fox to Sullivan, 8/29/30, GSA; "we attempted," Sullivan to Derr, 9/6/30, JPKP. Tambert's initial documenting of the rejected invoices had also been sent to the Pathé board. Even though the agreement had already been signed, it was put on the agenda of the September meeting. Kennedy formally recused himself from any actions, since he had "a connection" with both companies. Derr and Sullivan did too, but they stepped forward to say that Tambert should never have sent the new charges because they were "erroneous." Just the same, the board decided to assign Price Waterhouse to look into the matter and submit a report. Need to call board meeting, Sullivan to Scollard, 9/15/30, JPKP; JPK to board, 9/24/30; JPKP, Pathé minutes, Sindell Collection, 10/28/30.

307 The records show that for the preparation and shooting for those nine days, Pathé billed Gloria Productions over $20,000 for staff, construction, and electrical and sound equipment. That did not include cast salaries, most of the crew's salaries, or anything for Gloria, undated memo, Pathé/Swanson summary for 1929, GSA. Then there was another $6,000 charge for Paul Stein's brief nine-day stint as a director for what in retrospect was little more than a failed sound test. The bills for *The Trespasser* were small in comparison, yet there was still $25,000 for the construction of sets that Pathé kept and later "revamped" for use on four other Pathé pictures. Pathé summary memo for 1929, undated, GSA.

307 Wakoff to Fox, 8/16/30, GSA; loan agreement dated May 20, 1928, signed by Scollard as treasurer of Gloria Productions, JPKP.

307 triple her debt, Mashon, p. 116; "Stalin," Dufty/CB; "He saw," DKG, p. 223.

308 *Trespasser* accounts, JPK files, JPKP; "You should," Dufty/CB.

CHAPTER 25: "I AM NOW DEFINITELY OUT OF
THE MOTION PICTURE INDUSTRY"

309 "Up," Moore to Derr, 4/11/30, from Winslow, Arizona; Pathé Exchange Records, AMPAS; "He told me," Moore to Derr, 4/17/30, Pathé Collection, AMPAS.

309 Derr moving to the fore, V, 12/11/29; "personally," V, 3/5/30; move, Malone to Derr, 5/29/30, JPKP; writers, V, 2/5/30.

309 V, 2/12/30; selling, FD, 2/5/30. His plan was to screen seven or eight films quarterly for buyers.

310 "revolutionizing" V, 2/12/30; grosses, V, 10/15/30. *Holiday* would be remade eight years later starring Cary Grant and Katharine Hepburn. Ads, V, 7/23/30; "Derr the Doer," etc., FD, 10/13/30; "every celebrity," Derr to Ramsaye, 7/30/30, JPKP.

310 Multiple letters and cables, e.g., Scollard to Richards, 1/13/30; Scollard to Goldhar, 9/30/29; *Trespasser* file, JPKP. Each exchange needed precisely accurate continuity scripts so they could verify if indeed scene 18 was missing from reel 7. Of course there were problems, and in the process Scollard learned the difference between the negative length of a film, the scene footage length, and a flash print, as well as which film stock was the best, which was the cheapest, and which slicing machines to use to repair problem prints.

311 Various board minutes, e.g., 4/4/30, AMPAS; audit questions, minutes, 4/8/30, Pathé Collection, AMPAS; tax returns, 5/27/30.

311 stocks, V, 6/11/30; V, 4/17/29; "shed," V, 5/28/30.

311 Poole to JPK, 1/5/31, JPKP. Internal memos spelled out the reasons they should sell. First, there was the "severe" general business depression throughout the country at the time the motion picture business was still going through changes that demanded research and funding. Pathé was making fewer pictures and other companies were now in the newsreel business, "greatly increasing" competition and reducing profits. While their situation was not much worse than other small studios such as Universal and Columbia, their lack of theaters left them without bargaining power, allowing theater owners "to beat down our prices." (Unsigned memo, 10/27/30, JPKP. Mortgage spelled out in Pathé minutes, 2/4/30, Pathé Collection, AMPAS.)

312 Derr flying, V, 8/13/30; Pathé minutes, 8/18/30, Sindell Collection; Derr, Scollard, Milbank, Armbsy, Burton, Sheldon, and Webb were present. Transcontinental air flights had been introduced the year before, but they were actually two thousand miles by air and one thousand miles by train with several stops along the way. It reduced the time to cross the country from three and a half days to forty-eight hours; AH, 12/1975; Employees, V, 7/3/29; 13,000 shareholders, Innerarity to Stockholders, De Mille Collection; "hang," JPK to Poppe, 12/30/31, JPKP; multiple request letters, e.g., O'Leary to Simpson, 11/12/30, JPKP.

312 Hughes, Silverman to JPK, 8/19/30, 9/18/30, JPKP; V, 11/19/30; Schenck to JPK, 10/23/30, JPKP.

312 Details of K-A-O/Pathé contract, V, 10/15/30, 12/4/29; renegotiated contract and the fact that RKO had recently made distribution deals with smaller studios such as Universal and Columbia, V, 8/6/30. All together, Pathé was committed to paying Photophone over $100,000 a year for various contracts for sound equipment royalty and sound truck rentals; "much annoyance," LDA to JPK, 11/20/30, JPKP; "something," V, 11/9/30; Cimarron, V, 11/19/30.

312 "to bail," unsigned memo, 7/2/30, JPKP; Paramount, V, 7/30/30; separate sale, unsigned memo, 7/2/30, JPKP.

313 "equipment," "many," and "could arrive," Brown to Sarnoff, 10/8/30, JPKP; DuPont dividends, draft December memo to Pathé shareholders, JPKP.

314 Rockne was to make $500 a film and then 40 percent of the profits, Pathé minutes, 5/27/30, Pathé Collection, AMPAS; "featureless," V, 12/5/30; Scollard to Stone, 11/13/30, JPKP; V, 11/5/30, 11/19/30, 11/26/30; Derr internal memos, Pathé Collection, AMPAS; Derr's salary, V, 1/28/31; Brown to Sarnoff, 8/8/30, 8/24/30, 10/24/30, JPKP; V, 10/15/30.

314 Boards approving, V, 11/26/30; 6 percent notes, NYT, 1/6/31; "magnificent," JPK to Walker, 12/4/30, JPKP; JPK to employees, 12/9/30, JPKP; "I believe," JPK to Murdock, 12/9/30, JPKP.

315 two thirds approval, V, 11/26/30; Armsby to De Mille, 6/6/30, and Innerarity to Stockholders, DMC.

315 Meetings, Rowland to Ryan, 12/15/30, JPKP; Kaufman to JPK, 12/20/30, JPKP; "perfectly" and "tell me," JPK to Adkins, 12/22/30; "would seriously," JPK to Kaufman, undated, JPKP.

315 Wickham, Burton to Webb, 12/22/30, JPKP lawsuit, V, 12/24/30.

316 "the speculation," Sullivan to JPK, 12/29/30; "made a," JPK to Sullivan, 12/30/30; "I honestly" and "losing," JPK to Welsh, 12/19/30, all JPKP.

317 One exception was John Quinn, the fifty-five-year-old property man who had grabbed the drapes and died trying to put the fire out. He had been the sole support of his widowed mother, who was now receiving $8.31 a week from Pathé. Quinn was the only one of the dead whom the Pathé board specifically

mentioned by name in their meetings, and it was to agree to allocate $15 a week to his mother "for a couple of months" and then offer a final settlement of $5,000. *V,* 12/18/29; "for," Pathé board minutes, 12/30/30.

317 Flinn cleared, *NYT,* 4/27/32; "allowed to," Pathé Minutes, 12/30/30, Pathé Collection, AMPAS; "told," John Flinn III/CB.

317 "laden," *NYT,* 1/6/31.

318 *NYT,* 1/6/31.

318 "absolutely useless," Kane to JPK, 1/29/30, JPKP.

318 "she wouldn't," Marquis to JPK, 4/23/30, JPKP; "quixotic," quoted in *AD,* 4/94; bonus and contract changes, agreements of 9/10/30, Pathé board minutes, 1/13/31, Sindell Collection; salary, Pathé operating statement, 12/30, Pathé Collection, AMPAS.

319 Swanson, pp. 403–4. Derr had used the power of attorney back in 1928 and early 1929 when setting up Gloria Productions, establishing contracts and firing her personnel.

319 *V,* 7/2/30; *V,* 7/22/30; Bennett film, *V,* 8/13/30; *What a Widow* completed and shipped from the studio on September 5, 1930, Gloria Productions memo, undated but just after 2/31, JPKP; the contest was coordinated through twenty-four city newspapers and the price tag was put at $50,000; *V,* 7/25/30.

319 Bennett divorce, *NYT,* 1/17/30; Swanson divorce and Cohen, *NYT,* 10/22/30. Henri and Constance married in November of 1931, just days after his divorce was final, *NYT,* 11/23/31.

319 $300,000, *NYT,* 1/24/31.

320 "the making" and "more clearly," 12/3/30, Pathé minutes, Sindell Collection. Other contracts, various Pathé board minutes, e.g., 2/4/30, 3/4/30, Pathé Collection, AMPAS. Derr took the hint and within a week he was asking Kennedy to call a board meeting to "issue instructions" to him regarding a story option he wanted to exercise, Derr to JPK, 12/11/30, AMPAS.

320 All quotes, Pathé board minutes, 1/13/31, Sindell Collection. Bennett in turn notified Pathé that she was not only demanding another $10,000 under the agreement to share in the profits of her loan-outs, but if they tried to stop her from going with Warners, she would sue Pathé for breach of contract.

321 "fully explain" and "any unauthorized," Pathé minutes 1/13/31, Sindell Collection; "friendly," *V,* 2/12/30; "with or without," Pathé board minutes, 1/27/31, Sindell Collection.

322 Over the years, rumors have circulated that Derr taped Joe and Gloria together in her bungalow thinking it was funny, but Joe failed to find the humor. However, all of Derr's correspondence with Kennedy over the years verges on deferential and it is out of character for him to treat Joe as an equal, humorously or otherwise. Yet there is no question once Kennedy cut off the relationship, it was never repaired. When Joe received a particularly vitriolic anonymous hate letter in 1944 mailed from Beverly Hills, his friend Arthur Houghton suggested "uncharitably" that "our friend Derr" might have sent it, AJH to JPK 8/4/44, JPKP. After leaving Pathé, Derr remained in California and he and Sullivan worked with Howard Hughes on films such as *The Age for Love, Cock of the Air,* and the Howard Hawks–directed *Scarface.* Glazer to Wycoff, handwritten and undated but clearly early 1931, Glazer Collection, UCLA; MPPA files, AMPAS. By the mid-1930s, Derr had a production deal with Republic and created his own production company, Crescent Pictures, to make low-budget independent films with "historical backgrounds" that lasted through the late 1930s, producing over half a dozen films includ-

ing *My Old Kentucky Home.* He produced crime dramas in the late 1930s and early 1940s through Monogram Pictures and Producers Releasing Company, *V,* 4/8/36, 4/15/36; film credits, AMPAS.

322 Various letters to and from Kennedy and Poole, JPKP; Scollard's salary, Pathé board minutes, 5/28/29, Sindell Collection; Turner and Columbia Trust board, Scollard memo, 5/27/32, JPKP. Scollard kept a "large supply" of Columbia Trust deposit slips in his desk. Scollard to Turner, 11/29/30; nine floors, LDA to JPK, 11/20/30; nine employees, Webb to JPK, 7/2/31, JPKP. Eddie Moore had also shared a real friendship with Derr, but of all the letters in Moore's correspondence file, none after early 1931 are to or from Derr.

322 *V,* 2/4/31; "other Pathé," *V,* 2/4/31; *NYT,* 10/31/31. With Selznick's arrival, Bill LeBaron was moved from his role as overall production head to handle "six or seven specials a year."

323 "press," Vincent to Durkin, 3/5/31, JPKP; "too vague," Poole to JPK, 3/16/31, JPKP; "a toast," Poole to JPK, 1/30/31, JPKP; "I am now," JPK to Schulberg, 11/29/30, JPKP; "the only real," JPK to Moore, undated letter, staff files, JPKP; "Of course," Swanson, p. 408.

CHAPTER 26: "THE RICHEST IRISH AMERICAN IN THE WORLD"

324 "richest," 10/11/92; "conservatively," Looker draft, 5/37; *BG,* 9/25/32; "He already had," Krock oral history, JFKL.

324 Selznick, p. 130.

324 50 percent, JPK Paramount report, p. 6, Paramount Pictures Records, AMPAS. Moviegoing audiences had dwindled from a high of 110 million a week in 1929 to 60 million in 1933, Eames, p. 90; receiverships, Beauchamp, *Without,* p. 303; *NYDN,* undated clip, spring 1936, JPKP; "tremendous," Schenck to JPK, 10/23/30, JPKP.

325 "the condition" and "with deep," Pathé board minutes, 5/28/31; Webb to JPK, 7/2/31, JPKP; JPK to CF Adams, 4/13/29, JPKP; "there cannot," *SEP,* 1/16/37.

325 Only weeks after Teddy was born, the kidnapping of the Lindbergh baby on March 1, 1932, shocked and riveted the nation. The Kennedy personal staff was increased to include private guards to patrol their homes.

325 "financial fathers," Farley, *Behind,* 72; Nasaw, p. 455; Warm Springs weekend, *NYT,* 5/8/32; phone call to Hearst, Farley, *Behind,* p. 132. With Roosevelt campaign expenditures totaling $1.2 million between June 1 and November 2, 1932, Kennedy had contributed at least $15,000 outright, loaned another $50,000, and solicited funds from others, including $25,000 from Hearst, *NYT,* 11/1/32, 11/5/32.

325 Farley, *Story,* p. 28; "remarkably handsome," Krock oral history, JFKL; various cables between JPK and Gianninis, JPKP; campaign trips, *NYT,* 9/13/32; buses and tickets, DKG, p. 432. Hoover carried six states, Roosevelt the other forty-two, *NYT,* 11/10/32. The same *NYT* article by Arthur Krock puts Kennedy's name along with twenty others as possible cabinet members. AS, p. 103; various letters, JPKP; "Mr. Secretary" and "give me," JPK to Hays, 11/22/32; Christmas gifts, e.g., Kent to JPK, 12/28/32, JPKP.

326 *NYT* 5/8/32, 6/23/32; market conditions, Galbraith, *Crash,* p. 141; Moore's accounts, AS, p. 108; Paramount, Poole/Whitehead. Kennedy was also a victim of Depression-related bankruptcies. He was listed as a creditor to the tune of $32,000 in the bankruptcy of Palmer and Company Stock Brokers, *NYT,* 6/4/32. Palm Beach dates, Kresel memo 2/15/33, JPKP; stock pools

and Moore accounts, AS, p. 108; Kennedy joined the president's post-election celebration vacation in Florida, Whalen, p. 128. Kennedy was not alone in being disappointed. The financier Bernard Baruch, who had donated the largest individual amount to Roosevelt's campaign, $45,000, was said to want secretary of state, which was not offered him, NYT 11/1/32, 2/7/33.

326  James and Betsey Roosevelt had moved to Boston where her parents lived. BG, undated article, JPKP; AS, pp. 108, 127–28; "one of," SEP, 7/2/38.

327  JPK to Roosevelt, undated, AS, p. 108; "two enormous permits," SEP, 7/2/38; Jimmy Roosevelt Palm Beach visits, undated clips, JPKP; Goodwin, No Ordinary Time, p. 177; "surprisingly," SEP, 7/2/38. Alva Johnston's Saturday Evening Post article, entitled "Jimmy's Got It," raised serious questions about the wealth James Roosevelt accumulated while his father was president, but acknowledged there was no evidence that he had used undue influence to garner his impressive client list. Jimmy refused to make his tax records public or confirm his net worth, but his income was estimated to be between $200,000 and $2 million a year, DKG p. 444; JPK to JPK Jr., 12/4/33, JPKP. Jimmy later claimed he never intended to be a partner in the liquor business. It is doubtful he realized the amount of money at stake and instead viewed his assistance as a way to thank Joe for his help with his insurance business, which soon included clients such as the National Distillers Product Corporation, with their $70 million worth of coverage, as well as major policies covering the shipment of liquor. Roosevelt, My Parents, p. 210; A 1955 FBI memo noted it may well have been Jimmy who signed the contracts with the English distillers and then turned them over to Kennedy. AS, p. 109.

327  Kennedy bought the Palm Beach estate from Rodman Wanamaker, head of the Philadelphia-based department store chain, who had seen much of his fortune wiped out with the crash and ensuing Depression. Weiss and Hoffman, p. 78; house description, Lawford, p. 119.

327  "seriously," JPK to John Fitzgerald, 3/2/34, JPKP; "When," JPK to Poppe, 12/30/31, JPKP.

328  NYT, 4/3/34; JPK to Hearst, 12/23/33, JPKP; Rose letters, family files, JPKP.

328  "to eliminate," Milton Katz/Whitehead.

328  JPK memo, 4/34, AS, p. 129; "trying," Katz/Whitehead; "I had," SEP, 1/18/36.

328  "the bulk," JPK memo, 4/34, AS, p. 129; "be a credit," Ray Moley quoted in Whalen, p. 140; cruise, NYT, 7/1/34. Some were horrified, others laughed out loud at the news that Roosevelt was "setting a cat to guard the chickens," AS, p. 111. Many inside the administration were also upset and while Interior Secretary Harold Ickes called Kennedy a "former stock market plunger," he added that "the President has great confidence in him because he has made his pile and knows all the tricks of the trade. Apparently he is going on the assumption that Kennedy would now like to make a name for himself for the sake of his family, but I have never known many of these cases to work out as expected." Ickes, Diary, p. 273.

328  "to give," "remarkably," Baruch, and Swope, Krock oral history, JFKL;

329  "ability" and other quotes, NYT, 7/4/34.

329  Fortune, 9/37; NYT, 7/3/34; JPK memo, AS, p. 108, 138–39; "the days," NYT, 7/4/34; "no honest," NYT, 7/16/34.

329  Air-conditioning, salary, and Moore, Looker draft, 5/37; White House visits, Beschloss, p. 95; staff, Douglas, pp. 258–59; Katz/Whitehead; "confiden-

tial," *SEP,* 1/18/36; one dollar, Whalen, p. 14. A portion of the SEC was made up of the already existing Securities Division of the Federal Trade Commission, JPK to Wagner, 9/29/34.

330 Marwood was leased at $650 a month from Samuel and Mary Jane Martin, lease, 10/34, JPKP; house description and "amazing," Krock oral history, JFKL.

330 Attendees and menus, Marwood diaries, JPKP; "perfectly" and "all," JPK to Hays, 7/1/34, JPKP; DKG, p. 451; Beschloss, p. 95; AS, 154–55.

330 "at last" and "mere," quoted in Walsh, pp. 104–5, 115. An example of the changes the Production Code brought is that when Louis B. Mayer inquired about the possibility of remaking *Anna Christie,* in which the title character's past as a prostitute was alluded to, Breen informed him that in 1947 it was unthinkable to film such a story. MPPA production files, AMPAS.

331 Film prints, JPK to Murphy, 8/11/34; "I still," JPK to Houghton, 3/23/35; JPK to Feist, 4/6/35; *Variety,* Moore to Murphy, 9/26/34; JPK to Hays, 7/12/32; Kent to JPK, 12/28/32, all JPKP.

331 Paul Murphy was listed as a notary on several of Kennedy's corporate papers in 1928, Ford to Murphy, 12/19/34; JPK to O'Leary, 7/15/34, JPKP; O'Leary to JPK, 12/28/34, JPKP. O'Leary had moved his family to Scarsdale and Delehanty moved to Lynbrook on Long Island. Scollard had moved sometime before with his wife to Mount Vernon, New York, and Poole lived in Mount Kisco with his wife, unsigned letter to Sempf, 12/8/30, JPKP; Ford's longtime association with Maine and New Hampshire was recognized with the opening of the J. J. Ford Theater in Auburn, Maine, *MPN,* 11/3/28. Even if the gang was no longer together, others remembered those times fondly. James Seymour, whom Kennedy had brought from Harvard and put in the FBO publicity department, was now a successful writer and he wrote Kennedy that he looked back at his time at FBO as "the good old days" when "our close loyal little organization clung around your banner," Seymour to JPK, 5/17/34, JPKP.

331 Townsend to Murphy, 10/26/34; Moore to Murphy, 2/11/35; Ford to JPK, 8/26/35; Ford to Murphy, 12/19/34; Murphy to O'Leary, 5/7/35; "Sir Paul," JFK to JPK, 2/11/37; Rose, Joe, and cash dispersals, e.g., Murphy to JPK, 12/6/34, all JPKP.

332 JPK to RFK, 10/6/24; RFK to JPK, 10/6/24, AS, p. 143; discreet, Beschloss, p. 11.

332 Twelve hours, Looker draft, 5/37; swimming and 65,000 miles, *Time,* 7/22/35; friends in press, AS, p. 113; "two young," Vidal/CB.

332 *Time,* 7/22/35; "generally," Looker draft, 5/37; "firm," *NYT,* 9/18/35.

333 Sample of letters, JPK to Sulzberger, 9/23/35, JPKP. Joe also wrote an article under his own byline in the popular *Saturday Evening Post* entitled "Shielding the Sheep." He was now the paternalistic protector, claiming that his SEC "had saved the investing public a good portion of the billions it puts annually into business," *SEP,* 1/18/36.

CHAPTER 27: "WALL STREET AWAITS KENNEDY'S FINDINGS"

334 Memo re Ford testimony, 10/18/35, JPKP; Dinnes to Moore, 11/18/35, JPPK.

334 "the whole transaction," JPK memo to file, following 11/19/35 testimony, JPKP; Committee to JPK, 12/17/35, JPKP; "outside" JPK statement, JPKP.

335 "just," FD, 12/3/28; *Collier's,* 10/12/56. Sarnoff's plans to integrate his inter-

ests had played out in a variety of ways including the weekly *Radio-Keith-Orpheum Hour,* a nationally broadcast radio show featuring stars from the latest RKO films. RCA was also the country's major producer of phonographs and records under their Victor label, *NYT,* 1/16/29; *Time,* 9/18/39.

335 Sarnoff to JPK, 12/6/36, JPKP; "for the," draft release, JPK RCA file, JPKP.

335 JPK to Fayne, 3/4/36, JPKP; JPK recapitalization plan, 1/23/36, JPKP. Kennedy's plan was to keep the company's reserves, borrow $10 million at 2.5 percent, and expand rather than contract the number of common shares. JPK to board, 2/14/36, JPKP; "management," In re Radio reorganization, undated memo, JPKP.

336 Sarnoff to JPK, 3/20/36, JPKP. Kennedy was most pleased when another plan's chief proponent wrote him "to express my admiration and appreciation" because his new plan was "clever and ingenious and fair as possible to all interests," JPK to Sarnoff, 2/27/36; projections, *V,* 4/8/36.

336 "various," and "should," *V,* 4/1/36.

336 Paramount stock price, *V,* 4/8/36, 2/18/36, 3/25/36, 4/29/36; "a railroad," "a clean," "ill-assorted," *Fortune* 3/37; board makeup, *V,* 5/6/36.

337 calling in JPK, *V,* 5/13/36; no changes and other provisions, *V,* 4/29/36, 5/20/36, 5/6/36; minutes of special board meeting, 5/1/36, JPKP; Ford's work, Sabath hearings memo, 10/18/35, JPKP; theaters reduced, *Fortune,* 3/37; "I can always," Poole to JPK, 9/25/35, JPKP; Poole on Cinema Credits board, minutes, 3/12/32; JPKP; Pathé board meeting, 6/16/30, Pathé Collection, AMPAS. Rose Kennedy was in Europe and Russia that spring, taking along her daughter Kathleen, who was at school in France, Rose Kennedy, *Times,* pp. 205-8.

337 "unanimously," *V,* 5/6/36; contracts, *V,* 4/8/36.

338 Zukor power and personnel, *V,* 5/13/36; "How that," and office takeover, *V,* 5/6/36; "slate," *V,* 4/29/36.

338 913 North Bedford Drive; Shane to JPK, 5/25/36, JPKP; Dietrich, Bach, p. 202; "couldn't" and "running," JPK to DeFrasso [sic], 5/8/36, JPKP. Marlene Dietrich had used the home the year before. Di Frasso, née Dorothy Taylor, was in New York in May of 1936. Born in upstate New York where her father had a successful leather goods business, Dorothy married the English aviator Graham White and wed Count Carlo di Frasso in 1923. Her husband was content to stay in Italy while she roamed the globe finding loves like Gary Cooper, whom she reportedly met on board an ocean liner between New York and Europe when he was "recovering" from his affair with Clara Bow. The Hollywood jokes that resulted included Tallulah Bankhead's "he must be frassoed out" and Gene Fowler's "everyone knows the best way to go to Europe is on the Countess di Frasso." Cooper was followed by Bugsy Siegel in her affections and she introduced him to Hollywood society. She was a popular party giver, hosting events that brought together Clark Gable and Carole Lombard and Cary Grant and Barbara Hutton. The countess had a spectacular Rolls-Royce designed and named after her in the late 1930s and her brother Bert was president of the New York Stock Exchange. She continued her globe-trotting ways to the end, which came on a train between Las Vegas and Los Angeles on New Year's Day 1954. She had been partying the night before with Marlene Dietrich among others and when di Frasso was found in her cabin, she was still dressed in sequins and furs.

339 JPK to Ball, 5/11/36, JPKP; JPK to Brush, 5/8/36, JPKP; *V,* 4/8/36.

339 Jean Howard/CB, 8/1993; *VF,* 4/2003.

339 *V,* 5/13/36; Luce on board, *V,* 4/29/36; "destiny," CBL to JPK, 5/5/36, JPKP;

Luce had left his wife and two young sons to marry the already divorced Clare in November of 1935, Morris, p. 279. Washington dinners of Henry, Clare, and JPK, Morris, p. 259, AS, p. 113.

340 Flies to New York, V, 5/27/36; "deeply," JPK to Sabath, 6/2/36, JPKP; Sabath to JPK, 6/3/36, JPKP.

340 "Wall Street," V, 5/13/36.

340 "bookkeeping" and other quotes, JPK Paramount report, AMPAS; "shooting" and "costly," Fortune, 9/37.

341 "fixed," JPK Paramount report, AMPAS; "sway," Fortune, 9/37; Leonard Balaban/CB; JPK to Sabath, 6/2/36, JPKP; "had too many" and "did not know," V, 5/27/36; "outside," Shain to JPK, 5/25/36, JPKP.

341 V, 5/27/36; "letting," 5/28/36, quoted in DKG, p. 496; V, 5/13/36; "talked," Leonard Balaban/CB; "blunt," Gabler, p. 238. There was a quiet passion to Balaban. Where Louis B. Mayer would overtly proclaim his patriotism by celebrating his birthday on the Fourth of July, Balaban privately spent a portion of his increasing wealth on collecting original letters from the likes of George Washington and purchasing an original copy of the Bill of Rights, which he then donated to the National Archives. Balaban was given yet another reason to doubt Kennedy's sincerity after the end of World War II. Balaban had been to Europe as a government commissioner and returned home hand carrying a rosary that the pope had blessed and asked him to bring back to Joe. Judy Balaban recalls that her father "called Joe and left a message that he had the rosary from the pope and wanted to know whether Joe would like it sent or to have it picked up. When he heard nothing back, Dad had his secretary call again and leave the same message. I think there were about four to six calls with messages over the course of a year or more. But Kennedy never responded. I remember Dad being really shocked that such an allegedly devoted Catholic would treat the pope's personal gift with such contempt."

341 "distrusted" and "he craved," Leonard Balaban/CB.

342 Leonard Balaban/CB; "Since I," JPK to Paramount board, JPKP; "given," Griffis to JPK, 7/2/36, JPKP.

342 $50,000, secretary to Griffis, 7/24/36, JPKP. Kennedy was also reimbursed over $5,000 billed for his expenses and the seven associates he had hired to help him, including Scollard, Ford, Poole, and Kresel. Cokell to Murphy, 7/14/36, JPKP; "without," JPK to board, 7/14/36, JPKP.

343 "I have concluded," JPK to "Gentlemen," 7/14/26, JPKP; "mess," JPK to Krock, 6/24/36, JPKP. When Paramount began to turn around that fall, helped as all studios were by a rise in movie attendance, Kennedy received some of the credit. The financial press assumed that since Paramount had returned to being run by "picture men," they were "endeavoring to follow the recommendations made in the Kennedy report." The stock was selling at $17, up from the low of $8 when Kennedy came in, FDMR, 11/2/36.

343 One is reminded of the speeches of David Puttnam, the Oscar-winning producer who briefly reigned as head of Columbia. He blasted Hollywood's way of doing business to the point that the likes of Ray Stark and Bill Cosby objected so strenuously that Puttnam's tenure was aborted.

343 Burns as writer, Krock "help put," JPK to Krock, 6/24/36; "take a crack" and "had saved," Krock oral history, JFKL; Krock and JPK had been exchanging letters about Krock being unhappy and insecure in his current position at The New York Times and he sought Joe's ideas for other employment. Krock was being paid $25,000 a year so the extra $5,000 for a month's work was fairly

substantial, Krock to JPK, 3/2/36, JPKP. Krock later claimed he took no pay for the book, Blair and Blair, p. 43.

343 Thousands of copies and syndicated, Looker draft, 5/37; "a financier" and "father," cover of *I'm for Roosevelt*. Kennedy played another, less public, role in the reelection campaign by serving as a liaison between Roosevelt and the Catholic Church. The hateful Michigan-based Father Coughlin was becoming "a very dangerous proposition," fanning anti-Roosevelt sentiments on his Sunday radio broadcasts. To counteract Coughlin while not antagonizing more mainstream Catholics, Roosevelt allowed Kennedy to work behind-the-scenes with Bishop Spellman to arrange a Hyde Park lunch for Cardinal Eugenio Pacelli, the Vatican's secretary of state who would become Pius XII, when he "vacationed" in America. The papal visitor's next stop was the Kennedy home in Bronxville for afternoon tea. The results of the meeting were soon visible: President Roosevelt agreed to appoint the first official American representative to the Vatican since the Civil War and Father Coughlin ended his weekly broadcasts. Maier, pp. 104–110; REFK, pp. 204–5.

343 "he was given," Looker draft, 5/37; Delaware records; correspondence in Thomson Productions files, JPKP. Todd Shipyards and Pond Creek are examples of stock Joe held for years. The holding companies and trust helped him maintain the image that he had been "scrupulously correct, refraining from all trading, all market operations or advice" during his tenure at the SEC, Looker draft, 5/37. However, when Kennedy went to the Maritime Commission, Congress passed a special resolution approving his holding shares of Todd Shipyards, AS, p. 114.

344 Inauguration, AS, p. 190; "not well," DKG, p. 497.

344 Hearst breaks with Roosevelt, Beschloss, p. 111; Guiles, pp. 276–80, 403. Hearst also owned an opulent castle in Wales where he housed one of the largest private collections of armor, but he was in residence there for only a few weeks during the years he owned it. However, he was generous with allowing friends such as Joe Kennedy to use it when they wanted.

345 "corporate," Nasaw, p. 530; Poole memos, late 1936–early 1937, JPKP.

345 $14 million, Davies, p. 269; Poole memos, JPKP.

345 Guiles, pp. 292–97; Hearst would eventually agree to sell some of his assets, an apartment building, and a portion of his art collection. Some of his publications were merged.

346 "shocked" and "trusted," Hearst Jr., p. 328: "Kennedy's counsel was to sell the magazines; he planned to pick them up for little more than nothing. When Pop was informed about what Joe tried to pull, he was shocked. I don't think I ever saw him so taken aback. . . . Kennedy's attempted manipulation so dismayed the old man that the two were never close again." Marion, however, says while W.R. rejected Joe's offer, they all stayed on friendly terms and their correspondence verifies her version, Davies, p. 269. "there is nothing," JPK to Davies, 4/13/37; JPK to WRH, 8/3/38, JPKP. "irrevocable ten year term" as Hearst trustee went to Clarence Shearn, an old acquaintance of Hearst's who was associated with Chase Manhattan Bank.

346 "going," JPK to LeHand, 6/15/36, AS, p. 185; *Fortune*, 9/27; "see if," *Whalen*, p. 189; AS, p. 194; "give up," JPK to Boettiger, 3/22/37. John Boettiger was the publisher of a Seattle newspaper and, as the ex-husband of Anna Roosevelt, the president's former son-in-law, AS, 197; "very profitable," JPK to Byrnes, 3/15/37, AS, p. 196.

346 "hanging," Moore to Sheehan, 5/6/39, JPKP; reported settled $73 million worth of claims for a total of $750,000, *Fortune* 9/37.

347 "was a genius," Klemmer/Whitehead; newsreel clips "straight talking," Joseph Alsop, *BG,* 12/13/37.

347 "Chairman Kennedy," *Life,* 11/22/37; "permeated" and "inaccuracies," JPK to Davenport, 5/17/37, AS, pp. 199–210; "cheap" and remainder of quotes, JPK to Davenport, 5/25/37, AS, p. 211; "the brain child," JPK to Davenport, 5/28/37, AS, p. 211. *Fortune,* like *Life,* was a Henry Luce publication. Luce had first thought to call the magazine *Power,* as it was designed to praise "America's new royalty, businessmen and industrialists." Joe also claimed that the reporter was trying to "blackmail" him with the article in order to make "a sale of his book to a moving picture company."

348 Davenport to JPK, 7/15/37, JPKP.

349 "It is not," Whitehead/CB.

CHAPTER 28: "THE EMBERS OF TERROR, ISOLATIONISM, AND RACISM"

350 Krock quoted in Koskoff, p. 116; "the first," Collier and Horowitz, p. 86.

350 "Kennedy was," Tully, p. 157; Klemmer quoted in Collier and Horowitz, p. 88; Klemmer/Whitehead.

350 *BG,* 12/9/37, 12/22/37; *BH,* 1/8/38; *BG,* 12/10/37; "the President's insistence," *BG,* 12/10/37; "Today I," JPK diary, AS, p. 236. Fitzgerald was the only one to be overtly political, saying Joe was "dead set against war," *BG,* 12/9/37. Even the comments of Joe Junior and Jack, both currently at Harvard, were given their own account, *BG,* 12/9/37, 12/11/37.

351 "without the help," transcript, broadcast 12/11/36. The now former King Edward was given the title of Duke of Windsor, utilizing the name the royal family had assumed for themselves to replace their German surname during the First World War. King George's coronation was held on May 12, 1937, and Edward married Wallis on June 3, 1937, in the South of France. Wallis was to be called Duchess, instead of the sought after and denied "Her Royal Majesty."

351 Hitler's hatred was codified in the Nuremberg Laws of 1935, stripping Jews of their citizenship. Joe Junior had a rationale for Hitler's actions: Fifteen years after their defeat in the World War, Germans were at a point they "were divorced from hope. Hitler came in. He saw the need of a common enemy. . . . Someone, by whose riddance, the Germans would feel they had cast out the cause of their predicament. It was excellent psychology and it was too bad that it had to be done to the Jews." Joe allowed some emotion to enter his letter to his father when he added, "It is extremely sad that noted professors, scientists, artists, etc should have to suffer, but as you can see, it would be practically impossible to throw out only a part of them, from both the practical and psychological point of view." JPK Jr. to JPK, 4/23/34, AS, pp. 130–132; Shirer, pp. 26, 233.

352 "you and I," JPK to Cudahy, AS, p. 115; UPI press photos and newsreels; "installment," newsreels. Rose took the *Washington,* departing March 9, 1938. Eddie and Mary Moore sailed separately with Eunice and Rosemary. Eddie Moore was paid $2,500 a year by the State Department and they lived in an apartment attached to the embassy, Moore to Ford, 11/5/38, JPKP.

353 "tantamount" and "The press," *Independent,* 10/11/92; "extensive coverage," JPK diary, 3/38, AS, p. 245; newsreels and UPI photos.

353 "Private and Confidential," AS, p. 228.

353 Cliveden would become so political that those siding with appeasement of Hitler would be dubbed "the Cliveden Set." *The Spectator,* 6/3/36.

353–354 JPK diary example, 4/10/38, AS, p. 252; autograph example, Fast to JPK, 3/23/38, personal collection; letter sample, REFK to Patricia, 4/10/38, JPKP; "the happiest," DKG/Whitehead. Joe and Rose spent a weekend at Windsor Palace, where they made time to write over a dozen notes on the royal stationery to each of their children and friends such as Eddie Moore and Johnnie Ford. The Kennedys were in genuine awe to be staying at the palace and laughed together over being "one hell of a long way from East Boston," Beschloss/Whitehead.

354 salary, expenses, *BG,* 12/9/37; "not ones," Beschloss/Whitehead; "aeronautical," REFK diary, 5/17/38, AS, p. 258.

355 "long," REFK diary, 5/4/39. AS, p. 332.

355 JPK saw the royals on average of once a week; "she looked," JPK diary, 4/14/39, 4/13/39, AS, p. 326; "to have," Beschloss/Whitehead.

355 Hours at desk, Moore to Ford, 5/17/38; "a million," Moore to Ford, 7/20/38; termites, Ford to JPK, 5/5/38; Rose requests, Moore to Ford, 2/10/39; Hyannisport hurricane, Ford to JPK, undated cable, JPK to Ford, 9/23/38, all JPKP.

355 "Not soon again," *SEP,* 1/18/38; *Reader's Digest,* 4/39; "so he" and "it almost," Beschloss, p. 169. Joe had known Lord Beaverbrook, the owner of Britain's *Daily Express, Sunday Express,* and *Evening Standard,* since the late 1920s when the London press lord owned a small interest in Pathé. The two men were more than useful to each other, but they were also genuinely fond of each other and, in contrast to many of Kennedy's relationships, theirs would be maintained throughout their lives; AS, p. 162.

356 Morris, p. 318.

356 "Clare's," Selznick, p. 184; "not to live," Morris, p. 310; "his libidinous," Morris, p. 318; "made no," Morris, p. 322.

357 "the press," AS, p. 264; *Liberty,* 5/21/38. Joe timed his trip to witness Joe Junior graduate from Harvard, assuming that he would also be on the stage as one of those anointed for an honorary degree that year. The Boston papers had been saying for over a month he was to receive one, but it wasn't until the day before graduation that Kennedy learned the committee had decided against him. He arrived as planned at Cambridge, then abruptly told the press he needed to go to the Cape to be with Jack, who was ill. In fact, Jack was fine; it was Joe himself who was ill at the thought of watching Walt Disney and a dozen others receive the honor he believed he deserved. After all the years of long-distance effort Kennedy had put into his eldest son's upbringing, Joe Junior graduated from Harvard without his parents or any of his siblings in attendance. The young man who had spent much of his twenty-two years trying desperately to please his father must have felt that somehow he had let him down. Boston papers and degree, Koskoff, p. 139; DKG, pp. 535–36.

357 "I have," *I'm for Roosevelt,* p. 3; "He thought," Klemmer/Whitehead; "Yes, he did" and "He thought," Krock, oral history, JFKL. "inevitable," JPK memoir draft, AS, p. 264. Joe's visit home was hardly a rest; Johnnie Ford reported to Eddie Moore that Joe was "hopping around" the entire time and "the telephone calls were fast and furious," Ford to Moore, 7/27/38, JPKP. Joe unsuccessfully sought to speak before the Senate or at least a closed session of its Foreign Relations Committee, Hamilton, p. 230.

358 "chilling shadow," *Chicago Tribune,* 6/22/38. While James Roosevelt was on the list of receivers of the "Private and Confidential" letters, the president was given copies either by Krock thinking he was boosting Kennedy in the administration's eyes or through the various confidential, FBI, and intelligence channels; Hamilton, p. 231; AS, p. 228.

358 "helped Kennedy," *SEP,* 7/2/38; "a very imperious," Krock oral history, JFKL; Joe's expense, Hamilton, p. 230.

359 The family departed for the Riviera in waves. Joe and Jack, along with the cook and Joe's sister Margaret, were the first to leave in a three-car caravan. Rose and the younger children followed several days later; Moore to Ford, 7/20/38.

359 Dietrich's early success, *V,* 12/24/30; "box office poison," Bach, p. 236; "Queen," Bach, p. 230. Sternberg's first film with Dietrich, *The Blue Angel,* was released in America after *Morocco.*

359 Riva, pp. 469–70; "a beautiful," JPK to Land, quoted in Koskoff, p. 144; "gawky," "smiles," and "as used to," Riva, pp. 469–70. Sternberg, p. 37; "holding me," Jacobs, p. 139. Dietrich was born outside Berlin on December 27, 1901. Maria was born on December 13, 1924. Bach, pp. 13, 65. Douglas Fairbanks, Jr., had a celebrated affair with Dietrich two years before while they were making *Knight Without Armour* in England. Fairbanks had been raised by his mother in Europe and considered himself relatively sophisticated, so he coped with the framed picture of her recently deceased lover Jack Gilbert on her bedside table and the candle she lit for him nightly. What he could not comfortably adjust to was living with her when Marlene's daughter, her husband, and her husband's lover were all down the hall from them, Fairbanks/CB.

360 "the last," REFK diary, 9/28/38 and 9/30/38, AS, pp. 289–90. Within a week, the Germans took over the Sudetenland on the Czechoslovakia border. "In feverish," and gas masks and trenches, Moore to Ford, 9/28/38, JPKP. To Kennedy, the Munich agreement meant a prevention of war and he credited a variety of forces: the "German man and woman in the street" who did not want war, Chamberlain's "bull dog persistence," Mussolini's "middle, balance of power position," and Roosevelt's words of warning to Hitler, JPK to Hull, 10/5/38, AS, pp. 292–93.

361 "economic maladjustment" and "England can do," AS, p. 225; "The papers," and "he would," Joe Junior diary, 12/10/38, AS, pp. 305–6.

362 AS, pp. 306–9. Joe and Jack sailed together on the *Queen Mary.* His second son had made the Dean's List at Harvard and arranged to take the semester off to research his senior thesis on British policies that had led to the Munich agreement. Blair and Blair, p. 61. All the Kennedys attended Pacelli's "coronation" on 3/12/39. Eugenio Pacelli was elected Pope Pius XII on March 2, 1939, to replace Pius XI, who had died on February 10, 1939, oral history, Cardinal Montini, later Pope Paul VI, JFKL. "Personal" and "first," DKG, p. 581; Moore to Ford, 3/28/39 and 4/25/39, JPKP.

362 Checking in daily, Sherwood, p. 115; FDR invitation, Tully, pp. 313 and 317. Roosevelt, *Affectionately,* pp. 319–21; Berg, *Goldwyn,* pp. 331–33. Goldwyn had put young Roosevelt on the payroll to the tune of $25,000 a year and he loved telling people "the son of the President of the United States works for me." While Jimmy claimed that Goldwyn "never once asked anything of me that related to my parents," he brought his mother to dinner at the Goldwyns' home and to the Hollywood premiere of *Wuthering Heights.* Jimmy Roosevelt was hired as a vice president in January of 1939 and lasted less than a year with Goldwyn. Jimmy had divorced Betsey in 1940 and the next year he married the nurse who had tended him at the Mayo Clinic for a perforated ulcer. Betsey married the wealthy Jock Whitney, who among many other things was David O. Selznick's production partner in *Gone With the Wind,* and went on to serve as Dwight Eisenhower's ambassador to En-

gland, p. 317; "Kennedy's name," Morris, pp. 340–41; Rose in America, June 8, 1939, Moore to Ford, 5/18/39, JPKP.

363   "Papa Joe," Maria Riva/CB; Beauchamp and Béhar, pp. 43–44.

363   "ridiculous" and "the money," Riva, p. 486. Dietrich took Kennedy's suggestion that when she returned to Hollywood, she look up the agent Charles Feldman; he became a trusted advisor for years to come; Riva, pp. 486–87. Riva/CB.

363   "I can't" and "her family," Riva, pp. 487–89; trying to change Joe's opinions, Bach, p. 246; "advisable," American embassy release, 8/24/39. When the Kennedy family vacationed together, it was an opportunity for Eddie and Mary Moore to take off by themselves. During August of 1938, they went to Ireland and were joined by Johnnie Ford's wife and daughter, and then in August of 1939, the Moores drove through Belgium, France, Italy, and Germany, and found themselves struggling to get out of France in order to return to London. Moore to Ford, 7/26/38 and 8/31/39, JPKP.

364   Kennedys leaving on September 12, AS, p. 371; Kathleen to JPK, 9/18/39, AS, p. 381; *Time,* 9/18/39. The *Time* article came on the heels of an Arthur Krock piece claiming that Kennedy was the victim of a "propaganda campaign" that he was in "White House disfavor." In milder times, Roosevelt might have been amused, but now he called Krock "a social parasite" and wrote Joe that Krock's "distorted ideas of how to be helpful has done you more harm in the past few years than all of your enemies put together." "propaganda," *NYT,* 7/18/39; "distorted," FDR to JPK, 7/22/39, AS, p. 353.

364   Draft cable to Cohn and Capra, JPKP; "nothing short" and "one of," JPK to Hays, 11/12/39; AS, p. 400; "looking," JPK to Cohn, 11/17/39, JPKP; Houghton to JPK, 11/15/39; Parsons, *LAE,* undated; "an enthusiasm," *Cincinnati Post,* undated; "smash," "in a glow," *Springfield Daily News,* undated; "danger," JPK to Krock, 10/30/47, JPKP. Lewis Foster won the Oscar for best original story for *Mr. Smith,* but *Gone With the Wind*'s Sidney Howard won for best screenplay, Wiley and Bona, pp. 699–701.

365   Koszarski, *Von,* p. 329. Stroheim had returned to Europe to live and he died in Paris in 1957.

365   Hull and Farley, Goodwin, *No Ordinary Time,* p. 107; "Kennedy May Be," *BP,* 2/12/40; "The United States," Koskoff, p. 233; "the madhouse," Ford to Moore, 3/1/40, JPKP; Winchell and Runyon, photos, 12/39. Ford was also a trustee of the Kennedy children's trusts.

366   "his physical," Ford to Moore, 3/1/40, JPKP; Morris, pp. 353, 357, 364. The book Luce was working on was *Europe in the Spring,* Sylvia Morris/CB; "all morning," Morris, p. 372; JPK to Rose, 4/5/40, AS, p. 413. Joe had taken a country home near Ascot, reportedly to be close to Rosemary, who was at a school near there, but he kept it long after she returned home and his stays there during the London Blitz gave his critics more fodder. Pamela Harriman/Whitehead.

367   "terribly disturbed," Farley, *Story,* p. 199. JPK reportedly said of Churchill, "I don't have any confidence in a man who is always sucking on a whisky bottle," but James Reston points out this did not conflict with JPK continuing his role as a liquor importer, Reston, p. 68.

367   "every request," *HR,* 9/22/43; "to have" and "constantly," Hays, pp. 552–54; business trends, Reisman to JPK, 6/13/40, 7/11/40, JPKP; "rushed out," Jack Warner to Edward Kennedy, 2/12/65, Warner Bros. Collection, USC.

367   "I'll bet," Klemmer/Whitehead; "I told him," Swanberg, *Luce,* p. 430; "didn't understand," Pamela Harriman/Whiteside; JPK to Rose, 8/2/40, AS,

p. 455; "preempt," "we taped," Klemmer/Whitehead. At one point in September of 1938, Kennedy sent Johnnie Ford into Somerset Liquors to "save the business from going to pieces" and restructure the company. It was "the most important thing I know of" Joe told Ford, and while Kennedy believed the always affable O'Leary could be a "topside salesman," Ford was the businessman of the group, JPK to Ford, 9/27/38, JPKP.

368 "boomlet," AS, p. 264.

368 Beschloss, p. 16; text of JPK speech, AS, pp. 482–89, newsreels, Sherwood, p. 191; "our boys," AS, p. 489. There are a variety of stories of what happened when Kennedy met with Roosevelt and whom threatened whom with what remains a subject of discussion, but clearly Roosevelt had enough on Kennedy to make him think twice; e.g., Hersh, p. 78.

368 "Democracy," AS, p. 234; visits and "couldn't have been nicer," JPK to WRH, 11/26/40, AS, pp. 493–94; "are the" and "must assume," JPK to Cohn, 11/17/39, AS, pp. 108–109.

369 "there was no" and other JPK quotes, "made a," Douglas Fairbanks, Jr., to FDR, 11/26/40, Roosevelt Papers, Hyde Park; Berg, *Goldwyn,* p. 346; "they own" and "the embers," Fairbanks Jr., p. 309; "influential," Hecht, p. 520.

370 "the truth" and "I don't," JPK diary, 12/1/40, AS, p. 496; Roosevelt to Boettiger, quoted in Goodwin, *No Ordinary Time,* pp. 211–12. According to Joe's diary entries, the meeting covered a variety of issues. From the tone it is clear that Kennedy was already writing with an eye to posterity, putting himself in the role of the most reasonable of men, yet his vignettes include recounting that when the president asked him who he thought Churchill would take seriously and talk candidly with, Joe responded, "If there is a Chinese nigger, Churchill would talk to him now if you sent him."

### EPILOGUE: "THE FIRST AND ONLY OUTSIDER TO FLEECE HOLLYWOOD"

372 "would be," JPK to Houghton, 5/21/41; "It is one," JPK to Houghton, 3/13/41, JPKP. One of the exceptions to the novice status of much of Welles's cast and crew was the cinematographer Gregg Toland, who had filmed *The Trespasser.*

372 Houghton to JPK, 7/24/41; "I am delighted," JPK to Houghton, 8/4/41; "a terrible mess," JPK to Houghton, 6/8/42; box office down and "no prospects," JPK to Houghton, 5/21/41; "there is nothing," JPK to Houghton, 11/13/41, all JPKP.

373 Virginia, JPK to Houghton, 4/24/41, JPKP; selling Bronxville, JPK to Houghton, 11/13/41, JPKP; various hotel bills, JPKP.

373 "had carried" and "but he was," E. M. Kennedy, p. 221, Smith/CB; "back to" DKG, p. 641; "she must never" and "no mention" and "teaching," AS, pp. 515–16. While many biographers have Rosemary arriving at St. Coletta's School in Jefferson, Wisconsin, in 1941, Amanda Smith, who should know best, says Rosemary wasn't there until 1949. Joe was financially supportive of St. Coletta over the years and in the late 1950s he wrote them that "the solution of Rosemary's problem has been a major factor in the ability of all the Kennedys to go about their life's work." Doris Kearns Goodwin says when Rose visited Rosemary in the early 1960s and realized what Joe had managed to keep secret for so long, there was "an uncharacteristic bitterness" in her voice when she spoke of the situation. However, once the secret was out, the rest of the family visited Rosemary and even brought her to Hyannis Port for

visits, DKG, p. 643. Eunice Kennedy, who was always particularly close to her sister, would go on to found the Special Olympics and devote much of her life to the care and support of those with disabilities. Rosemary lived fifty-seven years at St. Coletta until her death at the age of eighty-six in January of 2005 "with her brothers and sisters at her side," *WP,* 1/8/2005.

374 Moore to Dowling, Koskoff, p. 46; "with your," JPK Jr. to JPK, 11/2/40, JPKP.

375 JPK diary, 4/10/42; AS, pp. 544–46; JPK to Houghton, 12/29/41, JPKP.

375 "wants," JPK to Houghton, 12/29/41, JPKP; "Kathleen," JPK to Houghton, 3/8/43, JPKP.

375 "I can't," JPK to Sarnoff, 2/2/42, AS, p. 539.

375 Hialeah, AS, p. 513; JPK to Houghton, 8/4/44; Houghton to JPK, 8/10/44; Scotch to Joe Breen, JPK to Houghton, 2/12/45, all JPKP.

375 "had a very hard," JPK to Houghton, 7/13/43, JPKP; "needed something," JPK to Houghton, 6/3/42, JPKP. As Kennedy put it to Arthur Houghton, who was still at the MPPA since Joe had asked Hays to hire him a decade earlier, "after some of the pictures I have looked at recently I am not at all worried" and besides, "we'll cross that bridge when we come it," JPK to Houghton, 7/13/43. Plot points, Houghton to JPK, 7/9/43; Houghton to JPK, 4/1/47, JPKP.

376 "magic touch," JPK to Houghton, 7/31/43; easily, JPK to Houghton, 8/17/43; "sure fire," JPK to Houghton, 8/4/43; JPK to Houghton, 9/14/43; "Clare Luce" and other quotes, JPK to Houghton, 10/5/1945, all JPKP.

376 Houghton to JPK, 6/24/42; Eunice at Stanford, JPK to Houghton, 1/7/42, Houghton to JPK, 7/28/43; "stunning," JPK to Houghton, 8/4/43, all JPKP.

377 "You are," JPK to Kathleen, 4/3/44, AS, p. 581; REFK cable, DKG, p. 544. Joe told Arthur Houghton on May 27, 1944: "We've had a little excitement over Kathleen's marriage, but I'm sure that whatever Kathleen does or will do for the rest of her life is just right by me." Rose recovered from her shock and tried to be supportive as Kathleen pleaded for her understanding. AS, pp. 583–93.

377 "was perfectly," Krock oral history, JFKL; *New Yorker,* 6/17/44; *Reader's Digest,* 8/44; REFK diary, 2/44: Jack was slow to return home after being hospitalized and Joe was convinced that "if he were John Doake's or Harry Hopkins' son he'd be home long before this," JPK to Houghton, 9/14/43, JPKP.

377 "it looks," JPK Jr. to JPK, 6/12/44, JPKP. It seems Joe Junior was also staying in England because he was in love with a woman who was not only Anglican but divorced, remarried, and a mother of three young children. Having witnessed his mother's reaction to Kathleen's marriage and knowing his father's plans for him wouldn't have made room for a twice-divorced mother of three, Joe had to realize that when he returned home his relationship with Pat Wilson would be at an end.

377 "expecting," JPK to JPK Jr., undated, JPKP.

377 "something" and "practically," JPK Jr. to REFK and JPK, 8/4/44, AS, pp. 598–99. "I quite," JFK to JPK Jr., undated, JPKP. "the burden," Red Fay/Whitehead. "all my plans," JPK to Houghton, 9/11/44, JPKP; "Harry," Miller, p. 186.

379 "I won't," JPK to Houghton, 5/26/45, JPKP. Joe's telegram of condolence was billed to Somerset Importers, JPK to Houghton, 5/9/45, JPKP.

379 "I probably," JPK to Houghton, 9/11/44; "I looked," JPK to Houghton,

1/21/44; Schenck, JPK to Houghton, 12/6/44; "Katharine," JPK to Houghton, 7/31/44, all JPKP.

379 JPK to Houghton, 11/21/44; "put her," Houghton to JPK, 11/15/44, JPKP; Merchandise Mart, DKG, p. 704.

380 "You could," Blair and Blair, p. 367. While the experts were confounded by many of Jack's illnesses, many seemed to have been intestinal in nature. The Mayo Clinic found that he showed an allergy to milk, but the clinic in Boston put him on a diet of milk shakes and cream soups to build up his weight. No one seems to have noticed the contradiction. It would not be until 1955, when Jack went to see Dr. Janet Travell, who would become his White House doctor, that he learned that he had been born with his left side slightly smaller than his right and the years of compensating for that had taken its toll on his lower spine. Travell oral history, JFKL.

380 Tierney, pp. 128–42; "the extras," Blair and Blair, pp. 334–35; 371–75.

380 DKG, pp. 704–5; Blair and Blair, p. 453; newspaper ads.

381 $8 million, AS, p. 521; bonus, Whalen, pp. 380–81. The new owners were listed as Joseph H. Reinfeld, Inc. and Ace Spirits, Corporate dissolution papers, Delaware Department of Corporations. Thomson Productions put in children's trusts, JPK to Copeland, 3/12/37, JPKP; AS, p. 52. Kennedy further enriched the family fortune by investing in Texas oil and gas as well as real estate. Joe now depended upon his New York office as the central station for his investments as well as handling his affairs and those of his family. As the children grew up, they became accustomed to using the office staff to get them show tickets, make travel arrangements, and even call girlfriends to confirm dates, e.g., Murphy to O'Leary, 12/21/43, JPKP.

381 "if there is," JPK to Houghton, 7/30/46; "I don't know," JPK to Houghton, 9/4/46.

381 "The first car," Pamela Harriman/Whitehead; "It never," Blair and Blair, p. 16; "Will Hays," McTaggart, pp. 18–19; "she thought," Blair and Blair, p. 143. Seymour Hersh recounts a tale Bobby Baker told him of being in Hyannis Port with then Senate Majority Leader Lyndon Johnson, sitting at the table with a gracious Rose, when Joe walked in with his female French caddie, didn't say a word, went upstairs and "engages in what, clearly and noisily, is sexual intercourse," Hersh, p. 27.

382 "became reluctant" and "pinch them," McTaggart, p. 18.

382 Other girlfriends, Blair and Blair, p. 354.

382 "Ambassador" and other quotes, Ogden, p. 309.

383 "regarded," Klemmer/Whitehead; "super-alpha-male," Vidal/CB.

383 Fontaine/CB; "Can you," Liz Smith/CB.

383 Fontaine/CB; procuring, multiple sources, including Liz Smith/CB; "had been so," Liz Smith/CB, "everything," JPK to Houghton, 5/4/47, JPKP.

384 "Joe Kennedy," Galvin/Whitehead.

384 Gentry, pp. 352–54.

384 "sounds more admirable," Navasky, *Matter of Opinion,* p. 123; "assist," letter dated 9/7/43, JPK FBI files; "the threat," 9/26/45 letter to Hoover from Boston agent re JPK, FBI files; letter to Hoover from Boston office, dated 12/27/43, FBI files. Joe was one of only two Special Contacts in the Boston area and quarterly reports were filed on him, usually noting that no contacts had been made. His Hyannisport agent was Carpenter and agent Richard Danner was his contact in the Miami office, letter to Hoover from Boston office, dated 12/27/43, FBI files. The Special Contact program ended in 1946, but was resurrected in a slightly different format in 1950 and Kennedy's name was reinstated at the head of the list.

385 Collective files, but sample is JPK to Hays, 7/18/34, JPKP; FBI files; JPK letters, JPKP.

385 *Spartacus,* Navasky, *Naming Names,* p. 327; Jacobs, pp. 118–19.

385 Tierney, pp. 128–42.

386 Dahl/CB; *VF,* 4/2003.

386 Dahl/CB. Another beautiful young actress Charlie Feldman set Jack up with was Nancy Olson Livingston. They saw each other several times, but Nancy too refused to sleep with him yet continued to see him throughout his life. Olson costarred with Gloria Swanson in *Sunset Boulevard* as Bill Holden's love interest and many other films through the fifties and sixties. Livingston/CB.

386 DKG, pp. 637–38, 723, 739; Evan Thomas, p. 56.

387 DKG, pp. 738–41; McTaggart, pp. 235–38. While McTaggart does not use endnotes, many sources and interviews are quoted within the text and hers is the only full-length book devoted to Kathleen. Billy's younger brother, who became the Duke of Devonshire, told Philip Whitehead that Joe made a pass at a girl at Kick's funeral. Her grave marker reads, "Joy she gave—joy she received."

388 "the Democratic party," JPK to Houghton, 8/22/46, JPKP; Houghton to JPK, 8/19/46, JPKP.

388 UA contract, Berg, *Goldwyn,* p. 215; "the only," Amon/CB; "wrecked," Klemmer/Whitehead; "All of it," Swanson/Kevin Brownlow; "What did," Dufty/CB. Swanson's last film appearance was in *Airport 1975* and she died in 1983.

389 Reimburse Billings, Evan Thomas, p. 50; "I am," JPK to Macdonald, 7/22/53, quoted in AS, p. 662. Johnnie Ford continued to work for Kennedy and manage the Maine and New Hampshire circuit until his death in Brookline on October 21, 1966, leaving a wife, three daughters, and four grandchildren. *V,* 11/2/66.

390 Hoover invitation, JPK FBI files. Hoover did not attend, sending the resident Hyannis Port agent in his place, who reported back to the director that both Joe and Jack took time during the reception to say nice things about him; tent, Vidal/CB; Davies, Guiles, p. 367. Davies and Brown also attended Eunice's wedding to Sargent Shriver that spring.

390 JPK to Hearst, 8/3/38, JPKP; Nasaw, p. 547.

390 Spada, pp. 63, 76. At the age of sixteen in 1939, Peter was parking cars on Worth Avenue in Palm Beach, and he remembered Kennedy because he usually tipped a quarter compared with the then customary 10 cents. There is an oft-repeated story that Kennedy caused Lawford to be fired or at least called on the carpet by reporting his displeasure over seeing the young Lawford relaxing in the company of young black men.

391 Crowther, pp. 234, 287–88. Mayer had gone to MGM corporate chief Nick Schenck and demanded that production head Dore Schary be fired. Schenck refused and Mayer was forced into resigning.

391 "Such," Spada, pp. 164–65.

391 "If" and "barefoot," Spada, p. 159; ring, *LAT,* 9/18/08.

392 *NYT,* 4/5/54; *NYT* 9/19/06; "one of," Spada, p. 175. After their honeymoon, Peter and Patricia returned to California where they soon purchased the former home of Louis B. Mayer on Santa Monica's "gold coast."

392 WRH Jr. to JPK, 1/26/61, JPKP; W. R. Hearst III/CB.

392 "sun box," Lawford, p. 119; wealth, *Newsweek,* 9/12/60; "The Kennedy fortune," Whalen, p. 411.

392 Fay, pp. 8–9; JPK to Dinneen, 8/6/55, AS, p. 667. Leonard and Judy Balaban/CB. Both Leonard and Judy Balaban clearly remember another incident

that stunned their father. Immediately following World War II, Balaban served on a government commission in Europe and "Dad came home hand-carrying a rosary which the pope himself had blessed and asked him to bring back to America for Joe. He called Joe and left a message and asked if Joe would like it sent or to have it picked up. When he heard nothing back, Dad had his secretary call again and I think there were four to six calls made over the course of a year or more, all leaving the same message. But Kennedy never responded. I remember Dad being really shocked that such an allegedly devout Catholic would treat the pope's gift with such contempt." Judy Balaban/CB.

392   Sampling of articles at JFK Library.

393   Carl Reiner/CB; "terrified," Spada, p. 172; "hovered," Spada, p. 174.

393   "You and I," etc., Sinatra, pp. 73–74; Tina Sinatra/CB; Cal Neva, Whitehead/CB; "cruder," Jacobs, pp. 118–19.

394   "had risked," REFK diary, 11/3/59, JPKL; DKG, p. 801; Davies, letter and homes, Guiles, p. 370; "in the," White, 1960, p. 179. As soon as she heard the convention was to be in Los Angeles, Marion wrote Joe inviting him to take over the estate as his "headquarters" and she and her husband, Horace, took a house at the beach so Joe could have the run of the place. She also encouraged her sister Rose to loan her Bel Air home to Bobby and his family.

394   "caddy," Leamer, p. 446; "crucial difference," Hersh, p. 155.

395   *Butterfield 8,* White, 1960, pp. 348–49.

395   Sammy Davis Jr., Spada, p. 262; tuxedo, Sidey, p. 21; Sheridan Park, Guiles, p. 371. Joe's one demand was that Bobby be made attorney general: "I want Bobby there. It's the only thing I'm asking for and I want it." After serving as his brother's campaign manager and giving his family two intense years of his life, Bobby Kennedy was thinking of moving back to Massachusetts, perhaps to run for governor or strike out on his own in some way. He had been the first of the children to marry and he and Ethel were looking at their tenth anniversary with seven of their eventual eleven children. He told friends that refusing the appointment "will kill my father," and, sure enough, Joe's plans trumped his son's. As Jack put it, "I need someone I know to talk to in this government . . . to tell me the unvarnished truth," and Bobby would be there as the first line of defense in case there were any legal challenges such as voter fraud in states like Illinois and "to protect Jack from his enemies, in and out of government." "I want," Reeves, p. 29; "I need," Evan Thomas, p. 109; "will kill" and "so he," Schlesinger, *Robert Kennedy,* p. 240. Jack's first announcement as president-elect was the reappointment of J. Edgar Hoover as head of the FBI, Hersh, p. 6.

396   Guiles, pp. 371–72; "She was," Saunders, pp. 37, 88.

397   "Certainly," Galbraith/Whitehead.

397   Sidey, pp. 219, 370–71.

397   "made a," Gentry, p. 488; Evan Thomas, pp. 163–64; Reeves, p. 272.

397   "given," Dallas, p. 2. Rose had noted in her diary of that Thanksgiving several weeks before his stroke that Joe had "an attack" ten days earlier and "is not at all himself" and "feels blah. For the first time I noticed he has grown old," AS, p. 699.

398   "he did not," Dallas, p. 27; multiple sources.

398   "my poor son," Dallas, p. 3. It is known that Jack met privately with Sam Giancana, to say nothing of the role of Judith Exner as a conduit for information.

399   "too open" and "Had the Kennedys," Sinatra, pp. 75–78.

399 Tina Sinatra/CB, Fontaine/CB.
400 "There were," Fay Kanin/CB.
400 Vidal/CB.
401 "Smell," Riva, p. 699.
401 Saunders, p. 223.
402 Saunders, pp. 225–32, Dallas, pp. 6–14. William Manchester in his *The Death of a President* has Teddy and Eunice waiting to tell him the next morning, but the thought of trying to outsmart Joe for that length of time stretches credulity and the nurse and chauffeur both say it was that night. "I know," Koskoff, p. 439.
402 Eisenhower funeral, Jack Newfield/CB.
403 "Joe Kennedy," Betty Lasky/CB.

# BIBLIOGRAPHY

BOOKS

Adams, James Truslow. *The March of Democracy: A History of the United States,* Vol. 4. New York: Charles Scribner's Sons, 1932.

Adams, Russell B. *The Boston Money Tree.* New York: Cromwell, 1977.

Allen, Frederick Lewis. *Only Yesterday: An Informal History of the 1920's in America,* 2 Volumes. London: Penguin Press, 1938.

Bach, Steven. *Marlene Dietrich.* New York: William Morrow, 1992.

Balio, Tino. *United Artists: The Company Built by the Stars.* Madison: University of Wisconsin Press, 1976.

Basinger, Jeanine. *Silent Stars.* New York: Alfred A. Knopf, 1999.

Beauchamp, Cari. *Without Lying Down: Frances Marion and the Powerful Women of Early Hollywood.* New York: Scribner, 1997.

————, editor. *Adventures of a Hollywood Secretary: Her Private Letters from Inside the Studios of the 1920s.* Berkeley: University of California Press, 2006.

————, and Henri Béhar. *Hollywood on the Riviera: The Inside Story of the Cannes Film Festival.* New York: Morrow, 1992.

Behr, Edward. *Prohibition: Thirteen Years that Changed America.* New York: Arcade, 1996.

Bennett, Joan, with Lois Kibbee. *The Bennett Playbill.* New York: Holt, Rinehart & Winston, 1970.

Berg, A. Scott. *Goldwyn: A Biography.* New York: Ballantine, 1989.

————. *Lindbergh.* New York: G. P. Putnam's Sons, 1998.

Berkman, Edward O. *The Lady and the Law: The Remarkable Story of Fanny Holtzmann.* Boston: Little, Brown, 1976.

Besas, Peter. *Inside Variety: The Story of the Bible of Show Business.* New York and Madrid: Ars Millerii, 2000.

Beschloss, Michael R. *Kennedy and Roosevelt: The Uneasy Alliance.* New York: W. W. Norton, 1980.

Birchard, Robert. *Cecil B. DeMille's Hollywood.* Lexington: University Press of Kentucky, 2004.

Blair, Joan, and Clay Blair, Jr. *The Search for JFK.* New York: G. P. Putnam's Sons, 1976.

Brazier, Marion Howard. *Stage and Screen.* Boston: Plimpton, 1920.

Brownlow, Kevin. *Hollywood: The Pioneers.* New York: Alfred A. Knopf, 1979.

————. *The Parade's Gone By.* New York: Ballantine, 1969.

Burk, Margaret Tante. *Are the Stars Out Tonight?* Los Angeles: Roundtable West, 1980.

Cameron, Gail. *Rose: A Biography of Rose Fitzgerald Kennedy.* New York: G. P. Putnam's Sons, 1971.

Caughey, John, and LaRee Caughey. *Los Angeles: Biography of a City.* Berkeley: University of California Press, 1977.

Chaplin, Charles. *My Autobiography.* New York: Simon and Schuster, 1964.

Chernow, Ron. *The House of Morgan.* New York: Atlantic Monthly Press, 1990.

Coffee, Lenore. *Storyline: Recollections of a Hollywood Screenwriter.* London: Cassell, 1973.

Collier, Peter, and David Horowitz. *The Kennedys.* New York: Simon & Shuster, 1984.

Cornwell, John. *Hitler's Pope: The Secret History of Pius XII.* New York: Viking, 1999.

Crafton, Donald. *The Talkies: American Cinema's Transition to Sound.* New York: Charles Scribner's Sons, 1997.

Creamer, Robert W. *Babe.* New York: Simon & Schuster, 1974.

Crowther, Bosley. *Hollywood Rajah.* New York: Henry Holt, 1960.

Cutler, John Henry. *Honey Fitz.* New York: Bobbs-Merrill, 1962.

Dallas, Rita, with Jeanira Ratcliffe. *The Kennedy Case.* New York: G. P. Putnam's Sons, 1973.

Dallek, Robert. *An Unfinished Life.* New York: Little, Brown, 2003.

Daniel, Clifton, ed. *20th Century Day by Day.* London: Dorling Kindersley, 2000.

DeMarco, Mario. *Tom Tyler and George O'Brien.* Compiled and self-published by Mario DeMarco.

De Mille, Cecil B., edited by Donald Hayne. *The Autobiography of Cecil B. De Mille,* Englewood Cliffs, N.J.: Prentice-Hall, 1959.

de Mille, William. *Hollywood Saga.* New York: E. P. Dutton, 1939.

Douglas, William O. *Go East, Young Man.* New York: Random House, 1974.

Dreher, Carl. *Sarnoff: An American Success.* New York: Quadrangle New York Times Books, 1977.

Edwards, Anne. *The DeMilles: An American Family.* New York: Harry Abrams, 1988.

Ellenberger, Allan R. *Celebrities in the 1930 Census.* Jefferson, N.C.: McFarland and Company, 2008.

Fairbanks, Douglas, Jr. *The Salad Days.* New York: Doubleday, 1988.

Farley, James A. *Behind the Ballots.* New York: Harcourt, Brace, 1938.

———. *Jim Farley's Story.* New York: Whittlesey House, 1948.

Fay, Paul B. *The Pleasure of His Company.* New York: Harper & Row, 1966.

Flamini, Roland. *Thalberg.* New York: Crown, 1994.

Fontaine, Joan. *No Bed of Roses.* New York: William Morrow, 1978.

Galbraith, John Kenneth. *A Life in Our Times.* New York: Ballantine, 1981.

Gentry, Curt. *J. Edgar Hoover: The Man and the Secrets.* New York: Plume/Penguin, 1992.

Golden, Eve. *Platinum Girl.* New York: Abbeville, 1991.

Goodwin, Doris Kearns. *The Fitzgeralds and the Kennedys.* New York: Simon & Schuster, 1987.

———. *No Ordinary Time.* New York: Simon & Schuster, 1994.

Goodwin, Richard N. *Remembering America: A Voice from the Sixties.* Boston: Little, Brown, 1988.

Grafton, David. *The Sisters: The Lives and Times of the Fabulous Cushing Sisters.* New York: Villard, 1992.

Guiles, Fred Lawrence. *Marion Davies.* New York: McGraw-Hill, 1972.

Gussow, Mel. *Edward Albee: A Singular Journey.* New York: Simon & Schuster, 1999.

Hamilton, Nigel. *JFK: Reckless Youth.* New York: Random House, 1992.

Hart, James D. *A Companion to California.* New York: Oxford University Press, 1978.

Hays, Will H. *The Memoirs of Will H. Hays.* New York: Doubleday, 1955.

Hearst, William Randolph Jr., with Jack Casserly. *The Hearsts: Father and Son.* New York: Roberts Rinehart, 1991.

Hecht, Ben. *A Child of the Century.* New York: Donald I. Fine, 1954.

Hersh, Seymour M. *The Dark Side of Camelot.* Boston: Little, Brown, 1997.

Higham, Charles. *Rose: The Life and Times of Rose Fitzgerald Kennedy.* New York: Pocket Books, 1995.

Hopper, Hedda. *From Under My Hat.* Garden City, N.Y.: Doubleday, 1952.

———. *The Whole Truth and Nothing But.* New York: Doubleday, 1963.

Howard, Jean. *Jean Howard's Hollywood.* New York: Harry Abrams, 1989.

Ickes, Harold. *The Secret Diary of Harold L. Ickes: The First Thousand Days, 1933–1936.* New York: Simon & Shuster, 1954.

Jacobs, George, with William Stadiem. *Mr. S: My Life with Frank Sinatra.* New York: HarperCollins, 2003.

Jacobs, Lewis. *The Rise of the American Film.* New York: Harcourt, Brace and Co., 1939.

James, Marquis, and Bessie Rowland James. *Biography of a Bank: The Story of Bank of America.* New York: Harper & Brothers, 1954.

Jewell, Richard B., and Vernon Harbin. *The RKO Story.* New York: Arlington House, 1982.

Johnson, Haines. *The Age of Anxiety.* New York: Harcourt, 2005.

Katz, Leonard. *Uncle Frank: The Biography of Frank Costello.* New York: Drake Publishers, 1973.

Kennedy, Edward M., ed. *The Fruitful Bough: A Tribute to Joseph P. Kennedy.* Privately printed, 1965.

Kennedy, Joseph P. *I'm for Roosevelt.* New York: Reynolds Hitchcock, 1936.

Kennedy, Joseph P., ed. *The Story of the Films.* Chicago: A. W. Shaw Co., 1927.

Kennedy, Matthew. *Edmund Goulding's Dark Victory.* Madison: University of Wisconsin Press, 2004.

Kennedy, Rose. *Times to Remember.* New York: Doubleday, 1974.

Kessler, Ronald. *The Sins of the Father.* New York: Warner, 1996.

King, Henry, edited by Frank Thompson. *Henry King Director.* Los Angeles: Directors Guild of America, 1995.

Kobal, John. *People Will Talk.* New York: Alfred A. Knopf, 1985.

Korda, Michael. *Charmed Lives.* New York: Random House, 1979.

Koskoff, David E. *Joseph P. Kennedy: A Life and Times.* Englewood Cliffs, N.J.: Prentice Hall, 1974.

Koszarski, Richard. *The Man You Love to Hate: Erich Von Stroheim and Hollywood.* New York: Ford University Press, 1983.

———. *An Evening's Entertainment: The Age of the Silent Feature Picture, 1915–1928.* New York: Charles Scribner's Sons, 1990.

———. *Von: The Life and Films of Erich von Stroheim.* New York: Limelight, 2001.

Lasky, Betty. *RKO: The Biggest Little Major of Them All.* Englewood Cliffs, N.J.: Prentice Hall, 1984.

Lawford, Christopher Kennedy. *Symptoms of Withdrawal.* New York: William Morrow, 2005.

Leamar, Laurence. *The Kennedy Men.* New York: William Morrow, 2001.

Leuchtenburg, William E. *The Perils of Prosperity, 1914–1932.* Chicago: University of Chicago Press, 1958.

Loos, Anita. *A Girl Like I.* New York: Viking, 1966.

Loy, Myrna, and James Kotsilibas-Davis. *Being and Becoming*. New York: Alfred A. Knopf, 1987.

Lyons, Eugene. *David Sarnoff*. New York: Harper & Row, 1966.

Maier, Thomas. *The Kennedys: America's Emerald Kings*. New York: Basic Books, 2003.

Marion, Frances. *Off with Their Heads*. New York: Macmillan, 1972.

Marx, Samuel. *Mayer and Thalberg: The Make Believe Saints*. New York: Random House, 1975.

McCartney, Laton. *The Teapot Dome Scandal: How Big Oil Bought the Harding White House and Tried to Steal the Country*. New York: Random House, 2008.

McTaggart, Lynne. *Kathleen Kennedy: Her Life and Times*. New York: Holt, Rinehart & Winston, 1983.

Miller, Merle. *Plain Speaking: An Oral Biography of Harry S. Truman*. New York: Berkley, 1973.

Morris, Sylvia Jukes. *Rage for Fame: The Ascent of Clare Boothe Luce*. New York: Random House, 1997.

Nareau, Bob, edited by Ed Berger. *The Films of Bob Steele*. Mesa, Ariz.: Robert Nareau, 1997.

Nasaw, David. *The Chief: The Life of William Randolph Hearst*. New York: Houghton Mifflin, 2002.

Navasky, Victor S. *Kennedy Justice*. New York: Atheneum, 1971.

———. *A Matter of Opinion*. New York: Farrar, Straus & Giroux, 2005.

———. *Naming Names*. New York: Penguin, 1981.

Noble, Peter. *Hollywood Scapegoat: The Biography of Erich Von Stroheim*. London: Fortune Press, 1950.

O'Brien, Lawrence F. *No Final Victories*. New York: Ballantine, 1974.

O'Connor, John E., and Martin A. Jackson, eds. *American History/American Film: Interpreting the Hollywood Image*. New York: Continuum, 1988.

Ogden, Christopher. *The Life of the Party*. Boston: Little, Brown, 1994.

Oppenheimer, Jerry. *The Other Mrs. Kennedy*. New York: St. Martin's, 1994.

Paris, Barry. *Louise Brooks*. New York: Alfred A. Knopf, 1989.

Parrish, Robert. *Growing Up in Hollywood*. New York: Harcourt Brace, 1976.

Persico, Joseph E. *Roosevelt's Secret War: FDR and World War II Espionage*. New York: Random House, 2001.

Polan, Dana. *Cinema and American Intellectual Life: The Beginnings of American Study of Film*. Berkeley: University of California Press, 2006.

Quine, Judith Balaban. *The Bridesmaids*. New York: Weidenfeld & Nicolson, 1989.

Ramsaye, Terry. *A Million and One Nights: A History of the Motion Picture Through 1925*. New York: Simon and Schuster, 1926.

Reeves, Richard. *President Kennedy: Profile of Power*. New York: Simon & Schuster, 1993.

Repetto, Thomas. *American Mafia: A History of Its Rise to Power*. New York: Holt, Rinehart and Winston, 2005.

Reston, James. *Deadline: A Memoir*. New York: Random House, 1991.

Rice, Grantland. *The Tumult and the Shouting*. New York: A. S. Barnes, 1954.

Riva, Maria. *Marlene Dietrich*. New York: Alfred A. Knopf, 1993.

Roosevelt, James, and Sidney Shalett. *Affectionately, F.D.R.* New York: Harcourt Brace, 1959.

Roosevelt, James. *My Parents: A Differing View*. Chicago: Playboy Press, 1976.

Rudnick, *Mabel Dodge Luhan*. Albuquerque: University of New Mexico Press, 1984.

Russo, Gus. *The Outfit*. New York: Bloomsbury, 2001.

St. Johns, Adela Rogers. *Love, Laughter and Tears: My Hollywood Story.* New York: Doubleday, 1978.

Sampson, Anthony. *The Money Lenders.* New York: Viking, 1981.

Sanders, Coyne, and Tom Gilbert. *Desilu.* New York: William Morrow, 1993.

Saunders, Frank, with James Southwood. *Torn Lace Curtain.* New York: Holt, Rinehart & Winston, 1982.

Schatz, Thomas. *The Genius of the System.* New York: Pantheon, 1988.

Schlesinger, Arthur M. Jr. *Robert Kennedy and His Times.* Boston: Houghton Mifflin, 1978.

Schlesinger, Arthur M. Jr., edited by Andrew Schlesinger and Stephen Schlesinger. *Journals: 1952–2000.* New York: Penguin, 2007.

Schulberg, Budd. *Moving Pictures: Memories of a Hollywood Prince.* New York: Stein & Day, 1981.

Searls, Hank. *The Lost Prince: Young Joe, the Forgotten Kennedy.* New York: World, 1969.

Selznick, Irene Mayer. *A Private View.* New York: Alfred A. Knopf, 1983.

Sherwood, Robert E. *Roosevelt and Hopkins.* New York: Harper & Brothers, 1948.

Shirer, William L. *The Rise and Fall of the Third Reich.* London: Secker & Warburg, 1960.

Sidey, Hugh. *John F. Kennedy, President.* New York: Atheneum, 1963.

Sinatra, Tina. *My Father's Daughter.* New York: Simon & Schuster, 2000.

Sinclair, Upton. *Upton Sinclair Presents William Fox.* Los Angeles: Upton Sinclair, 1933.

Slide, Anthony. *The American Film Industry: A Historical Dictionary.* New York: Limelight, 1990.

Smith, Amanda. *Hostage to Fortune: The Letters of Joseph P. Kennedy.* New York: Viking, 2001.

Smith, Page. *America Enters the World.* New York: McGraw-Hill, 1987.

Spada, James. *Peter Lawford: The Man Who Kept the Secrets.* New York: Bantam, 1991.

Spencer, Wilma Bell. *Palm Beach: A Century of Heritage.* Washington, D.C.: Mount Vernon Publishing, 2001.

Starr, Kevin. *Material Dreams: Southern California Through the 1920s.* New York: Oxford University Press, 1990.

Stenn, David. *Bombshell.* New York: Doubleday, 1993.

Summers, Anthony, and Robbyn Swan. *Sinatra: The Life.* New York: Alfred A. Knopf, 2005.

Summerscale, Kate. *The Queen of Whale Cay.* New York: Viking, 1997.

Swanberg, W. A. *Citizen Hearst.* New York: Macmillan, 1961.

———. *Luce: His Empire.* New York: Dell, 1972.

Swanson, Gloria. *Swanson on Swanson.* New York: Random House, 1980.

Sylvia. *Hollywood Undressed: Observations of Sylvia as Noted by Her Secretary.* New York: Brentano's, 1931.

Thackrey, Winfrid Kay. *Member of the Crew.* Lanham, Md.: Scarecrow, 2001.

Thomas, Bob. *Thalberg: Life and Legend.* Garden City, N.Y.: Doubleday, 1969.

Thomas, Evan. *Robert Kennedy.* New York: Simon & Schuster, 2000.

Thomas, Gordon, and Max Morgan Witts. *The Day the Bubble Burst: A Social History of the Wall Street Crash of 1929.* Garden City, N.Y.: Doubleday, 1979.

Thompson, Emily. *The Soundscape of Modernity: Architectural Acoustics and the Culture of Listening in America.* Cambridge, Mass.: MIT Press, 2004.

Tierney, Gene. *Self Portrait.* New York: Berkley, 1980.

Tully, Grace. *F.D.R. My Boss.* New York: Charles Scribner's Sons, 1949.

Tunney, Gene. *A Man Must Fight.* Boston: Houghton Mifflin, 1932.

Von Sternberg, Josef. *Fun in a Chinese Laundry.* New York: Macmillan, 1965.

Walsh, Frank. *Sin and Censorship: The Catholic Church and the Motion Picture Industry.* New Haven, Conn.: Yale University Press, 1996.

Walters, Barbara. *Audition.* New York: Alfred A. Knopf, 2008.

Weiss, Murray, and Bill Hoffman. *Palm Beach Babylon.* New York: Birch Lane, 1992.

Whalen, Richard J. *The Founding Father.* New York: New American Library, 1964.

White, Theodore. *America in Search of Itself.* New York: Harper & Row, 1982.

———. *The Making of the President 1960.* New York: Atheneum, 1961.

Wiley, Mason, and Damien Bona. *Inside Oscar: The Unofficial History of the Academy Awards.* New York: Ballantine, 1986.

Woon, Basil. *Incredible Land.* New York: Liveright, 1933.

Wyatt, Edgar M. *More than a Cowboy.* Raleigh, N.C.: Wyatt Classics, 1988.

Zukor, Adolph, with Dale Kramer. *The Public Is Never Wrong.* New York: G. P. Putnam's Sons, 1953.

*L'Eredità DeMille* (The De Mille Legacy). Pordenone, Italy: Le Giornate del Cinema Muto, 1991.

## UNPUBLISHED MANUSCRIPTS

Arrouge, Norma Shearer. "Norma Shearer Arrouge Memoir Notes." Unpublished autobiography. Courtesy of the Starlight Studio.

Colgan, Christine Ann. "Warner Brothers Crusade Against the Third Reich: A Study of Anti-Nazi Activism and Film Production, 1933 to 1941." Ph.D. diss., University of Southern California, 1986.

Looker, Harry. May 3, 1937, draft of *Fortune* magazine article that would appear in September by different author after Kennedy objected to Looker's version, 41 pages, JPKP.

Marion, Frances. "Hollywood." Original, much longer, manuscript for what would became *Off with Their Heads.* (If material is in the published book, it is cited from there, but more personal material is in "Hollywood.")

Mashon, Kenneth Michael. "Gloria Swanson at United Artists, 1925–1933." MA thesis, University of Texas, 1989.

## MAGAZINES AND TRADE PUBLICATIONS

*AD: Architectural Digest*
*AH: American Heritage*
*AM: American Magazine*
*Classic Images*
*Collier's*
*Daily Film Renter*
*EDR: Exhibitors Daily Review*
*EH: Exhibitors Herald*
*EHMPW: Exhibitors Herald and Moving Picture World*
*FD: Film Daily*
*FDYB: Film Daily Year Book*
*Film History*
*Film Mercury*
*Film Weekly*
*FGA: Films of the Golden Age*

*Fortune*
*HR: Hollywood Reporter*
*Liberty*
*Life*
*MPH: Motion Picture Herald*
*MPM: Motion Picture Magazine*
*MPN: Motion Picture News*
*MPW: Moving Picture World*
*Newsweek*
*NYMPN: New York Motion Picture News*
*PP: Photoplay*
*Picturegoer*
*Picture Play*
*Reader's Digest*
*SEP: Saturday Evening Post*
*Theatre Magazine*
*Time*
*V: Variety*
*VF: Vanity Fair*

NEWSPAPERS AND NEWS SOURCES

*BG: Boston Globe*
*BH: Boston Herald*
*BHC: Beverly Hills Citizen*
*Boston News Bureau*
*BP: Boston Post*
*Boston Transcript*
*Boston Traveler*
*Buffalo Courier-Express*
*Cincinnati Post*
*Dallas News*
*Davenport* (Iowa) *Democrat and Leader*
*FDMR: Fitch Daily Market Reports*
*Fitchburg Sentinel*
*The Guardian* (London)
*Hyannis Patriot*
*The Independent* (London)
*London Chronicle*
*LAE: Los Angeles* (Herald) *Examiner*
*LAT: Los Angeles Times*
*Miami Herald*
*NYDN: New York Daily News*
*New York Evening Post*
*NYHT: New York Herald Tribune*
*NYMT: New York Morning Telegraph*
*New York Sun*
*NYT: New York Times*
*NYW: New York World*
*Oakland Tribune*
*PI: Philadelphia Inquirer*
*Seattle Post*

*Springfield Daily News*
*The Spectator* (London)
*Standard Trade and Securities Service*
*Syracuse Herald*
*WSJ*: *Wall Street Journal*
*WP*: *Washington Post*
*Zanesville* (Ohio) *Signal*

## ARCHIVES AND COLLECTIONS

Academy of Motion Picture Arts and Sciences (AMPAS), Margaret Herrick Library, Beverly Hills: Pathé Exchange Records, Erich von Stroheim Papers, Paramount Pictures Production Records, Jesse L. Lasky Papers, Motion Picture Association of America, Production Code Administration Files; various biography and production records and files
American Film Institute Library, Los Angeles: Edmund Goulding Papers
Baker Library, Harvard Business School, Cambridge, Massachusetts: Hayden, Stone Collection, Louis Kirstein Collection
Beverly Hills Library, Historical Collections
Brigham Young University, Harold B. Lee Library, Provo, Utah: Cecil B. De Mille Collection
Bronxville New York Public Library, Historical Collections
Department of State Department of Corporations, Dover, Delaware
Franklin D. Roosevelt Presidential Library, Hyde Park, New York
George Eastman House, Rochester, New York
Indiana University: Will Hays Papers
John Fitzgerald Kennedy Library, Boston, Massachusetts: Joseph P. Kennedy Papers, Rose Kennedy Papers, various oral histories, papers, and texts
John Fitzgerald Kennedy Birthplace; National Historic Site, Brookline, Massachusetts
Library of Congress, Washington, D.C.
Los Angeles County Department of Records
Los Angeles Superior Court
Palm Beach, Florida, Historical Society
Peter Sindell Collection, privately held collection of several volumes of Pathé Corp. minutes, courtesy of Peter Sindell
Phillip Whitehead Collection, London: interview transcripts for his documentary, *The Kennedys,* London, private collection.
Santa Monica Historical Society
University of California at Los Angeles, Young Library: Benjamin Glazer Collection
University of Iowa, Iowa City: Keith/Albee Collection
University of Southern California Cinematic Arts Library, Los Angeles: Warner Bros. Collection, Frances Marion Collection
University of Texas, Austin, Harry Ransome Center: Gloria Swanson Archives

# INDEX

Page numbers in *italics* refer to illustrations.
Page numbers beginning 413 refer to notes.

A NOTE ON THE TYPE

The text of this book was set in Garamond No. 3. It is
not a true copy of any of the designs of Claude Garamond
(ca. 1480–1561), but an adaptation of his types, which set the
European standard for two centuries. It probably owes as much
to the designs of Jean Jannon, a Protestant printer working in
Sedan in the early seventeenth century, who had worked with
Garamond's romans earlier, in Paris, but who was denied their
use because of Catholic censorship. Jannon's matrices came into
the possession of the Imprimerie nationale, where they were
thought to be by Garamond himself, and were so described
when the Imprimerie revived the type in 1900. This particular
version is based on an adaptation by Morris Fuller Benton.

COMPOSED BY
*North Market Street Graphics, Lancaster, Pennsylvania*

PRINTED AND BOUND BY
*Berryville Graphics, Berryville, Virginia*

DESIGNED BY
*Iris Weinstein*